About the author

Alan F. Alford, B. Com., FCA, MBA, was born
1961 and educated at King Edward VI Grammar
School, Southampton and the Universities of Bir-
mingham and Coventry. Since he first visited the
Pyramids as a fourteen-year-old, he has travelled
extensively – to more than twenty-four countries –
in his quest to solve the riddle of humanity's mysterious past. His research includes field trips to Egypt,
Lebanon, Israel, Jordan, Mexico, Peru, Bolivia, China and Nepal. In addition, he has personally undertaken a ten-year study of the literature on the many
opposing theories that attempt to explain the anomalous history of mankind.

Gods of the New Millennium, Alan Alford's first book,
is the product of over a decade's research.

Gods of the New Millennium

Scientific Proof of
Flesh & Blood Gods

Alan F. Alford

NEW ENGLISH LIBRARY
Hodder and Stoughton

Copyright © 1996 by Alan F. Alford

First published in 1996 by Eridu Books

Published in 1997 by Hodder and Stoughton
First published in paperback in 1998 by Hodder & Stoughton
A division of Hodder Headline PLC

A New English Library paperback

10 9 8 7 6 5 4 3 2 1

Scripture quotations taken from the Holy Bible,
New International Version.
Copyright 1973, 1978, 1984 by International Bible Society.
Used by permission of Hodder & Stoughton Ltd,
a member of the Hodder Headline PLC Group.
All rights reserved.
"NIV" is a registered trademark of International Bible Society.
UK trademark number 1448790.

Pages 601–2 (credits and permissions) constitute
an extension of this copyright page.

British Library Cataloguing in Publication Data.
A CIP catalogue record for this title is
available from the British Library

ISBN 0 340 69613 3

Typeset by Hewer Text Composition Services, Edinburgh
Printed and bound in Great Britain by
Mackays of Chatham plc, Chatham, Kent

Hodder & Stoughton
A division of Hodder Headline PLC
338 Euston Road
London NW1 3BH

This book is dedicated to the Human Race –
that we might understand where we have come from
and where we are heading.

I have used male pronouns throughout this book, and I apologise to feminists and to anyone else who finds this practice offensive. I have done so purely to avoid the constant clumsiness of 'he or she', 'himself or herself', 'his or her' and so on. Readers should assume the alternatives whenever appropriate. I do not in any way wish to suggest an inequality between the sexes; indeed, the goddesses Inanna and Ninharsag will feature prominently in the events which I am about to relate.

CONTENTS

IMPORTANT FOREWORD

Around 200,000 years ago, the hominid known as *Homo erectus* suddenly transformed itself into *Homo sapiens* with a 50 per cent increase in brain size, together with language capability and a modern anatomy. How could this have happened so suddenly after 1.2 million years of no progress at all? It is anomalies such as these that have caused considerable discomfort to highly respected evolutionary scientists such as Noam Chomsky and Roger Penrose. When state-of-the-art evolutionary principles are applied to *Homo sapiens*, the logical conclusion is that we should not be here!

The religious view of Divine Creation suffers from equal scepticism. Who can take the Garden of Eden story seriously? Science and Religion are driving round in circles in a cul-de-sac. But mankind *is* here, and that fact needs to be explained.

The evolution of mankind is only one of the many mysteries that conventional science cannot explain. In recent years, the best seller lists have featured an increasing number of popular books which have dealt with these mysteries. One of the factors behind this trend has been the series of discoveries coming out of Egypt. The discovery of a secret doorway inside the Great Pyramid and the independent dating of the Giza Pyramids and Sphinx to the era 10500–8000 BC have captured the public's imagination. But these historical anomalies are not just confined to Egypt. All over the world we find sites such as Stonehenge, Tiwanaku, Nazca and Baalbek that do not fit the historical paradigm. A shadowy prehistory seems to exist as a legacy in the form of stone, maps and mythology, which our twentieth century technology has only just allowed us to recognise.

Against this background, many writers have grasped at the straw of Atlantis, and can be excused for doing so. But in fact the advanced knowledge of the Maya and the Egyptians can be traced back to the first civilisation of the Sumerians which suddenly and mysteriously emerged 6,000 years ago. The Sumerians claimed that their culture was a gift not from Atlantis but from the gods. In view of the physical evidence all around us, can we afford to dismiss what the Sumerians said?

The scientific establishment has an in-built aversion to the idea of 'gods', but this is simply a problem of terminology and religious conditioning. The fact is that man now possesses the genetic technology to create 'in his own image'. The beings we created might well call us 'gods'. The Sumerian and other Mesopotamian texts, discovered and translated only in the last one hundred years, do indeed credit flesh-and-blood gods with the creation of man. These texts closely parallel the Biblical account of Genesis, although the latter has been twisted towards a monotheistic interpretation.

Gods of the New Millennium is literally about the gods who created us, and is thus in complete contrast to other books which embellish their titles with the word 'gods', whilst continuing to treat those gods as mythology. Those other books have often been researched and written in less than a year by authors with little experience in the field. It is not surprising that such 'bandwagon' authors have simply rehashed existing material and offered only superficial explanations of the high technology which was used in ancient times.

This book, in contrast, is the product of a ten year personal quest, motivated by a pursuit of truth rather than a pursuit of short-term gain. During this time, I have personally visited the many anomalous places described in this book, rather than relying on second-hand reports, as many other authors have done. I have also had time to carry out a thorough review of existing literature myself, as compared to others who have had to use research assistants to meet tight publishing deadlines. The result is a book which at last provides some answers to the questions which everyone is asking.

Scientific progress is rarely possible without building upon the previous work of other scholars, and *Gods of the New Millennium* is no exception. In particular, I am indebted to an American scholar, Zecharia Sitchin, whose first book, *The Twelfth Planet*, I happened to discover in 1989. Sitchin's contribution to proving the intervention of flesh-and-blood gods in the creation of mankind cannot be overstated. His first book, the culmination of thirty years' research, not only explained who these gods were, but where they came from and why. Sitchin had amassed so much supporting evidence that much of it had to be held back, and subsequently published in four further books, referred to collectively as 'the Earth Chronicles'.

Why have Zecharia Sitchin's books had such limited impact? The first reason is his overwhelming attention to detail, which can be off-putting to many readers. The second reason is the immense scope of his research which has created a virtual monopoly of knowledge. Put simply, Sitchin is a difficult act to follow. By leaving so few stones unturned, he has placed other writers in a quandary. If they recognise his contribution, there is little they can add or amend, but if they ignore his theory they are guilty of intellectual neglect at best, a betrayal of truth at worst.

Sadly, few of the recent best sellers have made more than a passing mention of Sitchin, and some would appear to have gone to extreme lengths not to mention him, even to the point of crediting his ideas to someone else.

In contrast, my own research has been aimed purely at establishing the truth for my own personal curiosity. There was therefore no temptation for me to ignore Zecharia Sitchin; on the contrary, I embarked upon an exhaustive, perhaps unprecedented, critique of his theory. It quickly became apparent that there were several areas where his ideas needed to be revised. In addition, I began to examine how Sitchin's chronology – a central plank of his theory – could be reconciled to the Biblical time scales of the patriarchs. This was the 'holy grail' that would, to my mind, offer irrefutable proof that Sitchin was right. To my great disappointment, however, I was unable to reconcile his time scales to the Bible, no matter how I tried . . .

It was then that I discovered the simple mathematical key which solved the problem, and forced me to completely *revise* Zecharia Sitchin's chronology. As a result of my breakthrough, we now have for the first time a chronology which:

* matches the creation of mankind with the most recent scientific estimates;

* reconciles the arrival of the gods and the creation of mankind with the independently verifiable date of the Flood;

* reconciles the dates of the Biblical patriarchs from Adam to Noah;

* reconciles the dates of the later patriarchs from Noah to Abraham; and

   * reconciles with the infamous Sumerian Kings Lists of
     pre-Flood rulers.

This breakthrough forced me to tackle head-on the rather
unsettling question of the legendary life spans of the
patriarchs (numbering hundreds of years each), and the
Sumerian kings (numbering thousands of years each!).
Fortunately, my research coincided with some equally
dramatic breakthroughs in the field of genetic science,
which enabled me to explain the longevity of the patriarchs, and indeed the gods themselves, scientifically. It was
becoming apparent that I had some important new material, which ought to be published.

Because my new chronology is such a vital part of the
argument (and indeed central to any historical analysis), I
decided to set out *Gods of the New Millennium* as a one-
volume scientific proof of the ancient flesh-and-blood gods.
The discipline of writing down such a proof, without
leaving any loose ends whatsoever, led me into a number
of areas where I surprised myself by being able to throw new
light on ancient mysteries. I am delighted to share with my
readers my explanations of the Nazca Lines, Easter Island
and the lost city of Petra, and most importantly the Great
Pyramid. My study of the Pyramid, contained herein, is
aimed at validating what the ancient texts said about it –
that it was designed by the gods as a multi-functional
device. My analysis offers the first ever convincing explanation of its passages, chambers and shafts from a purely
functional perspective, and thus represents a major scientific breakthrough.

At the heart of this book is a new theory on the
importance of the 25,920-year precessional cycle. Other
writers have touched on the possible links between the
Sphinx and the precessional era of Leo 13,000 years ago,
but the full significance of these links runs far deeper than
the Sphinx. During the writing of this book, the British

authorities released new information on the dating of Stonehenge, and this proved to be highly significant. I am now able to offer a comprehensive solution to the Stonehenge mystery, tackling the fundamental question of why its design was so complicated if it was 'simply' a solar and lunar calendar, as is generally claimed. Armed with this new insight, I made a visit to Machu Picchu in Peru, and was able to confirm that this sacred site was used for exactly the same purpose as Stonehenge, both sites being connected to the precessional change from the era of Taurus to Aries over 4,000 years ago.

The conclusions of this book will undoubtedly prove controversial, since they challenge the established views of science. Cynics will ask how hundreds of years of establishment thinking can possibly be wrong. I need only point out that Ptolemy located Earth at the centre of the Solar System for 1,300 years before Copernicus corrected him. Unfortunately, one of our greatest weaknesses as a species is our tendency to rush into the construction of paradigms which are then defended at all costs.

The evidence contained in this book comprises scientifically verifiable facts. The scope of this evidence is worldwide (and indeed Solar System wide) and the science is multi-disciplined, covering fields as diverse as geology, geography, astronomy, mathematics, anthropology and genetics. I have linked together all of the mysterious places in the world as part of one *integrated* approach. There are no loose ends and no contradictory facts that are swept under the carpet.

As I mentioned earlier, my study of the gods indicates that the precessional cycle was symbolically important to them. One of the implications of this conclusion is that present millenarian expectations (in their many varied forms) may, for once, have some scientific basis, since the imminent arrival of the new millennium coincides approximately with a change to the precessional era of

Aquarius. I am sure my readers will be as fascinated as I am by the prospect of major changes being *directed* on Earth at that time.

So much for science, but what about our established religious institutions? Western religions may well be somewhat sensitive to my conclusion that the Hebrew 'God' of the Bible was a flesh-and-blood god, but in firmly identifying this god and his motives, I do not mean to cause any offence. I am solely interested in establishing the Exodus of the Israelites from Egypt as a real event in its proper historical context. Similarly, I do not mean to criticise monotheistic religion when I point out that its emergence has blinded us to the reality of the past.

As to the question of a Supreme Being, it is not my intention that intervention by flesh-and-blood gods should detract from anyone's belief in a supernatural divinity whom we might call God with a capital 'G'. The creation of the Universe is still shrouded in mystery, and the question of the creation of man needs to be redirected to the seed of the gods themselves. These mysteries, along with paranormal matters such as reincarnation and UFOs, are outside the realm of this book, which deals with the knowable, not the unknowable. Nevertheless, I believe that, by stripping away the prevailing myths of science and religion, we will all benefit from a clearer perspective on the yet greater mysteries of our existence.

CHAPTER ONE

BELIEVING THE UNBELIEVABLE

———◆———

Mountains of Knowledge

Where did we come from and why are we here? What is the nature of the path we tread and where does it lead? We entrust these deep questions to Religion and Science, the mainstays of modern society, but do they really offer us a path to the truth? Are we the product of a Divine Creation, did we evolve through natural selection, or is there another possible answer?

The evolutionary progress of an organism is sometimes compared to the perilous ascent of a mountain. Random genetic mutations cause the weakest individuals to fall to their deaths, while the strongest continue onwards and upwards. There is no turning back, no undoing of the evolutionary moves that eventually carry the organism to the mountain peak. Human knowledge works in the same way. How can science proceed other than to build on what has gone before? Theology – the study of religion – is no different. As the scientists ascend one peak of knowledge, the religious philosophers ascend another.

In modern times, the ascent of Religion seems to have

been stalled by dogma, whilst Science, in contrast, continues to race forever upwards towards higher peaks. The eagerness of the scientists is such that no time is allowed and no points awarded for an inspection of the mountain's foundations.

Five hundred years ago Nicolaus Copernicus was virtually lynched when he dared to suggest that the Earth revolved around the Sun.[1] If Religion and Science were to one day find someone like Copernicus waving from a higher mountain, a higher form of truth, they would hardly give a friendly wave back. The Mountain of Truth would be dismissed as the Mountain of Myth, or perhaps the Mountain of Fantasy.

This brings us to the crux of so-called myths and so-called truths, which can best be illustrated by playing a simple game. Which of the following is the myth and which is the truth?

* The Biblical account of Divine Creation.

* Darwin's theory of evolution by natural selection, as it applies to mankind.

* The Andean account of the creation of mankind by the *gods* at Lake Titicaca in Bolivia.

The scientist would say that only Darwinism can be scientifically proven, so the others are myths. The theologians would say that Andean creation was obviously a myth, that Darwinism was probably a lie, a mistake or at best only a theory, and that the only truth was the divine revelation.

Wrong and wrong again. *All* of the above statements are myths! Although the word 'myth' is synonymous with 'lie', the dictionary definition is actually 'a fictitious or unproven person or thing'. But in whose view does it need to be fictitious or unproven? Truth is thus totally in the mind of the beholder, and it all depends on the paradigm, or frame of reference, of the beholder. Let us briefly examine those paradigms.

If you have been brought up in a religious environment, your paradigm – or belief set – will strongly prejudice you against accepting anything that contradicts the firmly implanted notion that there is One Almighty God who created us from dust.

If you have undergone a scientific training and are encouraged to seek a rational explanation for everything, then a Divine Creation simply does not fit your preconceptions of a logical, comprehensible world. Perhaps Darwinism as a *general* principle does, but as we shall see later, it remains very controversial when applied to mankind.

If, on the other hand, you are a Peruvian who has never read the Bible or the theory of evolution, then the Andean legend is your supreme belief.

When we use the term 'myth' we must also remember that perspectives change with time. Atheism is a good example. Today the word 'atheism' means a belief that there is no God. But in ancient times it had very different connotations. To the Greeks who lived *c*. 400–200 BC, the atheists were the Jews who believed in *only one God*! Similarly, the first Muslims, who believed only in Allah, were labelled atheists. Their fellow-citizens, like the Greeks, had always sought the patronage of *many different deities*.[2] The definition of atheism thus changes in time according to historical perspective.

No-one believes in a myth as the truth – by definition! If we classify ancient civilisations as 'believing in myths', we are thus doing them a great injustice. The beliefs of these ancient people were founded on perceptions that had proper substance in their historical context.

Here is another dictionary definition of 'myth':

A story about superhuman beings of an earlier age taken by preliterate society to be a true account, usually of how natural phenomena, social customs etc came into existence.[3]

In common parlance we do call these traditions of super-human beings (or gods) 'myth', but to do so actually exposes our terrible prejudice. As we have seen, myths and truths are really in the mind of the beholder, dependent on his perspectives and historical context. What was the perspective of the Sumerians, the advanced city-dwellers who worshipped and wrote about their pantheon of gods 6,000 years ago? Did they invent all their tales to 'explain natural phenomena'?

Before we dismiss the Sumerians as a bunch of ignorant primitives, we should consider for a moment that their culture and institutions were so similar to those of the western world today that we would be hard pressed to tell the difference. It was the Sumerians who first used the wheel and, far from being 'preliterate', it was they who invented writing on clay tablets. I will have much, much more to say about the Sumerians in due course. As for their gods, the Sumerians believed they were real, not myth. Their paradigm was simply different from ours today. How arrogant it would be for us to automatically assume that the Sumerians were misguided.

Biblical Myths

In the beginning God created the heavens and the earth. Now the earth was formless and empty, darkness was over the surface of the deep, and the Spirit of God was hovering over the waters.[4]

How much truth and how much myth is there in the above statement? In a recent survey, 48 per cent of American respondents considered the Book of Genesis to be literally true and thought that mankind was created by God. But what does it mean to say that Genesis is 'literally true'? There are several modern versions, so which one is true? There are also progressive versions, catering for special interest groups, which often distort the literal meaning. And, more fundamentally, even the most conservative English Bible is a translation from Hebrew, and how many of us have read it in the original language? We are all therefore at the mercy of the translators.

Furthermore, even if we could read the Bible in Hebrew, we would still be reading a highly selective and edited version of events. It is not disputed that the bishops in the earliest Christian councils decided which texts should be included and which not. Texts which were considered unacceptable then, for whatever reasons, have always been regarded as outside the canon and therefore 'apocryphal' rather than the canonised 'holy' books.[5] There is little doubt that the 39 books of the Old Testament were the result of a protracted process of editing and collation. The religions deny this of course, but the first five books, known as the Pentateuch represent a collation of heavily edited material.[6]

In the nineteenth century, a group of German scholars, studying various Biblical inconsistencies, came to the conclusion that there were four sources behind the Pentateuch, and their explanation is regarded by many as the best available. The word of Moses, which was supposedly written in the Sinai desert in the fourteenth or fifteenth century BC, was thus being edited hundreds of years later, whilst the Book of Genesis was almost certainly an edited account of much earlier material.[7] This comes as a rude shock to those who believe that the Bible is a pure revelation of God, for in reality it has been edited by man. If there is any doubt about this, it should be obvious from the numerous contradictory statements and different accounts of key Biblical events such as the Creation and the Flood.[8]

The first myth of the Bible, then, is that it is a revelation of God. The second myth is that the Bible is about One Spiritual God. On the contrary, the kind and forgiving God of the New Testament is in complete contrast to the Old Testament's God of Wrath, an inconsistency that has caused many sleepless nights for the Christians. Consider the following episode which precedes the account of the Flood:

> The Lord saw how great man's wickedness on the earth had become, and that every inclination of the thoughts of his heart was only evil all the time. The Lord was grieved that he had made man on the earth, and his heart was filled with pain. So the Lord said 'I will wipe mankind, whom I have created, from the face of the earth . . . for I am grieved that I have made them.'[9]

Here we see a supposedly Supernatural God who is angry and ruthless, and there are literally dozens of further examples, particularly in the Book of Exodus, where the Lord shows an angry and vicious streak. But more importantly, if this God is all-powerful and omniscient, what is he doing making mistakes?

There are numerous examples in the Old Testament where the Lord makes appearances at a physical rather than a spiritual level. In the tale of Sodom and Gomorrah, the Lord needs to *physically go down* to the cities to ascertain the facts of the situation.[10] Then, instead of vaporising the people with a sweep of His Divine Hand, the Lord uses physical means (as evidenced by burning sulphur and smoke) to destroy not only the people but also the vegetation of the land. This is a God who, according to the Bible, personally helped the Israelites to conquer lands and destroy their enemies after the Exodus.[11]

It is thus a complete myth that the Old Testament God is the same as the kind, forgiving God described in the New Testament. Why has this myth arisen? Simply because there can be only One Spiritual God according to this religion. The truth, however, is an Old Testament God that sometimes acts like a man – he feels jealousy, anger and pleasure; he walks and talks;[12] he wrestles;[13] he is imperfect, not omniscient; he is harsh, cruel and intolerant;[14] and he exercises his power with physical manifestations.

But the myth also hides a more fundamental truth – for within the Old Testament the Lord is not the *only* God. Drawing on the Bible and other sources, Karen Armstrong has clearly demonstrated that the early Hebrews were pagans who also worshipped other gods:

> The idea of the covenant [with Moses] tells us that the Israelites were not yet monotheists, since it only made sense in a polytheistic setting. The Israelites did not believe that Yahweh, the God of Sinai, was the only God but promised, in their covenant, that they would ignore all the other deities and worship him alone. It is very difficult to find a single monotheistic statement in the whole of the Pentateuch ... The prophets would urge the Israelites to remain true to the covenant but the majority would continue to worship Baal, Asherah and Anat in the traditional way.[15]

Karen Armstrong points out that the Hebrew term *Yahweh ehad* meant 'Yahweh alone' – the only deity it was *permitted* to worship.[16] The clear implication is that these other gods must have existed as dangerous rivals to Yahweh. Were these other 'gods' simply idols and images, as Armstrong seems to think, based on her particular preconceptions, or were they 'walking, talking' rivals to the Old Testament God?

> Then God [Elohim] said 'Let us make man in our image, in our likeness, and let them rule over the fish of the sea and the birds of the air, over the livestock, over all the earth, and over all the creatures that move along the ground.'[17]

The question of whether there exists a kernel of truth in the above passage is the 64 million dollar one. But for the moment, I wish only to strip away what I call the 'Myth of the Elohim'. It might seem odd that God refers to '*us*' and '*our* likeness', but most people have ignored this as the 'royal we' or a mundane quirk of the translation from Hebrew. There is indeed a quirk with the translation of the above passage, but it is not what most people think. It is an established fact that the Hebrew word 'Elohim' is the *plural* of El, the Lord. This is well known in theological circles, but the general church-going public remains quite ignorant of this amazing little fact.

Further study of the Old Testament reveals a widespread use of the plural term Elohim, which is used on more than one hundred occasions when the Lord is not specifically named as Yahweh. In the vast majority of cases, the term appears in the Bible as a single God. How and where did the concept of Elohim emerge, and what was the meaning of its obvious pluralism? According to Armstrong, it was during the exile of the Jews in Babylon in the sixth century BC that the concept of monotheism based on Yahweh was enlarged to incorporate the God who had created heaven, Earth and mankind.[18] The resulting deity was known as Elohim.

God or Gods?

What is the truth behind the identity of Elohim? And who was he talking to when he said 'Let us make man in our image, in our likeness'? Could there have been more than one god present at the creation? And who were those other 'gods' whom the Israelites were forbidden to worship?

During the last one hundred years, tens of thousands of clay tablets have been excavated in ancient Mesopotamia (modern day Iraq),[19] dating back to 6,000 years ago. These clay tablets contain a wealth of information from the earliest civilisations, all of which believed in a bewildering variety of different gods. As a result of linguistic studies, it is now widely recognised that the original source of these ancient tablets (which I will call texts) were the Sumerian accounts, dating from the beginning of that civilisation in approximately 3800 BC. The existence of that civilisation, the existence of thousands of clay tablets and their translation is not in dispute.

Thanks to these archaeological and linguistic studies, the origin of the Elohim concept can now clearly be traced to a Babylonian epic text, known as the *Enuma Elish*. This epic, a tablet of which can be seen in Figure 1 (see black-and-white section), deals with the creation of the heavens and Earth by a Babylonian god named Marduk.[20] The amazing similarity between Genesis and the *Enuma Elish* is that one credits the creation of heavens and Earth to God, whilst the other makes exactly the same claim on behalf of Marduk.[21] Both are thus attempts to promote the achievements of an all-powerful god. It is almost as if one text is competing with the other. And there is no doubt at all that the Hebrews, having been exiled in Babylon, would surely have come into contact with, and been influenced by, the *Enuma Elish*, which had been the most sacred Babylonian ritual text for over a thousand years.

We should not be amazed to find that the Biblical account of the creation of mankind also has close parallels in the ancient texts. One Mesopotamian text describes the instructions given by the god in charge of the creation:

> 'Mix to a core the clay
> from the Basement of Earth,
> just above the Abzu—
> and shape it into the form of a core.
> I shall provide good, knowing young gods
> who will bring that clay to the right condition.'[22]

What is the significance of the 'clay' from which man was created? The Bible makes a similar claim that man was formed 'from the dust of the ground'.[23] An outrageous claim from a scientific viewpoint, but was it really 'dust' or 'clay' from which we were created? An internationally renowned scholar has pointed out that the Hebrew term used in Genesis is *tit*, which is derived from the earliest known language of the Sumerians. In the Sumerian language, the term TI.IT meant 'that which is with life'.[24] Was Adam created from *already living matter*?

What happened after the creation of the first man, Adam? The Bible states that God created 'man' first, followed by 'male and female', and suggests that a physical operation was carried out:

> So the Lord God caused the man to fall into a deep sleep; and while he was sleeping, he took one of the man's ribs and closed up the place with flesh. Then the Lord God made a woman from the rib he had taken out of the man . . . [25]

But was it really a 'rib'? In the Sumerian language the word TI stood for both 'rib' and 'life'.[26] Thus it would seem that it was Adam's life essence that was removed to create the first woman. Today we would recognise that life essence as the DNA in the human cell.

An ancient text commonly known by the name of its hero, Atra-Hasis, devotes one hundred lines to the creation of mankind, providing far more details than Genesis.[27] Instead of one god, however, we find various gods playing different roles. According to the *Atra-Hasis*, a god named Enki gives the instructions, assisted by a goddess whose name, Ninti, means 'Lady of the Rib' or 'Lady Life' in Sumerian:

> Ninti nipped off fourteen pieces of clay;
> seven she deposited on the right,

> seven she deposited on the left.
> Between them she placed the mould.
> . . . the hair she . . .
> . . . the cutter of the umbilical cord.
> The wise and learned,
> double-seven birth goddesses had assembled;
> seven brought forth males,
> seven brought forth females.
> The Birth Goddess brought forth
> the Wind of the Breath of Life.
> In pairs were they completed,
> in pairs were they completed in her presence.
> The creatures were People—
> creatures of the Mother Goddess.[28]

Only in the late twentieth century can we recognise the possibility that the production of males and females described in the ancient texts was achieved by the scientific process of cloning (see chapter 2).

The new creature was referred to in Sumerian texts by the name LU.LU literally meaning 'the mixed one'.[29] The earlier reference to the clay from the Earth, brought to the right condition by 'knowing young gods', suggests that mankind was created as a hybrid mixture of god and primitive hominid.

Why was mankind created? The Bible states only that 'there was no man to work the ground' prior to the creation.[30] But the *Atra-Hasis* gives additional detail:

> When the gods, as men,
> bore the work and suffered the toil—
> the toil of the gods was great,
> the work was heavy,
> the distress was much.[31]

The *Atra-Hasis* describes how the gods rebelled against their leader, Enlil. The father of the gods, Anu, was then called down from 'heaven' to attend a council of the gods. It was then that the god Enki (also known as Ea), provided the solution:

> 'While the Birth Goddess is present,
> let her create a Primitive Worker,
> let him bear the yoke,
> let him carry the toil of the gods!'[32]

The ancient versions of the Flood story similarly provide more detail than the Bible and place the event in a multi-god context. One such text is *The Epic of Gilgamesh*, a fragment of which is shown in Figure 2 (see black-and-white section).[33] In this text, the Flood hero is called Utnapishtim rather than Noah, but the basic story is the same. The only difference is that one god, Enlil, wishes to destroy man, whilst another, Enki, decides to save man. Scholars of these ancient texts do not dispute the roles of these gods, who are widely and consistently referred to, but it is difficult to find a single publication that does not implicitly or explicitly categorise these tales as mythology.

Are some of us guilty of bias when we treat 5,000-year old clay tablets as myth, but the 2,500-year old Genesis text as fact? After all, the subject matter is similar and the basic points are the same. The differences are purely theological – in the ancient texts mankind was 'created in the image and likeness' not of God, but of gods.

What factors drove rational and civilised ancient people to believe in plural gods? What kernel of truth might lie behind these Biblical and Mesopotamian myths? Our twentieth century paradigms make it difficult to ask, much less answer, these questions.

Monotheistic Conditioning

Why do we find the concept of 'gods' a difficult one? The problem lies in our perception and our terminology, the legacy from two thousand years of monotheism. The move to a belief in One God has not only distorted the original meaning of the Old Testament, but more importantly it has veiled our way of thinking.

The same problem exists with the Islamic religion, which is even more rigid. The God of the Muslims is known by the name Allah rather than the abstract notion of God that we have in the West. The Muslim holy book, the Koran, claims to be the word of God, spoken in divine revelation by Gabriel to the prophet Muhammad. However, the early history of Islam was far from straightforward. To our surprise, we find that it was not only in the West that monotheistic religion fought an uphill battle for acceptance. Karen Armstrong states that:

> For the first three years of his mission it seems that Muhammad did not emphasise the monotheistic content of his message and people probably imagined that they could go on worshipping the traditional deities of Arabia alongside al-Lah, the High God, as they always had. But when he condemned these ancient cults as idolatrous, he lost most of his followers overnight and Islam became a despised and persecuted minority.[34]

We in the West are all conditioned from early childhood to believe in One God. Through Bible studies at school and, for many, the ritual of prayers at home or Church on Sundays, the idea of a single all-powerful God is drilled into us. The mind of the child is enquiring, eager to learn, eager to please and therefore highly impressionable. Sociologists estimate that we absorb most of our cultural etiquette and moral values before the age of ten. And we are hardly encouraged, as children, to question what we are told.

In our mid-teens we begin to acquire scientific knowledge, which in some cases seems to conflict with our religious education. Sadly, however, this contradiction is explored by very few. After all, who can spare the time for philosophising when exhausted by the pressures of work, family and the trivia of everyday life? It is thus inevitable that the question of God is swept to one side. Most of us therefore take into our adulthood a firm idea of Jesus as the son of the One God, with in most cases only a vague notion of the Old Testament God. The paradigm of One God is therefore accepted by default and perpetuated through the generations. This is in stark contrast to other countries, where religions such as Hinduism continue to recognise a wide variety of different gods.

Against this background, it is hardly surprising that our preconceptions cause us to resist the suggestion that we were created by plural gods. It is a concept that seems alien and meaningless. But the problem is really one of terminology. Our dictionaries carry two main definitions of 'God'. The first is the Supreme Eternal Spiritual God, which we all perceive in subtly different but basically similar ways. The second, written with a small 'g' is seen as a 'supernatural being' or an image or idol thereof. The very word 'supernatural' suggests something unscientific and unreal. If we try to conceive of 'gods' being present at the scene of the Creation or the Flood, our minds automatically reject the idea.

In order to overcome the terminology barrier, let us briefly consider a myth of the gods from modern times – the amazing but true story of the 'Cargo Cult'.[35]

At various times in the 1930s, American and Australian servicemen landed in remote parts of the island of New Guinea, coming into contact with primitive local people who had been totally isolated from the outside world.

Cargo supplies were dropped off in the jungle for the advancing troops. From these cargoes, the visiting servicemen were able to bestow gifts of chewing gum, Coca-Cola and other trappings of modern day society on the local inhabitants. This generosity left an indelible mark on the people, who believed that 'big birds' would continue to deliver 'cargo' (manufactured items) to them. When the visitors departed, the locals tried to lure them back by building rough airstrips. Amazing as it may seem, the people constructed imitation radio transmitters out of bamboo, and crude model aircraft out of wood!

These people from New Guinea told legends of their 'gods' who came down from the sky bearing gifts and then departed. Beliefs akin to religious beliefs then developed, and the various 'gods' coalesced into a single deity called 'John Frum'. This is true! It would appear that the name of the deity was based on the names of the visitors who introduced themselves as 'John from Boston', 'John from New York' and so on. Despite having come into regular contact with western cultures in recent years, many of these people in New Guinea continue to believe in their god, 'John Frum'. Many more, however, have recognised the connection between their model aircraft cult and the real aircraft in the outside world, and thus realised that their 'god' or 'gods' were simply men.

What lessons can we learn from this strange but true case of the Cargo Cult? Perhaps that idols, myths and legends can represent the traces of a very real phenomenon and that flesh-and-blood men can be seen as gods by their less sophisticated fellow men. Indeed the Hebrew word for its unified godhead, Elohim, was derived from the Akkadian word *Ilu*, which meant 'Lofty Ones'. The terminology barrier has obscured whatever the ancients might have been trying to tell us.

From here on, all of my references to 'gods' should be taken to mean flesh-and-blood beings like ourselves, who simply have a technological advantage. After all, if we were to send some astronauts to a backward culture on another planet, who would doubt that they would be revered as 'gods'?

Ancient Myths

At this point a short detour around some ancient myths of the gods is in good order. Most of us are familiar with the highly embellished tales of the Greek and Roman pantheons, but their origins lie in earlier, more comprehensible versions from Egypt and Mesopotamia. The Mesopotamian accounts will be fully dealt with later in this book, so let us focus here on the Egyptians.

It is fair to say that the pharaohs of ancient Egypt were obsessed with a belief in the afterlife. This belief was inspired by their gods such as Ra and Horus, whom they seriously considered to be immortal. This seems very strange to us today, but it was their strongly held perception, which we must respect. Of course, they could not have lived long enough to establish the truth of whether the gods really were immortal, so we can safely call it a myth. Perhaps it contained a kernel of truth, perhaps not.

The Egyptian pharaoh-kings believed in a journey to a place called 'the Duat', a journey which took them across water and between two mountains to a place which they described as the 'Stairway to Heaven'. It was believed that, by reaching the heavens, they could achieve immortality like their gods. Now what could possibly have given the pharaohs such ideas?

Most of our knowledge of the ancient Egyptian afterlife cult comes from hieroglyphic[36] picture-writing, and in particular the so-called Pyramid Texts.[37] One of the most famous images is that of the Ani Papyrus (the Book of the Dead), where the dead pharaoh is being prepared for his journey alongside a rocket-type vehicle (see Figure 3, black-and-white section).

The Pyramid Texts describe a series of underground chambers in the Duat, through which the pharaoh travels, prior to his ascent to heaven. In one of these underground chambers he hears 'a mighty noise, like that heard in the heights of heaven when they are disturbed by a storm'. In another instance he encounters doors which open by themselves and 'gods', 'humming as bees', in cubicles. Sometimes the pharaoh encounters gods who keep their faces hidden, but on one occasion he sees the face (only) of a goddess. Next, the pharaoh sees gods whose task is to provide 'flame and fire' to Ra's 'celestial boat of millions of years', and other gods who 'order the course of the stars'.

The pharaoh then approaches his final destination, where he is required to shed his garments and dress in divine clothing. The 'Shem-priests', those who perform the mysterious 'opening of the mouth' ceremony, are now present. The text goes on to describe a long tunnel called 'Dawn at the End' and a cavern 'wherein the wind is brought'. The pharaoh reaches a point called the 'Mountain of the Ascent of Ra', where he sees an object called 'the Ascender to the Sky'. He steps into a 'boat' described as 770 cubits long (about 1,000 feet) and seats himself in a 'perch'.[38] After various further technical-sounding procedures, the 'mouth' of the mountain is opened and the Boat ascends:

> The Door to Heaven is open!
> The Door of Earth is open!
> The aperture of the celestial windows is open!
> The Stairway to Heaven is open;
> the Steps of Light are revealed . . .
> The double Doors to Heaven are open;

the double doors of Khebhu are open
for Horus of the east, at daybreak.

The Heaven speaks; the Earth quakes;
the Earth trembles;
the two districts of the gods shout;
the ground is come apart . . .
when the king ascends to Heaven,
when he ferries over the vault [to Heaven].[39]

Could this journey be the product of imagination? The description contains clues which have only become meaningful in the twentieth century. It is not difficult for us to visualise a modern-day NASA mission control centre, with computers humming and video-entry control systems. The rest of the details speak for themselves. When we read texts like this one on the walls of pyramids more than four thousand years old, it is rather challenging to our paradigms. We could conveniently dismiss it if it was an isolated case, but it isn't. Consider the following account, from a different culture, of an event which took place not far to the east of Egypt:

On the morning of the third day there was thunder and lightning, with a thick cloud over the mountain, and a very loud trumpet blast . . . Mount Sinai was covered with smoke, because the Lord descended on it in fire.[40]
And the glory of the Lord settled on Mount Sinai. For six days the cloud covered the mountain . . . To the Israelites the glory of the Lord looked like a consuming fire on top of the mountain.[41]

Is this simply the case of an over-active imagination? Hardly. After one of his meetings with the Lord on Mount Sinai, Moses returns to the Israelites with a 'radiant face' which frightens them.[42] How did this happen? A clue lies in Exodus 33:21–23:

Then the Lord said, 'There is a place near me, where you may stand on a rock. When my glory passes by, I will put you in a cleft in the rock and cover you with my hand until I have passed by. Then I will remove my hand and you will see my back; but my face must not be seen.'

The tale is accompanied by explicit instructions from Yahweh to Moses, warning of the potential danger to anyone coming up on the mountain.[43]

There is another intriguing aspect of the Exodus which cannot be ignored, and that is the Ark of the Covenant. The Lord tells Moses:

'Then have them make a sanctuary for me, and I will dwell among them. Make this tabernacle and all its furnishings exactly like the pattern I will show you.'[44]

There then follow clear and explicit instructions. The cover for the Ark is to have two 'cherubim', made out of hardened gold, one at each end of the cover, with their wings extended towards each other:

'There, above the cover between the two cherubim that are over the ark of the Testimony, I will meet with you and give you all my commands for the Israelites.'[45]

Why is it necessary to 'meet' at an appointed time in this way? The Lord explains that he cannot accompany the Israelites to the promised land in person;[46] instead he will use the Ark to communicate his commands. Surely this is twentieth century technology, there must be some mistake! But we also read that the Ark must be handled by priests equipped with 'sacred garments' and with a 'shielding curtain',[47] and when the proper instructions were not followed, the effects were potentially fatal.[48] Is it thus a coincidence that the chest of the Ark was to be made with gold inside and outside, representing two electricity-conducting surfaces, insulated by wood between? Similarly, was it a coincidence that it had to be moved using wooden staffs which would insulate those who carried it?

To find such references in the Book of Exodus, written around 2,500 years ago, describing events a thousand years earlier, staggers the imagination.[49] How can one dismiss the obvious references to aircraft and radiation on Mount Sinai, when there is an equally amazing description of an advanced communications device, operated by a powerful electrical system? It is difficult to comprehend how detailed technological descriptions such as these could have been dreamt up by the Israelites.

In this section I have illustrated my point with only two examples – from the Bible and ancient Egyptian Pyramid Texts – but I could have chosen from many more similar legends from cultures all around the world.[50] A common thread seems to run through all these myths and legends of ancient gods. What possible kernel of truth might they hide?

The Intellectual Cul-de-Sac

Is Darwinism a myth? The world's religions would have us believe so, but should we give any credence to their inevitably biased point of view? Their motives in attacking evolutionary science are obvious, and spring from the concept that God alone was the creator of all living things, including mankind. But although their belief comes from what the scientists would call an irrational faith, some of their arguments against Darwinism are highly rational. One of those arguments is that natural selection could never have produced man's incredibly complex brain. In the view of Religion, Darwinism is not a scientific fact but a weakly supported theory – thus, to the devout theologian, it is a myth that evolution is a fact!

Can we really believe that science – as rational seeker of

the truth, and the cornerstone of modern belief – has been misleading us? It is a formidable accusation. Surely we can rely on science and its systematic methods of observation, experimentation and measurement. Surely its theories are properly tested before being formulated into laws which govern the physical world. But how *can* Darwinism be properly tested? The scientists can prove that *in theory* a mutation and a change of species occurred, but in the absence of detailed fossil evidence, how can they say that it *actually did* occur?

What is the truth about Darwinism? For the answer we must turn to the arguments that are raging between the evolutionists themselves, and to a book which claims to 'lay out the current controversies' and 'expose the philosophical, even religious yearnings that have distorted disputes among scientists'.[51] Daniel C. Dennett, the author of *Darwin's Dangerous Idea*, is one of the leading philosophers of our time, with extensive experience in the field of evolution and genetics. In his book, Dennett attempts to kill the 'myth' (that dreaded word again) that the fundamentals of Darwinism, so well expressed by scientists such as Richard Dawkins, have been refuted by the eminent American scientist Stephen Jay Gould. The general theme of his book is that Darwinism is alive and well, but what Dennett actually does is expose the division among the scientists for us all to see.

Significantly, one of the main areas of controversy is something called 'adaptationism' – not a genetic process but rather an approach which some Darwinists have used to draw what are effectively short-cut conclusions by deductive reasoning. The question is whether this approach is *scientifically valid*. Dennett argues eloquently that adaptationism is a valid and useful approach in the field of evolution, but the fact that this argument exists at all indicates that it is not an approach which would normally be acceptable within other scientific disciplines.

Whilst the adaptationist controversy is one of semantics,

the main part of Dennett's book accuses some of the most distinguished scientists of our times, including Stephen Jay Gould, Roger Penrose, and the linguist Noam Chomsky, of being unable, ultimately, to accept the *very fundamentals* of Darwin's theory. This is a dramatic accusation.

Let us start with Gould. Dennett claims that Gould's comments have been hijacked and twisted in order to attack orthodox Darwinism. In trying to pin down the reasons why Gould has not corrected such misleading interpretations, he concludes that Gould ultimately lacks faith that Darwinian ideas can explain evolution in its entirety. Dennett then cites a similar reluctance on the part of Chomsky and Penrose, but here we get down to specifics.

Noam Chomsky is the world's leading expert on linguistics. His pioneering work has demonstrated that language structure – the ability to acquire language through parental communication – is innate in the newborn child. To the great disappointment of the psychologists, Chomsky has caused the question of language to change from one of learning theory to one of evolution theory – how did universal grammar evolve as an inbuilt biological function within the brain? As Dennett points out, there is no reason in principle why language acquisition should not have emerged through natural selection, yet Chomsky distances himself from this conclusion. Why?

To Roger Penrose, the brain as a whole poses an evolutionary mystery. Orthodox Darwinism attributes all of the functions of the brain to a collection of algorithms (step-by-step mechanical procedures), like an artificially intelligent computer. Penrose, however, sees the brain acting at a much higher level:

> I am a strong believer in the power of natural selection. But I do not see how natural selection, in itself, can evolve algorithms which could have the kind of conscious judgements of the validity of other algorithms that we seem to have.[52]

As incredible as it may seem, Roger Penrose has abandoned natural selection and, it would seem, is investigating a radical new approach to the mystery via quantum physics.

Clearly everything is not 'hunky dory' with Darwinism. Does this mean that Darwinism is dead? Not at all, for in the field of evolution generally it has much to offer. It is only when it applies to mankind that the battles begin. Why do top scientists such as Gould, who has been called 'America's evolutionist laureate', feel such discomfort with mankind's evolution? The great power of Darwinism, according to its proponents such as Dawkins, is that, *given enough time*, natural selection can explain anything and everything. Could it be that lack of time is the unspoken problem?

Stephen Jay Gould has referred to the 'awesome improbability of human evolution'.[53] If we use an ape as the starting point, a significant number of big evolutionary jumps are necessary to evolve into a man (a complete review of this will appear in the next chapter). The geneticists agree that mutation is the mechanism, but they also agree that the vast majority of mutations are bad. They also agree that the mutational mechanism must take a long time, because mutations which produce big changes are particularly dangerous to a species and thus unlikely to survive. Furthermore, they say, if a positive mutation is going to take hold in a species, it will do so only in the right circumstances, when a small population becomes isolated. Is it these improbable factors, allied to the short period of six million years allowed for man's evolution from the apes, which have caused our top scientists so much discomfort? To use an old adage, you can't get a quart out of a pint pot.

One thing is certain – mankind is here – and that fact needs to be explained. Religions raise many valid questions about Darwinism, such as how incredibly complex organs such as the eye, the ear and brain could have evolved simultaneously. They then turn to their holy books and find that God created man. But religions have no single positive rational scientific argument to support this claim. Religions accuse scientists of relying on the myth of Darwinism, but they themselves are guilty of relying on a myth – the 'revealed truth' of Divine Creation.

Science cannot ignore the fact that mankind is here on planet Earth. The only mechanism which has been put forward to explain this fact is Darwin's theory of evolution by natural selection. Since this appears to be the only alternative to Creation, the scientists have instinctively forced the theory to fit the facts and vice versa. It is a most convenient scientific paradigm. There is no doubt that Darwinism contains many truths in the animal kingdom, but severe doubts surround its practical application to man.

These two entrenched standpoints place us in an intellectual cul-de-sac. The religious and scientific arguments go round and round, but we are getting nowhere. How then to explain the fact that we *are* here? Is there an alternative which will get us out of this cul-de-sac? Sometimes a seemingly impossible problem has a simple solution – the problem becomes an 'evaporating cloud' which will quickly disappear. But invariably this requires a new way of looking at the problem, the removal of an incorrect assumption or constraint. Perhaps it is time to reconsider flesh-and-blood gods as the answer to the mystery.

Technological Perspectives

The Lord said 'Go out and stand on the mountain in the presence of the Lord, for the Lord is about to pass by'. Then a great and powerful wind tore the mountains apart and shattered the rocks before the Lord, but the Lord was not in the wind. After the wind there was an earthquake, but the Lord was not in the earthquake. After the earthquake came a fire, but the

Lord was not in the fire. And after the fire came a gentle whisper. When Elijah heard it he pulled his cloak over his face and went out and stood at the mouth of the cave.[54]

This is the account of Elijah's first encounter with the Lord, fortunately preserved in the Bible even though its meaning was surely not understood. It is not surprising that ancient tales such as this have been dismissed as myths. However, in our generation, for the first time, these myths can be seen to contain evidence of advanced technology. Only in the twentieth century have we developed the rocket engine and the aircraft, that enable us to interpret Elijah's 'vision'. Of course, we would not expect to find the correct technical terms used thousands of years ago, for the same reason that the American Indians referred to the railroad as the 'iron horse'. Imagine for a moment that *you* were asked to describe a computer using everyday terminology from one hundred years before it was invented!

Read Elijah's vision again with a technological perspective and ask yourself what kind of phenomenon is being described. If we had lived in his times, without a twentieth century vocabulary, we could surely find no better terms than his to describe the landing of a Harrier Jump Jet aircraft.

Alongside the widespread tales of flying gods, there are equally numerous tales of creation, where mankind was created by the gods, not God. One hundred years ago genetics was an unknown science, so it would have been ridiculous to suggest that the Divine Creation was actually a physical, genetic intervention. Nowadays the idea cannot be dismissed so easily. Furthermore, the twentieth century has witnessed a growing acceptance of the possibility of extra-terrestrial intelligence. The improvement of our telescopes, the findings from our space probes, and the use of powerful computers to process the data, have enabled us to reach out into our galaxy and understand it as never before.

Former sceptics, such as the famous scientist Carl Sagan, are now firm believers in the possibility of extraterrestrial life and intelligence. It is now thought that there are billions of stars with planets like Earth and that the universe contains an abundance of the basic ingredients of life. In 1989, the US space agency NASA announced a plan to embark on mankind's first systematic search for extraterrestrial intelligence (SETI), spending $100 million over ten years.[55] We can see how seriously the subject is taken by the fact that an established SETI code of conduct has been drawn up by the International Academy of Astranautics.

What will SETI find? Probably nothing – its search is the proverbial needle in a haystack. But if, as the Bible says, it was the Elohim, the *Ilu* 'Lofty Ones', who created us in their own image, then we should not be surprised to find *our own species* rather than bug-eyed monsters. It may well be that evolution to the point of self-awareness is so improbable that it has happened only once in our galaxy, and that we are an offshoot rather than the primary source. It may turn out that our whole concept of 'aliens' and 'extraterrestrials' has been based on a false premise.

The Old Testament Book of Ezekiel also records strange, technological visions.[56] Ezekiel was a priest among the Jews deported to Babylon in the first exile of 597 BC. Five years later he had the first of his amazing series of 'visions', which spanned a period of nineteen years. We can imagine Ezekiel's sense of frustration in trying to describe something which was beyond his comprehension and outside his vocabulary:

> I looked, and I saw a windstorm coming out of the north – an immense cloud with flashing lightning and surrounded by brilliant light. The centre of the fire looked like glowing metal, and in the fire was what looked like four living creatures. In appearance their form was that of a man, but each of them had four faces and four wings. Their legs were straight, their feet were like those of a calf and gleamed like burnished

bronze. Under their wings on their four sides they had the hands of a man. All four of them had faces and wings, and their wings touched one another. Each one went straight ahead; they did not turn as they moved.

As I looked at the living creatures, I saw a wheel on the ground beside each creature with its four faces. This was the appearance and structure of the wheels: they sparkled like chrysolite and all four looked alike. Each appeared to be made like a wheel intersecting a wheel. As they moved, they would go in any one of the four directions the creatures faced; the wheels did not turn about as the creatures went. Their rims were high and awesome, and all four rims were full of eyes all around.

When the living creatures moved, the wheels beside them moved; and when the living creatures rose from the ground, the wheels also rose. Wherever the spirit would go, they would go, and the wheels would rise along with them, because the spirit of the living creatures was in the wheels.[57]

Occasionally a scientist will break ranks with the establishment view. In 1968, following the publication of Erich von Daniken's *Chariots of the Gods*, a NASA engineer by the name of Josef Blumrich set about analysing the evidence in order to disprove von Daniken's suggestion that Ezekiel saw a spaceship:

I read *Chariots of the Gods* with the superior attitude of a man who knew in advance that it was all rubbish. From the wealth of material supplied by von Daniken, I found, when I came to the description of the technical characteristics of Ezekiel's visions, a territory in which I could join in the conversation, so to speak, as I have spent most of my life in the construction and planning of aircraft and rockets. So I got out a Bible to read the complete text, feeling sure that I would refute and annihilate Daniken in a few minutes.[58]

Josef Blumrich's credentials were first rate – a NASA chief engineer who was heavily involved in the design of Skylab and the Space Shuttle, and who had the rare distinction of a

NASA Exceptional Service Medal, awarded in 1972 for his outstanding contribution to the Saturn and Apollo projects. After a long period of intensive spare-time research, the cynical Blumrich became the converted Blumrich, and published in 1973 his book *The Spaceships of Ezekiel*.

Blumrich deduced both the shape and size of the craft seen by Ezekiel, and identified many key features such as rotor blades, fairing housings, landing legs and retractable wheels. He concluded that the shape of the ship was essentially the same shape that NASA engineers say is most compatible with the type of orbiting and inter-atmospheric descents and ascents that were described by Ezekiel. His drawing of the craft (Illustration 1) appears similar to a Gemini or Apollo capsule, with the addition of helicopter-like devices for the purpose of feathering descent and inter-atmospheric flight. Blumrich stated:

> The helicopter [devices] themselves are distinguished by such features as folding wings, ability to change their position and astute layout for the control rockets. All these properties fit together without any contradiction or unsolved questions; they are unmistakable indications of very able and sophisticated planning and design.[59]

Illustration 1

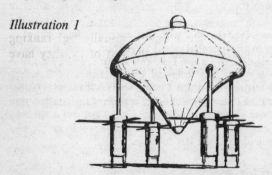

Modern devices such as those seen by Elijah and Ezekiel are not only described in the ancient texts, but also found depicted in drawings, paintings and cast in metal. Influenced by their own individual society and culture, the land-locked Hebrews referred to these craft as chariots, the sea-going Egyptians called them 'boats of heaven', whilst the Chinese saw them as dragons. In time, the references took on religious connotations such as the 'glory' or 'spirit' of the Lord. In the past it has been convenient to label as myth that which we do not understand; today we have no such excuses. If we are to continue blindly ignoring the evidence in front of us, then our thinking is no more advanced than the Cargo Cult of the New Guineans. It is time to recognise myths as the records of mankind's earliest prehistory and to seek out their hidden truths.

The Fear of Ancient Astronauts

There is a widespread perception that the idea of intervention by extraterrestrial gods – the so-called 'ancient astronaut' theory – has been entirely discredited. How has this lie been perpetuated? If we stop for a moment to consider how our beliefs are influenced – by books, newspapers, journals and television – it quickly becomes obvious that in many fields, science in particular, our perceptions are based on the views of the 'experts'. These experts, usually high-ranking scientists, are just as human as the rest of us; they have careers to follow and families to support.

The budding scientist is forced, early in his career, to choose a specialism in a field which is becoming increasingly specialised, as the body of human scientific knowledge expands. He becomes expert in a field which is usually long-established and which operates under very fixed paradigms. In each field there exist standard texts and theories which are so entrenched that nothing is to be gained (and everything lost) by the maverick who tries to challenge the status quo. Scientific progress is therefore achieved by building on top of what has already been established. It is not a good career move to tear down the 'Mountain of Knowledge' and start again.

Those scientists who appear in the media are usually ambitious, and their expert status comes only from a narrow focus in their field. They are not closed-minded but simply have little time for contact with other scientific disciplines. What are the belief sets of these people? Most fields of science have been studied for hundreds of years, during which they have evolved a number of fixed laws or assumptions. These include: life began on Earth and everything on Earth evolved from that beginning; life on Earth is unique so there can be no intelligence on other planets; every feature which we see on the planet and in the Solar System today formed gradually over millions of years, without any sudden catastrophes.

These few simple assumptions fundamentally influence dozens of vital scientific fields – biology, genetics, geology, geography, to name but a few. We stand at a point in history where it is only just becoming evident that some of these assumptions are incorrect. For example, it is now increasingly obvious that catastrophism has shaped many parts of the Earth and the Solar System. But even where the evidence is strong, the scientific establishment is incredibly conservative when it comes to new ideas which upset the old.

When we place our trust in the expert who appears on television we are actually placing our trust in the fixed laws and assumptions which have shaped his particular scientific field over the past few hundred years. We cannot blame the scientist for the set of beliefs which he must express to maintain the respect of his colleagues. Generalists, on the other hand, are more open-minded, but by definition they are not scientists; thus they are not regarded as 'experts' and not invited to speak. Thus our daily intake of knowledge is paradigms, paradigms and more paradigms.

It has not been difficult in the past to discredit the so-called 'ancient astronaut' theory. The very name itself conjures up images of a variety of space-suited aliens paying fleeting visits and quickly moving along for some more inter-galactic sightseeing. It is an image that vastly over-simplifies and demeans much of the good and varied work which is done in the field. I shall resist the use of the term in this book, in favour of the less racy title of 'interventionism', to borrow a political phrase. Its literal meaning is to 'come between' and it thus defines the role of the gods in genetically uplifting the hominid (ape-man) to the *Homo sapiens* (wise-man).[60]

The most famous proponent of interventionism is Erich von Daniken, whose views in *Chariots of the Gods* captured the imagination of the world's media in 1969.[61] Many of us who remember those heady days wonder what happened to von Daniken. There is a perception that some of his evidence was faked or at least in error, but who knows whether this is myth or fact? For more than ten years von Daniken appears to have been blacklisted by publishers in the UK and USA and until very recently his books have appeared only in the German language.

Erich von Daniken's ideas drew an immediate and vicious attack from all quarters. Who was orchestrating these attacks? The religious establishment – for obvious reasons – and the scientific experts, with all their entrenched and conservative ideas. Who dared to step into the ring and support von Daniken? Only the general public in their millions who bought his books – after all, they did not have precious academic careers on the line!

It is hardly surprising that the 'amateur' von Daniken appeared to have lost the argument, having been heavily outnumbered by such a formidable array of 'experts'. There never was a proper reasoned argument, just a barrage of abuse. Ever since then, a strong prejudice has existed against the interventionist theory. Visit some of the mysterious sites which von Daniken wrote about and you will find in the guide books a range of theories, one of which will be 'astronauts' – dismissed in tongue-in-cheek style. Similarly, most history books will mention the gods who assisted the earliest civilisations, but only to demonstrate their cultural mythology. They will have us believe that our primitive ancestors were in awe of the elements of nature, with rampant imaginations perhaps enhanced by hallucinogenic drugs. But these same books also tell us how advanced these societies were.

Thus today we find high ranking scientists and philosophers baldly stating that there is no evidence whatsoever to support an extraterrestrial intervention hypothesis. How can this howler of a lie be perpetuated? Partly through paradigms and prejudice, but also through simple ignorance. For the last twenty years, interventionists have maintained a low profile. With the exception of von Daniken in the German-speaking countries, interventionism has lacked a voice. Important breakthroughs have thus gone virtually unrecognised by the international academic community. This is not a conspiracy but simply a case of a soundly-based hypothesis being submerged in a thronging crowd of highly contrived theories.

Nevertheless, the resistance to interventionist theories runs a lot deeper than pure ignorance. One of the problems with it is that it can be used to explain just about everything. Surely that is a good thing – after all, we are in search of the ultimate truth, aren't we? Unfortunately it is not that simple.

Let us return to our 'Mountains of Knowledge' and play a game called 'Honesty'. The man on the highest mountain says to his rivals: 'come with me and I will show you a higher mountain – the mountain of the gods!' To the theologian he says: 'you may bring all of your holy books and beliefs with you'. What does the Honest Theologian say? 'Sorry, but if I come with you to the mountain of the gods, you will undermine the entire basis of my religion.

My Bible is the tool of my trade; if I rewrite it I am finished!'.

To the scientist the man offers the same invitation. What does the Honest Scientist say? 'Sorry, but we have been on this planet for 4.6 billion years and that gives me a firm timetable on which to base all my scientific theories. If I accept interventionism, that timetable goes out of the window. How can I then construct my theories and proofs? I will be out of business! I am making a good living out of science so I would prefer to stay just where I am'.

Darwin started a gravy train. The controversies on the origin of species, especially *Homo sapiens*, continue to sell millions of books and feather a fair few nests. It makes good commercial sense to keep the mysteries going. The Darwinists are trapped in an intellectual cul-de-sac but that just adds to the challenge – their inventiveness knows no bounds. Besides, there is plenty of mileage left in the cul-de-sac before anyone spots them driving round in circles. Erich von Daniken threatened to stop this gravy train in its tracks, not immediately but some way down the line. His ideas may have been speculative, but it was only a matter of time before someone else put the answers together. And yes there *are* answers – don't let us be sucked into the myth that life is supposed to be one big mystery.

Have you ever wondered why the bookshelves are stacked full of unexplained mysteries? Doesn't it strike you as odd that we can put a man on the Moon, but we cannot understand where the Moon came from? Isn't it strange that we are mapping the human genome, but we cannot say how the racial groups evolved? Conventional approaches have made negligible progress in solving these mysteries. What about the Pyramids, Stonehenge, the origin of the ancient civilisations and their remarkable knowledge, even the Earth itself and the Solar System – a whole publishing industry has evolved around these mysteries.

But it is an industry that has long given up trying to solve, and has resorted to mere description and speculation. It is rare today to find any serious attempt to explain the source of all these mysteries; it suits everyone to label the file 'unsolved' and close the case.

It is time to rethink our paradigms. Science and Religion, the cornerstones of our society today, are in a rut. Sometimes a scientific revolution is necessary. Ptolemy, an astronomer in Alexandria in the second century, thought that the Sun, the Moon and five planets revolved around the Earth. His 'scientific' theory held sway for an amazing 1,300 years before it was overturned by Copernicus. It is a poignant example of man's fallibility.

In the next 15 chapters, I will correct the myth about interventionism by setting down the best evidence in one volume. This is not going to be a generalised argument. In contrast to Darwinism, which has focused on the question of '*could it* have happened?', the interventionist theory is sufficiently advanced to answer the question of '*did it actually* happen?'. I will be dealing with the specifics of who, where, when and why. In the face of the controversy which will undoubtedly ensue, nothing less is acceptable.

Is my approach scientific? Definitions of 'scientific' vary, as we have seen with the adaptationist versus purist argument within Darwinism. I prefer to think of this book as the Interventionist's Day In Court. My approach is one of persuasion and accumulation of evidence which is 'beyond reasonable doubt'. It is for you – the jury – to decide.

Chapter One Conclusions

* Every myth – from science, religion or ancient tradition – contains an element of historical truth.

* The Bible and Pyramid Texts contain evidence of plural, flesh-and-blood gods, using technology comparable to that of the twentieth century.

* Natural selection works in theory, but in practice the time scale for the appearance of *Homo sapiens* causes serious discomfort to our top scientists.

* The term 'gods' is used in the remainder of this book to represent technologically advanced, flesh-and-blood beings, who created us 'in their own image' and thus physically resemble us.

CHAPTER TWO

MAN THE EVOLUTIONARY MISFIT

Dangerous Ideas

In November 1859, Charles Darwin published a most dangerous idea – that all living things had evolved by a process of natural selection.[1] Although there was almost no mention of mankind in Darwin's treatise, the implications were unavoidable, and led to a more radical change in human self-perception than anything before it in recorded history. In one blow, Darwin had relegated us from divinely-created beings to apes which had evolved by the impersonal mechanism of natural selection.

So dangerous was this idea to the religious establishment that, in 1925, a Tennessee schoolteacher, John Scopes, was put on trial, accused of teaching Darwin's new 'Theory of Evolution'. In a famous case, the theologians of the day scored a landmark victory. Since then, Darwinian thinking has staged quite a comeback. There is little doubt that the present-day evolutionists, zealously led by champions such as Richard Dawkins, are now winning the arguments. These scientists have refined Darwin's theory considerably, and are able to offer ever more elaborate evidence of the process of natural selection at work. Using examples from the animal kingdom, they have discredited the entire Biblical account of creation.

But are the scientists right in applying evolution to the two-legged hominid known as man? Charles Darwin himself was strangely quiet on this point,[2] but his co-discoverer Alfred Wallace was less reluctant to express his views.[3] Wallace clearly suspected an intervention of some kind, when he stated that 'some intelligent power has guided or determined the development of man'. One hundred years of science have failed to prove Wallace wrong. Anthropologists have failed miserably to produce fossil evidence of the 'missing link' with the apes, and there has been a growing recognition of the complexity of organs such as the human brain. It is as if science has come full circle, to a point where many feel severe discomfort with the evolutionary theory as it applies to *Homo sapiens*.

Here then is another dangerous idea. If we replace a creation by God, at a supernatural level, with a genetic enhancement by flesh-and-blood gods at a physical level, can the evolutionists survive a rational debate on a purely scientific basis?

Today, four out of ten Americans find it difficult to believe that humans are related to the apes. Why is this so? Compare yourself to a chimpanzee! Man is intelligent, naked and highly sexual, a species apart from his alleged primate relatives. This may be an intuitive observation but it is actually supported by scientific study. In 1911, the anthropologist Sir Arthur Keith listed the anatomical characteristics peculiar to each of the primate species, calling them 'generic characters' which set each apart from the others. His results were as follows: gorilla 75; chimpanzee 109; orangutan 113; gibbon 116; man 312.[4] Keith thus showed that mankind was nearly three times more distinctive than any other ape.

How do we reconcile Sir Arthur Keith's study with the

scientific evidence which shows a 98 per cent genetic similarity between man and the chimpanzee?[5] I would like to turn this ratio around and ask how a 2 per cent difference in DNA can account for the astonishing difference between man and his primate 'cousins'. After all, a dog shares 98 per cent of its genes with a fox, yet the two animals closely resemble each other.

Somehow we must explain how a mere 2 per cent genetic difference can account for so many 'value added' features in mankind – the brain, language and sexuality – to name but a few. Furthermore, it is a strange fact that *Homo sapiens* has only 46 chromosomes compared to 48 in chimpanzees and gorillas.[6] The theory of natural selection has been unable to suggest how the fusing together of two chromosomes – a major structural change – should have come about.

Is it credible that natural selection, via a random algorithmic process, could have focused our 2 per cent of genetic mutations into the most advantageous areas? The idea is, quite frankly, preposterous. It is an idea born of the paradigm that, since we exist, and since the chimp is our closest genetic relation, that we evolved from a common ancestor of the chimp. The missing possibility, which explains the highly focused change in human DNA, is the unthinkable idea of genetic intervention by the gods. But is it really so unthinkable? Fifty years ago, before the discovery of the genetic code, it may have been so. But in the late twentieth century, it is a fact that we now possess the genetic capability to act as 'gods' by creating life on another planet.

In this chapter, I submit in evidence mankind himself. As a wise man once said: 'since we are the result of events we seek, most answers will be found within ourselves'.[7] We will test the interventionist claims of the ancient civilisations against the current accepted wisdom of mankind's uninterrupted and gradual evolution. What we will find is missing evolutionary links, a too-rapid time scale and, finally, biological features that do not fit the known evolutionary history on planet Earth.

It is my intention that this chapter should in fact *strengthen* natural selection as a general theory. For, by relocating the evolution of *Homo sapiens* to the evolutionary home of the gods themselves, I will effectively be removing the biggest dilemma of the Darwinists from their frame of reference.

Darwinism Today

In order to throw down the gauntlet to the evolutionists, it is essential to conduct the fight in their own territory. A basic understanding of state-of-the-art Darwinian thinking is therefore essential.

When Darwin first put forward his theory of evolution by natural selection, he could not possibly have known the mechanism by which it occurred. It was almost one hundred years later, in 1953, that James Watson and Francis Crick discovered that mechanism to be DNA and genetic inheritance. Watson and Crick were the scientists who discovered the double helix structure of the DNA molecule, the chemical which encodes genetic information. Our school-children now understand that every cell in the body contains 23 pairs of chromosomes, onto which are fixed approximately 100,000 genes making up what is known as the human genome. The information contained in these genes is sometimes switched on, to be read, sometimes not, depending on the cell and the tissue (muscle, bone or whatever) which is required to be produced. We also now understand the rules of genetic inheritance, the basic principle of which is that half of the mother's and half of the father's genes are recombined.

How does genetics help us to understand Darwinism? It is

now understood that our genes undergo random mutations as they are passed through the generations. Some of these mutations will be bad, some good. Any mutation which gives a survival advantage to the species will by and large, over many many generations, spread through the whole population. This accords with the Darwinian idea of natural selection, a continuous struggle for existence in which those organisms best fitted to their environment are the most likely to survive. By surviving, their genes are more likely, statistically, to be carried into later generations through the process of sexual reproduction.

A common misconception with natural selection is that genes will *directly* improve in response to their environment, causing optimal adjustments of the organism. It is now accepted that such adaptations are in fact random mutations which happened to suit the environment and thus survived. In the words of Steve Jones, 'we are the products of evolution, a set of successful mistakes'.[8]

How fast is the process of evolution? The experts all agree with Darwin's basic idea that natural selection is a very slow, continuous process. As one of today's great champions of evolution, Richard Dawkins, put it: 'nobody thinks that evolution has ever been jumpy enough to invent a whole new fundamental body plan in one step'.[9] Indeed, the experts think that a big evolutionary jump, known as a macromutation, is extremely unlikely to succeed, since it would probably be harmful to the survival of a species which is already well adapted to its environment.

We are thus left with a process of random genetic drift and the cumulative effects of genetic mutations. Even these minor mutations, however, are thought to be generally harmful. Daniel Dennett neatly illustrates the point by drawing an analogy with a game whereby one tries to improve a classic piece of literature by making a single typographical change. Whilst most changes such as omitted commas or mis-spelled words would have negligible effect, those changes which were visible would in nearly all cases damage the original text. It is rare, though not impossible, for random change to improve the text.[10]

The odds are already stacked against genetic improvement, but we must add one further factor. A favourable mutation will only take hold if it occurs in *small isolated populations*.[11] This was the case on the Galapagos Islands, where Charles Darwin carried out much of his research. Elsewhere, favourable mutations will be lost and diluted within a larger population, and scientists admit that the process will be a lot slower.

If the evolution of a species is a time-consuming process, then the separation of one species into two different species must be seen as an even longer process. Speciation – which Richard Dawkins has termed the 'long goodbye' – is defined as the point where two groups within the same species are no longer able to interbreed. Dawkins compares the genes of different species to rivers of genes which flow through time for millions of years.[12] The source of all these rivers is the genetic code which is identical in all animals, plants and bacteria that have ever been studied.[13] The body of the organism soon dies but, through sexual reproduction, acts as a mechanism which the genes can use to travel through time. Those genes which work well with their fellow-genes, and which best assist the survival of the bodies through which they pass, will prevail over many generations.

But what causes the river, or species, to divide into two branches? To quote Richard Dawkins:

> The details are controversial, but nobody doubts that the most important ingredient is *accidental geographical separation*.[14] (emphasis added)

As unlikely as it may seem, statistically, for a new species to occur, the fact is that there are today approximately 30 million separate species on Earth, and it is estimated that a further 3 billion species may have previously existed and died out.[15] One can only believe this in the context of a cataclysmic history of planet Earth – a view which is becoming increasingly common.[16] Today, however, it is impossible to pinpoint a single example of a species which has recently (within the last half a million years) improved by mutation or divided into two species.[17]

With the exception of viruses, evolution appears to be an incredibly slow process. Daniel Dennett recently suggested that a time scale of 100,000 years for the emergence of a new animal species would be regarded as 'sudden'.[18] At the other extreme, the humble horseshoe crab has remained virtually unchanged for 200 million years.[19] The consensus is that the normal rate of evolution is somewhere in the middle. The famous biologist Thomas Huxley, for example, stated that:

> Large changes [in species] occur over tens of millions of years, while really major ones [macro changes] take a hundred million years or so.[20]

And yet mankind is supposed to have benefited from not one, but several macromutations in the course of only six million years!

In the absence of fossil evidence, we are dealing with extremely theoretical matters. Nevertheless, modern science has managed, in a number of cases, to provide feasible explanations of how a step-by-step evolutionary process can produce what appears to be a perfect organ or organism. The most celebrated case is a computer-simulated evolution of the eye by Nilsson and Pelger. Starting with a simple photocell, which was allowed to undergo random mutations, Nilsson and Pelger's computer generated a feasible development to full camera eye, whereby a smooth gradient of change occurred with an improvement at each intermediate step.[21]

This idea of gradiented, or incremental, change is central to the modern view of evolution. The key point is that for a mutation to successfully spread through a population, each step will only be as perfect as it needs to be to give a survival edge. Richard Dawkins uses the example of cheetahs and antelopes to demonstrate how this genetic rivalry works; the cheetah seems perfectly designed to maximise deaths among antelopes, whilst the antelope seems equally well-designed to avoid death by cheetah.[22] The result is two species in equilibrium, where the weakest individuals die but both species survive. This principle was first put forward by Alfred Wallace when he stated that: 'nature never over-endows a species beyond the needs of everyday existence'.[23] It is the same situation as the trees in a dense forest, which have over a very long time maximised their height in competition for the light.

And so we return to the vexed question of the evolution of mankind himself, and we throw down the gauntlet to challenge Dawkins and Dennett in their own academic back yard. For, in the remainder of this chapter, we will see astonishing examples of how we have evolved way beyond the requirements of everyday existence and in the complete absence of an intellectual rival. According to the modern theories of gradiented change and natural selection, many aspects of *Homo sapiens* are therefore an evolutionary impossibility.

In Search of the Missing Link

According to the experts, the rivers of human genes and chimpanzee genes split from a common ancestral source some time between 5 and 7 million years ago,[24] whilst the river of gorilla genes is generally thought to have branched off slightly earlier. In order for this speciation to occur, three populations of common ape ancestors (the future gorillas, chimpanzees and hominids) had to become geographically separated and thereafter subject to genetic drift, influenced by their different environments. The search for the missing link is the search for the earliest hominid, the upright, bipedal ape who waved a long goodbye to his four-legged friends.

Many scholars have had great difficulty accepting that our closest relations are the chimpanzees, which are culturally so different from us. However, recent studies have shown that one particular species of pygmy chimpanzee, known as the bonobos, is remarkably human-like in character.[25] Unlike other apes, the bonobos often copulate face to face and their sex life is said to make Sodom and Gomorrah look like a vicar's tea party! It is thought that the bonobos and chimpanzee species split 3 million years ago, and it seems likely that our common ancestor with the apes may well have behaved more like the bonobos than the chimpanzee.

I will now attempt to briefly summarise what is known about human evolution.

The search for the missing link has turned up a number of fossil contenders, dating from around 4 million years ago, but the picture remains very incomplete, and the sample size is too small to draw any statistically valid conclusions. There are, however, three contenders for the prize of the first fully bipedal hominid, all discovered in the East African Rift valley which slashes through Ethiopia, Kenya and Tanzania.

The first contender, discovered in the Afar province of Ethiopia in 1974, is named Lucy, although her more scientific name is *Australopithecus Afarensis*.[26] Lucy is estimated to have lived between 3.6–3.2 million years ago. Unfortunately her skeleton was only 40 per cent complete and this has resulted in controversy regarding whether she was a true biped, and whether in fact she may even have been a he!

The second contender is *Australopithecus Ramidus*, a 4.4 million year old pygmy chimpanzee-like creature, discovered at Aramis in Ethiopia by Professor Timothy White in 1994. Despite a 70 per cent complete skeleton, it has again not been possible to prove categorically whether it had two or four legs.[27]

The third contender, dated between 4.1–3.9 million years old, is the *Australopithecus Anamensis*, discovered at Lake Turkana in Kenya by Dr Meave Leakey in August 1995. A shinbone from *Anamensis* has been used to back up the claim that it walked on two feet.

The evidence of our oldest ancestors is confusing, because they do not seem to be closely related to each other. *Anamensis*, for instance, does not seem to be related to *Ramidus*. The inexplicable lack of fossil evidence for the preceding 10 million years has made it impossible to confirm the exact separation date of these early hominids from the four-legged apes. It is also important to emphasise that many of these finds have skulls more like chimpanzees than men. They may be the first apes that walked, but as of 4 million years ago we are still a long way from anything that looked even remotely human.

Moving forward in time, we find evidence of several types of early man, which are equally confusing. We have the 1.8 million year old, appropriately named, *Robustus*, the 2.5 million year old, more lightly built, *Africanus*, and the 1.5 to 2 million year old *Advanced Australopithecus*. The latter, as the name suggests, is more man-like than the others, and is sometimes referred to as 'near-man' or *Homo habilis* ('handy man'). It is generally agreed that *Homo habilis* was the first truly man-like being, which could walk efficiently and use very rough stone tools. The fossil evidence does not reveal whether rudimentary speech had developed at this stage.

Around 1.5 million years ago *Homo erectus* appeared on the scene. This hominid had a considerably larger brain-box (cranium) than its predecessors, and started to design and use more sophisticated stone tools. A wide spread of fossils indicates that *Homo erectus* groups left Africa and spread across China, Australasia and Europe between 1,000,000–700,000 years ago, but for unknown reasons disappeared altogether around 300,000–200,000 years ago. There is little doubt, by a process of elimination, that this is the line from which *Homo sapiens* descended.

The missing link, however, remains a mystery. In 1995, *The Sunday Times* summarised the evolutionary evidence as follows:

> The scientists themselves are confused. A series of recent discoveries has forced them to tear up the simplistic charts on which they blithely used to draw linkages . . . the classic family tree delineating man's descent from the apes, familiar to us at school, has given way to the concept of genetic islands. The bridgework between them is anyone's guess.[28]

As to the various contenders speculated as mankind's ancestor, *The Sunday Times* stated:

> Their relationships to one another remain clouded in mystery and nobody has conclusively identified any of them as the early hominid that gave rise to *Homo sapiens*.

The race to find the missing link continues. Rival anthropologists have raised millions of dollars to fund their searches. With stakes as high as this, there is no doubt that some major breakthroughs will have to be announced. And yet we should retain our sense of perspective. As one commentator has pointed out, there is no guarantee that any of these fossil discoveries actually left any descendants.[29] The evidence is so sparse that a few more sensational finds will still leave the scientists clutching at straws. Mankind's evolutionary history will remain shrouded in mystery. Only one thing is clear: the fossils spanning the period from 6 million to 1 million years ago prove that the wheels of evolution turn very, very slowly indeed.

The Miracle of Man

Why has *Homo sapiens* developed intelligence and self-awareness whilst his ape cousins have spent the last 6 million years in evolutionary stagnation? Why has no other creature in the animal kingdom developed an advanced level of intelligence?

The conventional answer is that we stood up, thereby releasing our two arms, and began to use tools. This breakthrough accelerated our learning through a 'feedback' system, which stimulated mental development.

The latest scientific research does confirm that electro-chemical processes in the brain can sometimes stimulate the growth of dendrites, the tiny signal receptors which attach to the neurons (nerve cells). Experiments with caged rats have shown greater brain mass developing where the cages are full of toys rather than empty.[30]

But is this answer too simple? The kangaroo, for instance, is extremely dexterous and could have used tools, but never did, whilst the animal kingdom is full of species which do use tools but have never become intelligent. Here are some examples. The Egyptian vulture throws stones at ostrich eggs to crack their tough shells. The woodpecker finch in the Galapagos Islands uses twigs or cactus spines in up to five different ways to root out wood-boring insects from rotten trees. The sea otter on the Pacific coast of North America uses a stone as a hammer to dislodge its favourite food, the abalone shellfish, and uses another stone as an anvil to smash open the shellfish.[31]

These are examples of simple tool use, but there is no sign of it leading anywhere. Our nearest relatives, the chimpanzees, also make and use simple tools,[32] but can you really see them evolving intelligence at our level? Why did we become intelligent whilst the chimpanzees did not?

Could our upright posture have made a telling difference? Anthropologists generally agree that one group of apes must have left their forest-dwelling cousins for the open savanna, possibly due to climatic change. There, the direct heat of the Sun favoured genetic mutations which better enabled these apes to stand up and protect their brain from the higher temperatures at ground level.[33] The vulnerability of these new hominids in the open savanna might then have led to the favouring of random mutations in the brain which increased the chances of survival by stealth.

The new upright posture may also have led to physical changes in the evolution of the brain. Advocates of the 'cranial radiator' theory, such as Professor Dean Falk, claim that fossilised remains show an enlarged occipital marginal sinus system and, in addition, tiny holes in the skull known as emissary foramina which allow blood vessels to penetrate the skull and enter the brain.[34] It is thought that these changes may have somehow accelerated the evolution of intelligence.

But these changes would not have happened overnight. It is unlikely that a group of apes suddenly became totally bipedal, for the simple reason that to do so would have made them less agile and more vulnerable to predators. As one wag suggested, if you put a hungry lion, a human, a chimpanzee, a baboon and a dog in a large cage, it is obvious that the human will get eaten first.[35]

What does the fossil record tell us about our evolving brain capabilities? Unfortunately the fossil record is not only sparse, but only tells us one half of the story. It is commonly assumed that a bigger skull implies greater cranial capacity and hence a bigger and better brain. This may be generally true, but size is not everything. After all, compare the intelligence of an elephant's 11 lb brain with our own 3 lb brain. Size alone misses the point that improvements can come from better wiring. A good analogy is the computer, which has been given vastly improved functionality, largely from better software. Unfortunately, our 'software' is the brain tissue, and it does not hang around to be studied by palaeoanthropologists.

What would we expect to see in the evolution of cranial capacity? According to the evolutionists, the development of our brain would have involved gradiented change, that is improvement via an extremely large number of very small steps. Natural selection would have favoured only those genes which produced an improvement in neural output which gave a useful survival edge. Would we therefore see incremental changes in *size and efficiency* going hand in hand, or would the efficiency increase first until it reached a capacity constraint? The latter might seem logical, but natural selection involves random genetic mutation and does not always achieve its ends via the most direct route. Irrespective of the route taken, we would expect a very slow increase in brain size and thus cranial capacity.

Now let us review the fossil evidence on cranial capacity. The data varies considerably and must be treated with care (since the sample sizes are limited), but the following is a rough guide. The early hominid *Afarensis* had around 500cc and *Habilis/Australopithecus* had around 700cc. Whilst it is by no means certain that one evolved from the other, it is possible to see in these figures the evolutionary effects over two million years of the hominid's new environment.

As we move forward in time to 1.5 million years ago, we find a sudden leap in the cranial capacity of *Homo erectus* to around 900–1000cc. If we assume, as most anthropologists do, that this was accompanied by an increase in intelligence, it represents a most unlikely macromutation. Alternatively, we might explain this anomaly by viewing *erectus* as a separate species whose ancestors have not yet been found, due to the poor fossil records.

Finally, after surviving 1.2 to 1.3 million years without any apparent change, and having successfully spread out of Africa to China, Australia and Europe, something extraordinary happened to the *Homo erectus* hominid. Perhaps due to climatic changes, his population began to dwindle, until he eventually died out. And yet, while most *Homo erectus* were dying, one managed to suddenly transform itself into *Homo sapiens*, with a vast increase in cranial capacity from 950cc to 1450cc. It is widely accepted that we are the descendants of *Homo erectus* (who else was there to descend from?) but the sudden changeover defies all known laws of evolution.

Human evolution thus appears like an hourglass, with a narrowing population of *Homo erectus* leading to possibly one single mutant, whose improved genes emerged into a new era of unprecedented progress. The transformation from failure to success is startling. Whilst Darwinists may well identify here the requisite small, isolated population, it nevertheless stretches the imagination to believe that our ancestor was a 'Clark Kent Super-Erectus' that suddenly expanded his brain size by 50 per cent!

In my view, the palaeoanthropologists are concentrating their search for the missing link in the wrong time frame. We constantly read about the search for our oldest ape ancestor, but it is the Super-Erectus missing link that is much more intriguing.

Against All Odds

Back in 1954, it was thought that the hominid leading to mankind split from the apes 30 million years ago, and that we had evolved gradually into our present form.[36] That period sets an unbiased benchmark of how long evolution possibly should have taken. Following the discovery that the split occurred only 6 million years ago, evolutionists have been forced to assume a much faster rate of evolution to explain our existence.

The other disconcerting discovery since 1954 is the shockingly slow evolutionary progress made by *Homo erectus* and his predecessors up to around 200,000 years ago. The evolutionary graph has thus changed from a nice straight line into an overnight explosion (Illustration 2).

Anthropologists have continually attempted to demonstrate a gradiented evolution from *Homo erectus* to *Homo sapiens*, albeit with sharp upward steps. However, their attempts to force the data to meet their preconceptions have been repeatedly exposed by new data.

Illustration 2: Evolution of Homo Sapiens

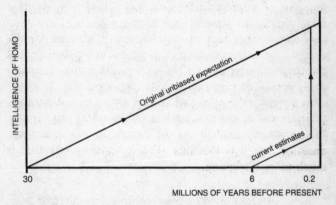

For example, it was originally believed that anatomically modern *Homo sapiens* (Cro-Magnon man)[37] appeared only 35,000 years ago, and had thus descended from Neanderthal who had died out at the same time.[38] At that time, one of the most dramatic events in human history appears to have occurred. Cro-Magnon man suddenly arrived in Europe, building shelters, organising himself in clans, wearing skins for clothing, and designing special tools and weapons using wood and bones. It is to this phase of *Homo sapiens* that we attribute the magnificent cave art such as that at Lascaux, France, dated to 27,000 years ago.[39]

But it is now accepted that, despite the behavioural differences, the European Cro-Magnons were no different anatomically from the *Homo sapiens* found in the Middle East 100,000 years ago. Both would be virtually indistinguishable from the population today if dressed in modern clothes. It is also clear that *Homo sapiens* did not descend from Neanderthal as was previously thought. Several recent discoveries in Israel have confirmed beyond any doubt that *Homo sapiens* co-existed with Neanderthal between 100–90,000 years ago.[40]

What then is our relationship to Neanderthal? We are used to seeing artists' impressions based on his known characteristics of clumsy limbs and crude features, but everything else, such as the liberal body hair, is pure supposition, designed to give us the impression of an evolutionary continuum. Recent discoveries have led to a major reappraisal of Neanderthal. In particular, a 60,000 year old Neanderthal's remains were found at Kebara Cave, Mount Carmel in Israel, with an intact hyoid bone, virtually identical to our present-day hyoid.[41] Since this bone makes human speech possible, the scientists were forced to conclude that Neanderthal had the capability to speak. And many scientists regard speech as the key to mankind's great leap forward.

Most anthropologists now recognise Neanderthal as a fully fledged *Homo sapiens*, who for a long time was behaviourally equivalent with other *Homo sapiens*. It is quite possible that Neanderthal was as intelligent and human-like as we are today. It has been suggested that his large and crude skull features may have simply been a genetic disorder similar to that of acromelagy. Such disorders are quickly spread in small, isolated populations due to the effects of inbreeding.[42]

As a result of the conclusive dating of contemporary Neanderthal and *Homo sapiens* remains, a new theory has emerged suggesting that both must have stemmed from an earlier 'archaic' *Homo sapiens*. Several fossils have been found of this so-called archaic species, which combine different aspects of primitive *erectus* and modern human anatomy. It is commonly cited, in the popular press, that these archaics emerged around 300,000 years ago, but once again this is pure supposition, based on a small sample size, preconceptions and guesswork. What are the real facts?

In 1989, an advanced seminar was held on *The Origins of Modern Human Adaptations*, dealing specifically with the archaic-modern interface. Summarising the results of the discussions, Erik Trinkhaus reported that:

> The key point of agreement in the course of the seminar was that sometime during the later Pleistocene [the last 1 million years], in a *relatively brief period* of transition, there was a transformation from archaic to modern humans – a transformation manifested in both culture and biology . . . the transformation from archaic to modern human witnessed not only the reorganisation of the brain and body and a shift in stone working from a simple, expedient technology to a complex and elegant craft, but also the first appearance of true art and symbolism and the blossoming of formal systems of language.[43] (emphasis added)

Erik Trinkhaus stated that the primary issue of the seminar was the distinction between late archaic and early modern humans, but on the timing of the transformation he had this to say:

> . . . our control of fine chronology is inadequate for periods prior to the finite limits of radiocarbon dating (*c.* 35,000 years BP) and from there back through most of the Middle Pleistocene.

A further seminar in 1992 also focused on the question of the transition from archaic to modern.[44] One of the papers presented included the following comment:

> The timescale of this transition lies beyond the dating range of C14 and therefore has necessitated the employment of a battery of new dating techniques.[45]

The various papers presented at the seminar were published by Aitken, Stringer and Mellars in 1993, and focused particularly on improved chronological dating methods. Significant progress was reported in a diverse range of new dating technologies – uranium-series dating, luminescence dating (thermal or optical) and electron spin resonance (ESR) – but each suffered various limitations in different circumstances. Nevertheless, many reliable datings, based on these methods (rather than radiocarbon, C14) were presented. Significantly, it was reported that all of the fossils of the archaics were poorly dated and could not be vouched by any of the new technologies.[46]

As for the moderns, the earliest definitive and reliable date was cited as 120–110,000 years Before Present (BP), at Qafzeh in Israel. None of the other dates, published by this esteemed group of scientists, was earlier than 200,000 years BP. The date of the emergence of the moderns could only be guessed at within a huge range from 500–200,000 years BP.

That is the true state of scientific knowledge on the subject. There is no proof that an archaic *Homo sapiens* existed 300,000 years ago, and no proof that Neanderthal dates back to 230,000 years ago.[47] The fact of the matter is that *Homo sapiens* fossils suddenly appear within the last 200,000 years, without any clear record of their origins. The *Atlas of Ancient Archaeology* sums up the situation as follows:

The contemporary history of *Homo sapiens (sapiens)* remains baffingly obscure . . . so little do we know about the approach to one of the great turning points of our global history.[48]

Meanwhile, Roger Lewin, writing in 1984, stated:

The origin of fully modern humans denoted by the subspecies name *Homo sapiens (sapiens)* remains one of the great puzzles of palaeoanthropology.[49]

The appearance of *Homo sapiens* is more than a baffling puzzle – it is statistically close to impossible. After millions of years of negligible progress with stone tools, *Homo sapiens* suddenly emerged *c.* 200,000 years ago with a 50 per cent larger cranial capacity, together with the capability for speech and a fairly modern anatomy. For unexplained reasons, he then continued to live primitively, using stone tools for another 160,000 years. Then, 40,000 years ago, he appeared to undergo what we might call a transition to modern behaviour. Having swept northwards, he expanded through most of the globe by 13,000 years ago. After another 1,000 years he discovered agriculture, 6,000 years later he formed great civilisations with advanced astronomical knowledge (see chapters 5 and 6), and here we are after another 6,000 years probing the depths of the Solar System.

The above scenario seems utterly implausible and flies in the face of our whole understanding of evolutionary theory as a slow and gradual process. Common sense would suggest at least another million years for *Homo sapiens* to develop from stone tools to using other materials, and perhaps a hundred million years to master mathematics, engineering and astronomy.

A Brain Teaser for Darwin

Earlier I pointed out that size is not everything, when it comes to brains. Nevertheless, size is clearly an advantage when combined with a high level of operational efficiency. A four litre BMW is always going to outpace a two litre BMW unless the latter happens to be a later-generation, higher technology design. In this section we will see that *Homo sapiens* has the best of both worlds – a relatively large brain *and* a highly efficient design.

During the last ten years, scientists have used new imaging technologies (such as positron-emission tomography) to discover more about the human brain than ever before. The full extent of the complexity of its billions of cells has become more and more apparent. In addition to the brain's physical complexity, its performance knows no bounds – mathematics and art, abstract thought and conceptualisation and, above all, moral conscience and self-awareness. Whilst many of the human brain's secrets remain shrouded in mystery, enough has been revealed for *National Geographic* to boldly describe it as 'the most complex object in the known universe'.[50]

Evolutionists see the brain as nothing more than a set of algorithms, but they are forced to admit that it is so complex and unique that there is no chance of reverse engineering the evolutionary process that created it. For these reasons, the *philosophers* are tending to lead the field in formulating theories for the brain's evolution.

The theologians have also had a field day with the discovery that the human brain is such a complex and perfect organ. However, leaving aside the irrational arguments for its divine creation, how might we disprove the gradualist evolutionary theory? After all, we cannot make all of those early hominids sit an I.Q. test. And we cannot make judgements about their intelligence based simply on their behaviour, for it is quite possible to have an advanced level of intelligence without adopting the material culture that we recognise as civilisation today. Fortunately, we can rely on a strong dose of armchair logic, an approach which is sometimes used by the eminent Richard Dawkins himself.

The human brain at birth is approximately one quarter of its adult size. The need for a large skull to house the fully grown adult brain causes human babies to have extremely large heads at birth (relative to other primates). Passing the baby's head through the birth canal is therefore the major problem of childbirth, and causes acute pain to the mother.

To many biologists, gynaecologists and anatomists, it is a mystery why the female did not evolve a larger birth canal. The answer is simple – engineering. Such a change would have required a radical redesign in bone structure, an impossibility within the limits of a body which is designed for bipedal walking.[51] The birth canal is thus the limiting factor to man's cranial capacity.

If we cast our minds back several hundred thousand years, before hospitals and midwives existed, it is not difficult to imagine that a large number of infants were stillborn or their mothers killed in childbirth. It therefore seems extremely doubtful that natural selection would favour a gene for large brain size, with its potential harmful consequences to both mother and child. Simply put, such a gene would not have successfully spread.

It seems much more likely that natural selection would have deselected the large brain and would have stumbled instead upon a better neural networking system, or alternatively a means to switch skull growth from pre-birth to post-birth. The fact that it did not, and the fact that the wiring of the brain also seems highly efficient in design, strongly indicates two essential evolutionary requirements. First, an incredibly long period, and secondly a pressing need to develop its optimum potential. Neither of these requirements is met by the established evolutionary circumstances.

Modern evolutionists agree that natural selection should only bestow as much of a new and better physical trend as is needed for survival. The cheetah and antelope which I mentioned earlier are typical of Richard Dawkins' world, where progress comes from a constructive tension between species – a critical balance between survival and extinction. According to this scenario, the genes which make good brains are favoured by natural selection only because they are critical to survival

Richard Dawkins illustrates his point with a story of how the motor car magnate Henry Ford instructed his staff to survey the scrapyards and find out which components of the 'Model T' did not wear out. As a result, the kingpins were re-engineered to a lower standard. According to Dawkins, the same principle applies to evolution by natural selection. It is worth quoting Dawkins in full, for we will turn this argument back against him:

> It is possible for a component of an animal to be too good, and we should expect natural selection to favor a lessening of quality up to, but not beyond, a point of balance with the qualities of the other components of the body.[52]

Here then is the evolutionary crunch. As efficient as the brain is, the average human being does not use it to anywhere near its full capacity. How then can Dawkins explain the massive *over-engineering* of the human brain? What useful survival skills did music and mathematical ability give to our hunter ancestors?

The evolutionists would argue that the algorithms of the brain did not evolve *for* music and mathematics, but were 'exapted' from developments for other purposes. No-one, however, can suggest what these other purposes might have been, that led to such a highly evolved mental *capability*.

Charles Darwin's partner, Alfred Wallace, clearly recognised the contradiction when he wrote:

> An instrument [the human brain] has been developed in advance of the needs of its possessor.

If we go back one million years to a time when man was fighting for survival, how can Richard Dawkins explain how evolution seems to have favoured non-essential abilities in art, music and mathematics? Why did the brain, which must have been at least partly evolved already, not benefit from *any* types of useful survival skills such as enhanced smell, infra-red vision, improved hearing and so on? The theory of evolution is supposed to explain *everything*, but it clearly does not explain the human brain. It is for this reason that some highly esteemed modern scientists have begun to search for a different mechanism to natural selection.[53] Alfred Wallace was the first to open this debate when he aired his suspicion that another factor, 'some unknown spiritual element', was needed to account for man's unusual artistic and scientific abilities.

The final nail in the evolutionists' coffin is this: where was the competitor that caused the brain of *Homo sapiens* to evolve to such an *extreme* level of size and complexity? What rival caused intellectual ability to be such an essential survival development? Who were we trying to outsmart?

Could inter-species competition be the explanation? In modern times our most significant achievements, space travel and nuclear weapons for example, have come from superpower competition. Did primitive men split into competitive, rival groups? Could Neanderthal have been a competitive threat to his fellow *Homo sapiens*? On the contrary, the evidence suggests that Neanderthal and Cro-Magnon peacefully co-existed. Discoveries at the cave of St Cesaire in France indicate that they lived in close proximity for thousands of years without fighting. Furthermore, early hominids continued to use simple stone tools for millions of years up to about 200,000 years ago – there is no sign of any escalation in tool use caused by an inter-species conflict. In the absence of an intellectual rival that fits the time frame, the evolutionary scenario for the human brain remains completely implausible.

Language Barriers

Many scientists believe that language is the key to mankind's great leap forward, since it uniquely enables us to communicate and transfer ideas and experiences from one generation to the next.[54] Until recently, this leap forward was associated with the behavioural changes which swept Europe around 40,000 years ago. Then, in 1983, came the shocking discovery of the 60,000 year old Neanderthal hyoid bone, mentioned earlier, which proved that Neanderthal could talk.

The origin of human language capability remains a controversial subject, and raises more questions than answers. Daniel Dennett sums up the state of confusion:

> . . . work by neuroanatomists and psycholinguists has shown that our brains have features lacking in the brains of our closest surviving relatives, features that play crucial roles in language perception and language production. There is a wide diversity of opinion about when in the last six million years or so our lineage acquired these traits, in what order and why.[55]

Most scientists now believe that *Homo sapiens* had speech from their very beginning. Studies of human mitochondrial DNA (mtDNA) suggest that, since speech is widespread today, it must have developed from a genetic mutation in 'mitochondrial Eve' (mtDNA Eve), 200,000 years ago (see chapter 11).

The pioneering work of Noam Chomsky has shown that newborn babies genetically inherit an innate and highly advanced language structure. According to Chomsky's recently-developed and widely-acclaimed theory of universal grammar, the child is able to subconsciously flick a few simple switches in order to comprehend and speak the language of its parents, wherever in the world it happens to be born. It is highly significant that Chomsky, the leading world expert in the science of linguistics, cannot see how the human language acquisition system *could possibly have evolved by natural selection.*[56]

One of the foremost evolutionists, Stephen Jay Gould, acknowledges the difficulties with the evolution of language by effectively admitting that it was a freak or chance development:

> The universals of language are so different from anything else in nature, and so quirky in their structure, that origin as a *side consequence* of the brain's enhanced capacity, rather than as a simple advance in continuity from ancestral grunts and gestures, seems indicated.[57] (emphasis added)

Why *did* man acquire such a sophisticated language capability? According to Darwinian theory, a few simple grunts would have sufficed for everyday existence, and yet here we are with more than 26 alphabet sounds and an average vocabulary of 25,000 words.

Moreover, speech capability was not such an easy or obvious target for natural selection. The human ability to talk resides in both the shape and structure of the mouth and throat, as well as in the brain. In adult humans the larynx (voicebox) is situated much lower than in other mammals, and the epiglottis (the flap of cartilage at the root of the tongue) is incapable of reaching the top of the roof of the mouth. Thus we cannot breathe and swallow at the same time, and are uniquely at risk from choking.[58]

This unique combination of features can have only one purpose – to make human speech possible. In all other respects it is an evolutionary disadvantage. Apart from the risk of choking, it causes our teeth to become crowded, so that, prior to the advent of antibiotics, septic impacted molars would often have proved fatal. Just as it is difficult to reverse-engineer the development of the brain and its language acquisition capability, so it is also difficult to reverse-engineer the development of speech capability.

Once again, we come back to the mystery of the human brain. We are expected to believe that, within a mere 6 million years, natural selection has caused our brains to expand to the physical limits of the birth canal. That is quite an evolutionary pace. And, at the same time, the brain has acquired an incredibly efficient design with capabilities that are light years away from our needs for everyday existence. In the words of Arthur Koestler:

> The neocortex of the hominids evolved in the last half a million years . . . at an explosive speed, which so far as we know is unprecedented.[59]

And here is the biggest mystery of all. We are not supposed to have become intelligent overnight, and evolution is supposed to be very slow. Therefore, if we go back one or two million years we should find a semi-intelligent being, using his newly-found abilities to experiment with primitive writing, basic art, and simple multiplication. But there is nothing. Without exception, all of the evidence shows that man continued to use the most basic stone tools for 6 million years, despite his increasing cranial capacity. This is very strange and highly contradictory. We deserve a better explanation.

A Sexual Revolution

I would like to round up my review of man, the evolutionary misfit, by focusing on some more mysteries and impossible time scales.

First of all, there is the mystery of the missing hair. Some anthropologists claim that we remain covered in tiny hairs, but such claims miss the point entirely. In his detailed study, *The Naked Ape*, Desmond Morris highlighted this strange anomaly:

> Functionally, we are stark naked and our skin is fully exposed to the outside world. This state of affairs still has to be explained, regardless of how many tiny hairs we can count under a magnifying lens.[60]

Desmond Morris contrasted *Homo sapiens* with 4,237 species of mammals, the vast majority of which were hairy or partly haired. The only non-hairy species were those which lived underground (and thus kept warm without hair), species which were aquatic (and benefited from streamlining), and armoured species such as the armadillo (where hair would clearly be superfluous). Morris commented:

> The naked ape [man] stands alone, marked off by his nudity from all the thousands of hairy, shaggy or furry land-dwelling mammalian species . . . if the hair has to go, then clearly there must be a powerful reason for abolishing it.[61]

Darwinism has yet to produce a satisfactory answer as to how and why man lost his hair. Many imaginative theories have been suggested, but so far no-one has come up with a really acceptable explanation. The one conclusion that can perhaps be drawn, based on the principle of gradiented change, is that man spent a long time evolving, either in water[62] or in a very hot environment.

Another unique feature of mankind may provide us with a clue to the loss of body hair. That feature is sexuality. The subject was covered in juicy detail by Desmond Morris, who highlighted unique human features such as extended foreplay, extended copulation and the orgasm.[63] One particular anomaly is that the human female is always 'in heat', yet she can only conceive for a few days each month. As Jared Diamond has pointed out, this is an evolutionary enigma that cannot be explained by natural selection:

> The most hotly debated problem in the evolution of human reproduction is to explain why we nevertheless ended up with concealed ovulation, and what good all our mistimed copulations do us.[64]

Many scientists have also commented on the anomaly of the male penis, which is by far the largest erect penis of any living primate. The geneticist Steve Jones has noted it as a mystery which is 'unanswered by science',[65] a point which is echoed by Jared Diamond:

> . . . we descend to a glaring failure: the inability of twentieth-century science to formulate an adequate Theory of Penis Length . . . astonishing as it seems, important functions of the human penis remain obscure.[66]

Desmond Morris described man as 'the sexiest primate alive', but why did evolution grant us such a bountiful gift? The whole human body seems to be perfectly designed for sexual excitement and pair bonding. Morris saw elements of this plan in the enlarged breasts of the female, the sensitive ear lobes and lips, and a vaginal angle that encouraged intimate face to face copulation.[67] He also highlighted our abundance of scent-producing glands, our unique facial mobility and our unique ability to produce copious tears – all features which strengthen the exclusive emotional pair-bonding between male and female.

This grand design could not be imagined unless humans also lost their shaggy coat of hair, and so it might seem that the mystery of the missing hair is solved. Unfortunately, it is not that simple, for evolution does not set about achieving grand designs. The Darwinists are strangely silent on what incremental steps were involved, but however it happened, it should have taken a long, long time.

Nobody has adequately explained the steps by which all of these major changes were achieved in a short time frame of only 6 million years. Instead of a long sexual evolution, we appear to have undergone an overnight sexual *revolution*, in total defiance of the laws of Darwinism.

There are three other interesting anomalies which are also worthy of note. The first is the appalling ineptitude of the human skin to repair itself.[68] In the context of a move to the open savanna, where bipedal man became a vulnerable target, and in the context of a gradual loss of protective hair, it seems inconceivable that the human skin should have become so fragile relative to our primate cousins.

The second anomaly is the unique lack of penis bone in the male. This is in complete contrast to other mammals, which use the penis bone to copulate at short notice. The deselection of this vital bone would have jeopardised the existence of the human species unless it took place against the background of a long and peaceful environment.

The third anomaly is our eating habits. Whereas most animals will swallow their food instantaneously, we take the luxury of six whole seconds to transport our food from mouth to stomach. This again suggests a long period of peaceful evolution.

The question which arises is *where* this long and peaceful evolution is supposed to have taken place, because it certainly does not fit the scenario currently being presented for *Homo sapiens*.

Genetic Engineering

Let us now examine the alternative to mankind's impossible evolution. Could we have been genetically created by the gods 'in their own image'?

The texts cited in chapter 1 do indeed suggest that a physical operation was carried out, as a result of which Adam's DNA was used to create Eve. Furthermore, the texts suggest that humans were then mass-produced by a process which we would today recognise as cloning. As for the first 'Adam', the evidence suggests that he was a hybrid mixture of god and *Homo erectus*. If this seems too unbelievable, let us stop for a moment, and reflect upon the science of genetics. It is an area which will crop up again and again in later chapters.

The gene is essentially a packet of chemical information consisting of DNA. It is now understood that the characteristics of a species are determined by the 4-letter DNA alphabet or 'bases' of A, G, C and T,[69] arranged in words of 3 letters, giving 64 possible words. These words mostly encode amino acids, which join together to form proteins, the building blocks of the body. In recent years, scientists have begun to 'read' these 'letters' and 'words' of the genetic code, thus isolating many genes and identifying their specific instructions.

The human genome comprises all of the genes on our 23 pairs of chromosomes. It is estimated that there are 3 billion chemical 'letters' in the entire human genome, representing data equivalent to a billion-page telephone directory. Scientists have referred to it as 'our inherited genetic message' or 'the biological recipe for man'. A commonly quoted statistic is that the DNA in each cell, unravelled, would stretch 6 feet, and that the DNA in the entire human body would stretch to the Moon and back 8,000 times.

Since Watson and Crick's discovery of DNA in 1953, discoveries in the field of genetics have flown thick and fast. Two major breakthroughs occurred in 1980, and were rewarded with the Nobel Prize in Chemistry. Walter Gilbert of Harvard and Frederick Sanger of Cambridge University jointly developed rapid methods for reading large segments of DNA, whilst Paul Berg of Stanford University pioneered the process of gene splicing.

How might flesh-and-blood gods have used genetics to physically intervene in mankind's creation? Let us briefly review the three main lines of applied genetic science, which have been discovered in the last twenty years: cloning, gene splicing and cell fusion.

Cloning of human beings has been a scientific possibility for many years, although for ethical reasons the practice has been confined to animals. The process would work by first removing the single set of 23 chromosomes from the female ovum.[70] The ovum could then be implanted with the complete set of 46 chromosomes from any human cell. This would lead to the conception and birth of a predetermined individual, an exact replica of the source of the unsplit set of chromosomes. An alternative to the removal of the female chromosomes is to deactivate the nucleus of the ovum either chemically or by radiation.

Gene splicing, also known as recombinant DNA technology, can take the form of inserting a new gene in, or removing an undesirable gene from, a DNA strand. The process involves the use of enzymes to allow DNA strands to be cut in the desired places, and then to either remove a 'sentence' that makes up a gene, or to insert a 'foreign' gene; afterwards the DNA is recombined. An example of gene splicing is the 'Mighty Mouse', created by researchers at the universities of Washington and Pennsylvania in 1982 by inserting the growth gene from a rat into a mouse; the mouse then grew to twice its normal size. Many 'improved' plant species have been designed in this way to resist disease, including the infamous example of the unrottable tomato. More recently we have seen the 'Super Salmon' from Swedish scientists, whilst future developments may even include the self-shearing sheep!

Whilst gene splicing attempts to enhance a selected aspect without changing the species, cell fusion even more controversially involves the creation of a new hybrid species. The process works by fusing cells from two different sources into a 'supercell', comprising two nuclei and a double set of the paired chromosomes. When this cell splits, a garbled mixture results. For example, in 1983 scientists combined a sheep and a goat (which cannot naturally mate), creating a 'geep' with a woolly coat and goat's horns. So far, it has not proved possible to predetermine the result of fusion, so the outcome of these experiments is an unpredictable chimera.

In 1989, the Human Genome Project was officially launched in the USA to co-ordinate international research at a cost of $3 billion. The aim of this international project is to track down, analyse and record the 3 billion chemical 'letters' of the human genome, and to map our 100,000 genes to specific regions on our chromosomes. In December 1993, a 'physical map of the human genome' was published by the Centre d'Etude du Polymorphisme Humain (Ceph) in Paris, representing a major landmark in this research. By making its map available internationally on the Internet, Ceph believe that it will enable gene hunters to move ten times faster in future, with a real prospect of deciphering all 3 billion chemical letters of the human genetic code early in the 21st century. Dr Daniel Cohen, director of Ceph, stated:

> Before today, a physical map existed for only 2 per cent of the human genome; our map covers about 90 per cent.[71]

When this research has been completed, mankind may have the power to create in his own image, in his own likeness. At that time, if we were to find a species on another planet which happened to have a similar DNA to ourselves, we could cross-breed with them, and select whatever traits we wanted to include, or indeed exclude. That species might well call us 'gods'.

One hundred years ago, it would have been science fiction to suggest that mankind could have been genetically engineered as a hybrid being and then cloned. It would also have been scandalous to suggest that the Biblical Elohim had actually resorted to such physical means. Today, such suggestions are scientifically valid and perfectly plausible. The question is, are we simply *re*discovering a technology that was used 200,000 years ago?

Chapter Two Conclusions

* *Homo sapiens* suddenly appeared around 200,000 years ago, with a 50 per cent increase in brain size, together with language capability and a modern anatomy. According to the theory of natural selection, this is statistically near-impossible.

* Human DNA shows signs of having passed through an extremely long and relatively peaceful evolution. This is inconsistent with an evolutionary split from the apes a mere 6 million years ago.

* The evolutionary anomalies within man are entirely consistent with the idea of a focused genetic intervention by flesh-and-blood gods.

* According to the ancient texts, the first Adam was a test-tube baby, created by the gods from already living matter. Adam's DNA (not his rib) was used to create the first woman. Humans were then cloned to ease the 'toil' of the gods.

CHAPTER THREE

SIGNS OF THE GODS

A Tour of the Evidence

According to the accepted history of mankind, we should not find examples of twentieth century technology being used thousands of years ago. And yet examples of this technology can be seen at sites all around the world, defying conventional scientific explanation. The fact that physical evidence of such technology does exist is highly disturbing and lends support to the idea that an advanced race of flesh-and-blood gods could have created us 'in their own image'.

This chapter covers a selection of sites which represent historical anomalies, based on my personal travels over the past few years. Many readers will already be familiar with places such as Tiwanaku and Nazca, whilst other readers will be totally unfamiliar. I will therefore attempt to strike a balance by keeping things reasonably brief, covering the essentials but also offering some fresh insights. As those who have visited these places will appreciate, there is no substitute for being there. Indeed, I cannot count the times that I have been surprised to find things to be quite different from how I had imagined them to be.

I am also including in this chapter some rather less familiar locations. Chavin de Huantar, for instance, is interesting for its original, highly advanced underground aqueduct systems, and I will be drawing a fascinating parallel between these and the waterworks of Tiwanaku.

Another little known site is that of Baalbek in Lebanon. As a result of war and terrorism, Baalbek has been a 'no go' area for more than twenty years. However, in May 1995, I finally managed to visit the Temple of Jupiter at Baalbek, and I am delighted to be able to share my first-hand impressions of the amazing 800-ton stones which have been miraculously transported and positioned in one of its foundation walls. The difficulties of performing these manoeuvres, even with twentieth century technology, are most enlightening.

Some of the sites not covered in this chapter are dealt with elsewhere. The pyramids of Giza, for instance, warrant a whole chapter in their own right (chapter 4), whilst the ancient astronomical observatory of Stonehenge is covered in chapter 5. A full discussion of the astronomical aspects of Tiwanaku and Machu Picchu is also held over until chapter 5.

In the pages which follow, I will be aiming to demonstrate a common pattern of anomalous technology in the pre-history of mankind.[1] In particular, I will be examining the weaknesses of the current scientific explanations for these anomalies, where such theories exist at all. In some locations, such as Nazca, we find a wide divergence of scientific opinion, which amounts to little more than a confession of ignorance. In most of the other locations, however, there is a complete void of scientific opinion, and a tendency to blatantly ignore crucial evidence. Puma Punku is a classic example of this approach, its precision-cut stones generally being excluded from the archaeologists' reports on the associated site of Tiwanaku.

One of the most frustrating areas of ancient technology is that of construction methodology. Almost every engineer has a theory on how his ancient precursors might have carved and erected huge precision-cut stones, but few such engineers have been brave enough to roll their sleeves up and put their theories to the test. On the few occasions where the experts *have* dared to venture forth into the field, the results have been dismal. For example, one of the most prominent Egyptologists, Mark Lehner, recently led a team which attempted to erect an Egyptian obelisk using ancient tools and materials.[2] The team had great difficulty explaining how the obelisk was transported up the Nile, since loading it onto a boat seemed to be physically impossible. The same team then had a dreadful struggle to erect an obelisk which was only one tenth the size and weight of the genuine article!

Mark Lehner belongs to a group of experts who believe that the ancient stonemasons worked granite (one of the hardest types of natural stone) by constantly pounding it with other, smaller stones. These experts typically demonstrate how the pounding technique can, after a few hours of effort, produce small indentations in the granite. They then claim this as proof that the pounding method does actually work. Unfortunately, not one of these experts has ever carried such a job through to completion, in order to show us how the stonemasons achieved perfect edges, especially the 'inner edges' of holes which are excavated into the face of the stone. In this chapter, we will see several amazing examples of such stonework, which could not possibly have been produced by the simple stone or copper tools which the ancient people supposedly used.

It is not my intention to speculate on exactly what kind of advanced technology was used to cut these stones, nor to answer the question of how they were moved over 'impossible' distances and gradients. We may never know. The question which I personally find more pertinent, and equally fascinating, is 'why did they do it?'. It is at this point that conventional scientists and historians attempt to distract us from their lack of understanding by vaguely referring to primitive religious beliefs. Some of the most curious anomalies in the world are thus conveniently labelled as temples, altars and ritual baths, when in fact their original purpose and function are totally obscure.

Unless we can understand the significance of an object, the question of 'why was it made?' will get us nowhere. For instance, asking why someone built a Stonehenge *temple* is a very different question from asking why someone built a Stonehenge *astronomical observatory*. It is therefore essential for us to cast off the religious interpretations and examine ancient objects with an open mind.

Nevertheless, the significance of some objects is sufficiently clear to frame the relevant questions. Among the questions which I will be asking are: why were 800-ton stones used in a wall at Baalbek when smaller stones would have been quite adequate; why were sophisticated waterworks so important to the original designers of Tiwanaku and Chavin? And why were the figures at Nazca designed only for viewing from the air?

Inevitably, I cannot avoid dropping a few immediate hints towards my answers to the above questions. However, readers must appreciate that a complete solution requires a fundamentally different frame of reference, which will be gradually introduced in the chapters which follow. In due course, and at the appropriate time, I will revisit nearly all of the sites in this chapter, to confirm their chronologies and to offer my explanations of their functions or meaning. In the meantime, I invite you to share my preliminary thoughts on our mysterious past.

Baalbek

The imposing ruins of Baalbek in Lebanon are situated in the fertile Bekaa valley at the foot of the Anti-Lebanon mountains, 53 miles north-east of Beirut. Baalbek was once one of the world's most sacred sites, and its temples one of the wonders of the ancient world. In modern times, however, Baalbek lies forgotten – wiped off the map by more than twenty years of warfare and terrorism. The site has become so neglected that some archaeology books omit any mention of it.

What a contrast from two thousand years ago, when Roman emperors would journey 1,500 miles to this remote location, to make offerings to their gods and receive oracles on the destiny of their empire. Indeed, it was here that the Romans built their grandest ever temples, crowned by the magnificent temple to their chief god, Jupiter. Only six pillars from that temple have survived the series of earthquakes which have laid the site to ruins, but these pillars, shown in Plate 1 (colour section), still form a spectacular sight today, rising to a commanding height of 66 feet. The size of this temple literally dwarfs the Parthenon of Athens.

However, as magnificent as the Temple of Jupiter certainly is, it stands on a pre-Roman terrace of colossal stones which is even more impressive. At the bottom of Plate 1 can be seen a row of nine blocks in the south-east wall of the terrace, each measuring approximately 33 by 14 by 10 feet, and thus weighing more than 300 tons apiece. At the same level in the adjoining south-western wall, we find six further 300-ton stones, above which are situated three enormous megalithic blocks, referred to as 'the Trilithon' or the 'Marvel of the Three Stones'. Plate 2 shows the three granite blocks of the Trilithon (the light coloured course), forming the sixth visible layer of the wall. Each of these stones measures an amazing 64 feet in length (on average), with a height of 14 feet 6 inches and a thickness of 12 feet.[3] They are estimated to weigh a staggering 800 tons each. Michel Alouf, the former curator of the ruins, notes that:

> . . . in spite of their immense size, they [the Trilithon stones] are so accurately placed in position and so carefully joined, that it is almost impossible to insert a needle between them. No description will give an exact idea of the bewildering and stupefying effect of these tremendous blocks on the spectator.[4]

The angle of the photograph in Plate 2 (hampered by the perimeter fence) (colour section) hardly does justice to the immense size of the Trilithon. Fortunately, however, its dimensions can be judged by a slightly larger block, known as the 'Stone of the South', which lies in a nearby hillside quarry, ten minutes walk to the south-west. Plate 3 demonstrates the huge scale of this stone slab, which measures 69 feet long by 16 feet wide by 13 feet 10 inches high. This block is estimated to weigh around 1,000 tons, the equivalent of three Boeing 747 aircraft.[5]

How were the 800-ton stones of the Trilithon moved from the quarry to the acropolis? The distance is not huge, no more than a third of a mile. Nor is the elevation very different between the two points. And yet, when one considers the size and weight of these stones and the fact that the route from the quarry to the acropolis is not entirely flat, transportation via any conventional means presents a seemingly impossible dilemma. Furthermore, an even greater mystery surrounds the manner in which the Trilithon stones were then fitted more than 20 feet high into the wall, without mortar and with perfect precision.

Some experts would have us believe that the Romans constructed this vast stone terrace at Baalbek as a foundation for their temples. However, it is a fact that no Roman emperor ever claimed to have accomplished this fantastic achievement, and as one authority has noted, there is a huge contrast in scale between the Roman temples and the size of the terrace on which they stand.[6] In addition, we have no evidence of any Roman technology that could have moved stones weighing 800 tons. In fact, there is no evidence of *any* known civilisation having the technology to erect the colossal stones which we see in the terrace at Baalbek.

Who could have built these huge stone foundations and why? It is a mystery that has inspired the imaginations of men for thousands of years.

The Arabs believed that Baalbek belonged to the legendary Nimrod, who once ruled this area of Lebanon. According to an Arabic manuscript found at Baalbek, Nimrod sent giants to rebuild Baalbek after the Flood,[7] whilst another tale relates that Nimrod rebelled against his god and built the Tower of Babel at Baalbek.

Other legends associate Baalbek with the Biblical figure of Cain, the son of Adam, claiming that he built it as a refuge after his god Yahweh had cursed him. According to Estfan Doweihi, the Maronite Patriarch of Lebanon:

> Tradition states that the fortress of Baalbek . . . is the most ancient building in the world. Cain, the son of Adam, built it in the year 133 of the creation, during a fit of raving madness. He gave it the name of his son Enoch and peopled it with giants who were punished for their iniquities by the flood'.[8]

The local Muslims also believed that it was beyond the capability of humans to move the enormous stones of Baalbek. Instead of giants, however, they credited the work to demons or djinn.[9] The English traveller, David Urquhart, in a similar vein, suggested that the builders used mastodons – huge extinct elephant-like mammals – as mobile cranes to help them move the stones![10]

It is sometimes claimed that modern cranes cannot lift stones as heavy as Baalbek's 800-ton monoliths.[11] This is actually incorrect. I posed the problem of the Baalbek stones to Baldwins Industrial Services, one of the leading British crane hire companies. I asked them how they might attempt to move the 1,000-ton Stone of the South and place it at the same height as the Trilithon.

Bob MacGrain, the Technical Director of Baldwins, confirmed that there were several mobile cranes currently available that could lift and place the 1,000-ton stone on a support structure 20 feet high. Baldwins themselves operate a 1,200 ton capacity Gottwald AK912 strut jib crane,[12] whilst other companies operate cranes capable of lifting 2,000 tons. Unfortunately, these cranes do not have the capability to move whilst carrying such heavy loads. How then might we transport the Stone of the South to the acropolis?

Baldwins suggested two possibilities. The first would use a 1,000-ton capacity crane fitted with crawler tracks. The disadvantage of this method would be the need for massive ground preparation works in order to provide a solid, level roadway for the crane to move.

The alternative to a crane would be a series of modular hydraulic trailers, combined to create a massive load carrying platform. These trailers raise and lower their loads using hydraulic cylinders built into their suspension. The initial lift at the quarry would be achieved by the use of a cut-out section beneath the stone, which the trailer would drive into. The final positioning in the wall, at a height of 20 feet, would be achieved by using an earth ramp.

There is, of course, one slight problem with Baldwins' solution. None of this twentieth century technology was supposedly available when Baalbek was built.

What happens if we fall back on non-technological methods? The usual suggestion is that megalithic stones were moved using a system of wooden rollers. However, modern experiments have shown such rollers being crushed by much lighter weights than 800 tons. Even if such a system was possible, it has been estimated that it would take the combined efforts of 40,000 men to move the Stone of the South.[13] It remains completely unproven that an 800-ton stone could have been moved using such primitive methods.

Another major weakness of the conventional explanation

is why the builders should have struggled with such a large weight, when it would have been far easier to split the giant monolith into several smaller blocks. According to my engineer friends, it would actually have been very risky to use large blocks in the Trilithon. This is because any vertical defects running lengthwise through the stone would have led to a severe structural weakness. In contrast, a similar fault in a smaller block would not have affected the overall construction.

It therefore makes no sense at all to imagine tens of thousands of men attempting to move and lift three 800-ton stones. How can we resolve this apparent dilemma and what can we deduce concerning the motivations of the Baalbek designers? On the one hand, it seems as if they were supremely confident their material had no defects. They might thus have favoured large stones for a specific structural reason, namely to provide a more stable platform which could withstand enormous vertical forces. An intriguing idea. On the other hand, it is possible that the builders were simply in a hurry, and it was therefore expeditious to cut and move one large stone rather than two small ones. This does of course presuppose a high level of construction technology being available.

Although the first of the above alternatives is the more enticing, in my opinion it is the latter alternative which provides the more likely explanation. My impression of the Baalbek platform, shared by others, is that it is incomplete. The Trilithon layer, for instance, rises above any of the other megalithic stones and does not form part of a level terrace. It thus appears to form part of an unfinished defensive wall. This theory is reinforced by the Stone of the South, which is still attached at one point to the rocky floor of the quarry. The physical evidence indicates a sudden abandonment of the construction project.

However, if the Trilithon layer represents a later addition, erected using high technology at an unknown time, then the layers below it must take us even further back into prehistory. These lower layers, in the south-western wall, have been carefully constructed of smaller stones, topped by a layer of 300-ton stones which have been shaped with an outward taper (Plate 2). If we now move to the same level in the adjoining south-eastern wall (Plate 1), we see a layer of megaliths, which although of similar size, are ill-matched: some are tapered, others are not, and the cut of the tapering does not match, even on adjacent blocks. The unavoidable conclusion is that this upper layer of the original platform has been reconstructed, having once sustained serious damage.

Let us now return to the sacred importance of Baalbek. Michel Alouf comments that 'nowhere is it clearly stated to what cause the religious importance of this town ought to be attributed'.[14] However, the Romans did leave us a clue with their temples to the gods Jupiter, Mercury and Venus. Why did the Romans, and indeed earlier civilisations of the Near East, worship this triad of gods? A major clue comes from the Greeks who called Baalbek 'Heliopolis' – the city of Helios. According to ancient legend, Helios was a Sun god who could traverse the skies in his 'chariot', and Baalbek was the alleged resting place of that chariot. Could this legend explain the need for such massive foundations in the original platform at Baalbek?

Tiwanaku

On the other side of the globe, the ruins of Tiwanaku in Bolivia have been described as the 'Baalbek of the New World'.[15] The site of Tiwanaku lies in a broad plain in the Rio Tiwanaku valley, one of several that cut back from the southern edge of Lake Titicaca into the huge plateau of the Bolivian altiplano. Its colossal stone blocks may not equal those of Baalbek in size, but they lie at an altitude of 13,000 feet. Here, the air is so thin that tourists struggle to catch their breath, and the high level of ultraviolet solar radiation poses a constant danger to human eyes and skin.

Thousands of years ago, the lichen-encrusted ruins of Tiwanaku were home to the highest urban settlement of the ancient world. Around AD 200, for reasons which are not entirely clear, Tiwanaku emerged as a sacred ceremonial centre. By AD 500, it was the capital of an expanding empire – the first empire of the ancient Americas. This empire, however, was not achieved by military conquest, but via economic power derived largely from huge agricultural surpluses. It was the collapse of the agricultural system, brought about by climatic change, that precipitated the end of the Tiwanakan era after 500 years of supremacy.[16]

The fact that Tiwanaku achieved agricultural surpluses at all is quite astonishing. Today, few farmers are brave enough to eke out an existence on the Bolivian altiplano, since hostile agricultural conditions bring total crop disaster every five years on average.[17] However, in ancient times this barren, windswept landscape had been transformed into a veritable oasis via a highly advanced agricultural technology. Archaeologists have found the remains of so-called 'raised fields' which protected crops from frost damage and allowed miraculous yields to be achieved. Experimental tests have shown this ancient technology to be far superior to modern methods using fertilisers.[18]

At its peak, the sacred city of Tiwanaku covered 2 square miles.[19] Its ceremonial core was surrounded by a moat, and the earth and clay which had been excavated from the moat had been used to construct a huge mound, known as the Akapana. The Tiwanakans also built a number of semi-subterranean temples alongside a much larger temple known as the *Kalasasaya*. Nearby, an equally huge temple, known as Puma Punku, was built to a quite different design. Illustration 3 shows the layout of all these principal structures.

Illustration 3

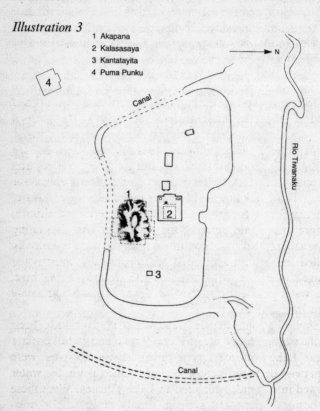

1 Akapana
2 Kalasasaya
3 Kantatayita
4 Puma Punku

Let us now take a closer look at these supposedly Tiwanakan temples, beginning with the most imposing structure, the Akapana. This artificial mound measures around 600 by 600 feet at its base, with a height of 50 feet. Although sometimes described as a truncated pyramid, it is in fact an irregular shape, with seven terraces and a large central depression. Inside the Akapana, archaeologists have found an amazing network of zigzagging stone water conduits.

Writing in 1993, anthropologist Alan Kolata, who had spent many years excavating at Tiwanaku stated:

> Our recent excavations at Akapana revealed an unexpected, sophisticated and monumental system of interlinked surface and subterranean drains.[20]

It is assumed that this 'drainage' system was designed to collect rainwater in the Akapana's central sunken court and feed it down to underground tunnels via the various terraces. The first component of this system was a major trunk line that led around the sides of the Akapana. Alan Kolata described this stone conduit as 'finely crafted' and 'precisely fitted', with the capacity to handle an 'enormous flow'. This trunk line fed the water to the next lower terrace, where it flowed for around 10 feet in an exterior stone drain, before once again entering the Akapana. The alternating internal/external route continued until the water eventually exited ten feet underground via 'beautifully constructed tunnels' – Figure 4 (black-and-white section). From here, the water drained into the Rio Tiwanaku and ultimately into Lake Titicaca.[21]

Similarly sophisticated waterworks systems have been found at the nearby site of Puma Punku and at Lukurmata (near Lake Titicaca), even though these 'temples' were otherwise quite different in design.[22] Once again, the water flowed into canals which led to Lake Titicaca. Were these elaborate waterworks systems simply designed for drainage? Alan Kolata acknowledged that the Akapana system was not a structural necessity:

> A much simpler and smaller set of canals would have accomplished the basic function of draining accumulated rain water from the summit. In fact, the system as installed by the architects of Akapana, although superbly functional, is completely over-engineered, a piece of technical stone-cutting and joinery that can only be called pure virtuosity.[23]

Did the Tiwanakans really build these waterworks systems, as the archaeologists would have us believe, or did they inherit them from a much earlier, more advanced but unrecorded culture? The evidence suggests the latter. One clue, which has mystified the archaeologists, is that the water systems of the Akapana had ceased to function at some time before AD 600, when the Tiwanakan empire was at its peak. This was proved by the discovery of undisturbed human and animal remains, buried at key points in the structure, where they would have been affected if the waters had still been flowing.[24] Another clue exists in the dating of human occupation at Tiwanaku to 1580 BC and 2134 BC using radiocarbon and obsidian dating respectively. Both dates tend to suggest that the Akapana was important prior to the Tiwanakan emergence in AD 200.

The anomalies continue if we move to the nearby site of Puma Punku, almost a mile to the south-west of the main ruins. Here we find the largest stones of Tiwanaku, some weighing over one hundred tons, representing the shattered remains of a partially excavated structure which is still not properly understood. Plate 4 (colour section) shows the scale of one of these huge red sandstone blocks, measuring approximately 26 by 16 by 2 feet and estimated to weigh 120 tons. Although badly eroded, the perfect lines of this and surrounding blocks can still be seen. They have amazed countless travellers such as the Spanish chronicler Pedro de Cieza de Leon who observed that:

> . . . some of these stones are very worn and wasted, and there are others so large that one wonders how human hands could have brought them to where they now stand . . . When one considers the work, I cannot understand or fathom what kind of instruments or tools were used to work them, for it is evident that before these huge stones were dressed and brought to perfection, they must have been much larger to have been left as we see them . . . I would say that I consider this the oldest antiquity in all of Peru'.[25]

Other stones at Puma Punku contain inexplicable grooves and niches, whilst some such as Figure 5 (see black-and-white section) bear the indentations of metal clamps which were used to fix the stones together. Some of these clamps have actually been found, although their whereabouts are now uncertain.[26] They were made of bronze – a metal that is not associated with any of the South American cultures at this time.

One of the most impressive stones at Puma Punku is shown in Plate 5 (colour section). This block, several feet high, contains a precision-cut groove approximately 6 millimetres wide. Inside the groove, all of the way from top to bottom, can be seen equidistant drilled holes. The question is, how could tiny grooves and holes have been made using crude stone hammers or soft copper hand tools? On the contrary, to cut and drill stone with this accuracy would require twentieth century technology.

Returning to the main site of Tiwanaku, we find one of the most famous sculptures of the ancient world situated inside the *Kalasasaya* temple. The 'Gateway of the Sun' is much smaller than one imagines, standing approximately 9 feet high. It is nevertheless, a most impressive monument, being carved from a single piece of grey andesite weighing around 15 tons. This stone is, like granite, one of the hardest and most difficult stones to work. On one side, the Gateway features a carving of the deity Viracocha and his winged attendants, but I would like to focus on the reverse side. Plate 8 (colour section) shows the Gateway's series of enigmatic niches, which include recesses for two hinges in the lower parts. These niches have been cut into the stone with great precision, forming perfect inside edges that could not possibly have been chiselled out using crude and primitive tools.

My final example of the precision workmanship at Tiwanaku lies to the east of the *Kalasasaya*, in a semi-subterranean temple known as the Kantatayita. Plate 9 (colour section) shows some of the precision-cut stones at this location, once again with perfectly cut inside edges. In the background of Plate 9, there lies a most unusual piece of curved architecture, once again made of the very hard grey andesite stone. Its front is elaborately carved and surrounded by nail holes, but its rear is stunning. It is difficult to find the superlatives to describe the perfect symmetry shown in Plates 6 and 7. Perfect edges are combined with a curved design which flares downwards and inwards simultaneously. Try carving that one with stone tools!

I have mentioned here only a few of the many incredible stones that lie strewn across the site of Tiwanaku, and it is worth emphasising that many more still lie buried in the ground under layers of sediment from thousands of years of human occupation and periodic flooding from Lake Titicaca.

How old might the site of Tiwanaku actually be? Unfortunately, no written records have survived (assuming they ever existed) to help us date the earliest phases. However, based on the astronomical alignments of the *Kalasasaya*, it has been suggested that that temple, and hence the site as a whole, was built at either 4050 BC or 10050 BC.[27] Although there have been no scientific appraisals of the age of the *Kalasasaya*'s stone pillars, the weathering of these stones has led many to agree with the earlier of the two dates. My own impression was that the 12-feet high standing pillars of the *Kalasasaya* looked older than those of Stonehenge (dated to 2700–2300 BC) but not by an additional 7,500 years. On the other hand, the huge blocks at Puma Punku may well be a lot older than the *Kalasasaya* pillars, since they have spent much of their life covered in mud and protected from the elements.

The little history that we do have of Tiwanaku has been filtered through numerous later cultures, including the Incas and the Spanish conquistadores who subjugated them in the sixteenth century. Cieza de Leon, mentioned earlier, was intrigued by Tiwanaku, and recorded the myths that were handed down by the local inhabitants:

> It is believed that before the Incas reigned, long before, certain of these buildings existed ... I asked the natives if these buildings had been built in the time of the Incas, and they laughed at the question, repeating what I have said, that they were built before they reigned, but that they could not state or affirm who built them. However, they had heard from their forefathers that all that are there appeared overnight.[28]

Similar legends claimed that Tiwanaku was built in a single night, after the Flood, by a mysterious race of giants – an explanation reminiscent of Baalbek. Other myths described lake Titicaca as the sacred spot where the god Viracocha created the world. Another legend, echoing the Bible, claimed Titicaca to be the home of a patriarchal couple who had survived a great Flood and propagated the Andean peoples. All of these tales are commonly cited to explain the religious mystique which allowed Tiwanaku to expand in later times.

In contrast to the legends, scientists are unable to explain why Tiwanaku suddenly emerged as a sacred centre.[29] They are unable to explain how huge stones were transported over tens of miles from the nearest quarries. They cannot explain the significance of the canals which surround the site,[30] nor the sophisticated waterworks systems inside the Akapana and elsewhere. And they cannot explain the existence of stones which have been cut and drilled using modern technology.

Chavin de Huantar

The ruins of Chavin de Huantar are located at an altitude of 10,500 feet in the Peruvian Andes, sandwiched between two ranges of rugged mountains, one cutting it off from the coast, the other separating it from the Amazonian jungle. It is difficult to find a more remote and better hidden location than Chavin de Huantar. And yet, 2,500 years ago, Chavin emerged as one of the most sacred cities in South America, exerting a profound influence on the distant coastal regions of Peru between 500–200 BC.

The main export from Chavin was religion, centred on the cult of a fanged jaguar. As a result of this strange cult, the remote city of Chavin developed into a most unlikely hub of regional trade, which carried the distinctive Chavin art-style throughout ancient Peru. At its peak, Chavin de Huantar covered 105 acres and its population numbered around 3,000 – small by today's standards, but an unusually large size for Peru at that time.[31]

The main ceremonial area at Chavin de Huantar covered 12 acres. Although referred to by the locals as 'El Castillo' (the Castle), the Chavin were never an aggressive people.[32] The ruined mounds of Chavin de Huantar have also been fancifully described as pyramids, which they were not. On the contrary, archaeological reconstructions of the site show a series of flat-topped temples, surrounding three sides of a square, sunken plaza. These unique 'temples' rank among the oddest buildings of the ancient world.

The principal temple, also known as the 'Old Temple', is designed in a U-shape, facing due east towards the sunrise. It contains a labyrinth of narrow subterranean passages, many of which inexplicably lead to dead-ends. One narrow passageway, however, allows access to an unusual vault in the form of a cross. At this juncture of passages, in the sacred heart of the temple, stands a stone in the shape of a knife or lance projecting from the ceiling into the floor. This carved stone, shown in Figure 6a (see black-and-white section) is known as El Lanzon – 'the Lance'.

The El Lanzon monolith, carved from one piece of granite 15 feet high, is assumed to be the main deity of the Chavin religion. Figure 6b (see black-and-white section) shows an exploded view of the carving, clearly showing the fangs and claws of this god. Although its fangs seem to be linked to the Chavin jaguar cult, the carving as a whole resembles a mixture of human and bull features, with serpents flowing from the head. The god has his right arm raised and left arm lowered, as if to convey some kind of message. Some commentators have noted the lack of a life line in the raised hand, suggesting that the god signifies death. Others see the image as benign and refer to it as 'the smiling god of Chavin'.

Whilst the precise meaning of *El Lanzon* is uncertain, it is clear that the carved statue was of great importance. The fact that its narrow, tapered upper section fits accurately through a tailor-made hole in the roof indicates that the temple must have been designed around the statue. It therefore seems as if this sacred relic was deliberately hidden away in the depths of the temple, in such a way that it could not be removed. Why did the priests go to such lengths to hide and protect their divine idol? A clue may exist in the irregular shape of the granite (especially at the front), which suggests that the stone was damaged *before* the carving was made. If that was the case, the stone may have already been sacred. It is possible that the Chavin priests carved *El Lanzon* and hid it to protect it from further damage.

The outside walls of the Old Temple were once adorned with more than two hundred frightening stone heads, some animal but mostly human. Only one of these gruesome heads remains in its original position (Plate 10, colour section). The fangs and large nose are typical of the Chavin heads, as is the strange knob-shaped protrusion on the top. The meaning of these features is a mystery. It seems particularly strange that such unwelcoming stone faces would have greeted the pilgrims who made the gruelling journey to Chavin.

Why did Chavin de Huantar suddenly emerge as a religious centre? Why did pilgrims trek through almost a hundred miles of extremely difficult mountain terrain to reach it? Clearly there was something very special about this place – something that is not readily apparent from the sprawling ruins of the temples which have been dated to around 500 BC. Does Chavin have a secret, earlier past?

Archaeologists have indeed found evidence of earlier occupation at Chavin de Huantar, radiocarbon dated to 1400 BC, suggesting that the importance of the site preceded the building of the temples by at least 800 years.[33] What was going on at this remote mountainous location? The answer perhaps lies in the earliest phase of construction – a *subterranean* network of finely constructed stone channels, which drew water from a nearby river and carried it underneath the site via an amazing hydraulic system. In her book *Chavin de Huantar – A Short Eternity*, archaeologist Nancy Abanto de Hoogendoorn described:

> . . . the large and complicated system of hydraulic channels in and around the temple. One of these takes in water directly from the Wacheqsa river . . . the water leaving the temple by another subterranean channel to the river Mosna.[34]

Figure 4 shows the flow of water from the Wacheqsa intake, a short distance to the west, underneath the site to the Mosna river immediately to the east. Several hydraulic channels brought the waters together in a subterranean gallery and fed it underneath a square sunken plaza. On one side of the plaza stood a large rectangular building known as the Northern Platform. Hoogendoorn has described the interior of the Platform as 'a large passage, completely made of sculpted stones and a quite profound hydraulic system'.[35] It is thought that the heavily damaged Southern Platform on the opposite side of the plaza had a similar function to its northern counterpart. The two platforms can be seen in Plate 11 (colour section), either side of the sunken plaza. Finally, all of the flowing waters converged underground at a point just beyond the plaza, where they were then drained by a single channel to the Mosna river.

Illustration 4

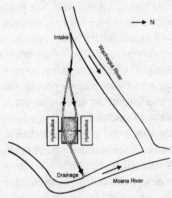

Why would anyone begin the construction of a settlement with such an advanced underground hydraulic system? The obvious answer is drinking water and sewerage, but if this was the case, then it was over-engineered on a massive scale, and would be quite without precedent in the ancient world. Another theory suggests that the builders designed the hydraulic system to counter the risk of flooding, supposedly by regulating the flow of the Wacheqsa river. It is difficult to see how this idea would have worked in practice, and if the risk of flooding was known in advance, why would anyone set down their roots in such a vulnerable position? There are plenty of other, safer locations in the vicinity.

On the contrary, it has been suggested that one of the few advantages of the Chavin location is its very proximity to these two water sources. This logical line of thought leads us to wonder whether the builders of Chavin deliberately chose this site specifically to make use of the flowing waters. It is difficult to believe that they were regulating the flow of waters between the two rivers for no apparent reason, so what might they have been doing? It is a fact that water is absolutely essential for most industrial processes. Few clues remain at the site to establish exactly what these processes might have been, but one authority has recently suggested the panning of gold as a possibility.[36] An old Incan legend indeed speaks of gold, silver and precious stones hidden somewhere beneath the temples.[37] Unfortunately, the first proper excavations of Chavin de Huantar, begun in 1919 by Julio Tello, were never completed, because in January 1945 an enormous flood buried the site under ten feet of mud and stones. Since then, archaeological efforts have concentrated on restoring the site to its previous condition.

Crucially, excavations stopped at the level of the sunken plaza which is located at the heart of the Chavin water-works. This plaza is dated to a later phase of Chavin, around 400–300 BC, and one wonders what earlier constructions might lie beneath it. Could Chavin have once been an industrial centre and could the key to its sacred importance lie in its secret past? It may be no coincidence that the over-engineering of the Chavin waterworks is mirrored by a similar level of unnecessary complexity in the Akapana waterworks at Tiwanaku . . .

Lost Secrets of the Incas

In AD 1532, the Spanish conquistadores arrived in Peru, under the leadership of Francisco Pizarro. The Incan empire which they found was huge and enormously wealthy, with gold reserves beyond the Spaniards' wildest dreams of avarice. However, it was also an empire plagued by internal strife, which made it extremely vulnerable. The

Incan gold proved to be a temptation that truly changed the course of history, leading to a long war in which the Spaniards brutally subjugated the native people. Remarkably, the Incan empire which they destroyed was totally devoid of writing, plunging the prior history of much of South America into an obscurity that can only be partially enlightened by oral traditions.

How long had the Incas been ruling the Andes before the Spaniards arrived? The Incan empire is commonly dated to the period AD 1100–1532, but its aggressive expansion is thought to have occurred after 1438 under the leadership of the famous Inca who came to be known as Pachacuti. It is believed that this Inca made a pilgrimage to a legendary mountain cave known as Tampu-Tocco, as a result of which he returned to the capital of Cuzco and adopted the name Pachacuti – 'the Shaker or Changer of the Earth'. From that point, it would seem, the Incas became oppressive dictators, building their empire by the ruthless enslavement of the surrounding tribes.

Why was the location of Tampu-Tocco so significant in Incan tradition? According to legend, the first Inca, named Manco Capac, had been born at Tampu-Tocco, where he disappeared one day, allegedly carried aloft by the Sun god. When he returned, he was wearing garments of gold and claimed a divine mandate to begin a new line of kings at Cuzco. Manco Capac thus became the first official Inca of the dynasty established at Cuzco in AD 1100.

However, according to an exhaustive analysis carried out by the Spanish historian Fernando Montesinos, the Incan Manco Capac was in fact named after an earlier Manco Capac, who had started civilisation at Cuzco thousands of years before the Incas. Montesinos recorded the local beliefs that 62 kings had reigned at Cuzco for approximately 2,500 years and that 28 kings had then ruled at Tampu-Tocco for around 1,000 years. This, the only chronological record of Andean prehistory, takes us back to a date of 2400 BC. At that time, the original Manco Capac had come to Cuzco from the sacred Lake Titicaca on the orders of the god Viracocha, who had given him a golden wand or staff. What exactly might this wand have been? According to one version of the legend, Manco Capac's instructions were to build a city where the wand sank into the ground, whilst in another version he had to use the wand to strike a particular stone.

Some historians believe that the later Incas appropriated the earlier tale of Manco Capac to their own dynasty, along with the creation legend of Titicaca which they had adopted from their conquest of Tiwanaku. The implication is that Peru once witnessed a long and unrecorded occupation by pre-Incan cultures. In the case of Cuzco, such a suggestion has now been confirmed by archaeology,[38] whilst other scholars have argued strongly that Cuzco had astronomical functions, which allow its origin to be dated to the era of 2200 BC or earlier.[39]

In the light of the above, it seems rather hasty to credit all of the impressive megalithic structures in Peru to the Incas, but nevertheless this has become the conventional wisdom. Curiously, advocates of this theory cannot explain why the Spaniards did not use the Incas' expert stonemasons to construct their own buildings following the conquest. It is a fact that, when earthquakes hit Cuzco in 1650 and 1950, most of the Spanish structures collapsed, whilst the supposedly Incan structures stood firm. One of these structures was a megalithic wall featuring an amazing stone with 12 angles (Plate 12, colour section). Its perfect, mortarless fit with the surrounding stones is typical of many examples all over Peru, where it is impossible to fit the thinnest needle or razor blade between the stones. The chronicles of the Spaniards repeatedly stressed their admiration for the megalithic walls of the 'Incan' fortifications. Is it therefore conceivable that the Spaniards would not have harnessed for themselves the skills of the Incas? Did these Inca stonemasons disappear into thin air . . . or did they never exist? In short, was the expertise *pre*-Inca?

How were stone blocks such as the stone of 12 angles cut and assembled with such accuracy? In 1996, field experiments were carried out to test a theory that 'scribing and coping' might have been used.[40] This technique utilises a simple wooden device with a string plumb-line, which enables the profile of a pre-cut stone block to be traced against an adjacent uncut stone. The adjacent block can then be carved with a matching surface, using smaller stones as hammers and chisels. The field experiment managed to produce reasonable results with small blocks of stone, but if we move from Cuzco to the nearby site of Sacsayhuaman, we find stones of a completely different magnitude.

The ruins of Sacsayhuaman (pronounced as 'sexy woman') occupy a ridge overlooking the city of Cuzco. The main feature of the site is a set of three parallel, zigzagging walls, as shown in Plate 13. These walls, when combined with the natural sheer drop on the opposite side, created a completely fortified area, that was used to good effect by the Incas against the Spaniards. But could the Incas really have built these massive fortifications using only stone hammers and muscle power?

The largest stones at Sacsayhuaman occur in the lowest wall, a magnificent 20 feet in height, where one stone in particular – Plate 14 – is estimated to weigh 120 tons. These zigzagging walls, more than 1,200 feet long, have rightly been called 'one of the most astounding megalithic structures of the ancient world'[41] and have repeatedly amazed all that have seen them. The Spanish historian, Garcilaso de la Vega, recorded his impressions that the walls were:

> . . . erected by magic, by demons and not by men, because of the number and size of the stones placed in the three walls . . . which it is impossible to believe were cut out of quarries, since

the Indians had neither iron nor steel wherewith to extract and
shape them.[42]

Leaving aside the enormous efforts which would have been
involved in dragging more than a thousand stones several
miles from the nearest quarry, let us return to the theory of
'scribing and coping'. In order to match the joints of the
Sacsayhuaman stones in this way, many stones weighing
10–20 tons would have had to be propped up in mid-air
while the scribing and coping was performed against the
stone positioned below. Faced with such a dangerous and
painstaking operation, the question which arises is not
whether the Incas could have done it, but why did they
bother? Why did they not use stones half the size? I asked
the same question earlier of Baalbek and was forced to
conclude that an advanced construction technology must
have been available.

A similarly advanced technology seems to have been used
on a rocky knoll at Sacsayhuaman, opposite the zigzag
walls. Here, we find the so-called 'Inca's Throne' – Plate 15
– where, for no apparent reason, a platform and series of
steps have been carved with great precision into the hillside.
The 'experts' claim that the perfect angles and edges of the
Inca's Throne were finished off using small stones as
precision tools. However, when one sees the accuracy of
this work first-hand, it seems ludicrous to suggest that such
primitive methods were actually used. The smooth, polished
faces of these steps, together with numerous other enigmatic
niches around Sacsayhuaman, appear instead to have been
machined using twentieth century technology.

Let us now move into the Urubamba Valley, the so-called
'Sacred Valley' of the Incas. This valley begins just north of
Cuzco and follows the Urubamba River north-west.
Among the numerous curiosities along this route, I would
like to focus in particular on just two – Ollantaytambo and
Machu Picchu.

Ollantaytambo is situated 40 miles north-west of Cuzco. Like Sacsayhuaman, it consists of a series of terraced levels, defended by huge megalithic walls. Like Sacsayhuaman and Tiwanaku, the site is littered with stone blocks in which mysterious niches have been cut with precise angles and perfect inside edges. Plate 19 shows an example of one amazing stone which stands at the bottom of these ruins.

Some of the megalithic walls at Ollantaytambo – Plates 18 and 20 – are among the finest in all of Peru. Curiously, one of the lower walls here has been repaired with inferior quality stones, which stand on top of their superior megalithic cousins. No-one but the Incas could have carried out these repairs. It is a feature repeated at other sites such as Pisac, and provides a further clue to the limited scope and quality of Inca constructions, contrasting their achievements to those from the pre-Inca period.

Above the fortified terracing at Ollantaytambo, there lies a mysterious building romantically known as the 'Temple of the Sun'. This 'temple' is fronted by six enormous monoliths, as shown in Plate 16, the largest stone measuring over 13 feet in height. These stones are unique, their straight sides and unusual spacers being in total contrast to the multi-faced joints and bevelled edges of other megalithic walls in Peru. Exactly how the stones were so perfectly shaped is unknown, since they were carved out of red porphyry, a stone as hard as granite.

The great mystery of Ollantaytambo is how these six 50-ton stones were moved to their present location, since the quarry from which they came has been definitively identified at Chachicata four miles away across the valley on the opposite mountainside![43] Having first quarried the stones, it would be necessary to take them down a steep mountain slope, across a river, and then up another steep mountain slope to the construction site. It seems to be an impossible task.

Nevertheless, in 1996, one group of experts boldly travelled to Ollantaytambo to demonstrate what was possible using human muscle power and traditional materials.[44] Their first task was to demonstrate how a relatively small one-ton stone (one fiftieth of the size of the genuine article) could be lowered down the mountain using ropes. The stone cascaded out of control, and it was fortunate that no-one was killed. The second task was to pull a stone of similar size across the river at a shallow point. Here, the team had a surprising success, the stone moving quickly across the gravelly river bed. In a similar manner, the stone was moved across a pre-prepared cobbled surface at a surprisingly rapid speed. At this point the project was abandoned, with the claim that the experts had illustrated how the stone could be pulled *up the mountainside*. Well, sorry chaps, it was a grand effort, but I fail to see how a 50-ton stone will overcome the power of gravity and shoot up a 50-degree mountain slope like greased lightning – even with a cobbled path and several thousand weightlifters.

Advocates of such push-and-shove methods point out that the remains of a ramp do exist, leading up the hillside at Ollantaytambo, and that, furthermore, numerous stones (the so-called 'tired stones' which never made it to the top) can be seen lying at the foot of the ramp. Unfortunately, this evidence only explains the stones that did *not* get up the ramp. It tells us nothing about the stones which we see at the top of the hill. It is not beyond the realms of possibility that the megalithic structures at Ollantaytambo already existed in Inca times, and that the ramp and tired stones represent the efforts of the Incas to emulate what they saw. It would appear that they failed, just as the 1996 team did. In support of this interpretation, Garcilaso de la Vega reported that one of the Incas had indeed attempted to enhance his reputation by ordering 20,000 men to pull a tired stone up a mountainside. The event ended in tragedy, with thousands of people being killed when they lost control of the huge stone.[45]

The greatest mystery of the Ollantaytambo 'temple', however, is its apparent lack of purpose. It does not seem to form part of a building, since the area enclosed by the walls consists of an outcrop of solid rock. It may be the case that a superstructure was intended, for there are clear signs that the building was abandoned in mid-course. However, the ultimate goal of the builders is quite obscure, for the ridge on which the stones stand is too narrow to have been of much strategic use. The so-called 'temple' reminded me of the J. F. Kennedy Memorial in Dallas, USA (Plate 17, colour section), simply because neither structure has any apparent purpose. Could this be the solution – was the structure intended as a memorial? It is noteworthy that the fourth stone from the left has been decorated with a relief carving of a four-sided step-pyramid, which is often associated with the afterlife and is commonplace at the sacred site of Tiwanaku in Bolivia (Plate 9). My memorial idea is as good a theory as any I have yet heard.

Machu Picchu, 25 miles north-west of Ollantaytambo, rivals the importance of Cuzco itself in Andean tradition. The ancient city is situated on a narrow, saddle-like ridge between two spectacular peaks – Machu Picchu and Huayna Picchu – as shown in Plate 21. At a height of 1,500 feet above the valley floor, the city of Machu Picchu was extremely well-hidden and thus eluded discovery by the Spanish conquistadores, only being 'discovered' in 1911 by the explorer Hiram Bingham.

Officially, Machu Picchu is a lost city, with no official history, and it is commonly assumed to have been built by the Incas during the last half of the fifteenth century. However, one of the main features at Machu Picchu, the 'Temple of the Three Windows', is unique and has enabled scholars such as Hiram Bingham to identify the site as the legendary location of Tampu-Tocco, the 'Resting Place of the Windows' which is also known as the 'Haven of the Three Windows'. If this identification is correct, then a line of 28 pre-Incan kings lived at Machu Picchu from around AD 100–1100, thus explaining the massive amount of construction at the site and the many varied styles that have been used. The official history, in contrast, implies (rather unrealistically) that everything was built in less than a hundred years.

As mentioned earlier, the later Incan stone masonry was no match for the earlier megalithic stonework, and Machu Picchu is another clear example of this. If we ignore the widespread later constructions, several key monuments stand out as vastly superior. The Temple of the Three Windows, shown in Plate 22 (colour section), is certainly the most beautiful of these and occupies a commanding position looking east. Alongside it is a mysterious 3-sided structure known as 'the Principal Temple', containing a series of niches and pegs – Plate 23. This temple is mainly built of very large blocks, with one of its adjoining walls featuring a stone with no less than 32 angles in its faces.

Behind the Principal Temple, a steep flight of steps leads to a natural viewpoint, where the rocky outcrop has been carved into a triangular platform. Here stands a precision-carved stone known as the *Intihuatana* – Plate 24. To the other side of the Principal Temple, at a similar distance, stands the *Torreon* (or 'Temple of the Sun'), a well-built tower with two windows and a doorway, as shown in Plate 25.

What was the purpose of all these strange buildings at Machu Picchu, with their assorted windows and niches? Why were they built in such a remote and inaccessible place? The general consensus is that Machu Picchu was not a defensive or strategic fortification, since there is little evidence of such a purpose. Some scientists have claimed that Machu Picchu was used as an astronomical observatory and calendar, citing as evidence its otherwise inexplicable windows, niches and pegs. However, they have so far failed to explain why it was necessary for these astronomers to go to so much trouble in such a remote location.

The more widely accepted view is that Machu Picchu, along with Cuzco, were sacred sites for religious and ceremonial purposes. Anthropologist Johan Reinhard is one of the strongest advocates of this theory, stating that Machu Picchu:

> ... is situated in the centre of sacred mountains and in association with a sacred river which is in turn linked with the Sun's passage, thereby forming a cosmological, hydrological and sacred geographical centre for the region in which it is situated.[46]

This religious interpretation noticeably links Machu Picchu and Cuzco to the other sites mentioned earlier in this chapter – Baalbek, Tiwanaku and Chavin de Huantar. All have become places of pilgrimage, and all exhibit unusual signs of high technology in prehistoric times. Is there a common factor that caused all of these places to become so sacred? We will now travel to Nazca to find another important clue.

The Nazca Lines

In the 1930s, archaeologists studying the 2,000-year old Nazca civilisation in southern Peru came across some very strange ruts in the ground. As they examined these ruts, they found to their astonishment that the brown crust-like surface of the desert had been deliberately removed to create furrows 4–6 inches deep. The lighter coloured sub-soil which had been exposed formed distinct lines which ran across the desert plain. In due course, it became apparent that the archaeologists had stumbled across a much wider phenomenon – the so-called 'Nazca Lines' – which cover a 30-mile long strip in the foothills of the Andes mountains. More than sixty years later, not one single theory has been put forward to explain all of the Nazca markings. A prominent scientist has called it 'one of the most baffling enigmas of archaeology'.[47]

Why have the Nazca Lines proved such an insoluble mystery? The reason lies in the sheer variety of designs, which include around 300 pictures, commonly referred to as 'geoglyphs'. Some of the better known of these figures are shown to scale in Illustration 5. The relative sizes of the spider, monkey, condor and lizard (among others) can be judged against the largest figure – a stylised heron with a zigzag neck, approximately 900 feet long. However, as diverse as these geoglyphs are, others are different again, consisting of totally abstract shapes. And even among the abstract designs, there is diversity. Whilst one design in particular contains no less than 365 angles, others, in the form of spirals, contain no angles at all.

Illustration 5

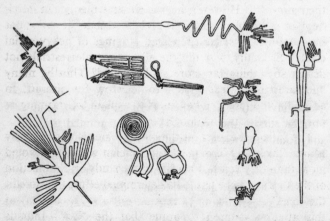

Adapted from M. Reiche, 1968.

Although the recognisable animal geoglyphs draw most of the attention at Nazca, they are in fact dwarfed by the huge trapezoidal (wedge-like) designs such as the one shown in Plate 27 (colour section). Some of these wedges have sides more than 2,500 feet long! The wedges, in turn, are outdone by the lines themselves, which run perfectly straight for up to 5 miles.

What could have been the purpose of all these diverse lines and geoglyphs? Seen as a whole, the Nazca Lines appear to be a jumbled mess, scattered seemingly at random over the desolate plain, crossing and intersecting for no apparent reason. In some places, carefully drawn geoglyphs have been partly obliterated by the huge wedges. Furthermore, there is a great contrast between some drawings which have been perfectly executed, and others which have been sloppily drawn. More puzzling still, many of the images are so big that they can only be viewed *from the air* at a height of 1,000 feet.[48] By whom were the lines and figures intended to be seen?

In 1969, Erich von Daniken floated the idea that airborne extraterrestrials might have laid out the lines as runways for their aircraft.[49] However, his imaginative theory ran into a number of problems. First, it is claimed that the soil is not hard enough to sustain repeated landings of heavy aerial craft.[50] Secondly, why did the alleged extraterrestrials not design something far more sophisticated? Thirdly, many lines are only 3 feet wide – too narrow for aircraft. In addition, von Daniken has failed to explain the meaning or purpose of the animal geoglyphs.

The foremost expert on the Nazca Lines is undoubtedly Maria Reiche, a German mathematician who has devoted more than fifty years of her life to the study and protection of the Lines. Reiche has led a determined effort to discredit the von Daniken theory of extraterrestrials. The strategy of this attack has been to argue that the Nazca Indians constructed the Lines relatively recently – some time between 300 BC and AD 800. In support of this possibility, some scientists have put forward ingenious ideas on how the geoglyphs could theoretically have been designed from the ground.[51] The more important evidence, however, is that which attempts to link the Lines definitively to the Nazcan culture. Here, neither of the two key pieces of evidence survives close scrutiny.

The first piece of evidence is a series of radiocarbon dates, based on ceramic and wood remains which were left at the Lines by the Nazcan people. It is claimed that this proves that the Nazcans constructed the Lines. On the contrary, the dating of these materials tells us only that the Nazcans lived in the area of the Lines. Since the Lines themselves cannot be radiocarbon dated, the possibility remains that they already existed when the Nazcan culture emerged.

The second piece of evidence is the alleged resemblance of the Nazca geoglyphs to certain features found on Nazcan pottery. This is an important issue because it potentially offers proof that the Nazcans had either designed the images or at least viewed them from the air.

Figure 7 (see black-and-white section) shows four examples of Nazcan pottery exhibited by the museum in the nearby city of Ica. The first supposedly matches the lizard in Illustration 5; the second supposedly matches the spider; the third supposedly matches the hummingbird (top left of Illustration 5); and the fourth supposedly matches the whale (bottom right of Illustration 5). In all cases the similarities are tenuous and key points of detail from the highly stylised geoglyphs are different or missing on the pottery. Five other examples (not shown below) are equally tenuous. In their eagerness to disprove the von Daniken theory, the experts seem to have forgotten that it is quite normal for ancient artists to reproduce figures of birds, insects, reptiles and sea creatures. If the judgement of these experts had not been so clouded, they might have wondered why the Nazcans did not decorate their pottery with the more unusual designs of the Nazca plain – the wedge shapes, the intersecting lines and the abstract shapes.

How does Maria Reiche explain the purpose of the Nazca Lines? Although Reiche claims not to have reached a definite conclusion, she leans heavily towards the theory that they represent an astronomical calendar.[52] She claims that the Nazcans used the lines and figures to measure the key points of the solar year to assist with agricultural planning. However, Reiche's theory, like von Daniken's, has collapsed under the overwhelming weight of logical argument stacked against it.

In 1968, a study by the National Geographic Society determined that, whilst some of the Nazca lines did point to the positions of the Sun, Moon and certain stars two thousand years ago, it was no more than could be expected by mere chance.[53] In 1973, Dr Gerald Hawkins studied 186 lines with a computer programme and found that only 20 per cent had any astronomical orientation – again no more than by pure chance.[54] In 1982, Anthony Aveni obtained similar results,[55] whilst in 1980, Georg Petersen pointed out that Reiche's theory did not explain the different lengths and widths of the lines.[56] More recently, Johan Reinhard has noted that the surrounding mountains provided a ready-made and much more effective mechanism for the Nazcans to use as a solar calendar; the lines would thus have been quite superfluous to them.[57] In addition to this avalanche of scientific opinion, we should also note that Reiche, like von Daniken, has failed to explain the significance of the animal geoglyphs.

How else might we explain the Nazca Lines? They were certainly not Inca roads, since many lines begin and end in mid-desert, and they were certainly not irrigation canals, since most of them do not lead to sources of water. With all possible *practical* purposes exhausted, many writers have begun to focus on the *symbolism* of the lines and figures. All manner of religious cults have now been suggested – ancestor cults, water cults, fertility cults and mountain cults.

The leading proponent of the cult theory is Johan Reinhard, who has identified many lines leading to religious shrines, water sources or mountains.[58] Reinhard has argued convincingly that the Nazcans worshipped the mountains, but why would they worship inanimate objects? Reinhard noted a widespread belief amongst ancient Andean cultures that various gods – whom they revered as their ancestors – resided in the mountains. These gods controlled the weather and hence the water supply which determined the fertility of crops and livestock. Reinhard added that the chief god Viracocha (mentioned earlier re Tiwanaku) was closely associated with both mountains and water.

How does the worship of mountain gods explain the Nazca Lines? Johan Reinhard has detailed various ancient traditions, according to which the mountain gods took to the skies in the form of eagles or condors.[59] As Reinhard explains, this cult theory explains the single most significant aspect of the Nazca Lines:

> That the figures can be best seen only from the air is explainable as being due to the *ability of the mountain deities to oversee the area*, such as appearing as birds or in the form of the flying feline.[60] (emphasis added)

Could this be a vital clue towards solving the mystery? The anthropologists attribute the belief in mountain gods to a sound ecological basis, since mountains are the source of rivers and rainclouds. But what if these mountain gods were not the product of human imagination? What if they were flesh-and-blood gods who sometimes flew in aircraft? It would be premature to reveal my unique proposal for solving the Nazca mystery at this point, but it is necessary for me to make two things quite clear – first, I am *not* saying that the Nazca Lines represented an airfield; secondly, I *am* saying that they do strongly indicate that aircraft technology was needed to observe them. This might seem a fanciful idea if it were not for the level of high technology seen earlier at Baalbek, Tiwanaku and the various pre-Incan sites of Peru.

A very strong pattern has emerged in this chapter. All of the sites we have studied indicate the existence of two distinctly different levels of culture – a prehistoric culture with advanced technology, and a later culture which gazed in awe at the miraculous stonework which the advanced culture had left behind. Were all of these sites adopted as sacred centres by later cultures, who created or preserved the legends of the gods?

The evidence cited earlier suggests that the Tiwanakans did not build the Akapana, but adopted it. They did not understand its purpose, but they made it their most hallowed spot. Nazca represents a parallel situation. It may be no coincidence that the Nazcan capital of Cahuachi functioned primarily as a ceremonial centre and is dated to *c*. AD 200, exactly the same time that Tiwanaku emerged as a sacred centre.[61] As at Tiwanaku, the Nazcans may have adopted the Lines, not understanding their origin or purpose, but worshipping them as sacred signs of the gods. As Johan Reinhard has noted, they built simple religious shrines at the end of many lines and worshipped mountain gods as their ancestors.[62] If we take these 'gods' to be the same flesh-and-blood beings that designed the waterworks of Tiwanaku and Chavin, the fortress of Sacsayhuaman and the platform at Baalbek, then the Nazca Lines signify another very important technology – they tell us that the gods could fly . . .

Chapter Three Conclusions

* Physical evidence suggests the existence of a very old, unrecorded culture, using advanced technology at Baalbek, Tiwanaku and various sites in Peru. Later cultures saw this technology as the handiwork of 'gods' and made these places sacred.

* The Nazca Lines indicate that one of the technologies possessed by these 'gods' was aeronautics. The existence of a huge prehistoric platform at Baalbek, along with the associated legend of the Sun god's 'chariot', supports this conclusion.

CHAPTER FOUR

THE PYRAMIDS OF GIZA

Gods and Pharaohs

In the last chapter, we marvelled at sites which cannot be explained by the accepted historical paradigm. Despite all efforts to convince us that these places were built by Tiwanakans, Incas and Nazcans, an air of mystery still surrounds the true identity of the original designers, who used technology equivalent to that of the twentieth century. Most significantly, the experts cannot explain why such huge, over-engineered monuments were built, often in the most remote locations. Due to the experts' lack of understanding, these mysterious constructions are dismissed as 'temples'.

This chapter deals with the most famous example of ancient high technology – the pyramids of Giza in Egypt. In the same way that the Incas have been credited with the prehistoric stonework in Peru, so have the ancient Egyptians taken credit for the pyramids of Giza. The only difference is that the pyramids are conveniently labelled as 'tombs' rather than temples. We are thus told that the three pyramids of Giza, as shown in Plate 28 (colour section), were built by three pharaohs from the third millennium BC – Khufu (whom the Greeks called

Cheops), Khafra (Chephren) and Menkaura (Mycerinus).

In this chapter, I am primarily concerned with the pyramid of Khufu. It is that pyramid which is commonly referred to as the Great Pyramid and which represents the last survivor of the Seven Wonders of the Ancient World. But does the Great Pyramid really belong to the pharaoh named Khufu, and was it ever a tomb?

In 1980, it was categorically proved that the pharaoh Khufu did *not* build the Great Pyramid, and yet, to this day, we continue to be fed the same old lies to the contrary. In this chapter we will be reviewing the damning evidence (as yet unchallenged) that the link to Khufu was a disgraceful archaeological fraud. First, however, let us examine the pyramids and the historical paradigm into which they are conveniently slotted.

There is a common perception that one Egyptian pyramid is very much like another. Few people realise just how special the Giza pyramids are, simply because no-one tells them. One reference book dismisses the entire site as a vast necropolis,[1] and it is difficult to find a book which *does* do full justice to all of the incredible features of the Great Pyramid in particular. This chapter will put the record straight, and in so doing it will become transparently obvious that it was not built as a tomb by the ancient Egyptians.

On account of its astonishing mathematical and geometrical design, the Great Pyramid has been described as 'the most accurately and comprehensively surveyed building in the entire world'.[2] And yet it still manages to surprise us. The secret doorway discovered by Rudolf Gantenbrink in 1993 – which I will be discussing in a later chapter – should make us all question what we are told. Yet ironically, it would seem that we, the public, should never have found out about *that* little discovery. The Egyptian authorities at Giza, who control the release of information, were so angry with Gantenbrink following his unauthorised press announcement, that they have since refused to allow him back into the Pyramid.

Most of us come away from Egypt completely perplexed. It is impossible for us to rationalise the confused images of that ancient culture against a complete absence of historical context. It is the role of Egyptology (the study of Egyptian history) to provide that context, but if we the public are the judge, then it clearly fails miserably. Egyptologists proudly claim their study to be the oldest scientific archaeology, but if it is so *old*, and so *scientific*, how is it that they cannot even explain how the Egyptian civilisation arose?

As one writer on Egypt, John Anthony West, put it:

> . . . every aspect of Egyptian knowledge seems to have been complete at the very beginning. The sciences, artistic and architectural techniques and the hieroglyphic system show virtually no signs of a period of 'development', indeed, many of the achievements of the earliest dynasties were never surpassed . . . [3]

According to the accepted chronology, Egyptian civilisation emerged independently from any other civilisation. It happened *c*. 3100 BC under the first pharaoh named Menes, who united, or possibly reunited, Upper and Lower Egypt (southern and northern respectively). Who was Menes? The experts can tell us nothing about him. What was the background to the battles he fought to unite Egypt? They cannot tell us. And why did the culture of ancient Egypt have so much in common with the Sumerian civilisation which preceded it by 700 years? They deny it! And yet it is completely naive to assume that the Sumerians, who were keen travellers and explorers, did not influence Egyptian culture.

Whilst Egyptian tour-guides and experts attempt to dazzle us with their expertise on ancient Egypt, the truth is that they know very little. They use a chronology which has largely been constructed from Manetho's Kings Lists, which were written long after the events occurred, and relied on fragmentary records which were thousands of years old.[4] Modern archaeology has provided precious little in the way of corroborative evidence to confirm the identities and dates of these kings. Therefore, the whole of Egyptian chronology is based on few facts and a whole lot of guesswork. However, it is not in the interests of the Egyptologists to admit to so many uncertainties.

It is rather intriguing that Manetho's Kings Lists recorded a long list of rulers prior to Menes. According to Manetho, the reign of Menes was preceded by a 350-year period of chaos (at last some background!) and, prior to that, a dynasty of thirty demi-gods had reigned for 3,650 years. That takes us back to around 7100 BC, well before any civilisation had begun. But the fun has only just started, because Manetho also listed two further dynasties of gods ruling for 13,870 years prior to that. This valuable clue to mankind's history is ignored, simply because the mention of gods does not fit the historical paradigm of the experts.

And yet this vast array of gods is the central focus of ancient Egyptian art and religion. Some of the Egyptians' god-legends are central to an understanding of their ancient cultural practices, but they are all studied under the banner of mythology.[5] Nor was Manetho alone in recognising these gods as historical figures. Greek and Roman historians, such as Herodotus and Diodor of Sicily, also gave detailed accounts of divine kingdoms dating back thousands of years before the pharaohs. All of these ancient historians are mocked by modern historians for being so naive as to believe what the Egyptian priests told them.

Having hopefully established at least some doubt regarding the reliability of Egyptian history, it is now time to take a closer look at the Giza pyramids, particularly the Great Pyramid, and to ask ourselves whether they really belonged to Khufu, Khafra and Menkaura.

First Impressions

Situated at the north-eastern edge of the Libyan plateau, the pyramids of Giza provide a commanding view of the horizon in all four directions. From the capital of Cairo, only a few miles away, the peaks of the two larger pyramids can be seen on the horizon to the north-west, above the sprawling city. From a distance, it is difficult to appreciate the huge size of these two pyramids. Only as one approaches, does the overwhelming scale of the construction become apparent. The Great Pyramid itself, missing its capstone, was designed with a height of 480 feet, reaching the same height as Khafra's pyramid but from a slightly lower base. This base covers an almost unbelievable area of 13 acres, with each side measuring 756 feet.

The exterior of the Great Pyramid now appears very roughshod and badly eroded, but it was once covered in an outer layer of fine white limestone casing blocks, giving it the totally smooth sides of a true pyramid. These casing stones were intact when Herodotus visited the site in the fifth century BC, but most were later removed for the construction of mosques in Cairo. Today, only a few remain in museums and at the top of Khafra's pyramid. These six-sided stones, weighing up to 15 tons each, were polished and precision carved to fit perfectly with each other and the core stones, with joints measuring less than one fiftieth of an inch!

Beneath the now-removed outer layer, the Pyramid's construction consists of approximately 2,500,000 dressed stones, mostly yellow limestone, but with harder granite for certain interior features. The total mass of the Great Pyramid is estimated at around 90 million cubic feet, which would weigh between 6–7 million tons. To put this into proper perspective, the highest cathedral nave in Europe would fit three times into its height, and its mass exceeds that of all the cathedrals, churches and chapels built in England since the beginning of Christianity. The Great Pyramid is often cited as the largest building on Earth, with twice the volume and thirty times the mass of New York's famous Empire State Building.

The Pyramid rests on an artificially levelled platform, which is less than 22 inches thick, yet is still almost perfectly level, with errors of less than an inch across its entire area, despite supporting such an enormous weight for thousands of years.[6] The base of the Pyramid is set out perfectly square – no mean feat of engineering in itself.

The internal construction of the Pyramid is believed to consist of a step-pyramid structure, superbly engineered to withstand great vertical stress. The stone blocks are precision-cut, and matched so perfectly that the entire Pyramid fits together without the use of mortar. The stones range in weight from 2.0–2.5 tons for the limestone core blocks to 50–70 tons for the huge granite monoliths. These larger granite stones were brought all the way from the quarry at Aswan, six hundred miles to the south. Needless to say, scholars have tried desperately hard to suggest how the ancient Egyptians might have moved and erected stones of this size, but without finding a convincing answer. As we noted in chapter 3, modern crane technology would cope with these weights, but no-one is seriously suggesting that the pharaohs could have designed and built such state-of-the-art machinery. Furthermore, it is difficult to imagine that even twentieth century technology would, in practice, be able to match the Great Pyramid's incredible precision.

Equal to the engineering precision, is the geographical precision with which all three pyramids at Giza have been laid out. Sir William Flinders Petrie found that the Great Pyramid had been aligned with True North within five minutes of arc, that is one twelfth of a degree![7] Those reference books which deign to mention this extraordinary fact are forced to admit that the alignment is too precise to be by chance.[8] The accuracy of the Great Pyramid's orientation is evidenced by the fact that Napoleon's engineers used it to triangulate and map northern Egypt.[9] Furthermore, the Great Pyramid is placed almost exactly on the 30th parallel north, a fact which will later prove highly significant.

Mysterious Niches

Whilst the exterior of the Great Pyramid is awesome in its size, the interior is awesome in its precision and unusual features (Illustration 6). One writer has described it as 'bizarre and obviously alien in design', an outrageous statement, but one for which any intelligent visitor could be reasonably excused.[10]

Illustration 6

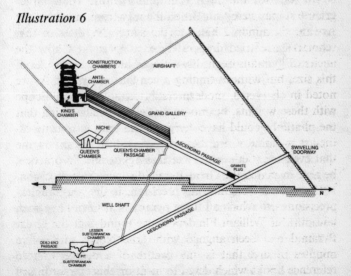

A swivelling stone doorway to the Pyramid is so cunningly disguised that it was never discovered from the outside, and the visitor today uses the artificial entrance to the Pyramid through its north face, where the Moslem Caliph Al Mamoon forced an entry in AD 820. This entrance leads directly to the Descending Passage and the Ascending Passage, each having an identical 26 degree angle to the horizontal. When Mamoon forced his entry, he burrowed through the stone into the Descending Passage, which led to a mysterious Subterranean Chamber, hewn out of the bedrock directly below the apex of the Pyramid (Plate 33, colour section). By chance, Mamoon's men dislodged a stone from the ceiling of the passage, revealing a large rectangular granite slab, facing down at an unusual angle. They tunnelled around what later became known as the Granite Plug, and became the first men to discover the Ascending Passage, which led to the upper chambers of the Pyramid.

The Ascending Passage is a unique feature, found in no other pyramid in Egypt. Bending double, one climbs up the passageway into the Grand Gallery (Plate 32) – another unique feature. Leading off from the Grand Gallery, a squarish room, romantically nicknamed the Queen's Chamber, lies precisely in the middle of the Pyramid's north-south axis. Its main feature is an incredibly large niche, cut into its eastern wall. This niche is technically described as a corbelled telescopic cavity, but neither this term, nor niche, do justice to the extraordinary shape and size of this feature which stands just over 15 feet high (Plate 30). Whatever it might have contained is unknown, for the Queen's Chamber was found totally empty. Needless to say, this remarkable niche is another totally unique feature in Egyptian pyramids.

The Grand Gallery continues to ascend at an angle of 26 degrees, for a distance of 153 feet, and with a height of 26 feet. It is difficult to find words to describe its intricate and precise design. It is best described as a corbelled telescopic vault, which is similar in pattern to the Queen's Chamber niche, but on a grander scale, and with seven corbelled overlaps rather than five. Each corbel overlaps the lower one by three inches, so that the Gallery narrows as it rises. Just above the third corbel, a curious and inexplicable groove runs the whole length of the Gallery, whilst on its floor, two ramps, one on each side, contain mysterious niches (Plate 32). The groove and the niches are rarely mentioned by the experts, since their symbolism is impossible to determine, and they could not, according to these experts, have had any practical purpose. Whatever they might have contained is unknown, but damage to the Gallery's walls, alongside each niche, strongly suggests that something was forcibly removed in ancient times.

The Grand Gallery ends with a small passageway into a complex Antechamber, which protects the entrance to the so-called King's Chamber. The walls of the Antechamber have been precision cut with grooves, one of which was found to contain a granite slab (or leaf), mysteriously cemented into position. Three other granite slabs, for which vertical grooves have been cut, are presumed missing. When lowered, these slabs would originally have descended to 3 inches beneath floor level. The uppermost part of the Antechamber contains unusual semi-circular hollows on one side, leading even the cautious experts to acknowledge some form of sophisticated portcullis device, which could lower the hard granite slabs to block access to the King's Chamber.

Passing through the Antechamber, one again bends double to gain access into the King's Chamber. The main feature is a mysterious granite box, nicknamed the 'coffer' (Plate 31), measuring 90 by 39 by 41 inches. This featureless and lidless box is often referred to as Khufu's tomb, but, whilst it is the right size for a body, it was in fact found totally empty. It is believed that this coffer once had a lid.

One text book states that the mummy of Khufu once lay in this sarcophagus, adorned with gold mask, jewellery and other material possessions.[11] This is a complete fabrication, and one despairs at such irresponsibility from an authoritative text book which many readers will accept without question.

Both the King's Chamber and the Queen's Chamber each contain a pair of so-called 'airshafts' – small rectangular shafts with a cross-section measuring approximately 8 inches by 8 inches. This is yet another unique feature, seen in no other pyramid in Egypt. Whilst the airshafts in the King's Chamber extend to the Pyramid's outer layer of masonry, those in the Queen's Chamber do not, thus disproving the myth that they really could have functioned as airshafts.

Recently, accurate measurements have been taken of some of these shafts, and it has been suggested that they were aligned to certain stars when the Pyramid was built. The evidence for this is somewhat tenuous, and will be covered in a later chapter. Suffice to say, for now, that the small doorway with metal handles, discovered by Rudolf Gantenbrink in one of the Queen's Chamber airshafts, suggests that it played a functional rather than a symbolic purpose.

Mathematical Excellence

The pyramids at Giza are sometimes called the only 'true' pyramids, because they are the only ones in Egypt with sides that rise at the 'perfect' angle of 52 degrees.

Why is 52 degrees so important? This angle embodies in the Pyramid the mathematical pi factor,[12] but more significantly, it is only at 52 degrees that the ratio of the height of the Pyramid to its base perimeter is exactly the same as that of the radius of a circle to its circumference.[13] Furthermore, the 52-degree pyramid also builds in the special geometric feature of the golden section.[14]

The technical difficulties with building at the extremely steep angle of 52 degrees are evidenced by the collapsed pyramid at Maidum and the Bent Pyramid at Dahshur, the latter having been changed in mid-construction to the safer angle of 43.5 degrees (Plate 29). This angle also embodies pi, but not in the perfect sense of the 52-degree pyramid.[15]

The mathematical symmetry of the Great Pyramid is such that the angles of the Ascending and Descending Passages, when added together, closely approximate the 52-degree angle at which the Pyramid itself rises from the ground.

All studies of the pyramids have confirmed the use of pi in their design, and caused a reassessment of the mathematical knowledge of the Egyptians. Unfortunately, the more measurements that are taken, the more likely that arbitrary or coincidental relationships will turn up, and this has certainly happened in the case of the Great Pyramid, where many researchers have been determined to find new relationships to fit their preconceived theories.[16] Nevertheless, the more outrageous and contrived claims should not be allowed to detract from the many genuine features of the Pyramid which are truly astounding. We have already covered its polar alignment and aspects of the amazing scale and features of the design; it is now time to get down to the nitty gritty.

Twentieth Century Engineering

Our first example of twentieth century engineering in the Giza pyramids is the six-sided limestone casing blocks, which were polished and precision carved to fit perfectly with each other and the core stones, with joints measuring less than one fiftieth of an inch. As if this was not incredible enough, all of these stones were found to be joined together with an extremely fine but strong cement, which had been applied evenly on semi-vertical faces across a surface expanse covering 21 acres on the Great Pyramid alone.[17] Sir William Flinders Petrie, one of the most eminent archaeologists to have studied Giza, commented:

> Merely to place such stones in exact contact would be careful work, but to do so with cement in the joints seems almost impossible: it is to be compared with the finest opticians' work.[18]

The second example is the internal passages of the Great Pyramid. These passages have been measured countless times and found to be perfectly straight, with a deviation, in the case of the Descending Passage, of less than one fiftieth of an inch along its masonry part. Over a length of 150 feet that is incredible. If one includes the further 200 feet of passage bored through the solid rock, the error is less than one quarter of an inch. Now this is engineering of the highest precision, comparable with twentieth century technology, but supposedly achieved 4,500 years ago.

Our third example is the machining of granite within the pyramids. One of the first archaeologists to carry out a thorough survey of the Pyramid was Petrie, who was particularly struck by the granite coffer in the King's Chamber. The precision with which the coffer had been carved out of a single block of extremely hard granite struck him as quite remarkable. Petrie estimated that diamond-tipped drills would need to have been applied with a pressure of two tons, in order to hollow out the granite box.[19] It was not a serious suggestion as to the method actually used, but simply his way of expressing the impossibility of creating that artefact using nineteenth century technology. It is still a difficult challenge, even with twentieth century technology. And yet we are supposed to believe that Khufu achieved this at a time when the Egyptians possessed only the most basic copper hand tools.

In 1995, an English engineer named Chris Dunn visited Egypt with the express intention of figuring out how their granite artefacts were produced. Dunn appeared to me to have the right qualifications for the task, including an open mind, for in his own words:

> When I look at an artefact with a view of how it was manufactured, I am unencumbered with a predisposition to filter out possibilities because of historical or chronological inequity. Having spent most of my career involved with the machinery that actually creates artefacts of the modern kind, such as jet engine components, I am fairly well equipped to analyse and determine the methods necessary for recreating an artefact under study. I have been fortunate, also, to have training and experience in some non-conventional methods of manufacturing, such as laser processing and electrical discharge machining.[20]

Dunn visited the Cairo Museum, the pyramids and the granite quarry at Aswan, in an attempt to figure out the processes that were used. It quickly became clear to him that many of the artefacts could not have been made without the use of very advanced machinery:

> We would be hard pressed to produce many of these artefacts today, even using our advanced methods of manufacturing. The tools displayed as instruments for the creation of these incredible artefacts are physically incapable of even coming close to reproducing many of the artefacts in question.[21]

Chris Dunn found that many artefacts bore the same marks as conventional twentieth century machining methods – sawing, lathe and milling practices.[22] He was particularly interested, however, in the evidence of a modern processing technique known as trepanning. This process is used to excavate a hollow in a block of hard stone by first drilling, and then breaking out, the remaining 'core'. Petrie had studied both the hollows and the cores, and been astonished to find spiral grooves on the core which indicated a drill feed rate of 0.100 inch per revolution of the drill. This initially seemed to be impossible. In 1983, Dunn had ascertained that industrial diamond drills could cut granite with a drill rotation speed of 900 revolutions per minute and a feed rate of 0.0002 inch per revolution. What these technicalities actually mean is that the ancient Egyptians were cutting their granite with a feed rate 500 times greater than 1983 technology!

Dunn was thus forced to consider more recent, and less conventional, machining methods. He asked himself what *single* method could explain *all* of the physical observations on the hollows and cores, including one particular mystery of how the spiral groove had cut deeper into the quartz content of the granite, which was harder than the surrounding rock (feldspar). Dunn posed the same challenge independently to another engineer, and eventually they both came to the same conclusion – the only possible method which fitted all the facts was *ultrasonic machining*.

In the late twentieth century, the ultrasonic tool-bit has found particular favour in the precision machining of unusually shaped holes in hard, brittle materials such as hardened steels, carbides, ceramics and semiconductors. Chris Dunn compares the drilling process to the motion of a jackhammer on a concrete pavement, but vibrating faster than the eye can see, at 19,000-25,000 cycles per second. Assisted by an abrasive slurry or paste, the tool bit cuts by an oscillatory grinding action. This feature, and only this feature, can explain the groove cut deeper into the harder quartz:

> In machining granite using ultrasonics, the harder material, quartz, would not necessarily offer more resistance, as it might

during conventional machining practices . . . the quartz [in the granite] would be induced to respond and vibrate in sympathy with the high frequency [ultrasonic] waves, and amplify the abrasive action as the tool cut through it.[23]

The unavoidable conclusion is that whoever built the Giza pyramids possessed extraordinary machinery and the capability to use it. Furthermore, the accuracy is such that the cutting tool alone is not sufficient. These tools must have been guided, not by the human eye, but by computer.

The Khufu Fraud

In April 1988, American television viewers were subjected to an outrageous programme on the Giza pyramids. The show, entitled *Mysteries of the Pyramids – Live* was hosted by Omar Sharif, interviewing a supposedly expert Egyptologist. In front of millions of viewers, the expert stated 'we *know* that the pyramids were built by the ancient Egyptians 5,000 years ago'. That sweeping statement was followed by the alleged proof – a royal cartouche of Khufu's name, painted inside the Great Pyramid. Upon hearing the expert's explanation of the cartouche, Sharif gratefully exclaimed: 'So. Proof that Cheops [Khufu] did build the pyramid – so much for ancient astronauts'.

As we shall soon see, the American public were provided with *total disinformation* by *Mysteries of the Pyramids – Live*. But before dealing with the alleged proof by cartouche, let us examine the other evidence often cited in support of 'Khufu's pyramid'.

In the fifth century BC, the Greek historian Herodotus returned from a visit to Egypt, claiming that the three pyramids at Giza belonged to Khufu, Khafra and Menkaura. Herodotus may have been a great historian, but evidently he relied on the word of his hosts – the Egyptian priests. How do we know that they told him the truth?

Herodotus' claims are recorded *as fact* by all of our history books, but what are the real facts? First, there is no evidence whatsoever to suggest that Khufu was a particularly well-known pharaoh. The text books admit that 'very little is known about Cheops [Khufu]'.[24] This is totally at odds with the suggestion that he built the Great Pyramid which, as I have demonstrated, is far superior to any other pyramid built in Egypt. Surely such a structure would have won Khufu respect and more than a passing mention in Egyptian history? And yet there are no exaltations, no records of mighty deeds, not even a single statue that can definitively be identified as representing Khufu.

The second fact is that, curiously, none of the other historians from antiquity who visited Egypt ever mentioned a pharaoh named Khufu, and none of those other historians claimed to know the name of the builder of the Great Pyramid.

The third suspicious fact is that, although Herodotus was able to name the builders of the Giza pyramids, and to state the time taken to construct the Pyramid and its causeway, he could offer no convincing explanation as to *how* it was constructed nor *the purpose* for which it was built.[25] He therefore left the most interesting questions unanswered.

Other than the word of Herodotus, there is only one single piece of evidence that the Great Pyramid may have belonged to Khufu – a painted cartouche of Khufu's hieroglyphic name, found inside the Pyramid by an English archaeologist, Colonel Howard Vyse.

When Colonel Vyse first went to Egypt in 1835, the *idea* that the Great Pyramid belonged to Khufu was already well established, although direct evidence was totally lacking. One can imagine Vyse's frustration, two years later, to have found no inscriptions whatsoever inside the Giza pyramids that would connect them to any of the pharaohs. Driven by frustration and ambition, Vyse then proceeded to have a cartouche of Khufu's name *forged* in a most unlikely place – an enclosed space between the giant granite slabs above the King's Chamber of the Great Pyramid. How do we know this? Due to a long-overdue and thorough investigation in 1980 by Zecharia Sitchin.[26] I will now summarise the overwhelming evidence cited by Sitchin.

How can we be so sure of a fraud by Vyse? The most damning evidence against him is a series of errors in the various markings and cartouches which were found daubed in red paint. Incredible as it may seem, the first suspicions of a fraud were raised in 1837, shortly after the discovery was made. Vyse had sent copies of the cartouches to the British Museum for confirmation. It has always been assumed that the opinion of its hieroglyphics expert, Samuel Birch, supported the reading of the cartouche as 'Khufu'. This was not the case, and in fact Birch expressed many doubts. In particular, he noted that many of the marks were curiously indistinct and that some of the symbols were highly unusual, never found in Egypt before (or since). He was also puzzled by the style of the script which did not begin to appear in Egypt until centuries later; some of the symbols could only be matched closely to ones appearing 2,000 years *after* the time of Khufu. Birch even found a symbol for an adjective used as a numeral – a basic grammatical error.

It is also little known that Birch found the names of *two* pharaohs in the inscriptions, a fact which he was totally unable to explain. He concluded that 'the presence of this (second) name, as a quarry mark, in the Great Pyramid, is an *additional* embarrassment' (emphasis added). This did indeed embarrass the Egyptologists, for it fundamentally called into question the authenticity of the inscription and their conclusion that the Pyramid belonged to Khufu. The matter has conveniently been left unresolved for over a hundred and fifty years.[27]

Subject to all the above provisos, Birch concluded that the royal cartouche could be read as that of Khufu.

The worst error made by the forgers was in the royal cartouche of Khufu itself. In the 1830s, Egyptology was in its infancy, and the forgers had to rely on the few specialist books which had been published. No-one was exactly sure what Khufu's cartouche should look like. One of these books, *Materia Hieroglyphica*, by Sir John Gardner Wilkinson, a standard reference work at the time, was constantly referred to in Vyse's diaries. Unfortunately for Vyse, Wilkinson's work was subsequently shown to contain various errors. In particular, it confused the sign for *Kh* with the sign for the solar disk representing Ra. The royal name found inscribed in the Great Pyramid contained exactly the same mistake.

With the benefit of hindsight, we now know that the name found by Vyse incorrectly used the solar disk, giving a reading of *Ra-ufu* rather than *Kh-ufu*. As Zecharia Sitchin has pointed out, this would not only have been an inconceivable error for an Egyptian scribe of the time, but would also have been blasphemy, since Ra was one of the foremost gods of the ancient Egyptians! Sitchin summarises as follows:

> Whoever daubed the red-paint markings reported by Vyse had thus employed a writing method (linear), scripts (semi-hieratic and hieratic) and titles from various periods – but none from the time of Khufu, and all from later periods. Their writer was also not too literate: many of his hieroglyphs were either unclear, incomplete, out of place, erroneously employed or completely unknown . . . The substitution of *Ra* for *Kh* was an error that could not have been committed in the time of Khufu . . . only a stranger to hieroglyphics . . . could have committed such a grave error.[28]

This undeniable proof of the forgery explains a number of other strange occurrences during Vyse's visit to Egypt: the firing of key members of his staff for no apparent reason; illogical instructions given to his staff at certain times; his first 'discovery' in the presence of two independent witnesses of markings which he had somehow overlooked when on his own; inconsistencies between his 'discoveries' and his diary records; manipulation of dates in his diaries; and suspicious circumstances surrounding a subsequent 'discovery' by Vyse of Menkaura's name in the third pyramid, which many suspect to have been a fraud. It also explains why no inscriptions were found in the first compartment above the King's Chamber, discovered by the earlier archaeologist Nathaniel Davison in 1765, but only in those higher compartments opened by Vyse.

Two further points are pointed out by Zecharia Sitchin. First, the markings found by Vyse are very large and crude compared to the neat and compact hieroglyphics normally used by the Egyptians. Secondly, and most suspiciously, no markings were found on the eastern walls of the compartments which Vyse had blasted through with explosives. The full story revealed by Sitchin is highly incriminating of Vyse and his loyal assistant Mr Hill. The motivation of Vyse to embark on such a fraud is not hard to fathom, given that he was running out of both time and money, finding nothing, and, by his own admission, 'I naturally wished to make some discoveries before I returned to England'.[29]

We are left with only two possibilities – either the markings were placed by an illiterate workman when the Great Pyramid was built, a workman who did not know for sure who his king was. Or the whole episode was a shameful archaeological fraud.

Having proved Khufu's (or should we say Ra-ufu's!) cartouche to be a fraud, there is absolutely no other evidence, other than the word of Herodotus, to identify the Great Pyramid with Khufu. The same applies to the other two pyramids, allegedly of Khafra and Menkaura. It is therefore hardly surprising that Zecharia Sitchin's evi-

dence has not been refuted, but rather ignored by the
Egyptologists. Who can blame them for such a tactic, since
if they were to admit the Pyramid does not belong to Khufu,
they would have to admit that they do not know who it
belongs to – an embarrassing admission for the so-called
experts.

Tombs of the Pharaohs?

The amazing Great Pyramid is supposed to have three
tombs, just in case the pharaoh died during the construction – this is seriously what the text books tell us! The
British Museum attributes the Great Pyramid's 'unusual
internal design' to 'the result of alterations in plan during
construction' – a direct reference to the traditional theory
that *each* of the chambers was intended as a tomb, and that
therefore the builders must have changed their minds
during the course of construction.

Is there any evidence to support the still commonly held
notion that the Great Pyramid was indeed a tomb, albeit a
high technology one? Such a suggestion – that the King's
Chamber (or the Queen's Chamber for that matter) of the
Great Pyramid was a tomb – flies in the face of the
evidence we have. To the surprise of many who have
taken the tomb theory at face value, no body, no mummy, nothing at all connected in any remote way with a
burial or a tomb, has ever been found inside the Great
Pyramid.

The Arab historians, who recorded Mamoon's entry into
the Pyramid, stated that there was no evidence of a tomb,
and no evidence of grave robbers, since the upper part of the
Pyramid had been very effectively sealed off and hidden. No
grave robber would have sealed a tomb after robbing it – he
would be more interested in a quick getaway. The unavoid-

able conclusion from this line of reasoning is that the Pyramid was designed to be empty.

Furthermore, the idea that the upper chambers of the Great Pyramid were ever designed for a burial is quite inconsistent with the fact that not one Egyptian pharaoh ever had his tomb placed high above ground level. In fact, a study of the numerous other pyramids in Egypt reveals no evidence that *any of them* were ever used as tombs.

According to convention, the obsession with pyramid building began with Djoser, an early pharaoh of the Third Dynasty *c.* 2630 BC, several hundred years after Egyptian civilisation began. For no reason which is apparent to us, he decided to abandon the simple mud-brick tombs of his predecessors and build the first ever pyramid of stone at Saqqara. It was an extremely ambitious project, supposedly unique and without precedent in Egypt (although similar ziggurats were being built in Mesopotamia centuries earlier). He was assisted in this task by an architect named Imhotep, a shadowy character about whom little is known.[30] Djoser's pyramid was built at an angle of approximately 43.5 degrees.

In the early nineteenth century, two 'burial chambers' were discovered underneath Djoser's pyramid, and further excavations revealed underground galleries with two *empty* sarcophagae. It has since been generally accepted that this pyramid was a tomb for Djoser, and also for members of his family, but in fact his remains have never been found, and there is no hard evidence that Djoser was ever buried in the pyramid.[31] On the contrary, many eminent Egyptologists are now convinced that Djoser was buried in a magnificent, highly decorated tomb, discovered in 1928, to the south of the pyramid. They can only conclude that the pyramid itself was never designed as a proper tomb, but represented either a symbolic tomb or an elaborate scheme to fool graverobbers.

Djoser's successor, it is believed, was the pharaoh Sekhemkhet. His pyramid also had a 'burial chamber' containing an *empty* sarcophagus. Whilst the official story is that the tomb was robbed, the truth is that the discoverer of the chamber, Zakaria Goneim, had found the sarcophagus fitted with a vertical sliding door which had been *sealed* with plaster. Again there is no evidence that this pyramid was intended as a tomb.[32]

Other lesser-known pyramids of the Third Dynasty follow a similar theme: the step-pyramid of Khaba was found *completely bare*; nearby was discovered another unfinished pyramid with a mysterious chamber, oval-shaped like a bath-tub, *sealed and empty*; and three other small pyramids contain no evidence of burials whatsoever.

The first ruler of the Fourth Dynasty, *c.* 2575 BC, was Sneferu. Here the pyramids-as-tombs theory takes another blow, for Sneferu is believed to have built not one but three pyramids. His first pyramid, at Maidum, was built too steep and collapsed. Nothing at all was found in the burial chamber other than fragments of a wooden coffin, believed to have been a later, intrusive burial. Sneferu's second and third pyramids were built at Dahshur. His second, known as the Bent Pyramid (Plate 29, colour section), is believed to have been built at the same time as that at Maidum, for the angle was suddenly changed in mid-construction from around 52 degrees to the safer angle of 43.5 degrees. The third pyramid is known as the Red Pyramid, after the local pink limestone which had been used, and this one rose at a steady but safe angle of around 43.5 degrees. These pyramids had two and three 'burial chambers' respectively, each of which was found to be *totally empty*.

Why did Sneferu require two pyramids close together, and what was the symbolism of the empty chambers? Having gone to such an effort, why would he be buried elsewhere? Surely one false tomb is enough to fool the robbers?

Now Khufu is believed to be the son of Sneferu, so we

arrive at the supposed construction date of the Great Pyramid at Giza without one shred of evidence that *any* pyramid was ever intended to be a tomb.[33] And yet all the books, all the tour guides and all the television documentaries state categorically and repeatedly that the pyramids at Giza, like all the other pyramids in Egypt, were tombs.

In summary, we have here an excellent illustration of how a nonsensical theory can take hold. Experts are eventually forced to defend the accepted theory with increasingly contrived explanations, such as the Giza builders 'changing their minds'. They are too arrogant to give us an honest 'don't know', and too weak to challenge the prevailing paradigm. Should we continue to blindly believe what these experts are telling us?

A New Theory

Egyptologists will undoubtedly cling to the argument that the Great Pyramid must be Khufu's because it dates to 2550 BC, when the only evidence that it was built in 2550 BC is the claim that Khufu built it. If we ignore this circular argument and examine the facts outlined so far, then the whole question of the builders and dates of construction of the Giza Pyramids is wide open. The only clue we do have is that twentieth century technology was used in their construction.

The official chronology starts with the 43.5-degree step-pyramid of Djoser, followed by pyramids such as those of Sekhemkhet and Sneferu. Within one hundred years of Djoser, we are expected to believe that a huge leap in technology enabled Khufu and his successors to build, with incredible precision, the 52-degree pyramids at Giza. Not only did they build pyramids in a different league to those which had gone before, but they also added unique design features which had never been seen before. The whole of the upper system of passages and chambers in the Great Pyramid is absolutely unique.

At this point the Egyptologists conveniently pass by Khufu's son Radjedef who, for unexplained reasons, chose not to use Giza, but selected a site some miles to the north.[34] Khafra and Menkaura then returned to Giza to build their pyramids.

According to the conventional chronology, the amazing peak of technology at Giza was immediately followed, for unexplained or contrived reasons, by a terminal technological decline. Egyptologists admit it is a mystery why Shepseskaf (the successor to Menkaura) built only a simple mudbrick tomb.[35] There then followed the Fifth and Sixth Dynasties of pharaohs, who did build some fine pyramids (once again featuring empty 'burial chambers'), such as that of Sahure, but never again on a par with Giza. The Sixth Dynasty saw a change in style with the pyramids of Unas, Teti, Pepy I, Merenre and Pepy II, which were elaborately decorated with the famous Pyramid Texts, but still included empty sarcophagae.[36]

I would now like to put forward a much more plausible theory – that the Giza pyramids *preceded* all of the other pyramids in Egypt and that they acted as a model for them. I would like to suggest that someone was once privy to the knowledge of the empty coffer which was hidden in the sealed upper section of the Great Pyramid. The later pharaohs then copied the empty boxes, which they believed to be symbolically important. Is there any evidence for the Giza-First theory?

Recent findings from an American archaeological mission have shown that Djoser's pyramid at Saqqara was originally cased with primitive mud bricks whitewashed to simulate white limestone, which soon crumbled to leave the impression of a step-pyramid.[37] Djoser's original pyramid would therefore have resembled those at Giza, with their gleaming white limestone casing stones.

It seems reasonable to believe that Sneferu may then have attempted to out-do Djoser by building two pyramids to match the two large pyramids at Giza. The attempted 52-degree angle which led to the collapse of his first pyramid at Maidum strongly suggests a familiarity with the pyramids at Giza. The theory is further strengthened by the fact that the angle of the Bent pyramid at Dahshur was altered in mid-construction, suggesting that it was being built simultaneously to that at Maidum.[38] It is therefore significant that, when the Maidum pyramid collapsed, Sneferu continued his ambitious two-pyramid scheme by constructing the Red Pyramid nearby. Protrusions on the side of the Red Pyramid indicate that it too may have been designed to support a white limestone casing, in emulation of Giza.

If the Great Pyramid already existed, then we cannot attribute any known pyramid to Sneferu's son, Khufu. It has been suggested that, in view of the difficulties in replicating the 52-degree angle, Khufu may have decided to forgo the hassle of building his own pyramid; instead he chose to 'adopt' the Great Pyramid as his own by building a temple nearby, whilst hiding his tomb somewhere in the vicinity.[39]

Khufu's son Radjedef may have thought his father's action was sacrilege, and this would explain why he resorted to a self-built pyramid, albeit a poor one. Khafra and Menkaura then copied Khufu's idea and 'adopted' the second and third pyramids at Giza.[40]

The apparent decline in technology after Khufu, Khafra and Menkaura, which has mystified the Egyptologists, now becomes understandable, since there was never a peak in technology at all, only a decline from the true 52-degree originals of Giza. When the pyramids on the Giza site had been fully adopted by the pharaohs, later pharaohs resorted to building their own pyramids.

The final test is, of course, to prove the age of the Great

Pyramid to be older then 2550 BC. We will return to this question in a later chapter. For now I will mention as evidence only the well known victory tablet of the very first pharaoh Menes (also known by the name Nar-Mer). This tablet, exhibited in the Egyptian Museum in Cairo, depicts the forceful unification of Upper and Lower Egypt by Menes *c*. 3100 BC. The tablet has been comprehensively studied by scholars, who are agreed that its symbols accurately represent the various places and enemies encountered during Menes' campaign. But, as Zecharia Sitchin has pointed out, one symbol has been conveniently ignored.[41] It is a *pyramid-shaped* symbol in the top left section of the tablet (Plate 34, colour section) which represents *Lower* Egypt – an accurate location for the Great Pyramid. This is only one piece of evidence, which does not constitute a proof, but it does seem to suggest that the Giza pyramids *already* existed in Egypt *c*. 3100 BC.

Finally, how do we explain the fact that Herodotus attributed the Great Pyramid to Khufu? If the pyramids already existed before civilisation began in Egypt, the Egyptian priests may simply not have known who built the pyramids, but knew they had been 'adopted' by Khufu and his successors. Could it be that an over-eager Herodotus, thirsting for knowledge as historians do, fell into the trap of pushing the priests so hard that they told him lies to shut him up? Human nature does not change, even over two thousand years. We should remember that Herodotus never answered the really interesting question of *how* the pyramids were built. It would have been quite easy for the priests to furnish Herodotus with an answer to the question of 'who', but much more difficult to explain the 'how' and the 'why', *if they did not know*.

A Trip to the Afterlife

Let us briefly step back from Egypt and resume a global viewpoint. In England, Stonehenge was built at a time before any society was supposed to exist. In South America, Tiwanaku was built thousands of years before history officially began. In Lebanon, the platform at Baalbek has never been dated, but legends place it, too, in a time before recorded history. The pyramids of Giza belong in the same category – before records began in Egypt. All of these sites have one other thing in common. They carry no inscriptions of any kind commemorating their builders.

It is as if – all around the world – there is a shadowy prehistory that precedes the official history of civilised man. Out of this history, a legacy has passed down to us – a legacy in stone, a legacy in mythology, a legacy in technology, which can only now be recognised in the twentieth century. It is not surprising that many people have therefore been drawn to the idea of Atlantis. But what kind of people were these Atlanteans who never left their names or those of their gods?

It is no coincidence that our open-minded study of the Great Pyramid has catapulted it back in time, before Menes, to the dynasties of the gods which were recorded by Manetho. But it leaves us asking many questions. Why a pyramid shape?[42] Why its unique grooves, niches and chambers? And what content or function of the King's Chamber was so important that it required protection by portcullises?

The ancient Egyptians texts record legends of flesh-and-blood gods. One legend describes the 'winged disc' of Ra, which was flown into battle by Horus. There is also reference to a foundry of 'divine iron' at Edfu and an underground complex known as the Duat, from which the pharaohs could soar heavenward. Are these tales the product of superstitious imagination, or memories of actual events and real locations?

The Ani Papyrus, housed in the British Museum, depicts the pharaoh's trip to the afterlife. The climax of the journey involves the 'opening of the mouth' ceremony, which I hinted in chapter 1 might refer to the 'mouth' of an underground chamber. At this ceremony, the Ani Papyrus shows the mummified body of the pharaoh accompanied by what appears to be a rocket (Figure 3, black-and-white section).[43]

Our preconceptions are so deeply ingrained that we want to laugh aloud at the notion, but how can we dismiss the incredible technology that exists within the pyramids at Giza – 'space age technology' in the words of the English engineer Chris Dunn? This state-of-the-art precision technology is not inconsistent with the ability to build rockets or aircraft. When we consider also the evidence from Nazca and Baalbek, some of the wilder theories of the pyramids as beacons for aerial navigation now do not sound so fanciful.

Let us consider once again the afterlife cult of the pharaohs. The deceased god Osiris was supposed to have made a journey between two mountains to the Duat, ascended to the stars and come back to life. The Pyramid Texts, cited in chapter 1, appear to describe technical aspects of an actual visit to the underground Duat. *What if the Egyptians knew that the pyramids at Giza played a role in the navigation to the Duat, where flesh-and-blood gods, perceived to be immortal, ascended to the heavens?* A religion could thus form (like the Cargo Cult) which required the building of a pyramid (or two) to emulate Giza, and an empty granite box to replicate the one in the King's Chamber.

If this seems unrealistic, then let us briefly consider the best alternative theory. The idea that the Great Pyramid was a *symbolic* tomb now seems to represent the new scientific consensus. According to this theory, the Pyramid's shafts pointed to the stars so that the soul of the pharaoh could be guided to heaven for eternal life. But why four shafts? Our mysterious pharaoh must have been quite a cosmic traveller! And why would Sneferu build himself three pyramids? What is the point of three eternal lives when you have one?

All of the establishment theories have their roots in Egyptian mythology, but at the same time they deny any reality within that mythology. And, in that denial, they lose credibility in explaining why such powerful religious beliefs came about. Thus we are expected to believe that the Egyptians' fear of death was so great that they *invented* a means to an afterlife. This is all very well, but would it really have inspired them to pile millions of limestone blocks one on top of the other? And where would the unique idea of a pyramid-shape have come from, for what possible connection is there, in an abstract sense, between a pyramid and everlasting life?

We will return in a later chapter to the subject of the Giza pyramids, and indeed to the Sphinx, which has recently been dated to thousands of years before the pharaohs. I will then summarise the evidence that establishes without any doubt the connection of these pyramids with the Duat. I will also establish the pyramids' date of construction and explain the motivation of the gods who built them. Finally, I will put forward a theory that explains *all* of the Great Pyramid's features based on a *functional* rather than a symbolic interpretation.

Chapter Four Conclusions

* The pyramids at Giza are totally distinct from any other pyramids in Egypt, with unique features such as

the Great Pyramid's upper passages, chambers, niches, shafts and Grand Gallery.

* The Great Pyramid was not a tomb. In fact, no evidence has been found in *any* of the pyramids in Egypt to suggest that they were originally constructed as tombs.

* The evidence linking the Great Pyramid to Khufu is based on an archaeological fraud. The identity of its builders and its age are therefore completely open questions.

* The pyramids show unmistakable signs of twentieth century technology – for example, ultrasonic machining.

CHAPTER FIVE

IMPOSSIBLE SCIENCE

———◆———

Nonsense from the Experts

In the third century AD, Flavius Philostratus declared that 'if the land be considered in relation to the entire mass of water, we can show that the earth is the lesser of the two'.[1] How could this have been known without an aerial survey of the Earth? In this chapter, I shall be reviewing some of the best documented, irrefutable examples of ancient science – examples which can be physically seen in situ or in museums.

I will be focusing particularly on several ancient civilisations which possessed advanced astronomical knowledge. This extraordinary knowledge can be ignored, but it cannot be denied. Some scientists have bravely tried to explain the existence of this knowledge with the suggestion that the ancient civilisations needed astronomy to tell them when to sow and reap their harvests. I am not joking! This idea is repeated ad nauseam in our text books. Here, for example, is one quote concerning the ancient Maya of Mesoamerica:

An obsession with the calendar, though not always to this marked degree, is a common feature of societies dominated by agricultural and religious festivals. An exact knowledge of the seasons and the period of maximum rainfall is, of course, essential to the timing of seed-sowing and harvesting.[2]

What preposterous nonsense! I am sure that farmers today would feel quite insulted at the suggestion of consulting an astronomer for guidance on the change in seasons. Here are a few basic truths that should squash this myth once and for all: first, whenever primitive societies have been found in the world they have managed to feed themselves and survive without astronomy or a calendar. Secondly, the calendar was invented by an urban society at Nippur in Sumer, not by an agricultural society. Thirdly, the astronomically aligned site of Stonehenge in England was originally laid out when no organised agricultural society is supposed to have existed in that area.

Necessity is the mother of invention. Surely our imaginary society would have been busy planting their crops, not hauling 50-ton stones across hundreds of miles of countryside. And why, as several experts have noted, should the Mayan calendars have emphasised long-term accuracy over hundreds and even thousands of years – are we to suppose that they were engaged in long-range weather forecasting for agricultural purposes?[3]

The suggestion that mankind developed advanced astronomy and built complex observatories for 'religious' reasons is equally intriguing. Somehow we are expected to believe that our ancient ancestors worshipped the wind, the rain, the Sun, the Moon, and so on, and built sophisticated observatories and temples to watch and to worship the movements of these 'gods'.

Primitive people may well have prayed to imaginary gods to grant them good crops, as aboriginal tribes do today, but would the Maya really have man-handled five million tons of material to construct the acropolis at Copan, to name but one example? To absorb thousands of man-years in such a task requires a proportion of idle time that is a feature of an advanced society, and advanced societies are not seduced by gods of the wind and rain. The Maya deserve more credit than that, and so do the Egyptians and the Sumerians.

As we take our tour through the 'impossible' ancient sciences of geography and astronomy, we must ask ourselves how and why these sciences arose, and we must reassess the motivations of our ancient ancestors.

Miracles of the Map-Makers

Modern mapping began with the 'Age of Discovery' – a period during which explorers achieved great fame from their expeditions into new territories. The Age began with the three voyages of Columbus, to the Bahamas, Puerto Rico and Haiti between 1492 and 1498. He was followed in 1500–1501 by the Florentine explorer, Amerigo Vespucci (after whom the American continent was named), who navigated the coastlines of Venezuela and Brazil, but turned back at Uruguay. Between 1519 and 1522, the Portuguese navigator, Magellan, sailed nearly all the way down the South American coast.[4] In 1530, Francisco Pizarro, the Spanish adventurer, sailed from Panama to Peru; he returned years later to conquer Peru and to explore inland and further down the coast.

These great journeys are supposed to have discovered new worlds and new coastlines which had never been seen or mapped before (we are supposed to ignore the fact that the local inhabitants lived there). But in the Topkapi Museum of Istanbul, there are two remarkably accurate maps known as 'Piri Re'is', which are contemporary with the Age of Discovery and therefore, according to the historical paradigm, should not have existed.

The first map bears a Moslem date equivalent to AD 1513, along with a note that it was partly based on maps used by Columbus. This map covers the Iberian Peninsula, the west coast of Africa, the Canary Islands, the Azores, the Atlantic Ocean, the West Indies, the eastern coast of South America and the Antarctica coastline to a point roughly underneath Africa.

The second Piri Re'is map, dated 1528, covers Greenland, Labrador, Newfoundland, the east coast of Canada, the east coast of North America as far down as Florida, and Cuba. It is suspected that a third map showing Europe, Asia and the Indian Ocean may also have existed.[5]

The most amazing thing about the Piri Re'is maps is their level of detail and accuracy. The eastern coast of South America in the 1513 map is charted all the way to the Patagonian tip, a coastline which, in its entirety, was supposedly unknown at that time.

A study by Charles Hapgood noted that the map also correctly depicted the Andean mountains and the rivers flowing eastward from them (such as the Amazon), areas which none of the 'discoverers' had attempted to explore.[6] Hapgood found that some parts of the South American Pacific coast had also been mapped, and stated that 'the drawings of the mountains indicate that they were observed from the sea, from coastwise shipping, and not imagined'.

Even more remarkably, the Piri Re'is maps accurately depicted the topography of Antarctica, together with its islands, rivers and coastline. Yet Antarctica has been covered by a one mile thick layer of ice for thousands of years.[7] Officially, this land was only discovered in 1820, and it was only between 1957 and 1960 that a comprehensive seismic survey revealed the true nature of Antarctica as a large continent with high mountains.[8] As the Piri Re'is maps were discovered in 1929, 28 years before modern science was able to probe the features beneath the ice, they cannot be accused of being fraudulent.

No less incredible than the depiction of Antarctica, was the amazing accuracy of the locations on the map. Gibraltar, for instance, was located at a longitude of 35 degrees north and a latitude of 7 degrees west; this is within 1 and 2 degrees respectively of the modern geographic position. Similarly, the Canary Islands were located within 1 degree in both directions.[9]

An investigation by the American cartographer Arlington Mallerey initially found all of the Piri Re'is features to be correct but in the wrong places. Subsequently, with the help of Mr Walters, a cartographer from the US Navy Hydrographic Bureau, he constructed a grid from the maps and transferred it to a globe. The perfect accuracy of the resulting map indicated an advanced knowledge of spherical trigonometry which stunned the scientists.[10] Following further studies of the maps, a press conference was held on 28th August 1958, supported by the US Navy Cartographer. The organisers stated:

> . . . we can't imagine how they could have made such accurate maps without the help of aircraft. The fact is that they did and what is more, they fixed the degrees of longitude absolutely correctly, something we couldn't do until two hundred years ago.[11]

The Piri Re'is maps are not alone. Other ancient maps of the world such as the Oronteus Finaeus map of 1531 and the Zeno map of 1380 have been subjected to similar scrutiny, with similar results. Regarding the Orontius Finaeus map, which also showed Antarctica's now hidden geographical and topographical features, Captain Burroughs, Chief of the US Air Force Cartographic Section concluded:

> It is our opinion that the accuracy of the cartographic features shown in the Orontius Finaeus map suggests, beyond a doubt, that it was compiled from accurate source maps of Antarctica.

Some of these ancient map-makers clearly attributed their knowledge to other even older maps, which once existed, and it is possible that they in turn date back to the time of the Phoenicians, the famous seafarers from the first millennium BC.[12] But where did the Phoenicians acquire their knowledge? All of these maps have caused a fundamental rethink of the knowledge possessed by ancient civilisations. Charles Hapgood summed up his findings as follows:

> It becomes clear that ancient voyagers travelled from pole to pole. Unbelievable as it may appear, the evidence nevertheless indicates that some ancient people explored Antarctica when its coasts were free of ice . . . The evidence presented by the ancient maps appears to suggest the existence in remote times, before the rise of any of the known cultures, of a true civilisation of a comparatively advanced sort, which either was localised in one area but had worldwide commerce, or was, in a real sense a worldwide culture.[13]

The Antikythera Computer

Whilst there is no doubt regarding the existence of sophisticated ancient maps, attempts are nevertheless made to undermine their credibility by raising doubts as to whether ancient seafarers actually could have *used* them.

Successful navigation at sea depends on a precise knowledge of latitude and longitude. Prior to the introduction of global satellite positioning in the 1990s, and before the first successful use of the marine chronometer in 1761,[14] the calculation of longitudinal position is thought to have represented an impossible problem. Whilst maps are clearly useful when in sight of land, how could they have been used for navigation when in the middle of the Atlantic? Charles Hapgood was severely criticised for daring to suggest that:

It is clear, too, that they had an instrument of navigation for accurately determining longitudes that was far superior to anything possessed by the peoples of ancient, medieval, or modern times until the second half of the 18th century.

However, in 1979, Maurice Chatelain, a former NASA scientist, came up with an ingenious solution to the mystery. Chatelain proposed that the ancient mariners took with them pre-calculated tables for sunset and moonrise time differences calculated for every day of the year.[15] They then established their longitudinal position at open sea by comparing the actual intervals of sunset and moonrise to those charted for their home port. The elapsed time was measured by batteries of hour-glasses. Thus, according to Chatelain:

Ancient navigators could easily determine their longitude by using every 2 minutes of sunset-moonrise difference for 15 longitude degrees of travel since the start of the voyage.[16]

In the National Archaeological Museum in Athens, there is an artefact which could well have been used in the navigational method described by Maurice Chatelain. The strange object was discovered in October 1900 just off the coast of the small island of Antikythera, which lies west of Crete in the eastern Mediterranean. At a depth of 180 feet, some Greek sponge divers came across the wreck of an ancient ship, complete with cargo. Among the cargo was a large collection of art in the form of vases, marble and bronze statues, which was retrieved and sent to a museum in Athens. In 1902, Valerio Stais, a young Greek archaeology student at the museum, was ordered to sort out the various broken and miscellaneous pieces. It was then that he found a small, calcified lump of bronze that, whilst drying, had split in half to reveal what looked like the inside of a large watch, with gears, pinions, dials and ancient Greek inscriptions.

After a further search, the young archaeologist found that there were four main pieces and some smaller lumps, which he cleaned and reassembled. Although some parts of the device were missing, presumably still on the sea bed, Stais was able to identify a sophisticated and complex mechanism, comprising about forty interlocking cog wheels (gears) of various sizes, nine adjustable scales and three axes on a base plate. The precision of the device can be judged by the fact that the central cog had 240 teeth, each only 1.3 millimetres high.

The inscriptions on the device were dated to 82-65 BC, whilst the sinking of the ship, based on the provisions aboard, was dated to between 83-75 BC. The ship itself was dated at around 200 BC. Inevitably, Stais's suggestion that the device was some kind of advanced astronomical clock was treated with ridicule, since it was considered impossible for such technology to have existed 2,000 years ago. The device was thus registered in the museum as a simple astrolabe, even though the medieval astrolabes a millennium later were mere toys in comparison.[17] The huge number of gears was conveniently overlooked, as was the fact that the device had been made in bronze rather than the more easily malleable brass which was used for medieval astrolabes.

In 1958, the 'simple' Antikythera 'astrolabe' was subjected to a thorough study by Professor Derek de Solla Price, an English scientist working for the Institute for Advanced Study at Princeton, New Jersey. Price published his findings in *Natural History*[18] and *Scientific American*, and later in his book *Gears from the Greeks*. Using the latest technology to photograph the separate layers of the device which could not be taken apart, Price found that each layer was, incredibly, only two millimetres thick. He found gears, dials and graded plates, assembled from at least ten separate parts; gears linked on several differentials that incorporated the cycle of the Sun and the 19-year cycle of the Moon;

gears fitted with tiny teeth, which moved on various axles – all made to an incredible precision (Illustration 7). Decipherment of the dials and graded plates suggested that the device was used to show the position of the Sun in the zodiac, the phases of the Moon and the movements of the planets. Price summarised his findings as follows:

> It appears that this was indeed a computing machine that could work out and exhibit the motions of the Sun and Moon and probably also the planets.[19]

Illustration 7

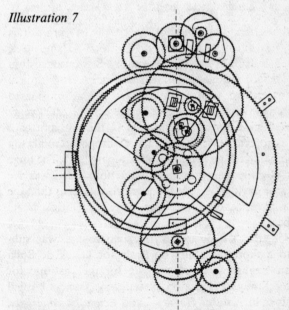

Whether this was indeed a navigational device for determining longitude, or perhaps a calendar or a planetarium, is unclear, but it is certain that it embodied an advanced knowledge of astronomy two thousand years ago, that should have been impossible. Furthermore, the construction of such a device in bronze at that time should also have been impossible. Who made the Antikythera Computer, and more importantly, who invented it? Could it have been a copy of an earlier, much older design?

Whatever its source, the Antikythera Computer will undoubtedly continue to perplex scientists as it has done over the last ninety years. In the meantime, the machine remains on display in the Athens Museum, accompanied by a plaque with the following bold statement:

> The mechanism is considered to be a calendrical Sun and Moon computing machine dated, after the last evidence, to circa 80 BC.[20]

Stonehenge

On Salisbury Plain in Wiltshire, England, 80 miles south-west of London, stands another calendrical computing machine, this time made of stone. I am referring to the most famous prehistoric monument in the whole of Europe, and possibly the world – Stonehenge.

Centuries of study have been unable to solve the mystery of who built Stonehenge and why, but modern science has been able to lift the veil on many of its secrets. It is now generally accepted that, from its beginning, Stonehenge was an astronomical observatory, aligned exactly to the stand-still points of the Sun and the Moon. Radiocarbon datings long ago confirmed that the original site was around 4,800 years old. This amazing date was initially regarded with ridicule, since according to the historical paradigm, no-one in England at that time had the expertise to design or build it.

In March 1996, English Heritage announced the results of an intensive two-year study of Stonehenge using inno-vative mathematical analysis and the latest radiocarbon dating technology, accurate to within 80 years.[21] This new study has dated the monument to *c*. 2965 BC (+ / − 2%), even earlier than previous estimates.

Following extensive surveys of the site, archaeologists now believe that the layout of the monument has been changed several times during its history. The earliest phase was a circular area, known as a 'henge', more than 300 feet in diameter, with a ditch and a raised bank around its circumference. One of the most exciting features of Stonehenge occurred during this earliest phase. Four Station Stones, positioned on the edge of the circle so as to form a rectangle, marked out a set of alignments to the highly complex 19-year cycle of the Moon.

Probably contemporary with the first phase is a series of 56 mysterious holes, which were made in a circle just inside the bank.[22] One of the most intriguing mysteries of Stonehenge is why these holes, known as Aubrey Holes after their seventeenth century discoverer John Aubrey, were filled in immediately after they were dug.

The initial henge was left basically unaltered for 300 years, but then underwent a series of dramatic changes. Around 2700 BC, 80 bluestones, each weighing 4 tons, were transported across a distance of 250 miles from Wales, and placed in a double circle of 'Q and R holes' inside the henge. The introduction of these stones literally made the site a 'stone henge' for the first time.

However, it is not clear whether the bluestone circles were ever completed, because *c*. 2665 BC (+ / − 7%) the builders adopted a radical new design.[23] The bluestones were removed, and substituted by huge sandstone boulders, known as 'sarsen' stones. These stones, weighing 40 to 50 tons each, were somehow transported over a river and steep gradients, from the Marlborough Downs, 12 miles to the north. They were then erected to form the Sarsen Circle, comprising 30 uprights, joined across the top by lintels. These lintels were carefully cut in a curved form to create a continuous ring when assembled, and stability was ensured by linking them to the uprights using the mortise and tenon joint which is familiar to carpenters. Many of these sarsen stones still stand today, allowing us to imagine Stonehenge in its full glory (Plate 37, colour section).

A 35-ton stone, known as the Heel Stone, may also date back to this phase of Stonehenge. It is believed that this stone, standing 16 feet high, and buried 4 feet into the ground, was used for astronomical observations, probably of the Sun. This would explain the origin of its strange nickname, which many believe to be derived from the Greek word *helio*. Exactly how it was originally used remains the subject of much dispute, but its current position, 100 feet away from the circle and opposite its entrance, is aligned along the site's axis to sunset at the winter solstice.

Some time later, the builders decided to bring even bigger stones onto the site. Five pairs of enormous sarsen stones, joined across the top by lintels, were erected inside the Sarsen Circle, in the shape of a horseshoe. The erection of these 13-feet high trilithons, for which the site is most famous, has been dated to *c*. 2270 BC (+/− 7%). Some remain in excellent condition today (Plate 35).

The bluestones were reintroduced to Stonehenge *c*. 2155 BC (+/− 6%). One, the 16-feet high Altar Stone, was set upright in the centre of the complex, directly on its axis. Two concentric circles of bluestones were then erected between the Sarsen Circle and the trilithons. Finally, *c*. 2100 BC (+/− 8%), 19 bluestones were set up to form a horseshoe inside the trilithons.

Circa 2000 BC, the builders turned their attention to the construction of a giant causeway, known as the Avenue. The first, and oldest, section of this Avenue is 600 metres long, and in later times two further sections were added, taking it to the banks of the River Avon two miles away. No-one has ever explained why such an extreme length was required. It is possible that the first straight section of the

Avenue is a widened version of an earlier avenue or pathway, which might well date back to the earliest phase of the site one thousand years earlier.

After this flurry of activity, all went quiet for around 500 years, followed by a minor addition of the so-called 'Y and Z holes'. Then the site was abandoned.

Stonehenge is an unusual site in the sense that it is the astronomers rather than the archaeologists who have led the research from the beginning. As early as 1740, William Stukeley discovered that the central axis of the site from the Altar Stone through the Heel Stone and the Avenue pointed to the position of sunrise at the summer solstice. This alignment was confirmed unequivocally by Sir Norman Lockyer in 1901.[24] The debate then shifted to other possible astronomical alignments, particularly since the site had many other features which could not be accounted for.

In 1963, it was suggested that the site could have been used for observing and predicting the equinoxes as well as the solstices. Then in 1964, Cecil Newham stunned the academic world with his proposal that Stonehenge was also used as a lunar observatory, based on the rectangle formed by the four Station Stones.[25] His findings were confirmed by Professor Gerald Hawkins in various studies between 1963–65;[26] using computer analysis, Hawkins proved that Stonehenge was not only aligned to certain key points in the cycle of the Moon, but also designed to predict lunar eclipses. These conclusions were simply too much for the scientific establishment, because lunar cycles are far more complex than solar cycles, and it was unthinkable that neolithic people could have had such an advanced knowledge of astronomy.

The fiercest critic to emerge was Richard Atkinson of the University College in Cardiff, who considered any lunar alignments to be purely coincidental. However, even Atkinson was forced to concede on this point following further investigation, first by Alexander Thom, an engineering professor at Oxford University, and secondly by the well-respected astronomer and mathematician Sir Fred Hoyle.

Alexander Thom published the most comprehensive survey of the site in the mid 1960s, which confirmed both lunar and solar functions for Stonehenge from its very beginning; it was clear, he said, that the site was in a *unique location*, for nowhere else would the lines formed by the rectangle of Station Stones point exactly to the eight key points of lunar observation. If the site had been positioned only a few miles further north or south, this geometrical relationship would not have worked.[27]

When Sir Fred Hoyle concurred with these findings in the late 1960s, the lunar theory suddenly became respectable. Hoyle declared Stonehenge to be not just an observatory but also a predictor of astronomical events; he felt that

> The builders of Stonehenge might have come to the British Isles from the outside, purposely looking for this rectangular alignment . . . just as the modern astronomer often searches far from home for places to build his telescopes.[28]

The indisputable conclusion is that whoever designed Stonehenge must have known in advance the precise length of the solar year and the cycle of the Moon. Even more impressively, these ancient astronomers had the skill to identify a unique location for the measurement of the Moon's 19-year cycle. Many reference books today are still, understandably, reluctant to cite the full evidence on Stonehenge, for conventional history simply cannot explain the advanced technology of the people who came here 5,000 years ago.

Astronomy in South America

Meanwhile, thousands of miles away from Stonehenge on an entirely different continent, we find evidence of similarly advanced astronomical knowledge. At Machu Picchu in Peru, there is a strange carved stone known as the *Intihuatana* (Plate 24 colour section), the word literally meaning 'the Hitching Post of the Sun'. As described in chapter 3, this stone has been precision-carved from a single natural rock, and is positioned at the highest point of the ancient city, on a rocky hill-top, which has been carefully worked into a platform. In the 1930s, Dr Rolf Muller, a professor at the Astrophysical Institute of Potsdam in Germany, made the first detailed astronomical study of Machu Picchu and published his findings concerning it and other sites in South America.[29] Muller determined that the various inclined surfaces and angled sides of the *Intihuatana* were perfectly designed (at that particular geographical position and elevation) to enable the determination of sunset at the winter solstice, sunrise at the summer solstice, and sunset at both equinoxes.

Moving to the nearby *Torreon* (meaning 'the Tower'), Muller found that the two trapezoid windows in the semi-circular wall (see Plate 25) enabled the observation of sunrise at the summer and winter solstices.

Applying the then controversial theory of archaeoastronomy, Rolf Muller arrived at the shocking conclusion that the astronomical alignments of the *Intihuatana* and *Torreon* were consistent with a 24-degree tilt in the Earth's axis, thus dating them to around 2300–2100 BC!

Muller's findings were later confirmed by subsequent studies using more precise instruments, particularly by the astronomers Dearborn and White from the University of Arizona, in the 1980s.[30] Another scholar has recently suggested that the Temple of the Three Windows (Plate 22) might also have had astronomical alignments – to sunrise on midsummer day, equinox day and midwinter day.[31] It has furthermore been suggested that the number of stone pegs in the *Torreon* and the Principal Temple (Plate 23) indicates a counting mechanism for a solar-lunar calendar.[32]

Three hundred and fifty miles south of Machu Picchu, lies the site of Tiwanaku in Bolivia (see chapter 3). One of the principal buildings at Tiwanaku is a temple known as the *Kalasasaya*, carefully constructed 4.5 degrees west of an exact east-west axis. This temple was designed with built-in sight-lines, enabling precise determinations of equinoxes and solstices by observing sunrises and sunsets from various focal points along the sight-lines (anchored at the temple's corners and the pillars erected at its western and eastern walls). It would seem that the *Kalasasaya* was nothing short of an ingenious celestial observatory. Moreover, the presence of thirteen rather than twelve pillars in the western wall has led some to believe that it was not just a solar observatory but also a solar-lunar calendar.

It is the dating of the *Kalasasaya*, however, which has caused the greatest controversy. Arthur Posnansky, the main researcher of Tiwanaku in the early twentieth century, found that the alignments of the temple did not conform to the 23.5 degree obliquity of the Earth in our present era. Using Sir Norman Lockyer's then recently published theories of archaeoastronomy, together with the formulas determined by an International Conference of astronomers in Paris in 1911, Posnansky dated Tiwanaku to around 15000 BC!

Intrigued by these findings, a German Astronomical Commission was despatched to Tiwanaku in 1926, comprising Dr Hans Ludendorff, Dr Arnold Kohlschutter and Dr Rolf Muller. They confirmed Posnansky's conclusion that the *Kalasasaya* was an astronomical-calendrical observatory, but found the date of construction to be either 15000 BC or 9300 BC, depending on the assumptions used.[33] Either date, however, was a shock to the scientific community who had previously thought the site to be no more than 2,000 years old.

Muller consequently joined forces with Posnansky in an attempt to resolve the dating issue. Eventually they settled on a date of either 10050 BC or 4050 BC. The latter date is thought to be the more likely and would happen to coincide exactly with the accepted date for the beginning of agriculture and animal domestication in the Tiwanakan region.[34]

It would seem that the expert builders and farmers of Tiwanaku were also highly skilled astronomers.

The Mayan Calendars

To the north of South America, in the region known as Mesoamerica, there existed an advanced civilisation, which was totally 'lost' to the outside world, prior to the arrival of the Spanish conquistadores in the sixteenth century. During its peak period, from AD 250–900, the civilisation of the Maya flourished in a region stretching from the southern United States down to the Isthmus of Panama, and covering present day south-western Mexico, Guatemala, Belize and parts of El Salvador and Honduras. However, by the time the Spaniards arrived, this extensive civilisation had mysteriously vanished.

The Maya left behind traces of an incredible culture, but one which the Spanish did their best to destroy. On one terrible night at Mani, in July 1562, Bishop Diego de Landa ordered the collection and burning of all the Mayan manuscripts and works of art, an act of vandalism which rivalled the burning of the Great Library of Alexandria:

> We found a large number of books . . . and as they contained
> nothing in which there was to be seen [but] superstition and lies
> of the devil, we burned them all, which they regretted to an
> amazing degree.[35]

It was fortunate perhaps that the jungle had already closed
in to hide from the Spaniards the full extent of the great
Mayan cities.

It was more than two hundred and fifty years later when
interest in the Maya revived, following the reports of great
travellers such as Lord Kingsborough and John Lloyd
Stephens.[36] It was only then that the incredible achievements of the Maya began to be recognised. Stephens saw in
the jungle-choked ruins:

> . . . the remains of a cultivated, polished and peculiar people
> who had passed through all the stages incident to the rise and
> fall of nations; reached their golden age, and perished, entirely
> unknown.

Attracted by Stephens' descriptions, archaeologists began
to reclaim from the tropical rainforest a series of extraordinary Mayan cities, with imposing palaces and eerie
pyramid temples soaring above the jungle canopy. Strug-
gling to decipher the unusually complex Mayan hieroglyphs, whose meanings had been lost in time,[37] these
archaeologists became more and more impressed by what
they found. Whilst Europe was in the Dark Ages, the Maya
had, in the words of George Stuart 'created one of the most
distinguished civilisations of all antiquity'.[38]

It is now known that the Mayan society comprised a
collection of city states centred on imposing ceremonial
cities such as Copan in Honduras, Tikal in Guatemala and
Palenque in Chiapas, Mexico. These cities were ruled by
priest-kings and controlled by dynastic families, linked by
trade and marriage alliances. The beautiful temples of the
Maya were matched by wonderful artistic achievements. In

addition to their writing system (formed of elaborate painted hieroglyphics), archaeologists have found exquisite jade jewellery, highly advanced sculptures and pottery, and sophisticated works of art, beautifully crafted from copper and gold.

Most impressive of all, however, was the Maya's knowledge of astronomy. Whilst scholars have tried to brush aside evidence of ancient astronomical knowledge at sites such as Machu Picchu and Tiwanaku, the Mayan knowledge is so extensively listed and in such great detail that it is widely recognised for what it is. For this we must thank three original Mayan books which are known to have survived to the present day.[39] Known as codices (picture-books), they are named after the cities in the museums of which they now reside: the Madrid Codex, the Dresden Codex and the Paris Codex. The first two deal with astronomy and divination, the latter with rituals, gods and astrology.

The experts admit that the Maya had in their possession astonishing facts concerning the Moon and the planet Venus, which they presume had been gleaned from long periods of observation. Mayan astronomical observatories have indeed been found, such as the *El Caracol* at Chichen Itza (Plate 38 colour section), where window-like openings in the tower were used to observe the equinoxes. It is worth briefly mentioning two examples which illustrate the amazing accuracy of the Mayan data. First, evidence from Copan (the astronomical centre) showed that the Maya had measured 149 lunar cycles as lasting 4,400 days; today's astronomers make it 4,400.0575. And secondly, in the Dresden Codex, the period of Venus' movement around the Sun was identified as a 584-day cycle compared to a current calculation of 583.92 days.

At the heart of the Mayan religion and science was an incredibly sophisticated calendar, which used three different time scales to date events in their history. The widespread use of this dating system on stone stelae (upright columns) enabled it to be deciphered quite quickly. The first dating system, known as the Long Count, expressed the date as a number of days since Day Zero, which occurred in 3113 BC.[40] The significance of this date – long before the beginning of Mayan civilisation – has never been established (but will be revealed in chapter 13).

The second system used the more conventional 365-day Solar Calendar, but with 12 months of 30 days and a thirteenth month of 5 days.

The purpose of the third, 260-day 'Sacred Calendar' remains a mystery. It appears to have been designed around the number 52, for it is not only divisible 5 times by 52, but coincides with the 365-day Solar Calendar every 52 years.[41] It is clear from the Madrid Codex that the Maya were fully aware of this interlocking cycle between the two calendars. The full significance of the number 52, however, remains a mystery.

Despite their use of the approximate 365-day solar year, it is clear that the Maya were fully aware of the principle of adjusting the solar calendar, as we do today in 'leap' years. It has been shown that they possessed accurate calculations of 365.2420 days for the solar year. Since modern astronomy calculates the actual length of the year at 365.2422 days, the Mayan calendar was in fact marginally more accurate than the Gregorian calendar which we use today, based on 365.2425 days.

In order to record the Long Count, the Maya used an elaborate 'base 20' mathematical system, which included the concept of zero and also the place concept whereby a '1' could represent 1, 20, 400 and so on (similar to our present day base 10 system). Just as we today have special terms to describe 'million' and 'billion', the Maya used a series of glyphs which culminated in the term *alau-tun* which represented 23,040,000,000. The only apparent explanation for such an advanced mathematical system is the Maya's fascination with the measurement of time, yet scholars are at a loss to explain why such large numbers were required. The term *alau-tun*, applied to the Long Count, represented a period of over 63 million years.

Conventional scientists have no satisfactory explanations as to how the Maya could have obtained such accurate astronomical measurements, nor what might have motivated them to do so. One book observes that:

> Such a degree of accuracy . . . is mysterious in a culture which had no way of measuring time, not even an elementary system such as an hour glass or a water clock – and no astronomical telescope or other optical instrument.[42]

Another book, devoted to the Maya, notes their 'obsession with time' and describes their complex interlocking calendars as:

> . . . one of the supreme intellectual achievements of the New World – their complexity reflected an esoteric importance in divination and a significance far greater than that of a simple device for marking the passage of time.[43]

Today, Mayan remains the first language of around 250,000 people, but the previous high culture is gone. It is as if a knowledgable elite disappeared from the scene, leaving behind their achievements to be consumed by the jungle. As to the origin of the Maya, that also remains an intriguing mystery. However, they were not the first high culture in Mesoamerica. Traces have been found of an earlier culture, known as the Olmecs, who possessed surprisingly advanced ceramics and jewellery. Few books have much to say about the Olmecs, since little is known about their rise and fall, but James and Oliver Tickell refer to their:

> . . . complex calendar from astronomical observation which underpinned their religion, mathematics and science.[44]

The Olmecs, like the Maya, appeared as if from nowhere with advanced astronomical skills. However, since the Olmec culture dates from *c.* 1500 BC, could it be that they, along with the Maya, were the recipients of a legacy which dates back to at least 2100 BC in Peru and to 4050 BC or earlier at Tiwanaku?

The Sirius Secret

In 1976, an American scholar, with interests in astronomy and ancient civilisations, published an astonishing book. In *The Sirius Mystery*, Robert Temple produced overwhelmingly detailed evidence that an African tribe, known as the Dogon, possessed an extraordinary knowledge of the Sirius star system.[45]

Robert Temple began his studies following an earlier report by two French anthropologists, Marcel Griaule and Germaine Dieterlen, who claimed to have found knowledge of Sirius in four Sudanese tribes.[46] The French scientists had focused their investigations on a people known as the Dogon, who lived in Mali, West Africa. Between 1946 and 1950, they gathered information from four Dogon priests concerning their sacred religious traditions. These traditions were apparently based on a myth which had been passed down orally from one generation to another.

Every sixty years, the Dogon practised a ceremony known as *Sigui*, which re-enacted the re-creation of the world by the god Amma, the crushing of the primitive Ogoman, and the subsequent granting of civilisation by Amma's son Nommo. The day of the gods' arrival was known to the Dogon as the 'day of the fish', and the gods themselves were regarded as amphibious beings.

According to Dogon tradition, these gods had come from a planet orbiting Sirius B, one of three stars in the Sirius star system.[47] The Dogon accurately described the 50-years orbit of Sirius B around Sirius A. This is quite amazing, because Sirius B is a 'white dwarf', the tiniest form of visible star in the universe. As such, it is invisible to the naked eye, and barely visible even with a good telescope. If the tale was a myth, why did the Dogon not worship Sirius A, the so-called 'dog star', which is one of the brightest stars in the sky?[48]

Robert Temple provides incontrovertible evidence that the Dogon knew of the existence of the invisible Sirius B. How could they have known? Some cynics have attributed this knowledge to visiting missionaries, but as Temple points out, these missionaries arrived more than a hundred years before Sirius B was photographed for the first time in 1970.

Nor was the Dogon knowledge of astronomy restricted to Sirius. Robert Temple also demonstrates that they knew of the Earth's rotation on its axis and its 365-day solar orbit, which they split into a calendar of 12 months. As for the Moon, the Dogon knew that it was dry and dead. And among their other remarkable knowledge (allegedly) is the existence of Saturn's ring and Jupiter's four largest satellites. Where did all this knowledge come from? Temple concludes his research as follows:

> The result, in 1974, seven years later, is that I have been able to show that the information which the Dogon possess is really more than five thousand years old and was possessed by the ancient Egyptians in the *pre-dynastic times* before 3200 BC.[49] (emphasis added)

Lessons in Astronomy

Few people realise that the 7 days of the week – Sunday to Saturday – were originally named after an astronomical source. Ironically, they derive from the time of Ptolemy in the second century AD and his incorrect theory that the Sun, Moon and five planets revolved around the Earth. Thus were the days named after the Sun (Sunday), the Moon (Monday), Mars (mardi), Mercury(mercredi), Jupiter (jeudi), Venus (vendredi) and Saturn (Saturday/samedi). Although based on an erroneous notion, it is fitting that our day to day lives are still linked so closely to astronomy, for it has been a continuing hobby, indeed obsession, of mankind since the earliest civilisation six thousands years ago.

It is therefore our duty, too, to understand at least the basics of astronomy, which will prove crucially important to an understanding of the gods. In the course of this chapter, I have made various passing references to equinoxes, solstices, precession and archaeoastronomy. What do these terms mean?

The starting point is the Earth's spin on its axis, which gives us the easily recognisable phases of night and day. The next step is to understand that the Earth's axis is tilted in its plane of orbit around the Sun (known as the obliquity of the ecliptic). This feature leads to the four seasons. The earliest civilisations were all quick to recognise four key points, by observation of the Sun's risings and setting relative to the Earth's horizon. These four points are the summer and winter solstices (solar standstills) when the Sun reaches its outermost positions north and south, seems to hesitate and then turns back; and the spring and autumn equinoxes (when day and night are equal) on the two occasions in the year when the Sun crosses over the Earth's equator.

In addition, the Earth has a wobble, like a spinning top. For general purposes, it is usually assumed that an arrow drawn through the Earth's axis, pointing to the heavens above the north pole,[50] remains fixed in its position. But this is not strictly true. Over a very long period (approximately 25,920 years), the Earth's wobble causes the arrow-point to move in the heavens, in a fashion which will eventually trace a 360-degree circle (Figure 8a (black-and-white section)).

As a result of this wobble, the starting points for the four seasons – when the Earth experiences its two solstices and two equinoxes – arrive slightly earlier each year. This effect, known as 'precession', amounts to only one month in every 2,160 years, so it is not something we would take much notice of. An important effect of the phenomenon, however, is to alter the backdrop of the stars at these four calendar points.

It is conventional to measure precession at the point of the equinoxes – thus the full astronomical term is the 'precession of the equinoxes'. From the most ancient times, this 360-degree circle in the heavens, representing 25,920 years, was divided into twelve sections of 2,160 years, each of which was associated with a house of the zodiac.[51] Thus we can use sunrise on the day of the spring equinox as a reference point to observe and measure the heavenly shift from one zodiac house to another. Right now, we are in the Age of Pisces and about to move into the Age of Aquarius (Figure 8b, black-and-white section), whereas in approximately 13,000 years time our descendants will be in the Age of Virgo, about to move into the Age of Leo (Figure 8c)

In the nineteenth century, the astronomer Sir Norman Lockyer noticed that some ancient temples had been realigned after they were built. Intrigued by the continual realignment of temples as time progressed, particularly at Thebes (Karnak) in Egypt, Lockyer began to develop a comprehensive dossier on the astronomical alignment of numerous temples and cathedrals. His conclusions, published in 1894 in his book *The Dawn of Astronomy*, caused a storm of controversy, for his theory suggested not only that the ancients had the astronomical knowledge, but also that the temple alignments could be used as a scientific method to date their construction. Like most revolutionary scientific breakthroughs, it took the best part of a century for his theories to gain wide acceptance.

How does the dating mechanism work? As well as causing the precession of the equinoxes, the Earth's wobble also affects its tilt. According to Norman Lockyer's calculations, the Earth's tilt is changed by 1 degree every 7,000 years. Subsequent refinements of Lockyer's work have suggested that the Earth's tilt varies between approximately 21 and 24 degrees to the perpendicular (it is currently around 23.5 degrees). This motion has been likened to the roll of a ship, but in slow motion, such that the horizons are raised and lowered almost imperceptibly.

By a close examination of the exact alignment of ancient temples, Lockyer's breakthrough has enabled us to make very close approximations of *some* construction dates. Those temples which are aligned to the solstices (and thus affected by the Earth's tilt) can be dated using detailed tables of the Earth's estimated tilt over the past several thousand years.

In his book, Sir Norman Lockyer cited a range of temples with all types of celestial alignments. As an example of a solsticial Sun Temple, he used the 'Temple of Prayer for Good Harvests', the most beautiful and most famous building in Beijing, China. It was here, at its south altar, that the most important state sacrifice was traditionally held on the day of the winter solstice. As examples of equinoctial temples, he cited the temple to Zeus at Baalbek in Lebanon, oriented on an exact east-west axis at its time of construction (Plate 1, colour section), the Temple of Solomon in Jerusalem and the great basilica of St. Peter's in Vatican city, Rome.

Lockyer's breakthrough enabled a new science, archaeoastronomy, to be founded, which could date the construction of stone temples which were outside the scope of radiocarbon dating.[52] Significantly, this science could not exist without implicitly recognising the astronomical knowledge of ancient civilisations.

Impossible Science

There is something not quite right with the received wisdom on the history of mankind. The general perception that the ancients were a backward lot is crumbling as we find out more about them. Scientists can no longer deny that ancient civilisations such as the Sumerians, the Egyptians, the Chinese and the Maya had extraordinary astronomical knowledge. As stated earlier, an entirely new branch of science – archaeoastronomy – has been founded upon it.

Most amazing of all, it would seem that our ancient ancestors knew of the 25,920-year precessional cycle. In a later chapter, we will be reviewing the widespread awareness of the precessional shift from Taurus to Aries over four thousands years ago. For now, we should note that in the second century BC, Hipparchus referred to 'the displacement of the solsticial and equinoctial sign' – a clear reference to precession. Where did Hipparchus acquire his knowledge? In his writings, he credited various mentors, especially the 'Babylonian astronomers of Erech, Borsippa and Babylon'. We now know that the ancient Babylonians, known as the Chaldeans, were indeed very advanced in astronomy, but they in turn acquired their knowledge from an earlier civilisation.

It was in Sumer – the very first civilisation – that astronomy began, and in Sumer that the various signs were first attributed to the twelve houses of the zodiac. It would seem that this earliest astronomy arose in a perfected form, right at the very beginning of the Sumerian civilisation nearly six thousand years ago. But instead of progressing, the level of astronomical expertise declined. Studies have shown that the Babylonians, who succeeded the Sumerians in Mesopotamia, used ephemerides (lists of planetary movements) which were less accurate.

Somewhere in the murky depths of history, this knowledge then went into a *further* decline. So much so that, two thousand years after the decline of Sumer, the Greeks and then the Romans somehow developed the idea of a flat Earth at the centre of the universe. It was as if someone was playing a joke on them, but it is no laughing matter that this new level of ignorance dominated the establishment thinking for around two thousands years.

When Copernicus placed the Sun at the centre of the Solar System, it might have seemed, at the time, a revolutionary suggestion. But Copernicus was not the first to identify the true picture – he was only *rediscovering* what had been known in ancient times. It may well be that Copernicus drew directly from ancient sources of information, for there is no doubt that pockets of ancient knowledge had survived, driven underground into secret religious traditions. For instance, the thirteenth century *Zo'har*, a central work in the literature of Jewish mysticism known as the *Kabbalah*,[53] stated quite clearly that the Earth turned around its own axis:

> The entire Earth spins, turning as a sphere. When one part is down, the other part is up. When it is light for one part, it is dark for the other part; when it is day for that, it is night for the other.

The source of the *Zo'har* was the third century Rabbi Hamnuna.

Another ancient epic, the Indian *Vishnu Purana*, repeated their long-held tradition that 'the Sun is always in one and the same place', whilst the *Surya Siddhanta* described Earth as 'a globe in space'.

In the sixth century BC, Pythagoras taught his students

that the Earth was a sphere. In the fifth century BC, the Ionian philosopher Anaxagoras explained that the Moon darkened the Sun during an eclipse, and that during a lunar eclipse the Earth's shadow fell on the Moon. In the third century BC, Aristarchus of Samos deduced that the Earth revolved around the Sun and the geographer Eratosthenes used geometry combined with astronomical knowledge to compute the circumference of the Earth with an error of less than 200 miles compared to modern geography. In China, during the second century AD, Chang Heng described the Earth as 'an egg' and explained that its axis pointed to the Polar Star. The list goes on.

These astounding examples of ancient science are conveniently swept under the carpet, for to recognise them is to raise the inevitable question of how these people could possibly have acquired their knowledge and, in particular, how the Sumerians could have acquired astronomical knowledge in such a perfected form, with no evidence of any period of intellectual evolution.

The mysterious source of Sumerian astronomy prompts a number of further questions: who could have mapped Antarctica before it was covered in ice? Who could have designed the amazing Antikythera Computer? Who could have laid out a temple at Tiwanaku *c.* 4050 BC? Who had the expertise to select the unique location of Stonehenge to build an observatory *c.* 3000 BC? Who designed the astronomical features of Machu Picchu *c.* 2300–2100 BC? These are only some of the mysteries which conventional science fails to answer.

The question of 'why' is even more intriguing than the question of 'who'. Why, for example, were the Sumerians, and almost every other ancient culture, obsessed with a calendar that would accurately record the movement of the Earth in the heavens? The Sumerians could not possibly have needed such a sophisticated level of astronomy for agricultural purposes. On the contrary, the Sumerian obsession with beginning the New Year on the exact day of the spring equinox was driven by religion.

Our survey of the 'impossible', and our search for a powerful motivating force, has brought us neatly back to what all of the ancient civilisations told us – that they were ruled by a technologically sophisticated race of 'gods'. The Sumerians called them by names such as Anu, Enlil and Enki. The Egyptians called them by names such as Isis, Osiris and Horus. The Babylonians focused on one god, Marduk. The Israelites were told to worship one god, Yahweh. The ancient people of the Americas worshipped gods called Quetzalcoatl or Viracocha. And in all of these lands there were so-called myths of the gods creating man and granting him civilisation and science. As we shall see in the following chapters, these flesh-and-blood gods were the primary reason why ancient man acquired such an obsessive interest in astronomy.

Chapter Five Conclusions

* The Piri Re'is maps could only have been produced using advanced technology – aerial surveys of the Earth and spherical trigonometry. They were either drawn before the Antarctic ice cap formed 6,000 years ago, or they made use of seismic survey technology.

* The historical paradigm cannot explain the amazing scientific knowledge possessed by the Maya, the Olmecs, the Dogon and the builders of Machu Picchu, Tiwanaku and Stonehenge.

* All of the ancient civilisations were obsessed with astronomy and recording the movement of the Earth in the heavens – but definitely *not* for agricultural purposes.

CHAPTER SIX

CIVILISATION –
A GIFT OF THE GODS

———◆———

The Sumerian Secret

Six thousand years ago, *Homo sapiens* underwent an incredible transformation. Man the hunter and man the farmer suddenly became man the city dweller, and within a mere few hundred years he was practising advanced mathematics, astronomy and metallurgy!

The place where these first cities suddenly arose was ancient Mesopotamia, in the fertile plain between the Tigris and Euphrates rivers, where the country of Iraq now lies. The civilisation was called Sumer, the 'birthplace of writing and the wheel',[1] and from its very beginning it bore a striking resemblance to our own civilisation and culture today.

The highly respected scientific journal *National Geographic* clearly recognises the primacy of the Sumerians and the legacy which they left to us:

There, in ancient Sumer . . . urban living and literacy flourished in cities with names such as Ur, Lagash, Eridu and Nippur. Sumerians were early users of wheeled vehicles and were among the first metallurgists, blending metals into alloys, extracting silver from ore, and casting bronze in complex molds. Sumerians were also the first to invent writing.[2]

The National Geographic also acknowledges:

> . . . the legacy of the Sumerians who . . . established the earliest known society where people could read and write . . . in all these things – in law and social reform, in literature and architecture, in commercial organisation, and in technology – the achievements of the cities of Sumer are the earliest we know about.[3]

All studies of the Sumerians have stressed the extremely short period within which their high level of culture and technology arose. One author described it as 'a flame which blazed up so suddenly',[4] whilst Joseph Campbell eloquently stated that:

> With stunning abruptness . . . there appears in this little Sumerian mud garden . . . the whole cultural syndrome that has constituted the germinal unit of the high civilisations of the world.[5]

Why then is there a widespread lack of public awareness regarding the Sumerians? A clue may lie in the fact that the *source* of their civilisation remains a complete mystery to conventional science.[6] History books are forced to gloss over Sumerian origins by simply referring to their emergence, as if no further explanation is necessary. This treatment is adopted by the highly respected *The Times Atlas of World History*, which is so embarrassed to admit its ignorance, that it ignores the Sumerians (the most important civilisation of all) and talks instead of the vague 'emergence' of a 'Mesopotamian' first civilisation.[7] The mystery is summed up by one National Geographic Society publication, which states:

Much has been written about where the Sumerian people may have originated, but no one knows.[8]

Nevertheless, many attempts have been made to portray the origin of the Sumerians as an *evolution* from pre-existing cultures in Mesopotamia.[9] These studies focus on pottery, and demonstrate that the people from Sumer had already lived in the area for thousands of years. However, they have little to offer on the question of why it suddenly became necessary for men to live in organised cites. The best explanations are inevitably vague and floundering:

> More complex societies derived from the increasing organisation needed to control the large populations supported by the productive lowland agricultural regimes.[10]

Such explanations are as contrived as the theories of mankind's sudden evolution. Whilst the brain is the Achilles heel of the evolutionists' arguments, so the Sumerians' *technology* is the Achilles heel of the historians' arguments. The scholarly obsession with creating a smooth and gradual cultural development ignores the amazing aspects of Sumerian metallurgy, mathematics and astronomy (inter alia) which all arose in perfect form at the beginning of their civilisation. Regarding the origin of that knowledge, it would seem that only the Sumerians themselves can solve the mystery that confounds the scientists. And the Sumerians attributed their success, indeed their very origin, to flesh-and-blood gods.

No wonder then that the text books are so vague on the origins of Sumer! The paradigm of modern science dictates that any accounts of gods are classified under mythology. Therefore, faced with only this one, uncomfortable explanation for the origin of the first civilisation, it is hardly surprising that the text books are lost for words.

This chapter, dealing with the Sumerian mystery, is an

appropriate point on which to conclude our round-up of the
mysteries of heaven and Earth, and to begin our study of
the solution. At a superficial level, Sumer provides scholars
with yet another unsolved mystery, but at a detailed level
there lie vital clues to explaining the many mysteries and
anomalies in the world today. This chapter is the tale of the
Sumerians and their gods.

The First Civilisation

Sumer was the first of the three 'great' civilisations of
antiquity, which all arose in the fertile areas of major
rivers – Sumer in the plain between the Tigris and Euphrates rivers, and the others by the Nile river (*c*. 3100 BC)
and the Indus river (*c*. 2800 BC) respectively. There was
without doubt, a strong Sumerian influence in those other
civilisations, for the Sumerians were keen travellers and
explorers. For the purpose of this book, it is not necessary
to prove that the earliest civilisations on Earth were off-
shoots from the first civilisation of Sumer, but there is
ample evidence that this was the case.

The discovery of ancient Sumer is an exciting story,
which begins in the nineteenth century – a rich period
for archaeology in the ancient Near East. In the once
fertile lands of ancient Mesopotamia, huge mounds were
all that remained of the world's earliest cities. For those
with the time and money to travel, fame was just then feet or
so underground – the only problem was knowing where to
dig. Spurred on by Biblical clues, the accounts of earlier
travellers and by local folklore, archaeologists such as the
Paris-born Englishman Sir Austen Henry Layard indeed
found their fame and fortune.

It was a Frenchman who made the first important
discovery. In 1843, Paul Emile Botta uncovered fantastic

temples, palaces and a ziggurat (step-pyramid) at a site identified as Dur-Sharru-Kin, the eighth century BC capital of Sargon II, king of Assyria. Today the site is called Khorsabad. Botta will always be remembered as the discoverer of the Assyrian civilisation.

Whilst archaeologists such as Botta and Layard continued to seek and explore new sites such as Nimrud and Nineveh, scholars such as Sir Henry Rawlinson and Jules Oppert began to shed light on the numerous clay tablets which the digs had uncovered. It soon became apparent that the ancient Mesopotamians were diligent record keepers, preserving information in a cuneiform script, inscribed on clay tablets. In 1835, Rawlinson had carefully copied a vital trilingual inscription on a stone slab found at Behistun in Persia; in 1846, he deciphered the script and its languages, one of which was Akkadian, common to the Assyrians and the Babylonians, who had inherited the Near East after the collapse of Sumer *c*. 2000 BC.

Sir Henry Rawlinson's timing was fortuitous. A few years later, Sir Austen Henry Layard began to excavate the mounds of the ancient Assyrian capital Nineveh, 250 miles north of modern-day Baghdad. As well as fantastic temples and palaces, he discovered in 1850 the library of Ashurbanipal, containing a collection of 30,000 clay tablets.

As more and more tablets were translated, the archaeologists became increasingly excited by the independent confirmation of Biblical rulers and cities. One inscription, listing the achievements of an earlier ruler, Sargon I, claimed that he was the 'King of Akkad, King of Kish', and that he had defeated in battle the cities of 'Uruk, Ur and Lagash'. Scholars were amazed to find that this Sargon had preceded his later namesake by nearly two thousand years, taking the Mesopotamian civilisation back to at least 2400 BC.

This was just the beginning of a series of tremendous finds which turned back the clock on the beginning of civilisation and enriched the museums of Europe and America with some of their prize exhibits. At this time, Sumer did not exist in the history books – it is only with hindsight that we now recognise it as the Biblical 'Shinar'.[11]

In 1869, Jules Oppert first proposed the prior existence of a 'lost' Sumerian language and people. As with all new ideas, it took some time to become fully accepted. Whilst the so-called 'Sumerian Question' raged through the latter part of the nineteenth century, the first Sumerian cities began to be excavated and speculation turned to established scientific fact.

The first Sumerian site was discovered by a French excavation team in 1877. It turned out to be the city of Lagash. American archaeologists were also attracted to the Sumerian ruins, and between 1887–1900 they excavated the city of Nippur, one of the most important religious sites. Today, the mounds of Nippur, with its ruined ziggurat, rise more than five storeys high and are clearly visible on the main road 93 miles south-east of Baghdad. Further south, the hot and dusty wasteland of Uruk yielded the world's first ever ziggurat, dedicated to the goddess Inanna, as well as examples of some of the earliest inscribed writing.[12]

The best preserved ziggurat in the whole of Mesopotamia was found at Ur, the birthplace of the Old Testament patriarch Abraham. The partly restored ruins of that ziggurat (Plate 39, colour section) still dominate the landscape today at the modern town of Muqayyar, 186 miles south-east of Baghdad. It was at Ur that the British archaeologist Sir Leonard Woolley discovered exquisite works of gold, silver and lapis lazuli including the 'ram in a thicket' (Figure 18, black-and-white section), the beautiful Queen's Harp (the oldest harp ever found, dating from 2750 BC) and a splendid headdress – all of which can now be seen at the British Museum.

It was at Eridu, however, almost 200 miles south-east of

Figure 1

Figure 2

Figure 3

Figure 4

Figure 5

Figure 6

Figure 7

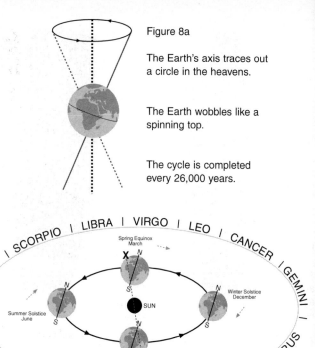

Figure 8a

The Earth's axis traces out a circle in the heavens.

The Earth wobbles like a spinning top.

The cycle is completed every 26,000 years.

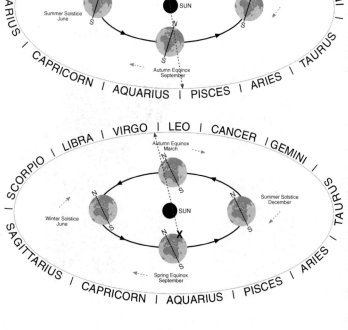

Figure 9

Figure 8b *(left)*

At the Spring Equinox an observer at Point **X** sees the Sun rise against the stars in the House of Pisces (just).

The Earth's wobble causes the Spring Equinox (etc.) to slowly slip forward in time.

Figure 8c *(left)*

13,000 years later, the Earth's axis is halfway through its cycle and the Spring Equinox now occurs in September. The Sun will rise against the House of Virgo.

Figure 10

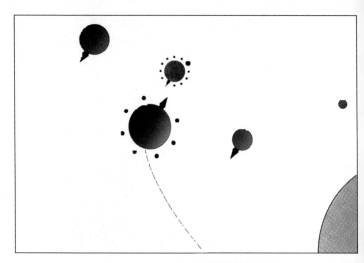

Figure 11a – Before Celectial Battle

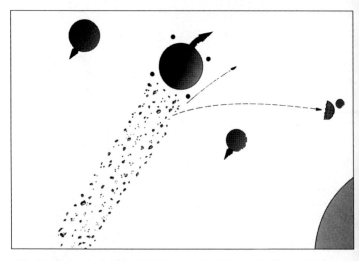

Mk Marduk; J Jupiter; T Tiamat; Mr Mars; K Kingu; E Earth
→ Direction of Orbit   -----► Path of Origin

Figure 11b – After Celectial Battle

Figure 12

Figure 13

Baghdad that the earliest Sumerian city was found. The city of Eridu is nowadays an abandoned, windswept wilderness, dominated by the ruins of Ur-Nammu's ziggurat. The city's ruins spread over an area measuring 1,300 by 1,000 feet. Here, beneath the foundations of its first temple, dedicated to the god Enki, archaeologists found virgin soil, marking the very beginning of civilisation on Earth. This temple was dated to 3800 BC, the same time that the world's first calendar began at Nippur.

By the early twentieth century, all but one of the Assyrian cities mentioned in the Old Testament had been found. The city of Babylon, too, had been excavated, although little remained of the ziggurat dedicated to its chief god Marduk. The royal city of Kish was also discovered, along with other important Sumerian sites such as Larsa, Shuruppak, Sippar and Bad-Tibira.

The full linkage between Sumer, Akkad, Assyria and Babylon remains a mystery to the historians, but the study of their written scripts has confirmed the primacy of the Sumerians. Many Akkadian texts directly stated that they were copies of earlier originals; one tablet, for example, found in Nineveh by Layard, referred to the 'language of Shumer not changed'. Scholars found that the Akkadian script used a large number of 'loan-words' in referring to subjects such as astronomy, science and the gods.[13] These loan-words indicated an earlier and fundamentally different writing system, known as 'pictographic', where single signs represented objects or concepts by the use of pictures. It has now been established that the original Sumerian writing system was indeed based on pictographic signs, similar to those later used in Egypt.

After one hundred years of translating the Sumerian texts, scholars have found no loan-words and no indication of any prior writing system. The invention of writing was truly a Sumerian 'first'. Consequently, it is now widely accepted that Sumer was the first advanced civilisation on Earth, and the date of its beginning is unanimously agreed to be 3800 BC.

Legacy of the Sumerians

The clay tablets uncovered by the archaeologists in ancient Mesopotamia are so numerous that a large number still remain untranslated today. Many deal with the humdrum routine of daily life – marriage and divorce records, school grammar and vocabulary texts, and commercial contracts, the latter dealing with matters such as the recording of crops, the calculation of prices and the movement of goods. Records such as these have given scholars a remarkable insight into Sumerian culture.

One of the foremost experts on Sumer is Professor Samuel Noah Kramer, who has travelled the world to study, copy and translate their texts. In his book *History Begins at Sumer*, he listed 39 Sumerian 'firsts'[14] In addition to the first writing system which we have already discussed, his firsts included the first wheel, the first schools, the first bicameral congress, the first historian, the first 'farmer's almanac', the first cosmogony and cosmology, the first proverbs and sayings, the first literary debates, the first 'Noah', the first library catalogue, the first money (the silver shekel 'weighed ingot'), the first taxation, the first law and social reforms, the first medicine, and the first search for world peace and harmony.

In Sumer we recognise many of the institutions which we cherish (or suffer) today. The world's first schools were wide ranging in their subjects and, by all accounts, very strict; flogging was common for pupils who were lazy, untidy or inattentive. The legal system was similar to our own, with laws to protect the employed, the unemployed, the weak and the vulnerable, and a judge and jury system similar to our own today. Evidently, society suffered from many of the same ills as ours, for *c.* 2600 BC it was necessary for a king named Urukagina to order the first legal reform to prevent the abuse of supervisory power, official status and monopoly position. Urukagina claimed that it was his god Ningirsu who had ordered him to 'restore the decrees of former days'.

In the field of medicine, Sumerian standards were extremely high from the very beginning. The library of Ashurbanipal, which Layard discovered in Nineveh, was carefully organised, with a medical section containing thousands of clay tablets. All of the medical terms were based on Sumerian loan-words. Medical procedures were outlined in text books, dealing with hygiene, operations such as the removal of cataracts and the use of alcohol for surgical disinfection. Sumerian medicine was marked by a highly scientific approach of diagnosis and prescription for either therapy or surgery.

Sumerian construction was also highly advanced, within the constraints of locally available building materials.[15] From the very beginning in 3800 BC, houses, palaces and temples were constructed of specially strengthened bricks, manufactured by combining wet clay with reeds.

The Sumerians were great travellers and explorers, and are credited with the invention of the world's first boats. An Akkadian dictionary of Sumerian words was found to contain no less than 105 terms for various types of ship according to their size, destination or cargo. One inscription, unearthed at Lagash, referred to docking facilities for ships and listed the materials which its ruler Gudea had imported to build a temple for his god Ninurta *c.* 2200 BC. The range of these materials is astonishing, including gold, silver, copper, diorite, carnelian and cedar wood. In some cases these materials were transported more than a thousand miles.

The first kiln is found also in Sumer. The use of a large oven, or kiln, allowed clay products to be fired, giving them extra tensile strength without contamination by dust or ashes. A similar technology was used to extract metals such as copper from its ore by heating the ore above 1,500 degrees fahrenheit in a closed, oxygen-starved furnace. This process, called smelting, became necessary at an early stage, when the supply of naturally occurring copper nuggets had been exhausted. Independent studies of early metallurgy have been surprised and baffled at the speed with which the Sumerians became expert in smelting, refining and casting.[16] These advanced technologies were being used within only a few hundred years of the beginning of the Sumerian civilisation.

Even more astounding was the Sumerian development of alloying, a process by which different metals are chemically combined in a furnace. The Sumerians mastered this process to produce the earliest bronze, a hard but malleable metal which changed the course of human history. The alloying of copper with tin was an incredible achievement for three reasons. First, it was necessary to use a very precise mixture of copper and tin (analysis of Sumerian bronze has established an optimum ratio of 85 per cent copper and 15 per cent tin). Secondly, tin was not available in any quantity in Mesopotamia. Thirdly, tin does not occur in a natural state and requires a complicated process to extract it from cassiterite ore. This is not the sort of thing one discovers by accident. The Sumerians used thirty different words to describe different qualities or types of copper, and their word for tin, AN.NA, literally meant 'Heavenly Stone', once again indicating that Sumerian technology was a gift of the gods.

Astronomy and Mathematics

In sharp contrast to the dark days between Ptolemy and Copernicus, the Sumerians clearly understood that the Earth revolved around the Sun and that the planets moved whilst the stars remained fixed. The evidence also suggests that they knew the planets of the Solar System before they were 'discovered' in modern times (see chapter 7).

Thousands of clay tablets, found at Nineveh, Nippur and other Sumerian sites, have been found to contain hundreds of astronomical terms. Some of these tablets included mathematical formulae and astronomical tables, which enabled the Sumerians to predict solar eclipses, the phases of the Moon and the movements of the planets. Studies of ancient astronomy have demonstrated the remarkable accuracy of these tables (known as ephemerides). No-one knows how they could have calculated such sophisticated data and we might well ask why they needed it.[17]

Several studies have suggested that the ziggurat, the hall-mark of Sumerian architecture, may have also served an astronomical purpose. These structures contained a square base with corners perfectly aligned to the four cardinal points of the compass. One scholar has therefore suggested that they were ideal for astronomical observation:

> Each stage of the ziggurat provided a higher viewing point and thus a different horizon, adjustable to the geographic location; the line between the east-pointing and west-pointing corners provided the equinoctial orientation; the sides gave solsticial views to either sunrise or sunset, at both summer and winter solstices.[18]

The Sumerians measured the rising and setting of the visible planets and the stars against the Earth's horizon, using the same heliacal system that is used today. We also owe to the Sumerians the division of the heavens into three bands – the northern, central and southern regions (corresponding to the ancient Sumerian 'way of Enlil', 'way of Anu' and 'way of Ea'). In fact, the whole concept of spherical astronomy, including the 360-degree circle, the zenith, the horizon, the celestial axis, the poles, the ecliptic, the equinoxes etc, all arose suddenly in Sumer.

The Sumerian knowledge of the Sun and the Moon was combined to form the world's first calendar, a solar-lunar calendar which began in 3760 BC in the city of Nippur.[19] The Sumerians recorded 12 *lunar* months amounting to approximately 354 days, and then added 11 extra days to match the *solar* year. This process, called intercalation, was continued each year, until the solar and lunar calendars realigned themselves after 19 years.[20] The Sumerian calendar was thus carefully constructed to ensure that key days such as New Year's Day always occurred on the spring equinox, and did not slip back as they do in other calendars.[21]

It is difficult to imagine a more complex calendar than that of the Sumerians, and later calendars were indeed much simpler.[22] It is quite improbable that the first calendar, at Nippur, was the most complex and yet there is no doubt whatsoever that this was so. Indeed, the whole subject of Sumerian astronomy is most intriguing, for the simple reason that it was not a necessity for an emerging society.

Allied to the Sumerians' interest in astronomy was the world's first known mathematical system. This system was highly advanced, and included the 'place' concept, whereby a digit could take on a different value depending on its place in the overall number (as '1' can mean 1, 10, 100 and so on). However, unlike our present-day *decimal* system, the Sumerian system was *sexagesimal*. Instead of base 10, it was a quasi base 60 system, which rather strangely alternated by 10, then 6, then 10 and so on. The place-digits thus ascended as follows: 1, 10, 60, 600, 3600, 36,000, 216,000, 2,160,000, 12,960,000.

As unwieldy as the Sumerian base 60 system might at first seem, it enabled the Sumerians to divide into fractions and multiply into the millions, to calculate roots or to raise numbers by several powers. In many respects it is superior to the base 10 system which is used today, due to the fact that 60 is divisible by ten integers whereas 100 is only divisible by seven integers. In addition, it is the only perfect system for geometry, and this explains its continued use in modern times – hence the 360 degrees in a circle.

Few people realise that we owe not only our geometry but also our modern time-keeping systems to the Sumerian base 60 mathematical system. The origin of 60 minutes in an hour and 60 seconds in a minute is not arbitrary, but designed around a sexagesimal system. Sumerian numerology is similarly evident in the 24 hours in a day, the 12 months in a year, the 12 inches in a foot and the dozen as a unit. Its legacy also appears in modern numbering systems which comprise separate, distinct numbers from 1 to 12, followed by expressions for 10 + 3, 10 + 4, and so on.

We should not be surprised at this point, to learn that the zodiac, too, was another Sumerian first, which later spread to other civilisations. However, the Sumerians did not use the zodiac on a month-to-month basis as we do for horoscopes today. Instead they used it in its *astronomical* sense, based on the Earth's wobble, to divide the great precessional cycle of 25,920 years into 12 periods of 2,160 years. As can be seen from Figure 8b, black-and-white section, the Earth's twelve month journey around the Sun changes the starry backdrop, forming a great 360-degree circle. The zodiac was created by dividing this circle into twelve equal parts (zodiac houses) of 30 degrees. The stars in each house were then grouped into constellations and given a name. The original Sumerian names of each house, paralleling the modern names, have now been found, proving beyond any doubt that the zodiac's first use was in Sumer. The nature of the zodiac signs (for which the star-pictures are wholly contrived), together with the arbitrary division into twelve, prove beyond any doubt that the identical zodiacs used in other, later, cultures, could not have been independent developments.

Various studies of Sumerian mathematics have pointed out, with some amazement, that the numerals are intimately connected to the precessional cycle.[23] The unusual alternating structure of the Sumerian sexagesimal system throws special emphasis onto the number 12,960,000, which represents exactly 500 great precessional cycles of 25,920 years. The lack of any connotations, other than astronomical, for the multiples of 25,920 and 2,160 can only suggest a deliberate design for astronomical purposes.

The uncomfortable question which the scientists have avoided is this: how could the Sumerians, whose civilisation only lasted 2,000 years, possibly have observed and recorded a celestial cycle that took 25,920 years to complete? And why did their civilisation begin in the middle of a zodiac period?[24] Is this a clue that their astronomy was a legacy from the gods?

Gods of the Shems

Why was the first civilisation on Earth, from its very beginning, so obsessed with a sophisticated study of the heavens? Why did the Sumerians go to such incredible lengths to build ziggurats aligned to the cardinal points of the compass? Why was the role of astronomer and priest combined? Furthermore, why was it so important to divide the Earth's celestial cycle by the number twelve? It is a number which brings us back to the Sumerians' central claim: 'whatever seems beautiful, we made by the grace of the gods'. Those gods, like the Greeks' gods millennia later, were organised in a pantheon of twelve.

So pervasive is the influence of the gods in Sumerian culture that one archaeologist was moved to comment that the 'gods bequeathed the Earth to mankind',[25] whilst Professor Samuel Kramer, one of the greatest authorities on Sumer, observed that:

With the help of their gods, especially Enlil, the 'King of Heaven and Earth', the Sumerians transformed a flat, arid windswept land into a blossoming, fertile kingdom.[26]

Naturally, we are not supposed to take Samuel Kramer's comment literally. Similar observations are found liberally spread throughout the academic press, presented, almost without exception, under a banner of Sumerian mythology and religious belief.[27] This belief system, like everything else in Sumer, was incredibly detailed and sophisticated. The whole of Sumerian life revolved around the gods, whom they regarded as flesh-and-blood immortals. Kings were chosen and could assume the throne only with the permission of the gods. In later times, battles were fought on the gods' behest. And the gods also provided specific instructions to build and rebuild temples in particular locations.

Why did the Sumerians spend thousands of man-years of effort to build and maintain hundreds of temples and ziggurats to their gods? The official explanation is that they invented their deities as an imaginative psychological response to a hostile, incomprehensible environment. The Sumerian beliefs are thus dismissed as a classic example of mankind's need for religion. However, such facile solutions leave unexplained the origin of the Sumerians' sophisticated scientific knowledge. Inventing gods is one thing, but inventing the technology to measure the movements of the planets and stars is another thing entirely.

If we give due recognition to the 'impossible' origin of Sumerian knowledge, as well as to the other mysteries of the world covered in chapters 1–5, a possible solution begins to emerge. Could all of these anomalous technologies have a common source? Can we continue to dismiss the Sumerians' claim that their civilisation was a gift of the gods?

Let us take a closer look at those Sumerian gods. Whilst the term 'gods' is full of awkward connotations for us, the Sumerians did not suffer from such problems, and referred to them as the AN.UNNA.KI, literally meaning 'Those Who from Heaven to Earth Came'.[28] They also described them pictographically as DIN.GIR.

What does the term DIN.GIR mean? In 1976, Zecharia Sitchin published a detailed etymological study of this, and other, terms used by the Sumerians and later civilisations to describe the rockets and craft of the gods. The pictographic sign for GIR (Illustration 8a) is commonly understood to mean a sharp-edged object, but an insight into its true significance can be gleaned from the sign for KA.GIR (Illustration 8b) which appears to show the aerodynamically-shaped GIR inside a shaft-like underground chamber. The sign for the first syllable DIN (Illustration 8c) makes little sense until it is combined with GIR to form DIN.GIR (Illustration 8d). The two syllables, when written together, make a perfect fit, representing, in Sitchin's words:

Illustration 8

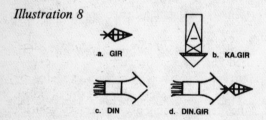

.a. GIR   b. KA.GIR

c. DIN   d. DIN.GIR

> . . . a picture of a rocket-propelled spaceship, with a landing craft docked into it perfectly – just as the lunar module was docked with Apollo 11.[29]

As with the Apollo rockets, three sections can be seen in the pictographic sign DIN.GIR – the lowest stage propulsion unit with the main thrust engines, the middle stage containing supplies and equipment and the upper stage command module. The full meaning of DIN.GIR, usually translated 'gods', is conveyed more fully by Sitchin's translation as 'The Righteous Ones of the Blazing Rockets'.[30]

Zecharia Sitchin's study also identified a second, different type of aerial vehicle. Whilst the GIR appeared to describe the rocket-like craft required for journeys beyond Earth's atmosphere, another vehicle known as a MU was used to fly within the Earth's skies. Sitchin pointed out that the original term *shu-mu*, meaning 'that which is a MU', later became known in the Semitic language as *shem* (and its variant *sham*). Drawing on the earlier work of G. Red-slob,[31] he pointed out that the terms *shem* and *shamaim* (the latter meaning 'heaven') both stemmed from the root word *shamah*, meaning 'that which is highward'.[32]

Because the term *shem* also had the connotation 'that by which one is remembered', it came to be translated as 'name'. Thus an unchallenged translation of an inscription on Gudea's temple reads 'its name shall fill the lands',[33] whereas it ought to read more literally as 'its MU shall hug the lands from horizon to horizon'. Sensing that *shem* or MU might represent an object, some scholars have left the word untranslated.

The Bible, too, has translated the term *shem* as 'name' and thus disguised the original meaning of the text. A particularly important example of this, as highlighted by Zecharia Sitchin, is the Biblical story of the Tower of Babel. If we substitute the literal meaning of *shem* as 'sky vehicle', the unintelligible tale in Genesis (the significance of which has always puzzled scholars) begins to take on a new meaning:

> Then they said, 'Come let us build ourselves a city with a tower that reaches to the heavens, so that we may make a *sky vehicle* and not be scattered over the face of the whole Earth.'[34]

The proper meaning of *shem* also casts new light on another section of Genesis which has always puzzled scholars, and which is highly significant to our study of the gods. In this example, the traditional translation of *shem* as 'name' is replaced by 'renown', on the basis that if one makes a name for himself, one is renowned. The passage which follows also includes reference to the mysterious Nefilim, a Hebrew word often mistranslated as 'Giants' but which actually comes from a root word meaning 'Those Who Descended'.[35] The meaning closely parallels the meaning of the Sumerian AN.UNNA.KI 'Those Who from Heaven to Earth Came':

> When men began to increase in number on the earth and daughters were born to them, the sons of God saw that the daughters of men were beautiful, and they married any of them they chose . . . The Nefilim were on the earth in those days – and also afterwards – when the sons of God went to the daughters of men and had children by them. They were the heroes of old, men of *renown*.[36] (emphasis added)

The Nefilim, then, were not the men of renown, but 'the people of the *shem*' – the gods of the sky vehicles.

There is one more example of linguistic confusion that I would like to cover, and that concerns the unfortunate association of gods with heavenly bodies. The association of gods with the Sun, Moon and visible planets has enabled scholars to dismiss the flesh-and-blood gods as a set of primitive beliefs. A classic example of this is the confusion which has arisen concerning the worship of a Sun god, both in ancient Egypt and the Near East.

According to Greek legend, Helios was a Sun god who traversed the skies in a chariot. The Greeks renamed the sacred Egyptian city of Leopolis in his honour, as Heliopolis – the 'City of Helios'. In the Near East, the same name Heliopolis was given by the Greeks to the city of Baalbek. Historians dismiss the ancient belief in these two sacred sites as a primitive form of Helios/Sun-worship. However, let us take a closer look at where the legend of Helios the Sun god came from.

Both Heliopolises were important sites for the gods, for

reasons which will become clear in chapter 8, and both were associated with a god known to the Akkadians as Shamash. Sumerian texts called him UTU, a god who controlled the sites of the *shems* and the 'eagles'.[37] The name Shamash, when spelled Shem-esh, literally means '*shem*-fire' and is thus often translated as 'He Who is Bright as the Sun'. The Sumerian name UTU indeed meant 'the Shining One', whilst Mesopotamian texts described Utu/Shamash as *rising* and *traversing* the skies.[38] It is not difficult to see how the accounts of these journeys could subsequently be misconstrued as the daily movement of the Sun.

Enki and Enlil

It is now time to lift the veil of mythology and identify some of the key members of the Sumerian pantheon of flesh-and-blood gods.

During the last one hundred years, scholars have been fascinated by the rich body of epic literature recovered by the archaeologists in Mesopotamia. That fascination has led to a determined and painstaking effort to piece together texts which are sometimes only recovered in fragments. Original Sumerian texts have been supplemented by later and similar Akkadian versions, allowing the full reconstruction of many ancient tales. What has emerged is a detailed and coherent picture of anthropomorphic gods with human-like emotions, intimately mixed up in human affairs. Scholars have been left in no doubt that the origin of the Greek tales of Zeus, Olympus and the pantheon of twelve gods lies in Sumer.

The names, family relationships, powers and duties of the Sumerian gods have emerged from the archaeological rubble to confront us with a highly detailed picture. Every major Sumerian city was associated with one or sometimes two gods. A review of these sites provides us with the most important names, to whom the temples were dedicated: to Enki at Eridu, to Anu and Inanna at Uruk, to Nannar at Ur and to Enlil at Nippur. The same names, or their Akkadian equivalents, also crop up again and again in the later Assyrian and Babylonian cities. It is clear that these names bestowed meanings which were based on human perceptions of certain aspects of these gods, and they thus appeared under different nicknames to reflect different attributes and powers.

The father of the gods was called AN (or Anu in Akkadian) meaning 'Heaven'. His name is preserved today in the Latin-English word 'annum'. AN played a remote part in the proceedings, residing in 'Heaven' and making only occasional visits to Earth with his spouse Antu. His temple at Ur was called the E.ANNA, the 'House of AN'. The Sumerians sometimes called it 'The House for Descending from Heaven'. When kingship was first granted to man by the gods (an antecedent for today's royal families), it was referred to as the 'Anu-ship'.

Anu had two sons who descended to Earth. Although they were brothers, they sometimes fought as bitter rivals. The firstborn son, Enki, was the first to take command on Earth, only to be displaced on Anu's orders by the second-born son Enlil. Ancient depictions of the gods Enki and Enlil are shown (seated) in Illustration 9a and 9b respectively, emphasising their flesh-and-blood nature and human-like appearance. The brotherly rivalry hinged on the gods' legal rules of succession, which were determined by genetic purity. Enlil, the offspring of Anu and his *half-sister*, thus preserved the father's genes through the male line far better than Enki.[39] This practice, of marrying half-sisters, seems rather incestuous to us today, but it was not always so. For example, it was also a common practice by the royal families in Egypt, whilst in the Bible, Abraham, too, boasted that his wife was also his sister.[40] The origin of this practice undoubtedly lies in the realm of the gods, and I will explain the scientific basis behind it in a later chapter.

Illustration 9

The name EN.LIL is usually translated 'Lord of the Wind', especially by those scholars who wish to belittle the Sumerian beliefs as mythology. A more literal rendering, however, is 'Lord of the Command',[41] a suitable name for one who became the principal god on Earth and carried the authority to bestow kingship to man. Enlil's city was Nippur, at which a magnificent E.KUR, a 'House like a Mountain',[42] was built, and fitted with mysterious equipment that could survey the heavens and Earth. Its five-storey ruins can still be seen today, one hundred miles south of Baghdad.

His brother EN.KI, meaning 'Lord of Earth' was also known as E.A, 'He Whose House is Water'.[43] His city was Eridu, on the waterfront where the Tigris and Euphrates meet the head of the Persian Gulf. He was the master engineer and chief scientist of the gods, and mankind's greatest benefactor. He often defended man in the council of the gods, and saved Noah and his family from the great Flood.

Why was Enki so friendly towards mankind? According to the Sumerians, it was Enki who played an instrumental role in man's creation.[44] Although regarded by scholars as myth, the Sumerians firmly believed that the gods had created man as a worker. The ancient texts describe a rebellion of the rank-and-file gods in protest at their heavy workload (the exact nature of this work will be discussed in chapter 14). Enki then settled the dispute by offering to create a primitive worker and 'bind upon it the image of the gods' so that it was intelligent enough to use tools and follow instructions.

Enki was assisted in the creation of man by his half-sister NIN.HAR.SAG, meaning 'Lady of the Head Mountain'.[45] She was the chief nurse in charge of the gods' medical facilities, and hence one of her nicknames was NIN.TI, 'Lady Life'. Together, she and Enki carried out genetic experiments, with varying degrees of success. The texts relate that Ninharsag was responsible for a man who could not hold back his urine, a woman who could not bear children and another being with no sexual organs. Enki also had his failures, including one man with failing eyesight, trembling hands, a diseased liver and a weak heart. Given our own twentieth century decoding of the human genome, we can understand the excitement and power felt by Ninharsag, who in one text exclaimed:

> 'How good or how bad is man's body?
> As my heart prompts me,
> I can make its fate good or bad.'[46]

Finally the perfect man was created. Ninharsag cried out 'I have created! My hands have done it!'. One text states quite explicitly that Ninharsag gave the new creation 'a skin as the skin of a god'. Having perfected the ideal man with a larger brain, enhanced digit ability and smooth skin, it was a simple next step to use cloning – now an established scientific process – to produce an army of primitive workers. This fantastic event was commemorated for all time by Ninharsag's symbol – the horseshoe-shaped cutter of the umbilical cord, an instrument that was used by midwives in ancient times. She also became known as the Mother Goddess, and became associated with numerous primitive religious cults throughout the ancient world. Archaeologists have long been puzzled by the sacred representation of the pregnant female form by the earliest societies.

In the first chapter, I described the meaning of terms such as 'clay/dust', 'rib' and the newly created being which the Sumerians called LU.LU – a term which literally meant 'one who has been mixed'. In the light of the fundamental contradictions of mankind's evolution, covered in chapter 2, the Sumerian account takes on a tremendous significance. Did Enki bind the image (the genetic blueprint) of the gods upon the lowly *Homo erectus*, which suddenly experienced the incredible evolutionary leap to *Homo sapiens* 200,000 years ago? A very detailed study of the ancient texts suggests that this was, indeed, exactly what happened.[47]

Wars of the Gods

The name Sumer was literally written as KI.EN.GIR,[48] meaning 'the Land of the Lords of the Rockets', but it also had the connotation 'Land of the Watchers', the latter term virtually identical to the term *neter* (*ntr*) by which the Egyptians referred to their gods.[49] These terms clearly indicate the role of the gods as Guardians or Lords over mankind. Scholars have tended to study the Sumerian and Egyptian civilisations as independent subjects, but as we shall see, the prehistory of mankind knew no such boundaries.

One of the best known and fascinating Egyptian legends is that of Osiris and Isis. Although generally regarded as myth, mainstream scholars *have* occasionally suggested that it *might* be based on historical events. According to Man-

etho, an Egyptian priest cum historian from the third
century BC, the god Osiris and his sister-wife Isis were
rulers over the land of northern Egypt more than six
thousand years *before* human civilisation began. As we
shall see, the tragic tale of Osiris sheds considerable light
on a key event in mankind's prehistory.

The tragic tale begins with Osiris being tricked by his
own brother Seth into lying in a large chest, which Seth
then seals and throws into the sea. Isis, overcome by grief,
goes in search of her missing husband. She is informed by a
divine 'wind' that the chest has been blown ashore at
Byblos in Lebanon. Whilst she is waiting for the help of
the god Thoth to resurrect the body, Seth appears again,
dismembers the body into fourteen pieces and scatters them
all over Egypt. Once again Isis goes in search of her
husband and manages to find all of the body parts except
his phallus. Some legends say that Isis then buried the parts
where she found them, others that she bound them
together, thus starting the tradition of mummification.
The tale continues with what appears to be an account
of cloning, as Isis extracts the 'essence' from the body of
Osiris and uses it to impregnate herself. She then secretly
gives birth to the child Horus, who grows up and returns to
avenge the death of his father.

The ensuing tale of Horus and the winged disc with which
he gives battle to Seth is yet another fascinating account of
ancient technology which deserves further study.[50] The
battle ends with the defeat and exile of Seth, a god who
was thereafter associated with chaos.

Prior to 1976, the Egyptian and Mesopotamian accounts
had been studied separately and largely from a mythological perspective. Then one scholar, Zecharia Sitchin, taking the translations at face value, linked the accounts
together into a consistent and credible sequence of
events.[51] In so doing, he turned Egyptian mythology into
the earliest period of human history, and showed how the

Horus-Seth conflict led to a ferocious war between the rival factions of Enlilite and Enkiite gods.

Why was there such hatred between the brothers Osiris and Seth? Applying the same rules of succession found in the Sumerian tales, Sitchin demonstrated that by marrying Isis, Osiris effectively prevented his rival Seth from producing an heir from the same half-sister. Until that time, the rivalry between Osiris and Seth had been solved by splitting the land of Egypt between them. Now Osiris had ensured that it would be a son of his, not Seth's, that would assume the future rule of the whole of Egypt.

Why should the defeat of Seth by the avenger, Horus, lead to a full scale war between the Egyptian gods and the eastern gods of Mesopotamia? The key to understanding the conflict lies in the division of lands and strategic sites between the two divine brothers Enlil and Enki. After the Flood – for the Sumerians recognised it as a genuine historic event – the texts state that the Earth was divided into four regions – a neutral zone of the gods on the Sinai peninsula, entrusted to the mother goddess Ninharsag; the African lands under the supervision of the Enkiite gods; and the lands of Asia, particularly Mesopotamia and the Levant,[52] under the supervision of the Enlilite gods.

As Zecharia Sitchin has shown, this division of lands accords with the legend that a great god named Ptah arrived in Egypt from overseas and undertook reclamation works, to raise the land above the waters. It was on this account that the ancient Egyptians named their country the 'Raised Land'. All of the evidence suggests, with little doubt, that this god was Enki.[53]

It is important to note that the descendants of Noah's son Ham were assigned to the African lands of the Enkiite gods, whilst the lands of the Near East and northern Asia were given to Noah's other two sons, Shem and Japheth respectively.[54]

It has been suggested by Zecharia Sitchin that the

mysterious cursing of Noah's grandson Canaan (the son of Ham) in Genesis 9 is connected with this division of lands.[55] Scholars have been mystified by the Biblical story which, whilst unintelligible, clearly appears to be of major importance. As one commentator notes, Genesis 9 'refers to some abominable deed in which Canaan seems to have been implicated'.[56] Citing the ex-biblical Book of Jubilees, Sitchin suggests that Canaan's abominable deed was to have strayed from the lands which had been pre-ordained for him:

> Canaan saw the land of Lebanon, to the river of Egypt, that it was very good . . . He went not into the land of his inheritance to the west of the sea; he dwelt in the land of Lebanon, eastward and westward of the Jordan.[57]

How could Canaan have so easily defied the instructions of the gods that assigned the *African* lands to the Hamitic people? As Sitchin points out, his action would surely not have been possible without the connivance of one or other major deity. It is therefore a strong possibility that Canaan's abominable deed coincided with the occupation of Lebanon by the god Seth and his supporters, fleeing from the battle with Horus.

In Zecharia Sitchin's view, it was this illegal occupation of Enlilite land that led to a full-scale war in which the Enlilites drove the Enkiite gods out of Canaan. The war is described in numerous Sumerian, Akkadian and Assyrian texts, which scholars collectively refer to as the 'Myths of Kur'. It is also alluded to in Egyptian ritual texts, one of which refers to 'Seth the rebellious on that day of the storm over the Two Lands'.[58] However, far from being myths, these tales represent a genuine account of one of the crucial events in the history of man, who was called up for the first time to fight for his gods.

The hero of the Enlilite clan was the god Ninurta, the

firstborn son of Enlil, who led the battle in a 'Storm Bird' with powerful weapons. Assisted by his brother Ishkur and his niece Inanna, he routed the enemy forces, which were led by the 'Great Serpent'. The texts describe a campaign which may have escalated far beyond its original objectives, with a merciless extermination of human armies deep inside African territories.[59] The final scene of the battle was the E.KUR, the 'House Like A Mountain', to which the Enkiite gods had fled, led by Enki, Ra and Nergal (and later joined by Horus). Although they were safe behind the Ekur's powerful protective shield, the Enkiite gods were effectively under siege, trapped with little food and water.

Why did one group of gods launch such a bitter and bloody war against their fellow gods? First, we should note the deep antagonism which divided the descendants of Enlil and Enki. As discussed earlier, the firstborn son Enki was extremely jealous of his brother Enlil, who was the legal heir to Anu. It should be recalled that, when the gods had first settled on Earth (aeons before kingship and civilisation were granted to mankind in Sumer), Enki had been displaced by Enlil, and we know from the *Atra-Hasis* epic that he was sent to a region known as 'the Abzu'. As we shall see in a later chapter, the term Abzu denoted the African lands, including Egypt. Enki was therefore resentful of his demoted status and relegation to the African lands.

The second major factor behind the war was the significance of the lands which were being occupied by Seth. As we shall see in chapter 8, these lands were of strategic importance to the gods who were planning to construct new facilities for their *shems* and eagles, to replace the sites destroyed by the great Flood. The planned locations for these new facilities included the future site of the city of Jerusalem, together with the Sinai peninsula.

The eventual outcome of the war was a humiliating surrender and one-sided peace conference, which was to have far-reaching repercussions. As for the fate of Canaan

and his clan, the Old Testament records that, instead of
being moved to their designated lands, they were allowed to
stay in the Middle East with a lower status,[60] as servants to
the Shemitic people,[61] whilst the lands of Japheth were to be
extended.[62]

Inanna – Goddess of Love and War

One of the most significant deities of the Near East
pantheons was a goddess whom the Sumerians knew as
IN.ANNA (meaning 'Anu's Beloved'). Her promiscuous
exploits were a favourite subject of the ancient scribes, and
her physical attributes were extremely popular with the
ancient artists. Hundreds of texts have been found dealing
with Inanna's love affairs, one of the best known examples
being *The Epic of Gilgamesh*. As the archetypal goddess of
love, she was known to all of the ancient civilisations under
a variety of different names. To the Assyrians and Babylonians she was known as Ishtar, to the Canaanites as
Ashtoreth, to the Greeks as Aphrodite and to the Romans
as Venus. According to the Sumerian texts, she was the
daughter of Nannar, the grand-daughter of Enlil and the
great-granddaughter of Anu. She was also known by many
other nicknames, such as IR.NI.NI 'The Strong Sweet-
smelling Lady'.

Inanna's sexual passions were rivalled only by her prow-
ess on the battlefield, hence she became known as the
archetypal goddess of war, as well as the goddess of love.
In many ways these two qualities went hand-in-hand. Her
tale, unfolded by Zecharia Sitchin in *The Wars of Gods and
Men*, is a tragic one, beginning with her marriage to
Dumuzi, a son of Enki. Whether this was a true love
match, or an attempt by Inanna to gain power in the rival
Enlilite lands, we cannot be certain. But in those early days,

her power in Enlilite country was certainly blocked by male domination. One does not need to be a feminist to sense her frustrated ambitions; her grandfather Enlil had overall command; her brother Utu was in charge of the key site at Jerusalem; her father Nannar was in charge of Sinai and her uncle ISH.KUR (meaning 'Far Mountain Land') had always been ultimately responsible for the important site at Baalbek. Her own power-base in Sumer was limited to the city of Uruk, which at that time carried very little status.

Shortly after her marriage to Dumuzi, Inanna incited him to beget an heir through the usual custom of his half-sister, Geshtinanna, an act almost certainly motivated by the gods' rules of heredity.[63] When his sister refused, Dumuzi, in the heat of the moment, raped her, a serious offence, even for the gods with their at times rather liberal code of conduct.[64] Ra, the elder brother of Dumuzi, and ill-disposed towards his relationship with the rival goddess Inanna, then ordered his arrest. The dramatic capture, escape and unfortunate death of Dumuzi are dealt with in the Sumerian text known as *His Heart Was Filled With Tears*. The ensuing trip by Inanna to Africa (the Lower World) is one of the most famous of all Sumerian texts, and was dutifully copied by the ancient scribes. Figure 9 (see black-and-white section) shows a tablet from the Akkadian version.

The death of Dumuzi, combined with the position of Africa in the Lower World (southern hemisphere), have naturally led to Inanna's 'descent' being viewed as a mythological tale of a trip to the underworld or realm of the dead.[65] This view has been reinforced by legends that it was a place from which men did not return, but in the case of Inanna, it was very much a land of the living from which she *did* return.

The furious Inanna blamed Ra for her husband's death and sought her revenge. We know from one text that Ra took refuge inside a 'Mountain' described as E.BIH 'The Abode of Sorrowful Calling'.[66] Another text describes it as the same E.KUR in which the Enkiite gods had been besieged by Ninurta. Zecharia Sitchin once again lifts the veil of myth to describe a historic event – the ensuing trial of Ra, his imprisonment inside the Ekur without food or water, and his subsequent escape.

There is little doubt that Inanna was left bitter and frustrated by the death of Dumuzi and the blocking of her ambitions in Africa. Her consolation prize, as suggested by Sitchin, was to be given control over a new civilisation, in the Indus Valley (modern Pakistan).[67] This mysterious civilisation first emerged at various sites c. 2800 BC and was in full bloom by 2500 BC.[68] The most striking feature of this culture, known as Harappan, was its homogeneity in all aspects of life, such as building, pottery and religious belief. Its principal cities, Harappa and Mohenjodaro, were laid out in a manner that has led archaeologists to think that they 'were conceived in their entirety before they were built'.[69] Significantly, the Harappan religious beliefs were very different from the Sumerians and Egyptians who worshipped many gods. In contrast, the Harappans worshipped a sole female deity (Figure 10, black-and-white section), whose depictions bore an amazing similarity to other images of the goddess Inanna.

However, Inanna was soon to grow bored with her new responsibilities, and she then turned her attention back to Sumer. During a visit to Enki at his home in the Abzu, Inanna got him drunk and tricked him into giving her certain divine objects known as 'ME's'.[70] Exactly what these objects were is unknown, but they bestowed great knowledge and power on Inanna.[71] Whilst her Harappan civilisation was busy repairing the damage from recurring floods, her Sumerian city Uruk suddenly became very powerful and Inanna herself became a major deity.

It was then, according to the ancient texts, that Inanna found the man who was to be the instrument of her ambitions, the man who established the city of Agade and subsequently founded the Akkadian empire. The man's name was Sargon the Great, and the archaeological date *c.* 2400 BC. The era of Inanna was about to begin, and in both love and war, she was to become more dangerous than ever before.

Is Sumer Atlantis?

What are we to make of the Sumerian civilisation and their astonishing accounts of the gods? Sumer is unable to impress us like the Egyptian pyramids – its ancient ziggurats are barely recognisable mounds – but the legacy of Sumerian technology reaches out and touches us continuously. Every time we check our watch, we should think of the Sumerian base 60 mathematics and its close connection with Sumerian astronomy. Whenever we drive our cars, we should remember the first Sumerian wheel. In all our established institutions, we should recognise the Sumerian legacy. Those thousands of tiny Sumerian clay tablets, which are quietly tucked away in our museums, speak far more lucidly than the hieroglyphics on public display in Egypt. The story they tell is powerful and compelling, offering solutions even to the mystery of mankind himself.

Let us examine some facts. First of all, it is an archaeological fact that the Sumerian civilisation began *suddenly*, nearly six thousand years ago. Secondly, it is a fact that the Sumerians had an unbelievable level of scientific knowledge, that did not appear to pass through any evolutionary period (who for instance could have observed and understood the 25,920-year precessional cycle?). Thirdly, the Sumerians explained everything in the context of their gods. Fourthly, the Sumerian tales of flesh-and-blood gods are echoed by the Hebrew tales of Yahweh and the Egyptian tales of Ra, not to mention the so-called myths from South America and the rest of the world.

Now let us examine some options: either the Sumerians were telling the truth, or they were lying.[72] If the Sumerians were lying (or at least being rather imaginative), then we still have to explain where they acquired their technology. If their teachers were not 'extraterrestrials' then they were terrestrials. The latter implies a prior civilisation, perhaps the popular idea of a lost civilisation of Atlantis, which taught itself over tens of thousands of years and then was destroyed in a cataclysm. We have a simple choice – gods or Atlanteans.

Here is some simple armchair reasoning. First, if the Sumerians were taught by Atlanteans, where did the Atlanteans come from? We still need to answer the mystery of *Homo sapiens*, which the Sumerians do so well. Secondly, there is no direct evidence of Atlantis – only plenty of speculation and a myth handed down by the Greek philosopher Plato. The Atlantis 'evidence', based on an oral tradition dating to around 350 BC, is infinitely less impressive than the Sumerians' textual evidence which has been lying undisturbed since 2000 BC. Thirdly, if we *were* to find an Atlantean site underneath the sea, we might well find texts showing that they too worshipped flesh-and-blood gods by the names of Anu, Enlil and Enki.

In previous chapters, we have studied many examples of ancient technology – in ancient maps, in the pyramids, in various other sites and their astronomical alignments. This same ground is covered by supporters of the Atlantis theory – the theory that everything can be explained by a lost civilisation. But at this point, chapter 6, we must part company with the supporters of Atlantis, for it is the intention of this book to deal in hard evidence, not unsubstantiated myth, rumour or speculation.

Putting armchair reasoning to one side, how can we adopt a scientific approach to corroborating the Sumerian accounts of the gods? As the famous Carl Sagan once said:

A completely convincing demonstration of past contact with an extraterrestrial civilisation will always be difficult to prove on textual grounds alone.[73]

The following chapters will therefore concentrate on *physical* evidence which corroborates the Sumerian texts. There are several crucial questions which we need to ask.

The first question is 'where did the gods come from?' This crucial matter is addressed as a priority in chapter 7.

The second question is 'what physical proof backs up the Sumerian accounts of the gods' presence on Earth?'. This will be addressed in chapters 8 to 10.

The third question is 'what was the purpose of the gods?' This is covered in chapter 14.

The fourth, and most vexing, question concerns the alleged immortality of the gods. The feasibility of very slow ageing, giving the appearance of immortality, is examined in chapters 12 and 13, based on the latest discoveries from genetic science.

Finally, in order to establish the role of flesh-and-blood gods in human *history*, we must satisfy the basic need for a *chronology* that will link all events together in a form that can survive the most rigorous of examinations. The basis for such a chronology is set out in chapter 11 and further developed in chapter 13.

If we can answer all of the above questions successfully, then we can put aside the red-herring of Atlantis, and focus on the only remaining question of 'where are the gods now?'. That question is taken up in chapters 15 and 16.

Chapter Six Conclusions

* The Sumerians possessed advanced knowledge of metallurgy and astronomy, the latter including the

Earth's 25,920-year precessional cycle.

* Scientists cannot explain how the Sumerian civilisation began so suddenly, nor how they acquired their amazing technology. The Sumerians called it 'a gift of the gods'.

* The origin of ancient technology can only be explained by a sophisticated race of 'gods' or a lost civilisation such as 'Atlantis'. However, it seems likely that the Atlantis legend is simply a sub-set of the greater mystery of Sumer and its gods.

CHAPTER SEVEN

PASSING TIME ON PLANET X

—————◆—————

The Epic of Creation

Where did the gods come from? According to the Sumerians, the gods came to Earth from a planet called Nibiru. Their descriptions of that planet match precisely the specification of the so-called 'Planet X', which is currently being sought by modern astronomers *within our own Solar System*. This planet is believed to have an elliptical orbit that takes it into the depths of space, well beyond the orbit of Pluto – hence it has not been seen in recent times. The scientific evidence and ongoing search for Planet X will be dealt with later in this chapter, but first we must review a mass of evidence that traces the history of that planet from the early days of the Solar System right up to the legendary Flood, which I will date to 13,000 years ago.

Our quest for Nibiru/Planet X begins with an extraordinary source – a 4,000 year old Babylonian text known as the *Enuma Elish*. In 1876, George Smith of the British Museum published his translation of this sacred Babylonian epic, pieced together from broken clay tables such as that shown in Figure 1 (see black-and-white section).[1]

Smith had already caused international headlines with his earlier translation of a Flood text which paralleled the Biblical tale. The *Enuma Elish* caused an equal stir, for it appeared to represent a creation myth that was far more detailed than the brief Biblical account of Genesis 1.

Nevertheless, for one hundred years, the *Enuma Elish* was dismissed as mythology – an imaginative account of a cosmic battle of good against evil – and the Babylonian New Year ritual which had developed around it was similarly regarded as meaningless superstition.

To the uneducated eye, the *Enuma Elish* is a tale of battles between one 'god' and another, the hero of which was Marduk, the chief deity of the Babylonians. The educated scholar, however, realises that the Babylonians were heirs to the Sumerian culture, and that the vast majority of Babylonian myths are politicised versions of Sumerian originals. The key question is this: if the very un-Sumerian ritual and political aspects are stripped away from the *Enuma Elish*, does the tale indeed represent an earlier Sumerian document with valid scientific credentials?

In 1976, Zecharia Sitchin came forward with an amazing, but as yet unrefuted claim, that the *Enuma Elish* is a cosmological epic, accurately describing the formation of the Solar System 4.6 billion years ago![2] Sitchin, an expert in Near Eastern languages, realised that the references to 'gods' were in fact references to 'planets', that 'winds' could be read as 'satellites'[3] and that the role of Marduk paralleled that of a planet known to the Sumerians as Nibiru.

The Babylonian epic begins: *Enuma elish la nabu shama-mu* – 'When on high the heaven had not been named'. It then lists the 'gods' which were begotten by AP. SU (the Sun),[4] with descriptions that match the planets of the Solar System in amazing detail. Then, 'in the heart of the deep', a new and more powerful god, called Marduk, was created:

> Perfect were his members beyond comprehension . . .
> unsuited for understanding, difficult to perceive.
> Four were his eyes, four were his ears;
> when he moved his lips, fire blazed forth . . .
> He was the loftiest of the 'gods', surpassing was his stature;
> his members were enormous, he was exceedingly tall.[5]

Marduk is interpreted by Sitchin as a wandering planet, thrust into the Solar System by an unknown cosmic event, perhaps ejected from a similarly unstable solar-planetary system. Its course, first via Neptune, then Uranus, indicates a clockwise direction, contrary to the counter-clockwise rotation of the other planets around the Sun. This factor will later prove highly significant. The combined gravitational effect of the other planets diverted Marduk into the heart of the newly developing Solar System – towards a collision with a watery planet named Tiamat:

> Tiamat and Marduk, the wisest of the 'gods',
> advanced against one another;
> they pressed on to single combat,
> they approached for battle.[6]

Armed with a 'blazing flame' and having acquired various 'winds' or satellites, Marduk 'towards the raging Tiamat set his face':

> The Lord spread out his net to enfold her;
> the Evil Wind, the rearmost, he unleashed at her face.
> As she opened her mouth. Tiamat, to devour him—
> he drove in the Evil Wind so that she closed not her lips.
> The fierce storm Winds then charged her belly;
> Her body became distended; her mouth had opened wide.
> He shot there through an arrow, it tore her belly;
> it cut through her insides, tore into her womb.
> Having thus subdued her, her life-breath he extinguished.
>
> After he had slain Tiamat, the leader,
> her band was shattered, her host broken up.
> The 'gods', her helpers who marched at her side,

trembling with fear,
turned their backs about so as to save and preserve their lives.
Thrown into the net, they found themselves ensnared . . .
The whole band of demons that had marched on her side
he cast into fetters, their hands he bound . . .
Tightly encircled, they could not escape.[7]

The planet Tiamat was thus 'extinguished', but the act of
creation was not yet finished. Marduk became caught in the
orbit of the Sun, forever to return to the place of the celestial
battle with Tiamat. On the first encounter, Marduk's
satellite-winds had smashed into Tiamat, but one orbital
period later, Marduk itself 'returned to Tiamat, whom he
had subdued' and the two planets did collide:

The Lord paused to view her lifeless body.
To divide the monster he then artfully planned.
Then, as a mussel, he split her into two parts.

The Lord trod upon Tiamat's hinder part;
with his weapon the connected skull he cut loose;
he severed the channels of her blood;
and caused the North Wind to bear it
to places that have been unknown.[8]

Zecharia Sitchin identifies the upper part (the 'skull') of the
watery Tiamat as the future Earth, shunted by one of
Marduk's satellites into a new orbit, along with its largest
satellite Kingu (meaning 'Great Emissary'). The final act of
creation then occurred on the second return of Marduk to
the celestial battle-site. This time Marduk collided with the
remaining half of Tiamat:

The [other] half of her he set up as a screen for the skies:
locking them together, as watchmen he stationed them . . .
He bent Tiamat's tail to form the Great Band as a bracelet.[9]

Figure 11 (see black-and-white section) shows the overall
effects of the celestial battle. Over the course of two orbits,

the planet Marduk/Nibiru had created both the heavens (the Asteroid Belt) and the Earth, in addition to the comets. As Sitchin points out, this is identical to Day One and Day Two of the Biblical Book of Genesis.[10] He failed to mention that the Muslims' holy book, the Koran, also parallels the *Enuma Elish*:

> Are the disbelievers unaware that the heavens and the Earth were one solid mass which We tore asunder, and that We made every living thing out of water?[11]

Scars of Genesis

Scientists are reluctant to admit that a 4,000 year old text could explain the origins of the Solar System – for that would raise the uncomfortable question of how the Babylonians could have acquired the knowledge – but nevertheless the *Enuma Elish* does explain virtually all the anomalies of the Solar System that puzzle modern astronomers.

The best example is literally under our feet – planet Earth herself. For thousands of years, we have taken it for granted that our planet has its land mass concentrated on one side of the globe, with the deep cavity of the Pacific Ocean bed on the other side. Now, as a result of late twentieth century space probes, there is a growing realisation that the continent-ocean distinction is unique to the Earth among the Solar System planets.

One particular mystery is that of the Earth's crust – the outer layer of material which forms the Earth's surface. On dry land, the continental crust is around 20 miles thick, with mountain 'roots' extending 40 miles deep.[12] Beneath the oceans, however, the oceanic crust is only 5 miles thick. This anomaly has been further compounded by the discovery of large slabs of crust, which have mysteriously 'dived' 250 miles beneath the Earth's surface. Even if this crust is taken into account, Earth still has less than half of the crust it ought to have relative to other planets.[13] And just to confuse things even more, the oceanic crust dates to no more than 200 million years old, whereas the continental crust dates to 4 *billion* years.

Why is the oceanic crust relatively fresh and what force caused the continental crust to 'dive'? Scientists have produced incredibly contrived theories to explain these mysterious anomalies. For instance, it is thought that the young age of the oceanic crust must be caused by it periodically diving into a 'subduction zone' in the mantle below, where it is then somehow recycled. The *Enuma Elish*, on the other hand, can explain everything perfectly, for it describes Earth as half of a planet that was catastrophically split into two – the surviving half of the watery planet Tiamat. The process of continental drift makes a lot more sense when seen in this manner as a catastrophic after-effect. The ancient Sumerians were well aware of this fact; as Zecharia Sitchin has pointed out, the term which they used for the Earth was KI, meaning 'to cut off, to sever, to hollow out'.[14]

Twenty years after Zecharia Sitchin offered the Sumerian solution to the Earth's origin, scientists have got no further in suggesting any alternative explanations. In fact, the evidence continues to support what Sitchin said. Recent improvements in geological dating have demonstrated a mystifying absence of crustal rocks from the Earth's earliest era, the so-called Hadean era between 4.6–3.96 billion years ago. Writing in the esteemed scientific journal *Nature*, J. Vervoort has recently described 'early large-scale chemical depletion of the mantle (presumably resulting from the extraction of continental crust)',[15] whilst fellow-research-er, Richard Carlson wrote:

Why did the Earth not form an extensive early crust or, if it did, where has all this old crust gone? . . . data taken in the early 1980s . . . showed clearly that, 3.8 billion years ago, the mantle had already been depleted by extraction of crust.[16]

Evidence from the Moon also offers confirmation of a cataclysmic event 4 billion years ago. The Apollo missions found a large number of rocks, known as breccias, which had been shattered and then fused together by a sudden, extreme heat. At the same time, the Moon's surface layer suddenly melted and its magnetic field declined to a negligible level.[17] We know that the Moon's craters, previously thought to be extinct volcanoes, were caused by massive impacts, around 4 billion years ago.[18]

According to the *Enuma Elish*, as deciphered by Zecharia Sitchin, the Moon (Kingu) was originally the main satellite of Tiamat, and was thus at the heart of the celestial battle. Its scars of battle can thus be explained. The origin of the Moon, as a satellite of a larger planet than Earth, also explains one of the greatest riddles of the Solar System. As surprising as it might seem, scientists are bitterly divided on the question of how the Earth came to acquire such a large Moon.

Relative to other planet-satellite relationships, Earth's Moon is far too large, and this has caused a particular problem with most theories on its origin. Its sheer size argues against the possibility of 'capture' by the Earth's gravity.[19] The fission theory (by which the Moon was ejected by the Earth in an over-spin condition) also fails to explain how such a large mass of material could have been ejected, and has hence led to a hybrid theory whereby a Mars-sized impactor planet might have struck the Earth with a glancing blow.[20] The fission theory is still favoured as the least-bad solution, but if the Moon was ejected from the larger planet Tiamat, then the size constraint on the fission hypothesis is eliminated.

Some experts have deduced from the Moon's size and composition that it is a bona-fide planet in its own right.[21] As pointed out by Zecharia Sitchin, the *Enuma Elish* does indeed state that the Moon was about to become a separate planet just prior to the encounter with Marduk.[22] It is thus no coincidence that the Sumerians always counted the Moon alongside the planets as a separate celestial body.

The *Enuma Elish* also explains a number of apparent contradictions in the composition of the Earth and Moon. Advocates of the fission theory have noted certain common properties in the Earth and Moon crusts, such as tungsten deficiency, which are highly unlikely to be coincidental. Other studies, however, have shown significant *differences* in the crust and mantle,[23] whilst radioactive elements found close to the Moon's surface are only found deep down within the Earth. The inevitable conclusion is that the Moon comprises a combination of terrestrial material and material from an external source, generally assumed to be an impactor planet.[24] That is exactly the scenario described by the Babylonian epic.

Scientific theories on the origin of the Asteroid Belt fare little better than those on the origin of the Earth and Moon. The official line is that the asteroids are small planetesimals (pre-planetary bodies), representing left-over debris from the beginning of the Solar System, that never finished accumulating into a planet. One theory supposes that, instead of forming a planet, these planetesimals collided too fast and shattered. Unfortunately, there is no underlying scientific theory to support such a contrived explanation.

On the other hand, there is scientific evidence to suggest that the asteroids are the remains of a cataclysmic collision. Apart from the fact that this appears intuitively obvious, there is an astronomical equation known as Bode's Law which predicts the existence of a planet at the exact distance where the Asteroid Belt orbits the Sun.[25] When the first asteroids were discovered at the beginning of the nineteenth century, an exploded planet was indeed regarded as the obvious explanation. In the twentieth century, however, astronomers have backed away from the catastrophic explanation due to a perceived lack of asteroidal mass to account for a suitably sized planet.[26] As Zecharia Sitchin has pointed out, the *Enuma Elish* solves the problem by locating the missing mass in the cleaved planet, Earth herself.

The comets too are a mystery to modern science. Despite a wealth of data and research, they remain one of the most enigmatic features of the Solar System. These icy planetesimals orbit the Sun with vast elongated, elliptical orbits, in contrast to the planets, which have approximately circular orbits. Some comets return to Earth only once every few thousand years, with the longest orbit being that of Kohoutek which is estimated at 75,000 years. They are regarded as the 'rebellious members' of the Solar System on account of their orbiting the Sun in many diverse planes, and in the *opposite direction* to the counterclockwise movement of the planets.

Like the asteroids, it was once believed that the comets were evidence of an exploded planet.[27] Science then regressed into increasingly contrived theories on how they were left-overs from the formation of the Solar System. According to the text books, the comets were somehow flung out by the gravity of the forming planets, generating a swarm known as the Oort cloud in the depths of space, beyond the planet Pluto.[28] After being 'stored' in the Oort cloud reservoir, some comets then for no apparent reason 'occasionally found themselves on trajectories back into the inner solar system'.[29]

One of the few open-minded modern astronomers, Tom Van Flandern, has recently questioned 'certain implausible aspects of the conventional theories' of comets, and particularly the 'unlikely Oort cloud hypothesis'.[30] Van Flandern questions fundamental aspects of the prevailing wisdom, which fail to explain why some comets orbit the Sun 1,000 times farther than Pluto, and why they all orbit in the same clockwise direction. The current theories also fail to properly explain how such an improbable thing as the Oort cloud could ever have formed.

Van Flandern explores the *only* possible alternative to the Oort cloud hypothesis – an exploded planet – and notes that mathematical modelling proves the comets to have a common point of origin.[31] He concludes that:

> [The] comets originated in the energetic breakup of a body orbiting the Sun in or near the present location of the Asteroid Belt . . .

Exactly as described by the *Enuma Elish*! As Zecharia Sitchin has shown, the direction followed by the planet Marduk did indeed take it in the opposite direction to the orbit of the planets. It was on the first passing of Marduk, as described earlier, that Tiamat's satellites were 'broken up' and numerous small planetary bodies ('gods') were thrust by the impact into new orbits, 'turning their backs around' to follow the clockwise direction of Marduk itself.

Studies of meteorites have also concluded that these cometary fragments were once part of a larger planet. In 1948, Brown and Patterson conducted an exhaustive survey and stated that:

> The conclusion appears irrefutable that meteorites at one time were an integral part of a planet.[32]

That conclusion has not been refuted since.

In addition to all of the evidence cited above, a number of further anomalies in the Solar System are now being attributed to a hypothetical intruder planet. These include the unusual tilt of Uranus,[33] the great red spot of Jupiter,[34] the retrograde rotation of Venus,[35] and the eccentric orbit of Pluto.[36] And then there are the moons of Mars, Uranus, Neptune, Saturn and Jupiter, which all show signs of unnatural evolution, whilst Charon, the tiny moon of Pluto, can only be explained by impact theory.[37] It is obvious that the Solar System bears the legacy of a very violent past. Tom Van Flandern summarises the case for catastrophism (and hence the *Enuma Elish*) as follows:

> The planetary breakup hypothesis explains the observations easily and well. Conventional models require the invention of numerous new explanations for numerous new observations.[38]

Evolution and Catastrophism

Did Nibiru/Planet X (alias Marduk) complete its acts of creation and then get thrown out into space, or did it get permanently caught in the Sun's orbit? Could its continued membership of the Solar System account for the step changes in the evolution of life on Earth, and could it even have seeded the very first life on Earth?

The planet Earth is believed to be 4.6 billion years old, but the fossil record shows a complete lack of 'life' in the first 600 million years.[39] Then, around 4 billion years ago, simple one-celled life forms began to appear (exactly how this happened is one of the hottest disputes in modern science). These one-celled creatures were surprisingly sophisticated[40] and, within another 500 million years, *multi*-celled organisms, with highly evolved genetic material, began to appear.

The speed of these evolutionary developments has prompted many scientists to suggest that life did not spontaneously develop on Earth, but descended from life which had already evolved elsewhere. Furthermore, due to the common genetic code of all life on Earth, scientists believe there was a *single* source. In 1973, Nobel prize winner Francis Crick, together with Dr Leslie Orgel, suggested that 'life on Earth may have sprung from tiny organisms from a distant planet'.[41] That view, initially treated with scepticism, is now widely accepted,[42] although the current consensus prefers a comet or meteorite impact as the likely source.[43]

In 1989, a team from Stanford University concluded that life on Earth had evolved in a very short window of time, between 4–3.8 billion years ago.[44] *Was the collision with Nibiru and its satellites the cause?* The ancient texts describe the planet Nibiru as watery, and thus suitable for the prior development of life as we know it. Nibiru is also described as 'glowing' and 'brilliant', with a 'shining crown'[45] – a likely reference to an internal source of heat, which would allow a temperate climate even when far from the Sun's rays.[46]

The mystery of the *origin* of life on Earth is equalled by the mystery of its *subsequent* evolution. It has recently become clear that catastrophism has played a major role in the mutation or extinction of different species. A recently published book by Richard Leakey and Roger Lewin suggests that on five occasions a major catastrophe has wiped out more than 65 per cent of all living species.[47] In addition, Leakey and Lewin make reference to ten or more lesser extinctions. The most recent of the Big Five was the event, dated to 65 million years ago, which killed off the dinosaurs.

Scientific evidence now supports the theory, first put forward in 1979 by the Nobel prize-winning physicist Luis Alvarez, that the 200 million year reign of the dinosaurs was ended by a huge meteorite impact.[48] Images taken by the American space shuttle have identified huge concentric circles, approximately 110–190 miles in diameter, beneath the sea in the Gulf of Mexico. The size of this ringed depression indicates an impact twenty times more powerful than all of the world's nuclear weapons. Measurements of rock density and the presence of iridium in the cretaceous/tertiary boundary in the rock strata, have enabled the crater to be dated to 65 million years ago.

Leakey and Lewin also date significant extinctions to 440, 365, 225 and 210 million years ago. In the most dramatic of these events, 95 per cent of marine species were killed at the end of the so-called Permian period, 225 million years ago. There is much controversy as to why these extinctions occurred – suggestions include changing sea levels, global climatic change, tidal waves and forest fires. But there is now a growing consensus that the root cause of these phenomena is impacts from space. In February 1996, the Russian scientist V. Alekseev put forward evidence that a group of meteorites originated from a parent body which suffered a collision in space approximately 380–320 million years ago.[49] This supports the theory that an impact from space caused the extinction at the end of the Devonian period 365 million years ago.

The emerging cataclysm theory dovetails neatly with Darwinian laws of evolution. As discussed in chapter 2, evolutionary progress, via mutation, depends on the geographical separation of small populations. In their aforementioned book, Leaky and Lewin review the recent evidence which suggests that the first simple life forms existed for billions of years (six sevenths of Earth's history) with little change; then, 530 million years ago, life suddenly exploded with vast diversity. Other writers have also noted this so-called Cambrian explosion, which witnessed 'the most spectacular rise in diversity ever recorded on our planet'.[50] At this time, a wide range of complex multi-cellular organisms suddenly appeared without any precursor species being evident in the fossil record.

It is curious to note that the vast majority of the Cambrian organisms disappeared within a relatively short period of a few million years, whilst those that survived are believed to have evolved into today's species. Were these former organisms ill-suited to the Earth's environment, and if so why did they suddenly appear at all? Was the Earth seeded for the second time, 530 million years ago, just as it was 4 billion years ago? And, in view of the identical genetic code, were both seedings from the same source?

The existence of Nibiru, on an orbital collision course with the inner Solar System, is fully consistent with the mysteries of mass extinctions and rapid evolution. Daniel Whitmire, an astrophysicist from the University of Southwestern Louisiana is convinced that Planet X explains the disappearance of the dinosaurs. He suggests that, when the approaching planet passed through the ring of comets, it would have sent some cometary fragments careering towards the Earth with the likelihood of a catastrophic collision.[51] Might a similar event be to blame for the legendary Flood?

Evidence of the Flood

From almost every culture around the world there emerge more than five hundred strikingly similar legends of a great Flood.[52] These legends all share a common theme – of mankind being swept away with the exception of one man and his family who survived. We in the West generally know the survivor's name as Noah, but to the Aztecs he was Nene, whilst in the Near East he was Atra-Hasis, Utnapishtim or Ziusudra. As for his means of escape, the Bible describes an 'ark' or boat, Mesopotamian records describe a submersible vessel, and the Aztec version refers to a hollowed-out log. According to the Aztec legend, men were saved by turning into fish.

Ancient texts from the Near East speak of the Flood as a

major catastrophe – not a local or trivial event, but a great time divider. The Assyrian king Ashurbanipal left us with the following inscription to illustrate the point:

> I can even read the intricate tablets in Shumerian;
> I understand the enigmatic words in the stone carvings,
> from the days before the Flood.

Most scientists believe the Biblical Flood to be a myth. Why is this? The deep schism between Science and Religion has caused many scientists to be deeply sceptical of anything which appears in the Bible. This is unfortunate, because the Bible contains a robust, albeit abbreviated, historical record – a record that has sadly been undermined by the drastic religious editing which it has received. The Flood is a prime example of how an actual physical event can be disguised by a heavy emphasis on monotheistic symbolism. How can we believe that God brought the Flood to punish mankind for his evil sins – for if God was a spiritual being, he would never have needed to use a Flood? Fortunately, the reliability of this particular story can be gleaned from other ancient texts which parallel the Bible.

As mentioned in chapter 1, the *Atra-Hasis* epic[53] clarifies the role of the Biblical 'God' as 'they' rather than 'He'. Furthermore, this account, inscribed in detail on tablets such as that shown in Figure 12 (see black-and-white section), states that 'they' did not bring it about deliberately. Instead, it was resolved in the council of the gods that the coming Flood, which the gods were powerless to prevent, should be kept secret from mankind.

The roles of the gods in the Mesopotamian Flood stories are fully consistent with their roles in other accounts. Enlil, the Biblical 'Lord' to whom mankind has become a nuisance, wishes to see him destroyed. His brother Enki, who was personally involved in the creation of the first Adam (the LU.LU worker), is sympathetic towards man and habitually antagonistic towards Enlil. Despite being pressurised into taking an oath of secrecy, Enki decides to warn one loyal follower and his family of the coming deluge. The chosen man is a priest from the city of Shuruppak (the city of Enki's sister Ninharsag), whose name in the Akkadian language is Atra-Hasis, meaning 'Exceedingly Wise'. It is worth noting that exactly the same meaning is applied to the hero Utnapishtim in the Flood account of *The Epic of Gilgamesh*.[54]

The god Enki, also known as Ea, speaks to Atra-Hasis from behind a reed screen, a detail which is also found in the original Sumerian text, where the hero is named ZI.U.SUD.RA. Detailed instructions are given by Ea for the construction of a submersible ship. *The Epic of Gilgamesh* provides a dramatic and vivid account of the final preparations, when the hero is told to watch for the departure of the gods themselves:

> 'When Shamash
> who orders a trembling at dusk,
> will shower down a rain of eruptions –
> board thou the ship,
> batten up the entrance!'[55]

Is there any tangible evidence that a huge deluge ever took place? Over the years there have been many false alarms, as archaeologists have found evidence of floods, which then turned out to be localised events. But would we really expect archaeologists to find signs of *The* Flood when they are excavating the sites of *post*-Flood cities? In fact, it is *other* fields of science that have provided the significant clues. And those clues all point to a global catastrophe approximately 13,000 years ago.

Whilst not counting as one of Leakey and Lewin's Big Five, the global extinctions which occurred 13,000 years ago were dramatic enough. In the Americas, scientists have dated to the period 11000–9000 BC the demise of around fifty major mammal species.[56] In contrast, the preceding 300,000 years witnessed an extinction rate of only one species in every 15,000 years. A similar pattern of mass extinctions *c.* 11000 BC is found across Europe, Asia and Australasia.[57]

In northern Alaska, gold mining activities have uncovered the bodies of thousands of dead animals from beneath the frozen ground. Experts have been unable to explain why these animals, acclimatised to temperate regions, should be found in Alaska.[58] Further examination reveals that the dead animals lie in a scene of utter carnage. Their bodies are found in a layer of fine sand, and lie twisted and torn in a confused mixture with trees and other fauna. One expert from the University of New Mexico has observed that:

> Whole herds of animals were apparently killed together, overcome by some common power ... Such piles of bodies of animals or men simply do not occur by any natural means.[59]

The destruction of these animals in Alaska was so sudden that their bodies were instantly frozen without decomposing, as evidenced by the tendency for local people to thaw the carcasses and use them for food.[60]

A similar story unfolds in Siberia, where the remains of numerous species, the majority from temperate climates, are found buried beneath the frozen landscape. Once again, we find the animal bodies mixed with uprooted trees and vegetation, amid signs of an unexpected and sudden catastrophe:

> The mammoths died suddenly, in intense cold, and in great numbers. Death came so quickly that the swallowed vegetation is yet undigested ...[61]

Considerable evidence points to substantial climatic change and major flooding *c.* 11000–10000 BC, possibly marking the end of an ice age:

The last 100,000 years of glacial expansion, as recorded by oxygen-isotope ratios in deep-sea cores from the Atlantic and the Equatorial Pacific, terminated *abruptly* around 12,000 years ago. A very rapid ice melt caused a *rapid rise in sea level* . . . (emphasis added)[62]

More recently, in January 1993, the highly esteemed journal *Science* also cited evidence for the 'Earth's greatest flood at the end of the last ice age'. The general consensus is that the end of that ice age, marked by a sudden and dramatic climatic change, occurred around 12,000 years ago.[63] The full evidence, however, suggests that this was not a Flood caused by a simple melting of the polar ice cap, but something far more dramatic.

In the Andes *mountains* of South America, geologists have found traces of *marine* sediments at a height of 12,500 feet. In the same region, some ruins at Tiwanaku (altitude 13,000 feet) have been found swamped under six feet of mud from an *unknown* source of flooding. Nearby, the waters of Lake Titicaca are slightly saline and studies have shown that its fish and crustacea are predominantly oceanic rather than fresh-water types.[64] Furthermore, in 1980, the Bolivian archaeologist Hugo Boero Rojo found extensive ruins, similar to the earliest Tiwanakan culture, 60 feet beneath the waters of Titicaca, close to the coast of Puerto Acosta.[65] All of these facts argue against the theory that the waters of Titicaca were lifted at the same time as the Andes mountains 100 million years ago. On the contrary, the source of the Titicacan sea waters must have been a much more recent event.

Another important clue to the nature of the Flood cataclysm is the evidence of simultaneous volcanic activity, which could only be caused by tectonic stress beneath the Earth's surface:

Interspersed in the muck depths, and sometimes through the very piles of bones and tusks themselves, are layers of volcanic ash. There is no doubt that coincidental with the [extinctions] there were volcanic eruptions of tremendous proportions.[66]

What force could have induced tectonic upheaval at the same time as raising the sea waters above the Andes? The melting of the Earth's ice caps is not a satisfactory explanation, and in any case, what caused the ice caps to melt so suddenly? No, we are instead faced with a sudden and violent event that swept trees and animals from one end of the globe to another. The unavoidable conclusion is that the Earth was moved by an extremely powerful *external* force.

Nibiru, Venus and the Flood

If the evidence of the Flood 13,000 years ago is as obvious as it appears, why is it taking so long for it to be recognised as scientific fact? The answer lies in the deeply embedded principles of modern science – nothing is 'possible' unless there is a scientific theory to explain it. It was for this reason that Alfred Wegener's idea of continental drift was neglected for around sixty years before it could be validated by the theory of plate tectonics. The failure to recognise the Flood cataclysm thus lies in the failure of scientists to find any plausible *cause* of the devastation which we have just examined.

However, the deciphering of the *Enuma Elish* and the evidence concerning Nibiru/Planet X, do now offer a possible cause for the Flood.

Zecharia Sitchin has suggested that Nibiru, having been caught in a solar orbit, caused the Flood by destabilising the Earth's ice caps. The Sumerian scribes indeed stated, repeatedly, that the Flood was caused by the planet Nibiru. Its effect was so powerful that the Earth was described as shaking to its very foundations. One text, quoted by Sitchin, identifies Nibiru quite clearly:

> When the sage shall call out: 'Flooding!' –
> It is the god Nibiru;
> it is the Hero, the planet with four heads.
> The god whose weapon is the Flooding Storm, shall turn back;
> to his resting place he shall lower himself.[67]

Is it scientifically feasible that Nibiru was the cause of the great Flood, raising the Earth's waters above both the Andes and Mount Ararat (where Noah eventually landed)? Everyday observation demonstrates that the combined gravitational effects of the Sun and the Moon are sufficient to pull the Earth's oceans sideways, creating a global bulge which equates to the high tides. Although these tides amount to only thirty feet in height, they do demonstrate an important principle – a bulging effect that could be highly exaggerated by the close passing of another planet. The Biblical record of the Flood states that 'the valleys of the sea were exposed and the foundations of the Earth laid bare',[68] suggesting that this is exactly what happened.

The orbit of Nibiru, as interpreted by Zecharia Sitchin, normally brings it to a point in the Asteroid Belt some 166 million miles from Earth at its closest point. At this proximity it would certainly be visible from Earth (as confirmed in a text describing Anu and Antu's visit to Earth) but would it be close enough to have caused the Flood? In my view, the answer is no. But before we discard Sitchin's theory, let us consider another possibility.

It is an established scientific fact that the orbits of planetary bodies are affected by the proximity of neighbouring planets. Therefore, when Nibiru pays its regular return visits to the inner Solar System, it would interact with the other planets and follow a slightly different course each time. Is it possible that Nibiru, instead of hitting its perihelion near the Asteroid Belt, could have been forced much closer to the Earth?

A Mesopotamian text translated by Alfred Jeremias indeed recounts an alignment of the planets which once brought Nibiru into close proximity with Venus and the Earth. The text, symbolically attributing deities to different planets, stated that the seven outer planets (Mars, Jupiter, Saturn, Uranus, Neptune, Pluto and Nibiru) 'stormed in upon the Celestial Bar' which separated them from the four inner 'planets' (the Sun, Mercury, Venus and the Moon).[69] As a consequence, Ishtar/Venus attempted to become 'queen of heaven' in a 'glorious dwelling place with Anu/ Nibiru'. And the Moon (Sin) was also 'violently besieged'. The text concludes that Nibiru saved the darkened Moon and made it 'shine forth in the heavens' once more, whilst Ishtar/Venus failed in her bid for glory. A close reading suggests that this text, in a similar manner to the *Enuma Elish*, is describing a celestial event rather than a battle of the gods.

Further corroboration exists in a statement by the Babylonian historian-priest Berossus in the third century BC:

> I, Berossus, interpreter of Belus, affirm that all the Earth inherits will be consigned to flame when the five planets assemble in Cancer, so arranged in one row that a straight line may pass through their spheres. When the same gathering takes place in Capricorn, then we are in danger of the Deluge.[70]

David Fasold, in his wide-ranging study of the Flood, quotes a fascinating clue which has been handed down in Chinese traditions. A pictograph translated by the Chinese scholars C. Kang and E. Nelson states enigmatically 'eight + united + earth = total . . . + water = flood'.[71] Fasold interprets this as eight survivors, but it strikes me as eight planets, including Nibiru and Venus. The reference to 'united' suggests an alignment of the planets in one line, as stated by Berossus, and as alluded to in the Mesopotamian reference to the 'storming of the Celestial Bar'.

Some writers have suggested a close passing of the planet Venus as the cause of the Flood, and it is curious in this context that the orbit of Venus was so closely studied and recorded by the Maya as well as by the Sumerian astronomers. The idea of a Venus 'fly-by' is perhaps driven by the many anomalies of that planet – in particular, its recently formed surface, its unexplained internal heat, and its unusual retrograde (clockwise) rotation.[72] The Venus fly-by idea does, however, suffer from one fatal flaw – what could have caused it to suddenly shift from its orbit?

We thus possess a number of clues which suggest that Nibiru occasionally makes an exceptionally close pass to both the Earth and Venus. Could this theory offer a scientific basis to explain the Flood? Compared to the theory of Zecharia Sitchin, Nibiru would, under this scenario, be much, much closer than the 166 million miles distance of the Asteroid Belt. At its conjunction with Earth, Venus is only 25 million miles distant. If, for the sake of argument, Nibiru had passed equidistant between the two planets, it could thus have approached Earth at a distance of 12.5 million miles – close enough for a planet three times the size of Earth to have a dramatic effect.

How was the Flood actually triggered? Most studies assume that the Flood was a tidal wave and have therefore searched the Earth itself for the cause. According to one theory, the Antarctic ice sheet periodically breaks loose and slips into the sea.[73] Another theory takes note of the Biblical reference to '*all* the springs of the great deep burst forth'[74] and thus suggests an outgassing of new oceanic water through rifts on the ocean bed.

If, however, we search for an external, celestial cause of the Flood, a much more plausible theory emerges. Scientists believe that the close proximity of two planets causes a 'space charge sheath', which involves tremendous electro-magnetic forces. The passing of Nibiru, three times the size of Earth, would thus have caused significant tectonic upheaval, accounting for the evidence of volcanism that accompanied the Flood. Its side-effects may well have included the melting or slippage of the ice cap, and the oceanic outgassing. As for the Flood itself, the Earth's waters would have been pulled to one side by gravitational attraction, causing an enormous bulge towards Nibiru as it passed Earth during the encounter. Finally, as Nibiru departed, the waters would have cascaded back to Earth, dumping a broken mass of trees and dead bodies in one location – exactly as described earlier.

One would also expect the encounter with Nibiru to have affected the Earth's rotation, tilt and spin. One ancient text, the *Erra Epic*, directly alludes to such changes in the Earth's orbit at the time of the Flood; the god Marduk complains that, due to the Flood:

> '[The] regulations of Heaven-Earth shifted out of their groove and the stations of the celestial gods, the stars of heaven, changed and did not return to their former places.'[75]

The magnetic field, it would seem, was also affected. In 1972, a team of Swedish scientists, studying geological core samples, concluded that a reversal of the Earth's magnetic field had occurred 12,400 years ago.[76] In fact, many such reversals are believed to have taken place during the Earth's long history, but no scientific explanation for the phenom-enon has ever been forthcoming.[77]

A close encounter with Nibiru would also have had dramatic effects on the planet Venus. Venus is a unique planet in the Solar System in having a retrograde or clockwise rotation. The speed of that rotation is also unusual, requiring no less than 243 days to rotate once on its own axis. Most planets take one day or less, with the exception of Pluto (6.4) and Mercury (58.6). The combination of these two quirks suggests that, in the words of astronomer Tom Van Flandern: 'something other than the Sun has robbed Venus of most of its spin'.[78] I suggest that it was the electromagnetic forces of Nibiru, which at some remote time first stalled the rotation of Venus, and later caused it to slowly rotate backwards. The *Enuma Elish* indeed confirms that Nibiru/Marduk had a clockwise rotation, opposite to that of the other planets. Such an encounter would also explain the extreme level of internal heat on Venus – a complete mystery to astronomers.

Is the turbulence on Venus a legacy from its origin or a relatively recent phenomenon? One scientist, Dr Stuart Greenwood, has demonstrated that the cloud cover on Venus has been increasing dramatically over the past few thousand years.[79] Using ancient astronomical records from the Maya and Babylonians, Greenwood has shown that the period of invisibility of Venus at its 'superior conjunction' (when it cannot be seen behind the Sun) has shortened significantly from 90 days to the present 50 days. Greenwood concludes that Venus must have recently possessed an atmosphere that contained significantly less cloud cover. This strongly suggests that it is currently 'on the rebound' from a recent encounter with Nibiru.

It is perhaps highly significant that the Aztecs preserved an ancient legend that called Venus the 'star that smoked.'[80] This ancient legend could very well be based upon an eye-witness account from the time of the Flood. If so, Venus may have lost its atmosphere in the encounter with Nibiru, and rebuilt it during the last 13,000 years. The Aztec legend makes an interesting comparison with a Greek legend, according to which a 'blazing star' almost destroyed the world, flooded it and was afterwards transformed into Venus. There may well be some historical basis for the Maya's apparently irrational fear that Venus could inflict death at a certain point in its orbit.

Science and legend thus come together to provide further support that the Flood was a historic event, caused by an external source that also affected Venus. The planet Nibiru is the missing link that can offer the long sought after scientific corroboration of the Flood legends.[81]

Planet of the Cross

Has Nibiru been seen since the Flood? The answer would appear to be yes, since the planet figures prominently in the records of the Sumerian civilisation which began six thousand years ago.

The Sumerians called the gods' planet NIBIRU, the 'Planet of the Crossing',[82] and to understand the significance of that name we must return to the ancient Babylonian epic of creation. According to the *Enuma Elish*, Nibiru was forever destined to return to the place of the celestial battle, where it had *crossed the path* of Tiamat – it was for this reason that it became known as the 'Planet of the Crossing'. In fact, in the earliest pictographic writing systems, Nibiru was represented by the sign of the cross. The religious significance of the cross, sacred to Buddhism as well as to Christendom, thus owes its origin to the celestial event which created the Earth and the heavens.

The Sumerian texts seem to claim that the chief god, AN (Anu), actually lived on Nibiru, from where he would make periodic visits to Earth, accompanied by his spouse, Antu. Sumerian records describe in detail the great pomp and ceremony that accompanied one such visit. Zecharia Sitchin has suggested that it occurred in the fourth millennium BC, when the gods decided to grant civilisation and kingship to mankind. On the seventeenth day of their visit, Anu and Antu were entertained in the city of Uruk, just prior to their departure. The assembled gods washed their hands in golden basins, and a grand banquet was served from seven golden trays. A priest then climbed to the top of the ziggurat-temple to watch for the appearance of Nibiru.

Various songs were then recited such as 'The Planet of Anu Rises in the Skies' and 'The Creator's Image has Arisen'. When the planet Nibiru appeared, bonfires were lit all over the land in celebration. There were more hymns to 'The Creator's Planet, the Planet that is Heaven's Hero', and finally the gods led Anu and Antu in a grand procession to their 'golden sanctuary for the night'. In the morning, the gods accompanied Anu and Antu to the 'holy quay', the 'place of the barque of Anu', where they received an elaborate ceremonial send-off.

The ancient belief in Nibiru is evidenced not only in the textual records, but also in the numerous depictions of a circular disc with two huge wings (Figure 13, black-and-white section). This symbol of the 'winged disc' was revered by the Sumerians, Assyrians, Babylonians, Egyptians and other later empires for thousands of years. Its presence adorned the temples and palaces of gods and kings, and it was often depicted symbolically hovering over ancient battle scenes. The significance of the wings has baffled scholars, who have tried to impose their preconceptions of a solar religion on these ancient civilisations. However, it does make sense in the context of a planet, whose ruler was the ultimate authority of human kingship on Earth.

If anyone believes that the Sumerian and Babylonian texts are elaborate inventions, and all similarities to the Solar System entirely coincidental, then they should reflect on one other piece of evidence deciphered by Zecharia Sitchin. It is an Akkadian cylinder seal from the third millennium BC, now on display at the State Museum in East Berlin (reference VA 243).

The Akkadian seal depicts eleven globes surrounding a larger six-rayed globe which clearly represents the Sun

(Plate 40, colour section). By starting at the three-o-clock position and moving anti-clockwise, we find an uncanny similarity to the Solar System in both relative size and position of the planets. With the exception of Pluto, which is shown in its original position as a satellite of Saturn,[83] the ancient depiction shows the planets as they existed following the collision of Nibiru and Tiamat. Between Mars and Jupiter, however, lies a large globe, around three times the size of Earth, which does not correlate with any known planet. It cannot possibly be coincidental that the *Enuma Elish* accurately identifies the position of this planet or 'god':

> God Nibiru:
> it is he who without tiring
> the midst of Tiamat keeps crossing.
> Let 'Crossing' be his name—
> the one who occupies the midst.[84]

A position between Mars and Jupiter is indeed the 'midst', with five inner planets and five outer planets (the Moon is counted as an inner planet since it evolved as a separate celestial body).

What did the ancient texts say about the orbit of Nibiru? The *Enuma Elish*, referring to Nibiru by the name of the god Marduk, described two 'abodes' which would equate to the perihelion and aphelion of the planet's orbit. These abodes were described using Sumerian terms – AN.UR meaning 'Heaven's Base' for the perihelion, the nearest point to the Sun – and E.NUN, the 'Great/Lordly Abode', for the aphelion. Zecharia Sitchin has clearly identified the heaven, and thus the perihelion, as the Asteroid Belt. The great lordly abode, on the other hand, was sometimes called 'the Deep', a term used also for the position of Pluto, and signifying a most distant position.[85] The Mesopotamian texts indeed described Marduk/Nibiru as the 'monitor' of the planets, with an orbit which was 'loftier' or 'grander' than the other planets, such that 'he scans the hidden knowledge . . . he sees all the quarters of the universe'.

These descriptions indicate a most unusual planetary orbit, coming close to the Sun at one extreme, and beyond Pluto at the other – an orbit which is highly elliptical. The only precedent for such an extremely elliptical orbit is the comets, which pass through the heart of the Solar System, but can then disappear for thousands of years before they are seen again. The *Enuma Elish* attributes the elliptical and irregular orbit of the comets to the break-up of Tiamat. Is it possible for a large planet to also possess such a strange orbit? The answer must be yes, but under extreme circumstances, and we should note that whatever accounted for the entry of Nibiru into the Solar System four billion years ago was, in itself, an extremely unusual event.

How long is Nibiru's orbit, and why has it not been seen in modern times? The answer, suggested by Zecharia Sitchin, lies in the Sumerian word SAR, which was sometimes applied to Nibiru. The term SAR meant 'Supreme Ruler', an association with its supreme deity Anu, but the term also signified the number '3,600', depicted as a large circle.[86] Furthermore, in some contexts, the term took on the meaning of 'a completed cycle'. Based on this, and other corroborating evidence, Sitchin has concluded that the orbit of Nibiru is approximately 3,600 Earth-years. This would explain why it has not been seen in recent times.

The Search for Planet X

Can modern science corroborate the existence of Nibiru, a planet with a size somewhere between that of Uranus and Jupiter, with a 3,600-year elliptical orbit, and with a perihelion that is normally close to the Asteroid Belt?

The discovery of new planets has, in the last two hundred years, owed more to the science of mathematics than it has to the design of bigger and better telescopes. The existence of Neptune, for instance, was originally deduced by irregularities in the orbit of Uranus. Similarly, Pluto was found following observations that an unknown gravitational force was affecting the orbit of Neptune.

Following the same principle, astronomers have become convinced that unaccounted-for irregularities in the orbits of Uranus, Neptune and Pluto (and to a lesser extent Jupiter and Saturn), imply the existence of a *further, undiscovered planet*. Astronomers are so certain of this planet's existence that they have already named it 'Planet X' – the Tenth Planet.[87] Despite recent attempts to debunk the evidence, the theory of Planet X is alive and well.

In 1978, the theory of Planet X took a giant leap forward, following decades of stagnation. The discovery of Pluto's satellite. Charon, enabled accurate measurements of Pluto's mass to be taken, and it turned out to be far less than expected. This allowed the deviations in the orbits of Uranus and Neptune to be mathematically confirmed, to a high degree of certainty. Two astronomers from the US Naval Observatory in Washington DC consequently resurrected the idea of Planet X. However, these astronomers, Robert Barrington and Tom Van Flandern, went much further, using mathematical models to suggest that Planet X had ejected Pluto and Charon from their previous positions as satellites of Neptune.[88] They proposed that the intruder planet was 3–4 times the size of the Earth, and that it probably would have been captured in orbit around the Sun 'in a highly eccentric and inclined solar orbit with a long period'.[89] It almost seems as if they used the *Enuma Elish* for their script.

In 1982, NASA themselves officially recognised the possibility of Planet X, with an announcement that 'some kind of mystery object is really there – far beyond the outermost planets'.[90]

One year later, the newly launched IRAS (Infrared Astronomical Satellite) spotted a large mysterious object in the depths of space. The Washington Post summarised an interview with the chief IRAS scientist from JPL, California, as follows:

A heavenly body possibly as large as the giant planet Jupiter and possibly so close to Earth that it would be part of this solar system has been found in the direction of the constellation Orion by an orbiting telescope . . . 'All I can tell you is that we don't know what it is,' said Gerry Neugebauer, chief IRAS scientist.[91]

Subsequent years saw little new information in the search for Planet X. However, scientists were evidently convinced that it existed, for they continued to carry out mathematical modelling of its characteristics. Their conclusions confirmed the theory that Planet X was three to four times the size of Earth and suggested that it had an orbit inclined to the ecliptic by a massive 30 degrees; also that its position was three times further from the Sun than Pluto.[92]

In 1987, NASA made an official announcement to recognise the possible existence of Planet X. The American journal *Newsweek* reported that:

NASA held a press conference at its Ames Research Center in California last week to make a rather strange announcement: an eccentric 10th planet may – or may not – be orbiting the Sun. John Anderson, a NASA research scientist who was the principal speaker, has a hunch Planet X is out there, though nowhere near the other nine. If he is right, two of the most intriguing puzzles of space science might be solved: what caused mysterious irregularities in the orbits of Uranus and Neptune during the nineteenth century? And what killed off the dinosaurs 26 million years ago [sic]?[93']

As the 1980s drew to a close, two things happened. First, the scientific journals began to witness a Planet X debunking campaign and, secondly, NASA began to put more and more resources into expensive space-based telescopes.[94]

The debunking campaign was led by scientists such as K. Croswell,[95] M. Littman,[96] E. Standish Junior,[97] and D. Hughes.[98] Their arguments ranged from the illogical to the bizarre. Croswell claimed the planet could not exist due to the lack of anomalous affects on the Pioneer and Voyager craft, ignoring the likely possibility that Planet X was below the ecliptic and close to its furthermost aphelion position. Littman attempted to ignore all astrometric observations prior to 1910, in order to eliminate the anomalies, despite the lack of any basis that these earlier records were incorrect.[99] Standish made minor adjustments to the data, thereby reducing the discrepancies that indicated a tenth planet – but, by his own admission, the anomalies were only reduced, not totally eliminated. Finally, Hughes attempted to disprove Planet X via a complex argument that, when the Solar System was born, there could not have been enough material for a further planet. Clearly, he had not been reading the *Enuma Elish*, which described Marduk/Planet X as originating from *outside* the Solar System.

All of these criticisms focused solely on the mathematical anomalies and ignored the other evidence which supported the existence of Planet X. In his 1993 update, Tom Van Flandern stressed that Planet X was still the only explanation for the strange origin of the Neptune satellite system and the unusual features of Pluto and Charon.[100] He also put forward important new evidence on deviations in several cometary orbits. Van Flandern emphasised that the perturbations in both the cometary and planetary orbits became progressively greater the further one went out into the Solar System, strongly suggesting a single body possibly twice as far from the Sun as Pluto.[101]

Van Flandern continues to be a supporter of the Planet X search. That search is now taking place in the southern skies, but it is proving incredibly difficult to spot such a distant object, which moves so slowly relative to the stars.[102] It is significant that in terms of size, orbital features and directional location, the specification of Planet X is identical to that of Nibiru as described by the Babylonians and the Sumerians.

Whilst the astronomers were hunting for Planet X, the American government began to pump unprecedented funds into the hugely expensive Hubble telescope. This space-based telescope was finally launched on April 20th 1990, only to be found defective. In November 1993, its vision was corrected by a giant 'contact lens', fitted in space at a cost of $700 million.

Meanwhile, the European Space Agency was building its Infrared Space Observatory, which it successfully launched in November 1995. Unlike Hubble, which is an optical telescope, the ESA's telescope is designed to detect *infrared* radiation. It can thus peek into the darkest depths of space, with a reputed ability to spot the heat from a snowman at a distance of 60 miles.

If that seems sophisticated, then what should we make of the latest plans from NASA? In December 1995, *Nature* magazine reported a NASA plan to launch a telescope into deep space, possibly as far as Jupiter. NASA attempted to justify such an extreme location by citing a need to reduce image degradation from atmospheric disturbance. Officially, this project is designed to detect large planets in *neighbouring* star systems. However, moving a telescope from Earth to Jupiter will make such marginal difference relative to 42 light years of space-distance (around one six thousandth of one per cent difference to be precise) that we must all scratch our heads and wonder why NASA wish to spend $1,000 million dollars or more in this way. On the other hand, if the search is not for planets 42 light years away, but for a distant planet *within our own Solar System*, then the plan begins to make sense.

Home of the Gods?

Thus far we have established an extremely strong case for the existence of Nibiru. We have identified its influence in the formation of the Solar System, in subsequent evolution on Earth and in the Flood 13,000 years ago. We have traced it even more recently to the era of the Sumerians, and reviewed the present day search for it in the depths of space. However, despite the strong association of Nibiru with the chief god Anu in the Sumerian texts,[103] can we state with certainty that it is, or was, the home of the gods?

An important clue may lie in the number '12', which has been sacred to mankind since time immemorial. It appears within Judaism in the twelve tribes of Israel, within Christianity in the twelve apostles and within Hinduism as a generally auspicious number.

In the complete absence of any other explanation for the sacred number twelve, it has been suggested that its roots lie in the realm of the gods, and specifically in astronomy.[104] As we discussed earlier, the planet Nibiru brings the total number of celestial bodies in our Solar System to twelve (counting the Sun and the Moon) and according to the Sumerians, the decision-making council of the gods also consisted of twelve 'olden' gods. The symbolic importance of this number has remained to this day in the division of the skies into twelve constellations, a division which split the Earth's precessional cycle into twelve periods of 2,160 years. It would seem that the gods' obsession with twelve, with astronomy generally, and with Nibiru in particular, had an almost religious significance, and it is possible to conclude from this that the gods were not strangers to the Solar System but residents from within.

A possible corroboration that Nibiru was the origin of the gods who came to Earth is found in the significance of the number '7'. The number seven, like twelve, was an important number to the gods, and has remained sacred to mankind ever since. The number is particularly evident in the Biblical seven days of creation, whilst in the New Testament we have the Book of Revelations with its seven seals, seven golden lampstands, seven angels with seven plagues, and the seven bowls of God's wrath. The number seven also appears in other religions and in the apocrypha. The Koran and the Book of Enoch both describe a journey through seven heavens, by Muhammad and Enoch respectively, whilst to this day, Muslim pilgrims must walk seven times around the Ka'bah in Mecca. Our modern cultures have also absorbed expressions such as the 'Seven Wonders of the Ancient World' (even though we could name a lot more) and the 'Seven Deadly Sins' (even though we could probably name a few more of those too!).

The divine legacy of '7' is also found in the otherwise unexplained origin of the seven days of the week. Most of us take the 7-day week for granted and assume it is a natural cycle. In actual fact, it is not a fixed cycle at all, and scientists have struggled for years to explain why this tradition should have originated. Theologians would claim that the answer lies in the Biblical seven days of creation, but the origin of the Biblical 'days' is almost certainly the seven tablets on which the *Enuma Elish* was written. This is evident from the contrast between the first six Babylonian tablets describing Marduk's acts of creation and the seventh tablet which is dedicated to a general exaltation of the god (and thus a parallel to the Biblical seventh day when God rested).

The 7-day week splits the solar year into 52 weeks and thereby unlocks the door to another mystical number from both Egyptian and Mayan tradition. According to an ancient papyrus found in a tomb in Thebes, Thoth the Egyptian god of magic, used to challenge mortals to a mysterious 'Game of 52', which they usually lost.[105] The number also appears in the Maya's enigmatic Sacred Round of 52 cycles (18,980 days), when their sacred year of 260 days would coincide exactly with their solar year of 365 days.

But what is the *ultimate* origin of the sacred number '7'? Why did the Babylonians write their creation epic on seven tablets? Whilst the seven stars of the Pleiades may ultimately be significant, Zecharia Sitchin has put forward a very interesting alternative theory, based on a literal acceptance of the ancient texts. Having already identified the association of twelve gods with twelve planets, he was intrigued by continual references to the god Enlil, known as the Chief God of the Earth, but also somewhat cryptically as 'Lord of 7'. This gave Sitchin the idea that Earth was somehow the seventh planet, and he quickly realised that Earth was indeed the seventh planet encountered by the gods as they travelled from Nibiru into the heart of the Solar System.[106]

Among the evidence cited by Zecharia Sitchin is a partly-damaged clay planisphere, which was found in the ruins of the ancient Library of Nineveh. This curved disc, thought to be a copy of a Sumerian original, bears a puzzling and unique array of cuneiform signs and arrows (Plate 41, colour section).[107] Studies of the disc have concluded that it represents technical or astronomical information. One segment shows two triangular shapes, linked by a line alongside which there are seven dots. One of the triangles then contains another four dots. Recognising the seven/four split as an ancient division between the outer and inner planets of the Solar System, Sitchin studied the disc a little more closely.

Along the sides of each segment of the disc were repeated

signs, which were meaningless in Akkadian, but sprang to life when they were read as Sumerian word syllables. Zecharia Sitchin found references to 'Enlil', to geographical features such as 'sky' and 'mountains', and to actions such as 'observing' and 'descending'. One reference was to 'deity NI.NI, supervisor of descent'. There were also numbers which would represent a mathematically perfect glide approach for a space shuttle landing. Sitchin was left in no doubt that the disc represented 'a route map, marking the way by which the god Enlil went by the planets, accompanied by some operating instructions'.[108] This disc seems to confirm that Nibiru was the home of the gods and Earth the seventh planet counting inwards.

Such a journey, by the gods to Earth, was also commemorated in the ancient Babylonian ritual of the 'procession of Marduk', the main event of the twelve day New Year Festival. Extensive excavations of Babylon, correlated with Babylonian ritual texts, have allowed scholars to reconstruct the holy precinct of the god Marduk, and bring to life the ancient ritual. The procession involves seven different 'stations' at which the god Marduk is praised with different names. Realising that the Babylonians had named the planet Nibiru as Marduk in honour of their national god, Zecharia Sitchin was able to decipher the names of the stations and the names of Marduk (which the text provides in both Akkadian and Sumerian). At this point it is worth quoting Sitchin in full:

It is our contention that the seven stations in the procession of Marduk represented the space trip of the Nefilim from their planet to Earth; that the first 'station', the 'House of Bright Waters', represented the passage by Pluto; the second ('Where the Field Separates') was Neptune; the third (mutilated), Uranus; the fourth – a place of celestial storms – Saturn. The fifth, where 'The Roadway' became clear, 'where the shepherd's word appears', was Jupiter. The sixth, where the journey switched to 'The Traveller's Ship' was Mars. And the seventh station was Earth – the end of the journey, where Marduk provided the 'House of Resting.[109]

Does all of the above evidence indicate that Nibiru was truly the home of the gods, or did they revere that planet because of its central role in forming the Solar System as we know it? Zecharia Sitchin has claimed that Anu really did rule a society on Nibiru, but let us consider whether that is a likely scenario. For instance, does Nibiru have a hospitable climate? Its orbit takes it so far from the Sun that sunlight would be perhaps only one sixtieth of that on the Earth; however, it is scientifically possible for planets to generate large amounts of heat internally. As mentioned earlier, Nibiru was indeed described as having ample heat (as well as water). Based on the few clues which we have, Nibiru's climate might be compared to a warm jacuzzi beneath a starry twilight – perhaps not as daunting as one might imagine, but nevertheless a raw deal compared to the luscious Earth. Why then would Anu, the ruler of the gods, wish to live there?

Could Zecharia Sitchin have misinterpreted the ancient texts? Two alternative possibilities spring to mind. First, it is by no means certain that the gods represented a *royal* bloodline and it is thus possible that they were acting under orders; in these circumstances, the presence of one or more gods on an inhospitable Nibiru can be explained. Secondly, it is possible that references to decisions emanating from Anu on Nibiru could refer to a transmitter – placed on Nibiru to relay messages from Anu who was elsewhere.

My point is this. Did the gods come to Earth not *from* Nibiru but *via* Nibiru? Was Nibiru used as a convenient travelling spaceship, racing across the Solar System, without any fuel, at a speed of around 10,000 miles per hour? The possibility is strengthened by the reference in the Babylonian re-creation of the journey. It is at the sixth station, Mars, where the journey switched to 'The Traveller's Ship'. This is exactly what one would expect if Nibiru itself was the spaceship until it reached its perihelion between Jupiter and Mars. Why switch ships otherwise?

Taking the argument one step further, it is highly unlikely that these gods evolved on Nibiru, for two reasons. First, the environment of Nibiru would be quite different from Earth, and yet the gods did, by all accounts, adapt remarkably well to Earth. Secondly, the regular cataclysms which would have been experienced as Nibiru passed through the Asteroid Belt, would have made it difficult for any species to have spent more than a few tens of thousands of years evolving.[110] On Earth, in contrast, the cataclysms only occurred at intervals of millions of years, and could thus have acted for the most part as a positive evolutionary force.

Where then might the gods, or shall we say 'intelligence', have evolved? In my view, a much more likely source than Nibiru would be an Earth-type planet in a nearby star system, in the direction of Nibiru's orbit (the southern skies). Based on the evidence of our own genetic make-up, as set out in chapter 2, we must look for an environment where a long and peaceful evolution could have occurred.

On the other hand, we must not discount the possibility that an intelligent species evolved on the Earth or Mars, left the Solar System, and then returned.

It is now widely recognised that Mars once had a different climate, with plentiful water that could have supported life. In addition, NASA images of seemingly artificial features on the Martian surface have caused intense speculation that an advanced civilisation was once based there.[111] The most intriguing evidence has come from an American team, Vincent Di Pietro and Gregory Molenaar, whose enhanced images of the monumental 'Face' in Cydonia have strongly suggested that it is an artificial construction.[112] It is quite possible that its inhabitants emigrated hundreds of millions of years ago specifically because of the environmental changes.

Alternatively, intelligence may have originally evolved on Earth. If we step back and reconsider the science of the Solar System, we find that the Earth might well be based in a rather unique corner of the universe. The periodic cataclysmic returns of Nibiru into the centre of the Solar System may have had very significant implications for the speed of evolution on Earth. The recurring sequence of partial extinctions would, according to the laws of Darwinism, have led to an accelerated development of those organisms which survived. If ever there was a place for intelligence to evolve, the Solar System must rank among the top contenders.

In 1993, Michael Cremo and Richard Thompson published a 900-page critique of conventional archaeology and anthropology entitled *Forbidden Archaeology*: *The Hidden History of the Human Race*.[113] Cremo and Thompson's 8-year investigation revealed evidence that hominids had been present on the Earth for hundreds of millions of years. Their well-referenced work includes a mass of anomalous material, such as manufactured items and human remains found in rock strata hundreds of millions of years old. The regular cataclysms described in this chapter shed some light on how such finds came to be embedded in solid rock. Cremo and Thompson's work deserves serious attention. It may shed light not directly on mankind's ancestry, but on that of our creators.

Chapter Seven Conclusions

* The *Enuma Elish* describes a scientifically plausible scenario for the formation of the Earth and the Asteroid Belt, the source of the Earth's Moon, the

origin of the comets, and many other unusual features of the Solar System, which are all unexplained by modern science.

* The Solar System includes a tenth planet, which has been mathematically discovered by astronomers and named Planet X.

* The Sumerians knew Planet X as Nibiru – the planet from which the gods came to Earth. It is most likely that the gods came *via* Nibiru and did not live or evolve there.

* Nibiru has an extremely long elliptical orbit lasting 3,600 years and its periodic returns to the inner Solar System have seeded life on Earth and accelerated its evolution.

* The Flood was a genuine historic event approximately 13,000 years ago, caused by a rare alignment of the outer planets which forced Nibiru into a close encounter with the Earth.

CHAPTER EIGHT

PROOFS OF
DIVINE GUIDANCE

———◆———

Cities of the Gods

Few people know why our planet is called the 'Earth'. The
origin of the name actually lies in the ancient city of Eridu,
where the archaeologists found the earliest evidence of the
Sumerian civilisation. However, Eridu was not only the first
city of the Sumerians, but also the first settlement of the gods.
Its name E.RI.DU echoed its earlier history, for it literally
meant 'Home in the Faraway Built', a most appropriate name
for the visitors from the planet Nibiru.[1] The Sumerian records
state that Eridu belonged to the god Enki, who was placed in
charge of Earth prior to the arrival of his brother Enlil. The
building of that first construction on Earth is commemorated
in a Sumerian poem *The Myth of Enki and Eridu*:

> The lord of the watery deep, the king Enki . . .
> built his house . . .
> In Eridu he built the House of the Water Bank . . .
> The king Enki . . . has built a house:
> Eridu, like a mountain,
> he raised up from the earth;
> in a good place he [had] built it.[2]

Why then did the archaeologists not find any evidence of earlier inhabitation by the gods? The simple explanation is that the earlier Eridu had been swept away by the Flood, and covered in a layer of mud so thick, that even if the archaeologists had known, it would have taken them a lifetime to excavate it. As it was, nothing remained to suggest any earlier occupation of the site, so the spades were set aside at the level of the Sumerian Eridu, c. 3800 BC.

The other sites of the gods were similarly inundated by the Flood and buried in mud. How are we able to draw these conclusions? In 1976, Zecharia Sitchin published a remarkable study, corroborating Sumerian claims that their cities had been built upon 'the everlasting ground plan' of the gods.[3] Sitchin realised that the locations of the ancient Sumerian cities did indeed follow a careful geographical plan, being equidistantly positioned on three lines, which converged at Sippar (Illustration 10).[4] Eridu itself was the most southerly city, situated close to the head of the Persian Gulf.

Illustration 10

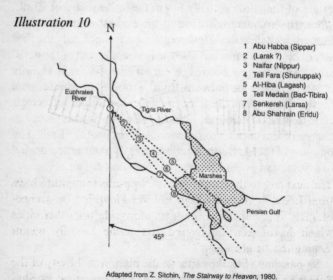

1 Abu Habba (Sippar)
2 (Larak ?)
3 Naifar (Nippur)
4 Tell Fara (Shuruppak)
5 Al-Hiba (Lagash)
6 Tell Medain (Bad-Tibira)
7 Senkereh (Larsa)
8 Abu Shahrain (Eridu)

Adapted from Z. Sitchin, *The Stairway to Heaven*, 1980.

Whilst such a layout was clearly not beyond the Sumerians' knowledge of geometry six thousand years ago, one key fact suggested a higher authority at work: the line through Bad-Tibira, Shuruppak, Nippur and Larak to Sippar intersected at exactly 45 degrees a meridian from the twin-peaked Mount Ararat, an outstanding landmark nearly 500 miles due north!

The full significance of the geometric plan became clear when Zecharia Sitchin studied the meaning of the names assigned to the cities.

At the centre of the plan was Nippur, the city of Enlil, chief of the gods. Its Sumerian name was actually NI-BRU.KI, meaning the 'Earth-Place of Nibiru'. The Sumerians identified it as the place of the DUR.AN.KI, the 'Bond Heaven-Earth'. Clues to the purpose of Nippur were found in references to a 'heavenward tall pillar reaching to the sky' and the pictographic sign for Enlil 'Lord of the Command', which resembled a tower and a radar net (Illustration 11).

Illustration 11

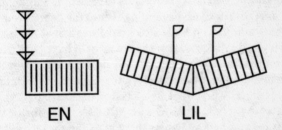

EN   LIL

The next city to the north-west of Nippur is thought to have been LA.RA.AK. Although not yet identified by archaeologists, it is named in the texts alongside the other cities which have been discovered. Its name literally meant 'Seeing the Bright Glow'.

Sippar, one of the key sites in the plan, was the city of the Sumerian god UTU, whom the Akkadians knew as Shamash. His name meant the 'Shining One', the 'One Who Lights Up'. In later Near Eastern languages 'Sippar' also came to mean 'Bird'. It is no coincidence that such connotations of flight should be connected with Utu/Shamash, for this was the god of the Heliopolises, who rose and crossed the heavens in his MU, and thus became known as Helios, the Sun god, who flew in a gleaming chariot.

What about the other cities? Larsa, or rather LA.AR.SA, meant 'Seeing the Red Light'. Lagash, or LA.AG.ASH meant 'Seeing the Glow at Six', perhaps a reference to the nearby industrial centre of BAD.TIBIRA, 'the Bright Place where the Ores are Made Final'. Finally there was Shuruppak/SHU.RUP.PAK, 'the Place of Utmost Well Being'; as the city of Ninharsag, it was undoubtedly the medical centre of the gods.

From all of these names, and the layout of the cities, Zecharia Sitchin concluded that, before the Flood, there had been a 'triangular landing corridor' with a 'spaceport' at Sippar and a 'mission control' at Nippur. Does this claim survive close scrutiny?

It is difficult in retrospect for us to assess the suitability of this area for shuttle-type landings, since the debris from the Flood would have totally obscured the original landscape. However, we do know that the area would have been rich in natural energy fuel, which seeped up through the ground even in Sumerian times. The idea that Sippar was an ancient space centre, where rockets ascended to 'heaven', is corroborated by its association with Utu/Shamash, for in later times he was well known as the god of the rockets. Sitchin notes that, when Utu's city was reconstructed at Sippar after the Flood, the Sumerian scribes reported a huge A.PIN inside his temple – an 'Object that Ploughs Through'. This term appears to describe a modern rocket, possibly a museum piece to commemorate Sippar's role as the first space centre.

If Zecharia Sitchin is right, then the cities of Sumer were

focused in very specific locations, in the southern part of Mesopotamia. Amazingly, this happens to neatly solve one of the most intriguing questions about the Sumerian civilisation, because historians have always wondered why northern Mesopotamia did not share in the early blossoming of the south.[5]

Baalbek Revisited

After the Flood had destroyed the pre-Flood space facilities, and after the waters had subsided, the gods returned to Earth. According to the Bible, this occurred on Mount Ararat, when Noah exited from the ark. His first action was to roast some animals as a sacrificial offering, and the Lord came down when he 'smelled the pleasing aroma'. *The Epic of Gilgamesh* also states that the gods 'smelled the sweet savour' and 'gathered like flies' for the feast.[6] The story hardly rings true, since Noah had just gone to great lengths to save each species of animal, and anyway, how were the gods supposed to have landed an aircraft on the side of a mountain? An elapsed time is therefore indicated, with the possibility that the feast took place some time later, at a different location. The exact details of how Noah and his family came from Ararat to their eventual lands further south have not been explored, but in my view the answer may well lie at the mysterious site of Baalbek in Lebanon.

As discussed in chapter 3, Baalbek was considered to be as old as time itself, and legend related it to the site where Helios brought his chariot to rest. Its lack of alignment to the cardinal points (in contrast to other ancient sites) suggests a pre-Flood construction in the most ancient of times. The mismatching stones at Baalbek (Plate 1, colour section) may thus reflect a reconstruction following damage from the Flood.

Whilst Baalbek's earliest history remains unrecorded, its usage by aerial vehicles in Sumerian times has been clearly described in *The Epic of Gilgamesh*. The epic relates the adventures of Gilgamesh, a ruler of the Sumerian city of Uruk *c*. 2900 BC, and his friend Enkidu. Gilgamesh, who considered himself to be two thirds god, one third human, was preoccupied with death and the possibility of immortality. A large part of the tale describes his expedition to find the abode of the gods in the 'cedar mountain'. His aim is clear from his boast: 'an everlasting *shem* I will establish for myself!'[7]

When Gilgamesh and his friend reached the cedar forests, they found it protected by an electrified fence:

> Enkidu opened his mouth and spoke, saying to Gilgamesh:
> 'my friend, let us not go down into the forest.
> When I opened the gate, my hand became paralysed.'[8]

Taking heart, the heroic pair continued, until they found their way barred by a mechanical monster, Humbaba, whose 'mouth is fire', whose 'breath is death':

> They stood still and looked at the forest.
> They beheld the height of the cedar.
> They beheld the entrance to the forest.
> Where Humbaba was wont to walk there was a path;
> straight were the tracks and good was the passage.
> They beheld the mountain of the cedar, the dwelling place
> of the gods, the throne-dais of Irnini/Inanna.[9]

The destination of Gilgamesh is clearly identified by the reference to the cedar forest. Today the cedar tree remains the national emblem of Lebanon (even though regrettably few cedars have survived) and there is no doubt that in ancient times Lebanon was famed for its ample supplies of cedars, which were used, for example, in the building of Solomon's temple. Readers of the

ancient epic have been left baffled as to why it was
necessary to guard these cedars five thousand years ago,
but the next quote makes it quite clear that it is an
abode of the gods, close to the cedar forest, which is
being guarded. The nature of the gods' abode becomes
clear when Gilgamesh is awoken from his sleep and says
to Enkidu:

'My friend, I saw a third dream;
and the dream which I saw was altogether frightful.
The heavens roared, the earth resounded.
Daylight failed, darkness came;
lightning flashed, fire blazed;
the clouds thickened, raining death.
The brightness vanished, the fire went out;
and that which fell down, turned to ashes.'[10]

Shamash, the god of the rockets, then appeared on the
scene, and assisted Gilgamesh in overcoming the mighty
Humbaba. However, he was destined not to reach his
goal beyond the cedar mountain. In tablet VI of the epic,
the goddess Inanna attempted to seduce Gilgamesh; the
latter, resisting her advances, recounted a long list of her
former lovers. The adventure then ended with an irate
Inanna chasing Gilgamesh and Enkidu back to the city of
Uruk.

The Epic of Gilgamesh not only confirms the use of
Baalbek in Lebanon as a platform for aerial vehicles, but
is consistent in all respects with our knowledge of the
Sumerian gods. It ties in with Sumerian records that
attribute the site to the god Ishkur (also known as
Adad), since Utu/Shamash, the god of the rockets, was
his nephew. The presence of Inanna is also to be expected,
first because she was renowned as a flying goddess, and
secondly because she was the twin sister of Utu. Moreover,
it is a fact that this triad of Ishkur, Utu and Inanna was
worshipped for millennia throughout the Near East, and

the temples of Baalbek are still dedicated to them as Jupiter, Mercury and Venus respectively.

How then does Baalbek relate to the legend of Noah and the Flood? Despite the legend of the ark landing on Ararat, all of the scientific evidence and legends suggest that post-Flood agriculture began in the Bekaa valley where Baalbek is situated. This supports the theory that Baalbek survived the great Flood and became the site of safe haven for the returning gods. How did Noah and his family make the trip from Ararat to the Bekaa valley? One version of the Mount Ararat rendezvous places the goddess Ishtar/Inanna at the scene. In the Babylonian version of *The Epic of Gilgamesh*, we find a remarkable parallel to the Biblical story of the rainbow and covenant with mankind. However, it is not the Lord, but the goddess Ishtar who:

> . . . lifted up the great jewels which Anu had made according to her wish [and said] 'O ye gods here present, as surely as I shall not forget the lapis lazuli on my neck, I shall remember these days and shall not forget [them] ever!'[11]

It may therefore have been Ishtar, in the course of surveying the flooded Earth, who was the first to spot the landed ark. Did she then bring Noah and his family safely back to Baalbek?

An unusual tomb in a mosque at Karak Nuh, 20 miles south of Baalbek, is said to be the tomb of Noah (Plate 42 colour section). A local legend relates that Noah was extremely tall and could stand across the Bekaa valley, with one leg on Mount Lebanon in the west and the other on the mountains of the Anti-Lebanon in the east. According to this legend, it is one of Noah's legs which is buried in the 'tomb', but the official line is that it contains 'merely a fragment of an ancient aqueduct'.[12] In view of the legend, and Noah's favoured position with the gods, it is quite possible that this unusually-shaped 'tomb', around sixty feet long by a few feet wide, might contain a wing from an ancient aircraft.

That Noah and his descendants initially settled in the region of the Bekaa valley is evidenced by the fact it was the first place where agriculture emerged. Scientists have been puzzled as to why agriculture began in the *mountains* of the Near East, but this should be no surprise in the aftermath of a great Flood, when the low-lying lands were nothing but lakes and marshes. The Bible itself states that Noah was 'a man of the soil' (a farmer), before he 'planted a vineyard'.[13] Professor Samuel Kramer also translated a Sumerian tablet which clearly identified the Lebanese mountains as the origin of post-Flood agriculture:

> Enlil went up the peak and lifted his eyes;
> he looked down: there the waters filled as a sea.
> He looked up: there was the mountain of the aromatic cedars.
> He hauled barley, terraced it on the mountain.
> That which vegetates he hauled up,
> terraced the grain cereals on the mountain.[14]

There is little doubt that Baalbek, and not Ararat, was the central focus for gods and men following the Flood.

Beacons to Baalbek

Confirmation that Baalbek was the main landing site of the gods following the Flood is provided by an amazing geographical clue, identified by Zecharia Sitchin. With hindsight it seems rather obvious, but, prior to Sitchin, no-one had ever noticed that the huge stone platform at Baalbek was equidistant from the pyramids at Giza and Mount St Catherine in the Sinai peninsula, as shown in Illustration 12.

Illustration 12

What is the significance of Mount St Catherine? Apart from the fact that it is one of the most sacred religious sites in the world, it is, more importantly, the highest mountain in the Sinai, at 8,700 feet above sea level.

The religious importance of Mount St Catherine dates back to AD 330. At this time, on the instructions of Helena, mother of Emperor Constantine, a small chapel was built over the roots of a bush. Tradition has it that this was the Burning Bush where God revealed Himself to Moses around 3,400 years ago, and the bush is so sacred that all attempts to transplant its branches to other places have failed. The name of the mountain comes from the martyrdom of Catherine, who converted to Christianity, but was tortured and beheaded in the early fourth century. Her body allegedly disappeared and was found hundreds of years later by monks on the mountain which now bears her name.

Adjacent to Mount St Catherine, to its south, stands Mount Sinai, at a height of 7,500 feet. It combines with Mount St Catherine to form an impressive double-peak, which mirrors those of the two main pyramids of Giza. In view of the geometric relationship with Giza, via Baalbek, can this mirror image possibly be a coincidence?

As described in chapter 4, the Giza pyramids were originally encased in polished white limestone casing blocks, which would have made them visible to the naked eye at a great distance. Maurice Chatelain, a former NASA scientist who played a key role in the Apollo Moon projects, has observed that:

> . . . in space, it [the Great Pyramid] shows on the radar screen much farther out because of its slanted sides that reflect radar beams perpendicularly if the approach angle is 38 degrees above horizon.[15]

Maurice Chatelain calculated that the Pyramid would originally have been 'a radar reflector with a directivity factor of over 600 million for a 2 cm wave length, for example'. In layman's language, that means an extremely powerful reflector.

Chatelain's thoughts are echoed in the words of an ancient Sumerian poem, which appears to describe the Great Pyramid in a navigational role, 'equipped' with a 'pulsating beam' for 'heaven to earth':

> House of the Gods with pointed peak;
> For Heaven to Earth it is greatly equipped.
> House whose interior glows with a reddish Light of Heaven,
> pulsating a beam which reaches far and wide;
> its awesomeness touches the flesh.
> Awesome house, lofty mountain of mountains—
> Thy creation is great and lofty,
> men cannot understand it.[16]

As for the platform at Baalbek, the need for its huge stones (see chapter 3) can now be understood in the context of the immense weights and vertical forces which they had to withstand. The textual evidence, the geographical evidence and the physical evidence all support each other to confirm that Baalbek was designed as a landing and launching platform for the rockets of the gods.

The Fate of the Great Pyramid

With the assistance of Zecharia Sitchin, we will now reconstruct some of the key points in the history of the Great Pyramid. Sitchin's research of ancient texts indicated that repeated references to an E.KUR ('House like a Mountain') were describing two separate places. One of these was quite clearly the ziggurat (step-pyramid) E.KUR of Enlil in Nippur. The other, however, was situated in the African lands of the Lower World. The evidence is contained in an Akkadian text known as *Ludlul Bel Nemeqi*, which mentions an evil god who has 'exited from the Ekur, across the horizon, in the Lower World'.[17] Can we confirm that the Lower World Ekur was indeed the Great Pyramid? A poem to the goddess Ninharsag states so quite categorically:

> House bright and dark of Heaven and Earth,
> for the *shems* put together;
> E.KUR, House of the Gods with *pointed peak*.[18]

Since the ziggurats in Mesopotamia had flat tops, only the Great Pyramid could possibly have fitted the description of a 'pointed peak'. Furthermore, anyone who has stood in awe at the foot of the Pyramid would indeed describe it as a 'House like a Mountain'.

The poem then continues to describe the Ekur with language that left Zecharia Sitchin in no doubt that it was accurately listing the Great Pyramid's major features.[19] Its foundation: 'clad in awe'. Its entrance: 'like a great dragon's mouth opened in wait'. The two gabled stones above the swivelling stone doorway: 'like the two edges of a dagger that keeps enemies away'. The Queen's Chamber: guarded by 'daggers which dash from dawn to dusk'. The Grand Gallery: 'its vault is like a rainbow, the darkness ends there; in awesomeness it is draped; its joints are like a vulture whose claws are ready to clasp'. The Antechamber: 'the entryway to the Mountain's top' with 'the bolt, the bar and the lock ... slithering in an awe-inspiring place'. All in all, a perfect description of the Great Pyramid's interior.

The identification of the Great Pyramid as one of two Ekurs has facilitated a new understanding of ancient texts, and in particular the so-called 'Myths of Kur', versions of which have been found in Sumerian, Akkadian and Assyrian. The Myths of Kur describe a major battle between Enlilite and Enkiite gods in various 'kur' or 'mountain' lands, with a dramatic climax at the Ekur or Great Pyramid. As discussed in chapter 6, this battle resulted from the occupation of Enlilite territories by the Egyptian god Seth and his followers, fleeing from the vengeant Horus.

We can now understand why Seth caused such a problem. By his occupation of Lebanon, he had caused all of the flight facilities – Baalbek, Giza and Mount St Catherine – to come under Enkiite influence. As we shall soon see, it also compromised plans which were in hand to build advanced space facilities in Jerusalem and central Sinai. The bitter conflict which ensued reflected the tension between Enlil and Enki, and between their heirs Ninurta and Marduk, for control and supremacy over the gods on Earth.

The war sounds more like a rout. Supported by Adad (Ishkur) and Ishtar (Inanna), Ninurta used powerful weapons to destroy the settlements of gods and men, and made the rivers run red with blood. The texts describe the retreat of the opposition into the mountainlands of Sinai and the land of Kush in present-day Sudan, where they were pursued and crushed without mercy.[20] It was a ruthless campaign, designed to remove human occupation from the lands of Sinai and to send a clear message that the Near East would remain Enlilite territory.

The final stage of the war was fought at the Ekur – the Great Pyramid. According to the Mesopotamian texts, the defending gods raised up a protective shield through which Ninurta's weapons could not penetrate. In a dramatic climax, the young god Horus was blinded trying to sneak out of the Ekur.[21] At this point, the mother goddess Ninharsag intervened and successfully negotiated a surrender. The peace conference is described in great detail in the text *I Sing the Song of the Mother of the Gods*.[22]

What evidence exists to suggest that the war of the gods was fact and not myth? One day, whilst reading the *National Geographic*, I came across a most unusual photograph of a mountain in Sudan. The mountain, Jebel Barkal, appeared to have been torn apart by a tremendous force, as can be seen in Plate 43 (see colour section).

Jebel Barkal is a strange and eerie mountain. It rises 300 feet above the flat desert plain of the Sudan, a mile from the Nile and close to Napata, the capital and sacred centre of ancient Nubia (also known as the kingdom of Kush). The mountain itself is regarded as especially sacred. At its base lies a ruined temple complex revered as the southern abode of the Egyptian god, Amen.

The National Geographic Society team were particularly intrigued by an isolated pinnacle of the mountain, where they found, at a height of 260 feet, inscriptions which had been 'carved at the highest, most inaccessible point on the pinnacle'.[23] In the words of Timothy Kendall, it was a 'tremendous engineering feat', for the inscriptions had been placed in an almost impossible position.

What had driven someone in remote times to erect a memorial on this remote mountain? Kendall and his team found at the site a depiction of Amen actually seated *inside* the mountain. They declined to comment on the catastrophic event that had obviously ripped apart the mountain at its centre and blackened its interior. But they did notice that the mountain had a 'broad undulating top, which was carpeted with pebbles'. These small blackened stones are a remnant of the powerful explosion that once devastated this site.

The other evidence we have to confirm the war of the gods is the physical condition of the Great Pyramid itself. We have already seen how its features correlate with the details of one Sumerian poem. Now we find further clues which prove that it was the same Ekur where the war of the gods ended in a frustrating siege.

The first clue is a mysterious well which has been excavated in the Great Pyramid's Subterranean Chamber. One Babylonian text confirms that this well was dug during the siege by Ra's brother Nergal, in order to boost the Pyramid's defences:

> The Water-Stone, the Apex-Stone,
> the . . . -Stone, the . . .
> . . . the lord Nergal
> increased its strength.
> The door for protection he . . .
> To heaven its Eye he raised,
> dug deep that which gives life . . .
> . . . in the House
> he fed them food.[24]

After the surrender of the Enkiite gods, the ancient texts describe how the victorious Ninurta entered the Ekur and disabled it. A detailed description of his actions, deciphered by Zecharia Sitchin, provides further corroboration to identify the Ekur as the Great Pyramid and thus to authenticate the war of the gods as a historic event.[25]

It is clear from the ancient text, known by its abbreviated name *Lugal-e*, that Ninurta was frustrated to see the conflict ended by peace settlement rather than a crushing defeat. He therefore vented his anger on the instruments left inside the Ekur. Inspecting its 'stones' (crystals?), Ninurta determined their destiny – to be destroyed or taken away. In what was probably the Queen's Chamber, he found the SHAM 'Destiny' stone, which had a red glow. Ninurta ordered it to be dismantled and destroyed, claiming that the stone's powers had been used 'to grab me to kill me, with a tracking which kills to seize me'.[26] The stone is described in the poem to Ninharsag as having 'an outpouring like a lion, whom no-one dares attack'. Today the enigmatic niche in the Queen's Chamber stands empty, its purpose otherwise unexplained.

Ninurta then passed up the Grand Gallery towards the King's Chamber. There he found the GUG 'Direction Determining' stone: 'then by the fate-determining Ninurta, on that day, was the Gug stone from its hollow taken out and smashed'. He also ordered the removal of the triple portcullises: the SU 'Vertical' stone, the KA.SHUR.RA 'Awesome, Pure which Opens' stone, and the SAG.KAL 'Sturdy Stone which is in Front'.[27]

On his return down the Grand Gallery, Ninurta destroyed or removed, as appropriate, the multi-coloured 'stones' which created the rainbow-like effect. The text clearly names 22 of these pairs of stones or crystals, whilst others are unfortunately illegible. Today, there are 27 pairs of empty niches in the walls above the ramps of the Grand Gallery and one further pair of empty niches on the Great Step.

Finally, the Great Pyramid's capstone, the UL 'High as the Sky' stone, was removed.[28] In the light of the *Lugal-e* text, it is rather amusing that some authors have interpreted the lack of a capstone as a deliberate design by the Pyramid's builders.

All in all, the details of the text correlate to a remarkable degree with the physical evidence which can still be inspected within the Pyramid to this day.

Thus did the era of the Great Pyramid come to an end. It was a fate which Ninharsag had anticipated as a necessary cost of securing the peace between the warring gods. In the *Lugal-e* text she exclaimed:

'To the House Where Chord-Measuring begins,
where Asar his eyes to Anu raised,
I shall go.
The chord I will cut off,
for the sake of the warring gods.'[29]

What was the chord-measuring function of the Great Pyramid, to which Ninharsag referred? A chord is defined as a straight line connecting two points on a curved surface, such as the surface of the Earth. The line from the Great Pyramid to Baalbek was a chord which measured exactly the same as the chord from Mount St Catherine to Baalbek.

The unavoidable conclusion is that the pyramids were visual markers for a pilot approaching towards Baalbek, but their role was surely more than just passive radar reflectors. Somewhere inside the Pyramid, the texts described a navigational beacon and/or radar system which spread a 'net' over heaven and Earth. Just as the Sumerians claimed, it was indeed a House Like a Mountain 'put together for the *shems*'.

We will leave the last word to the goddess Ninharsag herself:

'I am the mistress; Anu has determined my destiny;
the daughter of Anu am I.
Enlil has added to me a great destiny;
his sister-princess am I.
The gods have given unto my hand
The pilot-guiding instruments of Heaven-Earth;
Mother of the *shems* am I.
Ereshkigal allotted to me the place-of-opening
of the pilot-guiding instruments;
The great landmark,

the mountain by which Utu (Shamash) rises,
I have established as my platform.'[30]

Geometry of the Gods

The permanent disabling of the Great Pyramid led to the
immediate need for a new beacon site to guide the incoming
shems ('sky-chambers'). Baalbek had served its purpose
following the Flood, but the gods were now planning
something far more sophisticated.

Whilst work was in progress, Baalbek continued as the
central focus and a new beacon was established at Heliopolis, just 16 miles north-east of Giza.[31] The Heliopolis
beacon was located in a position where it could continue to
be used after the completion of the new space facilities, but
in the meantime it was used to point the way to Baalbek,
and this necessitated another equidistant beacon site to be
temporarily set up on the eastern coast of the Sinai peninsula.

It is no coincidence that Heliopolis was once the most
sacred city of Egypt, where its earliest kings were conse-
crated. This small city was the site of the enigmatic 'benben'
stone and the site from which the legendary phoenix rose
from the ashes. As with the Sumerian culture, the powerful
Egyptian priesthood at Heliopolis also safeguarded the
scientific knowledge bestowed by the gods, along with
the records of the divine succession which stemmed from
Ra.

The turbulent history of northern Egypt has left little
remaining at Heliopolis today, other than a single obelisk of
red granite, 170 feet high and weighing 350 tons. It is
generally believed that this obelisk, attributed to Senuseret
I in the early second millennium BC, replaced an earlier
construction.[32]

The Greek-given name Heliopolis meant 'City of the Sun', a reference to the Sun god, Shamash. In so naming it, the Greeks recognised its original link with the other city of Heliopolis, also known as Baalbek. The original name of the Egyptian Heliopolis was Annu – a clear reference to the Sumerian AN, representing both 'Heaven' and Anu, the heavenly father of the gods. Several writers have noted that Annu meant 'Pillar City'[33] and its hieroglyphic sign indeed resembled a high sloping tower (Figure 14a, black-and-white section), sometimes surmounted by a *mu* or sky-chamber. The original function of 'Pillar City' may also shed light on the mysterious djed symbol which is often associated with Heliopolis. The Egyptologists usually refer to this strange object (shown in Figure 14b, black-and-white section) as 'the backbone of Osiris', a meaningless expression of contrived symbolism. In fact, the djed symbol looks rather like a tower or lighthouse, and it was often depicted in pairs,[34] sometimes in the mysterious Duat, flanking the Gateway to Heaven. Did there once exist a second djed pillar with a similar function? The second, temporary, flight path would suggest that such a site must have once existed in the Sinai peninsula. It was almost certainly for this reason that the Pyramid Texts referred to the Heliopolitan gods as the 'Lords of the Dual Shrines'.

Let us now return to the final and most astounding flight path of the gods, where once again Zecharia Sitchin has discovered an amazing series of geometric, geographical relationships (Illustration 13). The new flight path was anchored on the two conical peaks of Mount Ararat – Little Ararat at a height of 13,000 feet and Great Ararat at 17,000 feet. These two mountains are particularly distinctive. Crowning a 25-mile wide massif, close to the Turkish-Iranian border, they rise either side of a deep natural depression. Significantly, the top few thousand feet of these peaks are permanently covered in snow – an ideal visual marker for the pilots of the *shems*.

Illustration 13

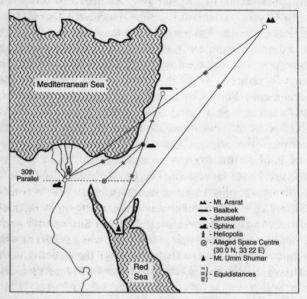

Mediterranean Sea

30th
Parallel

- ▲▲ - Mt. Ararat
- ▬ - Baalbek
- ▬ - Jerusalem
- ⚑ - Sphinx
- ⚑ - Heliopolis
- ⊗ - Alleged Space Centre
  (30 0 N, 33 22 E)
- ▲ - Mt. Umm Shumar
- ≣} - Equidistances

Red
Sea

Adapted from Z. Sitchin, *The Stairway to Heaven*, 1980.

The final flight path retained Heliopolis and added a new equidistant beacon point – the mountain of Umm Shumar, approximately 9 miles to the south of Mount St Catherine. Why did the gods change to Umm Shumar rather than retaining Mount St Catherine, which is the highest peak in the peninsula? Actually, there is little difference in height, Umm Shumar's 8,500 feet being only slightly lower than St Catherine. However, this deficit was more than offset by Mount Umm Shumar's brilliant natural prominence. Not only does it stand separately from the surrounding mountains, but it also shines like a beacon due to the presence of unusual mica particles in its rocks.

Other than the geometry, what other evidence suggests that Umm Shumar was a mountain of the gods? An unusual fact, which the experts have been unable to explain, is that Umm Shumar bears a Sumerian name, meaning 'Mother of Sumer'. Why would the Sumerians have a name for a remote mountain 750 miles to the west, beyond their field of vision? A study by Zecharia Sitchin noted that Umm Shumar was in fact a mountain with three main peaks, and the Sumerian names for the neighbouring peaks provided the clues to their function. One was named KA HARSAG, 'The Gateway Peak', and another was named HARSAG ZALA.ZALAG, 'Peak which Emits the Brilliance'.[35] No bets on which one contained the guidance equipment!

Having established the focal point at Ararat and the beacons in Heliopolis and Sinai, the gods proceeded to construct a sophisticated space centre and mission control centre, to replace the relatively crude platform at Baalbek. In order to identify these sites, Zecharia Sitchin followed a string of clues in the ancient texts and was amazed at what he found. It is not necessary to follow all the detective work, for the accurate alignment of the sites in Figure 13 speaks for itself.[36]

According to the geometrical plan, the space centre was built on the latitude line known as the thirtieth parallel north – a line which was symbolically important to the gods.[37] But where exactly on the thirtieth parallel? I decided to check for myself the geometry of the space centre, Heliopolis and Umm Shumar (and my readers are encouraged to get out their maps and rulers at this point). I was able to pinpoint the site of the space centre, alluded to by Zecharia Sitchin, at a longitude of 33 degrees 22 minutes east, 122 miles equidistant from Heliopolis and Umm Shumar. The nearest modern town is Nakhl, which in ancient times was called El Paran. The word Paran comes from a Hebrew root, meaning 'abounding in caverns or caves', an echo of the ancient Egyptian belief in the underground chambers of the Duat.

Remarkably, as shown in Illustration 13, the gods found

at Mount Zion, Jerusalem, a point that was exactly equidistant from the space centre and Baalbek (166 miles by my reckoning), and exactly equidistant from Umm Shumar and Heliopolis. It was there, at Jerusalem, that the mission control centre was constructed. But before we study Jerusalem, let us first follow the clues that identify the space centre in the Sinai.

The Sinai Space Centre

The Sinai peninsula is a desolate and forbidding place. From the granite mountains in the south to the limestone plateau in the centre, the landscape is a barren wilderness. However, despite the dry climate which makes the land unsuitable for farming, the Sinai occupies a strategic location, and has been a crossroads of world trade for thousands of years. Not only does it provide the bridge from the continent of Africa to the continent of Asia, but also it provides a link from the Mediterranean Sea to the Red Sea.

Did a space centre of the gods once exist in the central Sinai plain? Today there are no remains of such a site (for reasons which will be fully explained in chapter 10), but the uninterrupted 25-mile stretch between the Wadi El Agheidara and the Wadi el Natila would have presented an ideal hard, flat surface for landing shuttle-craft.

Although the Sinai is nowadays part of Egypt, the ancient chroniclers were in no doubt that it was previously a restricted area of the gods. The best record of this fact is that of Gilgamesh, the Sumerian king who was obsessed with eternal life. Following his failed attempt to gain access to the platform at Baalbek, he made a second expedition to the Sinai. His objective was to raise a *shem* and thereby gain immortality:

The lord Gilgamesh toward the Land of the Living set his
 mind . . .
'O Enkidu,
even the mighty wither, meet the fated end.
[Therefore] the Land I would enter,
I would set up my *shem* . . .
In the place where the *shems* have been raised up,
I, a *shem* would raise up.[38]

The route from Mesopotamia to Sinai is an indirect one, via
the Dead Sea to the north, due to the mountains which
protect the east flank of the Sinai peninsula. *The Epic of
Gilgamesh* indeed described his route via a low-lying sea,
where he asked a boatman named Urshanabi to ferry him
across. There is little doubt that these shallow waters were
those now known as the Dead Sea, which *The Epic of
Gilgamesh* refers to as the 'sea of the waters of death'.
Having crossed the sea, Gilgamesh eventually approached a
mountain pass which was guarded by 'Scorpion People'.[39]
The mountain has a Sumerian name MA.SHU, meaning
'Mount of the Supreme Barge',[40] which is identified in other
texts as 'Mount Most Supreme' and 'the Place from which
the Great Ones Ascend':

The name of the mountain is MA.SHU,
he arrives at the mountain of MA.SHU,
which every day keeps watch over the rising and setting
 of Shamash.[41]

Having sought the permission of Shamash, Gilgamesh was
allowed to proceed to the place where Shamash raised his
shems, but once again his quest was destined to fail, and the
rest of the plot does not concern us here. The question is
whether we can confirm that Mount Mashu was a mountain
in the Sinai. For the answer we have to cross the Sinai and
study the Pyramid Texts of the ancient Egyptians.

The Pyramid Texts represent the religion of the pharaohs.
They are essentially a statement of their obsessive belief in

the afterlife, and in particular a place called the Duat. The
Duat is usually thought of as the realm of the dead king
Osiris, a place in the starry skies where the dead pharaoh
ascended to the afterlife. Its purpose was clearly depicted by
the hieroglyph of a star and falcon. Yet the pharaoh's
journey to the Duat was described in terms of a *physical*
trip across land and water. The journey, described in the
Pyramid Texts, proceeded in an easterly direction; it began
with a crossing over water (a lake of reeds with a divine
ferryman) and proceeded over land between two mountains. At this point the pharaoh entered an 'underworld',
where the 'mouth' of the mountain was opened and the soul
of the dead king rose to heaven. One Sumerian poem almost
certainly refers to the same location as the 'Mount of
Howling Tunnels'.[42]

The Egyptian journey eastward mirrored the journey of
Gilgamesh westward – the Sinai lying between. As Gilgamesh reached a mountain pass, so too did the dead pharaoh
travel between two mountains, for central Sinai is indeed
surrounded by seven mountains and seven mountain
passes. Their common destination was not a mythical
underworld, but an underground space centre. The journey
to the Duat and thence to the stars was, for the Egyptians,
simply an imitation of the journeys of their gods – to
Nibiru, Baalbek or wherever. It was thus associated with
the perceived immortality of the gods. The pyramids of
Giza, and later Heliopolis, were perceived as part of the
gateway to the Duat and hence became a central part of the
pharaohs' afterlife cult. The tale of the Duat sheds new light
on the mysterious 'opening of the mouth' ceremony performed on the dead pharaoh. And it also sheds light on the
significance of the *scarab beetle* as a sacred Egyptian symbol
of life and immortality – the connection comes from that
insect's ability to burrow underground, and hence it was
symbolically associated with the *underground* base in the
Duat.

The textual clues to the past existence of a space centre in Sinai are completed by Zecharia Sitchin's identification of Sinai as the legendary location of Tilmun (sometimes referred to as Dilmun). Scholars have usually located Tilmun in Bahrain, where an ancient trading post has indeed been discovered.[43] From a careful reading of the Sumerian texts, however, Sitchin concluded that there were in fact two Tilmuns – a Tilmun city and a Tilmun land.[44] Furthermore, the search for the latter in the east was incorrect, since it was located not in the 'land where the Sun rises'[45] but in the land 'where Shamash rises'. Sitchin thus identified Tilmun land as the land of the gods, a restricted zone that was set up after the Flood. Its name, in Sumerian, was TIL.MUN, meaning the 'Land of the Missiles'.[46] A Sumerian poem entitled *Enki and Ninharsag: a Paradise Myth* describes Tilmun land as a quiet, forsaken place, with words befitting of the Sinai desert:

> The raven utters no cries,
> the *ittidu*-bird utters not the cry of the *ittidu*-bird,
> the lion kills not,
> the wolf snatches not the lamb,
> unknown is the kid-devouring wild dog.[47]

The meaning of Tilmun is echoed by the name 'Eagle Country', by which Sinai later became known.[48] The association of these fast, swooping birds with the Sinai and its space centre are highly revealing, since the Hebrew word for 'eagle' (*nesher*) is associated with a 'rushing sound' or a 'gleaming flash'.[49]

As noted in chapter 6, there is an important distinction between the *shems*, which flew in the Earth's skies, and the 'eagles', which were rockets for ascending beyond Earth's atmosphere. There is little doubt that ancient references to eagles referred to the rockets of the gods; in the *Epic of Etana*, for example, the Sumerian king Etana was carried aloft by an 'eagle', and he vividly described the Earth growing smaller and smaller until the oceans were the size of a 'bread basket'.[50] Etana's eagle (presumably its pilot) allegedly carried on a conversation with him during the flight, a detail which can no longer be dismissed as imaginative mythology.

After the Flood, the land of Sinai was initially assigned to Ninharsag, the sister of Enlil and Enki. In the Sumerian language, her name was spelled out as NIN.HAR.SAG, 'The Lady of the Head Mountain', almost certainly an association with the role of Mount St Catherine as a strategic beacon point in Sinai.[51] Zecharia Sitchin has demonstrated that Ninharsag is the same goddess as the Egyptian Hathor, who was also associated with Sinai. The name Hathor literally meant 'She Whose Home is where the Falcons are',[52] a name which once again echoes the meaning of Tilmum.

After the war of the gods, the stewardship of the Sinai changed hands. The intervention of Ninharsag to reprieve the besieged Enkites had called her impartiality into question. The Enlilites thus sought to bring the Sinai, with its planned space facilities, firmly into their own hands. The Sumerian poem *I Sing the Song of the Mother of the Gods* describes the debate which led to the appointment of Nannar (a son of Enlil and father of Utu/Shamash) in charge of Sinai.

The god Nannar was also known as Sin, an Akkadian name derived from the Sumerian SU.EN meaning 'Multiplying Lord'.[53] This nickname was almost certainly acquired from his fathering of the twins Inanna and Utu. Thus did the restricted zone of the gods become the land of Sin, a name which has been retained to this very day in the name Sinai. It is also worth noting that Sinai's Mount Umm Shumar, meaning 'Mother of Sumer', was named after Sin's wife Ningal, who was given the very same nickname in Ur. And the main oasis town of Nakhl, in the central Sinai plain, also bears the name of Ningal in the Semitic form of Nikhal.[54] As for Ninharsag, her earlier association of Sinai was not easily forgotten, and she continued to be known as the 'Lady of Sinai'.

Jerusalem

Jerusalem is the most sacred city on Earth, a holy place for the three largest religions of Judaism, Islam and Christianity. Its most hallowed spot, Mount Moriah, is nowadays dominated by the Dome of the Rock, with its striking golden cupola, erected by the Muslims. The 'Rock' of Mount Moriah is in fact a large horizontal platform known as Temple Mount. The Muslims identify it with *El Aksa*, the location from which the prophet Muhammad was taken aloft by the angel Gabriel through 'seven heavens' to meet God.[55]

According to Jewish legend, Jerusalem is the 'navel of the Earth' and Mount Moriah the place where Abraham saw 'a pillar of fire reaching from the Earth to Heaven, and a heavy cloud in which the Glory of God was seen'. The Bible reports that it was here, on the rock of Mount Moriah, that Abraham prepared to sacrifice his son Isaac to God over 4,000 years ago. It was also at this same, exact location that the Lord directed Solomon to build the first 'temple' to the Lord 3,000 years ago. That temple was destroyed, rebuilt, then destroyed again, and it is now marked by the site of the Muslims' golden cupola. What could possibly have triggered all of these legends to be associated with Jerusalem, and why has it become a place of such widespread religious veneration?

Ancient Jerusalem is nowadays hidden beneath the modern city. The only remaining feature of the Jews' second temple is the famous Western or Wailing Wall,

more than half of which is below the present day ground
level. Similarly the Rock of Temple Mount is all but hidden
from view. However, one outcrop can be seen beneath the
Dome of the Rock, with an amazing series of artificial levels
and niches (Plate 52 colour section). This rock is believed to
have magical powers and has been regarded as sacred from
ancient times. It is said that the hidden parts of the rock
contain unusual subterranean tunnels and chambers.[56]
Modern legends speak of secret excavations connected
with the Knights Templar and the search for the holy
Ark of the Covenant.

Both legend and history support the geographical evidence that Jerusalem was a space-related site of the gods. A
detailed etymological analysis by Zecharia Sitchin provides
further corroboration. First, the names of Jerusalem's three
hilly peaks have distinct literal meanings. In the north,
Mount Zophim is also known as Mount Scopus, which
literally means the 'Mount of Observers'; the middle hill,
Mount Moriah, means the 'Mount of Directing'. And
finally, in the south, Mount Zion means literally the
'Mount of the Signal'.[57]

The valleys around Jerusalem also provide significant
clues: one valley is named in the Book of Isaiah as the Valley
of Hizzayon, meaning the 'Valley of Vision'. Another
valley, Kidron, is named from a root word meaning 'to
glow, burn, radiate heat' and was thus known as the 'Valley
of Fire'. Its lower course is today known as Wadi-en-Nar,
or 'Fire Wadi'.

The Valley of Hinnom, *Geh Hinnom* in Hebrew, also has
associations with fire, hence the Greek *gehenna* is usually
translated as 'hell'.[58] According to legend, the Valley of
Hinnom contains a doorway to an underworld, marked by
a column of smoke rising between two palm trees.

Since time immemorial, Jerusalem has been an important
and sacred site, but the official reason for this is rather
obscure. Its importance cannot be traced to any advantage

of geographic position. Nor was it important as a trade centre. In fact, it lay on the edge of a barren wilderness, and was quite remote from the major international trade routes.[59] Its natural water supplies were limited, and yet its earliest inhabitants went to enormous trouble to construct unusually massive underground 'water cisterns'. Limited archaeological explorations have identified 37 such cisterns with a total capacity of about 10,000,000 gallons (37,850,000 litres). One cistern alone was capable of holding approximately 2,000,000 gallons (7,570,000 litres) of water.[60]

These massive water cisterns of ancient Jerusalem were well in excess of any possible requirements of an urban area which never covered more than three quarters of a square mile. Added to that, what possible motivation could there have been for people to congregate at this site when there were plenty of other less hostile places to live? Put simply, from a conventional geographical perspective, Jerusalem's location is a huge historical anomaly.

If, however, we adopt a less conventional scientific approach, then the location of Jerusalem becomes immediately obvious. From the gods' perspective, the site would make an ideal mission control centre. The hostile environment mattered little, since staffing would be minimal. The topography of the site was perfect – a small plateau, surrounded by a steep valley on three sides – defendable, should the need arise. And, finally, there were several springs which allowed water to be produced and stored for either industrial or space-related purposes.

If we examine the history of Jerusalem, we find that its earliest recorded name, recorded in Genesis 14, was Salem. The same passage of the Bible names the king of Jerusalem at the time of Abraham (c. 4,000 years ago) as Melchizedek, the priest of the Most High God.[61] What do we know of Melchizedek and his line of kingship at Jerusalem? Nothing whatsoever – he and his line of kings are a historical blank.[62] However, a clue to the meaning of the name Melchizedek is supplied by Paul, who refers to him as 'King of Righteousness'.[63] As we have seen, the gods were called DIN.GIR for which the first syllable meant 'Pure' or 'Righteous'. Thus Melchizedek was almost certainly an Enlilite god.

From all of the above evidence, and in particular the position of Mount Moriah at the centre of the flight path, it seems reasonable to accept Zecharia Sitchin's suggestion that Jerusalem's role was that of mission control. I will say no more, other than to quote the non-biblical Book of Jubilees:

> The Garden of Eternity, the most sacred,
> is the dwelling of the Lord;
> and Mount Sinai, in the centre of the desert;
> and Mount Zion, the centre of the Navel of the Earth.
> These three were created as holy places,
> facing each other.[64]

Clues from Jericho

When archaeologists began to excavate the famous Biblical site of Jericho around fifty years ago, they had no idea that they were about to uncover the world's oldest fortified settlement. As they sunk their trenches deep into the 70-feet high mound known as Tell es Sultan, they found a lowest level with items dating to 8000 BC.[65] This was an extraordinary find, for it occurred more than 4,000 years prior to the Sumerian civilisation, at a time when man was thought to be living a simple, nomadic life.

Stranger still was the fact that, from its earliest occupation, the site had been heavily fortified. Among the archaeologists' discoveries were a 30-feet high stone tower with an internal staircase, city walls with heights up to 20 feet, and an 8-feet deep ditch which extended over 20 feet beyond the outer walls. These constructions were of high quality, well-cut stones, fitted together without mortar.

Ancient Jericho was built on the site of a natural spring (Ain es Sultan) which still pumps 1,000 gallons of water per minute – a factor which clearly influenced its location. But what had driven ancient people to form a community of perhaps 2,000 people and then go to such lengths to fortify it? Who or what were they protecting themselves against? Why did the archaeologists find little more than walls and bones, why not the invention of writing and the wheel? What possible connection could there be between Jericho, the world's oldest urban settlement, and the emergence of civilisation in Sumer 4,000 years later? The mystery is aptly summarised by one book which refers to Jericho as 'the intriguing missing link that still awaits discovery'.[66]

The missing link has now been discovered. Just as the Great Pyramid marks the activity of the gods thousands of years before civilisation was granted to the Sumerians, so too does Jericho. The Jericho fortifications occupied a key strategic location just 15 miles east from Jerusalem, which we have just identified as the mission control centre of the gods. It therefore seems to have been a garrison to protect the eastern flank of the vital space facilities. As we have seen in *The Epic of Gilgamesh*, Jericho was indeed on the Dead Sea route which a land-based army would have to use to march on Jerusalem, or indeed to the space centre in the Sinai peninsula. As Zecharia Sitchin has pointed out, the original name of Jericho was Yeriho, literally meaning Moon City. As the Moon is satellite to Earth, so too was Jericho the satellite and protector of Jerusalem, the navel of the Earth.

A further ancient fortified site existed 12 miles *north* of Jerusalem. The modern town of Beitin marks the spot of ancient Beth-El, the 'House of God', where Jacob saw the angels of the Lord ascending and descending a stairway to heaven.[67] Half a mile to the east of Beitin, the site of Borj Beitin is described as 'one of the great viewpoints of Palestine',[68] where the patriarch Abraham once pitched his tent. Nearby, the modern village of Deir Diwan marks the site of the ancient Ai, where excavations have dated the earliest levels to *at least* 3000 BC. All of these sites stand on a stony plateau watered by four springs – an ideal fortification post for Jerusalem's northern flank.

Let us now leave Jerusalem and head south, back to the space centre in the Sinai. Here, too, we find the facilities protected by another fortified city. The place was known as Kadesh-Barnea, the site of an anomalous military expedition by Khedorlaomer *c.* 2100 BC, described in Genesis 14. Zecharia Sitchin has concluded that Kadesh-Barnea in Sinai was the same town which the Akkadians had referred to as *Dur-Mah-Ilani* in Tilmun land. The name *Dur-Mah-Ilani* meant 'the Great Fortified Place of the Gods'.[69] Its location matches the place where Gilgamesh was forced to seek the permission of the 'Scorpion People' to advance any further in his aim to raise a *shem*. Biblical scholars have always been mystified as to why a remote site in the Sinai desert should have been the target for an invading force, but Sitchin's explanation, in the context of a space centre in the Sinai, provides a significant clue.

In summary, it would seem that the gods' space facilities were protected by a series of fortified locations, all of which are otherwise quite baffling to scholars and archaeologists.

Message from the Sphinx

Alongside the pyramids at Giza lies the crouching figure of a lion with a human face, the whole monument carved out of the limestone bedrock. With dimensions of 240 by 66 feet, the Sphinx (Plate 47 colour section) must surely qualify as the world's greatest ever artistic achievement.

In order to obtain these monumental dimensions, the sculptor has excavated thousands of tons of solid rock. The experts are unable to tell us what motivated the unknown artist, and they have no clues, inscriptions or otherwise, to identify the date of its creation. And yet, despite the lack of any evidence whatsoever, the so-called experts are confidently able to tell us that the Sphinx was carved by one or other of the builders of the three nearby pyramids.

Much attention, recently in the form of computer simulation, has focused on the face of the Sphinx, in an attempt to identify it with one of the Giza pharaohs. The favoured choice is Khafra, whilst a minority attribute it to Menkaura. No-one, however, can be certain that the face depicted the artist, and no-one can say what changes might have been made to the face during later renovation work.[70] The small size of the Sphinx's head relative to its body may well indicate that some significant reprofiling has taken place.

Many scholars have drawn attention to the uniqueness of the Sphinx, for there is absolutely no precedent for the concept of representing the body of an animal with the head of a man. In fact, Egyptian art focused on the exact opposite concept, by showing their gods with the body of a man and the head of an animal. In addition, other representations of sphinxes, found in Egypt, combined the head of a *ram* with the body of a lion (Plate 49 colour section) – not a face of a pharaoh in sight. Furthermore, some commentators have expressed surprise that the concept of large-scale carving from solid rock was never emulated, despite its technical simplicity and plenty of suitable natural rock formations along the banks of the Nile.[71] It is these factors which have made the Sphinx such a mystery, for it appears totally distinct from the rest of ancient Egyptian culture.

We have already identified the Giza pyramids as part of

the gods' second flight path. Could the Sphinx also represent the handiwork of the gods rather than man? Like the pyramids, the Sphinx bears no inscription. Its perfect art form, like the perfect 52-degree angle of the Giza pyramids, was never reproduced anywhere else. We should not be surprised to find that these timeless monuments predate the rule of the pharaohs in Egypt by thousands of years. In the case of the Sphinx, this is now a scientific fact.

In October 1991, Dr Robert Schoch, a geologist at Boston University, presented detailed evidence that the Sphinx was thousands of years older than the commonly accepted date of 2500 BC.[72] His conclusion was based on the weathering profile of the limestone rock, out of which the Sphinx had been carved. Visitors to the Sphinx today can clearly see the vertical weathering profile in the limestone trench surrounding the Sphinx (Plate 48 colour section). This erosion, according to the science of geology, could only be the result of prolonged rainfall, in contrast to the dry weather experienced in Egypt since 2500 BC. Based on the climatic evidence, Schoch estimated that the Sphinx had to be between 9,000 and 12,000 years old, when the climate in Egypt was much wetter.[73]

Such an age is, of course, anathema to the experts – the same experts who state categorically that the Great Pyramid is the tomb of Khufu. Unable to disprove the geological findings (which have found widespread support among Schoch's scientific colleagues), the Egyptologists have resorted to the simple argument that it contradicts everything else that is 'known' about Egyptian history. Zahi Hawass, the curator of the Sphinx and the pyramids, stated 'we don't have any architectural evidence, we don't have any textual evidence at all to show that there was someone in Egypt at that time who can carve a statue like that'. Once again, hard, factual evidence is swept under the carpet in order to maintain the paradigm and avoid a rewrite of the history books.

These sceptics should now reflect on the fact that the Sphinx faces eastwards exactly along the thirtieth parallel north towards the Sinai, corroborating the textual and geographical evidence that a space centre once existed at this same latitude. Did the Sphinx once bear the face of a god? It seems highly likely. There is indeed a long-standing tradition that the Sphinx bears the features of Hor-Akhiti the 'Falcon of the Horizon', and one of the earliest Egyptian gods, Ra, was known by this name. It is surely no co-incidence that the easterly horizon did indeed mark the direction where the *falcons* landed.

Chapter Eight Conclusions

* Detailed geographical and textual evidence strongly suggest the prior existence of space facilities, built by the gods at Giza, Heliopolis, Baalbek, Jerusalem and in the Sinai peninsula.

* Jericho, along with Beth-El and Kadesh-Barnea, were built as fortified garrisons to protect access to the space facilities.

* The weathering of the Sphinx and the archaeological dating of early Jericho prove that these sites preceded the earliest civilisations by thousands of years.

* The physical evidence at Jebel Barkal and the Great Pyramid supports, in detail, the accounts of the gods as described in Sumerian texts.

CHAPTER NINE

THE GREAT PYRAMID REVISITED

──────◆◆◆──────

A Functional Approach

When I began writing this book, the last thing I expected was to find a solution to the mystery of the Great Pyramid. However, having covered all of the evidence in chapter 8, I was faced with a challenge which I could not ignore. Linking the Pyramid geographically to a flight path for the *shems* of the gods is all very well, but how does it explain such a huge and complex construction, when a simple Heliopolis-type pillar would have sufficed as a landing beacon? How can we explain the awe-inspiring Grand Gallery, the huge niche in the Queen's Chamber, the smaller damaged niches along the Grand Gallery and the series of portcullises outside the King's Chamber? All of these features suggested to me some mysterious purpose, not symbolic but purely functional.

If we turn to the ancient texts, we indeed find several descriptions of the Great Pyramid/Ekur's functional purposes. One function, that of guidance beacon, figures prominently, with numerous references to 'spreading a net', 'surveying Heaven and Earth' and 'pulsating a beam' throughout its 'field of supervision'.

However, there are also widespread references to the Pyramid's awesome powers. Texts dealing with the war of the gods state that the Enkiites retreated inside the Ekur, which was allegedly impenetrable to the attacking forces. The texts appear to describe a protective shield, which is curious, because the Mesopotamian name for Egypt was 'Magan', which indeed meant the 'Land of the shield'.[1] According to another intriguing reference, the god Ninurta claimed that the Pyramid's powers had been used during the war 'to grab me to kill me, with a tracking which kills to seize me'. And finally there are texts which, on a close reading, suggest that the Pyramid may also have included a communications facility to the planet Nibiru.

I therefore set about an examination of the Great Pyramid from an entirely *functional* point of view – an approach which has rarely, if ever, been undertaken before. My challenge was to use the physical evidence of the Pyramid to confirm what the ancient texts had said, and in so doing, to offer even stronger proof of flesh-and-blood gods.

Most of the theories which have been written about the Great Pyramid are, in my view, truly bizarre. We must dismiss all notions of tombs and suggestions of Khufu's statue being placed in the Queen's Chamber Niche. We must ignore the naive theory that the Pyramid is a symbolic representation of the Sun's rays descending to Earth. And we must discount romantic speculations of hidden treasures or secret repositories of information. What we are about to discover is far more exciting.

The ancient chroniclers relate that, after the Flood, Enki and his clan were given domain over the Lower World of Africa. It was there, in Egypt, that Enki was ordered to erect the beacons which would guide the *shems* in to Baalbek. And it was there, I believe, that Enki decided to use the opportunity to construct something far more sophisticated than a simple beacon, something which would enhance his power base and position.

If the texts are correct, we should find inside the Great Pyramid a beacon and radar system, a communications system and a powerful source of energy which can translate into an offensive capability. If we think of the Great Pyramid as a machine or factory, then its energy system should break down into a source of raw material or fuel, a processing system, an output-directing system and a control system. Let us now take an objective look at the evidence.

Red Herrings

Before we begin our examination of the Great Pyramid for possible clues to its function, it is first essential to strip away features that were not part of the original design. Many events have left their marks over thousands of years, creating numerous red herrings which have led other researchers astray. In order to eliminate these features, it is necessary to have a knowledge of the Pyramid's history. Many researchers, for instance, comment that the Great Pyramid is extremely hot and humid, forgetting that it was originally encased in polished white limestone blocks which would have reflected away the heat of the Sun. Similarly, much is made of the alignment of shafts which run from the King's Chamber to the outside of the Pyramid – yet no-one knows whether these shafts would originally have penetrated through the outer casing blocks which were removed by the Arabs.

Another red herring is the abundant amount of salt found within the Great Pyramid, particularly in the Queen's Chamber and in the limestone gable above the King's Chamber. Some very interesting theories have been put forward regarding this salt, but, in my view, it has simply come from rainwater – the same rainwater that has over thousands of years caused so much erosion near the Sphinx. My suggestion is based on a literal acceptance of the ancient texts which record the removal of the Pyramid's capstone, following Ninurta's victory over the Enkiite gods. Ninurta's action exposed the Pyramid's inner core to the elements and therefore the salt would have been washed out of the Pyramid's chemically impure limestone blocks.[2]

At the same time as the capstone was lifted off, many other items in the Great Pyramid were either destroyed or removed by Ninurta, as described in detail in chapter 8. In order to understand the functions of the Pyramid, it is necessary to mentally reinstall all of these items in their proper places. It is a matter of record that the god Ninurta dismantled a 'stone' from inside the Queen's Chamber, and destroyed or removed 'stones' within the Grand Gallery – hence the niches which are empty today. Ninurta also removed the triple portcullises from the King's Chamber Antechamber – its grooves now stand empty. The same incident most probably witnessed the damage to the coffer in the King's Chamber, and possibly the removal of its lid. We should be prepared to believe these ancient accounts since so many small details tie in to the physical condition of the Pyramid today.

Marduk's Imprisonment

An important set of clues to the Great Pyramid's features and functions comes from an ancient text describing the imprisonment of the Babylonian god, Marduk. The tale of the imprisonment, and subsequent escape, of Marduk from a mountain tomb has always been studied in a mythological context.[3] No-one seriously believed that it represented a historic event – until the tale was connected by Zecharia

Sitchin to another epic Sumerian tragedy, and the mountain tomb conclusively identified as the Great Pyramid.

The Sumerian tragedy has been compared to that of Romeo and Juliet, the major parts being played by Inanna, an Enlilite goddess, and Dumuzi, an Enkiite god. These two lovers were the subject of numerous Sumerian love poems. As discussed in chapter 6, Dumuzi had transgressed the laws of the gods by raping his own half-sister in an over-zealous attempt to obtain a male heir. His brother, Ra, may have regarded this as a threat towards the future sovereignty of his own offspring in Egypt, and took the fated decision to arrest Dumuzi. As Zecharia Sitchin has demonstrated at length, the Egyptian god Ra can be definitively identified with the Babylonian god Marduk.[4] It was Ra/Marduk who was therefore responsible for the accidental death of Dumuzi, which occurred during his arrest. Thereafter, Inanna became the bitter enemy of Marduk, whom she personally blamed for the death of her husband.

Against this background, a mysterious tale known as *Inanna and Ebih* begins to make some sense in the immediate aftermath of Dumuzi's death.[5] We can understand why Inanna is venting her fury against an evil god hiding inside a rather strange mountain, and we can now recognise that mountain as the Ekur or Great Pyramid. The grieving Inanna cries out:

> 'Mountain, thou art so high, thou art elevated above all
>   others . . .
> Thou touchest the sky with thy tip . . .
> Yet I shall destroy thee,
> to the ground I shall fell thee . . .
> Inside thine heart, pain I will cause.

> 'My grandfather Enlil has permitted me to enter inside
>   the Mountain!
> Into the heart of the Mountain I shall penetrate . . .
> Inside the Mountain, my victory I shall establish.'

> She ceased not striking the sides of *E-Bih*
> and all its corners,
> even its multitude of raised stones.
> But inside . . . the Great Serpent who had gone in,
> his poison ceased not to spit.[6]

Eventually Inanna was persuaded to allow the Great Serpent (clearly identified by Babylonian texts as Marduk) to come out from the Ekur and stand trial. It would seem that Marduk was indeed held responsible for the death of Dumuzi, perhaps for improperly authorising his arrest. Another Babylonian text records the guilty verdict, and a most severe sentence to imprison Marduk:

> In a great envelope that is sealed,
> with no one to offer him nourishment;
> alone to suffer,
> the potable water-source to be cut off.[7]

How was this imprisonment achieved? Having identified the prison with the Mountain, E.KUR or Great Pyramid, the answer would seem to lie in the granite blocks which once prevented access to the Pyramid's upper chambers. One of these granite blocks can clearly be seen on the left hand side as one enters the Pyramid through its modern entrance. It is one of three blocks of red granite which are commonly referred to as the 'Granite Plug'. The top block of these three is unusual in having a roughly-shaped top, as if the stone had been fractured by a powerful force.

Conventional Egyptology attributes the Granite Plug to a safety measure to protect the pharaoh's tomb. Other commentators believe it was built into the Pyramid from the beginning and may have had a symbolic purpose. The rather more practical answer is that the granite blocks were slid into place to imprison the god Marduk. But what was the *original purpose* of the Plug?

It is generally assumed that the granite plugs were indeed dropped into their current position in order to seal the Pyramid. The tight fit of the plugs in the bottom of the Ascending Passage has led some engineers to think they were built in situ, exactly where they now are.[8] However, such a theory makes little sense from a design point of view. One Pyramid expert, Peter Lemesurier, helps us to resolve the issue. He states that the Passage suddenly narrows from an upper width of just over 41 inches to 38 inches at the bottom, and that the granite plug is *tapered precisely* to fit into the lowest section of the passage.[9] The fact that they are now embedded in the bottom of the Ascending Passage would thus not be fortuitous. Furthermore, the broken upper part of the Plug suggests that it must have been forcefully lowered into the passage from somewhere above it in the Pyramid.

Where was the Plug originally situated? The Plug's width of 41 inches (2 'royal cubits') is identical to the width of the Queen's Chamber Passage and the King's Chamber Passage, perhaps suggesting them as a likely source. On the other hand, the floor of the Grand Gallery, between the ramps either side, is also 2 royal cubits.

It is difficult to see why the Granite Plug would have been used to seal the entrance to the Queen's Chamber – why use granite when that chamber is otherwise constructed of limestone? Could it have therefore been located so as to block access to the King's Chamber? Even though the King's Chamber is made entirely of granite, its entrance was *already* equipped with a series of granite portcullises, so this location made little sense.

The Great Step outside the King's Chamber was an intriguing possibility; this large limestone platform has clearly suffered explosive damage, which has now been repaired to facilitate access for tourists. Measuring approximately 5 feet in depth and 7 feet in width, it was a feasible location, but again I could fathom no possible purpose for any further protection of the King's Chamber beyond the existing portcullis system.

By a process of elimination, I arrived at a location for the Plug on the Grand Gallery floor. It would thus follow that it was moved up and down to either allow or prevent access to the Gallery from the Ascending Passage. Connecting the physical evidence with the ancient texts, I deduced that the upper Plug was probably designed with a protruding lip in order to seat it at the top of the Ascending Passage. The imprisonment of Marduk was achieved by exploding the Plug, probably by use of a short fuse, to send it crashing all the way down from near the top of the Gallery into the Ascending Passage. The explosion had broken off the protruding lip of the Plug and blown a dozen cubic feet of limestone out of the Great Step (minor damage to the Antechamber entrance behind the Step and to the roof at the top of the Ascending Passage supports this proposition). As we shall see later, the Plug may well have been designed in two separate parts – one to seal the top of the Passage and one to seal the bottom. The two parts of the Plug would originally have been connected with a strong cable.

There are two points that I now need to cover briefly, in order to prove that all of this was quite feasible. First, where is the mechanism by which these heavy granite plugs could have been lifted and lowered? A mysterious but little known feature within the Grand Gallery is a pair of 6-inch wide grooves which run the whole length of its walls. They can be seen running along the fourth overlapping section in the corbelled walls of the Gallery. Peter Lemesurier's book refers to this groove as being used for a 'sliding floor',[10] and it is clearly a major embarrassment to those who see symbolism rather than functionality within the Great Pyramid's design. My more practical suggestion is that this pair of grooves supported a travelling overhead gantry crane, as is commonly used in modern engineering factories.

Exactly when this equipment was removed from the Pyramid, we do not know, but in all probability it was among the items destroyed or removed by Ninurta.

Secondly, how did the granite blocks jump the gap above the Ascending Passage, where the rising floor is interrupted to allow access to the Queen's Chamber? This 'gap' is around 16 feet long and requires visitors to climb up the *side* ramps, before continuing to the higher parts of the Pyramid on the *central* staircase (originally a perfectly smooth floor). Within the gap, where the floor is missing, there are five pairs of holes or 'wall sockets', perfectly aligned from the Ascending Passage to the Gallery floor, as seen in Illustration 14. There is even a supporting step carved out where the floor commences. Detailed descriptions of the Great Pyramid have therefore surmised that there once existed an 8-inch thick 'bridging slab' of limestone, which once completed the floor of the Gallery.

Illustration 14

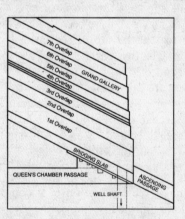

In summary, there was no problem with sliding the Granite Plug from the top of the Grand Gallery down to the bottom of the Ascending Passage.

Marduk's Release

According to the Babylonian New Year ritual, Marduk was saved from his fate only *after* his imprisonment, when the real guilty party was identified and captured. Marduk's sister-wife Sarpanit and his son Nabu appeared on the scene and a plan was hatched to release him. It was decided that they would bore a shaft and release Marduk through a SA.BAD – a 'chiselled upper opening':

> At the vortex of the hollowing, into the insides,
> a doorway they shall twistingly bore.
> Getting near, into its midst they will break through.'

The description of the rescue tallies precisely with two mysterious and otherwise inexplicable features of the Great Pyramid. The first evidence of the escape is clearly visible in the missing 'ramp stone', a large gap which has now been boarded up at the bottom western side of the Grand Gallery. Experts who have studied the surrounding rock have concluded that the missing stone was blown apart from below.[12]

The second crucial piece of evidence is the so-called Well Shaft – unfortunately not accessible to tourists – but fortunately documented in great detail. The Well Shaft, so named by the Arabs, is actually a series of vertical shafts which connect the upper and lower parts of the Great Pyramid – see Illustration 6. It comprises seven sections: four long 'finished' sections, one mysterious rough section, and two short sections which connect into the Descending Passage and Grand Gallery respectively. It has been conclusively proved that the straight sections of the Well Shaft were an integral part of the Pyramid's original design.[13] The only unaccounted for section is therefore the rough tunnel, the origin of which cannot be conventionally explained. This tunnel fits the description of the 'doorway they shall twistingly bore'.

The odds against two pieces of physical evidence – the tunnel and the exploded ramp stone – agreeing by pure chance with an ancient Babylonian text are astronomical. There seems little doubt that the ancient text describes a genuine attempt to rescue Marduk from within the Great Pyramid.

When the Arabs, led by Mamoon, broke into the upper chambers of the Pyramid in the ninth century, they encountered an unspecified amount of limestone rubble above the Granite Plug; they also found a layer of white dust inside the Grand Gallery, which made their ascent somewhat slippery. These observations can now be explained. The limestone rubble and the dust were caused first by damage to the Great Step, pieces of which followed the Plug into the passage; secondly by the explosion of the missing ramp stone to rescue Marduk; and thirdly by the probable destruction of the bridging slab at the same time.

Where was Marduk actually imprisoned? One's instinctive reaction is to suggest the King's Chamber, and there is indeed various damage in its vicinity which might indicate evidence of a rescue attempt. But is that damage in fact caused by other events?

The King's Chamber has suffered what the experts call 'subsidence', which has caused minute cracks to appear in the granite beams. Explosive force seems a more likely explanation than subsidence, but this need not have arisen through a rescue of Marduk. A more likely explanation is that this damage was caused when the top of the Granite Plug was exploded close to the King's Chamber passage, in order to imprison Marduk. Alternatively, it may have been caused in much later times by explorers such as Vyse, who is known to have blasted his way crudely around the Pyramid with liberal amounts of explosives, and is known to have explored above the King's Chamber in 1837.

There is also a third possibility. According to the ancient texts, Ninurta removed the granite portcullis from the Pyramid's Antechamber. At the furthermost southern end of this Antechamber there is noticeable damage at the top of the passage to the King's Chamber, as shown in Figure 15 (see black-and-white section). It is very likely that this was caused by Ninurta's removal of the largest granite slab which, due to its size, required explosive force to loosen it from its position.

In the light of the above, plus the earlier explanations for the damage to the Great Step and the mouth of the Antechamber, there is little evidence to suggest that Marduk's imprisonment was confined to the King's Chamber. The only possible evidence is the damage to one corner of the King's Chamber coffer, but it is likely that this was another act of vandalism by Ninurta.

My conclusion is that Marduk was not confined to the King's Chamber, for two reasons. First, it was not necessary to confine him within one section of the upper Pyramid, which was already blocked in its entirety. And secondly, the text cited earlier described his imprisonment inside a 'great envelope', a very apt description of the Pyramid's upper parts as a whole rather than one particular chamber. This conclusion will prove to be very important, in due course.

After Marduk's escape, he fled Egypt, becoming a legendary god who was remembered by the name Amen-Ra, 'the Hidden One'.[14] He subsequently became the god of the Babylonians, whose New Year rituals described his exile and made great play of his innocence.

However, one anomaly of Marduk's escape still remains to be explained. Why did his rescuers choose a route which required them to climb up the Well Shaft and bore through *32 feet* of limestone when they could have achieved their aims much more directly using the 'Mamoon method'? A tunnel through the limestone around the granite plug would have halved the distance and more than halved the time.

The only sensible answer to this enigma is subterfuge. The discreet entrance via the Well Shaft (a route known only to those familiar with the Pyramid's design) was intended to ensure that no-one detected the escape until Marduk had safely fled from Egypt. Marduk was surely not an exiled god, as the Babylonians were led to believe, but a god who was regarded as a criminal on the run.

Gantenbrink's Breakthrough

The so-called 'airshafts' of the Great Pyramid have in recent years become the focus of much research, and hence become the basis for several revisionist theories on the significance of the Pyramid itself. In 1994, Robert Bauval and Adrian Gilbert put forward a theory that the shafts were aligned to certain stars when the Pyramid was built. I will discuss their findings in due course, in the context of the Pyramid's construction date. Bauval and Gilbert's theory is replete with mystic symbolism of the pharaoh's soul ascending to heaven, and thus follows what is becoming a fairly conventional way of thinking. However, if we leave all the symbolic suggestions to one side, what do the physical features of these shafts actually tell us?

The King's Chamber contains two airshafts, one exiting towards the north and one towards the south. The existence of these shafts has been known since AD 820. In 1872, however, our understanding of the Pyramid took a major step forward, with the discovery by the British engineer Waynman Dixon of two sealed shafts in the Queen's Chamber. These shafts exited the chamber to the north and south, but unlike those of the King's Chamber they did not pierce the outer masonry of the Pyramid. Thus the theory that these shafts were airshafts was finally disproved. This conclusion was highly embarrassing since it meant that the real purpose of the shafts was totally obscure. The term 'airshafts' has stuck only because no-one has a clue why they exist.

Another major breakthrough in our knowledge of the shafts occurred in April 1993, when it was announced that a mysterious doorway had been found within the southern shaft of the Queen's Chamber[15]. A team from the German Archaeological Institute in Cairo, led by the engineer Rudolf Gantenbrink, had been tasked with improving the ventilation inside the Great Pyramid. Their work had initially concentrated on improving airflow by clearing the northern shaft inside the King's Chamber. This had involved the design and construction of a miniature robot which could be sent up inside the tiny shafts which are only 8 inches square. Their work was most successful – the blockage was cleared, a fan installed and humidity duly fell from a stifling 90 per cent to 60 per cent.

However, for reasons that are not entirely clear, Rudolf Gantenbrink's work shifted to the Queen's Chamber. It would seem that he had become involved in using his robot to measure the shafts with a degree of accuracy never before obtained. With the northern shaft apparently blocked by an obstruction, Gantenbrink focused on the southern shaft. After travelling the 84-inch long horizontal section, his robot UPUAUT 2 ('Opener of the Ways' in ancient Egyptian) began to ascend at an angle of almost 40 degrees. After travelling around 130 feet, it crossed a mysterious metal plate. Finally, after 210 feet, a sensation – UPUAUT 2 was forced to a stop by a limestone slab with two metal handles (Figure 16, black-and-white section).

The robot was able to aim a laser beam under the doorway, indicating that it was not firmly resting on the floor. At the bottom right hand corner of the doorway, a small piece appeared to have been drilled through, and a stream of black dust or sand could be seen along the edge of the shaft.

Bauval and Gilbert were as excited about this strange doorway as they were about their star correlations, but in reality the find cast significant doubt on their theory of symbolic alignments. Instead, the stone doorway suggested a much more fundamental and functional purpose. Its position, approximately 80 feet from the outer masonry of the Pyramid, and 64 feet higher than the level of the King's Chamber, inevitably suggested the existence of a hidden chamber.

We still do not know what lies behind the doorway, since the Egyptians have appeared strangely reluctant to pursue any further investigations (at least publicly). Gantenbrink, however, is convinced that a concealed chamber lies behind the door, and he quotes a long list of engineering clues in support of his claim. The physical evidence revealed by the robot includes the following: a change in the last 16 feet from rough-hewn limestone to highly polished white limestone (not found in any other 590 feet of shafts so far explored); signs of some structural damage (found nowhere else), suggesting internal stress, possibly due to the presence of a cavity; and the presence of stress relieving techniques, using vertically-laid blocks in the walls of the passage near the door.

Even more curious is the fact that the walls of the southern shaft appear to comprise *mortared* blocks, despite the tightly-fitted stones. Why would the Pyramid builders go to such lengths to seal the walls of this shaft? What could the shaft possibly have carried which required such a sealant? It was a major clue which would soon enable me to solve the mystery of the Great Pyramid.

King's Chamber Fire

During the summer of 1995, a major clue fell into my lap. Following an article which I had written on the Great Pyramid's shafts, I received a most interesting package from Canada. The author, Bernd Hartmann, claimed to have solved the mystery of the Pyramid by taking an engineering approach.[16] His unpublished theory suggested that the Pyramid was a giant limestone sponge which somehow sucked water from the Nile and then converted it into hydrogen and oxygen; the purpose was to burn the hydrogen gas to create energy in the form of heat. Hartmann's theory hinged on an unknown 'gasification' process in the Grand Gallery, based on the special 'crystal' powers of the Pyramid. The theory seemed unscientific, left several features of the Pyramid unexplained, and did not fit the evidence from the Mesopotamian records. Nevertheless, there was something disturbingly perceptive about Hartmann's claim. I had a feeling that he might be close, and I was particularly intrigued by his interpretation of the King's Chamber.

The question which arose in Bernd Hartmann's mind was this – why go to the trouble of building the floor, walls, doorway and roof of the King's Chamber out of granite, yet build the rest of the Pyramid out of limestone? His answer focused on the main practical difference between the two stones, granite being harder and thus a better heat conductor. Hartmann concluded from this that the King's Chamber was an enormous oven. An especially convincing aspect of his theory was his claim that the five so-called Construction Chambers, situated above the King's Chamber, were designed as a chimney to reduce the heat to a level which could be accepted by the surrounding limestone.

The five granite beams forming the Construction Chambers are the largest and heaviest stones in the entire structure, weighing up to 70 tons. They possess smooth polished bottoms and rough tops. It seems inconceivable that the Pyramid's builders would not have finished off one side of these granite beams. On the other hand, could it have been a deliberate design? As pointed out by Hartmann, granite is an excellent heat conductor, and the combination of a smooth bottom and rough top would enable each beam to conduct away the heat very efficiently. The gradually reducing size of the beams was also a perfect mechanism for dissipating the heat, assisted by four air spaces, with an average height of around two and a half feet, in between the beams.

Whilst not accepting Bernd Hartmann's overall theory, I felt he was on to something with the King's Chamber. No-one had come up with a better theory as to why it was necessary to build the Construction Chambers. For example, if, as is generally believed, the Construction Chambers were designed for strength, why were they not also placed above the Queen's Chamber, lower in the Pyramid? The Queen's Chamber has just one roof – a *limestone* gable, formed of twelve blocks – but has not suffered any ill consequences. And above all, why use five layers of granite above the King's Chamber when surely one would have sufficed?

Water is the Solution!

As I sat contemplating the possibilities of hydrogen fires and shafts that may have been mortared for the transport of gas, fate intervened in the form of Channel 4's *Equinox* programme to give me the final clue. On 17th December 1995, *Equinox* reviewed the work of various researchers around the world who were trying to produce a super-efficient energy device – a machine that would produce more energy output than input, and hence be more than 100 per cent efficient. This is of course contrary to the accepted laws of physics, particularly that of the 'conservation of energy'. Nevertheless, several researchers were claiming to have made important breakthroughs.

Among these researchers is an American inventor, Stan Mayer, who has designed what he calls a 'water fuel cell'. Mayer claims that his device splits water into its hydrogen and oxygen components. The heat energy created by burning the hydrogen gas has been measured at more than 100 per cent of the energy which was input to stimulate the splitting of the water. Mayer's machine comprises a strange assembly of alloy rods immersed in water inside a perspex container. The chemical reaction is stimulated by the passing of electronic pulses through the water.

Despite the criticisms which are always made of mavericks by the official scientific community, Mayer is taking his work extremely seriously and has registered dozens of patents all over the world to protect his invention. Furthermore, he claims to be working with NASA scientists on developing future technology for the American space programme. Mayer's water fuel cell would not only revolutionise the space programme, but also would create almost unlimited energy on tap. Needless to say, the threat to multi-billion dollar petrochemical investments and the potential threat arising from terrorist access to unlimited energy have caused the veil of national security to fall over Mayer and NASA's research.

Could a similar water fuel cell have once existed inside the Great Pyramid, thus accounting for its awesome capabilities? It was an exciting possibility that tied in with the theory of burning hydrogen gas in the King's Chamber. My mind turned to the southern shaft of the Queen's Chamber where Gantenbrink's robot had revealed the unusual mortared finish. Was this a clue to the location of the gas production? I decided to study the ancient texts for any references to the use of water inside the Great Pyramid. Lo and behold – there were indeed several unexplained references.

The first clue is found in the text dealing with the siege of the Ekur, when it is reported that Nergal, a brother of Ra/ Marduk, attempted to boost the Ekur's defences. The partly damaged tablet states:

> The *Water-Stone*, the Apex-Stone,
> the . . . -Stone, the . . .
> . . . the lord Nergal
> increased its strength.
> The door for protection he . . .
> To heaven its Eye he raised,
> dug deep that which gives life . . .
> . . . in the House
> he fed them food.[17] (emphasis added)

In addition to the above reference to a Water-Stone, it is highly significant that the siege was ended only when the attacker Ninurta ordered Utu/Shamash to cut off the Pyramid's *water supply* – a watery stream that ran near the Pyramid's foundations.[18] In all other details, the Mesopotamian texts have been quite accurate and here too the suggestion of a water supply is highly plausible, for the level of the River Nile is only marginally below the site of the Giza pyramids.

In a poem to Ninharsag, I found another tantalising clue to the importance of water beneath the Pyramid. The text, illegible in places, referred to the Great Pyramid, with which Ninharsag was originally associated, and stated:

> House of Equipment, lofty House of Eternity;
> its foundation are stones which . . . *the water*.[19]
>   (emphasis added)

Finally, I found another vital clue in the text dealing with the sentencing of Marduk, as cited earlier:

> In a great envelope that is sealed,
> with no one to offer him nourishment;
> alone to suffer,
> the potable *water-source* to be cut off.[20] (emphasis added)

As we have already identified, the 'envelope' was the Pyramid's upper chambers and Grand Gallery. Why would the gods record a decision to cut off a water-source from Marduk unless there definitely was a water-source in that upper area of the Pyramid? Was it possible that water was being pumped from the watery stream, an offshoot of the Nile, up inside the Pyramid? And where was the location of the Water-Stone which Nergal had increased in strength? As I searched every recorded nook and cranny of the Pyramid, one solution presented itself – the empty niche in the east wall of the Queen's Chamber.

The Queen's Chamber Niche (Plate 30, colour section) is an astonishing 15 feet in height and 3.5 feet deep. Its shape is best described as a corbelled telescopic cavity, with five sections, each smaller than the one below it. Its purpose has always mystified the experts. To my mind, however, there are two significant factors which immediately suggest this empty niche to be the home of the Water Fuel Cell. First, its size. If such a cell is going to produce the kind of power that this 6 million-ton structure was allegedly capable of, then there has to be a powerful engine, and there is no substitute for cubic capacity. Secondly, this niche is the most easterly feature which has yet been discovered in the entire Pyramid (Illustration 15) and east is the direction of the waters of the Nile. Furthermore, a line drawn directly downward from the niche arrives just a short distance to the north-east of the well in the Great Subterranean Chamber – a well which was dug in search of water.

Without further excavations inside the Great Pyramid, we can only speculate as to how the water was pumped up to the Water Fuel Cell in the Queen's Chamber, but many possibilities spring to mind. As to the pipe which must have delivered the water, it seems highly significant that the rear of the Queen's Chamber niche has been subjected to a determined excavation, resulting in a rough-hewn hole about 3 feet square and 30 feet deep (Plate 30, colour section). This excavation is attributed to 'unknown treasure seekers' at an unknown time. The question is, what prompted them to start digging in this precise location, and in an easterly direction?

Illustration 15

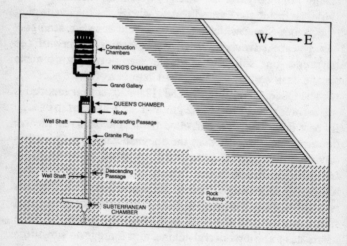

The Gas Chamber

It is now time to start testing my emerging theory against the physical evidence around the Pyramid, starting with the Queen's Chamber, where a Water Fuel Cell was used to split water into its chemical constituents of hydrogen and oxygen gas. Before we proceed, however, it is essential to establish a few brief facts about these two gases.

Oxygen is a colourless, odourless gas with an atomic structure larger and more complicated than the simple hydrogen atom. It is highly reactive and essential for almost all known forms of combustion.

Hydrogen is a flammable colourless gas, the lightest known element in the universe and 14.4 times lighter than air. When burned, it produces a very high temperature flame, and is commonly used in industry for welding and cutting metals. Experimental car engines have been made which burn pure hydrogen gas; the exhaust is pure water and nitrous oxide (laughing gas), the latter produced from the nitrogen content of the air.

It is also important to understand that when we make a fire with wood, for example, it is not the wood which is burning but the hydrogen attached to the wood, using oxygen from the air for combustion. The burning of pure hydrogen, in contrast, does not produce side-effects such as smoke and solid waste, which we normally associate with fires. Furthermore, the flame of a hydrogen fire is virtually invisible since the fire does not contain carbon and other impurities.

When these two gases are first produced in the Queen's Chamber, the much lighter hydrogen gas will generally rise above the oxygen, but the turbulence of the process will result in a mixing of the two gases. As we now know, the southern shaft in the Chamber is mortared and leads upwards to a doorway and, the evidence suggests, a hidden chamber. It would thus seem that one of the gases is to be transported and stored. Is it possible to fill with gas a chamber 64 feet higher than the King's Chamber? This would have created no problem, since the original bridging slab in the Grand Gallery could have been used as a valve to seal off the Chamber and its passage. This would have created sufficient back-pressure to force the gases upwards along the Queen's Chamber shafts. The small doorway discovered by Rudolf Gantenbrink could have been opened and closed by remote control, thus acting as another valve in the system. The handles of this door would have been used for emergency over-ride in the case of electronic failure.

Returning to the bridging slab valve, it would, when opened, have released gas into the Grand Gallery. But how was this bridging slab opened and closed? Instead of physically moving the slab itself, a much more efficient system would have been to drill holes through its middle and use the Granite Plug to cover and uncover the holes. A very neat system. The opening of this valve would be achieved by lifting the upper Granite Plug clear of the slab. The lower Granite Plug, to which it was connected by a wire rope, would have continued to seal the bottom of the Ascending Passage in order to achieve operating pressure of the gas in the Grand Gallery.

Beneath the bridging slab, as I mentioned earlier, there are five pairs of holes, which would have held supporting cross-beams. The pair of holes in the centre of the bridging slab were significantly larger than the others. This backs up my theory, since it would have been necessary to support the slab at its weakest point to carry a heavy granite plug, acting as a valve.

Does this theory literally measure up to reality? The Granite Plug would originally have been around 15 feet long. The gap in the Grand Gallery, where the bridging slab would have been, is around 16 feet long. These facts are consistent with the theory. As mentioned earlier, it is likely that the Plug comprised two sections, an upper and lower plug which blocked the top and bottom of the Ascending Passage respectively. Assuming that this was the case, the Grand Gallery would require sufficient clearance to pull both plugs, connected by the wire rope, above the Passage, to permit access for repair or maintenance. The measurements do indeed allow this as a possibility, since the total length of the Grand Gallery is 153 feet compared to 124 feet in the Ascending Passage.

Valves and Nozzles

Before we examine the final destination of the hydrogen gas in the King's Chamber, it is worth studying the important clues in the Antechamber which is situated in the approaching passageway.

The Antechamber is around 9.5 feet long and 12.5 feet high. Most attention is usually focused on the portcullis system which once existed there (Illustration 16). Nowadays, only the first part, 'the Granite Leaf', can be seen. Its top has been broken off but its other dimensions are 15.75 inches thick and 41.2 inches wide. Curiously, it was never designed to descend to the floor. The position of the other three portcullises is marked by three large retaining grooves in the granite side walls, which extend 3 inches below the floor level. These were designed to hold granite slabs, each measuring 21.5 inches thick by 41.2 inches wide, with their respective heights unknown.

Illustration 16

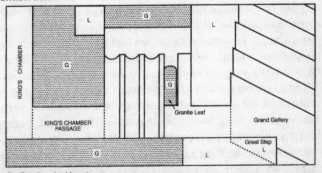

G - Granite   L - Limestone

The most interesting feature of the Antechamber, which is rarely mentioned, is the set of vertical grooves running down the south wall to the top of the King's Chamber's inner passage (Figure 15, black-and-white section). These four rounded grooves, 4 inches wide and 2.8 inches in depth, are not in any position to form part of the portcullis system. When combined with a tightly fitting granite slab in front of the wall, they would effectively form a series of pipes which would squirt the hydrogen gas into the King's Chamber. The slab which stood here would thus have remained fixed in position, except where access was required for maintenance purposes. Its function tallies with the SAG. KAL stone ('Sturdy Stone which is in Front') which Ninurta removed only with great difficulty (see chapter 8).

A fundamental law of physics states that a gas will travel more quickly (for a given pressure) when it is forced through a smaller hole. This is the principle by which water-pistols cover surprising distances. Therefore, if a sufficient pressure was applied to push the gas in the Grand Gallery upwards towards the King's Chamber, the narrow passageway at the top of the Gallery would have accelerated the gas through into the Antechamber. In order to enter the King's Chamber, the gas would then have to pass through the small pipes at the top of the far wall of the Antechamber. By the same principle, this would cause another vast increase in velocity. It is no coincidence that, in between the pipes and the passage entrance, we find four granite slabs or portcullises which could be raised to narrow the access; in this way the velocity of the gas could be varied, with five different speeds for any given pressure. Note also that a by-product of the Antechamber valve system would have been heat – in the same way that the valve of a bicycle pump becomes hot with vigorous use. This explains why even the outer slabs of the King's Chamber Antechamber were made of granite.

How were the portcullises raised and lowered? The mechanism can no longer be seen, but there is plenty of evidence to suggest that it once existed. Above the grooves which held the portcullises, there is an empty space measuring approximately 38 inches in height on the west side and 46 inches on the east side, and running the whole 9.5 feet length of the Antechamber. The only clue to the nature of the apparatus once situated there is a series of three semi-circular hollows on the western wall, each with a diameter of 17.25 inches (see Figure 15, black-and-white section).

Fuel for the Fire

Inside the King's Chamber we find only two items of any distinction. One is a rectangular granite coffer, found lidless and empty. Its interior dimensions are approximately 78 by 27 by 34 inches, and its walls and base are 6–7 inches thick. It is generally believed that the coffer once had a lid, measuring approximately 90 by 39 inches.

The other interesting feature is the pair of shafts, which would have been at the same height as the coffer's missing lid. The experts state that these shafts penetrate the outside of the Pyramid, which indeed they do today, but they tend to forget that the Pyramid was once fitted with casing stones, so no-one knows for sure whether they truly vented to the atmosphere or not. Although the coffer is today situated at the far end of the Chamber, it is movable, and its original position in the Chamber is not known.

What would we expect to find if we were burning pure hydrogen gas to generate energy? First, we would need a receptacle to burn the gas under controlled conditions. Second, we would need a source of oxygen, without which combustion cannot occur. Thirdly, we would need a way of removing the energy output (heat).

The coffer was clearly the location of the fire, but how did the gases enter the coffer under controlled conditions? The squirting of hydrogen gas into the King's Chamber can be compared to placing your thumb on the end of a hosepipe; the water accelerates but the same amount of water exits the hose. By the same principle, there would be no point in squirting hydrogen gas into the King's Chamber unless it went *directly* into the coffer. We must therefore suppose either that the coffer was positioned directly at the entrance to the King's Chamber, or that some connection apparatus once existed and has since been dismantled.

Is there any evidence that the coffer was once fitted with connections for entry of gases and exit of heat energy? A major clue remains in the damage to one corner of the coffer. It has been a mystery how this occurred, since granite is an extremely hard stone. However, this feature is fully consistent with the theory of the coffer as a receptacle for burning hydrogen gas. The connection holes would have created a potential weak spot in one corner – a vulnerable target for vandalism. The damage which we see today was not caused by tourists (as is sometimes suggested) but by the angry god, Ninurta.

Assuming for the moment that the Grand Gallery gas was the hydrogen, where did the oxygen come from, and how did it enter the coffer?

The King's Chamber's southern shaft has the most unusual entrance of any shaft in the Pyramid. Nowadays it is fitted with a fan, but prior to that it had already been mutilated by 'unknown treasure seekers'. Whilst the upper shaft is a standard 9 by 9 inch rectangular section, its bottom entrance is an extraordinary dome shape, as can be seen in Illustration 17. The depth of this 'dome' is a massive 70 inches, its height varying from 12 to a maximum 28 inches, and its width varying from 6 to a maximum 18 inches. It is thought that the badly mutilated opening may have originally been circular, with a 12 inch diameter.

Illustration 17

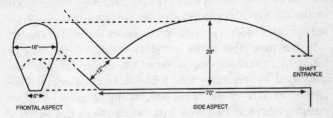

This physical evidence strongly supports the notion of a large valve or filtration unit originally fitted in the southern shaft. Its purpose would have been to control the pressure of the oxygen, and possibly to purify it. There would probably have been a physical connection from this valve to the coffer, but any such pipework was long ago removed.

It is interesting to compare these findings with the Mesopotamian texts which state that, following the war and siege at Giza, Ninurta entered the King's Chamber, and:

> Then, by the fate-determining Ninurta, on that day
> was the GUG stone from its hollow taken out and smashed.[21]

The literal meaning of GUG, as interpreted by Zecharia Sitchin, is 'Direction Determining'. He assumed, incorrectly, that it was some guidance equipment removed from the coffer. As we have seen, the coffer had a different purpose, and no 'stones' were located inside it. The mystery is solved when we imagine Ninurta quizzing his advisers on the function of the mysterious valve in the wall. They might have said: 'it directs the oxygen into the coffer'; and so it became known as the 'Direction Determining Stone'.

How was the heat energy from the fire removed and how was it used? Although the lid of the coffer is now missing, it is reasonable to assume that it contained an outlet which carried the heat energy away from the coffer. Several surveys of the Pyramid's King's Chamber have commented on the blackened appearance of the northern shaft, suggesting that this shaft was used to transport the heat energy.[22]

Somewhere above the northern shaft of the King's Chamber, the heat energy from the hydrogen fire was converted by generator into a usable form of energy. We cannot be sure of the exact process, but it may not have been very far removed from late twentieth century technology. The generator may have been situated close to the outer face of the Pyramid, or it may have been located in the capstone. We have no way of knowing the nature of the capstone (Apex Stone) which was removed by Ninurta – it may not have been made of stone at all. All we can say is that the square summit platform has four base sides of 48 feet and the missing capstone would have been approximately 30 feet high. Its functional importance is indicated by its removal.

Secret of the Hidden Chamber

If Rudolf Gantenbrink is correct, and a chamber lies behind the mysterious stone doorway, what could have been its purpose? Did the Pyramid builders intend it to be a gas tank to hold reserve supplies of hydrogen or oxygen, as a company or factory might keep a ready stockpile of raw material? The idea seemed plausible.

Gantenbrink's robot found the entrance to the hidden chamber 64 feet above the King's Chamber. Bauval and Gilbert, in their detailed study of the Pyramid's shafts, commented that the Queen's Chamber's southern shaft ran almost parallel to the one emerging from the King's Chamber. Coincidence? It would not take a great feat of engineering to equip the gas tank with an exit, a pump, and a flap-valve connection to the King's Chamber shaft, thus enabling gas to be routed into the King's Chamber.

Does such a connection and flap-valve exist in the King's Chamber southern shaft? It is curious that this was the shaft which Gantenbrink was brought to Giza to unblock. The nature of the blockage and its exact location have never been revealed, but suffice to say that one would expect any foreign matter falling into a smooth-sided shaft to fall straight to the bottom where it could easily be removed. It is a fair bet that the blockage was caused by the ancient valve.

Which gas was stored in the hidden chamber? As I tested various scenarios, it became clear that the hidden chamber was not used for gas storage. The answer suddenly clicked. It was only necessary for the Pyramid to use a fraction of its potential power in everyday use. The complicated system which I have described so far is one which squirts hydrogen into the fire with variable speed control.

A simpler and more direct system, on the other hand, would operate under low pressure, at a fixed slower speed, to keep things ticking over. In fact, the more I thought about it, the more essential such a system became. If I was designing it, that's what I would have done. Under this scenario, we would create a tremendous pressure of gas in the Grand Gallery, and then store that energy as compressed hydrogen, just as a service station will store compressed air to quickly inflate motorists' tyres. On the occasions when a blast of extra power was needed, the portcullises would be opened and the huge pressure differential would cause a powerful surge of hydrogen into the King's Chamber's coffer.

As I reviewed the limited options available for the rather less exciting low-pressure system, it became clear that the hidden chamber must be a crucial aspect of what I was looking for.

Let us briefly return to the starting point of the process,

where the operation of the Water Fuel Cell in the Queen's Chamber produced two gases. Initially, we would release hydrogen into the Grand Gallery, using a filter to allow only the small hydrogen atoms to pass through.[23] Once the Gallery was at full pressure, we would close the bridging slab, and the back-pressure would force oxygen and hydrogen to enter the Queen's Chamber shafts. If we wished to separate these two gases in order to run a low-pressure system, how would we do it? Since the hydrogen atom is much smaller than the oxygen molecule, the first step would be to fit a filter over one shaft to allow only hydrogen to pass through. The other shaft would then carry oxygen, inevitably mixed with hydrogen due to the turbulence of production. However, this oxygen mixture could be purified by allowing the mixed gases to settle, and venting the lighter gas (hydrogen) to the atmosphere. It is rather amusing to think that one of the shafts may have been an 'airshaft' after all.

The solution thus presented itself quite logically. The hidden chamber was used as a Gas Settlement Chamber, using the King's Chamber southern shaft to vent the excess hydrogen. The remaining pure oxygen could then be passed down the same shaft into the King's Chamber.

In order to run this low-pressure system, the other shaft in the Queen's Chamber had to carry the filtered hydrogen up to the King's Chamber. Is there any evidence that this was the case? It is time to pay a visit to the mysterious northern shaft of the Queen's Chamber.

The Kinky Shaft

It is commonly believed that the northern shaft in the Queen's Chamber heads directly upwards in a northerly direction. This, however, is a complete speculation, which has been repeated so often that it appears as fact. The truth is that this shaft has never been completely explored, and since it does not reach the Pyramid's outer core, *no-one knows* where it really goes to.

In 1993, Rudolf Gantenbrink made the first ever attempt to fully explore this shaft. Sure enough, his robot began by proceeding upwards in a northerly direction. After a short distance, the shaft temporarily kinked to the west in order to avoid running straight into the Grand Gallery.[24] But then UPUAUT 2 came across something very strange. Instead of reverting to its northward course, the shaft kinked backwards in the opposite direction, upwards and towards the *south*.[25] Due to an obstruction on the floor of the shaft, Gantenbrink was reluctant to allow the robot to continue, lest it become stuck. The ultimate destination of the Queen's Chamber northern shaft therefore remains a mystery, but all previous assumptions about this shaft have now been thrown into confusion. It is a discovery which, whilst not as dramatic as the southern shaft's secret doorway, is equally as intriguing.

Needless to say, the experts confidently predict that the kinky shaft will kink back once again to its original northern course. However, according to my theory, this shaft must lead to the King's Chamber.

At this point, Pyramid-experts will be raising two objections. First, that my kinky shaft cannot connect to the King's Chamber, because there is no possible entry point. And secondly, that both of the Queen's Chamber shafts were originally sealed.

Let us take the second point first. The experts tell us that the Queen's Chamber shafts were only discovered in 1872, and that the first 5 inches of shaft were not pierced through to the Chamber. Let us take a closer look at how these shafts were discovered. Charles Piazzi Smyth, the Astronomer Royal of Scotland, explains:

> Perceiving a crack ... in the south wall of the Queen's Chamber, which allowed him at one place to push in a wire to a most unconscionable length, Mr Waynman Dixon set his carpenter man-of-all-work, by name Bill Grundy, to jump a hole with hammer and steel chisel at that place.[26]

I find it difficult to believe that a permanently closed shaft would have cracked and then been discovered in the above manner. It is much more likely, in my view, that these shafts were sealed as yet another act of vandalism by Ninurta who was determined to take the Pyramid out of service. The discovery of the hidden chamber above the 'sealed' shaft supports this interpretation, based on my functional approach. The sealing of the shafts is yet another red herring.

As for a physical connection between the Queen's and King's Chambers, yes this is a controversial claim, and initially I, too, was sceptical. But, instead of dismissing the possibility, I decided to revisit the evidence. I was immediately struck by something so obvious that it is habitually overlooked. In one corner of the King's Chamber is an excavation in the floor which is attributed to Caliph Al Mamoon in AD 820. A mutilated lump of granite from this excavation still remains in the chamber, whilst the hole in the floor is covered with a metal grille, as can be seen in Plate 31 (colour section). This hole lies near the north-west corner of the King's Chamber – the exact location for a connection with the kinky shaft.[27]

As amazing as it seems, my quest for a functional explanation of the Great Pyramid has located two vitally important connecting shafts (or pipes) in the two precise locations where ancient 'treasure hunters' have butchered the Pyramid. What prompted Mamoon to hack his way into the King's Chamber floor? Why did he think there was something hidden there? And what prompted unnamed treasure hunters to burrow so determinedly behind the Queen's Chamber Niche? Why did they choose that particular location? What are the odds against both of these locations being selected for vandalism to the exclusion of any others?

The only loose end is an unusual feature in the Queen's Chamber – its sunken floor, which lies 21 inches beneath the level of the approaching passage. No-one has been able to explain why this floor appears rough and unfinished, in

Illustration 18

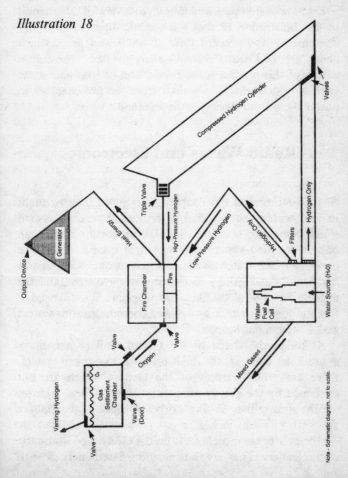

Note - Schematic diagram, not to scale.

complete contrast to the rest of the Pyramid. My interpretation of this floor is that it was used to drain water, which occasionally recombined from oxygen and hydrogen gases at high temperatures. The rough finish may have been designed to allow the water to soak down through the limestone floor, rather than flooding the passageway into the Grand Gallery.

Let us now step back and take an overview of this chapter so far. Illustration 18 uses a schematic diagram to clearly demonstrate the upward flow of water and gases which constitute the Great Pyramid's energy system. The culmination of this process is the production of heat and water vapour, which travels in a shaft from the fire chamber to power the output device at the Pyramid's apex.

Radio Waves and Electronics

At the beginning of this chapter, I suggested that we ought to find within the Pyramid a tremendous energy system which comprised a source of fuel, a processing system, an output-directing system and a control system. So far we have identified water as the fuel, the passageways, chambers, shafts and gallery as the processing system, and the missing capstone as the likely output point. We still need to find the control system, as well as a communications system and a directional beacon.

Although the shape of the Grand Gallery may have assisted in creating the high-pressure hydrogen system, there are other features of the Gallery which are not explained by the energy-producing system. These features are the strange overlapping, corbelled shape of the Gallery and its mysterious niches.

One pair of these niches sits on the Great Step at the top of the Gallery. They are thus positioned extremely close to the Pyramid's centre line, directly beneath the apex. Of these two niches, the eastern one is located above the Queen's Chamber Niche or Water Fuel Cell – at the Fuel Cell's mid-depth but slightly off centre. It may therefore have been involved in supplying electronic pulses to assist the water splitting process.

As for the western niche on the Great Step, it is positioned exactly above a small cut-out in the western side of the Lesser Subterranean Chamber (just outside the Great Subterranean Chamber at the bottom of the Pyramid). We will return to this niche in a moment.

Below the Great Step, the Grand Gallery contains 27 further pairs of niches, cut vertically down against the base walls of the Gallery (Plate 32, colour section). Each niche consists of a hole measuring 6 inches wide, 10 inches deep and 20.6 inches long. Above the niches are cross-shaped features, each comprising a vertical mark crossed by a slanted depression running parallel to the ramp. These marks strongly suggest that some objects, once affixed to the wall, have been torn out. This damage, we know from Mesopotamian texts, was inflicted by Ninurta.

I would welcome suggestions from electronic engineers, but here is my interpretation of the above features. In view of the level of technology generally being used by the gods, the transmitting of messages either on Earth or from Earth to Nibiru would not require more than a small box of sophisticated electronics, with messages being beamed upwards through the apex of the Pyramid. However, the reception of incoming messages from vast distances is another matter entirely.

It is evident from the vast radio-telescopes which are used in the SETI search for extraterrestrial signals that size matters. The reason for this is that radio waves are one million times longer than light waves. The size and shape of the Grand Gallery therefore suggest to me a powerful listening post for amplification of incoming signals. The niches positioned along this listening post would have contained apparatus (possibly crystals) which resonated to different frequencies. The information would then be transmitted electronically from the top of the Grand Gallery, western side niche, to a relay device situated directly below in the Lesser Subterranean Chamber.

Where was the directional beacon which the texts described as the main function of the Pyramid? The most likely location would have been a small transmitter, located in the capstone which was long ago removed.

Finally, we have to ask, where was the base from which all of these functions were controlled? By a process of elimination, the only chamber not included in the functions so far is the Great Subterranean Chamber. This Chamber was originally sealed off at the bottom of the Descending Passage by a stone doorway; old drawings confirm the damage caused when someone blasted through long ago.[28] The western side of the Great Subterranean Chamber consists of limestone bedrock, cut into strange grooves and protrusions, but disfigured by erosion, perhaps by rainwater passing through the Pyramid over thousands of years. Although disfigured, the features are certainly not natural. It is thus likely that this was the location of the control room and its equipment.

In addition to the central control room, other localised controls may also have existed. One of these may still be hidden inside the Pyramid today. For reasons that have rarely been questioned, the two-part Granite Leaf, mentioned earlier, has been cemented into the grooved walls in its *lower* position, and bears an irregular shape as if broken off from above. Whilst the damage can be attributed to Ninurta, the cement is a mystery. It is also a mystery how the portcullis system was operated. Furthermore, the two-part Leaf is an anomaly, since it was never designed to descend to the floor, but instead rests in its lowered position at chest height. It also contains an inexplicable 'boss' or 'seal' on the upper part. Putting all these clues together, and considering them in the light of a functional explanation of the Pyramid, the obvious conclusion is that these two granite slabs contain a hidden control panel. It seems strange that no-one has ever attempted to separate and open them . . .

Giza's Chronology

As promised, I will now pass a few comments on Robert Bauval and Adrian Gilbert's claim that the 'airshafts' were aligned to certain stars, and thus fulfilled a symbolic purpose. Using Rudolf Gantenbrink's measurements of the slope of the shafts, they found that c. 2450 BC the southern shaft of the Queen's Chamber had been aligned with Sirius, the northern shaft of the King's Chamber had been aligned with Alpha Draconis and the southern shaft of the King's Chamber had been aligned with the lowest star in Orion's Belt.

The first point to note is that the date 2450 BC has no particular significance, since Khufu's reign is generally accepted to be 2550 BC. More importantly, however, it must be recognised that 2450 BC is a convenient average adopted by Bauval and Gilbert; their precise results showed three different dates: 2400 BC for the alignment of the Queen's Chamber and 2425 and 2475 BC for the alignments of the King's Chamber. This is not very convincing. First, the lower Queen's Chamber must have been constructed first and should therefore align at the earlier date and not at the later date. Secondly, the King's Chamber shafts, which should have been constructed simultaneously, aligned at two different dates, with an unexplained 50 years difference.

One of Bauval and Gilbert's findings which does interest me, however, is the exact mirror image of the three Giza pyramids with Orion's Belt at 10450 BC, both in relative position and size.[29] Several writers have claimed that the Pyramid has alignments to stars, but their claims are unconvincing, since the Earth's wobble causes the positions of stars to move, and there are bound to be random alignments from time to time. Bauval and Gilbert's discovery is in a different league, because what they found was a mirror image rather than a chance alignment. The fact that they found that mirror image to be exact at 10450 BC is all the more convincing because they did not go looking for it (in contrast to a deliberate search for alignments around the time of Khufu). Indeed, they have not been able to offer a satisfactory explanation of this remote date.[30]

According to Khufu, the alleged builder of the Pyramid, its owner was the goddess Isis, whom he referred to as the 'Mistress of the Pyramid'. The evidence concerning Isis is in the form of an inscription on a stele, found in the 1850s in the temple, or 'House', of Isis near to the Great Pyramid. It has been translated as follows:

> Eternal life to Horus Mezdau.
> To King of Upper and Lower Egypt,
> Khufu, eternal life is given!
> He founded the House of Isis,
> Mistress of the Pyramid,
> beside the House of the Sphinx.[31]

The stele on which this inscription was found came to be known as the 'Inventory Stele', and is today exhibited in the Cairo Museum. Ironically, the experts have proclaimed it a forgery, because it contradicts the evidence from Vyse's fraudulent inscription just over a decade earlier! Whilst it is true that the writing style on the stele may indicate that it was produced some time after Khufu, it is perfectly possible that it was a copy of an earlier original. Scholars have been unable to suggest why such a forgery would have been made 4,000 years ago in a manner which praised Khufu and yet attributed the Pyramid to the ancient goddess, Isis.

Whilst not constituting a chronological proof, the Inventory Stele has all the hallmarks of authenticity, since Manetho's history of Egypt dates the rule of Isis and Osiris in Egypt to around 10000 BC. Furthermore, it corroborates Bauval and Gilbert's dating of the Giza pyramids to 10450 BC.

As we have seen in chapter 7, the Flood occurred *c*. 11000 BC, shortly before the above dates for Isis and the Giza Pyramids. All of this evidence corresponds to the ancient texts, as interpreted by Zecharia Sitchin, which link the pyramids to a flight path built by the gods as soon as practical following the Flood.

Chapter Nine Conclusions

* Ancient texts describing the siege and ransacking of an 'Ekur', along with the imprisonment and release of the god Marduk from that Ekur, explain in extraordinary detail many features found inside the Great Pyramid.

* The Great Pyramid possessed a tremendously powerful source of energy, and could be operated with offensive capabilities. In addition, it functioned as a directional beacon and as a sophisticated communications system.

* The Pyramid's enigmatic chambers and shafts have a functional explanation. The Queen's Chamber Niche contained a Water Fuel Cell, the King's Chamber coffer was used to burn hydrogen gas, the Grand Gallery functioned as a cylinder for compressed hydrogen gas, and the 'airshafts' transported hydrogen and oxygen accordingly. The mysterious doorway, discovered by Rudolf Gantenbrink, is a valve leading to a Gas Settlement Chamber.

CHAPTER TEN

NUCLEAR CATASTROPHE 2024 BC

Sumer's Sudden Downfall

The mysterious beginning of civilisation in Sumer, nearly six thousand years ago, was matched by its equally sudden and mysterious demise. The circumstances behind this demise are generally brushed over by the general history books. They tell us that this magnificent civilisation begot a rival in the neighbouring and equally mysterious Akkadian empire, and that around 2000 BC both the Sumerians and the Akkadians disappeared for no particular reason. We are then told that two new civilisations, the Babylonians and the Assyrians, arose as if from nowhere to dominate Mesopotamia. With this huge over-simplification, the matter is left to rest.

And yet a mass of evidence does exist, describing the downfall of Sumer, so why does this evidence not appear in the history books?

The answer is that the nature of the final disaster which struck the Sumerians mystified them as much as it mystifies scholars today. The Sumerians' description of the disaster is so strange that it is conveniently regarded as mythology and brushed to one side. It is archaeological fact, however, that Sumer's demise came suddenly.

In 1985, Zecharia Sitchin put forward a credible scenario for the use of nuclear weapons to the west of Sumer, at a date which coincided with its mysterious downfall.[1] We will deal with that scenario in due course, but meanwhile let us consider Sitchin's claim that the Sumerians were decimated by the nuclear fall-out. The evidence is contained in various texts, known as 'lamentations' over the destruction of various Sumerian cities. The following translations have been published by the foremost expert on Sumer, Professor Samuel Kramer.[2]

> On the land [Sumer] fell a calamity,
> one unknown to man;
> one that had never been seen before,
> one which could not be withstood.

> A great storm from heaven . . .
> A land-annihilating storm . . .
> An evil wind, like a rushing torrent . . .
> A battling storm joined by a scorching heat . . .
> By day it deprived the land of the bright sun,
> in the evening the stars did not shine . . .

> The people, terrified, could hardly breathe;
> the evil wind clutched them,
> does not grant them another day . . .
> Mouths were drenched with blood,
> heads wallowed in blood . . .
> The face was made pale by the Evil Wind.

> It caused cities to be desolated,
> houses to become desolate;
> stalls to become desolate,
> the sheepfolds to be emptied . . .
> Sumer's rivers it made flow
> with water that is bitter;
> its cultivated fields grow weeds,
> its pastures grow withering plants.

The nature of the disaster was such that even the gods were powerless to resist it. A tablet named *The Uruk Lament* states:

> Thus all its gods evacuated Uruk;
> they kept away from it;
> they hid in the mountains,
> they escaped to the distant plains.[3]

In another text, named *The Eridu Lament*, Enki and his wife Ninki also fled their city of Eridu:

> Ninki its great lady, flying like a bird, left her city . . .
> Father Enki stayed outside the city . . .
> For the fate of his harmed city he wept with bitter tears.[4]

Numerous Sumerian lamentation tablets have been found and translated in the last hundred years, covering Uruk, Eridu, Ur and Nippur. These tablets suggest that all of the cities simultaneously experienced the same phenomenon. However, there is no mention of warfare – a subject with which the Sumerian chroniclers were quite familiar. On the contrary, the disaster appeared not as a destruction but as a *desolation*. One scholar, Thorkild Jacobsen, concluded that Sumer had been struck not by invaders, but by 'a dire catastrophe' which was 'really quite puzzling'.[5]

As cited above, what struck the Sumerian cities was an 'evil wind' that brought death like an invisible 'ghost' that had 'never been seen before'. No wonder that nuclear fallout has been suggested as the cause. What are the alternatives? Could it simply have been an unprecedented killer disease? Whilst this must remain as a possibility, the Sumerians' detailed descriptions of water turning bitter, people retching blood, and the effect on animals as well as humans, suggest that this was not any type of disease known to us today.

Furthermore, several lamentation texts, such as the one

cited above, refer to a 'storm' which accompanied the invisible 'ghost'. Those who have experienced the unseen radioactive fall-out of a nuclear explosion could surely find no better terms to describe it. Let us now review the evidence of that explosion.

Sodom and Gomorrah

The Biblical tale of the destruction of Sodom and Gomorrah by fire and brimstone is familiar to most of us. But how many of us take it literally? Like many other important events in human history, the story has been relegated to 'myth' or religious symbolism. However, the Biblical account in Genesis 18–19 describes a premeditated, controllable act, by a god who did not differentiate between the people and the vegetation of the plain. This was a real event, as evidenced by the description of dense smoke rising from the land the following morning.

If we accept the story of Sodom and Gomorrah as an eye witness account, there occurred an explosion so powerful that it can be compared to the use of nuclear weapons at Hiroshima and Nagasaki in 1945.

This story is treated as myth because our paradigms do not allow the existence of nuclear weapons four thousand years ago. It is also tempting to dismiss the tale on account of the reference to Lot's wife, who turned back and became 'a pillar of salt'. However, it does not sound so ridiculous when we learn that several studies have suggested the term 'salt' to be a mistranslation. If we were able to read an original Sumerian version of the event, we would find the word NIMUR, meaning both salt and vapour.[6] Thus Lot's wife may have become 'a pillar of vapour'.

Several ancient texts have now been discovered, paralleling the Biblical narrative, but predating it. These accounts

provide additional background details which are lacking in
the Old Testament. One of the earliest Sumerian texts
clearly parallels the Biblical destruction of the evil cities
by fire and brimstone:

> Lord, bearer of the Scorcher
> that burnt up the adversary;
> who obliterated the disobedient land;
> who withered the life of Evil Word's followers;
> who rained stones and fire upon the adversaries.[7]

Who were the 'disobedient adversaries', and what was the
'Evil Word' that they followed? The full significance of the
Sodom and Gomorrah incident was revealed in a detailed
study by Zecharia Sitchin in 1985.[8]

The background to Sodom and Gomorrah was a heated
argument concerning the right of the god Marduk to return
to his city, Babylon, and assume supremacy over the gods.
Whilst Marduk's father, Enki, defended the rights of his
first-born son, the other gods were bitterly opposed, for
reasons which will become clear in due course. One god,
named Erra, vowed to use force against Marduk. A long
text known as the *Erra Epic*,[9] describes what happened
next, as a furious Erra exited from the council of gods with a
defiant promise:

> 'The lands I will destroy,
> to a dust-heap make them;
> the cities I will upheaval,
> to desolation turn them;
> the mountains I will flatten,
> their animals make disappear;
> the seas I will agitate,
> that which teems in them I will decimate;
> the people I will make vanish,
> their souls shall turn to vapour;
> none shall be spared . . .'[10]

The gods, locked in dispute, asked Anu to resolve the conflict. Anu agreed to the use of seven powerful weapons to attack Marduk, but Gibil, a brother of Marduk, warned him of Erra's plan:

> 'Those seven, in the mountain they abide,
> in a cavity inside the earth they dwell.
> From this place with a brilliance they will rush forth,
> from Earth to Heaven, clad with terror.'[11]

A god named Ishum, meaning 'Scorcher', was then appointed to join Erra in the Lower World (Africa) to prime the weapons and deliver them to their targets. Zecharia Sitchin has identified this god as Ninurta.[12] As the son of Enlil by his half-sister Ninharsag, Ninurta was the direct rival of Marduk, the son of Enki. As for Erra, there is little doubt that this god was Nergal, a god who was often referred to in ancient texts as the 'raging king', 'the violent one' and pointedly 'the one who burns', a god of war and hunting and a bringer of pestilence.[13]

It was Erra/Nergal, an embittered and jealous brother of Marduk, who assumed the most aggressive role, vowing to destroy not only Marduk and his supporters, but also his son Nabu. Erra suggested that the weapons be used against the cities of Sodom and Gomorrah where Marduk and his son Nabu were thought to be hiding, and, for reasons which will later become clear, against the Sinai space centre itself:

> 'From city to city an emissary [weapon] I will send;
> the son, seed of his father, shall not escape;
> his mother shall cease her laughter . . .
> To the place of the gods, access he shall not have;
> the place from where the Great Ones ascend
> I shall upheaval.'[14]

Ninurta tried to calm Erra with words almost identical to those used by Abraham to God in the Biblical account:

'Valiant Erra,
will you the righteous destroy with the unrighteous?
Will you destroy those who have against you sinned,
together with those who against you have not sinned?'[15]

Having agreed on a plan, the two gods then carried out the
devastating attack, Ishum to the space centre and Erra to
Sodom and Gomorrah:

Ishum to Mount Most Supreme set his course;
the awesome seven, without parallel,
trailed behind him.
At the Mount Most Supreme the hero arrived;
he raised his hand –
the Mount was smashed.

The plain by the Mount Most Supreme
he then obliterated;
in its forests not a tree stem was left standing.

Then, emulating Ishum,
Erra the King's Highway followed.
The cities he finished off,
to desolation he overturned them.
In the mountains he caused starvation,
their animals he made perish.[16]

The *Khedorlaomer Texts*[17] confirm the details of the *Erra
Epic* and summarise the destruction:

He who scorches with fire,
and he of the evil wind,
together performed their evil.
The two made the gods flee,
made them flee the scorching.

That which was raised towards Anu to launch
they caused to wither:
its face they made fade away,
its place they made desolate.[18]

According to the *Erra Epic*, the attack by Erra not only destroyed the evil cities of Sodom and Gomorrah but also created the Dead Sea as we know it today:

> He dug through the sea,
> its wholeness he divided.
> That which lives in it,
> even the crocodiles,
> he made wither,
> as with fire he scorched the animals,
> banned its grains to become as dust.[19]

Did crocodiles once live in the Dead Sea? It is no coincidence that nine hundred years earlier Gilgamesh was warned not to let his hand touch the 'waters of death', as his boat approached the far western shore of the 'Sea of the Waters of Death'.[20] In modern times it is known as the Dead Sea for a different reason – because its concentration of salt is so high that marine life cannot live in it.

Geographical Evidence

Where did the events of Sodom and Gomorrah take place? The Bible clearly identifies the Valley of Siddim with the Salt Sea, suggesting that there had once been a valley where the waters now lie.[21] Modern reference books state that the destroyed cities were indeed once situated in the area of the Dead Sea, drawing this conclusion from Greek and Roman historians, who stated that the valley was inundated after the event. It is no coincidence that the name Gomorrah came to mean 'submersion' in the Hebrew language, nor that the Bible refers to the Salt Sea as the Sea of the *Arabah*, the latter term in Hebrew meaning 'dry or burnt up', and thus commemorating the attack.[22] Can all of these sources be wrong?

More specifically, scholars locate the evil cities in the *southern part* of the Dead Sea, which to this day is called 'Lot's Sea', commemorating the man who was allowed to escape the disaster. The Bible provides a number of further clues which pinpoint the exact location: references to salt, bitumen and tar pits all fit the southern part of the Dead Sea.[23] First, this area still remains, in places, a flat salt marsh. And secondly, to this day, lumps of bitumen still float to the surface of the Dead Sea, which for this reason was called Lake Asphaltites in ancient times. In addition, the south-east shore of the Dead Sea is indeed 'well-watered' and rich in vegetation, in accordance with the Biblical description.

What *physical* evidence might prove that a nuclear explosion occurred at the Dead Sea in ancient times?

The geology of the Dead Sea is unusual. It is divided into two parts by a large peninsula called the Lisan ('the Tongue'), which reaches to within two miles of the western shore. North of the Lisan, the Dead Sea is up to 1,310 feet deep, the lowest landlocked point on Earth. To the south, in complete contrast, the waters are shallow, from only three to fifteen feet deep. Could this unusual geological feature be attributed to an explosion which breached the original Lisan and caused the previously dry 'valley of the fields' to become submerged under water?

To this day, unnatural levels of radioactivity are found in the water of springs around the southernmost edges of the Dead Sea. One study confirmed that this radioactivity was sufficiently high to 'induce sterility and allied afflictions in any animals and humans that absorbed it over a number of years'.[24] Further evidence of an explosion is being revealed by the falling level of the Dead Sea, which has in recent years dropped from 1,280 feet to 1,340 feet below sea level.[25] The shrinkage of its surface area has exposed bizarre fissures, described by one observer as 'almost architecturally articulated rock fissures'.[26]

1 Temple of Jupiter at Baalbek, Lebanon, showing lower wall of 300-ton monoliths.

2 The 3 x 800-ton Trilithon at Baalbek. Modern technology would struggle to emulate such a construction.

3 The 1,000-ton Stone of the South lies abandoned in a quarry at Baalbek. Size does not appear to have been a constraint to the builders.

4 The shattered ruins of Puma Punku near Tiwanaku, Bolivia.

5 Carved stone block at Puma Punku. The precision-made 6 mm wide groove contains equidistant, drilled holes. I defy anyone to reproduce this using stone or copper tools.

6 & 7 Engineering precision at Tiwanaku, Bolivia. Perfect edges are combined with a symmetrical curved design which flares downwards and inwards simultaneously.

8 Gateway of the Sun, Tiwanaku. The niches of this 15-ton monolith have perfect inside edges, as if carved by modern technology.

9 Another enigmatic carved stone at Tiwanaku.

10 A menacing head stares from a wall at Chavin de Huantar, Peru.

11 The Chavin de Huantar sunken plaza, looking east. A sophisticated hydraulic system moved water underneath the site.

12 A 12-angled stone in Cuzco, Peru. If the Incas built walls such as this, where did all their expert stonemasons disappear to?

13 Sacsayhuaman, Peru. Did these walls protect a site of the gods?

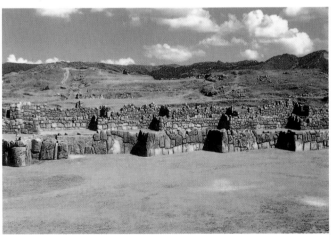

14 A 120-ton stone in a wall at Sacsayhuaman. Why did the builders not make their lives easier with two smaller stones?

15 The precision-carved Inca's Throne at Sacsayhuaman.

16 This huge structure at Ollantaytambo, Peru, has no apparent purpose.

17 JFK Memorial in Dallas - another piece of architecture with no apparent purpose. Was Ollantaytambo (above) a memorial to a god?

18 Megalithic stonework on the mountainside at Ollantaytambo. The stones were miraculously transported from the opposite mountain.

19 An amazing monolith at Ollantaytambo. Carved with stone tools?

20 The Terrace of Ten Niches, Ollantaytambo. One of the most elegant examples of pre-Incan stonework.

21 Machu Picchu, Peru. In the background stands the mountain of Huayna Picchu.

22 The Temple of the Three Windows at Machu Picchu - an important location in Andean prehistory.

23 The Principal Temple at Machu Picchu, with its enigmatic niches and pegs.

24 The Intihuatana at Machu Picchu. Astronomers believe it was aligned to the Sun in the era 2300-2100 BC.

25 The Torreon at Machu Picchu is also thought to have astronomical alignments.

26 V-shaped groove pointing due south from Huayna Picchu to the Intihuatana.

27 The Nazca Plain, southern Peru. Until now, no single theory has explained all of its strange markings.

28 The Pyramids of Giza, Egypt c. 10450 BC.

29 The Bent Pyramid at Dahshur c. 2600 BC. The steep 52-degree angle of the Giza pyramids was never successfully copied by the pharaohs.

30 The 15-feet high Niche in the Queen's Chamber of the Great Pyramid. Until now, it has been assumed that this niche once contained a statue.

31 King's Chamber coffer, Great Pyramid.

32 The author in the mysterious Grand Gallery of the Great Pyramid. The corbels and niches are not decorative, but form part of a highly functional design.

33 Great Subterranean Chamber of the Great Pyramid. Its carved features have been highly eroded by rainwater.

34 Narmer Tablet, Cairo Museum, showing pyramid symbol in top left corner.

35 A huge Trilithon at Stonehenge, England c. 2300 BC. Each upright weighs around 50 tons.

36 The distant Heel Stone marks the axis of Stonehenge, aligned to the summer solstice.

37 The Sarsen Circle c. 2700 BC. If Stonehenge was simply a solar-lunar observatory, why did the builders go to so much trouble?

38 A Mayan observatory at Chichen Itza, Mexico.

39 Sumerian ziggurat at Ur, third millennium BC. The Sumerians claimed their knowledge was a "gift from the gods".

40 Akkadian cylinder seal showing undiscovered planet in the Solar System.

41 Ancient planisphere, British Museum, showing route map of the gods into the Solar System.

42 The unusual "Tomb of Noah" at Karak Nuh, Lebanon. The tale of Noah and the Flood now has a scientific basis.

43 The sacred mountain of Jebel Barkal in Sudan. Geologists cannot explain the huge scar and blackened stones - evidence of an unnatural catastrophic impact.

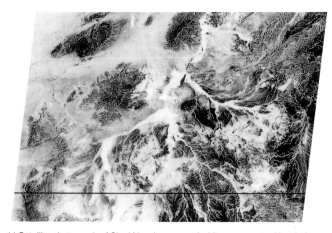

44 Satellite photograph of Sinai showing unusual white scar, centred just below the 30th parallel (marked).

45 Blackened boulders, Sinai.

46 Burnt stones cover the lighter-coloured subsoil, Sinai.

47 The Sphinx at Giza marks a new era c. 8700 BC.

49 Ram-headed sphinx at Karnak, Egypt.

48 Geological weathering provides a major clue to the Sphinx's antiquity.

50 St Catherine's Monastery.
The nearby Mt St Catherine is
geographically related to Giza
and Baalbek.

51 Naram-Sin Stele, Louvre
Museum, showing capture of
rocket-like object.

52 Dome of the Rock at
Jerusalem, Israel. This sacred
site dates back to c. 8700 BC.

53 The beautifully carved
Treasury at Petra, Jordan, may
have its roots in the Biblical tale
of Lot.

54 The moai statues of Easter Island. No-one knows how 10-ton hats were fitted onto their heads.

55 The Candelabra/Trident at Paracas, Peru. The trident is a well-known symbol of an ancient god.

56 Olmec head weighing 24 tons at La Venta Park, Mexico. Negroid features seem far from home in the Americas c. 1500 BC.

57 Olmec carving at La Venta shows a helmeted figure emerging from a cave.

58 Sarcophagus lid from the tomb of Pacal at Palenque, Mexico. A crouching figure operates a complex machine.

59 Teotihuacan, Mexico, showing the Street of the Dead and the Pyramid of the Moon.

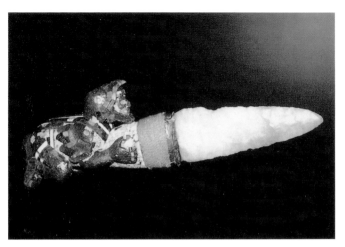

60 Aztec ceremonial knife, British Museum. The handle depicts a flying god.

61 Aztec Sun Stone records the catastrophes of the past and predicts a future destruction by fire.

62 El Castillo pyramid at Chichen Itza, Mexico.

63 Sleeping god on a raft of snakes at Budhanilkantha, Nepal. The arrival of this god in Nepal matches the departure of an identical god from Mexico.

What about the high salt concentration, more than five times the normal level? This is actually caused by the absence of any outlet from the Dead Sea other than by evaporation. The 6.5 million tons of fresh water which pour in every day from the Jordan River erode natural salt from the Dead Sea floor, which cannot evaporate, and this increases the salt concentration. But here is a strange fact. In October 1993, it was announced that Israeli and German scientists would attempt to take samples of sediments from beneath the Dead Sea, using the latest drilling technology. Previous attempts had failed due to an extremely hard layer of rock salt, only a few feet beneath the bottom of the Sea.[27] What unnatural event could have formed a crust of rock salt so hard that modern technology struggled to penetrate it?

Now let us move south to an even more dramatic proof of ancient nuclear weapons. Zecharia Sitchin has highlighted an enormous geological scar on the Sinai peninsula, exactly where the space centre of the gods ought to be.[28] This scar is visible from high above the Earth, appearing as a mysterious white patch. Following up on Sitchin's claim, I obtained a *close-up* satellite photo of the scar, showing an area 112 by 112 miles – Plate 44, colour section. Whilst the thousands of tiny lines are wadis (dry riverbeds), no scientific explanation of the bright scar (situated bottom, left of centre) has ever been forthcoming.

Furthermore, in the eastern Sinai, millions of blackened stones are found strewn for tens of miles. These stones are, without any doubt, unnatural. The expeditions to the Sinai by Nelson Glueck in the 1950s highlighted the existence of numerous blackened rocks, scattered across the landscape.[29] These rocks have more recently come to the attention of Emmanuel Anati, who was attracted to the region by his interest in rock art. Following his first expedition in 1955, Anati carried out several field trips to the site of Har Karkom (Jebel Ideid), a sacred mountain from the third millennium BC. Anati's book, *The Mountain of God*, shows many boulders, several feet in diameter, on which ancient travellers have etched various signs and symbols (Plate 45). Anati's photographs clearly demonstrate that the rocks are blackened only on the surface.[30]

Emmanuel Anati also describes the large mountain plateau of Har Karkom as covered in an expanse of black stone fragments, known as 'hamada'. In some places, the hamada has been cleared in ancient times to form so-called 'hut circles'. Again, Anati's photographs (Plate 46) demonstrate that the blackened stones are a thin surface layer. The ground beneath is a hard light-brown coloured surface, which from the air reflects the sunlight to create the appearance of bright white patches.

What do the geologists have to say about the blackened rocks in the Sinai? They admit that they resemble *volcanic* rock, and yet this cannot be so, since there are no volcanoes anywhere near the Sinai. These stones are an anomaly – an impossibility that cannot be explained by conventional science. Due to the perceived 'impossibility' of nuclear weapons four thousand years ago, the debate goes no further.

But it cannot be denied that the black, charred rocks are there in the Sinai, as is the enormous scar. The only possible explanation is that provided by Zecharia Sitchin – an unnatural explosion. In this context, everything begins to make sense. The incontrovertible physical evidence not only confirms the reliability of the *Erra Epic*, but also the reliability of all the other evidence in chapter 8 which identified the Sinai as the geographic location of the space centre.

Chronologically, the destruction of the space centre, Sodom and Gomorrah and the fall of Sumer can all be tied together *c.* 2000 BC (the era of Abraham). The Sumerian lamentation texts clearly link the 'evil wind' to the events in Sinai, by their references to 'a great storm directed from Anu', a 'storm in a flash of lightning created' and by stating '*in the west* it was spawned'.[31] The Dead Sea and the space centre in Sinai are indeed located to the *west* of Sumer. Other references pinpoint the Sinai specifically: 'from the midst of the mountains it had descended upon the land, from the Plain of No Pity it hath come'.[32]

It only remains to offer a convincing explanation of why the gods permitted such extreme force to be used. In order to understand the full story of how the gods decided to sabotage their own space facilities, we must begin with the Tower of Babel incident in which the god Marduk attempted to rebuild his pre-Flood city in Sumer.

The Tower of Babel

I have, in earlier chapters, described the succession rules of the gods, which caused such deep resentment between the two brothers Enki and Enlil, and consequently between their respective descendants. Prior to the Flood, this resentment appears not to have broken out into open conflict. After the Flood, however, when the Earth was redivided, territorial disputes arose to prompt a bitter war of the gods, the evidence for which we have seen at the Great Pyramid and Jebel Barkal.

As a result of that war, supremacy among the gods lay with Enlil and particularly his firstborn son Ninurta. In due course, when the flooding had subsided sufficiently from the Tigris-Euphrates plains, the gods decided to re-establish there the olden cities in their original locations. But this territory was now assigned to the Enlilite gods. Of the Enkiites, only Enki himself, by prior agreement, was allowed to rebuild his pre-Flood city (Eridu). Marduk's pleas to rebuild his pre-Flood city of Babylon were met with no sympathy whatsoever.

It would appear that the Biblical account of the Tower of Babel has its roots in this conflict.[33] Marduk, as the chief god of Babylon in later times, is the likely perpetrator, but what was the nature of the 'Tower'? Remembering (from chapter 6), that a *shem* means 'sky vehicle' rather than 'name', let us re-examine what Marduk's supporters were up to, by correcting the translation of the Biblical account:

> 'Come let us build ourselves a city,
> with a tower that reaches to the heavens,
> so that we may make a *shem* for ourselves.'[34]

It now becomes apparent that Marduk's plans were both ambitious and controversial. Furthermore, Zecharia Sitchin has highlighted the existence of an Akkadian text, which parallels the Bible's account of what happened next.[35] Various clues in that text confirm that Marduk was the rebel, whilst the most telling verse identifies the Biblical 'God' as Enlil, who:

> To their stronghold tower, in the night,
> a complete end he made.
> In his anger, a command he also poured out:
> to scatter abroad was his decision.
> He gave a command their counsels to confuse.
> . . . their course he stopped.[36]

It is not at all clear whether the languages of mankind were actually changed during this incident, but the Akkadian tale does confirm that Marduk's people were indeed scattered. However, in contrast to general perceptions of the Biblical account, the Tower of Babel must be seen here as a fairly localised incident, which only affected one relatively small group of people.

What was the chronology of the Tower of Babel incident? Zecharia Sitchin dates it shortly prior to Marduk's return to his Egyptian homelands, where he was known by the name Ra. The latter event can be dated very roughly to around 3450 BC, the time when Egypt entered 350 years of chaos prior to the beginning of its civilisation *c.* 3100 BC.[37] The incident at Babylon would certainly not have been any earlier than that of the first Sumerian cities of Eridu and Nippur. Thus we can place it with some confidence between 3800–3450 BC.

Following the war of the gods, in which Marduk led the Enkiite forces, a condition of the peace treaty was that his pacifist brother, Thoth, be placed in charge of Egypt. By now, however, Thoth had long stepped down, allowing various other gods and demi-gods to rule the land. The opportunity existed for an embittered Marduk to return to Egypt and vent his frustration. It is highly likely that Marduk/Ra's return to Egypt coincided with the death of Dumuzi, whose tragic tale was related in chapter 6. If Marduk assumed power in Egypt at that time, he was doing so in defiance of the peace treaty, and his authority was arguably illegal. We can now begin to understand why Dumuzi's accidental death resulted in such a harsh punishment for Marduk.

It would seem that, following his escape from the Pyramid, Marduk went into a self-imposed exile as Amen ('the Hidden One') to his supporters and *persona non grata* to his enemies. His principal enemy was Inanna, who, as a result of her husband Dumuzi's death, had turned from a goddess of love to a goddess of war, with a bitter hatred of Marduk. Inanna had always had ambitions, but now those ambitions were intensified. As described in chapter 6, she was not satisfied with her dominion over the new Indus Valley civilisation, nor with her low-ranking Sumerian city of Uruk. In approximately 2350 BC, her powerful ambitions were fulfilled. Armed with the enigmatic 'MEs' which she had dispossessed from Enki, she found a man whom she named Sharru-kin ('Righteous Ruler'). This man, known to us as Sargon, was the founder of the Akkadian empire and its capital city Agade.

As Inanna strove to build a powerful new kingdom in Mesopotamia, Marduk could only watch from the sidelines with growing frustration. Convinced of his own innocence, and angry at the refusal of the gods to permit his city to be rebuilt at Babylon, he consoled himself with the belief that a 'destiny-determining time' would come, when he would return to Babylon, overturn Inanna's supremacy, and claim Lordship over the gods. As we shall see in the next chapter, this 'destiny-determining time' was not a whimsical dream but a scientific reality. And the timing of the Akkadian empire can thus be seen as a deliberate attempt by Inanna to counter the ambitions of her arch enemy.

Inanna's Conquests

Circa 2350 BC, Sargon, assisted by Inanna, began to build a mighty empire throughout Mesopotamia. In so doing, he took great care not to alienate the other gods of the Near East. Initially, his conquests avoided Enlil's city of Nippur, Ninurta's city of Lagash, the disputed site of Babylon and the strategic sites of the gods at Jerusalem and Baalbek. Then, in his old age, he made the fatal mistake of removing 'sacred soil' from Babylon to somehow 'legitimise' Inanna's city of Agade.

It would seem that this sacrilegious act prompted Marduk's return to Babylon. The ancient texts state that Marduk destroyed Sargon's people by hunger, and afflicted Sargon himself with a 'restlessness' that led to his death after a reign of 54 years.[38]

Reassembling his scattered people, Marduk rebuilt Babylon and, according to the ancient texts, constructed a sophisticated waterworks system. This is an interesting detail, since the site of eighteenth century BC Babylon does indeed lie underneath the present-day water table, preventing its excavation.[39] It is my view that Marduk avoided this flooding by pumping water out of Babylon into the surrounding areas. The surrounding cities quickly grew reliant upon these fresh supplies of water from Babylon, since the average rainfall in Babylonia has been negligible since time immemorial.[40] Indeed, without irrigation canals and the flooding of the rivers, Babylonia would have been a barren desert.

Marduk's supporters continued to fight fierce battles with Sargon's successors, and the council of gods, in a bid to avoid further armed confrontation, sent Nergal, a brother of Marduk, to persuade him to leave Babylon. Nergal provided Marduk with convincing evidence that his 'destiny-determining time' had not yet come.[41] Marduk eventually agreed to leave, but on the condition that no-one interfered with Babylon's waterworks system:

> 'On the day I step off my seat,
> the flooding shall from its well cease to work . . .
> The waters shall not rise . . .
> the bright day to darkness [shall turn] . . .
> Confusion shall arise . . .
> the winds of draught shall howl . . .
> sicknesses shall spread.'[42]

After Marduk's departure, Nergal entered the secret chambers of Babylon and, in a surprising act of animosity, upset the precious waterworks. As forewarned, there was a serious drought in the surrounding cities. Nergal ended up being severely chastised by the elder gods.

Around 2250 BC, following Marduk's departure from Babylon, and the ensuing drought, Inanna once again decided to flex her muscles – this time with the grandson of Sargon, called Naram-Sin.[43] His name clearly indicates that Inanna had won the support of her uncle, the god Nannar/Sin.

This time it would seem that Inanna was determined to see just how far she could extend her powers. The Mesopotamian texts provide a long list of Naram-Sin's conquests, including Jericho, Baalbek, Dilmun-land (Sinai) and finally Egypt.

Is there any historic corroboration of Naram-Sin's conquests? Archaeology has confirmed that the era of Jericho in the third millennium BC ended in destruction.[44] The attack upon Baalbek, where Inanna reportedly burned down its gates and held its defenders under siege, could well explain the abandoned quarry work which can still be seen at the site today – a feature that no-one has ever ventured to explain. In Egypt too, an incursion by foreigners is confirmed at this time in history by a long poem known as 'the Admonitions of Ipuwer'.[45]

As for Naram-Sin's alleged conquest of the Sinai space centre, could this incident be the one commemorated on the famous stele of Naram-Sin, now on display at the Louvre Museum in Paris?[46] The central feature in Plate 51 (see colour section), which many believe to be a mountain, looks more like the rockets with which Dilmun land was associated. The horned tiara, worn by the victorious Naram-Sin, was a symbol of the gods, and suggests that this was a victory in the most sacred region where gods alone were allowed to rule.

It would seem, however, that Naram-Sin made one conquest too many. Whether it was the space centre, the Enkiite territories or both, we cannot be sure, but the council of the gods decided to arrest Inanna and put an end to her aggrandisement. A Sumerian poem known as *The Curse of Agade* relates that Inanna fled from her city Agade. The gods then stripped the city of its powers, possibly including some of the 'MEs' stolen from Enki:

The crownband of lordship, the tiara of kingship,
the throne given to rulership,
Ninurta brought over to his temple;
Utu carried off the city's 'Eloquence',
Enki withdrew its 'Wisdom'.
Its Awesomeness that could reach the Heaven,
Anu brought up to the midst of Heaven.[47]

The texts state that Marduk's brother Nergal had also assisted the conquests of Naram-Sin, and thus acted in an unlikely alliance with Inanna to prevent Marduk's return.[48] We can only guess at the reasons for this brotherly enmity. Shortly afterwards, Inanna and Nergal staged a major revolt against the authority of the elder gods, a revolt which ended in failure and the catastrophic destruction of Agade.

The Curse of Agade blames the destruction of Agade on Naram-Sin, who allegedly attacked Enlil's city, Nippur, desecrating its sacred Ekur.[49] We know from a Sumerian poem entitled *Hymn to Enlil* that this Ekur was the resting place for 'a fast stepping bird' from whose 'grasp no-one can escape', and the spot from where he could 'raise the beams that search the heart of all the lands'.[50] The attack was thus not just a symbolic insult to the highest god on Earth, but also a physical disabling of his powers.

According to *The Curse of Agade*, the gods wiped Agade from the face of the Earth. The hordes of Guti were then ordered by Enlil to leave their homelands in the Zagros Mountains and subjugate Inanna's supporters. The Akkadian empire disintegrated and the central administration fell into a state of anarchy. Did the gods really have a hand in this? It is a fact that Agade is one of the few ancient Mesopotamian cities whose location has never been discovered by the archaeologists,[51] whilst historians are puzzled at the fall of such a mighty empire which collapsed *c.* 2200 BC as suddenly as it had once begun.[52]

Battles of the Kings

The Guti occupied Mesopotamia for around a century, but left little trace of their culture.[53] Meanwhile, between 2200–2100 BC, several Sumerian and Elamite cities declared their independence, and entered a new era of prosperity that would prove to be their swansong.

The Elamite state of Ninurta was first to emerge as a dominant force, centred on its capital city of Susa in southeast Mesopotamia. Its powerful defences and highly-trained army had enabled it to escape conquest by military alliance with Naram-Sin.[54] However, after Naram-Sin's death, its ruler Puzur-Inshushinak declared independence and, to emphasise the point, assumed the title 'King of the Universe'.

The Sumerian renaissance began at Lagash, whose famous ruler, Gudea, reigned early in the 22nd century BC. This king embarked on a massive programme of temple restoration, and took Sumerian culture to new heights.[55] Lagash, however, was destined to remain a religious centre, with no aspirations for political control over a new Sumerian empire.

Shortly afterwards, the city of Ur arose as the new Sumerian capital. The famous (and final) Third Dynasty of Ur took Sumerian achievements to new heights in art, foreign trade and temple-building. The god in charge was Nannar/Sin, a move perhaps aimed at keeping his niece Inanna in check.

We now enter a period where historic dates can be established with a high degree of accuracy. Ur's first ruler Ur-Nammu is generally dated to *c.* 2112 BC.[56] Ur-Nammu instigated a new legal and moral code, and began a restoration programme throughout Sumer which returned the temples of the gods, including the Ekur at Nippur, to their former glories. Not only the temples had to be restored but also the trust of the people in their gods. After two hundred years of chaos, the people of Mesopotamia had become independent and unruly. Sumerian texts record that Ur-Nammu was given a remit by Enlil to bring these rebellious city-states to heel.[57]

Unfortunately, just as the Sumerians began to find new faith in their gods, disaster struck again. Their king, Ur-Nammu, fell from his chariot in the middle of battle, and was 'abandoned on the battlefield like a crushed vessel'.[58]

The new ruler of Ur, c. 2094–2047 BC, was named Shulgi.[59] Towards the end of his reign we see the first signs of trouble for the last Sumerian dynasty. Shulgi became engaged in a series of battles to put down uprisings in the outer provinces, c. 2054–2047 BC. In order to strengthen his position, he obtained by the marriage of his daughter, an alliance with the Elamites.[60] In exchange for control of the city of Larsa, Shulgi engaged the services of the notorious Elamite troops as a kind of foreign legion under the command of Khedorlaomer.[61]

Where was Marduk at this time? According to Zecharia Sitchin's chronology, in 2048 BC Marduk was about to enter the land of Hatti (the land of the Hittites in Anatolia) where he would rest for 24 years, awaiting a 'favourable omen' for his return to Babylon.[62] The presence of an Egyptian god in Anatolia at this time is indeed confirmed by the archaeological record. At the site of Alaca Huyuk (an important city dating to at least 2500 BC) the entrance to the city was found to be flanked by Egyptian-style sphinxes, dating to around 2000 BC.[63]

After Shulgi's death c. 2047 BC, his son Amar-Sin[64] faced a continuing struggle to assert the authority of Ur, and the Sumerian texts record in the seventh year of his reign, c. 2040 BC, a major campaign to subdue an uprising in four western lands.[65] The despatch by Amar-Sin of troops under Khedorlaomer to quell the rebellion is dealt with both in the

Old Testament and in the *Khedorlaomer Texts*, which both confirm the rebellion as taking place in the thirteenth year of rule from Ur.[66]

What was the cause of the rebellion? The *Khedorlaomer Texts* make it clear that the rebellion was a change of allegiance from Sin, the god of Ur, to Nabu, the son of Marduk. Sin's son, Shamash claimed that the people had betrayed their covenant with his father:

> 'The faithfulness of his heart [the king] betrayed
> in the time of the thirteenth year
> a falling-out against my father [he had];
> to his faith-keeping the king ceased to attend;
> all this Nabu has caused to happen.'[67]

The change of allegiance to Nabu in Canaan is commemorated today by the various names in the region – Mount Nebo to the north-east of the Dead Sea, and the large town of Nabulus to the north-west. In later times, the name Nabu took on the meaning 'speaker/announcer/prophet',[68] reflecting the role that Marduk's son had played in stirring up the rebellion.

But what was the nature of this rebellion that caused it to be preserved in history as such a major event? The answer comes from a scrutiny of the battle which took place in the following year. According to Genesis 14:

> In the fourteenth year, Khedorlaomer and the kings allied with him went out and defeated the Rephaites in Ashteroth Karnaim, the Zuzites in Ham, the Emites in Shaveh Kiriathaim and the Horites in the hill country of Seir, *as far as El Paran near the desert*. They then turned back and went to En Mishpat (that is, Kadesh), and they conquered the whole territory of the Amalekites, as well as the Amorites . . .[69] (emphasis added)

This sequence of battles is also confirmed by the *Khedorlaomer Texts*. It is only *after* this gruelling tour that the kings of the east finally confront the kings of the evil cities whom they had been sent to punish. So why the delay, and why waste their time with a long out-of-the-way excursion into the desert?[70] As Zecharia Sitchin has pointed out, the only possible significance of El Paran (Nakhl) and Kadesh-Barnea is their strategic location in the restricted land of the gods – the space centre in the Sinai desert. Why else would the invaders target an oasis town in the middle of nowhere?

A Sumerian cylinder seal cited by Zecharia Sitchin (Figure 17, black-and-white section, with emphasis added) gives a remarkably accurate visual portrayal of the space centre incident, although my interpretation differs from that of Sitchin.[71] It is my conclusion that the Canaanite kings, incited by Nabu, had marched south to occupy the space centre. Then, when they heard of the formidable strength of the approaching eastern alliance, led by Khedorlaomer, they fled to Kadesh-Barnea. Thus did the invaders turn back from Nakhl to Kadesh, as described in Genesis 14, in order to pursue their fleeing enemy.

From Kadesh, the kings of the east chased the kings of the west back to the Valley of Siddim, where the latter were forced to make a stand in their homeland and were heavily defeated.[72] The cylinder seal shown in Illustration 17 identifies the space centre location by the sign of Sin's crescent moon and a tower with wings. However, there is no battle scene (as suggested by Sitchin) but only a depiction of four kings marching in and five kings marching out in the opposite direction.

My interpretation of these events illustrates the desire of Marduk to take possession of the space centre in addition to his return to Babylon. This is vital to an understanding of the extreme actions which were later taken against him and his son Nabu. According to Zecharia Sitchin's chronology, it was a mere 16 years later that Marduk returned to Babylon and the nuclear weapons were used. During those sixteen years, the last two kings of Ur, Shu-Sin c. 2037–2029

BC[73] and Ibbi-Sin *c*. 2028–2024 BC[74] turned to desperate defensive measures to protect a crumbling empire in times of great uncertainty.

Significantly, Shu-Sin put down an uprising at Mardin in southern Turkey – by now Marduk's territory. *Circa* 2034 BC, he then built a fortress to assist the defence of Sumerian territories against the Amorites.[75]

Early in the reign of Ibbi-Sin, the Third Dynasty of Ur literally disintegrated.[76] The last records of Sumer describe numerous oracles of imminent invasion from the west, the cessation of tributes from the outer provinces and finally the cessation of foreign commerce in the third year of Ibbi-Sin's reign.[77] No inscriptions of his reign have been found beyond the fifth year, *c*. 2024 BC. In that year, a prince by the name of Ishbi-Irra instigated a rebellion in the key city of Mari, which protected the western approach to Sumer. Ibbi-Sin's last records spoke of a deep penetration by the Amorites into Sumerian territories.[78]

Marduk's Return

The Sumerian texts state that the chaotic final battle for Sumer was fought and lost by Elamite troops against the overwhelming numbers of invading Amorites. These Amorites were destined to become the first dynasty of the new kingdom of Babylon. Who were these Amorites, and why did they support Marduk?

Since the invasion of Sumer came from the west, it is not very helpful to find that the term Amorite, derived from the Akkadian word *Amurru*, simply means 'Westerners'. Biblical studies, however, have identified the Amorites as the dominant tribe among the Canaanites, and thus descended from the line of Ham.[79] The final battle was thus based on racial loyalties – Shemitic easterners[80] defending their territory against Hamitic Africans who were supporting an African god, Marduk.

By the same token, we would expect the native Egyptians to rally to Marduk's cause. What then was happening in Egypt *c*. 2024 BC? This date falls between the end of the Old Kingdom *c*. 2100 BC and the beginning of the Middle Kingdom *c*. 2000 BC.[81] Egyptologists refer to this time gap as the 'First Intermediate Period' (FIP), signifying a time of chaos, during which the country was divided between rival dynasties. The collapse of the Old Kingdom is generally attributed to 'social revolution',[82] and as I shall suggest in a later chapter, it is likely that these first Egyptian pharaohs were in fact Sumerians. Was the timing of the FIP simply a coincidence, or could it have signified an internal rebellion by the native Africans in preparation for Marduk's return to power?

Closer inspection of the Egyptian situation confirms that the rebels were based in the south at Thebes, which was indeed the centre of worship of Marduk as Amen, 'the Hidden One'. Their faithful support of Marduk has been commemorated in the world *aman*, which was preserved in the Hebrew language with the literal meaning 'to build/ support' and figuratively 'to be firm/faithful'. Geographically, these supporters were expanding northwards, towards the delta area and *the Sinai peninsula*. Would Marduk once again attempt to take control of the space centre?

The exile of Marduk is described in a partly damaged tablet, found in the great library of Ashurbanipal. Its significance went unnoticed until Zecharia Sitchin placed it into historical context – a final countdown of 24 years from 2028 to 2004 BC, at which time Marduk finally returned to Babylon:

'I am the divine Marduk, a great god.
I was cast off for my sins,
to the mountains I have gone.

In many lands I have been a wanderer:
from where the sun rises to where it sets I went.
To the heights of Hatti-land I went.
In Hatti-land I asked an oracle
[about] my throne and my Lordship;
in its midst [I asked] 'Until when?'
24 years in its midst I rested.

'My days [of exile] were completed;
I raised my heels toward Babylon,
through the lands I went to my city;
a king in Babylon to make the foremost,
in its midst my temple-mountain to heaven raise.'[83]

The ancient texts record a short-lived victory for Marduk. In the chaos of battle, various temples were destroyed, including the shrine of Enlil at Nippur. Enlil, who was somewhere 'loftily enthroned', sped back to Sumer and demanded an explanation. Although the Babylonian accounts blamed the desecration on the god Erra (Nergal), other gods accused Marduk of the sacrilegious act.

It was at this time that the council of gods met to decide what action to take, and at this council that the god Erra stormed out with a promise of vengeance. And, chronologically, it was at this time and in this context, that another deity, the Biblical 'God', decided to drop in on the city of Sodom 'to see if what they have done is as bad as the outcry that has reached me'.[84] The outcome, as discussed earlier, was the destruction of Sodom and Gomorrah, and the Sinai space centre.

At this point it should be recalled that the change of allegiance of the 'evil cities' had occurred 17 years previously, in 2041 BC, and been dealt with by Khedorlaomer. The destruction of Sodom and Gomorrah was thus a different punishment for a separate incident.

What was the second crime of Sodom and Gomorrah, the 'outcry' of which had reached the ears of God? In view of the previous attempt of the Canaanite kings to seize the space centre, and in view of the expansionist threat from Marduk's supporters in northern Egypt, there can surely be only one conclusion – the kings of Sodom and Gomorrah were once again preparing an army to march on the space centre.

It is against this background that one must understand the radical decision of the gods to use nuclear weapons against Marduk and his son Nabu. We can only speculate on what Marduk might have intended to do with the space centre, but the texts related that he and Nabu must be stopped at all costs.

What happened to Marduk and Nabu? One of the aims of Erra/Nergal was to kill them both, but according to the ancient texts they were both warned of the attack on Sodom and Gomorrah and thus escaped. Nevertheless, it would seem that Nergal may have had another attempt. A mere 50 miles to the north, in a separate incident, also dated to *c.* 2000 BC, the town of Tell Ghassul was utterly destroyed. So powerful was the force used, that this town was once thought to be the site of ancient Sodom.[85] Archaeologists have been unable to explain the cause of the extensive damage and the thousands of blackened stones which they found strewn across the site. Once again, however, Marduk and Nabu escaped. According to legend, Nabu became the god of a Mediterranean island, whilst Marduk himself was finally allowed to assume the Lordship of the gods from Babylon.

Abraham the Spy

Earlier we noted the presence of Abraham at Sodom and Gomorrah, and he was also in Canaan during the Battle of the Kings. Who exactly was the Biblical patriarch, Abraham, and what role did he play in this crucial period of the world's history? Most scholars have overlooked or discarded the possibility that, since Abraham came from Ur, he might actually have been a native of Ur. Several studies have indeed concluded that he was a Sumerian.[86]

A major clue to Abraham's Sumerian origin is his original name AB.RAM, which carried a clear meaning, 'Father's Beloved', in the Sumerian language.[87] Another clue exists in the Biblical term 'Ibri' with which Abraham's family identified themselves.[88] This term, the origin of the word 'Hebrew', is usually translated as 'wanderers' or 'those who crossed over', but in Sumerian it meant 'natives of IBR'.[89] The place name IBR is indeed linked to the verb ibri, meaning 'to cross', but as one authority has pointed out, it is also closely connected to the original Sumerian name for the city of Nippur, NI.IB.RU, literally translated as 'The Crossing Place'.[90] We encountered this city in chapter 8 as the original mission control centre of the gods, and it thus took its name from the planet NI-BIRU, the 'Planet of Crossing'.

The Biblical Ibri are therefore the Sumerian 'ni-ib-ri' – the natives of Nippur. And Nippur was Sumer's foremost religious city. Nor did Abraham come from a family that were typical Nippurians. On the contrary, the evidence suggests that he was from the most noble, priestly class.[91] The ease with which Abraham commanded respect, even in foreign lands, tends to support this view.[92]

What was a Nippurian priest doing in Ur? The obvious conclusion is that the move coincided with the rise of the Third Dynasty of Ur under Ur-Nammu in 2113 BC. The Sumerian texts record that Enlil, the god of Nippur, had entrusted the safe-keeping of his city to Sin, the god of Ur. The timing of Terah and Abraham's departure from Ur to Harran would have been close to the time when Ur-Nammu came to his untimely end, c. 2095 BC.

Let us take a closer look at Abraham's role after he left Ur. First, his family was ordered to Harran – a town which has been identified by archaeologists in the foothills of the Taurus Mountains.[93] Then, when he was 75, Abraham was told by 'God' to leave Harran.[94] His route took him through Canaan, where God appeared to him, and he then built an 'altar' where he 'called on the name of the Lord'.[95] His journey then continued to the Negev – the arid region bordering on the Sinai – and from there into northern Egypt.[96] According to the Book of Jubilees, his stay in Egypt lasted 5 years. Working backwards from Abraham's age of 99 in 2024 BC, he was born in 2123 BC, and thus his period in Egypt encompassed the years 2048–2043 BC.

According to the Old Testament, Abraham's first action back in Canaan was to approach the altar he had built and again 'call on the name of the Lord'.[97] The year was approximately 2042 BC, just one year before the Canaanite kings rebelled against Sin, and thus a time when Nabu would have been actively lobbying for their support.

In 2040 BC, following the Battle of the Kings, Abraham demonstrated the alliance he had forged with the local nobility. He took 318 trained Amorite soldiers and rescued Lot from the homebound kings of the east – quite an achievement at the grand old age of 83! Three years later Hagar bore him a son, Ishmael. The Biblical record is then blank until 13 years later, when at age 99, Abraham entered a covenant with God, who promised him a child the following year (another fine achievement!). Before that year had passed,[98] Sodom and Gomorrah were destroyed; the date was 2024 BC.

Thus, as the Amorites invaded Abraham's homeland to the east, God promised to Abraham's descendants the lands of the west. Was Abraham simply a pawn in the game, or did he earn his prize? Let us now review his movements in the context of the threat from Marduk.

First, Abraham moved to Harran, the northernmost outpost of Ur, on the border with the Hittite lands, where Marduk was shortly to arrive. In 2048 BC, the same year that Marduk arrived for his 24-year stay, Abraham left Harran but his father stayed behind. This move may have been prompted by the death of Shulgi, king of Ur, and the prospect of further turmoil in his empire's western provinces. In any event, Abraham headed for Egypt and consulted with the northern pharaohs who were desperately resisting Marduk's supporters in the south. Can it then be a coincidence that Abraham returned to Canaan only one year before the rebellion of the kings?

I do not subscribe to the view which has been expressed by Zecharia Sitchin that Abraham played a military role in the Battle of the Kings.[99] As I suggested earlier, there was no battle in the Sinai, only a tactical withdrawal. Abraham's military involvement, as it appears in the Bible, is restricted only to the subsequent rescue of his nephew Lot, in what was probably a surprise raid. There is nothing to suggest anything beyond that. However, there *is* evidence to suggest that his role was one of *espionage*.

At a time of great uncertainty for the Third Dynasty of Ur, its god, Sin, would have found it extremely useful to have a trusted pair of eyes and ears in the lands of the unstable western provinces, particularly as he feared an imminent return of Marduk from the west. There is no doubt that such a spy existed in Canaan, for the Bible records the fact:

> Then the Lord said: 'The outcry against Sodom and Gomorrah is so great and their sin so grievous that I will go down and see if what they have done is as bad *as the outcry that has reached me*.'[100] (emphasis added)

Having gained the confidence of the Canaanite kings, Abraham was in a perfect position to report on the political situation and possible troop movements. I have suggested earlier that Nabu motivated the kings of the west to form an army to capture the space centre in the Sinai in 2041 BC. It was at that exact time that Abraham returned to Canaan to watch what they were up to. The 'altar' which Abraham built in Canaan, where he called on the name of the Lord, was thus a means to keep Sin informed of events.

The Petra Connection

After the destruction of Sodom and Gomorrah, the other cities of the plain, and the space centre, the repercussions spread far and wide. The nuclear fall-out in Sumer caused many survivors to become refugees. Their migrations were accompanied by a high level of culture and technology, hence explaining many of the mysterious breakthroughs *c.* 2000 BC which archaeologists have uncovered all over the world. We will discuss some of these migrations further in chapter 15. However, whilst some Sumerians fled thousands of miles, others preferred to stay closer to home. One such refugee was Abraham's nephew Lot:

> Lot and his two daughters left Zoar and settled in the mountains, for he was afraid to stay in Zoar. He and his two daughters lived in a cave. One day the older daughter said to the younger: 'Our father is old, and there is no man around here to lie with us, as is the custom all over the earth. Let's get our father to drink wine and then lie with him and preserve our family line through our father.'[101]

This incestuous tale of Lot and his daughters demonstrates the scale of the catastrophe which had befallen the region. Although the gods sometimes practised similar acts of incest, it was not a widely accepted custom of the people at that time. It can be understood only in the aftermath of a nuclear explosion. We ourselves might contemplate unthinkable acts only in the most extreme circumstances; examples of cannibalism by survivors of plane crashes in remote areas prove the point. Lot and his daughters, who witnessed the nuclear holocaust, may well have believed that they were the only survivors.

Where are the 'mountains' and the 'cave' where Lot lived with his daughters? As far as I am aware, no-one has attempted to locate them, perhaps because the whole tale, being connected with Sodom and Gomorrah, is regarded as a Biblical myth. However, there *is* a site hidden deep in the mountains of that area that fits the bill – a site which I visited in 1994.

The mysterious lost city of Petra is located less than sixty miles directly south from the southern part of the Dead Sea where Sodom and Gomorrah are believed to have once stood. It was thus within reach of, and a safe distance from, Lot's initial destination of Zoar, the small town which had been spared from the destruction.[102] As I studied the maps of the area, it was clear that Petra was located in a mountain range that extended all the way south from the Dead Sea almost as far as the Gulf of Aqaba, which is then surrounded by mountains on both sides. Anyone fleeing south had little choice but to seek refuge in these mountains. *Hachette's Guide to the Middle East* describes Petra as:

> . . . not so much a town as a natural stronghold where one could seek refuge without having to build walls, and where one could live in the *caves* as comfortably as one could in man-made houses.[103] (emphasis added)

Petra, literally meaning 'Rock', is entered via a narrow Siq one mile long and as narrow as six feet across, beneath two cliffs which rise up to 260 feet in height. This dusty trail was featured in the film *Indiana Jones and The Last Crusade*. As one exits the Siq, one enters what has rather aptly been described as a 'fairy city of pink sandstone'.[104] Over a site of eight square miles, a fantastic array of temples and tombs has been carved out of the sandstone rock.

As I studied the history books on Petra, I came up against a complete blank. Having been 'discovered' in 1812 by a young Swiss explorer named Johann Ludwig Burckhardt, little progress has been made in our knowledge of this once important site. As one book admits: 'almost nothing is known about its origin or nature'.[105]

Nevertheless, the extensive collection of carved temples and tombs at Petra is generally attributed to the Nabateans, a people of mysterious origin, who gradually infiltrated the area around 500–400 BC.[106] These Nabateans became wealthy on account of Petra's position as an important crossroads of two important trade routes, and it is thus naive to think that previous travellers and occupants did not also leave their mark. Indeed, Petra contains a bewildering variety of different styles and different cultures. On the one hand there are numerous depictions of steppyramids, indicating a Mesopotamian link, on the other obelisks and serpents indicating an Egyptian connection. The Romans, too, could not resist the urge to build a huge amphitheatre here.

My impression of this unique site was of a tremendous contrast in the quality of the workmanship. Most of the tombs and temples are very simple designs – natural clefts enlarged to form cavities, surmounted on the outside face of the cliff by two-dimensional relief work of mediocre quality. Many of these facades are badly eroded due to their exposure to the elements.

The *Ed Deir* ('the Monastery'), in contrast, is impressive, standing 135 feet high and 150 feet wide. Its upper parts are carved in three dimensions, and the main artistic feature is a splendid urn which is itself 30 feet high. The Monastery is dated to around AD 40, which may be a reasonable estimate, since it has suffered little erosion despite its exposed position in the side of a hill. However, although well-carved and well-preserved, the simple style and imposing size of the Monastery bear no comparison to 'the Treasury'.

To me, *El Khazneh* ('the Treasury') stands out clearly from the rest of Petra as a work of vastly superior quality. As shown in Plate 53 (see colour section), the detailed three-dimensional carving is stunning, and would be unthinkable for an artist to undertake today. It bears comparison with the great Sphinx of Egypt. Once again, an urn is the main feature and accounts for the name of the Treasury.

Elsewhere in Petra, there are many poor quality and badly eroded reliefs which appear to be copies of the Treasury. In contrast to these later copies, however, the builders of the Treasury took great care to undertake a preliminary excavation deep into the cliff face prior to carving. This technique, combined with a careful position-ing of the Treasury in a sheltered spot surrounded by cliffs on all sides, has minimised the risk of erosion. For this reason, it is possible that archaeologists have under-esti-mated its age by more than a thousand years.

Could the Treasury mark the cave where Lot and his daughters lived *c.* 2000 BC? Inside there is indeed a large natural cave of great height which has been squared off to create ample living quarters for a small family. The interior is stark and functional, the only features being large empty niches. In contrast, the exterior facade of the Treasury is incredibly ornate – a 'labour of love' that was built to last. The question is: who might have had the motivation to dedicate so much time and care in this secluded location?

When one tries to research into the history of Petra, all discussions of its inhabitants begin with the Edomites. These are the people descended from Esau, who are thought to have occupied the area from around 1000 BC. No-one claims that the Edomites actually founded Petra, and yet the historians seem reluctant to search any further back in time. Why?

Here is my theory of Petra. After the nuclear destruction in 2024 BC, Lot and his daughters travelled south and discovered the entrance into the mountains. In those days,

Petra was surrounded by forests of cedar and pine, in contrast to the arid desert of today.[107] At the end of the Siq, they found the cave in which, according to the Bible, they took up residence. After the death of Lot, his sons (by his daughters) Moab and Ben-Ammi dedicated themselves to commemorating their father (and perhaps their father's wife who was turned to vapour) by the elaborate carving of the building now known as the Treasury. The urn (the symbolism of which no-one has explained) signified the ashes of their dead father, and was perhaps also a memorial to their father's wife.

After this task was completed, the sons' curiosity led them into the outside world. As recorded in Genesis, one son Moab formed the tribe known as the Moabites, who lived in the mountain range where Petra lies. The other son, Ben-Ammi, became the father of the Ammonite tribe – the city Ammon today stands just 90 miles north of Petra.

In later times, the Edomites and Nabateans came to the area. Some emulated what they saw, sometimes with their own artistic, cultural bias, but none applied the same diligence as the original artists. Over thousands of years, the site lost its importance and the knowledge of its origins was restricted to a chosen few. Those few clues which *were* handed down then became enshrined in the Biblical myth of the destruction of Sodom and Gomorrah. Could this be the reason why scientists are reluctant to search for the *origins* of Petra?

Chapter Ten Conclusions

* The Biblical 'fire and brimstone' destruction of Sodom, Gomorrah and the other 'evil' cities of the plain was caused by the nuclear weapons of the gods in 2024 BC. A simultaneous nuclear strike destroyed the space

centre in Sinai, leaving the geological scar and blackened rocks which can still be seen today. The nuclear fall-out brought the Sumerian civilisation to its knees *c*. 2000 BC.

* The 'evil' of Sodom and Gomorrah was a change in allegiance to a 'foreign' god, Marduk. Nuclear weapons were used against the space centre to prevent its capture by Marduk. The background to these events was Marduk's ambition to assume 'Lordship' at the city of Babylon.

* Abraham acted as a spy for his god. His reward was the Biblical 'covenant' which promised prosperity to his bloodline.

* The 'cave' where Lot and his daughters fled following the attack on Sodom and Gomorrah is nowadays known as 'the Treasury' in Petra.

CHAPTER ELEVEN

THE STAR-CLOCK

---◆---

Secrets of the Zodiac

Thousands of years ago, ancient astronomers divided the starry skies into twelve sections, using the same contrived names and symbols that we still use today. The Greeks called this band of stars the zodiac. Today, the relative position of the Sun and the Earth at a person's birth-date are used to determine their astrological 'star sign', in order to determine their personality and to assist the preparation of detailed horoscopes. Such practices are highly popular and entertaining, but have little or no scientific merit. Astrology has come a long way from its roots.

If we travel back into earlier Sumerian and Egyptian times, we find the existence of the zodiac in a different field altogether. For there is no doubt that these ancient civilisations used the signs of the zodiac *on a scientific level*. Incredible as it may seem, it is now widely accepted that the ancients knew of the 25,920-year cycle of the precession of the equinoxes and divided that cycle into 12 periods of 2,160 years. How can we be so certain of this?

In chapter 6, we noted that the Sumerian mathematical system had been carefully designed around the number 3,600, such that their highest number, 12,960,000, was equal to exactly 500 precessional cycles of 25,920 years. Whilst 25,920 years represents 360 degrees of the celestial 'circle', 2,160 years represents 30 degrees, and 72 years represents just one degree. The number '72' is thus very significant, and its prominence in an ancient Egyptian legend has prompted one Egyptologist, Jane Sellers, to suggest that the Egyptians, too, were aware of precession. The legend in question is the Osiris myth, where 72 conspirators engage in a plot, led by Seth, to kill Osiris. Sellers is a rare individual – a multi-disciplined scientist who understands astronomy as well as archaeology. She is convinced that the 4,000-year old Pyramid Texts display unmistakable knowledge of astronomy, even though the Egyptians themselves may not have understood the significance. Sellers states:

> I am convinced that for ancient man, the numbers 72 . . . 2,160 and 25,920 all signified the concept of the Eternal Return.[1]

Sellers is not the only respectable scientist to recognise the Egyptians' knowledge of precession. The eminent Carl Jung (1875–1961) took a barrage of criticism when he suggested that the ancient Egyptians knew the transitions between one zodiac house and another.[2] Jung was particularly struck by the chaos in Egypt at the collapse of the Old Kingdom, which coincided with the end of the age of Taurus and the beginning of Aries. He described these periods as 'transitions between the aeons', which sometimes marked calamitous change, and even saw the uncertainties of his own times as marking the passage of Pisces to Aquarius.[3]

Modern astronomers date the era of Taurus to c. 4360–2200 BC, the age in which the Egyptian civilisation began. Initially, the Egyptian pharaohs of the Old Kingdom worshipped the bull, the sign of Taurus.[4] Then, after the chaos of the First Intermediate Period, a new era began in Egypt c. 2000 BC. At that time, the pharaohs began to depict sphinxes with *rams' heads* (Plate 49 colour section), signifying the era of Aries, which had recently begun. The monuments of ancient Egypt are thus testimonies to what Carl Jung was saying.

Amazingly, the Egyptian ram has a counterpart in Sumer. One of the most famous finds in the Sumerian royal city of Ur is the so-called 'Ram in a Thicket' (Figure 18, black-and-white section),[5] but a close examination of this ram shows it to be covered in *feathers*. It should therefore be seen as a symbolic interpretation of a god, waiting for the age of Aries to arrive. Such an interpretation is highly consistent with the Sumerian texts *c.* 2100 BC, which describe omens of imminent invasion from the west. Furthermore, shortly after 2000 BC, the widespread emergence of bull sacrifice was a symbolic sign that the age of Taurus had finally ended.

What possible use or significance did a zodiac age of 2,160 years have to man, as he emerged in his new civilisations? There is no readily apparent answer to this question. The inevitable conclusion is that the zodiac was designed not by man, but by the gods, and that it was intended purely for the use of the gods.

This piece of inductive reasoning can also be argued directly from the evidence. Although the zodiac first appeared in Sumer some time after 3800 BC, some studies have demonstrated its prior existence.[6] One Sumerian tablet actually lists the zodiac constellations beginning with Leo, hinting at a much earlier origin *c.* 11000 BC, when man was barely a farmer.[7] Furthermore, the number 12, which was used to divide the precessional cycle into 12 'houses' of the zodiac, was based on the 12 bodies of the Solar System. This knowledge was not invented by man but bequeathed by his gods.

In the previous chapter, I described how Marduk was waiting for a 'destiny-determining' time before returning to Babylon. One text, dealing with his return, describes how Nergal persuaded him to leave Babylon, suggesting that he had returned 'too early'. Can it be a coincidence that this dispute arose just as the precessional 'clock' was about to announce the beginning of a new precessional age?

In this chapter, I will demonstrate how the zodiac, in its *astronomical* sense, is a 'star-clock', which helps us to date the Flood, the Sphinx and the Pyramids. And I will reveal how these clues have led me to develop a new chronology which finally provides a complete reconciling link between Science, the Biblical Book of Genesis and the Sumerian Kings Lists.

The Flood, the Sphinx and the Pyramids

In chapter 7, I presented overwhelming evidence that the Flood occurred approximately 13,000 years ago. According to modern astronomers, the zodiac era which began at that time was that of Leo. If one of our ancient ancestors had wished to preserve for us the approximate date of the Flood, what better way to do it than to associate it with the position of the stars at the time of Leo? Are there any such zodiac clues to the date of the Flood?

Two such clues have come to light. One, contained in the ancient Babylonian New Year ritual, makes reference to 'the constellation Lion that measured the waters of the deep'.[8] The other, found in a miniature cuneiform tablet, refers to the Flood occurring when the planet Nibiru was in the constellation of Leo:

Supreme, Supreme, Anointed;
Lord whose shining crown with terror is laden.
Supreme planet: a seat he has set up
facing the confined orbit of the red planet.
Daily *within the Lion* he is afire;
his light his bright kingships on the lands pronounces.[9]
  (emphasis added)

Could the great Sphinx of Egypt, built with the body of a lion, possibly signify the first age of the zodiac *c*. 10900–8700 BC?

Earlier, we reviewed the geological evidence which proves the Sphinx to have been built between 9,000 and 11,000 years ago, and concluded that this unique carving, totally unrelated to the rest of Egyptian culture, might be the handiwork of the gods. We also saw, in chapter 8, that the Sphinx was aligned to a space centre in Sinai, which was geometrically related to a mission control centre at Jerusalem. Jerusalem, in turn, was geographically protected by Jericho which, according to the archaeologists, was founded *c*. 8000 BC. The chronological evidence of Jericho and the Sphinx therefore support each other, with a date of around 9000–8000 BC.

Could the Pyramids at Giza date to the same era? The lack of any Flood damage to the Pyramids suggests that they were built *after* the cataclysm of 11000 BC. However, the first flight path, in which the Pyramids were a key component, clearly preceded the later space centre to which the Sphinx was aligned along the thirtieth parallel. Thus the Pyramids must have predated the era 9000–8000 BC, but not any earlier than 11000 BC. This narrows things down considerably.

The experts have always been obsessed with trying to date the Pyramids to the time of Khufu. Any attempt to suggest an earlier date meets with a sarcastic smile and a confident assertion that there was no-one in Egypt to build it at that earlier time. No marks are awarded to the archaeologist who tries to buck this consensus. This means that vital evidence dating the Pyramids has been continually overlooked. As mentioned in chapter 9, this evidence includes an inscription attributing the Pyramid to Isis, a goddess whose reign is listed by Manetho at 10000 BC, and the surprise finding by Robert Bauval and Adrian Gilbert that the three Giza pyramids were exactly aligned with the three stars of Orion's Belt in 10450 BC.

As we have seen, a detailed study by Zecharia Sitchin has concluded that the flight path based on Giza (Figure 12) was set down by the gods as soon as practical after the Flood, to replace their pre-Flood flight path which had been destroyed. All of the evidence thus hangs together. It is my conclusion that the Flood occurred *c.* 11000 BC, at the *very beginning* of the Age of Leo, just as the Sumerian texts suggested; that the Pyramids were constructed shortly afterwards, in 10450 BC; and that the Sphinx was also built to signify the Age of Leo. It would appear that the lion-bodied Sphinx is the most obvious clue to the star-clock which was adopted by the gods, based on the Earth's precessional cycle – a wobble that may well have begun with the Flood cataclysm itself.

Lordship Begins

How and why did it become necessary to divide a 25,920-year precessional cycle into twelve houses of 2,160 years each? And why did Marduk believe that he had been promised a divine rule at Babylon, commencing from the age of Aries? How and why might such an agreement have been reached? Here is my theory.

After the Flood, the chief scientist of the gods, Enki, took up dominion over Egypt and the lands of Africa. The time was 11000 BC. Nibiru had just passed the Earth, and its gravitational forces had caused a huge dislocation of the oceans, which had bulged out and then crashed back to Earth in a massive tidal wave. The effect was to create, or at least change, the Earth's wobble, leading to the precessional effect as we know it today.[10]

Fascinated by astronomy, and being a master of the sciences, Enki quickly set about measuring the effect of Nibiru on the Earth's movement. As we now know, the retardation of the stars amounts to approximately one degree every 72 years. Thus, within 108 years, Enki could have measured exactly one and a half degrees and felt sufficiently confident to make an announcement in the council of the gods. The announcement he made was scientifically rather exciting, because the 25,920-year cycle which he had discovered miraculously matched the long-term cycles of Nibiru.

What happened next? As described in chapter 6, the succession dispute between Osiris and Seth, and the latter's occupation of Canaan, led to an all-out war in which Ninurta was victorious over the Enkiite gods. We know from the ancient texts that this war of the gods ended with a surrender and peace conference. One of the conditions imposed by the Enlilites was that Thoth (a pacifist) should be appointed in charge of Egypt.[11] This vital detail enables us to date the war of the gods, based on Manetho's history of Egypt. By adding the reigns of Thoth and his successors (5,570 years) to the approximate date of the first pharaoh Menes (c. 3100 BC), the war of the gods can be dated to around 8700 BC.

Amazingly, the war of the gods occurred precisely 2,160 years after Enki's announcement of the 25,920-year cycle. Could it be that Enlil's son. Ninurta, using the sacred number 12, had deliberately timed the war to coincide with a one twelfth division of the celestial cycle?

As we have seen with Seth and Osiris, the Flood had symbolically marked a new era on Earth, in which the younger gods such as Enlil's son, Ninurta, were ambitious for power. The olden gods had perhaps finally realised the need to take a back seat. Thus it was, in my view, that the great cycle of 25,920 years was divided into twelve – to give each of the younger gods, the first two generations below Enlil and Enki – a fair and democratic opportunity for 'Lordship'.

Of the two olden gods, Enlil and Enki, the former would

have remained in overall command of Earth, but delegated the Lordship. The latter, as the discoverer of the precessional cycle, would naturally have sought an association with the first zodiac house. Thus Enki retrospectively adopted the sign of the Lion, the king of the animals in his African territories. The implication is that the Sphinx was carved for Enki, in commemoration of the war (which ended at Giza) shortly after 8700 BC.

Returning to the peace conference, it was, like many in modern times, an agreement of concessions by the losers to the victors. Despite the decimation of the people and the ransacking of the Great Pyramid, Enki was expected to yield something further. One of these concessions was that none of the Enkiites who took part in the war should in future be allowed to rule Egypt. But was this enough? One text records that Enki negotiated the right to rebuild his city Eridu in the Enlilite territories, and the right for his descendants to be able to come and go as they pleased.[12] But was there another part of the deal that went unrecorded by the ancient scribes?

A reference in the *Lugal-e* text suggests that the surrender of the Enkiites was subject to a future '*destiny determining time*'.[13] It was, I suggest, a concessionary deal under which Enki granted three successive zodiac periods of 'Lordship' to the Enlilites. The 'destiny-determining' time, when 'Lordship' would return to Enki via his first-born son Marduk, would thus be *c.* 2200 BC.

Signs of the Gods

Do the signs of the zodiac support my theory that the age of Marduk followed three Enlilite zodiac periods? It is my belief that they do. Many of the clues can be decoded using the signs themselves (see the Egyptian versions in Illustration

19), the known history of the gods, and the Sumerian meanings assigned to each age.

The first age, Leo was called UR.GULA 'The Lion' by the Sumerians. As explained earlier, it symbolically represented Enki, the 'king' of the African lands. The goddess Inanna who stole the MEs from Enki was often portrayed by her supporters riding on the back of a Lion, thus signifying her subdual of the mighty beast. In Egypt, Enki was known as Ptah, and his goddess-wife Sekhmet was represented with the face of a lioness.

The Age of Cancer, which followed around 8700 BC, was depicted by the Crab, which the Sumerians called DUB, meaning 'Pincers'.[14] The title is befitting of the warlike role played by the god Ninurta, Enlil's son and heir, who won the pyramid war and was also the hero of an earlier mythical struggle against a god named Ullikummi/Zu, whose chariot he crippled by cutting its pinions.[15] Furthermore, the Egyptians depicted Cancer as the scarab beetle, signifying the role which Ninurta must have taken in the construction of the underground chambers of the Sinai space centre which was constructed *c*. 8000 BC, following the decommissioning of the Pyramid.

Cancer is followed by the Age of Gemini, which the Sumerians listed as MASH.TAB.BA meaning the 'Twins'. There is no mistaking the association with Nannar/Sin, the firstborn son of Enlil, commemorating the twins Inanna and Utu (Shamash) who were born to him after his arrival on Earth. The Egyptian zodiac sign does indeed show the twins as male and female.

Gemini is followed by Taurus, named by the Sumerians GU.ANNA, meaning the 'Heavenly Bull'.[16] This sign represented the god Ishkur, also known by the names Adad and Teshub (the Storm God). The name Ishkur in Sumerian meant 'Far Mountain Lands', befitting his domain in the Taurus Mountains and – as we shall see later – in South America. The Egyptian zodiac showed the bull

Illustration 19

with a disc on its back, representing the return of Nibiru and a ceremonial visit of Anu to Earth which coincided with this age.

Thus the first three signs of the zodiac, following Enki's Leo, can be definitely identified with each of Enlil's three sons.

The age of Marduk, represented by the Ram of Aries, at first appears to be an enigma since the sign of the ram has no obvious association with Marduk. It is my suspicion that the sign was originally elsewhere in the sequence and has been moved. The puzzle can be solved by recognising Marduk's possible guilt in the death of his brother Dumuzi *c.* 3450 BC. As we have seen, this was a major event in the history of the gods, and caused the widowed Inanna to turn from love to war. Her ambitious conquests came to an end with the destruction of Agade *c.* 2200 BC, but we have not explained how the bitter Inanna was eventually pacified. For, in the final analysis, she was not involved in the resistance fought by Ninurta against Marduk in 2024 BC. Why was this?

The answer, I believe, lies in a concession offered by Marduk to name the next sign of the zodiac after Inanna's dead husband, Dumuzi, thereby ensuring that Dumuzi would be remembered for all time. The latter's association with the ram of Aries is clear from his nickname 'the Herder' (on account of his domain in the African lands of present-day Sudan). This nickname closely matches the meaning of the Sumerian name for Aries – KU.MAL, meaning 'Field Dweller'.[17] Such a political concession, in order to neutralise Inanna, may have been a key component of Marduk's strategy in preparing his return to Babylon. In addition, it was an honourable and generous act of respect for his dead brother.

What of the remaining seven signs of the zodiac? The five dealt with so far can be identified with great certainty. After 2000 BC we must be more careful, for it is highly possible that Marduk or his rivals politically interfered with the sequence of ages which had not yet come to pass. Nevertheless, there does seem to be evidence of an alternating sequence between Enlilite and Enkiite gods, which is what we would expect to find.

The sign of Pisces is listed in Sumerian as SIM.MAH meaning 'Fishes', often depicted by two fishes astride a watery stream or river.[18] In my view, the sign was given to Ereshkigal, a sister of Inanna, who was married to Marduk's brother Nergal. She lived with Nergal in his African domain at a site which has not yet been located, but is described in texts as the 'prairie country of the River Habur' – the 'river of fishes and birds'.[19] Various other clues suggest a location possibly near Lake Victoria or Lake Malawi. The cichild fish of these lakes are well-known to evolutionists for defying Darwinism by evolving into hundreds of different types within the last 200,000 years.[20] Is this really an inexplicable phenomenon, or could there have been an artificial breeding programme by Ereshkigal, the goddess of the fishes?

The sign of Aquarius is an oddity. Depicted as the 'Water Bearer', the Sumerian term GU carries no connotation of water. It is possible that the sign may have been used by Marduk to insert his loyal son Nabu into the zodiac, in precedence to the other, elder Enkiite gods. Nabu was indeed associated with waters as a result of a Mediterranean island to which he had fled following the nuclear attack on the Canaanite cities.[21]

Capricorn was listed by the Sumerians as SU-HUR.MASH, the 'Goat Fish'. It is most likely the symbol for Ninharsag, the Mother Goddess who was also nicknamed NIN.MAH, meaning 'Lady Fish'. In Egypt she was known as Hathor, and was also depicted as 'the Cow', bearing some similarity to the image of the goat-fish; Egyptian artists sometimes linked the sign of Capricorn with the umbilical cutter, a symbol of Ninharsag from her days as Mother Goddess. She was neutral from the Enlil and Enkiite camps.

The next sign of Sagittarius is clearly an Enkiite sign. In Sumerian it was listed as PA.BIL, meaning 'the Defender',[22] whilst it was pictorially represented by the Archer. Both terms are identifiable with Marduk's brother Nergal, who played a heroic role as Defender of the Great Pyramid and played the Archer as Erra, the god who fired the nuclear weapons at Sodom and Gomorrah.

The sign of Scorpio was called GIR.TAB, the first syllable GIR being a reference to rockets and thus to the Enlilite god Utu/Shamash, who was in charge of the space centre and Baalbek. The sign was depicted by the ancient Egyptians as a scorpion – with pincers and a sting in the tail. The soldiers who defended the space centre were indeed described in ancient texts as 'scorpion-men', whose weapons sometimes 'stung' unauthorised trespassers.[23]

Libra was named ZI.BA.AN.NA, meaning 'Heavenly Fate'. Its depiction of a god between two scales strongly suggests Thoth, a brother of Marduk. As we shall see, it was Thoth who played a fair and impartial role to both sides in the weighing of the heavenly signs which determined whether Marduk's destiny-determining time had come.

Finally, Virgo was depicted as the beautiful Maiden. The Sumerians called her AB.SIN, a clear reference to Inanna – she 'whose Father was Sin'. As her city Agade was wiped out, so too has her name been curiously depersonalised, perhaps as part of the punishment for her rebellion which went too far. Furthermore, it may be that, in exchange for the repositioning of Dumuzi's sign, Inanna's sign too was repositioned – as the last in the pantheon of twelve.

What is Time?

According to my theory, as set out above, the change of Lordship to Marduk *c*. 2200 BC was unprecedented – the first such change in the history of mankind. It was also the first such change since the beginning of civilisation, and for that reason we have so much documentary evidence of the event. The result, as we saw in the last chapter, was a nuclear cataclysm, but the years leading up to that tragic climax can tell us much about the culture of the gods and the process behind the star-clock.

In the matter of Marduk's return to Babylon and 'Lordship' over the gods, a close reading of the ancient texts suggests that the star-clock was of critical importance. The various texts, dealing with Marduk's return, imply that both his right to rule, and the timing of his rule, were in dispute. The question of his right to rule probably hinged on his illicit escape from imprisonment. Arguably, he was still an escaped convict in the eyes of some. The question of the timing, however, is the area I wish to concentrate upon.

When Marduk first returned to Babylon, the date (based on the era of Sargon I) was *c.* 2320 BC. The ancient texts state that Marduk's brother Nergal travelled to Babylon to persuade Marduk that his time had not yet come. It would seem that Marduk was persuaded without too much difficulty, but in the course of discussion he complained 'where is the oracle stone of the gods that gives the sign for Lordship?'[24] What was this 'oracle stone' and why should a simple count of 2,160 years have proved so problematical?

Let us consider how the precessional ages would have been measured. First, one would need to adopt a fixed observation point, the usual convention being the spring equinox, when night and day are equal. Then the position of the stars which rise above a fixed point on the horizon on that day each year would need to be recorded. The completion of a zodiac house would then be measured by the retardation of the stars through 30 degrees (one twelfth of the 360-degree circle of the zodiac). In order to calculate accurately the movement from one house to another, two things would therefore be essential – first, a starting point, and secondly, a map of the heavens. Was the starting point measured by the Flood, or a later date (I have suggested a 108 year delay)? That may well have been one source of misunderstanding. As for the map of the heavens, that could well have been the 'oracle stone' which had gone missing.

Nevertheless, readers may well ask why the gods did not simply invent a quartz clock and count 2,160 years electronically. A good question, that goes right to the heart of the issue! The answer which I will shortly set out provides a final solution to the mysteries of Stonehenge and Machu Picchu.

Did the gods use the star-clock for a practical purpose?

Zecharia Sitchin has suggested that the unusual structure of the Sumerian mathematical system, rising by alternate factors of 10 and 6, is linked to the 10:6 ratio of 3,600:2,160, where 3,600 represents the orbital period of the gods' planet Nibiru. Sitchin proposed that, *in order to keep track of time* on their home planet, the gods sought a long cycle on Earth which produced a manageable relationship to 3,600 years.[25] He suggested that 2,160 years represented that convenient measure, and the precessional cycle was therefore divided by 12 to produce 2,160. Unfortunately, this argument fails the 'quartz clock question'.

On the contrary, all of the evidence suggests that the star-clock performed a strictly symbolic rather than practical function. The gods' almost religious obsession with the Solar System, evident from the use of 12 celestial bodies as a sacred number, demonstrates that they were obsessed with cosmic equilibrium. The perpetual beat or pulse of a quartz clock would have been a meaningless measure of time to them. Instead, they saw time in terms of great cosmic cycles, in which the Earth's precessional cycle of 25,920 years was only a representation of even greater cosmic cycles. Time in this symbolic sense was not a constant rate of change; it was measured by the movement of the Earth relative to the stars, and in theory its cycles could vary.

The gods' concept of time could not be magically distilled into simple numbers and tables – it was manifest only in the heavens and determinable only from the floating observatory of Earth itself. Time was a concept of aesthetic beauty, a reflection of nature, indeed almost of the divine nature of the universe. To construct a quartz watch would be akin to putting the cart before the horse, for time did not determine the heavens – rather, the movement of the heavens determined time.

The Era of Marduk

How did Marduk determine the timing of his moves to Babylon? The first move occurred toward the end of Sargon's reign, and is therefore datable to the latter end of the 24th century BC. But, as I suggested in the last chapter, the timing of Inanna's conquests under Sargon strongly hint at a deliberate manoeuvre to thwart Marduk's return. It is thus possible that his return may have been planned for the *beginning* of the 24th century BC.

At this point, it will prove useful to construct some tentative dates, which we will later compare to developments at Stonehenge. Whilst 2,160 is a mathematically convenient approximation of a precessional age, the latest scientific estimates suggest 2,148 years.[26] I will use the latter date in the illustrations which follow, but with the *caveat* that these ages were not necessarily constant, but were in practice determined by the Earth's wobble which was theoretically subject to variation.

According to my analysis, Marduk counted four precessional ages from the date of the Flood, producing an initial return date of *c*. 2400 BC. At that time, political and military developments in the Near East dissuaded him from returning. When he did eventually return, *c*. 2320 BC, the Enlilite gods, assisted by Nergal, did everything they could to persuade him to leave. They argued that the zodiac had commenced 108 years later than the Flood date which Marduk had used. I also believe that they contrived an argument in order to penalise him by a further 3 degrees of celestial time. This penalty of 3 degrees, added to the standard division of the skies into 12 segments of 30 degrees, may have led to the origin of 33 degrees as a mystic number, which is nowadays reflected in the ranks of freemasonry.[27] A compromise was then reached which did allow the Flood as the zodiac starting point, but postponed his return from *c*. 2400 BC by the 3 degrees (215 years) to *c*. 2185 BC.

When Marduk finally reinstalled himself in Babylon in 2024 BC it would seem that he was around 160 years late. Why the delay when he was so anxious to return? The answer, for once, lies not in the stars but on the Earth. We saw in the last chapter that he had to take control of the Near East by force, with a mass invasion of Amorite supporters. In the final battle, he was fiercely opposed by Ninurta and the Elamites. His delay almost certainly lies in military preparations and diplomacy, such as the move which successfully kept Inanna out of the final conflict. The oracle which Marduk sought in Hatti-land was surely of a practical nature, recommending the timing of his invasion. During this delay, his son Nabu was busy building political and military support in Canaan.

We can now understand why the Third Dynasty of Ur was so unsure of itself, why it suffered one tragedy after another, why it was obsessed with omens of invasion, why it needed to use Elamite troops to quell rebellion in the outer provinces, and why it was necessary to send Abraham to opposite ends of the empire to spy on Marduk's military strength and intentions.

Stonehenge Revisited

How did Marduk attempt to determine his 'destiny-determining time'? It was a time which was written in the stars, perhaps encoded on star maps, such that Marduk knew in advance which star must rise on the day of the spring equinox. However, in order to plan for his new era he needed to know *when* that day would come – how long would he have to wait? As I described earlier, the gods' concept of time occurred in the heavens, so the only way to measure time was to build an observatory – one that would *measure* the retardation of the stars with a very fine accuracy, and one that would *predict* the future movements of those stars. And the key to that prediction was the *rate of change* in the stars. Only by measuring the speed of precession could the future be forecast. One place in the ancient world clearly stands out as meeting these requirements. It is time to revisit the unique site of Stonehenge in England.

A new and detailed study by the British authorities has determined that the first phase of the Stonehenge site was commenced *c.* 2965 BC (+/− 2%).[28] In the absence of any other plausible explanation of who could have laid out such a sophisticated observatory, we must look to the needs of Marduk, who would at that time have been turning his mind to the coming new age. But something rather strange happened at Stonehenge. No sooner had work commenced, than the 56 carefully excavated Aubrey Holes were immediately refilled, and the site was inexplicably abandoned for approximately 300 years.

The secret to this mystery lies, I believe, in a poorly understood Egyptian myth concerning a dispute between Marduk and Thoth. The 175th chapter of the Book of the Dead describes the 'return' of Ra and his subsequent anger at Thoth. 'O Thoth, what is it that has happened?' cries Ra. He accuses Thoth of 'destruction of hidden things', apparently relating to the calendar, and accuses Thoth of cutting short the years and curbing the months.[29] The calendrical significance of the encounter has been highlighted by Zecharia Sitchin, who mistakenly thought that it marked a return of Ra/Marduk to Egypt.[30] On the contrary, there is little doubt that the encounter occurred at Stonehenge.

The presence of Thoth at Stonehenge can be determined by its lunar functions, which act as a virtual 'fingerprint' of this god, who is known as the Moon god and credited with the introduction of Egypt's first, *lunar* calendar.[31] As noted in chapter 5, Stonehenge was uniquely chosen for its ability to mark the *eight* key points of the Moon in its 18.6-year cycle. And Thoth was indeed known in Egypt as Khemennu, meaning 'Lord of Eight'.[32] When it came to astronomy, Thoth was the expert to whom Marduk would naturally have turned for advice. My conclusion is that Thoth was therefore the designer of the Stonehenge observatory.

When Marduk arrived at Stonehenge to see how work on his observatory was progressing, he found that Thoth had designed it around *lunar* measurement and predictions. What Marduk found was a ditch, 4 Station Stones positioned in a rectangle that marked the movements of the Moon, and 56 Aubrey Holes that also appeared to have a lunar purpose (since 3 lunar cycles of 18.6 years equal approximately 56).[33] The fact that Thoth had ingeniously positioned these holes for a dual purpose[34] was of little consolation to Marduk, who needed and had specified a solar calendar.[35]

As related by the Book of the Dead, Thoth had indeed 'curbed the months', from 30 days to the lunar month of 29.5 days, and hence 'cut short the year', from the 360-day Egyptian calendar to the 354-day lunar calendar (comprising 12 months of 29.5 days). Furthermore, the Book of the Dead records that, after the argument, Thoth left for a distant land. The physical evidence at Stonehenge shows that the Aubrey Holes were indeed quickly filled in and the site abandoned.

Why was the lunar calendar such a problem for Marduk? What Marduk required from Thoth was a prediction of star-time, converted into an easily measurable cycle of Earth-time. Marduk wanted a portable clock that he could consult anywhere on the globe – a simple solar year countdown was therefore the most suitable. How could he count down a prediction expressed in 18.6-year lunar cycles, unless he kept travelling back to Stonehenge?

Why was Thoth so obsessed with lunar time? The answer

lies in a purist's need for an accurate prediction of precession. In order to *predict* future precession, one first has to *measure* the current *rate of change* against a *stable* yardstick. However, if the measurement is based on the yardstick of solar observations (from one spring equinox to the next) then it contains what one is trying to measure in the first place. A systematic error is therefore introduced, amounting to one month every 2,160 years. If you have had difficulty following this argument, or consider such an error to be immaterial, then you are experiencing the same frustration that Marduk must have felt 5,000 years ago!

Now let us move forward to the next phase of Stonehenge, when the Sarsen Circle and the Avenue were constructed. The latest datings suggest that the first Sarsen stones began to arrive *c.* 2665 BC (+/− 7%) and that the Avenue was being worked on *c.* 2500 BC. The number of Sarsen uprights (30) and the alignment of the Avenue to the summer solstice suggest that this phase was not the work of Thoth, but of Marduk. The timing of these developments is highly significant, given Marduk's expectation of a return to Babylon *c.* 2400 BC. We should note that all of the work in this phase was completed prior to Marduk's return to Babylon *c.* 2300 BC.

The next phase of Stonehenge is marked by the erection of the huge trilithons, which has now been dated to *c.* 2270 BC (+/− 7%). Significantly, this date immediately follows Marduk's departure from Babylon, having accepted a later compromise return date. No-one has ever explained the need for the immense size of these trilithons, but it could reflect an anti-vandalism measure, perhaps prompted by damage to the Sarsen Circle in his absence (some of these Sarsen stones are missing).

Also, at about this time, work was being carried out on the Avenue, which was realigned to the winter solstice. It is amazing that so little attention has been paid to the Avenue at Stonehenge, for its 600-metre long first section literally dwarfs the site of the stone circle itself. The significance of the length of the Avenue can only be put down to the need for extreme *accuracy* of measurement of precessional change, just as a rifle with a long barrel facilitates a more accurate aim at a target.

I have estimated that Marduk's new compromise date may have been *c*. 2185 BC. Once again, this date matches a development at the monument of Stonehenge, and this time it would seem that Thoth had returned, with the supreme accuracy of his lunar calendar. How do we know this? Because the lunar number '19' crops up in the 38 stones of the Bluestone Circle and the 19 stones of the Bluestone Horseshoe. The latest date for the Bluestone Circle is *c*. 2155 BC (+/− 6%), and for the Horseshoe *c*. 2100 BC (+/ − 8%). Perhaps Thoth had the foresight to begin the process of recording Marduk's new era.

After these developments, Stonehenge was abandoned until the sixteenth century BC. Again, the date of abandonment, some time after 2100 BC, is significant, given that Marduk had finally returned to Babylon in 2024 BC.

There is just one further note to add on the role of Stonehenge as a star-clock. In June 1996, English Heritage announced a newly-discovered phase of the Stonehenge site, dating back to 8000 BC. A thesis published by the chief archaeologist, Dr Geoffrey Wainwright, suggests that 20-feet high wooden 'totem poles' were erected and worshipped.[36] The evidence consists of charcoal from pine trees, which was found in numerous circular pits measuring 4 feet across and 5 feet deep. This charcoal has been radiocarbon dated to approximately 8000 BC. Allowing the usual latitude for error, the *actual* date of 'Woodhenge' would lie in a range 8600–7400 BC. As noted in chapter 4, Stonehenge is situated in a unique position for the eight key points of lunar observation; therefore the 'totem poles' of Woodhenge must surely have been astronomical markers. It is not yet clear whether Woodhenge also measured stellar time, but its chronology places it right at the time when the precessional eras were assigned to the gods, *c.* 8700 BC.

Machu Picchu's Star-Clock

At first glance, it might seem that the site of Machu Picchu in the Andes *mountains* has little in common with Stonehenge, which is located on the *flat plains* of southern England. On the contrary, as we shall now see, both sites fulfilled exactly the same functional purpose.

At Stonehenge the rate of precessional change was measured by observing the rise of stars on the distant horizon, with a 2-mile long Avenue assisting the accuracy of the observations. At Machu Picchu, an Avenue was not required, for mother nature had supplied a series of jagged mountain peaks which formed perfect, ready-made markers for stellar observation.

How do we know that Machu Picchu was actually used for such a purpose? The evidence is centred on the enigmatic *Intihuatana* stone (Plate 24 colour section), which is positioned on an exact north-south axis with the mountains of Huayana Picchu and Salcantay.[37]

Salcantay mountain dominates the skyline at Machu Picchu and, with a height of 20,600 feet, is one of the two largest mountains in the entire region. This mountain has been regarded as sacred since pre-Inca times and continues to be worshipped today by the local people.[38] It stands exactly due south of the *Intihuatana*.

Huayna Picchu mountain stands just to the north of Machu Picchu, overlooking the site from a 700-feet higher elevation (Plate 21 colour section). It lies within a horseshoe formed by the Urubamba river. The steep gorge around Huayna Picchu has been known since time immemorial as 'the Gateway of Salcantay', signifying its close relationship with that sacred mountain.[39] Huayna Picchu stands exactly due north of the *Intihuatana*.

At the highest point of Huayna Picchu there lies an artificial platform (now dilapidated) and a v-shaped groove cut into the stone (Plate 26 colour section). This groove points exactly due south towards both the *Intihuatana* and the distant peak of Salcantay.[40] Slightly below this groove lies another artificial triangular platform; its v-shaped angle also points exactly due south.

Figure 19 (see black-and-white section) shows how the Machu Picchu star-clock worked. First, it is necessary to identify the star that appears above the tip of Salcantay. Then, at a fixed point during the year, a measurement can be taken to show how far that star has moved to the left as a result of precession. Adjacent mountain peaks provide ideal reference points to determine when a particular number of celestial degrees has been reached. By co-ordinating these observations with a solar or lunar calendar, the rate of precessional change can be expressed in terms of so many degrees in so many years (it will be approximately one degree in 72 solar years).

Since Salcantay cannot be seen from the *Intihuatana*, the purpose of the *Intihuatana* seems to be two-fold. First, it could have maintained, in a convenient location, a record of the stellar positions seen from Huayna Picchu. Secondly, it could have been used to establish an accurate alignment of the measuring equipment used on Huayna Picchu. I am referring here to the need to ensure that the angle of precessional change is measured exactly from the original starting position. This would be achieved by using an electronic signal from the *Intihuatana* to confirm the *exact* bearing which had been used from Huayna Picchu for the earlier measurements. In addition to these functions, it should also be noted that the *Intihuatana* has been carved to produce a symbolic representation of the profile of Huayna Picchu, specifically in the way the Sun and shadows contrast on the two faces of the mountain when seen from below.[41]

What then should we conclude of the claimed *solar* alignments of the faces of the *Intihuatana* ('Hitching Post of the *Sun*') as outlined in chapter 5? The validity of these alignments actually remains unaffected, since the solar and stellar functions can easily co-exist within the same stone. Indeed, measurements of the annual solar cycle would have been essential to determine the exact day when the stellar observations were taken. I must stress, however, that the *primary purpose* of the *Intihuatana* was stellar. We should perhaps rename it as the 'Hitching Post of the *Stars*'.

The sacred traditions of the Machu Picchu region provide an extremely strong corroboration of my star-clock theory. First, it should be noted that the Incas and their Andean predecessors worshipped stars in two different types of constellations.[42] The first comprised star-to-star formations, named after animals in a similar manner to the zodiac. The second were based on so-called 'dark clouds' – the clouds of interstellar dust *between* the major stars. The worship of the latter constellations is highly unusual and indicates an obsessive interest in tracking the precessional movements.

The names of the Inca constellations, which are still used to this day, are also highly revealing. One of the most prominent, known to us as Scorpius, is named 'the Serpent changing into the Condor'[43] – a reference perhaps to Marduk flying to or from Babylon. Amazingly, the Quechua name for the Serpent is *Amaru*,[44] echoing the *Amurru* 'westerners' or Amorite supporters of Marduk (see chapter 10). Adjacent to that constellation was Alpha and Beta Centauri, which the Quechua called 'the Eyes of the Llama'.[45] Could this be a reference to Marduk watching and waiting for the ram of Aries to signify the beginning of his era? The parallels are startling.

The most impressive support for the Machu Picchu star-clock, however, comes from Johan Reinhard, an expert in Andean mythology. Reinhard discusses the sacred traditions of Peru in a symbolic context and makes the following comment only in passing, but to me it appears a ringing endorsement of Figure 19 (see black-and-white section:

> Still today stars . . . are believed to acquire a greater amount of power when they become associated with a sacred mountain.[46]

Who was the mastermind behind the ingenious selection of Machu Picchu as a stellar observatory? As stated earlier, the only comparable construction was at Stonehenge, which I have concluded was designed by the god Thoth. A clue to Thoth's involvement at Machu Picchu has indeed been found in the Principal Temple, where archaeologists uncovered 56 vessels along with a mysterious layer of fine white sand.[47] The number 56 signifies three lunar cycles, in a similar manner to the 56 Aubrey Holes at Stonehenge. It is thus highly likely that the vessels and sand were used in the measurement of a lunar calendar, with which Thoth was closely associated.

One ancient Egyptian text states that, following his dispute with Marduk/Ra, Thoth left Stonehenge for a distant land, referred to as *Hau-nebut*.[48] Could this destination have been Machu Picchu? The date at which Thoth left Stonehenge is likely to have coincided with the earliest ditch phase, which archaeologists have dated to *c.* 2965 BC. Amazingly, we find that the pre-Incan traditions recorded by the Spanish historian Montesinos place the beginning of the Andean calendar at an almost identical date of 2900 BC.[49] I suggest that this is not a coincidence.

Counter of the Stars

There can be little doubt that Thoth was the mastermind behind Stonehenge and Machu Picchu, but was he also behind some of the other legendary calendars and astronomical observatories of the ancient world?

The Egyptian Book of the Dead records a journey by Thoth to 'the desert, the silent land' where 'sexual pleasures are not enjoyed'.[50] Could this explain yet another mysterious calendar which began in China at the date 2698 BC? Chinese legend associates their ancient calendar with the legendary reign of Huang Ti and the arrival of 'Sons of Heaven' in 'fiery-tailed dragon ships'.[51]

The most sacred spot in China is Tian Tan (the Temples of Heaven) in Beijing. Whilst Stonehenge is aligned to the summer solstice, Tian Tan is aligned to the winter solstice. At this time of year, a spectacular procession would set out from the Forbidden City, carrying the emperor to the Altar of Heaven, a 3-tiered circular white marble terrace known as the 'Huanki'. The emperor would recite words from a 5,000-year old tradition and, in a practice no doubt dating to the change in the zodiac, sacrifice a bull calf.[52]

The comparison of Tian Tan to Stonehenge is intriguing. As at Stonehenge, the main temple of Tian Tan is circular in shape with concentric rings of pillars within – an unusual design in ancient times. The Huanki Altar is also circular and is situated to the south at the end of a 1,000-feet long causeway – another unusual feature similar to the Avenue at Stonehenge. To the north-west of the site, we find a temple of the Moon, called the Yuetan.[53] All of these places have been built and rebuilt countless times, with remarkable devotion and skill, to mark the spot where the Chinese calendar began.

Moving forward in time, we find Thoth constructing

another astronomical observatory in Mesopotamia early in the 22nd century BC. Appearing under the guise of Nin-gishzidda,[54] Thoth appeared in a 'vision' to the Sumerian king Gudea and instructed him to build a fabulous structure known as the E.NINNU.[55] In 1887, the German archaeologist Koldewey discovered the Eninnu – a mysterious structure built on a circular platform at Lagash (modern-day Al Hiba/Tello). Although the purpose of this enigmatic structure is much disputed, the detailed descriptions which are recorded in ancient texts leave us in no doubt concerning its astronomical functions.[56]

Why was it necessary for Thoth to build so many observatories? It would seem that the answer lies in the need to satisfy both Enkiite and Enlilite gods regarding the latest position of the star-clock. Whilst Stonehenge was built for Marduk, the Eninnu was built for Ninurta and Machu Picchu was, in all probability, built for Ishkur.[57] Thoth thus assumed an impartial position in the debate, simply providing advice and facilities to those gods who were interested. For this reason, his Egyptian name was Tehuti, meaning 'He who Balances'.[58] The Pyramid Texts were even more explicit, describing Thoth as 'he who reckons the heavens, the counter of the stars and the measurer of the Earth'.

All of these observatories appear to have peaked at the time of Marduk's return to Babylon c. 2200 BC. This is the date ascribed to the solar calendar alignments at Machu Picchu; it is the date attributed to Gudea's Eninnu in Mesopotamia; it is the time at which the Bluestone Circle and Horseshoe were erected at Stonehenge; and it is the date at which a strange rounded 'temple' was constructed at Barbar in Bahrain.[59]

This unprecedented spate of observatory building seems to have gone unnoticed by historians, for the reason that they are trained *not* to make connections between distant locations. Each individual site is therefore linked dismissively to primitive religious cults. One authority, for instance, suggests that the *Intihuatana* was 'perhaps used in connection with Sun worship'.[60] On the contrary, all of these sites had a stellar significance, coinciding with a precessional shift from Taurus to Aries *c.* 2200 BC. It is clear that, all around the world, the gods were watching the skies. No other theory can explain the physical evidence.

Towards a New Chronology

My spirit will not contend with man for ever, for he is mortal; his days will be a hundred and twenty years.[61]

This statement is made by the Lord shortly before the Flood and in the context of wishing to utterly destroy mankind. It has therefore perplexed the Biblical scholars, whose best explanation is that the Lord was offering a period of grace for man to amend his ways.[62] And yet nothing in the Bible or other ancient texts suggests that man was given such a reprieve. If it was so, then Noah would have been entrusted to communicate this message to his fellow-man. Instead we find that Noah's family alone were saved and immediately afterwards offered an *everlasting* covenant. According to the Bible, Noah then proceeded to live for 950 years rather than the supposedly allotted 120.

If, however, the original verse is translated literally, we find the past tense being used rather than the future tense. Thus:

And his days *were* a hundred and twenty years.[63]

In 1976, Zecharia Sitchin concluded that this count of years should be applied not to mankind but to the deity. The Bible was thus recording the periods that the Lord had been on Earth. This enormous conceptual breakthrough enabled Sitchin to attempt a chronology of the gods.

How could the deity have lived only 120 years when Adam, a mere human, had lived 930 years? The answer is that the Bible recorded not 120 'years' but 120 'periods'. How long were these periods? The Sumerians counted sacred periods known as 'sars', which they depicted as a circle, representing, 3,600, the central number in their mathematical system. Zecharia Sitchin logically concluded that the Sumerian sar represented the 3,600-year orbit of the gods' planet Nibiru.[64]

The next major breakthrough in Sitchin's chronology of the gods came with the decipherment of Akkadian tablets describing the creation of mankind. Experts regard as pure myth the claim that the senior gods created a primitive 'LU.LU' worker to undertake the 'toil' of the rank-and-file gods, but the ancient scribes repeatedly made reference to events when the gods alone were on Earth and when man had not yet been created. If we take their claim literally, then we find that the creation of man was preceded by 40 periods of suffering by the rank-and-file gods.[65] The events are recorded in detail in the text entitled *When the gods like men bore the work*:

For 10 periods they suffered the toil;
for 20 periods they suffered the toil;
for 30 periods they suffered the toil;
for 40 periods they suffered the toil.[66]

It was then, after these 40 periods, that the rank-and-file gods staged a rebellion, which coincided with a visit to Earth by Anu. In order to placate the rebels, Enki and Ninharsag offered the ingenious solution of genetically engineering a slave worker.[67]

The above text, combined with the Biblical '120 periods', provides the basis of a chronology for dating the creation of

Homo sapiens. How long were the 40 periods of toil? The term used in the Mesopotamian texts was 'ma', which most scholars translate as 'year', but its literal meaning is 'a repeating cycle that completes itself'.[68] Zecharia Sitchin thus concluded that the ma was another manifestation of the 3,600-year cycle of Nibiru.

Working backwards from a Flood date of 11000 BC – with which I concur – Zecharia Sitchin proceeded to use the 120 sar and the 40 ma to date both the arrival of the gods and the creation of mankind. This was the first serious attempt at dating the gods in modern times and thus deserves credit.

But did Zecharia Sitchin get it right? He had *apparently* reconciled his dates to the Sumerian and Babylonian Kings Lists, which also spanned 120 sar; and he had very approximately tied his chronology in to the latest palaeoanthropological evidence regarding early *Homo sapiens*. However, in an attempt to prove Sitchin's theory correct, at least to my own satisfaction, I set several further objectives. First, his chronology should reconcile to the eras of the Biblical patriarchs from Adam to Noah. Secondly, it should reconcile to the legendary reigns in the Sumerian Kings Lists. And thirdly, it should dovetail with the reigns of the pre-Flood gods in Egypt, as recorded by Manetho. Sitchin had made only a superficial examination of these matters.

The Bible carefully preserves the ancestral line of Adam through to Noah in its records of the ages at which each father begot a son. These years, including allowance for Noah's age at the time of the Flood, add up to 1,656, suggesting that mankind was created 1,656 years before the Flood. In addition, the Bible similarly records the ancestral line after the Flood from Noah to Abraham, amounting to a period of 292 years. Whether we use 2123 BC for the date of Abraham's birth (see Appendix A) or any other commonly accepted date, these numbers simply do not stack up, for they suggest that the Flood took place in 2415 BC and that man was created in 4071 BC. The scientific evidence – of advanced civilisation in 3800 BC and *Homo sapiens* 200,000 years ago, in addition to the lack of any Flood evidence *c.* 4000 BC from archaeology – suggests that the Biblical data is fundamentally understated.

Zecharia Sitchin suspected that the ages of the early patriarchs may have been reduced by a factor of 60.[69] I adjusted for this, but the figures still did not reconcile. Another commentator suggested that the Biblical figures were months rather than years, but by his own admission this continued to give 'contradictory results'.[70] Treating these numbers as 'days' has also been considered, but without success.[71] Clearly I was not the first to search for a solution to one of the Bible's greatest mysteries. Nevertheless, I began to work on a theory that the Biblical data had been drawn from earlier Sumerian sources, and that somewhere along the editorial line, someone had misunderstood the Sumerians' unusual sexagesimal (base 60) system.

As I experimented with the Sumerian sexagesimal system, I made the breakthrough that was to solve all of the chronological problems. In order to understand this, and to follow my arguments in a later chapter, it is essential that the reader pays close attention at this point to a quick lesson in Sumerian mathematics.

The decimal numbering system which we use today consists of units rising by a factor of 10 each time. Thus 5,000 for example, is written as follows:

UNITS:	10,000	1,000	100	10	1
	N/A	5	0	0	0

So far so good. Now for the Sumerian sexagesimal system, which rises by *alternating* factors of 6 and 10, thus 5,000 becomes 1–2–3–2–0:

UNITS:	3,600	600	60	10	1
	1 –	2 –	3 –	2 –	0

Whilst the Sumerian system might seem a little strange at first, it is ideal for geometry and calculation with fractions. It has also been found to match the celestial heavens, both in its use of 3,600, the orbital period of Nibiru, and in the manifestation of the precessional cycle. To quickly illustrate, as the units alternate above 3,600 we see: 36,000 . . . 216,000 . . . 2,160,000 . . . 12,960,000. The last number, which was highly symbolic to the Sumerians, represented exactly 500 great precessional cycles of 25,920 years. The preceding units represented 100 and 1,000 multiplied by the precessional period of 2,160 years.

If that seems like a miracle, then here is the really magic part. If we write the precessional number 2,160 in Sumerian numerals, this is what we get:

UNITS:	3,600	600	60	10	1
	N/A	3 –	6 –	0 –	0

These two numbers, 3,600 and 2,160, represented the two important cycles of the gods. One was the orbital period of their planet, which in practice meant a ceremonial visit from the leader Anu, and an opportunity to transfer resources between the planets. The other determined the rotation of the Lordship over the gods on Earth. Amazingly, these two cycles precisely coincided every 10,800 Earth-years, at which point exactly 5 precessional ages were completed, and exactly three orbits of Nibiru.

Returning to the basis of Zecharia Sitchin's proposed chronology, we find that the key measurements of time – the 40 periods of toil and the 120 periods of the Lord – are exactly convertible between sars of 2,160 and 3,600. For example, 10, 20, 30, 40 and 120 sars of 2,160 years would translate exactly into 6, 12, 18, 24 and 72 sars of 3,600.

What is the relevance of this? It means that dates of Nibiru's return which marked key points in one calendar, could be exactly translated into precessional periods which preserved the same key dates in another calendar. And, as I have suggested, the star-clock came into use only *after* the Flood, when the Earth's present wobble was created. It was then, after civilisation was given to mankind, that the gods told the priests to pick up their tablets and write.

Since the meaning of SAR ('Lord/Ruler') applied equally to both cycles, could it be that the history of the gods had been recited using sars of 2,160, which had become even more sacred than the sars of 3,600? And could it be that, at some point thereafter, the sars of 2,160 years, written as 3–6–0–0, had become confused with sars of 3,600 years? I decided to construct a new chronology based on a sar of 2,160 and put it to the test:

	SITCHIN (sars of 3600)	ALFORD (sars of 2160)
Arrival of the gods (Flood – 120 sar):	443,000 BC	270,183 BC
Rebellion of rank-and-file gods (Arrival + 40 sar)	299,000 BC	183,783 BC
The Flood	11,000 BC	10,983 BC (see chapter 13)

Dating Homo Sapiens

Zecharia Sitchin dates the arrival of the gods to 443,000 BC, which he supports with a claim that they arrived in the Age of Pisces. According to my analysis, however, the precessional ages as we know them only began 13,000 years ago. It is therefore invalid to count back beyond that time using

precessional periods of 2,160 years. The gods may well have
arrived in an age of Pisces (the evidence is tenuous), but we
cannot possibly date it.[72]

As can be seen above, my chronology gives a much more
recent date for the creation of mankind, shortly after
184,000 years ago versus Sitchin's 299,000 years ago.
Which date is more likely to be correct?

As discussed in chapter 2, the question hinges on the
appearance of the so-called *archaic Homo sapiens*, which the
experts believe must represent an earlier evolutionary step
toward fully-fledged, anatomically modern *Homo sapiens*.
Since the latter is dated to around 200,000 years ago, the
archaics, it is assumed, must have appeared around 300,000
years ago. The latter is a convenient figure which also
matches the 'accepted' date for the demise of *Homo erectus*. A cynic would suggest that the scientists have interpreted the data to match their preconceptions of a smooth
evolutionary progression, and drawn their conclusions
accordingly.

How reliable is the dating of the archaic specimens? As I
pointed out in chapter 2, the accuracy of radiocarbon
dating is limited to 40,000 years ago. There is *not one*
reliable dating to suggest that the archaics preceded the
moderns. Added to which, the archaic specimens represent
such a small sample size that no-one is quite certain exactly
what they are. They combine features of modern man with
other, more archaic features, but with considerable varia-
bility in the combination of archaic and modern features.[73]
This can mean one of three things. Either this group had
been evolving for a long time (and if so, where is the fossil
evidence?), or they were the result of inter-breeding (genetically impossible?), or they represent unnatural genetic
experiments by the gods, as indeed described in the ancient
texts.

What reliable datings of *Homo sapiens* do we have? A
conference held in 1992 summarised the most reliable

evidence then available.[74] All of the dates I shall cite are the ranges of different specimens found at each location, and all dates are subject to an accuracy of $+/-$ 20 per cent. The most definitive dating is 115,000 years BP (Before Present) at Qafzeh in Israel. Other specimens at Skhul and Mount Carmel in Israel are dated at 101–81,000 BP. In Africa, specimens in the bottom layers of Border Cave are dated to 128,000 BP (confirmed to at least 100,000 BP using ostrich eggshell dating). At Klasies River Mouth, South Africa, the dates ranged from 130–118,000 BP. And finally, at Jebel Irhoud, South Africa, the dates went back the furthest of all, from 190–105,000 BP. The conclusion is that *Homo sapiens* appeared *less* than 200,000 years ago, and there is not one shred of evidence to date any modern or part-modern fossil any earlier.

Now let us take a look at the genetic evidence. In 1987, Allan Wilson, Mark Stoneking and Rebecca Cann, from the University of California at Berkeley, declared that all women alive today must have had a common genetic ancestor who lived between 250–150,000 years ago.[75] How did they arrive at this conclusion?

This genetic dating has been made possible by the discovery of mitochondria – the tiny bodies within a cell that are responsible for production of energy through breakdown of sugars. Unlike our other DNA, which is scrambled by sexual recombination, mitochondrial DNA (mtDNA) is inherited virtually unchanged through the female line and is thus a perfect marker to trace ancestral relations.[76] Moreover, it mutates at a predictable rate. The number of differences between the mtDNA in a worldwide sample of 135 different women allowed Wilson, Stoneking and Cann to compare how far back the ancestors of these women had diverged.

In order to calibrate the divergences, the researchers used a comparison of mtDNA between man and chimpanzees, based on a separation 5 million years ago. And that led to the conclusion that a common ancestor named 'Mitochondrial Eve' must have lived 250–150,000 years ago.

This genetic evidence has been challenged, due to its calibration with the chimpanzees, whose separation date from man is not known with certainty. Consequently, in 1992, the geneticists returned with an improved methodology. Working with other associates, Mark Stoneking this time used an intraspecific calibration, based on different human populations.[77] In order to validate the results, the team utilised two different approaches, which gave remarkably similar results. The revised date for the common mtDNA ancestor, with a 95 per cent degree of confidence, is now either 133,000 years or 137,000 years ago, using method 1 or method 2 respectively.

This new genetic evidence does not undermine the fossil evidence dating back to 190,000 years BP, but simply proves that surviving female variation dates to an ancestor who lived somewhat later. As Richard Dawkins has pointed out, this does not mean that Eve was the only woman on Earth at that time, just that she is the only one who has an unbroken line of female descendants.[78] The chances are that many earlier Eves have descendants alive today, but their ancestry has passed, at some point, through the male line only.

Despite the new mtDNA dates, most studies still tend to support and cite the 200,000 BP common ancestor. It is, after all, a date remarkably similar to the fossil evidence for the emergence of *Homo sapiens*. As for the 137–133,000 BP dating, I will return to this in chapter 13. It may have an extraordinary significance.

As a final comment, I would note that the Bible states that the gods 'created man in their own image'. Thus it would be impossible to tell apart the skeletal remains of a god from that of a man. The areas where *Homo sapiens* first emerged have been identified as Ethiopia, Kenya and South Africa. In chapter 14, I will identify the 'toil' of the gods as taking place in that exact same region. Therefore, if the palaeoanthropologists did one day discover what appeared to be a *Homo sapiens*, and dated it reliably to around 300,000 years ago, they could well be mistaking the remains of a god for the remains of a man. The ancient texts recorded that some of the rank-and-file gods did indeed die. During their mutiny, they complained that 'the excessive toil has killed us'.[79]

According to my chronology, this back-breaking toil began 272,000 years ago. Forty sars later, the rebellion of the rank-and-file gods led to the genetic creation of mankind. In due course, I will use Biblical data to prove that these sars lasted 2,160 years, and that man was therefore created shortly after 184,000 years ago. First, however, it is essential to revisit our genetic origins and reconsider the longevity which the Bible claimed for the early patriarchs. This is the subject of the next chapter.

Chapter Eleven Conclusions

* The Flood occurred *c.* 11000 BC, and the Pyramids at Giza were constructed shortly afterwards, *c.* 10450 BC.

* The tidal wave from the Flood affected the Earth's wobble, and initiated the 25,920-year precessional cycle. The gods measured time by the motion of the Earth and created a 'star-clock' by dividing the precessional cycle into 12 periods of 2,160 years.

* The Sphinx was built *c.* 8700 BC to commemorate the end of a war between the gods and retrospectively marked the first precessional age of Leo. The war led to a surrender by the Enkiite group of gods, who

agreed that their rivals would assume 'Lordship' over the Earth for three consecutive precessional periods.

* The shift from Taurus to Aries *c.* 2400–2300 BC marked the time when Marduk was *controversially* due to resume Lordship for the Enkiite gods. Antipathy towards Marduk led to a bitter dispute over the exact date for the beginning of his reign.

* Stonehenge was built by Thoth for Marduk as a sophisticated observatory, to measure the rate of change of the precessional cycle, and to make predictions of future star positions.

* A second star-clock was built at Machu Picchu in Peru, where Thoth initiated the Andean calendar in 2900 BC. Other observatories were built at Tian Tan (China), in Lagash (ancient Sumer) and at Barbar (Bahrain).

CHAPTER TWELVE

ADAM'S DESIGNER GENES

———◆———

The Gods of Eden

Our journey has taken us back in time to events nearly 200,000 years ago, when the rank-and-file gods rebelled and mankind was created. But how do these events tie in with the Biblical tale of the Garden of Eden, and what really happened there? Who was the 'serpent' that spoke to Eve? What was the fruit which Adam and Eve ate from the Tree of Knowledge? And why did it then become so important to block their access to the Tree of Life? In this chapter, we will lift the veil of mythology and cast aside the religious symbolism in order to gain a full scientific understanding of these events.

We will start with the location and meaning of Eden. Genesis 2 states that Eden was watered by four rivers. Two of these rivers are named as the Tigris and the Euphrates, leading most scholars to locate the tale of Eden in Mesopotamia. The other two rivers, however, the Pishon and the Gihon appear to have African connections. This has caused Biblical scholars a great deal of confusion for a long time. Could there in fact have been two Edens?

In chapter 6, we saw that the Sumerian name for their gods, DIN.GIR, literally meant the 'Righteous Ones of the

Rockets'. In the Sumerian language E.DIN would therefore literally mean the 'Home of the Righteous Ones'. There is little doubt that E.DIN and Eden are one and the same. Eden was the abode of the gods.

Having thus identified the meaning of Eden, we would indeed expect there to be more than one abode of the gods. In chapter 6, I described the division of the Earth between the two major groups of gods, descended from the two brothers Enlil and Enki. We have identified the Enlilite lands as Mesopotamia, in the east, and the Enkiite lands in the Lower World of Africa, in the west. The idea of two Edens enables us to solve certain inconsistencies which have long been recognised in the Biblical creation account. For instance, both Genesis 1 and Genesis 5 suggest that male and female were created together by Elohim on the 'sixth day':

> He created them male and female and blessed them. And when they were created, he called them 'man'.[1]

But in Genesis 2, it states that man was created *first*, and a female helper was *later* created *from* man to keep him company.

Furthermore, there is a strong suggestion that the man *already* existed when he was placed by God in the Garden of Eden:

> Now the Lord God had planted a garden in the east, in Eden; and *there he put the man he had formed*.[2] (emphasis added)

These texts sit uncomfortably with the account which follows in Genesis 2, when the creation of Eve appears to take place in the eastern Eden. Could this Biblical passage have been recorded out of sequence? Was there in fact an earlier creation of both males and females in the west?

At this point we should recall the *Atra-Hasis* text (cited in chapter 1), which claimed that fourteen birth goddesses simultaneously produced seven males and seven females in order to relieve the 'toil' of the gods.[3] And we should also note that all of the Mesopotamian texts attributed the creation of man to Enki, the chief god of the *African* lands.

Was it thus from the *western* Eden of Africa that the Lord God acquired the man, whom he subsequently placed in the eastern Eden? A text named by Professor Samuel Kramer *The Myth of the Pickaxe* begins to shed some light on the matter, and identifies the Lord God as Enlil:

> The Anunnaki [rank-and-file gods] stepped up to Enlil . . .
> Black-headed Ones they were requesting of him.
> To the Black-headed people
> to give the pickaxe to hold.
>
> The Lord Enlil,
> whose decisions are unalterable,
> verily did speed to separate Heaven from Earth;
> in the DUR.AN.KI he made a gash,
> so that the Created Ones could come up
> from the Place-Where-Flesh-Sprouted-Forth.
>
> The Lord called forth the AL.ANI, gave its orders.
> He set the earth splitter as a crown upon its head,
> and drove it into the Place-Where-Flesh-Sprouted-Forth.
> In the hole was a head of a man;
> from the ground, people were breaking through towards Enlil.
> He eyed the Black-headed Ones in steadfast fashion.[4]

In other texts, the Place-Where-Flesh-Sprouted-Forth was referred to as *Bit Shimti* – the 'House' of Shimti. The Sumerian syllables SHI.IM.TI literally translate as 'Breath-Wind-Life'. *Bit Shimti* was thus the 'House Where the Wind of Life was Breathed In'.[5] The wording is directly comparable to Genesis 2:7, where the Lord God formed man and 'breathed into his nostrils the breath of life'.

Why was it necessary for Enlil to use force to acquire the

Black-headed Ones? The text makes it clear that there was a dispute between Enlil and his brother Enki. Enki wished to keep the exclusive use of the workers to reduce the toil of the gods in the African lands, whilst Enlil felt obligated to ease the toil of the gods in Mesopotamia.

Thus it was that *the Adam* came to be taken, by force, and placed in the Garden of Eden. Against this background we can begin to understand the ensuing events.

Identity of the Serpent Gods

Who or what was the Serpent in the Garden of Eden? Since it spoke to Eve, it would be logical to conclude that it was not a snake, but a god – a rival god to Enlil. It is a fact that all over the world there are examples of ancient people worshipping the serpent as a positive force. This appears strange only due to the fact that Western theologians have used the Genesis story to depict the snake as a satanic force.

In Mesoamerica, Aztec myth describes the creation of man by the Feathered Serpent god, Quetzalcoatl, who was assisted by the Serpent Woman, Cihuacoatl. At the ancient Aztec capital of Tenochtitlan (present day Mexico City), the sacred precinct was decorated with the heads of feathered serpents and, in the centre, the entrance to the temple of Quetzalcoatl was guarded by the gaping fangs of a giant serpent. These Aztec serpent designs dominate numerous other sacred sites such as Teotihuacan in Mexico. The ancient Maya also revered the Feathered Serpent god, this time by the name of Kulkulkan. All over Mesoamerica, Aztec, Mayan and Toltec sites were dominated by the serpent motif, which can still be clearly seen to this day.

To the east of Mesoamerica, the country of Haiti has legends of the serpent going back to the beginning of creation. The native voodoo people believe in a god called

Damballah Wedo, whose image is the serpent. Damballah Wedo is seen as the Great Serpent, the Creator of the Universe, Heavens and Earth. According to a curious voodoo Flood tradition, the Serpent let go the waters upon the Earth, the Rainbow arose and the Serpent took the rainbow, named Ayida Wedo, as his wife.[6]

In North America, too, serpents were a key feature of the native Indian cultures. The serpent symbol dominates the art of the Hohokam Indians at sites such as the famous Snaketown, Arizona in the south-west USA, dating from *c.* 400 BC to AD 1200. Meanwhile, in the north, an unknown culture left a huge and mysterious serpent-shaped mound in Ohio.[7]

On the opposite side of the world, in the Far East, we again find gods associated with serpents. In Tibet, for example, the serpent adorns the sacred trumpets of the monks. And in Nepal, at a site called Budhanilkantha, a mysterious statue known as the Sleeping Vishnu lies on a bed of snakes in a water tank (Plate 63, colour section).

We should not leave out Iraq, the cradle of civilisation. Just north of Mosul, near the town of Sheikh Adi, is the Shrine of the Yezidis, where the serpent symbol is proudly emblazoned on the main door. This site is an important place of pilgrimage for thousands of the nomadic Yezidis.[8] In western eyes they are seen as devil worshippers, but the Yezidis regard the serpent as the most powerful force in the world, the dispenser of good as well as evil.

In Australia, the aboriginal people have carefully preserved legends of the serpent in their so-called 'Dreamtime' myths of the Earth's creation. In the central region of Australia, ancient drawings can be found of the Rainbow Serpent, who created rivers, mountains and people on his legendary journey down from the north coast.[9]

The numerous examples cited above are hardly examples of satanic worship. If the serpent is satanic, then perhaps the theologians could explain why the serpent is the symbol of medicine and healing to this day. As one authority notes:

> Ancient statues frequently depict the god [Aesculapius] as bearing a staff round which is entwined a sacred snake. But the association of the serpent with healing is a very old belief; and it is worthwhile to note that to this day the symbol of the profession of healing is a snake entwined around a staff, although it is connected with supernatural healing and not with rational medicine.[10]

This belief is traceable to the Roman god Aesculapius, the father of medicine and healing, whose marble statue from the Capitoline Museum in Rome (Figure 20, black-and-white section) clearly shows the serpent and staff symbol.[11] It would seem that the legend ultimately traces back to the Greek Hermes, who is identified with the Egyptian god Thoth. However, that god learned everything from his father, Enki, the god who masterminded the genetic creation of mankind.

Could all of these serpent tales have evolved independently, or do they have a common source in the Enkiite gods of Africa? The latter seems the more plausible scenario. In ancient Egypt, for example, there is no doubt that, of the many animals depicted in their art, the serpent was the most auspicious and sacred. Two serpents were commonly depicted wearing the royal crowns of Upper and Lower Egypt respectively. The pharaohs, too, were often shown with a serpent on the forehead. And, most sacred of all, two serpents were usually depicted flanking the winged disc of Nibiru.

In the rival land of Kush, to the south of Egypt, the serpent was equally revered. Kushite and Meroite kings and queens were depicted wearing crowns with the royal emblem of the cobra. The symbol of the winged serpent is a typical feature on local pottery.[12]

There is no doubt that the ancient African civilisations

were the home of the serpent gods – the only question is how and why these gods first became associated with serpents.

The Meaning of the Serpent

So the Lord God said to the serpent,
'Because you have done this,
Cursed are you above all the livestock
and all the wild animals!
You will crawl on your belly
and you will eat dust
all the days of your life.
And I will put enmity
between you and the woman
and between your offspring and hers;
he will crush your head,
and you will strike his heel.'[13]

At first glance, it might seem that the Lord God's curse was extremely effective. Studies of human likes and dislikes of animals show that the snake is the overwhelmingly least popular animal, amassing 27 per cent of the vote, compared to only 9.5 per cent for the spider in second place.[14]

The reason why the snake is so hated appears, however, to have more to do with human psychology than a divine curse. Desmond Morris attributes it to an inborn aversion which has less to do with the danger of being bitten, and more to do with their almost complete lack of anthropomorphic (human-like) features.

In view of our innate dislike of snakes, it becomes particularly intriguing why it should have been a sacred symbol for the ancient civilisations. If we take the Aztec Feathered Serpent, for example, the feather symbolism would seem to represent the gods' flight capability. But the origin of the snake itself as a symbol seems to have eluded most writers on the subject.

Did the Enkiite gods have a penchant for wearing snake skins, or did they have an obsession with pet snakes who accompanied them on their travels? These ideas seem far-fetched. Tracking down the origin of the symbol is fraught with difficulty. Take for example the following extract from a Sumerian poem known as *Enki and the World Order*, in which Enki himself is the narrator:

> When I approached Earth
> there was much flooding.
> When I approached its green meadows,
> heaps and mounds were piled up at my command.
> I built my house in a pure place . . .
> My house – its shade stretches over the *Snake Marsh*.[15]
>   (emphasis added)

This text describes Enki's return to Earth after the Flood, and the rebuilding of his original house at Eridu.[16] But what does the Snake reference really mean? Does it signify the actual presence of snakes in the marsh, and thus a possible origin of their association with the Enkiite gods? Or does it simply apply an *already existing* nickname which had its origin elsewhere?

A major clue lies in the literal meaning of the Hebrew word for the Biblical Serpent – *nahash*. This term comes from the root NHSH which means 'to find things out, to solve secrets'[17] – a fitting description of Enki, the chief scientist of the gods, and of his sons to whom he passed on his knowledge. Once again, however, we must still question how the snake came to be associated with the gods of wisdom. The Garden of Eden tale does not provide a convincing answer as to why the serpent symbol was *proudly* adopted by the Enkiites and the civilisations with which they were connected.

On the contrary, there is a much better explanation. The

connection of the serpent symbol with the Enkiite gods (which as far as I know no-one has yet explained) lies in the African lands. It is so obvious that many writers have commented on it without realising the significance. The following quote from the *Art and History of Egypt* hit me like a lightning bolt.

> As time passed, the Nile gradually evolved into its present form, *a gigantic serpent* that began in the heart of Africa and wound its way, for thousands of kilometres along the Red Sea, until it found an outlet in the Mediterranean.[18] (emphasis added)

The effect of the Nile is the same on all who see it. Another writer stated:

> . . . seen from the air, it looks like *a gigantic snake*, lazily slinking northwards to the cool Mediterranean.[19] (emphasis added)

The Nile does indeed *crawl along the ground*, just like a snake, regularly reversing direction (200 miles south at one point) and then rediscovering its northwards route. The significance of this river to Africa cannot be overstated. Today, it flows through ten countries and provides 97 per cent of Egypt's water.[20] To the ancient Egyptians, and to their gods, the Nile meant life, in a land almost totally devoid of rain. The regular annual flooding of the Nile's banks left behind a highly fertile soil, creating a six mile wide swathe of green through a landscape of total desolation. The words of Herodotus remain true today: 'Egypt is a gift of the Nile'.[21]

By recognising the Nile as the Serpent, we can explain why *all* the Enkiite gods, whose domains were in Africa, were associated with the sign of the snake or serpent.[22] In the earliest times, there were no negative connotations of snakes. On the contrary, it was a favourable symbol – of the god Enki who created mankind, of the same god who saved man from the Flood, and of all the Enkiite gods who possessed advanced scientific knowledge which was bequeathed to man.

We have only the Bible to thank for the association of the serpent with evil. And it now becomes clear that the Garden of Eden story was simply a political put-down by one god of another – based on a dispute which we will shortly examine. It would seem that whatever the serpent-god did to Adam and Eve was a retaliation for the forced raid by Enlil on the African LU.LU workers. Enraged by this retaliation, Enlil cursed his brother Enki by applying his epithet NHSH 'the solver of secrets' to the humble snake, an animal which is naturally detested by man. It was an appropriate choice of animal due to its resemblance to the flowing Nile – the latter symbol having *already* been adopted by the Enkiites.

That the events did indeed occur in this manner is supported by the juxtaposition of the Eden story in Genesis 3 to the naming of all the animals by man in Genesis 2:19–20. In my view, the latter passage appears out of sequence, and properly belongs with the tale of the cursing of the serpent in Genesis 3.

Immortality of the Gods?

According to the Sumerians, immortality was the preserve of the gods alone, and was not granted to mankind. As one poet eloquently put it:

> Only the gods live for ever under the sun,
> as for mankind, numbered are their days,
> whatever they achieve is but wind.[23]

Was it always so, or did mankind, too, experience a brief golden age of immortality? The very presence of the Tree of

Life in the Garden of Eden *can* be interpreted as showing that man originally had *conditional* immortality.[24] This Tree is seen as having the power, bestowed by God its creator, to impart imperishable physical life, for as long as He permitted man to partake of it. By eating the forbidden 'fruit', Adam and Eve gave up their immortality – as the Bible said: 'to dust you will return'.

Some religions attribute this penalty to Adam and Eve's disobedience, but it is more likely a trade-off for their acquisition of sexual knowledge.[25] In any event, to have retained immortality would have resulted symbolically in man continuing to sin forever, thus precluding any possibility of redemption, which is a basic tenet of Christianity. The blame for man's loss of immortality, and gaining of sexual knowledge, is ultimately placed on the snake, or serpent-god, that caused Adam and Eve to eat the fruit.

Could there just possibly be a real phenomenon hidden within all the religious symbolism concerning immortality? Could it be that there was some physical substance to the Tree of Life? Could its 'fruit' have been a drug which delayed the ageing process? It is a curious coincidence that, from the very beginning of human history, the flesh-and-blood gods were perceived as immortal beings.

The apparent impossibility of immortality has caused most scholars to reject the ancient tales as romanticised myths, but what if we are dealing not with immortality but with *extended longevity*? If this was the case, the gods may well have appeared to man to be immortal because they aged so slowly. Immortality would thus have been perceived and not real.

With the benefit of hindsight, we do indeed find textual clues to suggest that the gods did suffer the effects of ageing over the very long term. Ninharsag, for instance, a goddess who was instrumental in the creation of man around 180,000 years ago (by my chronology) was later known in Egypt as 'the Cow' – an unflattering reference with definite ageing connotations. The Canaanite god El, meanwhile, was described as having a grey beard; the goddess Asherah said to El 'thou art great indeed and wise; thy beard's grey hair instructs thee . . . wisdom and everlife are thy portion'.[26] Did the gods have extended longevity?

Our sceptical twentieth century scientists would get a satisfactory answer to this question only by rediscovering the longevity drug or capturing one of these super-beings and marching him into the laboratory for genetic testing. The first is a possibility, but it would prove nothing. The latter is a most unlikely scenario. The truth is that we would not expect to find any scientific evidence of the gods' longevity in a form that could be objectively tested. On the other hand, we would expect to see a really major impact on the cultural beliefs of the humans who lived alongside these gods. This is the only testable theory – and it is exactly what we find.

From the earliest times of civilisation six thousand years ago, humans have been obsessed with immortality and have searched far and wide for a 'Land of the Living' or a 'Fountain of Eternal Youth'. Examples include the adventures of the Sumerian kings Gilgamesh and Amar-Sin in the third millennium BC, the journeys of Alexander the Great in the fourth century BC and, in more recent times, the voyages of Columbus.

Amazing as it may seem to us with our twentieth century preconceptions, these powerful historic figures took the quest for immortality extremely seriously. The sceptics would view this obsession as an understandable social response to the daily struggles and tragedies of human existence. On the contrary, the evidence suggests that the obsession with immortality was not an abstract phenomenon, but a targeted quest.

In the cases of the Sumerian kings, and possibly in the case of Alexander the Great too, they knew the exact physical locations which were associated with the perceived immortality of the gods. We saw these locations in *The Epic of Gilgamesh* (chapter 8), when Gilgamesh travelled to the west – first to the gods' platform in Baalbek, and thereafter to the boundary of the Sinai space centre. Meanwhile, on the other side of the Sinai peninsula, the Egyptians located the Land of the Gods *in the east*.

The cultural impact of the gods' longevity is best seen in Egypt. Most people today are fascinated, but confused, by the ancient Egyptians. It is almost as if they had some secret, esoteric knowledge which we cannot quite grasp. By the time the pharaohs came to rule Egypt, their two main gods Thoth and Ra/Amen were both absent. But the traditions and memories of these gods, and the legends of their immortality, were still fresh. These pharaohs were men who were blessed by the gods with a high level of scientific knowledge, but little comprehension. In life they, like Gilgamesh, were forbidden to enter the Land of the Gods, but in death they imagined their 'ka' or spirit-double following the journey of the gods, via a pyramid, across water and between two mountains to the Duat, from where they would ascend to heaven and everlasting life. It was an emulation of a physical journey undertaken by the god Osiris six thousand years earlier.

Wherever one goes in Egypt, there are obvious marks of a cultural impact which is comparable to the effect of Christianity in the churches and cathedrals of the western world. Whether it be giant obelisks, huge pyramids, temples, statues, tombs or papyrus texts, the entire culture of the early Egyptians is indelibly stamped with the immortality cult of the pharaohs.

Is it possible for us to accept some scientific basis for these cultural beliefs? How can we rationalise the possibility that the gods lived for hundreds of thousands of years? As tempting as it is to retreat behind our cosy paradigms, let us keep our minds open.

Let us imagine for a moment that we genetically capped

the life span of all future human offspring at a mere 50 years (though I hasten to add that I am sure there are better ways of cutting the social security budget!). After two generations, the last human centenarians would die off. The first few generations with artificially capped life spans would initially be perplexed by their own short lives. However, after a hundred or so generations, the reduced life span of 50 years would be regarded as perfectly normal. And – here is my point – any recollection of people living to 120 would then be dismissed as sheer myth. The 20th century history books which diligently recorded the lives of our statesmen would be regarded as the work of liars or imbeciles. Our future ancestors in the 40th century might even decide to edit the history books to conform to their accepted norms.

I hope the point of principle has been established. It is now time to examine what science has to say on the subject.

What is Ageing?

What exactly is the ageing process? In the past we might have been forgiven for thinking that our bodies simply wore out through the stresses of everyday life. However, we now understand that ageing is genetically pre-programmed into the cells of the human body.

We all started our lives as a single cell, namely the female egg known as the ovum. After fertilisation, the ovum contained a complete set of chromosomes (the human genome), half from our mother and half from our father. This genome can be compared to a recipe for building the human body. Shortly after fertilisation, the building of our bodies began through a process of cell division, which culminated in hundreds of millions of cells – blood cells, bone cells, muscles, flesh, organs and so on – all necessary to make us the complete human beings that we are.

Even into adult life, most of our cells continue to divide. This splitting of one cell into two involves a duplicating of the genetic message (the human genome) which is carried on the 46 chromosomes in every human cell. But instead of an exact duplication, our genetic programme is being gradually eroded by an imperfect copying process. And, when enough of these mistakes have accumulated in our cells, the effects of ageing become visible.

It is these genetic errors (or mutations) that cause the greying of our hair when the pigment cells in the scalp cease to function. Similar factors cause our bones to weaken, our joints to shrink and our spines to curve. Geneticist Steve Jones describes it as a 'biological identity crisis' and explains that our ageing bodies are working from 'an imperfect instruction manual, full of printing errors'.[27] Professor Rajinder Sohal of the Southern Methodist University in Dallas states that: 'after the age of 55 human beings go to hell very fast because the rate of deterioration doubles every six years'.[28] So serious is this escalation in the rate of genetic degradation that, by the time we are 80, a critical one third of our protein has been damaged.

Why should nature have evolved such an imperfect copying system? On the contrary, it would seem that the problem lies not in the genes themselves but in the air that we breathe. Doug Wallace, head of genetics at Emory University in Atlanta, USA, has spent 25 years studying minute organisms called mitochondria, which exist inside every human cell. These mitochondria are the power plants of the cells, and thus of the body, synthesising oxygen (provided by our red blood cells) and other nutrients to provide energy for the cells' various functions. Wallace, along with many other eminent scientists, believes that excess oxygen, often referred to as 'free radicals', causes corrosive damage to the cells in the same way as oxygen causes cars to rust and butter to go rancid.

Geneticists believe that our genes have evolved maintenance systems in the form of enzymes, built in to the cells, which specify the repair of damage caused by the free radicals. The primary purpose of these enzymes is to constantly travel up and down the chromosomes, checking and correcting any damage.[29] This process is facilitated by the double-stranded nature of the DNA which forms the chromosome. The DNA double helix is like a spiral ladder with two twisting side-rods linked together by numerous rungs in between. The rungs comprise *pairs* of the DNA letters – A, G, C and T, such that the sequence down the side-rods spells out the DNA words or instructions. Significantly, the rungs can exist only in the combinations of A/T or C/G. This rule enables the enzymes to proof-read the DNA and repair any missing letters. The system may not be foolproof, however, in the rare event that opposite pairs are simultaneously damaged.

It would appear that the process of cell division must be a key feature of the body's defence system against the attack from free radicals. At a certain point in time, something in the genes instructs the cell to divide into two and thereby renew its defences. This involves the simultaneous division of every chromosome within the cell. Ironically, the chromosomes are at their most vulnerable at this time, for the process involves the breakdown of the protecting membrane of the cell nucleus. Thus exposed, the chromosomes uncoil themselves into straight ladders and divide. The rungs of the ladder are snapped apart, and the two strands of DNA separate. Any damage to the single strands of DNA at this moment, *before* they form a new partner strand, may be irreparable. However, studies of mutations show that they are much more common in the non-active or junk DNA,[30] suggesting that the cells contain a defence mechanism that highlights the *active* genes as the priority target for protection.

Recent research has begun to provide clues as to the exact process of cell ageing. Scientists at the Geron Corporation, whose Board of Advisers includes James Watson (from the famous Watson and Crick partnership that discovered the DNA molecule), believe they may have discovered the biological clock, the mechanism that controls life and death in the cell. It is called a telomere – a repeating DNA sequence found at the tail of every chromosome, and often compared to the protective plastic tip of a shoelace. Every time a cell divides, and the DNA in the chromosome replicates, this tail grows a little shorter. In a baby it is about 20,000 letters long, whilst in a 60-year old it is less than half this.[31] When the telomere has been reduced to a certain point, the cell stops dividing and enters a stage called senescence. At this point, the cells and their functions suffer an escalating amount of damage.

Human cells divide at different rates, and genes have different mutation rates, for reasons that are not entirely clear to scientists.[32] Certain sequences of DNA bases mutate more often than others and this genetic damage occurs at different rates in different parts of the body. Large genes with more interspersed pieces of DNA are more prone to damage than simpler genes,[33] and, to complicate matters further still, if the genes which specify the self-maintenance system are themselves attacked, the cells will become less effective at repairing the damage, and the speed of deterioration will thus increase.[34]

Ageing is clearly a complex process, with many different body systems going wrong at different times. Two of the most crucial systems are thought to be the brain and the immune system. The brain is unusual in the fact that cell divisions cease at an early stage, followed by a long process of gradual cell deaths.[35] This affects critical faculties such as hearing, sense of smell and memory. The immune system, on the other hand, has (rather curiously) the highest mutation rate of all body cells, and is among the first to fail with age, leaving us susceptible to all manner of diseases.[36] The combined deterioration of these two systems is central to the ageing process which ends in natural death.

Some scientists believe that all aspects of ageing will ultimately be traced to a single gene, named the Methuselah Gene. The vast majority of scientists, however, believe ageing to be far more complex. Hundreds of genes are generally thought to be involved, although some may be more crucial than others. In the end, ageing may come down to just a few dozen critical genes.

The Science of Longevity

Longevity is the latest genetic science. Whilst our ancestors such as Gilgamesh and Alexander the Great sought it in the land of the gods, today our scientists seek it in the laboratories. Whereas previously it was thought that all organisms had a maximum life span fixed by the rate of ageing of their body cells,[37] now it is thought that the body's genetic programme can be changed. Is immortality thus within our reach?

In June 1995, it was announced that scientists had found a longevity gene that could prolong the life of microscopic earthworms by up to 65 per cent. A team led by Tom Johnson of the Institute for Behavioural Genetics at the University of Colorado discovered a gene, which they named 'Age-1', that regulated the worms' *ability to repair their cells*. By experimenting with mutations of this gene, they found that one mutation caused a remarkable improvement in the worms' resistance to toxins, temperature fluctuations and ultraviolet radiation. The team believe that this major breakthrough represents the first step towards understanding how cells that degenerate in later life can be repaired. They hope that, within the next decade, the human equivalent of Age-1 will be understood, enabling human life to be prolonged by more than 40 years.

In December 1995, it was reported that Dr Barbara Bregman and a team from the Universities of Zurich and Georgetown in Washington DC had also made another major breakthrough, which was hailed as 'the holy grail of neurobiology'. It had been thought that it was biologically impossible to regenerate the nerve cells in the brain and spinal cord (unlike other body tissues), once they were damaged. However, Bregman discovered that, by using antibodies, she could block the action of inhibitor chemicals which prevented the nerve cells of rats from growing. In this way, she successfully managed to restore the growth potential which the rats' cells had when they were young.[38]

Meanwhile, a team of scientists in France, led by Dr Francois Schachter, has been studying the human immune system – identified earlier as a genetic weak link – by a painstaking comparison of French centenarians' DNA to a control sample of the general population. Schachter has already found one gene, named 'HLA-DR', which is far more prevalent in the centenarian group.

Schachter's colleague Marie-Laure Muiras is one of many scientists who are studying ways to reduce the damage caused by free radicals. Muiras has found in the centenarian group a gene, named 'PARP', which may be responsible for specifying the DNA repair process. If we could fully understand this genetic system, we could consider the creation of genes which specified a super-efficient maintenance system.

An alternative defence against ageing is to fend off the free radicals *before* they cause any damage. Professor Rajinder Sohal (mentioned earlier) has injected fruit flies with genes which protect their cells against oxygen attack, and has already successfully increased their life spans by one third. Doug Wallace (also mentioned earlier) thinks it may be possible to overcome the effect of the free radicals by assembling a cocktail of chemicals which form a barrier around the cells.[39]

Finally, we return to the telomeres, where further research may stand the best chance of a *revolutionary* breakthrough. Scientists working for the Geron Corporation are confident that the telomeres are the clocking mechanism that determines the life of the cell. They are also quietly confident that it may be possible to influence the *length* of a telomere. This would be a dramatic development, with the possibility of preventing the vast majority of genetic copying errors arising in the first place, as well as enabling the restoration of youth to already senescent cells.

If we can eliminate the effect of the free radicals, indefinitely extend the number of cell divisions, and possibly even restore growth to nerve cells in the brain and spinal cord, what limits would there be to human life? Even if we were to suffer disfiguring accidents, new breakthroughs in tissue engineering could step in to preserve our bodies.

Are these dreams of human longevity just pie in the sky, or do the mechanisms exist to make the dream come true? It is all very well experimenting with rats, but how do we get new genetic material into the human cells where it really matters? The solution lies in another new technology of the late twentieth century – gene therapy.

What is gene therapy? The basic concept is to introduce corrective genes to cure damaged cells. Almost every illness is due to the improper functioning of one or more genes. Gene therapy would provide a cure by inserting a new gene into the damaged cells; the new gene would take whatever corrective action was necessary. In cancer patients, for example, it might instruct the production of the protein which would kill off the malignant cells. The challenge for the genetic scientists is to deliver the gene to the right cell location. Research is now focusing on the use of *viruses* to act as the delivery mechanism. Due to their innate ability to attack and invade cells, the virus is the perfect natural carrier. In theory the virus can be reprogrammed to neutralise the viral infection and to carry instead a new cargo of corrective genetic material. A team of British scientists recently announced the use of the herpes virus to target the central nervous system (including the brain), thus offering a potential delivery system for the treatment of Alzheimer's and Parkinson's diseases.

Expectations from gene therapy are running high. Up to four thousand illnesses are caused by damage to a single gene. Laboratory trials are being conducted all around the world on how to deal with a number of the more serious conditions, including Aids, Haemophilia, cystic fibrosis, rheumatoid arthritis and vascular disease, as well as various forms of cancer. Impatient critics are quick to point out that no-one has yet had a disease cured solely by the use of gene therapy, but in truth the research is still in its very early stages, and a number of challenges still need to be overcome.[40] *The Sunday Times* probably struck the right note of realism when it described gene therapy as a: 'burgeoning area of medicine that is destined to become a commonplace treatment over the next 50 years'.[41]

Although primarily designed for the treatment of illnesses, gene therapy offers the potential delivery mechanism for some of the longevity improvements which we have discussed. The perfection of this treatment is proceeding alongside the deciphering of the human genome and the search for the entire sequence of longevity genes, with a potential coming together in the early part of the 21st century. In the words of one of the most eminent scientists in the field, Dr Francois Schachter:

There is no reason why we should not extend the maximum human life span. We are very close to having the technology, and the pieces of the jigsaw are rapidly falling into place.[42]

Pure Genes of the Gods

As we stand on the threshold of a huge breakthrough in ageing science, we have to ask ourselves whether the gods, who created us, have been here before us.

In chapter 2, I set out clear evidence that our genes – the genes we inherited from the gods – have evolved over a long and peaceful period – elsewhere. However, although the laws of natural selection would statistically favour the development of longevity genes, it is difficult to imagine that the gods *naturally* acquired life spans of hundreds of thousands of years. The feasible solution to this puzzle must lie in the artificial mutation of their genes, a process which we ourselves are now beginning to contemplate for the first time. We are thus at a point in history where we can – for the first time – begin to take seriously the textual evidence that the gods *appeared* to be immortal.

A strange feature of the Mesopotamian texts dealing with the affairs of the gods is their preoccupation with having offspring by a *half-sister*. Under the gods' rules of succession, the progeny of such an alliance became the legal heir in preference to the first-born son. As we have seen, it was this practice that caused bitter rivalry between the brothers Enlil and Enki. One text describes the manoeuvres of Enki in attempting to produce a male heir by his half-sister Ninharsag.[43] This rule of succession also led to the rivalry between the Egyptian gods Osiris and Seth.

Such a practice seems strange to us because it verges on incest, and indeed there are good scientific reasons why incest is prohibited. Once again the answer lies in the genes. Most harmful genes are recessive by nature – that is to say that they are dominated by an equivalent safe gene. Generally speaking, we need to inherit two copies of the recessive gene, one from each parent, for the disease to have any effect. Producing offspring from a close relative thus increases the risk of the child receiving two copies of the same recessive.

Why then were the gods not only unconcerned about inbreeding, but positively in favour of it? The answer can only be that the genes of the gods were *pure* and contained no harmful imperfections. Furthermore, we could go so far as to speculate that the genetic improvements in longevity were reserved only for the ruling elite among the gods.[44] This assumption explains the rather strange meaning of the name of the Babylonian god MAR.DUK – 'Son of the Pure Mound'[45] – indicating the genetic purity of his father Enki, and in particular those genes associated with longevity.

Our ancestors were unfortunately not aware of the dangers of inbreeding, and continued to emulate the gods' practice of marrying half-sisters. Abraham, for instance, boasted that his wife was also his sister,[46] whilst the Egyptian pharaohs and the Inca rulers are also thought to have carried out similar practices.

Earlier I recounted examples which showed that the gods *did* seem to suffer the effects of ageing. This idea is further supported by the retirement phase which Enlil and Enki went through when they set up the precessional ages to give the younger gods the chance to govern. It would thus seem that whatever genetic improvements they had made, there was still an inexorable state of deterioration.

If this was the case, then we would expect to find evidence of further attempts to slow down the ageing process – steps above and beyond the original, artificial creation of the genes and their ancestral preservation through incest. We are talking here of a *maintenance* system, directly equivalent to the modern fight against free radicals. And that is exactly what we find.

It has long been assumed that Egyptian depictions of gods being served with cups (contents unknown) symbolised their immortality. The ancient artist would hardly bother to commemorate the even if it was not important. The symbolic importance of the cup of immortality is also evident from numerous Mesopotamian tombs, where archaeologists have found bodies lying with the hand holding a cup to the mouth, as if the dead were about to drink. These burials included various other accoutrements for day-to-day life, implying an association of the cup with eternal life in the hereafter.[47] The cultural comparison with Egypt hardly requires elaboration.

Does the ancient Egyptian association of gods and cups represent an eye-witness account of the gods consuming anti-ageing substances? Such observation may have occurred not necessarily in Egypt but in nearby Mesopotamia, where the kings and high priests lived alongside their gods. One source of this esoteric knowledge may have been the Sumerian king Gilgamesh. Tablet X of *The Epic of Gilgamesh* describes his journey to the land of the gods, where he meets Utnapishtim (Noah). In Tablet XI, Utnapishtim relates to Gilgamesh the story of the Flood, and then gives to the departing hero a plant called 'the old man becomes young':

> 'Gilgamesh, I will reveal unto thee a hidden thing,
> namely, a secret of the gods I will tell thee:
> there is a plant like a thorn . . .
> Like a rose its thorns will prick thy hands.
> If thy hands will obtain that plant, thou wilt find new life.'[48]

Another Sumerian text, dealing with the tale of Adapa – a 'Model Man' created by Ea/Enki – describes his trip to Nibiru, the planet of the gods. Here, we find references to 'the water of life' and 'the bread of life'.[49] Finally, there is the Garden of Eden with its Tree of Life which offered potential immortality to Adam and Eve. Let us now return to the Garden of Eden, where all of the legends, ancient texts and depictions join with the latest scientific evidence to allow, for the first time, a full understanding of this historic event.

The Adam's Designer Genes

Now the serpent was more crafty than any of the wild animals the Lord God had made. He said to the woman 'Did God really say, "You must not eat from any tree in the garden?"'

The woman said to the serpent, 'We may eat fruit from the trees in the garden, but God did say, "You must not eat fruit from the tree that is in the middle of the garden, and you must not touch it, or you will die."'

'You will not surely die', the serpent said to the woman. 'For God knows that when you eat of it your eyes will be opened, and you will be like God, knowing good and evil.'[50]

In the absence of the original Mesopotamian story, it is difficult to know how literally to take the highly symbolised Biblical account. The basic essence of the story, however, is clear – a fruit or drug is forbidden, but then consumed, leading to sexual 'knowledge'. In the context of the Bible this 'knowledge' is clearly sexual knowledge.[51]

Why was sexual knowledge such a dangerous thing for the newly emerging humans to have? The answer lies in the earliest creation of man before he was placed in the Garden of Eden – the *Atra-Hasis* account of the creation using fourteen birth-goddesses. In chapter 2, I compared this process to the cloning of a genetically engineered hybrid of *Homo erectus* and a god. A common feature of hybrids, whether natural such as the mule or unnatural (in the laboratory), is sterility.[52] Whilst two different species with similar chromosomal structure can produce offspring, the biological process is not sufficiently accurate to specify the special characteristics of the sex cells which permit further procreation by those offspring. It is thus extremely likely that the original combination of *Homo erectus* and god was a sterile hybrid – unless the gods wished it otherwise.

In chapter 2, I mentioned that humans have 46 chromosomes, whilst chimpanzees and gorillas have 48. This fundamental difference is a mystery to evolutionary science. In the words of geneticist Steve Jones, it is as if 'two chromosomes are fused together in the line leading to humans'.[53] Given the clear signs of sophisticated genetics, it was not impossible for the gods to create a hybrid with full sexual capability. The question is – did Enki *wish* mankind to have sexual knowledge? To answer that, we have to revisit the question of why man was created in the first place.

As uncomfortable as it may seem, all of the Mesopotamian texts indicate that man was *originally* created as a slave race to relieve the 'toil' of the gods. These claims are indeed repeated in our encyclopaedias, under the heading of religious myth, but it is a fact that the Hebrew word for worship, *avod*, literally means 'work'.[54] The Sumerian texts consistently called these earliest beings LU.LU, which also had the connotation of worker or servant.

Before Adam acquired sexual knowledge and was expelled from Eden, the Bible speaks of man as 'The Adam'. In Genesis 1:26, for example, the Hebrew word for 'man' is *Adama*. This is derived from the Hebrew words for blood (*adamu*) and red (*adom*), and thus means 'the red blooded one'.[55] These Biblical references to 'The Adam' as a general category carry clear connotations of the earliest LU.LU.

What was the required genetic design for these LU.LU? I would like to save a discussion of the gods' 'toil' until chapter 14, but suffice to say for now that he had to pick up tools and follow simple instructions. He therefore needed to be strong, obedient and easy to control. Sexual desire would not have been a helpful trait and would thus have been genetically repressed.

Whilst Zecharia Sitchin can largely be credited with providing the breakthrough in our understanding of the LU.LU creation process and its background, he does not explain the need for creation of the woman to work alongside the man. Without wishing to be sexist, the 'toil' *was* hard, even for the gods. The answer I believe lies in the reference to Eve in Genesis 2 as 'a helper'. As I asked myself how could the woman 'help', the answer became clear. She was intended to relieve the toil, not of the gods, but of the birth-goddesses.

As mentioned in chapter 1, the creation of Eve took place not from the man's rib but from his essence – his DNA. The operation thus involved an adjustment to the 23rd chromosome pair that defines the human sexual characteristics. Males carry a 23rd chromosome which is known as X-y, whilst females carry an X-X. As a hybrid, it is possible that the original male LU.LU may have possessed an X-X-y, a rare condition that exists today in some men and causes them to be sterile. If this was the case, then woman may have literally been taken out of man, as the Bible claims, by deleting a 'y' from the 23rd chromosome.

By thus creating a female with maternal (but presumably not sexual) abilities, further females could be cloned to take on the role of receiving implanted cloned eggs to bring forth the required number of cloned males.

One further point merits discussion at this juncture. What life span was Enki to grant to the newly created workers? If we accept that one half of the LU.LU's genes came from a god, then the potential existed to use the gods' longevity to the full. In my view, for reasons which will become clear in the next chapter, the LU.LU's longevity was initially fixed at around 100,000 years.

Eden and the Forbidden Fruit

We now have a detailed background from which to interpret the Biblical events of the Garden of Eden. Immediately
several things become clear. First, the creation story of Eve
from Adam has been recorded out of sequence in the Bible,
and belongs to the preceding period when The Adam was
created in the *western* Eden. This must be so, because there
would have been no point in Enki repeating his original feat
of genetic engineering, from scratch, in a second location.
Secondly, mankind's acquisition of sexual knowledge in
Eden fits perfectly with his original status as a sterile hybrid.
And thirdly, the presence of the Serpent, representing the
scientific genius of the Enkiite gods, is a stunning detail of
consistency, which suggests that a deliberate *genetic* change
bestowed sexual knowledge on Adam and Eve.

Furthermore, the background to Eden, described in *The
Myth of the Pickaxe*, provides a clear motive for the
serpent-god, generally thought to be Enki himself,[56] to
act against Enlil, who had seized the Black-headed Ones
from Enki without his permission. Having established the
motive, did Enki have the *opportunity* to carry out the act?
In my view he did, and here is my theory.

Although he had obtained some male workers by force,
Enlil remained powerless to expand his newly acquired
labour force to the required numbers. For that he required
females. Even if he had also seized some females (who were
fewer in number and would have probably been secured
inside Enki's medical facilities), he needed the knowledge of
Enki to carry out the cloning procedure. Thus it was
inevitable that Enlil should try to persuade Enki to come
to Mesopotamia and grant him an independent genetic
laboratory. Enki thus had the opportunity to plan a spite-
ful trick on Enlil.

When he arrived in the eastern Eden, Enki brought with him the necessary equipment and medical staff, and oversaw the construction of a medical centre. Most importantly, he brought a female, or more likely two females, to set up the cloning operation. When everything was prepared, Enki then suggested (as one would) that he carry out the first two operations to show Enlil how it was done. One male and one female embryo were then implanted into the two female LU.LUs. But little did Enlil realise that Enki had genetically altered these two embryos to give them full sexual awareness and reproductive capabilities. At this point we shall call these two individuals Adam and Eve.

When Adam and Eve began to grow up, they were as children sexually unaware, and would have played innocently in 'the Garden', which more accurately would have been a secure wing of the hospital facility. Then one day the sex genes kicked in (as they do) and the two pubescent children realised that they were naked, and clothed themselves to hide their embarrassment. They then hid from the Lord God (Enlil) who was walking in the Garden 'in the cool of the day'[57] – possibly a reference to the building's air-conditioning. When Enlil saw Adam and Eve, he immediately realised the genetic trick which had been played on him.

The conversations with the Serpent and with the Lord God, which are recorded in Genesis 3, are in my view attempts to impart some fictitious meaning to a text which was beyond the comprehension of those who wrote it. The Biblical editors reconstructed the basic plot to carry a symbolic meaning, and that required the treatment of Adam and Eve as 'husband' and 'wife', together with the insertion of a dialogue which never existed.

What was Enlil to do with Adam and Eve? Their ability to reproduce independently had totally removed the control which he had sought over the worker population. Furthermore, if they were allowed to partake of the fruit of the Tree of Immortality, he would soon have a huge population explosion on his hands. This explains the very real danger that forced Enlil to expel Adam and Eve from their secure surroundings, into the wilderness where they should fend for themselves. Without the heart to murder the blameless pair, he took the most acceptable option of placing them in a hostile environment where they themselves might survive, but would hopefully never successfully master the unlearned art of independent childbirth. And in order to prevent unauthorised access to the medical facility and the Tree of Life, Enlil positioned there a 'cherubim and a flaming sword'[58] – yet another Biblical reference to high technology.

Sumerian depictions of the events in Eden suggest that the serpent-god was Enki himself, and that he was temporarily arrested for his unauthorised act.[59] As for Adam and Eve, the Bible states that they successfully mastered the practice of midwifery, but perhaps with some further Enkiite assistance, for Eve states that '*with the help of the Lord* I have brought forth a man'.[60] The symbol of the Sumerian goddess Ninharsag was the umbilical cutter, a reference that may reflect her assistance to Eve as well as her initial role in producing the LU.LU.[61] The Book of Jubilees relates that, after their expulsion from Eden, Adam and Eve returned to 'the land of their creation' i.e. to Africa.[62]

The rest, as they say, is history. The political bias of the gods ensured that mankind received two conflicting accounts of the rights and wrongs of what happened in the Garden of Eden, depending on whether they learned of it from Enkiite or Enlilite sources. The Bible happens to be based on a text that blamed Enki for man's loss of immortality – a fairly predictable line of criticism from an Enlilite source. No doubt the blame attached to Eve also reflects a political or sexist bias at some remote point in time.

Thus it was that LU.LU the hybrid became Adam the

man. As the progenitor of the human race, he was deprived of the chance to extend his years, but nevertheless managed a 93,000-year life span that might well be an inspiration to our twentieth century geneticists.

Chapter Twelve Conclusions

* The latest scientific findings demonstrate that ageing is purely a matter of genetics.

* The gods lived hundreds of thousands of years but only *appeared* to be immortal.

* The gods used gene therapy to enhance their longevity genes; they used half-sisters to prevent genetic drift; and they used cocktails of drugs to slow down the ageing effect of free radicals.

* Adam and Eve possessed *some* of the gods' longevity genes.

CHAPTER THIRTEEN

A NEW CHRONOLOGY

---◆---

Patriarchs, Kings and Pharaohs

In chapter 11, I suggested that a star-clock, based on the Earth's precessional cycle, might be the key to dating the arrival of the gods 120 'sar' before the Flood and the creation of mankind 40 'sar' after their arrival. We have already seen that this new chronology is consistent with the fossil and genetic evidence of early *Homo sapiens*. I also set several further objectives which had to be achieved by the proposed chronology. First, it must reconcile with the Biblical time scale from Adam to Noah. Secondly, it must reconcile to the Sumerian and Babylonian Kings Lists. And thirdly, it should dovetail with the pre-Flood gods of Egypt, as recorded by Manetho. This chapter will offer a complete reconciliation of all these dates based on a sar of 2,160 years.

I will also use Sumerian mathematics to reconcile exactly the Biblical ages of the patriarchs after the Flood, from Noah to Abraham, with a Flood date of 10983 BC. And finally, I will reconcile Manetho's dates of Egyptian god-kings after the Flood to a date of 3113 BC, and thus reveal the long sought-after origin of the mysterious date which was so sacred to the Maya.

The most challenging aspect of these proofs is the implicit acceptance that the patriarchs possessed a longevity which has subsequently been lost. In the previous chapter, I provided the scientific basis for my claim that the first patriarch, Adam, lived for 93,000 years. That longevity was directly due to the genes inherited from The Adam (the LU.LU), whose genes had in turn been inherited from the gods. In this chapter, I will explain exactly how those genes were lost, and why mankind ended up with 'three score years and ten'.

Sceptics may try to argue that no human skeleton aged to 100,000 years has ever been found. This would be a ridiculous argument, since the age of death can only be estimated by comparing to a yardstick based on the modern life span. To illustrate my point, there is in Mexico a tomb which contains the skeleton of a Mayan king named Pacal. Inscriptions state that the king died at the age of 80 but archaeologists have concluded that he could not have been more than 40.[1] Their conclusion is based on the observation that his skeleton showed the signs of midlife wear and tear. Thus, if 50 per cent of his years had expired, he must have been only 40. Wrong! What if his life span was all set to reach 160? This is a classic example of preconceptions getting in the way of good science.

In this chapter, I will show how the Biblical editors divided the pre-Flood life spans by a factor of 100. Nevertheless, they *were* able to cast off at least some of their preconceptions by recording ages in excess of 900 years for the early patriarchs! As tempting as it is for us to compound the problem by reducing these figures again, we must instead go back to the beginning, to Adam's 'designer genes', and start from a completely fresh paradigm.

Pre-Flood Chronology

The genetic breakthroughs of the last 50 years, and in particular the most recent discoveries of longevity genes, allow us to see the Old Testament in a light that has not been possible before. Whether it is a question of gods living 300,000 years or man living 100,000 years, the same point of principle is at issue. Was it possible for a human body, made in the genetic image of the gods, to live beyond our current average life spans? Given sufficient scientific advancement, which the gods certainly possessed, the answer has to be yes, and significantly so. We are thus not dealing in speculations but in soundly-based scientific theory.

As a starting point, let us examine the ten patriarchs before the Flood, as recorded in Genesis 5. Table A shows the age at which each patriarch begot the other, allowing us to date precisely the elapsed time from Adam to the Flood as 1,656 years.[2] Today, the sciences of anthropology and genetics tell us that the ancestry of *Homo sapiens* is a lot more ancient than this time scale suggests, but when the Bible was compiled this knowledge was not known. The Biblical editors would thus have had no qualms at all about drastically reducing the Biblical time scales, which ran through the ages of the patriarchs, to match their own preconceptions. In so doing, they would assume that the higher dates recorded by their ancestors were somehow in error. They would not have divided the figures by a random number, but by a convenient factor which was a credible explanation of the perceived discrepancy. A factor of 100, for instance, springs readily to mind.

If we multiply 1,656 years by 100 we arrive at a date 165,600 years before the Flood, as shown in Table A. In chapter 11, I suggested a chronology that dated the rebellion of the gods to 80 sars of 2,160 years before the Flood. This calculates to 172,800 years. The difference between 172,800 and 165,600 is 7,200 years. The fact that this is exactly twice 3,600 – the orbital period of Nibiru – does not seem to be coincidental.

According to the Sumerian texts, the rank-and-file gods rebelled 80 sar before the Flood, coinciding with the visit of Anu and hence the orbit of Nibiru. Enki then created the LU.LU in the Lower World (Africa), a genetic feat that in its final stages may well have required some further equipment from Nibiru. Thus one period of 3,600 years would have passed.

Table A   Pre-Flood Ancestry

	Years of Age	
	Per Bible	Original
Adam had Seth	130	13,000
Seth had Enosh	105	10,500
Enosh had Kenan	90	9,000
Kenan had Mahalalel	70	7,000
Mahalalel had Jared	65	6,500
Jared had Enoch	162	16,200
Enoch had Methuselah	65	6,500
Methuselah had Lamech	187	18,700
Lamech had Noah	182	18,200
Noah at time of Flood	600	60,000
Total Elapsed Time (Years)	1,656	165,600

Source: Genesis 5–7.

Another orbital period of Nibiru then ensued, during which the LU.LU workers toiled only in the Lower World. It was then that Enlil grabbed a share of the Black-headed Ones, as related in *The Myth of the Pickaxe*. The reference in that text to Enlil breaking the DUR.AN.KI, the 'Bond Heaven-

Earth', indicates the close proximity of Nibiru once again, for it would have been meaningless to break this link at any other point in Nibiru's orbit. Furthermore, the timing of Enlil's raid may have been deliberately timed to coincide with Anu's visit, in order to gain support for the action he was about to undertake.

The Garden of Eden incident, which immediately followed Enlil's raid, would thus have occurred two orbital periods (7,200 years) after the rebellion of the rank-and-file gods. Table B shows how this chronological gap perfectly matches an overall timetable based on a sar of 2,160 years, where the pre-Flood Biblical time scales are multiplied by a factor of 100 (to reverse the earlier editorial division by 100).

Table B Reconciliation of Biblical Time Scales (Pre-Flood)

Arrival of the gods	(Flood – 120 sar)	270,183 BC	
Rebellion of the gods	(Flood – 80 sar)	183,783 BC	
			} 3,600
Genetic creation of LU.LU		180,183 BC	
			} 3,600
Genetic creation of Adam & Eve		176,583 BC	
			} 165,600
Flood		10,983 BC	
Total Elapsed Years (since Rebellion)			172,800

Notes: Sar = 2,160 years. 3,600 years = orbital period of Nibiru. Flood date based on Table C and Abraham's year of birth 2123 BC (Appendix A). 165,600 matches the Biblical years × 100 (Table A).

If Adam and Eve were born in 176,583 BC, with life spans *c.* 90,000 years, then Eve may indeed be one and the same as mtDNA Eve who has now been dated between 137–133,000 years ago. However, in order to determine the date of the genetic separation of the family of mankind, we should instead look for a clue as to when Adam and Eve's clan began to leave their African homelands (to which they had emigrated after their ejection from Eden in the east). That clue is provided by a key marker in the Bible:

> Adam lay with his wife again, and she gave birth to a son and named him Seth, saying, 'God has granted me another child in place of Abel, since Cain killed him'. Seth also had a son, and he named him Enosh. *At that time men began to call on the name of the Lord.*[3] (emphasis added)

Where did men 'call on the name of the Lord'? A likely possibility is the *pre-Flood* cities of Mesopotamia. The Bible might thus be pinpointing the first time that some of Adam and Eve's descendants left Africa to live a separate existence in Asia. The fact that the Bible records the above event at all, indicates that it was important, and it is difficult to think of a more important milestone in the history of man. The geneticists would agree – this separation is exactly the type of event which would cause the female mtDNA to begin diverging. As mentioned in chapter 11, Mark Stoneking has dated mtDNA Eve to 137–133,000 years ago. A parallel study by Luigi Cavalli-Sforza has estimated that the genetic separation of Africans and non-Africans occurred slightly later, just over 100,000 years ago.

When, according to my chronology, was the time of Enosh, when the Biblical migration out of Africa occurred? If we reconstruct the era of Enosh by multiplying by a factor of 100, then he was born 23,500 years after Adam (see Table A). He then lived for 90,500 years. Since Adam was born in 176,583 BC, Enosh's lifetime can be dated to precisely 153,083–62583 BC. The early part of Enosh's life thus tallies well with the genetic evidence from Stoneking and Cavalli-Sforza.

Dating the Flood

I would now like to use the Bible to confirm the exact date of the Flood, which I have suggested was *c.* 11000 BC. Table C shows the sequence of patriarchs after the Flood, with the ages at which they continued the line through to Abram (Abraham).

It is my contention that this data originally existed in Sumerian base 60 format, as shown in *column b*. This is logical if, as concluded in chapter 10, Terah and Abraham were Sumerians.

Table C   Post-Flood Ancestry

	ELAPSED YEARS		
	(a) Per Bible (b/50)	(b) True Base 60	(c) True Base 10
Shem had Arphaxad 2 years after the Flood	2	2–0–0	120
Arphaxad had Shelah	35	1–7–5–0	1,070
Shelah had Eber	30	1–5–0–0	900
Eber had Peleg	34	1–7–0–0	1,020
Peleg had Reu	30	1–5–0–0	900
Reu had Serug	32	1–6–0–0	960
Serug had Nahor	30	1–5–0–0	900
Nahor had Terah	29	1–4–5–0	890
Terah had Abram	70	3–5–0–0	2,100
Total Elapsed Years	292		8,860

Source: Genesis 11.

Notes: Converting the Sumerian data to modern base 10 is covered at the end of chapter 11. The date relating to Shem was written in Sumerian but considered by the Biblical editors in the context of the pre-Flood chronology and thus divided by 100, not 50. Some Biblical authorities say that Terah fathered Abram at 130 based on Genesis 11:32, 12:4 and an incorrect assumption that Terah died in the year he arrived in Harran.

In order to record the ages of Table C, column b, at an 'acceptable' level, it was necessary to reduce them by a common factor, which I suggest was 50. Why was it decided to divide the Sumerian numbers by 50? The answer is actually quite simple.

The numbers in Table C, column b, can only be divided sensibly by 25,50 or 100. No other divisor would produce whole numbers. It can be seen that a divisor of 50 results in Nahor becoming father to Terah when he was 29 years old. If a factor of 100 had been used, Nahor would have fathered Terah at the age of 14! If, on the other hand, 25 had been used as the divisor, Terah would have fathered Abram at the age of 140! Fifty was thus the best compromise by far. In support of this conclusion, it should be noted that 50 was a sacred number for the Hebrew editors of the Bible; every 50th year was celebrated by the Hebrews as a Jubilee Year, in which slaves were freed and debts waived.[4]

Now, in order to calculate the real elapsed time from the Flood to Abraham, all we have to do is to convert the Sumerian numbers in Table C from base 60 to base 10. The result, shown in column c, is a duration of 8,860 years.

If we use a date for Abraham's birth of 2123 BC (see Appendix A), the Flood can then be dated precisely to 10983 BC.

Calculations of Longevity

So far, we have worked only on the ages at which each patriarch fathered the son who continued the line to Noah and onwards to Abraham. However, in order to prove my genetic longevity theory, we need to look at the trend in their *total* life spans.

In the case of the *pre*-Flood patriarchs, the figures quoted in Genesis 5 show the number of years from father to first-named son, the number of years afterwards when the father had 'other sons and daughters' and finally a total life span. Having already concluded that the years from father to son were divided by 100 (Table A), there is no reason to doubt that their *total life spans* were also divided by 100.

However, the lives of the *post*-Flood patriarchs from Shem to Abraham, are another matter entirely. The data is summarised in Genesis 11 in a similar way to Genesis 5, but with one significant difference – the Biblical editors were *reluctant to add together the ages to reach a total life span*. Why should this be?

It is nowadays widely accepted that the Old Testament drew its accounts from a number of different sources. I have already suggested that the years making up the *family tree* from Noah to Abraham were recorded in Sumerian base 60. It is quite likely that the source of this data dealt solely with the ancestral links from Abraham back to Noah.[5] It is a fact of life that records of births are much easier to maintain than the record of deaths. But did the details of the *additional years* come from a different source, in a different numerical format? If there was indeed a different source that provided fuller details of the patriarchs' lives, including their total life span, and if this data was *not* recorded in base 60, then the Biblical editors would have had great difficulties in reconciling the two sets of figures. Could this be the reason that they did not add the figures together to reach total life spans?

My line of reasoning assumes that the Hebrew compilers of the Bible had lost their knowledge of the 'archaic' and unusual Sumerian base 60 system. How could this have happened? The Jewish people spent an extremely long exile in Egypt for 400 years prior to the Exodus. Later they spent around 60 years exiled in Babylon. And, even when they were freed by Cyrus in 539 BC, the vast majority of Jews stayed in Babylon rather than returning to Jerusalem. Therefore, throughout their history they were subject to the influence of foreign cultures – Egyptian, Babylonian and later the Persian culture. During this time, many traditions were abandoned or forgotten. It is known, for example, that after the Babylonian exile, the Jews had adopted the Babylonian names for the months of the year.[6]

There is also evidence to suggest that the Jews were forbidden to record numbers during their exile in Babylon because, during this period, they evolved a code of accenting certain alphabetical letters in order to represent numerals – a practice which does not appear after the exile.[7] Significantly, the numbering system which they developed at this time was decimal with special symbols for figures such as 100, whilst their highest number was a 'myriad', which represented 10,000.

The Jews were thus a long way from the Sumerian origin of their patriarch Abraham, and had lost the knowledge of the sexagesimal system in which their ancestry through to Abraham was recorded.

The Biblical editors therefore had a problem. They had three sets of numbers which did not reconcile, for reasons they could not understand. The easiest solution would have been to leave out the total life span, and this is exactly what we find in Genesis 11.

Let us now try some alternative theories to reconstruct the life spans of the *post*-Flood patriarchs. We have already established that the line of ancestry (from each father to first-named son) was a Sumerian source divided by 50 (Table C), that divisor being by far the best available compromise. Let us now focus on the *additional years* which make up the remainder of each life span. First, let us confirm my hypothesis that the additional years were *not* derived from Sumerian numerals divided by 50. If this had been the case, then Eber, who was born in 8893 BC[8] and who had Peleg in 7873 BC, would have lived an additional 8,100 years (a further 430 years in the Bible × 50 = 2–1–5–

0–0 in Sumerian = 8,100). This seems highly unlikely as he would still have been alive when the Bible was written. Thus we can discount a Sumerian source for the additional years.

Should we take the additional years at face value? If so, then Peleg, who was born in 7873 BC and who had Reu in 6973 BC, would have died 209 years later in 6764 BC. That would mean fathering a child 81 per cent through his life (and similar results are found for all of the other patriarchs). Whilst not impossible, this is in sharp contrast to the pattern established before the Flood, where we find equivalent percentage ratios of 17 for Jared, 19 for Methuselah and 23 for Lamech.

How else might the additional years have been derived? The most acceptable solution turns out to be the neatest one. If we multiply the additional years by 10, this gives ratios of first-named son to total lifetime which are very similar to the early patriarchs cited above. It is highly feasible that the Biblical editors did indeed divide the original figures for additional years very neatly by 10 in order to fit the picture which they were trying to present.

The only remaining problem is to decipher the true life span for Noah, whose recorded life span of 950 years included 600 before the Flood and 350 after the Flood. In contrast to most of the other later patriarchs, the Bible *does* add together his years to arrive at a total of 950. Whilst the 600 before the Flood would represent 60,000, can we apply the same method as the elder patriarchs and multiply his post-Flood 350 also by 100? If we did, then Noah would live 35,000 years after the Flood, which according to my chronology is impossible, since the Flood occurred only 13,000 years ago.

One possibility is to multiply Noah's 350 post-Flood years by 10, as with the younger patriarchs. That would give Noah a true life span of 63,500. My best guess, however, is that the Biblical editors were in possession of

Noah's total life span written in Sumerian as 1–9–0–0–0–0, which is 68,400 in the decimal system. Dividing this figure by 50 or 100 would have produced a life span inconsistent with the other patriarchs, and would have meant Noah living alongside Moses and David. Therefore, Noah's age was fudged to 950 by dividing 1–9–0–0–0–0 by 200. If I am correct, then the claim of the Sumerian king Gilgamesh to have met Noah (of which I have previously been cynical) may have indeed been true, for Noah would not have died until 2600 BC.

In my view, the whole approach of the Biblical editors was based on smoothing the age reduction all the way from Adam through to Abraham, much as a good accountant will smooth the trend in his profit figures, in order to please his boss by giving added credibility to the numbers. They would have worked backwards from Abraham, whose life span they were fairly certain of and, due to the constraints mentioned earlier, they would have agreed upon 50 as a necessary divisor *after* the Flood. Then, respectful of tradition that lives had been longer before the Flood, they would have got pre-Flood and post-Flood life spans to meet in the middle by using a divisor of 100 for the former and combining 10 with the existing 50 for the latter. A classic piece of book-keeping.

Table D shows, in my view, how the figures would have appeared to the Biblical editors and how the smoothing exercise was undertaken.

A good example of the fancy accounting footwork performed by the Biblical editors occurs in Genesis 11:28. The Bible, which is usually so accurate in recording the ages when events take place, suddenly becomes rather woolly:

While his father Terah was still alive, Haran died in Ur of the Chaldeans, in the land of his birth. (emphasis added)

Table D   Summary of Total Life Spans

	Became Ancestor	Additional years	Total	Age per Bible	Revised Ages
Adam	13,000	80,000	93,000	930	93,000
Seth	10,500	80,700	91,200	912	91,200
Enosh	9,000	81,500	90,500	905	90,500
Kenan	7,000	84,000	91,000	910	91,000
Mahalalel	6,500	83,000	89,500	895	89,500
Jared	16,200	80,000	96,200	962	96,200
Enoch	6,500	N/A	N/A	N/A	N/A
Methuselah	18,700	78,200	96,900	969	96,900
Lamech	18,200	59,500	77,700	777	77,700
Noah	50,000		1–9–0–0–0	950	68,400
Shem (+ yrs post-Flood)	10,000				
	2–0–0	5,000		600/602	15,120
Arphaxad	1–7–5–0	4,030		438	5,100
Shelah	1–5–0–0	4,030		433	4,930
Eber	1–7–0–0	4,300		464	5,320
Peleg	1–5–0–0	2,090		239	2,990
Reu	1–6–0–0	2,070		239	3,030
Serug	1–5–0–0	2,000		230	2,900
Nahor	1–4–5–0	1,190		148	2,080
Terah	3–5–0–0	135		205	2,235
Abram	100	75	175	175	175

Source: Genesis 5–7,9,11,25.
Notes: Left-hand columns are a reconstruction of what the
Biblical editors saw. Dashed numerals are Sumerian base 60.
Converting the Sumerian data to modern base 10 is covered at
the end of chapter 11.

I will now demonstrate why the Bible is so vague. According
to my chronology, Terah had Haran when he was 2,100
years old, but he only lived to 2,235 in total (a very late child
for good reasons – see later). The Sumerian dates would
have been shown as: 3–5–0–0 and 3–7–1–5 respectively.
These figures, divided by 50, produced ages of 70 and 74.

Thus, it would have appeared to the Biblical editors that for Haran to have died whilst his father was alive, Haran could not have been more than 4 years old at the time. Why is this a problem? Because Haran had already fathered Lot! Thus the age of Terah when Haran died has been removed in a classic fudge. This corroborates my theory that the ages shown in the Bible have been drastically reduced and were based on original Sumerian data.

The River of Pure Genes

According to my chronology, Adam and Eve's designer genes were successfully passed undiluted through the nine pre-Flood generations of patriarchs from Adam to Noah's father Lamech. Table D shows seven of these first nine patriarchs living for an average of 93,000 years. How was this longevity maintained?

Since all human life flowed from Adam and Eve, the earliest humans had little alternative but to marry their close relatives. Initially, the longevity genes would have remained intact. Inevitably, however, these genes were susceptible to gradual damage from free radicals (minute amounts of surplus oxygen inside the cells). This process of deterioration would have led to genetic copying errors in the sex cells (particularly of the male, whose sperm is constantly renewed). The genetic risk was particularly great for children who were fathered in later life. The enormous orgy of human reproduction which followed the granting of sexual knowledge to Adam and Eve would have gradually led to genetic mutations which spread through the population and decreased life spans.

In contrast, the evidence suggests that the line of patriarchs from Adam to Lamech was a priestly line who carefully isolated their pool of genes from the rest of mankind. Although the Bible gives little information on the marital practices of the patriarchs, we can surmise from the case of Abraham and Sarah that the tradition of marrying a half-sister was maintained. Ex-biblical sources support this assumption. The Book of Jubilees, for example, states that:

> In the eleventh jubilee Jared took to himself a wife; her name was Baraka (Lightning Bright), the daughter of Rasujal, *a daughter of his father's brother* . . . and she bare him a son and he called his name Enoch.[9] (emphasis added)

In addition to the practice of marrying close relations, my chronology indicates that all of the early patriarchs were born to a relatively youthful father (compared to modern customs). This would be a key requirement in minimising the mutational effects arising in the sex cells.

Elsewhere, in contrast, 165,600 years would have allowed the human genes to have divided and recombined through more than 6,000 generations. The river of human genes (to borrow a Richard Dawkins expression) was thus split in two – one a narrow channel that carefully preserved the genes, the other a swirling rapids where sexual pleasures were the foremost consideration.

It would seem that, at least for a while, a new branch of genes joined those of the humans. The Bible records a time when the 'sons of God saw that the daughters of men were beautiful' and 'had children by them'.[10] The Biblical tale is closely echoed by the non-biblical Book of Enoch, which states that Enoch had 'testified about the Watchers who had sinned with the daughters of men'.[11] The Bible does not record the death of Enoch but simply states that he was 'taken away' by the Lord. According to my chronology, Enoch was born in 114,400 BC, 'walked with God' from 107,900 BC and was 'taken away' in 77900 BC. It appears to me that, by assisting the Lord with his testimony, Enoch became a spy long before Abraham, and moreover it sounds as if he was the first human to ever be given a witness protection programme. As for the progeny of the Watchers (the rank-and-file gods) and the daughters of men, it seems highly likely that they perished in the great Flood.

The one apparent exception to the average pre-Flood life span of 93,000 years is Noah's father Lamech, who seems to have had a somewhat premature death at the age of 77,700. His death occurred shortly before the Flood, and could have been accidental. There is no other evidence to suggest that he was genetically any weaker than his predecessors.

The Curse of the Lord

Noah's birth was far from normal. According to the Book of Enoch, when Noah was born, his father Lamech was extremely perturbed to find that 'his body was white as snow and red as the blooming of a rose'. Lamech was so shocked that he asked his father Methuselah (meaning 'Man of the Missile') to make enquiries of Enoch who was staying among the sons of the gods (the Watchers or Nefilim), because:

> 'I have begotten a strange son, diverse from and unlike man, and resembling the sons of the God of Heaven; and his nature is quite different, and he is not like us . . . And it seems to me that he is not sprung from me but from the angels.'[12]

Enoch's response was to assure Lamech that Noah was indeed his son, but his unusual disposition was part of a plan to save Noah and his family in a coming deluge. It would seem that Noah's father may have become known as Lamech, meaning 'He who was Humbled', as a result of this rather embarrassing accusation against his wife.

Noah's name, on the other hand, is generally accepted to

mean 'Respite' or 'Comfort', the origin of this name being explained by Genesis 5:29:

> When Lamech had lived 182 years, he had a son. He named him Noah and said 'He will comfort us in the labour and painful toil of our hands caused by the ground the Lord has cursed.'

According to my chronology, Noah was born in 71000 BC, and the Biblical reference to the ground which had been cursed by the Lord may well refer to the beginning of the last ice age, which scientists believe began 75,000 years ago. Once again, we find a corroboration of my chronology, based on a sar of 2,160 years.

Lamech's hope for better times was not to come true, for mankind's problems were only just beginning. According to the *Atra-Hasis*, some time before the Flood, the god Enlil decided to punish man with infectious diseases and a series of droughts. Why did Enlil do this? The text explains that mankind was fornicating loudly like wild cattle in the field:

> Enlil held a meeting.
> He said to the gods, his sons:
> 'Great is the noise of mankind.
> Because of their noise I am disturbed;
> because of their tumult I cannot catch any sleep.
> . . . let there be malaria.
> Instantaneously the pestilence shall put an end to their noise!
> Like a storm let it blow upon them,
> sickness, headache, malaria, disease!'[13]

Man's excessive fornications are also alluded to in the Biblical reference which precedes the great Flood:

> The Lord saw how great man's wickedness on the earth had become, and that every inclination of the thoughts of his heart was only evil all the time.[14]

Enlil's pestilence, however, did not achieve its ends. Following supplications by the 'Exceedingly Wise' Atra-Hasis (Noah), Enki decided to come to mankind's assistance. Enlil then complained that:

'The people have not become fewer, but are more numerous than before.
Because of their noise I am disturbed;
because of their tumult I cannot catch any sleep.
Let the fig tree be cut off from the people;
in their bellies let vegetables be wanting.
Above let Adad make scarce his rain . . .'[15]

According to the *Atra-Hasis*, there then followed seven harsh periods of severe famine. The tablets are badly damaged at this point, but by the sixth period the people had turned to cannibalism to survive.[16] In the seventh period Enki angered Enlil once again, by releasing provisions to the starving people. It was only then that the gods become aware that the next return of Nibiru would cause a great Flood in which mankind would perish anyway.

Scholars have translated these harsh 'periods' of famine as 'years', but in fact the proper meaning is 'passings', presumably of the gods' planet Nibiru. In total then, mankind suffered for approximately eight or more periods of 3,600 years before the Flood.[17] This takes us back to a date of at least 40000 BC – a highly significant date. According to the anthropologists, it was at this exact time that men migrated into Europe with new inventions (tailored clothes, improved shelters and so on). The anthropologists have also found evidence of a similar, earlier leap in technology in the Near East.[18] It all suggests a desperate migration away from the harsh conditions inflicted by Enlil in Mesopotamia. Indirectly, this migration helps to explain the mysterious demise of Neanderthal man at around the same time, 40,000 years ago. In contrast to the neat explanation provided by the *Atra-Hasis*, scientists have made a desperate attempt to explain this mystery by suggesting that anatomically modern humans benefited from a sudden brain mutation![19]

Did these diseases, dating from around 40000 BC, have any effect on man's genetic disposition? Atra-Hasis/Noah claimed to have lived in the temple of Ea (Enki), and may thus have avoided exposure, but other members of Noah's family may well have passed down the effects of the diseases even into modern times. Geneticist Steve Jones, commenting on the mysteries of the human genome, notes that:

> . . . much of the inherited landscape is littered with the corpses of abandoned genes . . . at some time in their history a crucial part of the machinery was damaged . . . bizarrely enough there even seems to be a gene within a gene . . . most remarkably it seems that a few haemophiliacs have suffered from the insertion of an extra segment of DNA into the machinery, a segment which seems to have moved from somewhere else in the recent past.[20]

Origins of Racial Diversity

According to the *Atra-Hasis* and parallel texts, Enki was forced to swear an oath of the gods not to warn mankind of the coming Flood of 10983 BC. Fortunately for us, he found a way to break that oath and unilaterally saved Noah and his family. The Flood thus acted as a gateway or bottleneck through which the genes of man were transmitted to the post-Flood generations.

According to the Bible, the three sons of Noah – Shem, Ham and Japheth – took separate territories and fathered everyone in the world alive today. Did these three sons represent three distinct races? Modern studies of human racial diversity are unfortunately few and far between. As Jared Diamond notes:

The subject of human races is so explosive that Darwin excised all discussion of it from his famous 1859 book *On the Origin of Species*. Even today, few scientists dare to study racial origins, lest they be branded racists simply for being interested in the problem.[21]

Genetic scientists, however, have projected backwards from all of the human racial diversity which exists today and found a common point, known as mtDNA Eve (Mitochondrial Eve) around 135,000 years ago. These findings suggest that racial diversity must have been preserved on Noah's Ark if the Flood occurred only 13,000 years ago. Biblical scholars would agree with this conclusion. A major clue lies in the names of Noah's sons, particularly the name Ham which literally means 'He who is Hot', implying a dark coloured skin. Furthermore, the location of the Hamitic tribes in the Table of Nations (Genesis 10) has been clearly identified by Biblical scholars as the African lands. The Koran, too, is explicit in referring to separate *nations* on board Noah's Ark, when it states 'blessings upon thee and on the nations with thee'.[22]

The scenario of preserving mankind's racial diversity on Noah's Ark is entirely consistent with the Biblical record that *all* living creatures were saved. Unfortunately, most people have regarded the tale of the Ark as a myth, due to the logistical problems of confining so many types of animals and birds in such close proximity, added to the practical difficulties of gathering together so many different species.

However, if we were to be forewarned of a Flood tomorrow, we would, with the benefit of modern scientific knowledge, not round up the animals themselves but *their genes*. And there are two clues which suggest that this is exactly what happened 13,000 years ago. The Utnapishtim legend of Noah states that Utnapishtim loaded aboard whatever he had of '*the seed* of all living creatures'.[23]

And in the *Atra-Hasis* (Fragment III), the god Ea (Enki) tells Atra-Hasis 'game of the field and beasts of the field, as many as eat herbs, *I will send unto thee*'.[24] An echo of this is found in Genesis 6:20 which states that 'two of every kind . . . *will come to you*'.

If the seed or genes of all living animals were kept alive in the Ark, why not also the genes representing *human* diversity?

However, the problem of human races goes much further back in time, prior to Noah's Ark, for no-one can explain how the races evolved. As Jared Diamond points out, *all* of the current theories on the origin of racial characteristics have fundamental weaknesses.[25] Despite the overwhelming evidence that we are all descended from a common *Homo sapiens* ancestor around 200,000 years ago, the problem of racial diversity has forced many scientists to persist with the so-called 'multi-regional model', which proposes that *Homo sapiens* evolved from several geographically separate *Homo erectus* groups 1,000,000 years ago. This contrived theory has appeared only because of sheer disbelief that our racial differences could have evolved over a mere 200,000 years.

Can the Bible, in the context of plural gods, solve the racial mystery which has perplexed the scientists? Is there a way to explain how Shem, Ham and Japheth might represent the three lines of human diversity whilst still being the sons of Noah? In my view, the answer is yes, and the key to the mystery is genetic science.

Furthermore, it turns out that the answer to the mystery of our racial origins is closely connected to another mystery – the reducing longevity of the Biblical patriarchs following the Flood. In fact, my recalculations of these life spans (Table D) show that the reductions were even steeper before they were smoothed out by the Biblical editors. It has generally been assumed that this phenomenon was in some way connected to the physical event of the Flood itself.[26] On the contrary, we shall see that reduced longevity *and* racial differences were *both* caused by genetic engineering.

By the time Noah was born, mankind had spent 105,600 years in a frenzied orgy of reproduction and genetic division. The resulting explosion in population was exponential (our twentieth century population growth gives us a good idea of the problem). One can possibly sympathise with Enlil's attempts – recorded in *Atra-Hasis* – to reduce mankind's numbers through starvation and disease. In the face of Enlil's hostility and the oath of the gods to let man be destroyed by the Flood, what was Enki to do? How could he save the diversity of mankind, whom he had created, without risking his own neck in a flagrant breach of the gods' decision? If Enki simply placed three different families in the Ark, they would get little mercy from Enlil afterwards. His only chance was to genetically redesign the human species to remove the longevity which had largely caused the over-population problem. At the same time, Enki decided to create three diverse races, perhaps to give the other gods some sense of ownership in a distinct branch of mankind. Here is my theory on how he did it.

Thousands of years before the Flood. Enki, as the scientific genius of the gods, was able to predict the planetary alignments which were to cause it. The unusual birth of Noah, discussed earlier, was the first step in his far-sighted strategy. Subsequently, ten thousand years before the Flood, Enki secretly brought Noah – by then a trusted and high-ranking priest – to his medical facilities. At the same time, Enki selected and brought three women from three diverse races of mankind to the same location. There, the eggs of each of these women were fertilised by Noah's sperm, and implanted into three surrogate mothers. This genetic mixing was designed to cause a 50 per cent dilution of Noah's longevity genes.

Nine months later, Noah became the father of three sons, Shem, Ham and Japheth, as recorded in the Bible. Due to the 50 per cent dilution of the longevity genes, Shem lived only 15,120 years compared to 68,400 for Noah.[27] This disproportionate effect is not surprising, since Noah was very old when he fathered these sons and thus his sex cells were registering a high level of mutations. Furthermore, it is possible that the genes of the three ethnic women had been attacked by viruses.

This life span, however, was still far too long for Enki's purposes, and a further disintegration of the longevity genes was required. Accordingly, he gave instructions that the three ethnic mothers of Shem, Ham and Japheth were to marry their own sons. These, then, were the three women who accompanied Noah, his unnamed wife and his three sons onto the Ark (some texts allow also for a boatman or navigator). Using this strategy, Enki caused a further significant dilution of Noah's 'pure' genes and a significant increase in the proportion of 'ethnic' genes in the next generation. Whilst Shem, Ham and Japheth had retained 50 per cent of the pure seed, their sons and daughters became 25 per cent pure seed and 75 per cent ethnic.

The effects on longevity were striking – as we would expect them to be. Arphaxad, for example, lived only 5,100 years. Meanwhile, three separate races emerged with nearly 200,000 years of mitochondrial diversity – preserved through the matriarchal line – exactly in accordance with modern scientific findings.

There are several further factors which tend to corroborate the above theory. First, the location. The Akkadian version of the Flood refers to Noah as Utnapishtim, the son of Ubar-Tutu, and locates both of them in Shuruppak.[28] Shuruppak has been firmly identified as the medical centre of the gods. It was also referred to as the city of Sud, who has been identified as Ninharsag – the same goddess who had assisted Enki with the genetic creation of the LU.LU.[29]

Secondly, the independent account in the Book of Enoch

of Noah's unusual white/red pigmentation describes a deliberate step in Enki's strategy for obtaining a greater range of colour variation in the three new lines of mankind.[30] Without Noah's whiteness, Enki could only have blended three shades of black.

Is it possible that Lamech's fathering of Noah was really subject to genetic intervention? In January 1996, British and American scientists announced that men with blocked sperm tubes (the biggest single cause of male infertility) could bear children through a new technique which removed sperm from the tube area immediately above the scrotum. This technology, using a syringe and butterfly needle, could have been combined with artificial insemination without Lamech's knowledge. A fragment from the Book of Noah, discovered at Qumran, records an ambiguous response from Lamech's wife, when questioned about the conception of Noah. She implored her husband to 'remember my delicate feelings' – perhaps a sign that she was keeping a secret of the gods.

Thirdly, the idea of using genetics to limit the human population is strongly supported by other measures recorded at the same time. The Mesopotamian versions of the Flood end with new instructions for the human race – the exclusivity of man to woman (in contrast to their previous conjugations like 'wild bulls'):

> Regulations for the human race:
> let the male . . . to the young maiden . . .
> Let the young maiden . . .
> The young man to the young maiden . . .
> When the bed is laid,
> let the spouse and her husband lie together.[31]

At the same time, a genetic fault was introduced (which we would recognise as the menopause or possibly a recessive gene) which prevented childbirth in some women:

> Ea [Enki] turns to Mami, the mother-goddess and says:
> 'O Lady of Birth, creatress of the Fates . . .
> let there be among the people bearing women and barren women,
> let there be among the people a *Pashittu*-demon,
> let it seize the baby from the mother's lap,
> establish *Ugbabtu*-priestesses, *Entu*-priestesses and *Igisitu*-priestesses.
> They shall indeed be tabooed, and thus cut off from child-bearing.'[32]

Whilst both of these changes occur immediately following the Flood in Mesopotamian accounts, the later Biblical texts appear to have relocated the passage to the Garden of Eden, where the instructions of the Lord hint at both man-woman exclusivity *and* child-bearing problems:

> To the woman he said,
> 'I will greatly increase your pains in childbearing;
> with pain you will give birth to children.
> Your desire will be for your husband,
> and he will rule over you.'[33]

The fourth corroborating factor is the apparent birth of all Noah's three sons in the same year. The King James Version of the Bible (KJV) translates the original Hebrew literally:

> And Noah *was* five hundred years old: and Noah begat Shem, Ham and Japheth. (emphasis added)

The New International Version of the Bible (NIV), on the other hand, has attempted to conceal the impression of three sons in the same year by altering the translation:

> *After* Noah was 500 years old, he became the father of Shem, Ham and Japheth.[34] (emphasis added)

The deliberate vagueness of the word 'after' suggests a fudge. However, in order to make the illusion succeed, it is also necessary to disguise the fact that all three sons were 100 years old when the Flood occurred 100 years later. Therefore the NIV states:

> Two years after the Flood, when Shem was 100 years old, he became the father of Arphaxad.[35].

However, the KJV retains the original and literal meaning of the Hebrew:

> Shem was a hundred years old, and begat Arphaxad two years after the Flood.[36]

Whilst the NIV fudge conveniently allows 24 months for the birth of three separate children, the reality is that all of Noah's sons were born in the same year. Why did the NIV Biblical revisionists find this idea so offensive that they tried to hide it? Could it have implied to them that Noah's three sons came from three different wives within the same year?

A Split in the Genes

Following the reduced life spans of Shem and Arphaxad, the next drop in life spans occurred several generations later with Peleg who, along with his immediate successors, lived approximately 3,000 years compared with a previous norm of around 5,000 (see Table D).

According to my chronology, Peleg lived from 7873–4883 BC. He was thus the first of the patriarchs to be born after the war of the gods which marked the beginning of the Age of Cancer c. 8700 BC. His name, 'Peleg', meant 'Division', which is usually thought to refer to a division of land. Genesis 10:25 indeed states that he was named Peleg because 'in his time the earth was divided'. According to my chronology, however, the division of the Earth between the gods, or at least the decision to divide it, was taken around 800 years before Peleg was born.

Could Peleg's name have referred to a division in the priestly genes? The sons of Shem had been able to maintain their albeit reduced longevity by inter-marrying with their sisters or half-sisters. If, however, someone was to marry outside the family – a risk as the number of eligible population rose – then the longevity genes would be further diluted. Could that 'someone' have been Peleg's father?

In chapter 10, we discussed the origin of the term Hebrew/Ibri which meant native of Nippur and traced it to NI.IB.RU 'The Crossing Place'. It was a reference to the gods' planet Nibiru which was known as the 'Planet of Crossing', due to its return to the Asteroid Belt where it had collided with Tiamat 4 billion years previously. Nippur was the location of the DUR.AN.KI, the Bond-Heaven-Earth, which we have identified as the mission control centre of the gods' pre-Flood space facilities. After the Flood, the city which became the new mission control centre was Jerusalem, which I have concluded was built *c.* 8700 BC.

It is no coincidence that, according to my chronology, Peleg's father lived from 8893–3573 BC. Nor that his father's name was Eber, meaning 'Crossing'. His name must surely commemorate his role in supervising the construction of the new mission control centre at Jerusalem – a project that would have taken him far away from the land of the Shemitic people (Mesopotamia) for an extended period. According to my calculations, Eber fathered Peleg in 7873 BC. Could it be that the division of the Earth took Eber away from his homeland and forced him to dilute the royal genes with a foreign wife? This scenario would explain both the naming of Eber's son, Peleg ('Division') and the reduced life spans which followed.

More Genetic Engineering

Finally, we have to explain the 175-year life span of Abraham, which shows a very steep decline compared to those which we have so far discussed. His days were truly decimated and yet the Bible is adamant that he died 'at a good old age, an old man and full of years'.[37] We can thus attribute his relatively short life span only to a genetic factor. However, the decline in Abraham's age is so great that it cannot be dismissed as genetic drift; indeed the Bible confirms that he kept with tradition by marrying Sarai who was a half-sister. What exceptional circumstances might have affected Abraham's genes?

Amazingly, if we study the Old Testament, the clue is right there. It is curious that no sons are listed to Terah prior to the age of 70. This is very old for fatherhood relative to the other patriarchs (see Table C). According to my recalculations, Terah was 2,100 years old when he had Abraham, and then he died at the age of 2,235 – a comparable life span to his predecessors. Terah's date of birth, 4223 BC, would probably have made him the first high-priest of Nippur after Sumerian civilisation began *c.* 3800 BC. How did Terah become a father at such a mighty age? The wording used in the Bible is exactly the same as that used to describe the anomalous birth of Shem, Ham and Japheth to Noah:

> *After* Terah had lived 70 years, he became the father of Abram, Nahor and Haran.[38] (emphasis added)

It is curious that the Old Testament uses this vague language in only two places – the birth of three sons to Noah and the birth of three sons to Terah. We have already seen that the circumstances of Noah's unusual fatherhood were embarrassing to the Biblical editors, who tried to disguise the suggestion that he had three sons simultaneously. Surely it is more than a coincidence that this same vague expression is followed by another steep fall in longevity for Abraham?

The logical conclusion is that there was a genetic intervention in the birth of Abraham and his brothers. In the light of Abraham's subsequent espionage exploits, and with the 'writing on the wall' for the Third Dynasty of Ur, this conclusion takes on a powerful significance. Was Abraham, right from the beginning, even before the covenant with God, part of a divinely-inspired plan?

Did this plan include a deliberate reduction of Abraham's years, to relegate his genetic status to that of his new compatriots? Or did Abraham lose his father's longevity simply because the genetic engineer was, in this case, working with very old and highly mutated sperm cells? Whilst we should not rule out the former, the latter is the scientifically more plausible solution. In summary, genetic engineering allowed Terah to father three sons in the twilight of his life, but natural genetic degradation determined their reduced life spans.

Proving the 'Impossible'

I would now like to return to my overall chronology and discuss how it fits the Sumerian and Babylonian Kings Lists. These lists summarise the reigns of different 'kings' and their cities from the beginning of time to the date of the Flood. They represent the most sacred Sumerian and Babylonian traditions, and yet modern scientists attach little value to them. Why is this? Because all of the scholars regard the dates on these kings lists as 'impossible'. We will now reconsider the evidence.

In the third century BC, the Babylonian historian-priest Berossus, in an attempt to impress the Greeks, painstakingly wrote down a complete list of the kings of Babylon. His original work has not survived, but we can study it today through the works of Greek historians such as Alexander Polyhistor, Abydenus and Apollodorus. Polyhistor, for example, wrote:

> . . . in [Berossus's] second book was the history of the ten kings of the Chaldeans, and the periods of each reign, which consisted collectively of a hundred and twenty shars, or 432,000 years; reaching to the time of the Deluge.[39]

Other ancient historians also wrote of 120 saroi, sars or shars, which they believed to represent 3,600 years each. Consequently, it was claimed that ten kings had reigned for a total period of 432,000 years. But did these sars really represent 3,600 years each or are we, once again, dealing with a *post*-Flood sar of 2,160 years? For the answer, we need to go back in time to study the earlier *Sumerian* Kings Lists. The following quote is from one of the earliest, well-preserved and thus most reliable Sumerian lists:

> When the kingship came down from heaven,
> the kingship was in Eridu.
> A.LU.LIM was ruler in Eridu.
> He reigned 8 sar.
> A.LAL.GAR reigned 10 sar.
> (Two kings they ruled it 18 sar)
> In Bad-Tibira, EN.MEN.LU.AN.NA ruled 12 sar;
> EN.MEN.GAL.AN.NA ruled 8 sar.
> Divine DU.MU.ZI, the Shepherd, ruled 10 sar.
> (Three kings they ruled it 30 sar)
> In Larak EN.ZIB.ZI.AN.NA ruled 8 sar.
> (One king he ruled it 8 sar)
> EN.MEN.DUR.AN.NA was king in Sippar,
> he ruled 6 sar.
> (One king he ruled it 6 sar)
> In Shuruppak UBAR.TUTU was king,

he ruled 5 sar.
Five cities, eight kings,
they ruled 67 sar.
The Deluge came down.[40]

This Sumerian list makes it quite clear that there were 8 kings before the Flood, not 10, and 67 sar, not 120. Why are there such large discrepancies between this and the 10 Babylonian kings? The simple answer is that the two lists recorded different lines of kings from two different geographic locations. Interestingly, the Chinese also claimed ten emperors before the Flood, but again the location could have been different. For this reason, any attempt to adjust the Sumerian 8 kings to match 10 kings recorded elsewhere is fundamentally incorrect. Unfortunately, many scholars appear to have fallen into this trap, enticed no doubt by the similarity in legendary life spans between the 10 Babylonian kings and the 10 Biblical patriarchs. Once again such a comparison is invalid.

Incidentally, the term 'king' in this context is misleading, since kingship was only lowered from Heaven to man for the first time in Sumer c. 3800 BC. It is thus more accurate to use the term 'governorship' – an administrative role for *junior gods* (the names of senior gods such as Enlil and Enki do not appear in the lists).

In addition to the preoccupation with ten kings, there has also been an obsession with the number 432,000. Many studies have shown that this number had a symbolic importance to our ancient ancestors. By way of example, it is a remarkable fact that the Rigveda, the Sacred Book of Verses in the Sanskrit language, uses 432,000 syllables to record its tales of gods and heroes. This obsession with 432,000, drawn from 120 sars of 3,600, has caused some scholars to fudge the Sumerian Kings Lists to bring them up from 241,200 years to the required 432,000 years.[41] This is despite the fact that to get from 8 kings and 67 sar to 10 kings and 120 sar requires some extraordinary reigns for the two extra kings.

Such an approach is unfortunately encouraged by a number of discrepancies between Kings Lists recorded in different Sumerian cities. One list, for example, made in the city of Larsa by Nur-Ninsubur, inserts a king from Larsa itself between the three kings at Bad-Tibira. Our suspicions should be alerted. This Kings List was prepared around 2200–2100 BC – the time when the Sumerian empire sought the assistance of Elamite mercenaries to subdue instability in the outer provinces. We know from ancient texts that the price of this military support was the city of Larsa. It is not at all surprising that the Elamites should have sought some prestige by adding their own legends into the Sumerian records.

In chapter 11, I pointed out that the number 2,160, written in Sumerian, appears as 3–6–0–0, and suggested that a sar could be based on *either* 2,160 or 3,600 years, with the 2,160-year sar coming into favour after the Flood (which caused the Earth's wobble). How might this explain the difference between the Sumerian list of 67 sar, and the Babylonian list of 120 sar?

The chronology of gods and man which I have put forward in this chapter (Table B), allows a period of 259,200 years between the arrival of the gods and the Flood. This represents 120 sar of 2,160 years each. However, we would not expect the Kings Lists to have begun immediately, since there were no cities to be governed. How long did it take for the gods to construct their pre-Flood space facilities, from scratch, after their first arrival on Earth? One Sumerian text gives us a rough idea, claiming that Enlil waited 6 sar whilst Nippur was under construction.[42]

In Table E below, I have broken down the first 259,200 years of the gods on Earth into two periods – an initial period of 5 sar (18,000 years) before governorship began, and a second period of 241,200 years, which reconciles to the Sumerian list of 8 kings and 67 sar cited above. Crucially, these figures are based on the *pre*-Flood sar of 3,600 years. The total period amounts to 72 sar.

Table E The Confusion of the Sumerian Kings Lists

	SARS	YEARS
Pre-Flood – Sars of 3,600 years		
Rule of elder gods during construction of cities	5	18,000
Governorship of cities by junior gods	67	241,200
Total Elapsed Time from Arrival to Flood	72	259,200
Post-Flood – Sars of 2,160 years		
The gods converted the figure	120	259,200
The Sumerians recorded only the sars	120	–
Berossus and others then reconstructed the time scales incorrectly using pre-Flood sars of 3,600	120	432,000

Following the Flood, which caused the commencement of the precessional cycle, the 2,160-year sar became more important. The 72 sars would therefore have been translated by the gods into 120 sars, still representing the same period of 259,200 years. Table E shows, in my opinion, what happened next. The Sumerian historians ignored the years and simply remembered the pre-Flood period as '120 sars'. Then, along came Berossus (or perhaps one of the earlier Babylonian historians) and resurrected the idea of a sar being 3,600 years, hence calculating a totally mythical period of 432,000 years. Oops! It is time that the record was put straight.

I submit my chronology as proof of the 'impossible' Sumerian Kings Lists.

Egyptian Chronology
and the Maya Connection

In the third century BC, an Egyptian priest named Manetho was ordered to set down the histories of Egypt.[43] His claims are almost as astounding as the Sumerian Kings Lists. According to Manetho, there were four periods (which he called dynasties) before the pharaohs ruled in Egypt – two dynasties of gods, one of demigods and a transitional dynasty.

Manetho stated that, in the beginning, seven great gods ruled Egypt for 12,300 years: Ptah for 9,000, Ra for 1,000, Shu for 700, Geb for 500, Osiris for 450, Seth for 350 and Horus for 300 years.

The second dynasty of gods comprised twelve divine rulers – Thoth, Maat and ten others, who ruled for 1,570 years.

The third dynasty consisted of thirty demi-gods who reigned 3,650 years.

The fourth period, lasting 350 years, was a period of chaos, when Egypt was disunited and had no ruler. It ended with a reunification under Menes, who is widely regarded as the first pharaoh of Egypt.

As far as his more recent dynasties are concerned, Manetho has yet to be contradicted by archaeological evidence. However, when it comes to the earlier, legendary reigns of the gods, sometimes spanning thousands of years, scholars have found it difficult to accept that his list has any historical value.

Manetho, however, was not alone in his views of Egyptian prehistory. The Greek historian Herodotus visited Egypt and also recorded the rule of gods in an era before the pharaohs. In view of the scientific basis which I have put forward for longevity, it is time to suspend our disbelief and take a closer look at Manetho's histories.

First, it is necessary to anchor Manetho's chronology at a point in time. Typically this is done by working backwards from Menes, who is generally held to have ruled from *c.* 3100 BC. Instead, let us start by dating the reign of Thoth. Numerous references in Mesopotamian texts suggest that Thoth was appointed in charge of Egypt following the war of the gods. In chapter 11, I dated this event to the end of the first precessional period in approximately 8700 BC.

If we count back the years from Thoth in 8700 BC through Horus (300), Seth (350), Osiris (450), Geb (500) and Shu (700), we find that the dates match perfectly to the date of the Flood *c.* 11000 BC. Manetho's chronology can thus be anchored on the point of 10983 BC which I have derived from the Biblical patriarchs.

So far Manetho's chronology seems reliable, but what kind of records could he have used to cross the threshold into the days before the Flood? Can we rely on his suspiciously round numbers of 9,000 years for Ptah and 1,000 years for Ra? These two gods can be identified with certainty as Enki/Ea and his son Marduk, but according to the ancient Mesopotamian texts, the Lower World, including Egypt, was assigned to Enki shortly after the gods arrived on Earth. In my chronology that would be hundreds of thousands of years. Once again it would appear that the original time scales have been subjected to editorial reductions.

The alleged reigns before the Flood total 10,000 years or 100 centuries. What happens if we replace the centuries by sars of 2,160 years? The rule of Ptah (Enki) in Egypt would then stretch back 216,000 years before the Flood – to a date of 226,983 BC. This date represents an exact mid-point between the arrival of the gods on Earth in 270,183 BC and the rebellion of the gods in 183,783 BC. Could it be that this was the time when Enki was controversially relegated to his duties in the Lower World? Once again, the 2,160-year sar offers a very plausible scenario.

When we use Manetho's histories to roll the date of the Flood forward to the time of Menes we find something even more remarkable. Using my Flood date of 10983 BC, derived from the patriarchs, the beginning of the reign of Menes and hence of Egyptian 'civilisation' can be pinpointed as follows:

Date of Flood	10,983 BC
First Dynasty of Gods (excluding 10,000 years pre-Flood)	2,300
Second Dynasty of Gods	1,570
Third Dynasty of 30 Demi-gods	3,650
Period of Chaos	350
	3,113 BC

Many scholars have been intrigued by the date 3113 BC, which represents the mysterious starting point of the Mayan calendar in Mesoamerica.[44] Those scholars have also been fascinated by the numerous cultural similarities between the Egyptians and the Maya. Now – according to my chronology – even the Mayan calendar can be tied in to the Egyptians. As tempting as it is to explore the subject further, I must, reluctantly, defer that discussion to another day and another book.

Chapter Thirteen Conclusions

* My chronology of gods and mankind, based on a sar of 2,160 years, reconciles with:

   – the Biblical patriarchs from Adam to Noah
   – the Sumerian and Babylonian Kings Lists
   – Manetho's history of Egyptian gods before the Flood

* The longevity which is claimed in the Bible, the Sumerian Kings Lists and Manetho's History of Egypt, can be explained by genetic science. The longevity recorded in the Bible has been *considerably understated* due to editorial intervention.

* The ages of the later patriarchs can be used to date the Flood precisely at 10983 BC. This date then enables the beginning of Egyptian civilisation to be dated to 3113 BC. This is exactly the same as the beginning of the Mayan calendar in central America.

* The three sons of Noah – Shem, Ham and Japheth – represent three different races of mankind. This racial diversity was genetically engineered by the god, Enki.

CHAPTER FOURTEEN

THE TOIL OF
GODS AND MEN

Nimrod The Slave

Why did the gods create mankind? According to the Bible, man was created to 'work the ground'.[1] As to the Sumerian version of events, it is summed up by the National Geographic Society's *Splendors of the Past*, which acknowledges that 'the gods of Sumer rebelled at such drudgery – and invented man to dig and tend.'[2]

Should we continue to dismiss the Sumerian and Biblical accounts as mythology? In the previous three chapters, I have put forward a scientific basis for dating the rebellion of the gods, after 40 periods of toil, to 183,783 BC. As a result, man was genetically created *as a slave* 3,600 years later. But what exactly was the 'toil' of the gods, to which I have repeatedly referred in earlier chapters? What evidence can demonstrate the nature of the toil and the purpose of the gods on Earth?

Inevitably we will achieve little by searching in vain for evidence hundreds of thousands of years old. Instead we must focus on the last 13,000 years since the Flood, and examine the relationship between the gods and mankind.

Only then can we assess the reasons why the gods first came to Earth.

Our search begins with the legendary figure of Nimrod. The Biblical Table of Nations states that Noah's son Ham fathered Cush and that:

> Cush was the ancestor of Nimrod, who grew to be a mighty warrior on the earth. He was a mighty hunter before the Lord ... The first centres of his kingdom were Babylon, Erech, Akkad and Calneh, in Shinar. From that land he went to Assyria, where he built Nineveh, Rehoboth Ir, Calah and Resen ...[3]

This passage has always puzzled Biblical scholars. It is widely acknowledged that the line of Ham (meaning 'He who is Hot') represents the darker-skinned Negroid race,[4] but the lands of Mesopotamia were dominated by the *Shemitic* people. Scholars have therefore interpreted the Biblical text as an invasion by Nimrod of the Shemitic lands. Unfortunately, despite numerous archaeological excavations, no evidence whatsoever has come to light to identify Nimrod or a Negroid kingdom in any of the cities named by Genesis. As one authority comments:

> Nimrod has not been identified with any mythical hero or historic king of the [cuneiform] inscriptions ... the most admissible correspondence is with Marduk, chief god of Babylon.[5]

The second slightly puzzling point is the Biblical description of Nimrod as a 'hunter before the Lord'. However, as explained by the M'Clintock and Strong Cyclopaedia, the term 'hunter' should not be taken literally:

> Hunting and heroism were of old specially and naturally associated ... The Assyrian monuments also picture many feats in hunting, and the word is often employed to denote *campaigning*.[6] (emphasis added)

Nimrod was therefore 'a mighty *campaigner* before the Lord', but still the meaning of the statement does not shine through. In order to decipher Nimrod's role, we must examine the sense of the Hebrew word *liph-neh* which is commonly translated as 'before'. In fact, its use elsewhere in the Bible signifies a meaning of *opposition*.[7] Suddenly, the significance of Nimrod's first venture, at Babylon, becomes clear. If we translate 'Lord' as Enlil (rather than the Bible's retrospective use of Yahweh), then Nimrod becomes the perpetrator of the Tower of Babel, in opposition to Enlil.

In chapter 10, however, we noted that the Tower of Babel incident was an act of defiance by *Marduk* – an attempt to rebuild his pre-Flood city in Babylon. Who then was the guilty party, Nimrod or Marduk? As one commentator has pointed out, Marduk and Nimrod were *both* cited by ancient myths for their acts of rebellion.[8] Some authorities have therefore mistakenly come to the conclusion that the rebel Nimrod and the rebel god Marduk were one and the same person.

Unfortunately, such a theory is immediately sunk by the second and third cities named by Genesis, for Erech and Akkad were the cities of Marduk's arch enemy, Inanna. How can we resolve this strange contradiction?

The most likely explanation is that Nimrod was not a warrior-king, but a slave.[9] His campaign began at Babylon, in support of Marduk, and ended with an assignment to Inanna (Marduk's arch-rival) in punishment for his rebellion. Only this conclusion can explain the archaeological invisibility of Nimrod's presence in Mesopotamia, an invisibility which is entirely characteristic of an enslaved people.

Why would slavery have been practised by the gods six thousand years ago? If we review the timing of events, the answer becomes clear. For seven thousand years after the Flood, the fertile crescent of Mesopotamia had been water-logged. Eventually, the situation improved and the gods decided to rebuild their cities on the sites of the pre-Flood flight path. The first city to be rebuilt, we know, was Eridu *c.* 3800 BC. The second was probably Nippur. But despite this sudden urge for new cities, no-one seems to have asked who physically built them. The technology may have come from the gods, but who provided the muscle power?

The list of cities built by Nimrod encompasses Babylon in 3450 BC, Agade in 2400 BC and Nineveh probably around 2300 BC.[10] These dates span a period of over a thousand years, once again corroborating the human longevity that existed during this era. It is thus possible that the legends of Nimrod rebuilding Baalbek immediately after the Flood may have some historical basis.

What happened to Nimrod and his clan, once their city-building programme was complete? Were some of his followers scattered around the world following the earlier incident at the Tower of Babel, and was their language changed? And was there another group of slaves, perhaps related to Nimrod, who built the cities which *preceded* Babylon? Our study of Nimrod is about to take us to some very strange places indeed.

The Mysterious Olmecs

The history of the ancient peoples of Mesoamerica is a mystery wrapped in an enigma. Thousands of years ago, incredibly advanced civilisations emerged as if from no-where, and often they vanished again just as quickly. With the exception of the Maya, the Mesoamerican cultures left no written clues to their history, and even the Mayan glyphs remain largely undeciphered. These ancient peoples possessed complex calendars and astronomical knowledge, they built pyramids similar to those in Egypt and Mesopotamia, and they spoke of their ancestors arriving by sea.

And yet archaeologists continually ignore all these clues and study Mesoamerican civilisation as an entirely separate subject, searching in vain for a *home-grown* story line. There is no greater embarrassment to these archaeologists than the earliest of all the Mesoamerican people – the Olmecs.[11]

The Olmecs mainly inhabited the Gulf Coast of Mexico. Today, their cities are found in swampy lowland areas, making travel and excavation particularly difficult. As a result, we know frustratingly little about these people. However, what we *do* know comes as a total bombshell, for their main legacy to us is a collection of huge stone heads, with *Negroid* features.

Sixteen of these unusual Negroid heads have so far been found at the sites of San Lorenzo, Tres Zapotes and La Venta. Many of these heads have been moved to museums, including the splendid open-air jungle museum at La Venta Park.[12] Plate 56 (colour section) shows a typical head from La Venta Park, with flattened face, thick lips, broad nose, almond-shaped eyes – indisputable Negroid characteristics. This particular head is 7-feet high and weighs an incredible 24 tons. The rest of the heads range from 5–10 feet in height, with the largest weighing around 30 tons. As astounding as it is to find African features in Mesoamerica, it is equally astounding how these huge basalt stones could have been transported over distances of 40–80 miles from the nearest quarries.

In addition to the carved heads, the Olmec sites contain numerous unfinished stone balls, indicating that their work was abandoned in mid-course. But why did they ever begin such a huge project? Why expend so many man-hours on a seemingly pointless exercise?

Needless to say, the discovery of African features on these Olmec heads has the archaeologists completely stumped. Their embarrassment has only grown as a result of radiocarbon dating tests at San Lorenzo which have dated the site at which the heads were found to *at least* 1200 BC.[13] *National Geographic* is now openly conceding a date of 1400 BC for the Olmec site of Teopantecuanitlan,[14] whilst other authorities are suggesting 1500 BC as the most likely date of their emergence.[15]

The culture of the Olmecs is revolutionary, having no precedent whatsoever in Mesoamerica. Whilst they are most famous for their legacy of the giant Negroid heads, there are other features of Olmec society which are equally intriguing. As one expert points out:

> Almost nothing is known of the Olmec language or origins . . . [they] created sophisticated ceramics and jewellery of precious stones . . . Most significantly, they devised a complex calendar from astronomical observation which underpinned their religion, mathematics and science.[16]

This sudden, advanced culture inevitably reminds us of the Sumerians.[17] Professor Walter Krickeberg has suggested that the Olmec culture is like a legacy, which must have had an 'external impulse'.[18] Almost without exception, however, the academic community looks the other way. Are they uncomfortable with the concept that a *Negroid* people could have been the source of the earliest Mexican cultures? This racial aspect is certainly de-emphasised by many of the books on ancient civilisations, who prefer to blandly label the Olmecs as a 'race of precursors'.[19] Other books, meanwhile, ignore these anomalous people altogether or craftily focus attention on the Zapotecs, a later culture which may have been geographically connected to the Olmecs.[20]

If we study the Olmec culture without any prejudice or preconceptions, what can we conclude? First, several clues are provided by surviving Olmec works of art. For example, a carved block of basalt found at La Venta (Plate 57, colour section) depicts a crouching figure emerging from what appears to be an underground cave. The man holds in his right hand a rope which is connected to the wrist of a colleague carved on the side panel. This stone is conventionally interpreted as an 'altar', but if we use our eyes, rather than our preconceptions, what we see is either a prisoner or a miner.

If we now return to the giant Olmec heads, we notice that, without exception, they are fitted with protective helmets with side-straps. This is a significant clue, not to be dismissed as decorative headgear or fancifully linked to astronauts, but highly indicative of a *mining* helmet. Indeed, another Olmec carving at La Venta supports this conclusion. Figure 21 (see black-and-white section) shows a 9-feet high stone slab known as the King's Stele. The main feature is a man with Negroid features, grasping a tool shaped like a hockey stick. The religious interpretation of this tool is 'a crook' (to go with the 'altar'!), but it seems to me to be some kind of tool. Furthermore, above the central figure are two smaller figures, one on each side, again wielding tools – a pole and an axe respectively.[21]

It would be too simple, however, to suggest that the Olmecs were purely engaged in mining. Archaeological excavations of their settlements have indicated a sophisticated, but unidentified, technology. The site at La Venta, for instance, is dominated by a strange volcano-shaped pyramid, which suggests a practical rather than a symbolic purpose. Excavations have discovered a series of trenches, paved with tiles of serpentine, a green-blue coloured precious stone. The purpose of these trenches is unknown.

Meanwhile, at the site of San Lorenzo, archaeologists have been completely mystified by a network of artificial reservoirs which are connected by subterranean conduits and sluices. These elaborate earthworks and stone constructions are probably typical of the forty or so known Olmec settlements, many of which have never been properly excavated. It all smacks of a purposeful, functional design. What could the Olmecs possibly have been up to? And how did this Negroid people end up in Mesoamerica?

Could these Negroid Olmecs have come to Mesoamerica

directly from their African homelands, or were they a remnant of Nimrod's people who were scattered from Babylon *c.* 3450 BC?[22] If the latter, what were they doing during the intervening 2,000 years? And where did they learn their mining and other technological skills? The answers can be deduced from the mysterious sites of *South* America, but first I would like to take a small detour *northwards* to the famous site of Teotihuacan.

Teotihuacan – City of the Gods

Thirty miles north-east of present-day Mexico City lies Teotihuacan, known to the Aztecs as the 'Place of the Gods' and undeniably one of the most sacred sites in the ancient Americas. According to Aztec legends, it was here, in the central highlands of Mexico, that the Sun and the Moon were born and time itself began. These legends are reflected in Teotihuacan's two principal monuments, the Pyramids of the Sun and the Moon, which dominate the landscape with heights of 212 feet and 140 feet respectively.

Most books tell us that Teotihuacan dates from 200 BC, but in fact it already occupied 4.5 square miles by that date; therefore the city's origin must have been much earlier. This vast metropolis is thought to have been a magnet for surrounding cultures, but despite identifying the presence of many diverse peoples, the archaeologists are still not at all clear who the *original* Teotihuacanos were. Unfortunately, they are concentrating their search around the date 200 BC.[23]

Could the Maya have built Teotihuacan? Despite the Maya having an advanced civilisation by 200 BC, they were based a long way to the south, in Yucatan, Guatemala and Honduras. There *were* clear cultural links between the Maya and Teotihuacan, but these date to later times.[24]

No-one is seriously claiming a Mayan origin for this city.

Who else in Mesoamerica might have built Teotihuacan? Could it have been the Zapotecs, a mysterious people identified with the city of Monte Alban, where they emerged into the history books *c.* 500 BC? A *National Geographic* update on Teotihuacan acknowledges the presence of the Zapotecs, but describes them as latecomers, strangers who settled near the city limits, possibly for trading purposes.[25]

Could it have been a city of the Toltecs? This mysterious people are associated with the city of Tula (also known as Tollan), which is close to Teotihuacan geographically, but is dated to a much later period, *c.* AD 500–700. Nevertheless, a culture does not appear overnight, and it is a fair bet that the Toltec culture was originally established at Teotihuacan.[26] However, that does not mean that the Toltecs built it.

So far, only small sections of Teotihuacan's eight square miles of temples, palaces and residences have been excavated. Further clues to its origins may still lie buried in the ground. In the absence of any form of writing at Teotihuacan, the archaeologists are shooting in the dark. Karl Taube, an archaeologist from the University of California sums up our current state of knowledge:

> We still don't know what language the Teotihuacanos spoke, where they came from, or what happened to them.[27]

What we *do* know about Teotihuacan only adds to the mystery. The site appears to have been laid out with amazing technology. The Street of the Dead, the main axis of the site, runs perfectly straight for 2 miles, and archaeological evidence suggests that some form of sophisticated direction-determining device was actually used in its construction.[28] Furthermore, the layout of the site was based on a 15.5 degree tilt from the cardinal points, a tilt which some experts believe was a deliberate alignment with the Pleiades star constellation.[29] One study of Teotihuacan has even suggested that the entire site was laid out mathematically to represent the orbits of planets in the Solar System.[30]

Archaeologists have found the whole site of Teotihuacan – pyramids, streets and floors of houses – to be inexplicably paved with water-resistant stucco.[31] Excavations in the Atetelco part of the city reveal apartments with sunken courtyards or patios open to the sky, apparently designed to capture rainfall. *National Geographic* reports:

> Throughout the compound, carefully graded stucco floors funneled water to hidden reservoirs. An intricate drainage system below the floor led excess water to the street.[32]

At the Pyramid of the Sun, archaeologists have discovered a sunken space or channel surrounding it on three sides. Underneath the pyramid, a mysterious underground cave has been found, along with a complicated network of subterranean chambers, passages and drainage pipes. Some of these chambers contain a thick layer of mica. This mica has natural insulating properties, which make it resistant to water, heat and electricity. Experts have traced the source of the Teotihuacan mica 2,000 miles away in Brazil![33] Meanwhile, the rerouting of the San Juan river away from its normal course and towards the city provides another vital clue.

Could *water* have played a vital role at Teotihuacan? It has been suggested that an underground water source once existed, close to the Pyramid of the Moon (Plate 59 colour section). That pyramid, like the Pyramid of the Sun, is surrounded by a mysterious sunken channel and once featured a prominent status of a 'water-goddess'. It is possible that water from the Pyramid of the Moon flowed down the Street of the Dead and was ultimately carried away by the San Juan river. These flowing waters, together with the subterranean drains and sluices, bring to mind the sites of Tiwanaku and Chavin de Huantar, which we studied in chapter 3. It may be no coincidence that Tiwanaku also has natural springs which still produce to the south of the site, as a result of a high groundwater level in that region. We can only surmise that all of these sites used the flowing waters to support an unidentified industrial process (or processes). Unfortunately, no experts have ever studied Teotihuacan from such a controversial perspective.

The Builders of Teotihuacan

The dating of Teotihuacan to 200 BC enables the archaeologists to dismiss the possibility that it was built by the Olmecs, for at that time the Olmecs were in terminal decline, far to the south. But have they written off the Olmecs too soon? The popular scientific press seem to quote only the more 'acceptable' radiocarbon datings, whilst ignoring the more controversial evidence. Little mention is made, for instance, of the 900 BC radiocarbon dating at Teotihuacan, established by Miguel Covarrubias in the 1950s, nor the more recently confirmed radiocarbon dating of 1474 BC. Open-minded archaeologists are now joining the growing consensus that much of Teotihuacan was built as early as 1400 BC.

Amazingly, Aztec legends can corroborate a date of 1400 BC for the beginning of Teotihuacan in its present layout. The Aztec legends tell of a day when the Earth fell into total darkness except for Teotihuacan, where a sacred flame continued to burn. The gods then gathered together at Teotihuacan and attempted to move the Sun and the Moon, which were stationary. According to various versions of the legend, an arrow was fired or the wind god blew into the sky. In any event, the Sun and the Moon continued their course and the world was saved. From this legend, the Aztecs drew their notion that time had stopped and then begun again, and the pyramids of Teotihuacan were thereafter associated with the Sun and the Moon. These Aztec legends strongly suggest that the pyramids of the Sun and Moon were built to commemorate the day when the Sun failed to rise. Was this a real event and, if so, when did it occur?

Fortunately, Zecharia Sitchin has established for us a chronology which links the day when the Sun failed to rise in the Americas with a day when the Sun *stood still* on the opposite side of the world! The event in the Americas is recorded by the chronicles of Montesinos, which describe a day when the Sun failed to rise in the Andes. This unusual event occurred in the third year of the reign of the pre-Incan monarch Titu Yupanqui Pachacuti II, when 'there was no dawn for twenty hours'. Sitchin has dated this observation to precisely 1391 BC.[34]

Meanwhile, on the *opposite* side of the world, in the east, the same event is recorded in the Biblical Book of Joshua:

> On the day the Lord gave the Amorites over to Israel, Joshua said to the Lord in the presence of Israel: 'O sun, stand still over Gibeon, O moon, over the Valley of Aijalon.' So the sun stood still, and the moon stopped, till the nation avenged itself on its enemies, as it is written in the Book of Jashar. *The sun stopped in the middle of the sky and delayed going down about a full day*.[35] (emphasis added)

Based on an Exodus date of 1433 BC (see Appendix A), Sitchin has dated the Israelite entry into Canaan 40 years later in 1393 BC, and the day the Sun stood still would thus have occurred shortly afterwards, exactly in agreement with the Andean chronology.[36]

The consistent details of the duration of the event ('twenty hours') rule out the possibility of an eclipse. Instead, the most likely scientific possibility is that the

Earth's spin was temporarily affected by the close passing of a large comet. It is an established fact that comets have counter-clockwise orbits, and would hence act as a force *against* the Earth's direction of rotation. This suggestion is supported by the Book of Joshua 10:11 which refers to 'large hailstones' coming down from the sky – fragments of the comet which had broken off and entered the Earth's atmosphere.

The Aztec creation legend, like most other myths, thus appears to have a solid scientific basis. Furthermore, the legend indicates that Teotihuacan *already* existed in 1391 BC, allowing for the possibility that it was then *enlarged* to commemorate the 'rescue' of the Sun and the Moon. Such a conclusion is supported by the earliest radiocarbon datings of the site to *c*. 1400 BC. We must therefore look to much earlier cultures to identify the builders of Teotihuacan.

At 1400 BC there were few cultures in Mesoamerica to choose from. The Maya are recognised to have emerged around 1200 BC[37] and they were based too far south. The style of the pyramids at Teotihuacan is also quite different from anything which the Maya ever produced. We are thus left with only one apparent solution – the mysterious Olmecs who emerged in Mesoamerica around 1500 BC.

I shall now return to the question I posed earlier. Why would the Olmecs go to such enormous lengths to move 30-ton basalt balls over distances up to 80 miles, and then carve them with such disapproving, indeed frightening, faces? Here is my suggestion, based on the theory that the Olmecs were slaves.

Within a hundred years of settling in to their Gulf Coast homeland, the Olmecs were ordered by the gods to leave their cities and build Teotihuacan. The Olmecs therefore set about an urgent project to erect fierce-looking stone heads around their cities. The purpose was to mark their territory and frighten off any potential settlers during their absence. Each head was thus carved with unique features, and with a size that played up to their image as men of 'giant' stature. In mid-construction, time ran out and the Olmecs were forced to head northwards on their new quest.

Other than the chronology, which fits perfectly, is there any evidence to place the Olmecs at Teotihuacan? In view of my earlier comments on Nimrod as a slave, the comments of Linda Manzanilla, an archaeologist at the National Autonomous University of Mexico, are particularly pertinent. Manzanilla was fascinated to find that most of the site at Teotihuacan comprised approximately 2,000 one-storey stone apartment compounds. Struck by the scale and uniqueness of these compounds, Manzanilla hinted at the notion of a massive enslaved work force:

> There's no other civilisation in Mesoamerica that had these multi-family houses . . . maybe it was a state decision to control the labour force, but we don't know.[38]

Manzanilla has also studied a labyrinth of caves surrounding the site, which she believes are the result of the mining of the volcanic rock which was used to build the pyramids. Who were the people of this huge labour force, who mined, moved and constructed *35 million cubic feet* of rock for the Pyramid of the Sun alone? Who else in Mesoamerica but the Olmecs fit this profile?

We should recall that the grid-pattern of Teotihuacan was carefully pre-planned from the very beginning. We should recall the many inexplicable features of that city, which bring to mind Olmec sites such as La Venta, which had similar subterranean tunnels and waterworks systems. We should also note the widespread examples of Olmec art found at Teotihuacan.[39]

And finally, we should take note of the Teotihuacan chronology *c.* 1400 BC, and the presence of the Olmecs in Mesoamerica at that time, commemorated by one of the central themes of Olmec art – Negroid figures, in clay or stone, peering upwards to the sky. The symbolism of this has baffled the experts, but to me the meaning is quite clear. The anxious skyward gaze marks the day in 1391 BC when the Sun did not rise, a day so unique in human experience that the Bible states 'there has never been a day like it before or since'.[40] Once again, the evidence confirms the presence of the Olmecs in America *c*. 1400 BC.

Tiwanaku and the Kassites

Where were the Olmecs before they arrived in Mesoamerica? In chapter 3, we marvelled at the incredible megalithic stonework of Tiwanaku in Bolivia, which, based on the alignment of the *Kalasasaya* temple, has been dated to at least 4050 BC. We were also intrigued by the findings of subterranean enclosures, particularly the over-engineered water conduits inside the Akapana. We found at Tiwanaku a site built for an obscure functional purpose, devoid of any writing that might provide a clue to its history. It is a picture that bears many similarities to Teotihuacan in Mexico. In fact, one team of scientists has found incredible similarities between the Akapana in Tiwanaku and the Pyramid of the Moon in Teotihuacan.[41]

Whilst the purpose of Teotihuacan remains a mystery, there are many clues to suggest that the product of Tiwanaku was *bronze*, an extremely hard and useful alloy comprising 85 per cent copper and 15 per cent tin.[42]

Evidence of *copper* at Tiwanaku is evident even to the casual observer. On my visit to the site, I found that patches of a greenish-white coppery residue had appeared at the side of the pond inside the Akapana. A similar greenish-white residue had also appeared in a long stripe on the ground inside the *Kalasasaya*. In addition, the entire site is covered with mysterious green pebbles, possibly discoloured by exposure to copper. The purpose of this gravel is a mystery to the archaeologists. Alan Kolata believes that it has a natural origin, being washed down from a nearby mountain, although he admits it is a mystery why the Tiwanakans went to so much trouble to bring billions of these tiny pebbles to the site.[43] As usual, the gravel is dismissed as a weird religious cult. My own impression, in contrast, was that this green gravel is the legacy of a *very* ancient phase of Tiwanaku, perhaps from before the Flood; only flooding would account for the widespread occurrence of the pebbles over such a large area and to some considerable depth in the soil.

If copper was indeed used at Tiwanaku, it did not have to come far, for the Andes mountains contain rich copper deposits. However, the more important component of bronze is tin, a metal obtained by a difficult extraction process from cassiterite ore. Whilst copper deposits are quite commonplace, cassiterite ore is relatively rare.

It is thus highly significant that Tiwanaku is situated directly on top of one of the world's largest belts of cassiterite. This massive belt stretches from the eastern shore of Lake Titicaca around its southern basin and then south, parallel to the River Desaguandero, as far as Oruru and Lake Poopo, a total distance of around 200 miles. This abundant supply of cassiterite is surely the reason why Tiwanaku was originally founded in such a remote and hostile environment.

Further corroboration of Tiwanaku as an ancient centre for the production of bronze is found in numerous linguistic references to either tin or copper. The Sumerian word for tin was AN.NA, literally meaning 'Heavenly Stone'.[44] It is surely no coincidence that the name Tiwanaku is derived from the Sumerian TI.AN.NA, meaning 'Life, Tin'. Similarly, the Sumerian word for copper was URU, a significant clue perhaps to the role of the mysterious Uru tribe of Lake Titicaca. As Alan Kolata has pointed out, the Uru Indians were at one time proliferous along the rivers connecting Titicaca to Lake Poopo and the nearby town of Oruru.[45] Perhaps their origin is connected with the transportation of copper, as the name which has been given to them suggests.

Assuming that Tiwanakan bronze production commenced *c.* 4050 BC,[46] the obvious question to ask is why it was not started thousands of years previously, when the space facilities of the gods were being constructed. If Tiwanaku was not functioning, then the bronze for those constructions must have come from elsewhere. What happened to that earlier source of bronze, and why did production then shift to Tiwanaku? Did that earlier source become exhausted or did it, for some reason, become unworkable?

An intriguing possibility is that the earlier centre of metallurgy was in Antarctica, where there are extensive mountain ranges, rich in mineral deposits. Sedimentary core samples, taken from the Ross Sea by the 1949 Byrd Expedition. have proved that rivers flowed freely in Antarctic prior to 4000 BC, when it then became glaciated.[47] Any mining activity in Antarctica would have had to cease in 4000 BC. It may be no coincidence that this date precisely matches the beginning of Tiwanaku.

Were there Negroid miners present at Tiwanaku? Could this be the place where the Olmecs learned mining and perhaps mineral processing techniques? The bridge to make this connection is a mysterious people from Mesopotamia, known as the Kassites.

The Kassites are most famous for their occupation of Babylon in the sixteenth century BC, after that city fell to the Hittites. Prior to that, the Kassites had lived in the Zagros Mountains, to the north-east. Curiously, just like Nimrod and his followers, the Kassites were virtually an invisible people. Even when they occupied Babylon, they made no cultural changes whatsoever. Their contemporaries regarded them as a barbarous people, but in ancient times the word 'barbarian' had no negative connotations. The origin of the term is actually the Greek word *barbaros*, which was used to describe a 'non-Greek foreigner' – someone who could not be understood due to their babble or unintelligible language.[48]

The Greek word *barbaros* is, in turn, ultimately derived from the Sumerian word BAR, meaning 'metal'. The repeated syllables in BAR.BAR may thus have originally signified a foreigner who was associated with various metals. The Kassites were therefore not barbarians in the modern sense, but foreigners who worked with metals. One scholar has indeed suggested that the name Kassite derives from a common origin with the term cassiterite (tin ore), and has linked the appearance of the Kassites *c.* 2200 BC with a dramatic increase in the previously dwindling tin content of bronze products in Mesopotamia.[49]

Other scholars have compared the term Kassite to Cushite, noting that the Akkadian name for the Kassites was *Kashshu*.[50] Geographically, the Kassites were associated with the region of ancient Elam known as Kush-an. It was in this region of the Zagros Mountains that cassiterite was mined in ancient times, passing from the Zagros to Mesopotamia via the ancient city of Susa. The earliest phase of Susa is dated to around 4000 BC, the same time as Tiwanaku, and like Tiwanaku it suddenly appeared as a mature culture.[51]

Now we come to the more interesting part – various authorities have established that the earliest inhabitants of ancient Elam were *Negroid*:

> Sculptural remains discovered in the region [of Elam], and other evidences, point to its habitation at a very early date by *Negroid* peoples . . .[52] (emphasis added)

This is not the only example of a Negroid presence in the mountain regions of the Near East. In 1959, the *Journal of*

Near Eastern Studies published an article claiming evidence of a Negroid population in ancient times in the region of the south-east corner of the Black Sea and later in the Caucasus region further north.[53]

All of the above evidence – the 'barbaric' language, the cultural invisibility, and in particular the geographical connections, tend to suggest that the Kassites were Negroid slaves, who were involved in cassiterite mining and production of bronze. The etymological connection between the Biblical Cushites (of dark-skinned Hamitic origin) and the Kassites is therefore more than coincidence. It is extremely important to note, however, that the term Kassite describes an activity rather than a race. Several commentators have indeed suggested that the Kassites were once *led by* an Indo-European elite, based on the Indo-European names of their gods.[54] The available evidence suggests that the Kassites were thus a mixed group of Africans and Indo-Europeans.

If tin was one of the products of Tiwanaku, along with bronze, then it is highly likely that the sudden appearance of both tin and Kassites in the Near East *c.* 2200 BC coincided with the shutdown of Tiwanaku. As discussed in chapter 11, the gods in South America were at this time awaiting Marduk's final controversial return to Babylon. *Circa* 2255 BC the gods had inflicted a devastating punishment on Inanna's city Agade – a turn of events that could only hasten the return of her rival, Marduk. It is possible that not just the Kassites, but the gods too, returned to the east, resulting in the shutdown of Tiwanaku at the time.

The intriguing question that arises from the above discussion is 'how do the Olmecs fit in?' What might have caused one group of Negroes to become separated from the Kassites and literally miss the boat home from Tiwanaku *c.* 2200 BC? And that raises another interesting question – if the Olmecs, who emerged *c.* 1500 BC, did learn their skills at Tiwanaku, where were they between 2200–1500 BC?

The Nazca Incident

Four hundred and fifty miles north-west of Tiwanaku, along the Pacific coast, lies the plain of Nazca in Peru. In chapter 3, I concluded that the mysterious lines and drawings at Nazca could only have been designed for *viewing from the air*. Are the Nazca Lines somehow connected with Tiwanaku? For the answer we must travel 120 miles north-west of Nazca and revisit one of the largest geoglyphs of all – the famous 700-feet high trident on the mountainside at the Bay of Paracas (Plate 55, colour section). This mysterious geoglyph is etched into the ground to a depth of around 2 feet, and outlined by stones which may have been placed at a later date. No-one knows for certain the age of the original carving. However, an expedition by the French writer Robert Charroux in 1969, noted that, although the mountainside was exposed to the wind, the wind contained no dust or sand. Charroux thus concluded that the trident carving could have been drawn millennia ago and yet still have avoided any significant erosion.[55]

The trident symbol at Paracas is a major clue to its origin. According to local legend, this carved trident represents the lightning rod of the god Viracocha, who was worshipped throughout South America under various names such as Rimac (Illustration 20).

Illustration 20

Figure 14a

Figure 14b

Figure 15

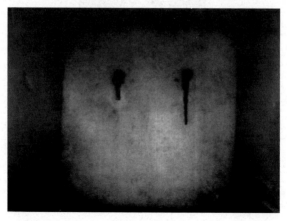

Figure 16

Figure 17

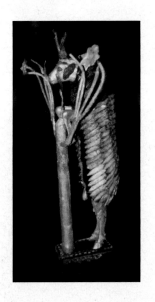

Figure 18

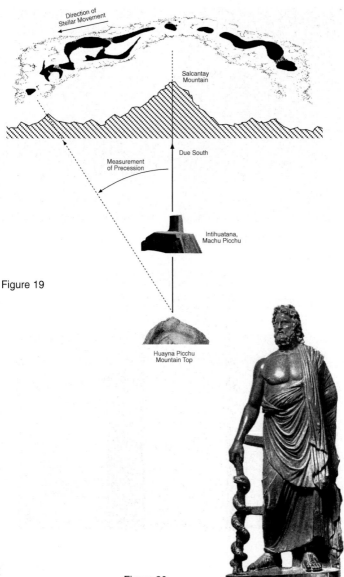

Direction of
Stellar Movement

Salcantay
Mountain

Measurement
of Precession

Due South

Intihuatana,
Machu Picchu

Figure 19

Huayna Picchu
Mountain Top

Figure 20

Figure 21

Figure 22

Figure 23

Figure 24

Figure 25

Figure 26

Figure 27 *(right)*

Figure 28

Figure 29

Figure 30

Figure 31

Figure 32

Figure 33

Figure 34

Figure 35

Figure 36

The depiction of a god with forked lightning is, however, not unique to this region. We find similar depictions of such a god in Mesopotamia. Scholars of Near Eastern divinities will immediately recognise him as 'the Storm God'. The largest temple at Baalbek once contained a golden statue of this Storm God, who was recognised as the head of the triad worshipped there.[56] The Roman historian Macrobius described the statue of the god as:

> . . . hold[ing] in his right hand a whip, charioteer-like, and in his left a thunderbolt *with ears of corn*.[57] (emphasis added)

Amazingly, the Paracas trident shows exactly the same features interpreted by macrobius as 'ears of corn', although their real purpose may be somewhat more functional.

The Storm God was known to the Sumerians by the name Ishkur, meaning 'Far Mountain Lands', and this god was usually shown with a tool in one hand and a forked lightning in the other (Illustration 21 a, b & c). The people of the Near East knew him by a variety of other names such as Teshub, Ramman[58] and Hadad, and showed him with a thunderbolt in his left hand and an axe in his right hand (See Figure 22, black-and-white section). Did this axe signify mining for the production of bronze, were the 'far mountain lands' the distant Andes, and was the 'thunderbolt' of the east the same as the 'trident' of the west?

Illustration 21

A remarkably similar Storm God appears in Mesoamerica. The *National Geographic* update on excavations at Teotihuacan, referred to earlier, stated that depictions of a Storm

God, wielding a huge and fearsome weapon, appeared everywhere the archaeologists dug (Illustration 22). Surely it is no coincidence that, according to legend, a god *blew* into the sky at Teotihuacan on the day the Sun did not rise, for the Hittite people of Anatolia (modern day Turkey) indeed called Ishkur by the name of Teshub, meaning 'the Wind Blower'.

Illustration 22

As seen in Illustration 21 and Figure 22, Ishkur the Storm God was commonly depicted on top of a bull. This symbol is also found in the Americas, particularly at the sacred centre of Chavin de Huantar in Peru, where it was the focus of a religious cult. In addition to the fanged, bull-like features of the *El Lanzon* god (Figure 6, black-and-white section), we also find a fanged, human-like bull on another famous stele from Chavin – the 6-feet high Raymondi Stele.[59] Figure 23 (See black-and-white section) shows this bull-god with a sceptre in each hand standing beneath a machine-like device.

Other South American cultures also worshipped the bull. What is the significance of this animal? In chapter 11, we noted that the association of the Storm God Ishkur/Teshub with the bull had its roots in the precessional cycle, specifically the zodiac sign of Taurus. For this reason, the lands of Ishkur in modern-day Turkey contain the *Taurus* Mountains. It is generally recognised that the era of Taurus commenced 4380 BC and ended in

2220 BC – *exactly* the time scale we are concerned with at Tiwanaku.

At Tiwanaku, the Gate of the Sun depicts a god holding a weapon in one hand and a forked lightning in the other (Figure 24, black-and-white section). If this god is Viracocha, as local legends claim, then Viracocha is simply another name for the Storm God, Ishkur, who was associated with both the bull and the trident.

From all of the above, we can conclude that Ishkur/Adad/Teshub was the deity called Viracocha who had set up Tiwanaku for the production of tin and bronze, and later been instrumental in the design of Teotihuacan for some other unknown industrial function.

One of the most prominent legends of Tiwanaku is that of a weeping god, commonly depicted on statues with three tear drops below each eye (see the highly stylised version in Figure 24, black-and-white section). The legends of the weeping god are vague and diverse, and may have been invented by the people who found the statues with the mysterious tears. No-one really knows the significance of these tears. Could it be that the god Ishkur was desperately sad to leave Tiwanaku, or could it be that he cried for the loss of Agade, the city of his niece Inanna? I do not find either of these scenarios very convincing. It is necessary to seek a much more dramatic event, closer to 'home', that would bring such an emotional outburst from this powerful god. The solution, I believe, lies on the plains of Nazca.

First, however, it is necessary to appreciate the symbolic meaning of the huge trident at Paracas. The presence of this trident on the coastal hillside clearly states to anyone arriving by sea that they are entering the territory of the Storm God. The fact that the symbol exists at all tells us two things – one, that Ishkur possessed the skill and technology to etch the figure into the mountainside, and, two, that he felt it necessary to do so. The latter point strikes me as odd, for I do not subscribe to the theory expressed by some

writers that the gods, with all their technological capabilities, *needed* to leave marks on the desert as directional
indicators.[60] Why then would a powerful god leave such a
statement behind?

Now let us turn our attention to the plain of Nazca. But
instead of being distracted by its random designs, let us
focus on some underlying facts. The Nazca plain is virtually
unique for its ability to *preserve* the markings upon it. This
property comes from the combination of the Nazca climate
(one of the driest on Earth, with only twenty *minutes* of
rainfall per year) and the flat, stony ground which mini-
mises the effect of the wind at ground level. With no dust or
sand to cover the plain, and little rain or wind to erode it,
lines drawn here tend to stay drawn.[61] These factors,
combined with the existence of a lighter-coloured subsoil
beneath the desert crust, provide a vast writing pad that is
ideally suited to the artist who wants to leave his mark for
eternity.

Who was the Nazca artist? Given that Ishkur's symbol
appears a short distance to the north-west at Paracas, surely
it was he. Who else but Ishkur could have flown in the
vicinity of Nazca, and who else but Ishkur possessed a
technology that could direct a cutting beam into the desert
plain below?

Why then does the Nazca plain appear to be such a
jumbled mess of figures, with lines and broad bands that
seem to serve no artistic purpose? In my view, the answer
lies in the tale of the weeping god. Here is my theory.

Towards the end of the Tiwanakan era, some of the slaves
rebelled. A group of them seized one or more aerial craft
belonging to Ishkur, and took turns to deface the Nazca
plain in a wanton act of vandalism. In some places they
gouged broad bands that perhaps erased the art that Ishkur
himself had drawn earlier. In other places they drew
pictures that were designed to mock and insult the god.
Some of the rebels drew impressive images, others took the

controls and could only draw amateurish doodles. The whole incident was so chaotic that in places they intersected each other's work. When Ishkur saw the desecration of the plain and the vandalisation of his own artwork, he wept. And thus was born the legend of the weeping god.

Figure 25 (see black-and-white section) provides an overview of the intersecting marks at Nazca, showing how the huge wedges are wide enough to have eradicated the geoglyphs. Studies have confirmed that the earlier phase of Nazca was indeed 'more advanced'.[62] My theory explains why many of the lines at Nazca point towards mountains, since it is a natural human tendency to fly an aircraft towards a reference point on the horizon. It also explains why the lines sometimes cross perfectly straight over deep ravines – a virtually impossible task without an aircraft. Finally, and most importantly, my theory explains *all* of the features at Nazca – the lines *and* the geoglyphs, the random distribution of drawings, the overlapping patterns and the variable quality of the drawings. No other theory has emerged from 50 years of study to explain everything that we see at Nazca today.

What evidence is there to confirm that Nazca was desecrated by a rebellion of slaves? It is time to pay a visit to another mystery of the Americas – the enigmatic statues of Easter Island.

Exile on Easter Island

Easter Island lies in the Pacific Ocean 2,300 miles west from the coast of Chile and around 2,500 miles from Tiwanaku and Nazca. This small volcanic island, only 45 square miles in area, is dominated by its unique *moai* statues (Plate 54, colour section). Three hundred *moai* are thought to have once stood around the coastline on stone platforms, gazing outwards, whilst a further four hundred partly-finished statues have been found in the nearby quarry at Rano Raraku.

The size of the Easter Island statues is impressive, as are the clean-cut lines produced by the artist. In height, the moai range from 15–30 feet, the tallest of which is reputed to weigh 89 tons. These statues are supposed to have been carved out of an extinct crater, and then erected, by men equipped only with the simplest of stone tools. To cap this incredible achievement, the artists then managed to lift and fit 10-ton hats on to the statues' heads.

Many fanciful theories have attempted to describe how these statues might have been erected, but nobody really knows. Thor Heyerdahl has spent years on this mystery and got nowhere, other than demonstrating that it is possible to 'walk' the statues along the ground, as we might move a refrigerator. To suggest, as some do, that Heyerdahl successfully 'carved and erected' a statue on Easter Island is pure myth. The truth is that he employed a group of locals who, with simple tools, managed to work a relief only a couple of inches into the rock face.[63] They eventually managed, over several weeks, to re-erect a *small* statue, but they did not attempt to lift it onto a stone platform, nor to fit a 10-ton hat onto its head.

Another Easter Island myth is that, based on radiocarbon datings, the statues have been dated no older than AD 400. Radiocarbon dating, by definition, cannot date stone, and thus relies on dating organic material left at the site *after* the stonework. It therefore proves nothing about when the statues were *originally* constructed.

The truth is that no-one has the faintest idea *when* the Easter Island statues were erected, *who* erected them or *how* they managed to cut them out of the volcanic rock. Perhaps it is time to study them with a different paradigm – a paradigm that accepts the presence of gods in South America in ancient times and recognises the many connections between Easter Island and the South American mainland.

In 1991, an article was published by the Ancient Astronaut Society, illustrating the uncanny similarities between the masonry from a *moai* platform on Easter Island and a wall at Ollantaytambo in Peru.[64] The stones appeared to have been cut and assembled in an identical fashion and in neither case could a thin blade be inserted between the huge, accurately fitted blocks. According to the so-called experts, this masonry was an independent Easter Island development, but is it really likely that two *independent* cultures learned how to slice through rock like a hot knife through butter?

The hats and chiselled facial features of the Easter Island statues also bear a similarity to statues found on the South American mainland. Figure 26, shows two statues from Aija in Peru, which in turn resemble a depiction of an Indo-European ruler from the Indus Valley (Figure 27, black-and-white section).

There are also some similarities between the statues of Easter Island and those of Tiwanaku. Figure 28 (see black-and-white section) shows the statue of Pachacamac situated within the *Kalasasaya*; its 2-tier hat can still be discerned despite the attempt to vandalise it, and it bears some resemblance to the two-tier hats of the *moai* (Plate 54, colour section).

As with the trident at Paracas, the most revealing question to ask of Easter Island is 'why?'. Why did someone go to all the trouble of erecting hundreds of statues around the coast, and then carefully fit them with hats? I have only ever found two plausible answers to this question. One, that they were designed to scare people away (like the Olmec heads). Or two, that they were designed to catch someone's attention to remind them 'we're still here, please rescue us!'

The fact is that, when the builders of these statues disappeared from Easter Island, they left so suddenly that their work was abandoned in the quarries. I therefore favour the second scenario – a marooned people who sought help and were rescued. Now how does a group of expert stonemasons just *happen* to get stuck on a remote island at a great distance from the South American coast?

The answer must surely lie in a deliberate exile of workers from Tiwanaku. As I suggested earlier, the Nazca Lines include the vandalistic efforts of a rebellious group of slaves. The weeping god, Ishkur, reasserted his authority, first by carving his trident on a mountainside quite separate from the desert plain, and then by punishing the guilty parties. We know from ancient texts that a typical punishment of the gods was banishment or exile. Easter Island would have made an ideal and convenient location.

I therefore suggest that, when most of the slaves returned to Mesopotamia *c.* 2200 BC, one group was exiled on Easter Island. The *moai* statues were modelled with the serious features of their custodians in an attempt to attract their attention and sympathy. It was an act of dedication that we might even view as an apology in stone.

After the Easter Islanders were rescued, where did they go to? As we look to the nearby continent of the Americas, two obvious solutions present themselves – Mesoamerica and Chavin de Huantar in Peru. Both sprang to life at the same time, *c.* 1500–1400 BC.

At Chavin de Huantar, an early settlement has been radiocarbon dated to around 1400 BC. A pre-Incan legend, recorded by Montesinos, describes the arrival of foreigners on the shores of Peru at this time. According to the legend, which can be dated to *c.* 1500 BC, these men of 'giant stature' headed into the *mountains* where they later angered their god and were destroyed.[65] The question which arises in *my* mind is how these settlers managed to find the remote and well-hidden mountainous site of Chavin. The answer which occurs to me is that they had been involved in its *original* construction, implying that the builders of the underground waterworks at Chavin were one and the same as the builders of Tiwanaku.

Meanwhile, another group of rescued Easter Islanders turned up in Mesoamerica as the *Negroid* Olmecs, whose civilisation has also been dated to around 1500 BC. The logical implication of this is that the Easter Island stone-masons were Negroes, and hence the Tiwanakan workers were also Negroes. Everything ties together. The evidence of the Kassites being a mixture of Africans and Indo-Europeans neatly explains why Indo-European features appear on the *moai* statues, as well as at Aija on the mainland. These 'elite' Indo-Europeans were, it would seem, the supervising workforce.

There remains just one loose end to address. How did the Olmecs come to be based on the *east* coast of Mesoamerica, whereas Easter Island is off the *west* coast of South America.

In actual fact, there *is* an Olmec city on the west coast, and it is thought to be one of the earliest, if not *the* earliest of the Olmec settlements. It has only been belatedly recog-nised that the site of Izapa, radiocarbon-dated to approxi-mately 1500 BC, is the largest Olmec site of all and shows the longest period of occupation.[66] Contrary to the popular opinion that the Olmecs emerged on the Gulf coast, archaeological evidence is increasingly emphasising a ma-jor Olmec presence in the south-west, at sites such as Pijijiapan, La Blanca, Abaj Takalik, Monte Alto and Chalchuapan.[67] These discoveries have been so impressive that John Graham, an archaeologist from the University of California at Berkeley, has now gone on record with his view that the Pacific coast may have been the original Olmec heartland.[68]

To the cynic who suggests my theories are too conveni-ently simple, I would cite the famous scientific principle of 'Occam's Razor' – invent no unnecessary hypotheses.[69] In other words, the more complex and convoluted a theory, the more implausible that theory is likely to be. At Teotihuacan, Tiwanaku, Nazca and Easter Island we have extraordinary phenomena, that have defied explanation by any other means. Is it really likely that there should be several separate extraordinary causes of these mysteries?

Mysteries such as these are actually illusions, caused by a prejudice that treats gods as myth and precludes us from making connections between distant sites in ancient times. We have all grown a little too attached to the existence of these mysteries, but if we apply a *proper* scientific approach, they should, by definition, not exist at all. A 'proper approach' means a *non-dogmatic* search for the truth, with an open mind which will constantly challenge the prevailing wisdom and consider all possible explanations.

According to the principle of Occam's Razor cited earlier, it is illogical to assume that two or more *independent* ancient cultures appeared in the Americas with advanced stonemasonry or metallurgy skills. According to Occam's Razor, we should *expect* the mysteries to disappear by reducing our assumptions to the absolute minimum. My simple explanation that connects the Olmecs to Tiwanaku, Nazca, Easter Island and Teotihuacan is therefore a powerful signal that the new paradigm, presented in this book, is on the right track.

Fallen Giants

If some of the Tiwanakan workers returned to the east as the Kassites, who were prominent for most of the second millennium BC, then we ought to find mention of them in the Bible. So where are they? The names Olmec and Kassite are, of course, non-Hebrew terms, which we would not expect to find in the Bible. Nor do they appear as Cushites, since that name signifies the many diverse Hamitic tribes descended from Cush himself. Furthermore, the Old Testament makes no specific reference to skin colour, preferring to identify tribes by geography, political allegiance and ultimately to their race via the Table of Nations.

On the other hand, there are several groups of people described in the Bible whose origin is a mystery – peoples who cannot be traced back to the Table of Nations. These peoples appear from time to time as the mythical 'giants'. Could there be some truth behind these legendary folk? Goliath, for instance, the famous giant defeated by David, is described as 9-feet tall – well within the bounds of scientific possibility.[70] He was described as a Gittite[71] and sometimes as a Philistine, but these terms only tell us that he came from the Philistine city of Gath, and throw no light on his racial origin. Goliath's brother is also named by the Bible, in a passage which intimates that he and others from Gath were also of giant size.[72]

Another prominent Biblical giant was Og, king of a region called Bashan,[73] whose bed measured 13 by 6 feet,[74] not inconsistent with Goliath's height of 9 feet. Og was sometimes described as an 'Amorite',[75] this term simply meaning a westerner. Elsewhere, however, Og was referred to as 'one of the last of the Rephaites'[76] or the last of the 'remnant' of the Rephaites.[77]

Who were the Rephaites? Biblical references identify them as a group of giants descended from Rapha.[78] The Ammonites called these people 'Zamzummim', a term which is thought to mean 'gibberish'. As for the meaning of the name Rephaites, this term is used elsewhere in the Bible to describe the dead, in the sense of being 'sunken, powerless, impotent in death'.[79]

From all of these clues, we can make a number of deductions concerning the Rephaites giants. First, their giant appearance was due to a commonly inherited genetic disposition. Secondly, they were a *remnant*, indicating that they had once been numerous. Thirdly, they spoke a language that could not be understood (i.e. they were foreigners in Canaan). Fourthly, they were either sterile or lacked female companions with whom to interbreed, and were thus ultimately doomed to extinction.

Could the Rephaites have been a remnant from the Tiwanakan slaves? We have traced the Tiwanakans to the Kassites, who were described as barbarians, with a language that could not be understood. We have also traced the Tiwanakans to the Olmecs, whose art typically depicted all-male groups, with sad and lonely expressions, as noted by the *National Geographic*: 'a trait typical of Olmec art is the long face with downturned mouth'.[80] Another common Olmec art theme is a *male* figure holding an inactive helmeted child, indicating an unusual obsession with childbirth (or lack of).[81] Indeed, the Olmecs disappeared from the Americas in a manner which is fully consistent with a sterile male-only population. Many Olmec and Kassite characteristics are therefore similar to those of the Biblical Rephaites.

The only reservation that we might have in making this connection is the geographical distance between the Rephaites in Canaan and the Kassites who lived eight hundred miles to the east, in the Zagros Mountains. However, there is no reason why those Kassites who returned from Tiwanaku could not have subsequently split into two groups. Can we positively make such a connection?

A major clue comes from a second group of giants identified in the Old Testament. In addition to the Rephaites, there is another group known as the Anakim. The origin of these people is obscure. The Bible names some of their leaders as Ahiman, Sheshai and Talmai, from the town of Hebron.[82] These people were so big that they made the Israelites seem like 'grasshoppers' in comparison (certainly an exaggeration!). In ancient times, Hebron was known as Kiriath-Arba, the 'city of Arba', and Biblical authorities believe that Arba was a great man of the Anakim, possibly their forefather.[83]

The Anakim, like the Rephaites, inhabited the mountainous regions of Canaan and some of the coastal areas. This geographical coincidence suggests that the Anakim and the Rephaites were one and the same people, or at least two groups from the same genetic race. The principle of Occam's Razor suggests that we do not invent two races of giants when one is a sufficient explanation.

What is the clue, then, that connects these Anakim giants to the Kassites? The name Anakim is thought to derive from the Sumerian AN.NA meaning 'tin'. As we discussed earlier, there is also a strong case for believing that the Kassites were associated with the mining of cassiterite ore and the production of tin. Thus we can make the link between the Anakim giants and the Kassites.

The terms Anakim and Rephaite are also, in my view, two descriptive attributes of one people – a people of large stature who were, on the one hand, associated with tin and, on the other, doomed to die. Whereas the Bible does not comment on the origin of the Rephaites, it *does* give us a direct hint on the origin of the Anakim. The information comes from the Israelite spies who were sent from the Sinai prior to the invasion of Canaan *c.* 1400 BC. The spies returned with a disturbing report that: 'we saw the Nefilim there (the descendants of Anak come from the Nefilim).'[84] In chapter 6, we identified the Nefilim as 'Those Who Descended' – the gods themselves.

To summarise this chapter so far, we have followed a chain of clues that connect the Olmecs to Tiwanaku, Tiwanaku to the Kassites, the Kassites to the Anakim/ Rephaites, and the Anakim to the Nefilim. We might dismiss all this as coincidence, if it was not for the evidence of the gods in the other 15 chapters of this book. We might also dismiss the idea of 9-feet tall giants if the Biblical legends of giants in the east were not supported by similar

South American legends of giants in the west.[85] Was this race of giants a special creation of the gods?

The infamous account of Genesis 6 states that the daughters of men bore children to the Nefilim. However, this event occurred before the Flood. Therefore, the question of 'giant' offspring from the Nefilim is an academic point, since according to the Bible, they all would have been destroyed by the Flood. How then could the Anakim have 'come from' the Nefilim *after* the Flood?

In chapter 13, I dealt in some detail with the genetic creation of the three races of mankind by the gods. This threefold division of mankind between the tribes of Shem, Ham and Japheth does not allow for a fourth, distinct race of 9-feet tall 'giants'. But could these men have been created *subsequently* as a special race to carry out the physical labour required to build the pyramids, construct the space facilities, and rebuild cities such as Nimrod's Babylon?

Here is another pertinent question. Where did the metals come from to build the gods' space facilities after the Flood? The mining and refining of minerals must have been an essential requirement. Who was to carry out all this work? Not the gods themselves, but an enslaved human workforce. Given the genetic science which the gods possessed, why not engineer a special race of strong, tall people, endowed with long life spans but unable to procreate – a pre-Eden style, controlled population?[86] Is this the secret behind the 'giants' who, according to the Bible, died out *c*. 1300 BC?

Even if we recognise the prior existence of a 9-feet tall race of giants, it is clear that brute force alone would not have been sufficient to move stones weighing hundreds of tons. This could only have been achieved with the use of the gods' technology. The chosen race therefore had to be intelligent and skilled in the operation of sophisticated technologies.

There is indeed a pictorial record of a technology that

was once used in the Americas, possibly for mining and stone quarrying operations. The Toltecs of Mesoamerica depicted sophisticated tools, that may not have been used by them, but were certainly known to them. At their main city of Tula, they carved 13-feet high statues (known as the Atlantes) which held modern-looking tools (Illustration 23a). A Toltec relief carving on a stone column at Tula shows exactly how these tools were used on the rock face (Illustration 23b). Similar tools, known as Thermo-Jets, have been used in modern times to cut the giant monument at Stone Mountain in Georgia, USA.

Illustration 23   a.

b.

A further record of ancient technology is found at Palenque in Mexico, where a stone sarcophagus lid, found in a royal tomb, shows a Maya king working a complex mechanical device (Plate 58, colour section). Some have interpreted the figure as an astronaut in a rocket-propelled vehicle, but it is much more likely that the device represents a boring machine that had been used in much earlier times for mining purposes. The equivalent twentieth century machine would be a recent invention known as the 'Impact Ripper' – a hydraulically powered chisel mounted on rails, which attacks the rock face with a hitherto unknown accuracy. I am not claiming that the Maya used this device themselves, for they were not miners, and, even if they had been, a king would not have commemorated such an activity in his tomb. Instead I am suggesting that the machine (or drawing thereof) existed as a legacy from the Olmecs, and had over time become a mystical tradition to the Maya. It is a known fact that the early Maya were in close contact with their Olmec neighbours in Mesoamerica.

Our study of the post-Flood era has identified one chosen race, perhaps even a created race, of Negroid people who were trained by and controlled by the gods. We saw them building Mesopotamian cities from 3500 BC. We saw them at Tiwanaku, engaged in bronze production and associated activities from 4050–2200 BC. We saw them as Olmecs building Teotihuacan c. 1390 BC and occupying Chavin de Huantar c. 1500 BC. We saw them amongst the Kassites in later Mesopotamian history, and as Rephaim and Anakim in Biblical history, when the last remnant were defeated by the Israelites c. 1400–1300 BC. The evidence suggests that Nimrod, too, was one of these Negroid giants, the one who became particularly famous due to his act of rebellion against Yahweh.

Having gained an understanding of the relationship of men and gods in the post-Flood era, it is now time to go back to the beginning, to assess the 'toil' for which man was originally created.

African Genesis

According to my chronology, the gods arrived on Earth 259,000 years before the Flood, and shared the Earth with mankind for 165,600 of those years. Did man get lumbered in these earlier times with a similar toil to that which I have described so far – a mixture of mining, metallurgy, construction and industrial processing? Did these activities exist *before* the Flood?

In terms of physical evidence, we cannot hope to find

evidence equivalent to sites such as Tiwanaku. Nevertheless, in 1980, Hugo Boero Rojo did discover extensive ruins *underneath* Lake Titicaca, indicating that something occurred here before the Flood.[87] This is supported by Arthur Posnansky's claim that human skeletons were discovered in the alluvia from a mysterious inundation at Tiwanaku.[88] For what reason other than mining would an advanced society have existed in the Bolivian altiplano, with all its mineral wealth, *before the Flood*?

Turning to the textual evidence, we find in the Bible a reference to the existence of metallurgy from the earliest times before the Flood. According to Genesis 4, Tubal-Cain (from the accursed line of Cain) 'forged all kinds of tools out of bronze and iron'.

Mesopotamian texts provide much greater detail. The Sumerians claimed that, when the gods first arrived on Earth, they built a number of cities that were later destroyed by the Flood and that these cities were subsequently rebuilt. One of those original cities, established around 250,000 years ago, was named BAD.TIBIRA, meaning 'Foundation Place of Metalworking'.[89] It was the place to which mineral ores were brought by ships which the Sumerians called MA.GUR UR.NU AB.ZU, 'Ships for Ores of the Lower World'.[90]

Metallurgy is but one aspect, however, of a much wider 'toil' for which mankind was used after the creation. Mesopotamian texts describe the activity of the rank-and-file gods in the Eden of the east, where Enlil was supervising the digging of canals, the raising of dykes and the construction of accommodation and other facilities.[91] All of the pre-Flood cities, such as Nippur (mission control) and Shuruppak (the medical centre) required ongoing construction and maintenance. *The Myth of the Pickaxe*, cited in chapter 12, clearly describes the 'toil' of the gods which drove Enlil to steal 'Black-headed' slaves from Enki.

All of these forms of toil ultimately depended on raw

materials, in the form of minerals that had to be mined before they could be processed and put to use. According to the *Atra-Hasis*, this was the task supervised by Enki, who was sent to the Abzu in the Lower World – the Eden of the west *c.* 250,000 BC. The *Atra-Hasis* states:

> The gods clasped hands together,
> then cast lots and divided:
> Anu to heaven went up;
> to Enlil the Earth was made subject;
> that which the sea as a loop encloses,
> they gave to the prince Enki.
> To the Abzu Enki went down,
> assumed the rulership of the Abzu.[92]

One of Enki's nicknames was *nahash*, the solver of secrets, indicating his scientific knowledge. He was also known, however, by the nickname BURU, the pictograph for which resembles a mine-shaft and bestows the meaning, according to Zecharia Sitchin, of 'God of the Deep Mines'.[93]

Egyptian hieroglyphs also support the theory of mining activities in the African continent. Several scholars have noted the resemblance of the ancient Egyptian sign for the gods, *neter*, to an axe (Illustration 24).[94] Since no-one else has come up with a satisfactory explanation why a flag on the end of a stick should signify gods, the axe theory is currently the best available, and symbolises the primary purpose of the gods' presence in the African continent.

Illustration 24

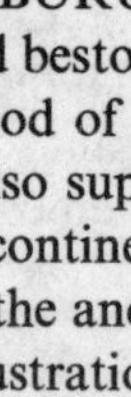

What is the meaning of the Abzu, or AB.ZU in Sumerian, to which Enki was sent? The common translation of the term is 'primeval deep source', carrying clear mining connotations, but sometimes misinterpreted as a sea of deep water to the south of Sumer.[95] The full meaning, however, has been amply demonstrated by Zecharia Sitchin, who points out the similarity between its pictographic sign and a mine shaft, as can be seen in Illustration 25.[96]

Illustration 25

Can we prove that mining occurred on Earth 200,000 years ago? The best proof would come from the pre-Flood mine shafts themselves, but, not surprisingly, there has never been a detailed search for such evidence. In fact, there is little enough information on more recent prehistoric mining, as noted by one of the few such surveys carried out by a British engineer in 1980, in which the author stated:

> Very few sites are available for inspection or photography and most, in fact nearly all, are backfilled and nothing remains of the original excavation to be seen. So in most cases we must depend on old reports, papers and articles.[97]

Searching for such remote evidence therefore appears to be an utterly futile task. Nevertheless, we do occasionally hear anecdotal reports of ancient mine shafts uncovered by modern mining explorations, and there are indications that these may go back to at least 100,000 BC.[98]

There is one alternative approach to corroborating the ancient texts, and that is to search for the miners themselves rather than the mine shafts. This might initially sound rather ridiculous, but genetic science actually provides us with the tool to prove or disprove textual claims that the LU.LU slaves were created in Africa, where the main mining activities were located. One such text records the divine instructions from Enki to Ninharsag, the Mother Goddess:

> Mix to a core the clay
> from the Basement of the Earth
> [just] above *the Abzu*.[99] (emphasis added)

What do the genetic scientists say? During the last ten years, more and more evidence has pointed to human origins in Africa, not just for *Homo erectus* and his precursors, but most significantly for *Homo sapiens* too. Some scientists have resisted this so-called 'Out of Africa' theory, but the evidence appears overwhelming. In particular, a study by Wilson, Stoneking and Cann found that the greatest genetic distance in mtDNA is to a group of Africans, concluding logically that the earliest tribal separation took place from an African source.[100] The same conclusion was reached using fundamentally different genetic data by Luigi Cavalli-Sforza of Stanford University.[101]

At a conference on the origin of modern humans, held in 1992, every contributor, without exception, supported the theory that Mitochondrial Eve was an African, confirming the established fossil evidence of our earliest origins in Ethiopia, Kenya and South Africa.[102]

What minerals might the gods have been seeking? To this day, the lands of southern Africa are a rich source of iron, cobalt, gold, cassiterite, copper and diamonds, to name but a few. These remote times do not yield their secrets easily, and more than one item may have been on the gods' 'shopping list'. As noted earlier, at least one of these minerals was shipped to Bad-Tibira for refining. The location of that pre-Flood city suggests that the refined products were transported to Nibiru when that planet approached Earth on its orbit every 3,600 years. This, then, was the primary purpose for which the gods came to Earth, and the reason for which mankind was created.

Chapter Fourteen Conclusions

* Flesh-and-blood 'gods' came to Earth to exploit its abundant mineral wealth.

* Mankind was originally created as a slave race, to relieve the gods of their 'toil' in underground mine shafts. Subsequently, man was used for various other labour-intensive and dangerous activities. The gods created man in Africa, in accordance with the scientific evidence.

* All races of mankind continued to serve the gods after the Flood. One group of Negroes was selected (possibly created) and trained for mining, mineral processing and construction activities.

* Tiwanaku was constructed for the gods c. 4050 BC by highly skilled Negroes, supervised by Indo-Europeans. It functioned as a centre for the production of bronze. The god in charge of Tiwanaku was Ishkur. His symbol, the trident, is carved on the mountainside at Paracas near Nazca.

* Nimrod was the leader of an enslaved Negroid population which was used to build the cities of the gods in Mesopotamia. He rebelled against Yahweh by building Babylon for the African god Marduk c. 3450 BC.

* The Nazca Lines in Peru represent an act of vandalism by rebelling Negroid slaves.

* The Easter Island statues were erected by a group of Negroes, who were exiled there as punishment for their defacing of the Nazca plain.

* The Olmecs of Mesoamerica came from Easter Island
  c. 1450 BC. They were used by the gods to build
  Teotihuacan as a mineral processing centre *c.* 1390
  BC. Giant stone Negroid heads were hurriedly carved
  and erected by the Olmecs to act as territorial markers
  during their absence in Teotihuacan.

* Tiwanaku was shut down *c.* 2200 BC, coinciding with
  the threat from Marduk in Mesopotamia. The mysterious Kassites who appeared in Mesopotamia at that
  time were workers returning from Tiwanaku.

* The Kassites included Negroes who became known as
  the Biblical Anakim and Rephaim. These Negroes
  were the legendary 'giants', with large stature and
  long life spans, but with a doomed bloodline.

CHAPTER FIFTEEN

GODS OF A
NEW WORLD ORDER

━━━◆◆◆━━━

Lifting the Veil

Where are the gods now and what are the implications for
the future? These questions lead us inevitably into a
reconsideration of world history, particularly the period
from 2000–200 BC.

This period began in the aftermath of the nuclear
destruction of Sodom, Gomorrah and the Sinai space
centre. It is a period which encompasses the Biblical figures
of Isaac, Jacob, Joseph and Moses, where we have detailed
textual accounts but little archaeological evidence. Elsewhere, however, it is the opposite – archaeological evidence
but few textual accounts. A veil of darkness descends over
an era of widespread chaos and warfare. By the time that
era had ended, most of the cities of the ancient world had
been razed to the ground.

Prior to 2000 BC, the Sumerians wrote down everything,
even the most trivial day-to-day events. However, in the
period 2000–200 BC, few records were made, and even
fewer survived. Archaeology thus becomes our prime tool
of knowledge, but it is a blunt tool – a laborious process of

hard work and guess work, which is a long way from being an exact science. As a result, we have only the flimsiest understanding of events in this key period of mankind's history.

Whilst I am not a recognised historian, it quickly became apparent to me that, for this particular period, there are no experts. On the contrary, empires rose and fell for no apparent reason, mysterious 'Hyksos' people conquered Egypt, mysterious 'Sea People' appeared from nowhere to ravage the Near East, and advanced civilisations arose in the New World of the Americas, as if out of thin air!

As I attempted to peer through the veil of history to identify the continued presence (or otherwise) of the gods, I found that many mysterious historic events began to make sense. Unintentionally, I was putting the revised paradigm of *Gods of the New Millennium* to the test – and it was scoring rather highly, to put it mildly. My main objective, however, was to search for the activities of the gods, and that presented me with quite a challenge. How can one verify the presence of gods in such a chaotic period?

Surprisingly perhaps, there were numerous clues to follow. For instance, the name of a king or pharaoh would, more often than not, commemorate their allegiance to a specific god. Similarly, a work of art would depict a recognisable symbol of a god, whether in the image of a serpent, a bull or even a bare-breasted goddess. Finally, there were some useful inscriptions which directly evoked the names of particular gods for particular nations. In this way, it was possible to construct a political overview of world events. But how could I verify the *physical* presence of these gods? How could I be sure that kings did not call upon *absent* gods?

The first reliable indicator was technological intervention. Sometimes this is described in texts, such as the Ark of the Covenant in the Bible. Sometimes it appears in a physical form, such as the pyramids which still exist at Teotihuacan.

The second indicator was also a physical one – the sheer scale of destruction in the ancient cities. This scale of destruction stares archaeologists in the face every time they excavate, but how could so many cities have been razed to the ground using only fire, swords, bows and arrows?

The greatest problem I faced in writing this chapter was that of chronology. Following the publication of David Rohl's *A Test of Time* in 1995, big question marks hang over the conventional chronology of the Egyptian pharaohs.[1] Furthermore, Rohl's new chronology proved to have knock-on effects elsewhere, particularly as a result of dating the Babylonian king Hammurabi more than two hundred years later than previously thought. I personally find Rohl's new chronology rather convincing and have therefore chosen to use it throughout this chapter, indicated where appropriate by the initials 'NC'. Nevertheless, whilst this debate remains unsettled, some caution must be in order.

Back to the Beginning

Before embarking on our search for the presence or absence of the gods after 2000 BC, it is appropriate to remind ourselves briefly of the historical context established so far, with particular emphasis on man's tribal origins and allegiances.

Our revision begins with the Flood, when three lines of mankind emerged from Noah's Ark. The dark-skinned tribes of Ham went south to the African lands, the tribes of Shem settled in the Levant and the highlands around Mesopotamia, and the tribes of Japheth went north, to the Anatolian plateau (modern-day Turkey) and beyond. There was, however, one important exception. Prior to the war of the gods *c.* 8700 BC, Canaan, a son of Ham, had illegally occupied the land of Lebanon. Although his Canaanite tribe was allowed to stay, the Bible records that they were relegated to a servile status.

Between 11000–4000 BC, man possessed the same latent intelligence he possesses today, but was generally confined to living a nomadic lifestyle. Human populations quickly spread throughout the world. Then, from 3800 BC onwards, a series of developments created a new elite of civilised men. It began with the cities of Sumer, which were rebuilt in their pre-Flood locations, coinciding with the return of the planet Nibiru and the royal visit of Anu. At the same time, the god Ishkur began a new phase of construction at Tiwanaku for the manufacture of bronze.

In 3113 BC, civilisation was extended to Egypt – a decision which was necessary to restore the chaos caused by the exile of Marduk and the ensuing power vacuum. From its beginning, Egyptian civilisation embraced the Minoan culture of nearby Crete, where archaeologists have found extensive evidence of close trading ties.[2] The first Egyptian pharaohs, beginning with the legendary Menes, were in all likelihood Sumerians, imposed on Egypt with the consent of its highest god, Enki.[3] It is surely no coincidence that the name Menes is mirrored by the legendary first ruler of Crete, named Minos.[4] These two mysterious characters are almost certainly the same person. The native people of Egypt were also closely related to those of Crete, the Cretan natives being one of the tribes descended from Ham's son Mizraim, the father of the Egyptians.[5]

Some three hundred years later, *c.* 2800 BC, civilisation was granted to the people of the Indus Valley, under the aegis of the goddess Inanna. The Indus region quickly became an important supplier of grain to Sumer,[6] but suffered a serious setback when its main port city, Lothal, was engulfed by a flood *c.* 2400 BC.[7] It may be no coincidence that, at the same time, the Akkadian empire arose under Inanna via the conquests of Sargon the Great.[8] Inanna's move began a sequence of events that destroyed the Sumerian 'golden age', and which climaxed with the return of Marduk to Babylon in 2024 BC. Historians believe that Marduk's supporters, who began a new dynasty of kings in Babylon, were the Amorites, a major tribe among the Canaanites and thus of Hamitic stock.[9]

It was then, as Marduk occupied Babylon and threatened to capture the space facilities, that Nergal and Ninurta unleashed nuclear weapons to destroy Sodom, Gomorrah and the space centre in Sinai. As the nuclear fall-out cloud descended on Sumer, man and his gods stood at the brink of a new age of further death and destruction.

World Migrations 2000 BC

It is no coincidence that history books refer repeatedly to the year 2000 BC as a major turning point for many regions of the world. The 'Big Picture', which the books do not identify, includes the fall of Sumer (the Third Dynasty of Ur) to the 'evil wind' and the unprecedented wave of human migration which followed – caused not so much by the nuclear fall-out *per se*, but by the political aftermath of the invasion of the Amorites and the consequent upheaval. Prior to 2000 BC, civilisation was restricted to those areas already mentioned. Then, after 2000 BC, agriculture, astronomy, metallurgy and most significantly, writing, suddenly appeared all over the world.

First, however, we must deal with the exception. From around 2000 BC, the Indus Valley civilisation entered what is described as a decadent phase. The reasons for this are identified by archaeologists as the widespread flooding of its major cities in 2000 BC and 1900 BC respectively.[10] For

Lothal, it was the second such disaster, and its docks were completely silted up. Interestingly, one of the foremost experts on Indus archaeology, S. Rao, attributes the 2000 BC flood to 'tectonic disturbances', which are quite possibly a side-effect of the nuclear strike in Sinai.[11]

The Indus disaster may well account for the appearance of the Aryans ('Noble Ones') who migrated into northern India at this time, bringing with them the sacred Sanskrit language.

Meanwhile, the refugees from Sumer passed by the flooded Indus region and headed east toward Thailand and China. The history books record the mysterious arrival of technology in those regions:

> The record of East Asia's movement into the metal Ages is cloudy. About 2000 BC, peoples of the Khorat Plateau of present-day Thailand, the Red river region of Vietnam, and the North China Plain appear to have moved *directly* from the Stone Age into the Bronze Age.[12] (emphasis added)

> The advent of bronze in China is peculiar for the *advanced technology* which was operated *from the very beginning*, as seen in the vessels and weapons from Cheng-chou and Anyang.[13] (emphasis added)

Writing, as highlighted earlier, is also a big clue to these migrations. Studies have proved conclusively that the earliest form of Chinese writing, which arose shortly after 2000 BC, was derived from Sumerian. The pictographic signs not only looked similar, but were pronounced the same way, whilst terms which had various meanings in Sumerian often had the same multiple meanings in Chinese.[14]

Elsewhere in the Far East, the Tibetan language is one of many that have also been traced to Sumerian, whilst the Hsing Nu people of northern Tibet are reported to be of Mesopotamian origin, and claim to have fled from a fiery cataclysm.[15]

Migrations also took place to the west, as evidenced by massive changes on Crete dating to 2000 BC. The spectacular 5-acre, multi-storey palace at Knossos is dated to this time, together with the palace at Phaistos. Even further west, some historians believe that the earliest Mayan settlement at Dzibilchaltun may have occurred around 2000 BC. The starting point of the Mayan calendar in 3113 BC indicates that the Maya were emigrants from somewhere in the Egyptian/Cretan sphere of influence.

Meanwhile, in Babylon, a quasi-monotheistic movement was set in motion by the god Marduk, to whom all of the other gods officially became subordinate.[16] In order to signify his hero status, the name Marduk was substituted for that of Nibiru in the *Enuma Elish*, whilst the name of his spouse Sarpanit replaced Inanna/Ishtar, who was Marduk's traditional enemy. Under Marduk's guidance, Babylon rose to became a great city, its name meaning the 'Gateway of the Gods'.[17] Its Amorite leaders built a huge 7-storey ziggurat in Marduk's honour, naming it the E.TEMEN.AN.KI – 'Temen's House of Heaven and Earth', which was also known rather intriguingly as the *E-sagila* – 'The Temple that Raises its Head'.[18]

A New World Order

The rise of Babylon as a major world power could not have been achieved without international trade. The presence of Amorites at the key Mediterranean port of Byblos from 2000–1700 BC confirms the role of that city within a Babylonian-Egyptian-Cretan trade axis.[19] First, however, it was necessary for Marduk's supporters to gain the upper hand in Egypt. In the aftermath of a huge wave of migration, northern Egypt was being ruled by pharaohs of the 11th Dynasty, bearing foreign names such as Inyotef and

Montuhotep. One of these pharaohs, Montuhotep II, had reunited the whole of Egypt in an enormously long reign of 51 years.

Shortly after 1800 BC (NC), however, a new line of 12th Dynasty pharaohs was begun by *Amen*emhat I, his name signifying worship of the hidden god Amen/Marduk. It was at this time that the Israelites were prospering in Egypt, having arrived during the reign of Montuhotep II. A later pharaoh, Senuseret I, saw these Israelites as a threat and thus enslaved them. The Bible records that they were forced to build the cities Pithom and Rameses.[20]

Marduk's 12th Dynasty marked a renaissance of Egyptian achievement, which included the conquering of Nubia, the region to the south which was famous for its gold and trade with the African interior.[21] It was almost certainly this expansion that caused one group of Nubians to migrate permanently to Mali, West Africa, where they became known as the Dogon (see chapter 5).[22]

As Marduk attempted to build his new world order from Babylon, other, rival kingdoms began to emerge elsewhere. One independent power arose at Mari, a city already established on the River Euphrates, where archaeologists have found an impressive palace, library and archives, and more significantly a series of shrines dedicated to Marduk's great rival Inanna/Ishtar.

At around the same time, another city, Ashur, was founded on the River Tigris, with Inanna once again being the major deity. Mari and Ashur were both strategically positioned on two major trade routes, one from Babylon to the Mediterranean, the other from the Zagros Mountains to Anatolia bringing supplies of tin to the Hittites. From their initially peaceful beginnings, these people would eventually coalesce into the cruel and ruthless might of Assyria.[23]

Another independent power emerged to the south of Babylon, where Ninurta regathered the Elamite forces which had been defeated by Marduk's Amorites, and began to rebuild a military force centred on the cities of Larsa and Susa.

Last but not least, a long way to the north, in Anatolia, the kings of the Hittites set down their roots at Kanesh (modern day Kultepe) and fortified the city of Hattusas (Boghaskoy) to become the new capital of a powerful kingdom that would play a major role in the ancient Near East for around a thousand years.[24]

Hittites, Hurrians and Indo-European Origins

Who exactly were the Hittites of Anatolia? Some scholars have confused them with the Hittites of the Bible – a Hamitic tribe according to the Table of Nations. However, the Anatolians' written language was a distinctive mixture of archaic Indo-European script and Sumerian loan-words, leading most scholars to believe that they were of Indo-European origin. The name 'Hittite' came only from their geographical association with the land of Hatti (Anatolia) and its capital city Hattusas.[25]

The Hittites became close neighbours to an equally intriguing and powerful people known as the Hurrians, who have been labelled the world's first Indo-Europeans.[26] Both of these peoples are destined to play an important role in the history I am about to unfold. But in order to understand the background to these two great powers, and hence their motivations, it is first necessary to make a quick detour into the science of linguistics. We must understand what the term 'Indo-European' actually means.

The languages of mankind are divided by linguists into two distinct branches – Indo-European and Non-Indo-European. The Indo-European branch includes English, German and 138 other languages. These languages, spoken by nearly half the world's population, are incredibly similar in structure and form.[27] The Non-Indo-European branch, in contrast, represents a more diverse variety of tongues. All of the evidence suggests that the latter diversity is 'normal', arising from the separation of man after the Flood into numerous small, parochial and self-sufficient communities.

The homogeneous nature of the Indo-European languages is therefore regarded as an anomaly – a very important anomaly, which can shed light on the origins of the so-called 'white Caucasian' people. Scientists agree that, at some point in the past, a huge migratory wave must have brought the Indo-European language to most of northern Europe. Even more intriguing is the fact that the cradle of civilisation – the first international city-state of Sumer – spoke a Semitic rather than an Indo-European language.[28] So where did the latter come from? It is a question which has caused deep confusion and bitter disagreement among scholars.[29] Once again, it is a mystery which can be solved only by reference to the gods.

Linguistic scientists believe that an Indo-European mother-tongue must have existed *c.* 3000 BC and began to break up around 2500 BC.[30] This matches the date at which a new civilisation was begun in the Indus Valley by the goddess Inanna *c.* 2800 BC. A long Sumerian text known as *Enmerkar and the Lord of Aratta* describes how the god Enki was angered by this development and decided to change the language of the Indus people.[31] It would seem that his plan was to sabotage communication between the Indus and Inanna's city of Uruk in Sumer,[32] an action undoubtedly motivated by the manner in which Inanna had stolen his precious ME's (see chapter 6). This intervention by Enki is remarkably consistent chronologically with the scientific theory.

How did the Hittites manage to migrate from the Indus to Anatolia? No-one knows for certain, but there are two important clues. One clue is the Hittites' use of Sumerian loan words, suggesting a prior stay in Mesopotamia. The other clue is a connection with the goddess Inanna, indicated by the oldest Hittite traditions in Anatolia.[33] Inanna had two main cities in Mesopotamia, which are possible points of Hittite origin. One is Uruk, the other Agade, and both were founded before the Hittites first settled at Kanesh in Anatolia *c.* 2300 BC. Uruk is thought to have had the closest links to the Indus civilisation, and it is thus possible that the Hittites came from an Indo-European colony, established there to overcome the bilingual difficulties of the Indus-Sumerian agricultural trade. Alternatively, it is possible that the Hittites represent a remnant from Agade, the city of Inanna which the gods wiped from the face of the Earth *c.* 2250 BC (see chapter 10). The presence of the Indo-European Hittites in Agade might in turn be connected to the catastrophic flooding of the Indus port city of Lothal, which occurred very soon after the rise of Agade as a new power *c.* 2400 BC.

Did the Hurrians also originate from the Indus? Studies of the Hurrians have highlighted the Indo-European names of their gods and kings, whilst stressing that their language, like the Hittites, made extensive use of Sumerian/Akkadian loan words. All of the evidence suggests that the Hurrians were the great traders of the ancient world. They were highly prominent in Ur, where they were associated with the garment industry, and they also controlled major trade routes through cities such as Harran. It would seem that, from the earliest times, the Hurrians plied the trade routes all the way from the Mediterranean to the Indus Valley.

How far did the Hurrians travel? In chapter 14, we noted Indo-European racial features on the statues of Easter Island. An archaic Indo-European script has also been found there.[34] It is possible that the Hurrians may have been the supervisors of Tiwanaku, based on my belief that the Easter Islanders were Negroes exiled from Tiwanaku. This view is strengthened by the fact that the main Hurrian deity was none other than Teshub – the master of Tiwanaku and Nazca.[35]

Solutions from Santorini

We will return to the Hurrians and Hittites in due course, but first let us move forward chronologically. One of the most significant historic events in the period 2000–200 BC was undoubtedly the massive eruption of Santorini. When this volcanic Greek island exploded, 192 million tons of sulphuric ash fell as acid rain to the east – the biggest volcanic explosion in more than 4,000 years. Experts believe that the effects of Santorini would have included global climatic cooling and a famine in the east lasting at least seven years. The affected lands included Egypt, Anatolia and the Levant – basically the whole of the ancient world with the exception of Mesopotamia.

On what date did Santorini erupt? Improved scientific methods, correlating tree ring and radiocarbon dating, have now established that the explosion occurred *c.* 1628 BC, much earlier than previously thought.[36] This dating ties in well with events in the ancient Near East.

The climatic change resulting from the Santorini eruption could help to explain why the Egyptians began to closely monitor the annual levels of the Nile inundations under Amenemhat III *c.* 1660–1615 BC (NC), as evidenced by the so-called 'High Nile Inscriptions'. Santorini might also explain the claim by Herodotus that the same Amenemhat III was the legendary King Moeris, who constructed the Nile flood catchment hydraulic system in the Faiyum region. The High Nile Inscriptions demonstrate a concern that was soon justified by events, for the flood levels rose to almost double the ideal level for a period of twelve years.[37] The consequence was catastrophic damage and a long-lasting famine.[38] It is not surprising that, under David Rohl's new chronology, Egypt's 12th Dynasty went into a decline, marked by the Second Intermediate Period of chaos. It was at this time that Nubia, the land conquered three hundred years earlier, finally threw off the Egyptian yoke.

Santorini also explains the mysterious rise *c.* 1600 BC of a new world power – that of Mycenae – just outside the affected zone. The Mycenaeans worshipped a bare-breasted mother-goddess, identifiable without a doubt as Inanna. Under her influence, the Mycenaeans suddenly enjoyed a powerful trading position, and were able to build a powerful military machine.

Finally, the date of Santorini ties in to the era of Hammurabi, 1565–1522 BC under the new chronology.[39] Under the old, established chronology, this renowned Babylonian king ruthlessly set about subjugating his former allies for no apparent reason. It has thus been assumed that his conquests must have signified the beginnings of the Babylonian empire. Under the new chronology, tied in to Santorini, his actions were instead necessary to re-establish control during a time of great chaos, when famine was driving waves of migrants eastwards into Mesopotamia. The famous 'Law Code' stele which Hammurabi erected at Sippar, just north of Babylon, may well have been a warning to these immigrants to watch their conduct.[40] This scenario also sheds light on the Law Code's reference to three classes of people – free men, slaves, and a category known as *mushkenu*. The latter word, of uncertain meaning, is understood to imply a category of state-dependants, and would neatly describe the new group of immigrants.[41]

The huge influx of migrants placed an unbearable pressure on the established Babylonian infrastructure. Under these circumstances, the opportunity arose for several cities to make their bids for independence from the central authority at Babylon. The threat to the status quo was so intense that Marduk decided to arm Hammurabi with a powerful weapon in order to reunify the empire:

> With the powerful weapon
> with which Marduk proclaimed his triumphs,
> the hero [Hammurabi] overthrew in battle
> the armies of Eshnuna, Subartu and Gutium . . .
> With the 'Great Power of Marduk'
> he overthrew the armies of Sutium, Turukku, Kamu . . .[42]

An early target for Hammurabi was the city of Mari, which in 1531 BC (NC) was totally annihilated.[43] The scale of the destruction at Mari confirms the textual account of Marduk's powerful weapon. It also provides a clue to the power behind the independence movement, for Mari was a city that had long been associated with Inanna. The signs therefore suggest that Marduk was faced by a renewed threat from Inanna – not just from Mari, but also from her new kingdom of Mycenae in the north.

Catastrophe on Crete

In approximately 1450 BC, a major catastrophe simultaneously struck all of the cities on the island of Crete. The beautiful palaces at Knossos, Phaistos and Kato Zakro were utterly destroyed. The towns which had been powerful centres of international trade for five hundred years were burned to the ground.

The scale of destruction was so great and so widespread that archaeologists have searched in vain for a powerful natural phenomenon as a cause.[44] The mystery is summed up by *The Times Atlas of World History*, which admits quite frankly: 'the cause of this havoc is unknown'.[45]

Some experts, however, have reluctantly come to the conclusion that the fiery destruction of Crete was indeed the work of human hands. The National Geographic Society admits that 'the evidence now points to conquest by the warlike Mycenaeans of the Greek mainland'.[46]

This half-hearted attempt to pin the blame on Mycenae is a perfect demonstration of the uncertainty which surrounds this dark age of human history. Clearly it must have been the Mycenaeans, but no-one can explain why they carried out such a violent act of state vandalism.

Can the history of the gods provide us with the missing historical context? As mentioned earlier, the Mycenaeans worshipped the bare-breasted goddess, Inanna. She was an Enlilite and a rival of the Enkiite gods. Could Crete have previously been an Enkiite stronghold? The evidence in favour of such a hypothesis can be seen in the new Cretan religion which portrayed a bare-breasted goddess holding two serpents. Figure 29 (see black-and-white section), an example from Knossos, graphically symbolises Inanna's victory on Crete against the Enkiite serpent gods.

As for Inanna's motive, the destruction of Mari by Hammurabi is an obvious contender, but was there a further motive? The Cretan/Minoan culture has left us a possible clue in one of the most powerful legends of the ancient world – the tale of the Minotaur. This half-man, half-bull was supposedly the offspring of a bull from the wife of King Minos. However, if we recognise the symbol of the bull as that of an Enlilite god, then the tale may represent the imprisonment in a labyrinth, not of a Minotaur, but of an illegitimate flesh-and-blood god. The Greek tale of Theseus and the Minotaur includes an account of the burning of the King's palace, suggesting that this story may have originated with the destruction of the Minoan palaces *c.* 1450 BC. Although the tale has been embellished to describe a mythical creature, it may have its roots in an assault by Inanna to rescue an imprisoned god.

Massacre at Mohenjo-daro

At around the same time that Crete was destroyed by
Inanna, Mohenjo-daro, the capital city of her Indus Valley
civilisation, suffered a mysterious catastrophe.

Seventy years of archaeology have shed little light on the
history of Mohenjo-daro. It is widely agreed that this city,
along with others in the Indus Valley, suffered a progressive
decline after 2000 BC, due to a series of floods. Its final
downfall, however, came suddenly. According to the National Geographic Society:

> Skeletons scattered in the streets during its final stage . . .
> suggest that the final blow to the city was delivered by
> invaders.[47]

The foremost authority on the Indus civilisation, Sir Mor-
timer Wheeler, came to a similar conclusion:

> Looking back on the macabre scene we may perhaps conclude
> that, since seventeen of these skeletons seem definitely to
> belong to the latest occupation and the remainder present
> the same aspect . . . we have here in fact the vestiges of a
> final massacre, after which Mohenjo-daro ceased to exist.[48]

Who carried out the 'final massacre'? Wheeler suggested it
was the Aryans, but according to my reading of events the
Indus *were* the people who became the Aryans. Furthermore, all of the archaeologists have confirmed the lack of
any foreign occupation of Mohenjo-daro, together with the
lack of any assault on the city of Harappa, 350 miles to the
north.[49]

In 1979, David Davenport and Ettore Vincenti published
a major clue to the Mohenjo-daro mystery.[50] Davenport
and Vincenti were intrigued by the thousands of so-called

'black stones' which littered the site. When they analysed these 'stones', they turned out to be fragments of pottery, fused together by extreme heat.[51] According to their updated calculations, these clay vessels had been briefly exposed to a blast of heat measuring between 1400–1600 degrees centigrade![52] Davenport and Vincenti then studied the site of Mohenjo-daro in some depth, and pinpointed three distinct waves of devastation which had spread out up to one mile from the epicentre of the explosion. According to their conclusions, the only reason archaeologists did not find far more skeletons at Mohenjo-daro was the intense heat which had vaporised anyone standing near the epicentre.

When did the destruction of Mohenjo-daro occur? Archaeologists' best estimates suggest a date of around 1500 BC, the same time at which Harappa too was finally deserted.[53] By then, the cities of the Indus were already in severe decline,[54] so why would anyone bother to destroy Mohenjo-daro? The only logical answer comes from the rivalry between Inanna and Marduk and the events on Crete. The singling out of Mohenjo-daro is highly suggestive of a limited tactical retaliatory strike. Just like two modern super-powers, a full exchange of weapons made no sense for the divine powers of ancient times.

A New Wave of Migration

The conquests of Hammurabi, the conflagration on Crete and the destruction of Mohenjo-daro set in motion a fascinating chain of events that no-one, to my knowledge, has yet unravelled. All of these events coincided, c. 1500 BC, with the rescue of the Olmecs from Easter Island, the emergence of various cultures in the Andes, and possibly the first arrival of the Maya in Mesoamerica.[55]

First, I would like to deal with the most straightforward migrations from Crete to the coast of the Levant. The Hebrew scriptures state that the Philistines – the avowed enemies of Israel – were the remnant from the coasts of Caphtor.[56] Scholars generally identify Caphtor with Crete, and in particular with the name *keftiou*, given by the Egyptians to the Cretans. It was thus from Crete that the Philistines emigrated to the coastal plains of Canaan, and it is believed that this migration occurred *c*. 1500 BC, coinciding with the conflagration on Crete.[57]

Who were these Philistines and what role did they play on Crete? Being from Caphtor makes them Caphtorim only in a geographical and not a racial sense. Similarly, being called Philistines may also indicate a geographical reference, since Genesis 10 records an earlier line of people called Philistines who gave their name to the land of Palestine.[58] It is for these reasons that the Philistines are generally considered to have been from Indo-European rather than Hamitic stock.[59] If so, then the Philistines were related to the Hurrians, and we can guess that their role on Crete was that of traders. Archaeological and textual evidence indicates that the Philistine immigrants into Canaan were well-organised, militarily strong and commercially astute – all characteristics of an Indo-European elite.[60]

The Phoenicians too are thought to have originated from Crete. Their name comes from *phoi-nix* meaning 'date palm', and was applied by the Greeks to distinguish this great sea-faring people from the other Canaanites.[61] The Phoenicians settled to the north of the Philistines, along the coast of modern-day Lebanon, where they founded important trading cities such as Sidon and Tyre. Sidon was their first city, and indicates their Hamitic tribal origin from Sidon, the first-born son of Canaan.[62]

We shall now travel across the globe and examine the migrations which occurred into the Americas, also *c*. 1500 BC. All of these migrations occurred on the west coast, and we must therefore look to an origin from the Indus or Mesopotamian regions. The former would have been fleeing the destruction from Mohenjo-daro, whilst the latter would have been either driven out by Hammurabi or voluntarily escaping the strains of over-population.

Where did the migrants land in the Americas? Archaeologists have highlighted 1500 BC as a crucial period in South America, when advanced settlements emerged as if from nowhere. Alan Kolata has described an 'explosion' in Titicacan culture at this time,[63] whilst on the Peruvian coast a huge palace was built by a previously unknown culture at Sechin.[64] Archaeologists also date to this time the site of Chavin de Huantar in Peru and the appearance of the Olmecs in Mesoamerica. The mystery of this sudden and widespread change was noted by Professor Walter Krickeberg:

> The oldest American high civilisations appear on the scene suddenly, apparently without roots or preliminary stages, for example the Olmec culture in Mesoamerica and the Chavin culture in the Andes. This remarkable phenomenon can probably only be satisfactorily explained if we postulate one or more *external impulses* which affected ancient America.[65] (emphasis added)

As I explained in the last chapter, the Olmecs and Chavin cultures were the result of a rescue from Easter Island, and were thus a by-product of the wave of migration. Who were their mysterious rescuers? Of the many interesting South American legends, one happens to confirm Alan Kolata's comment on the cultural explosion at Titicaca. The legend concerns a King Atau, who arrived by sea with two hundred men and women, and marched from Rimac to Lake Titicaca. A related legend recalls that invaders arrived at Titicaca and slaughtered the white men whom they found there. And the Uru Indians who live at Lake Titicaca still maintain a tradition that their ancestors were seized by invaders and used for sacrifice; according to the Uru, this occurred some time 'before the Sun was hidden',[66] i.e. before 1390 BC.

Finally, we should not ignore a similar external impulse which affected Australasia *c*. 1500 BC.[67] Since this continent is situated on the easterly sea route to South America (prior to crossing the Pacific Ocean), it can be no coincidence that it experienced a wave of colonisation by a sophisticated group of people at this time.

Yahweh's Secret Identity

Having dated the catastrophes at Crete and Mohenjo-daro to *c*. 1450 BC, the timing of the Exodus of the Israelites from Egypt, in 1433 BC (see Appendix A), now takes on a new significance. Can a proper historical context of the gods help us to understand why one god, named Yahweh, went to the assistance of the Hebrews?

The meaning of the name Yahweh (sometimes pronounced Jehovah) has puzzled theologians for thousands of years – so much so that the Jewish Publication Society now leaves the name untranslated, with the footnote 'meaning of the Hebrew uncertain'. This is not a true statement, however, because the meaning of the Hebrew '*ehyeh asher ehyeh*' is actually quite clear – it literally means 'I am who I am'. As Karen Armstrong has suggested, in common parlance it equates to 'mind your own business'![68]

Why was Yahweh so evasive about his identity, and what were his motives in leading the Israelites out of captivity into the Sinai desert? A review of Near East politics at 1433 BC can answer both of these questions.

Shortly after the destruction of Crete, severe over-crowding afflicted the Levant coast, following the immigration of Phoenicians and Philistines. Archaeological excavations at

Byblos have confirmed a massive destruction of that city *c.*
1450 BC (NC), followed by severe over-population.[69] The
Byblos experience was repeated all along the coast, and was
to prompt the movement into Egypt of the mysterious
'Hyksos' people, who would rule northern Egypt for two
hundred years. The Israelites were about to become em-
broiled in an all-out war for the Nile delta.

Yahweh therefore acted to urgently move the Israelites
into the only available safe haven – the Sinai desert – an
area which was generally considered off-limits, due to the
lingering fear of radioactive contamination. Was this evacuation part of the earlier covenant with Abraham – a
payback for his espionage activities – or was there more to
it?

Yahweh's plan certainly went far beyond saving the
Israelites. It is possible to deduce, from his emphasis of
the ten commandments and the detailed new laws set out in
Exodus 20–23, that he was disaffected with mankind. In
particular, it would seem that Yahweh was disgusted at the
worship of idols and the widespread use of divination. His
actions suggest a desire to return to the traditional values,
from the earliest days of Sumer. But times had changed. The
earliest Sumerians had been quite innocent and trusting in
the gods who had always protected them. Now, after one
thousand years of chaos and warfare, the people were
confused, uncertain and superstitious. The only way forward for Yahweh was to create a new covenant of trust and
a loyalty to one god alone. It was for that reason that he
took the Israelites into a forty year isolation in the Sinai
desert. Only in that way could he bring forth a new
generation that was untainted by the polytheism of the
Egyptians. Only through monotheism could men recapture
their long-lost golden age.

Now let us return to the name Yahweh, with all its
evasive connotations. A close reading of the Book of
Exodus indicates that Yahweh was following a carefully

executed plan, which had three further objectives beyond the simple release of the Israelites. The first of these objectives was to weaken Egypt so fundamentally as a world power that it could not rise up and challenge the new monotheistic kingdom. The second objective, by Yahweh's own admission, was to build a reputation that would frighten Israel's enemies.[70] And the third objective was to win the sympathy and/or fear of the Egyptian people, in order to acquire silver and gold. These precious metals were required to build the Ark and the Tabernacle, the essential means by which Yahweh would communicate to his chosen people.[71]

In order to achieve all of these objectives, it was necessary to gradually escalate the scale of the 'plagues' on Egypt.[72] And in order to play this psychological game successfully, it was essential that the Egyptian pharaoh did not recognise the name, and hence the reputation, of the god who opposed him.

Pharaoh's ignorance of the divine name Yahweh caused him to dismiss the threats of the Israelites.[73] If he had recognised his true enemy, the game would not have been played out to its conclusion. As it was, Pharaoh persistently ignored the increasing desolation that was being inflicted upon his country. By the time this psychological game was over, Egypt had lost most of its livestock, most of its crops and fruit trees and even most of its first-born children.[74] The Egyptians were then so incensed that they chased after the fleeing Israelites and lost six hundred of their finest chariots, which were swept away by the sea.[75]

There was another powerful reason why Yahweh did not disclose his real name. Let us suppose that Yahweh was indeed a major god, well-known in the Near East. If that god wanted to make a fresh start by reintroducing traditional values via a monotheistic kingdom, then the *worst thing* he could do would be to retain his old name, especially if he was already worshipped under that name by the neighbouring people. Imagine the reaction of the Israelites, upon entering Canaan, to find their special god being worshipped by their enemies, as one of many gods. And which of those enemies would fear the Israelites, if the Hebrew god was one of their own gods?

What was the name of the most commonly worshipped deity in the region of Canaan? Although Inanna was worshipped there as Astarte, and an unknown god was worshipped as Dagon, the most prominent god was certainly Hadad, who many believe to be identical with Baal. The popularity of Hadad is evident from the common usage of his name by various kings – for example, Ben-Hadad of the Aramaeans, Hadad the Edomite and Hadadezer, the enemy of David, to name but a few. In addition, the main deity of the Hurrians, who held prominent positions in the Levant, was Hadad under the name Teshub. And finally, the Hittites, who had a strong presence in Canaan, were also big devotees of Teshub. The most powerful deity in the Israelites' promised land was definitely the Storm God.

Now let us follow the clues as to the real identity of Yahweh. Our first port of call is Exodus 6, which states:

> God also said to Moses, 'I am the Lord. I appeared to Abraham, to Isaac and to Jacob as *El Shaddai*, but by my name Yahweh I did not make myself known to them.'[76]

The above passage is confirmed by the Bible's account of the earlier meeting with Abraham:

> When Abraham was ninety-nine years old, the Lord appeared to him and said, 'I am *El Shaddai*; walk before me and be blameless. I will confirm my covenant between me and you and will greatly increase your numbers.'[77]

These passages leave no doubt that the name Yahweh was first used during the Exodus.[78] There is no basis whatsoever for religious claims that the name Yahweh existed at the time of the covenant with Abraham, the Flood, Adam and Eve, or even at the creation of heaven and Earth. These represent a rather predictable attempt at retrospective monotheistic editing.

What is the meaning of Yahweh's earlier name of *El Shaddai*? The word *shaddai* is stated in the plural and is usually translated as 'omnipotent' in the sense of a divine level of excellence, befitting of the plural Elohim. In recent years, however, it has become apparent that its root is the Akkadian word *shadu*, which means 'mountains'. Therefore *El Shaddai* should not be translated as God Almighty, but more accurately (and indeed literally) as 'God of the Mountains'.[79] Does this provide a clue to Yahweh's real identity?

There was indeed a god in the Sumerian pantheon who was known as a god of mountains. His name was ISH.KUR, the youngest son of Enlil, and his name literally meant 'He of the Far Mountain Lands'. As we discussed in chapter 14, Ishkur was also known by the name Adad, or Hadad in Hebrew.[80] Since Hadad/Teshub was the pre-eminent god in Canaan, a new monotheistic religion under the name Ishkur or Adad would have been a non-starter. Ishkur is thus a perfect match for the mountain god *El Shaddai*, who by necessity became the anonymous god Yahweh.

In the previous chapter, we identified Ishkur's mountain lands as the Taurus and later the Andes Mountains, and noted that he returned from Tiwanaku to the Near East *c.* 2200 BC. He was thus in the right place at the right time to appear as *El Shaddai* at Sodom and Gomorrah in 2024 BC. At that time, his elder brother Nannar/Sin was the god ruling over the Third Dynasty of Ur.

Does the Biblical *character* of Yahweh match that of Ishkur? First, as an Enlilite god, Ishkur fits the bill for the Biblical God, who was anti-Babylon, anti-Egypt and anti-

Marduk. Secondly, Ishkur was, under his various names, consistently represented as the Storm God, with his famous symbol of the thunderbolt, trident or forked lightning. This symbolism is remarkably consistent with the manner in which Yahweh caused Egypt to release the Israelites:

> When Moses stretched out his staff towards the sky, the Lord sent thunder and hail, and lightning flashed down to the ground.[81]

This was no ordinary storm, but the worst ever experienced in Egypt, pre-arranged to strike at an exact time. A similar phenomenon was used to enable Samuel to defeat the Philistines:

> But that day the Lord thundered with loud thunder against the Philistines and threw them into such a panic that they were routed before the Israelites.[82]

Secondly, both Ishkur and Yahweh were emotional gods with a violent streak. Ishkur was identified in chapter 14 as the Weeping God of Tiwanaku. Yahweh was also a highly emotional god, a jealous god by his own admission,[83] who quickly lost his temper. During the Exodus, Yahweh often threatened to destroy his own people:

> 'But I will not go with you, because you are a stiff-necked people and I might destroy you on the way.'[84]

Both Yahweh and Ishkur were occasionally prone to violence. On some occasions, Yahweh ordered disobedient followers to be put to death,[85] whilst on other occasions he sent fire or a plague to consume the grumbling Israelites.[86] Ishkur could similarly be incited to violence. His cult symbol was the bull, which was feared throughout South America as a sign of death and destruction. Certain South

American legends describe a day when terror came from the skies, when 'wild animals' overran mankind – an incident which I will later connect with Ishkur.

In summary, we have a perfect match between Ishkur and Yahweh. We also have an understanding (after several thousand years of waiting), of the reason for the anonymous name 'I Am Who I Am'. And furthermore, we have a good understanding of Yahweh's motives. Here we have the youngest son of Enlil, whose Tiwanakan followers had scattered, returning to find his original lands in Anatolia occupied by the Hittites. Here we have a god who never had a *permanent* city and people to call his own, returning to find his name being misused and abused by a bunch of soothsayers and idol-worshippers.

And finally, to remove any last vestige of doubt, we can explain why the Lord said to Moses: 'no-one may see me and live',[87] and why only Yahweh's 'glory' was ever seen.[88] The first reason Yahweh's face could not be seen was to prevent the Israelites from recording his image and hence exposing his secret identity to their enemies. And the second, more practical, reason was that he was absent on business elsewhere.

Ishkur was, after all, a god of the Americas, and the presence of his Storm God image at Teotihuacan (*c.* 1390 BC) demonstrates his continuing presence in that region at the time of the Exodus. This absence explains why the Ark of the Covenant was built and used for communications in the Sinai desert from 1433–1393 BC. It is time that we used our twentieth century eyes to recognise that Yahweh spoke to Moses through a radio transmitter. Unlike the Omnipresent Spiritual God, flesh-and-blood gods cannot be in two places at the same time!

Absent Gods

Thus far, we have seen striking physical evidence of the continuing presence of the gods on Earth c. 1500 BC. The cataclysmic destructions at Crete and Mohenjo-daro can be dated to around 1450 BC, whilst Hammurabi's earlier destruction of Mari (1531 BC NC) should perhaps also be included on this list of divinely inspired disasters. Shortly thereafter, in 1433 BC, the gods' intervention becomes obvious once again, through the technological aspects of the Exodus. The reality of Yahweh's intervention at that time is clear from references to the 'pillar of fire' that led the Israelites,[89] the smoke and fire of the landing on Mount Sinai, and the powerful communications device known as the Ark of the Covenant.

However, it is of crucial importance that Yahweh himself was *not physically present* during the Exodus and continued to be absent as the Israelites entered the 'promised land' of Canaan. During this time, the fourteenth century BC, Yahweh always relayed any instructions via the Ark, and any physical interventions were carried out on his behalf by divine emissaries – the so-called 'angels' of the Bible. These angels were not mythical or ethereal entities but flesh-and-blood walking, talking beings of a subsidiary status to the higher gods. The wings with which they were commonly depicted in later times represented artistic interpretations of their mode of transport.[90]

These 'angels' assisted the Israelites, led by Joshua, in their partial conquest of the Canaanite lands, beginning with the defeat of Jericho c. 1390 BC. The collapse of Jericho's walls is an event now confirmed by archaeology, and may well be the result of another divine technology which was described in non-technological language as a 'trumpet blast'.[91]

Yahweh's instructions to the Israelites had been to mercilessly wipe out the inhabitants of the conquered lands,[92] and the reasoning behind this can be seen from the problems which were encountered soon after Joshua's death, when the Israelites began to inter-marry with their enemies. This practice quickly led to the worship of other gods, in blatant disregard of Yahweh's first and second commandments, resulting in a premature end for Ishkur/Yahweh's monotheistic experiment. The lands of the Philistines. Canaanites, Sidonians and Hivites all remained unconquered.

During the time that Yahweh/Ishkur acted as the absent god of the Israelites, it is noticeable that other gods, too, were absent from the affairs of mankind.

The promiscuous goddess Inanna, for example, usually inspired a tell-tale legacy of bare-breasted statues wherever she went, but after Crete the trail goes cold.

Similarly, it would seem that her rival, Marduk, had also withdrawn from the scene. Marduk's Egyptian homeland, once a mighty power, was left weak and vulnerable by Yahweh's escalating series of 'plagues', and the northern delta was occupied soon afterwards by an invading force of 'Hyksos'. Conventionally, we know little about these Hyksos, the only clue being their name which literally means 'chieftains of a foreign hill country'.[93] According to my analysis, however, they were almost certainly Hurrians of Indo-European descent, driven south by over-population in the Levant. The fact that these Hyksos kings subjugated Egypt for around two hundred years is crucial, because it suggests that Marduk and his clan were not physically present to expel them.

Meanwhile, Marduk's city of Babylon, in Mesopotamia, was also left surprisingly defenceless. At the same time that his Egyptian lands were being subjugated by the Hyksos, the vital city of Babylon, for which Marduk had fought so hard, was attacked in a surprise raid. The Hittite king

Mursilis carried off its treasures, including the solid gold statues of Marduk and his spouse Sarpanit. The reaction to this sacrilegious act suggests an *indirect* intervention by Marduk, for Babylon was immediately repossessed by the Kassites, a mysterious people who suddenly swept down from the Zagros Mountains. In the conventional chronology, this occurred in 1595 BC and the Kassites ruled the Near East for a long era of 438 years. This length of reign is in apparent contradiction to the negligible cultural impact of the Kassites.[94] Under David Rohl's new chronology, however, the puzzlement of the scholars can be resolved, for the event occurred *c.* 1250 BC and the Kassites ruled for less than a century.

The origin and motivation of these Kassites has always perplexed the historians, for they made no changes to Babylonian culture (which they were supposed to have conquered), but simply maintained the status quo. As we have seen, however, these Kassites were almost certainly ex-miners from Tiwanaku, and the Negroid element were racially loyal to Marduk. These Kassites were not 'invading' Babylon, but rather occupying it, presumably on the instructions of the absent Marduk.

The weakness of Babylon prompted a major change in the political balance of the eastern lands. A growing threat began to emerge from the Assyrians, who under Shalmeneser I established Nimrud as their new capital and set up a military post at the ruined site of Mari *c.* 1250 BC. The Elamites too were recovering from their annihilation by Hammurabi, as evidenced by the construction of a superb ziggurat at Choga Zanbil, dedicated to their god Inshushinak, also *c.* 1250 BC. These Elamites began to make successful raids into Babylonia and *c.* 1170 BC sacked Babylon itself, together with the city of Aqar Quf, which the Kassites had built just to the north.

Meanwhile, Egypt began to experience a renaissance, with the 18th Dynasty pharaohs successfully expelling the Hyksos *c.* 1183 BC (NC).[95] The first pharaoh of that dynasty was called Ahmose – a name which means 'from the god Ah emanated'. Ahmose was followed by successors who bore the name Thutmose, meaning 'from the god Thoth emanated'. These two gods were one and the same since Ah signified the Moon god, which Thoth most certainly was.

Whilst it *is* possible to read into this Egyptian renaissance a *physical intervention* by Thoth, there is no hard evidence to support such a conclusion. Indeed, it should be recalled that Thoth was a pacifist god, a god of balance, who did not take sides in the disputes between the gods. If Thoth *had* been allowed to intervene to redress the damage caused by Ishkur in 1433 BC, it would surely have happened much earlier than the twelfth century BC. It seems more likely that the 18th Dynasty pharaohs were calling upon an *absent god*, and expelled the Hyksos by their own efforts.

The overall conclusion from the available evidence is that, during the period 1450–1000 BC, the gods had withdrawn from the Near East (the Old World) and gone to the Americas (the New World), where there *are* signs of divine activity at Teotihuacan *c.* 1390 BC. The lack of direct intervention in the Old World suggests that Marduk, Inanna and Yahweh (Ishkur) were all side-lined by a deliberate policy of non-interference. Could it be that, in the aftermath of the escalating conflict which had destroyed the Cretan palaces and Mohenjo-daro, the olden gods had brought the younger, warring gods to heel?

The Temple of Jerusalem

After a fifty-year period of worshipping Thoth, the Egyptian pharaohs once again began to call upon the name of Amen (Marduk). There is nothing, however, to suggest that

Amen was physically present. On the contrary, in 1022 BC (NC) a remarkable thing happened. After three years on the throne, the pharaoh *Amen*hotep IV suddenly changed his name to Akhenaten and made a revolutionary conversion to monotheism. During Akhenaten's reign, all references to the god Amen ceased, and were replaced by 'DINGIR.A', thought to represent the worship of Aten, the solar disc.

Our understanding of this remarkable period in history is assisted by the so-called 'Amarna Letters', which were exchanged between Akhenaten and his allies in Gath, Ashkelon, Gaza, Ashdod, Ekron, Jerusalem and the Kassite city Kar-Duniash.[96] These were the cities of the Philistines – Indo-Europeans who were ruling the Levant from their confederacy of city-states. The closeness of this alliance is demonstrated by Akhenaten taking among his wives both a Hurrian, named Tadu-Hepa, and a daughter of the Kassite king Burnaburiash II.[97]

This back-door attempt by the Philistines to conquer Egypt via Akhenaten would last only thirteen years. Tutankh*amen* then reversed the policies of Akhenaten and denounced him as a heretic. During this brief period, however, the power balance of the Levant was substantially changed. Prior to Akhenaten, Egypt had embarked on a policy of defensive expansionism, and had forged a successful alliance with the Hurrians.[98] Now, the Levant had become a battlefield between the Philistines and a roaming army of bandits known as the 'Habiru'. As David Rohl has so convincingly demonstrated, these well-organised Habiru of the Amarna Letters were led by David – the future king of the Israelites and, most significantly, the future conqueror of Jerusalem.[99]

Who was occupying the site of Jerusalem prior to its conquest by David? According to the Amarna Letters, the inhabitants were the Jebusites, and their king was allied to Akhenaten and the other Philistine rulers. This alliance can be explained by a common Indo-European origin, for the king of Jerusalem was named Abdiheba, meaning 'servant of Heba', who was a Hurrian goddess.

Furthermore, it can be demonstrated that the Jebusites were one and the same people as the Hyksos. The Egyptian historian Manetho explains that the Hyksos, after they were expelled from Egypt, went and 'built a city in a country now called Judaea . . . and gave it the name Jerusalem'.[100] According to the Amarna Letters, the Jebusite name for Jerusalem was 'Tianna' – a giveaway to their partly Sumerian culture, for the name is so clearly rooted in the Sumerian TI and AN, meaning 'Life' and 'Heaven' – a fitting name for the sacred site of Jerusalem. Amazingly, the name TI.ANNA echoes the name of Tiwanaku, suggesting that the Jebusites might have been the former supervisors of operations at that site.

According to the new chronology, David captured Jerusalem during Akhenaten's last year, when Egypt was impotent as a military power. Did the god Yahweh have a hand in this conquest? The ease with which David took the city via its water tunnel system does suggest that he had a source of inside information. Furthermore, it may be significant that, whilst David's rival King Saul never once called on Yahweh via the Ark of the Covenant,[101] David himself apparently did. In the Book of Samuel I, verse 30, David used a special garment known as an *ephod* to call the Lord and successfully received a reply.[102] Was the capture of Jerusalem a divinely orchestrated plot?

With hindsight, it would seem that the main purpose of the capture of Jerusalem was to build a 'temple' for Yahweh. The detailed plans for that temple, described in Kings I verse 7, are quite mystifying, and suggest to me some obscure technical purpose far beyond a simple altar for the worship of an absent god.

The plot thickens when we date the construction of the 'temple', by Solomon, to 953 BC.[103] For in 952 BC (NC), Marduk/Ra reappeared in Egypt! After an absence which I have suggested lasted 450 years, a pharaoh suddenly adopted the name Ramesses, meaning 'begotten by Ra'. He was soon followed in 936 BC (NC) by the most famous pharaoh that ever lived – Ramesses II (Ramesses the Great). And Ramesses the Great's first task, having driven the Hittites back to Kadesh, was to sack Jerusalem. This ransacking of the 'temple's treasures' can be dated to 925 BC (NC), just 21 years after the temple was completed.[104]

Unless we believe in coincidences, the inevitable conclusion is that Yahweh/Ishkur broke the gods' policy of non-interference and was then punished by an equal and opposite intervention by Marduk (via Ramesses). It is evident from the Bible that the Ark of the Covenant was being used to keep Yahweh up-to-date with events, and it is possible that David's successful campaigns, facilitated by the political weakening of Egypt under Akhenaten, provided a tantalising opportunity for him to reassert his authority in the Old World. What better target than Jerusalem, which as the former site of the gods' mission control centre, was arguably more sacred than Babylon itself.

The Assyrian Mystery

The next major incident in the history of Jerusalem came more than two hundred years later, in 689 BC. At this time, the Assyrians were masters of the Old World. They had conquered the Babylonians and the Elamites, and had deported the Israelites from their northern kingdom of Samaria. Meanwhile, the Hurrians had finally packed up and left the Levant for a hopefully more peaceful existence in the north-east, near Lake Van. It seemed as if no-one could withstand the onslaught of the Assyrians' military might, which would soon come to its peak with a brutal invasion of Egypt under Esarheddon and later by his successor Ashurbanipal.

Who were the Assyrians and why did they suddenly pursue such a vicious programme of expansionism? Originally they were migrants from Sumer, and mainly supporters of Inanna. However, that was more than a millennium previously, and their religion was now based on the first holy trinity – a composite god named Asshur, formed of a triad of Anar, Bel and Ea (the Sumerian Anu, Enlil and Enki). Beneath this triad, the Assyrians worshipped a secondary triad of Sin, Shamash and either Ramman or Ishtar.

The Assyrians' belief in an ancient trinity of gods from Sumer suggests that they were not being supported by the direct intervention of any specific god. The absence of the gods in Assyrian affairs is confirmed by an attempted attack on Jerusalem by the Assyrian king Sennacherib in 689 BC. It was then that Sennacherib made his infamous boast that no god was more powerful than the mighty Assyrian army. But, no sooner had Sennacherib spoken these words, than the gods *did* intervene . . .

> That night the angel of the Lord went out and put to death a hundred and eighty-five thousand men in the Assyrian camp.[105]

Once again it was the emissaries of the gods, rather than the gods themselves, who carried out the divine mandate. Could the extermination of the Assyrians, as recorded in the Bible, have been an actual historic event, representing another example of the gods' awesome technology? One important detail suggests that it may have been. Prior to the angel's attack, the king of Jerusalem had approached the communications device known as the Ark of the Covenant (at this time safely installed inside the 'temple' and referred to as 'the Lord'), and said:

'O Lord, God of Israel, enthroned between the cherubim . . .
  listen to the words Sennacherib has sent to insult the living
  God . . .'[106]

In the same year as his disastrous attack on Jerusalem,
Sennacherib faced the latest in a long-running series of
rebellions by his appointees in the city of Babylon. This
time his soldiers brutally sacked Babylon in an unprecedented manner.[107] However, even this ruthless act of
suppression failed to prevent Babylon from bouncing back
fifty years later. It was then that the Assyrian empire
suffered a mysterious demise:

With the year 639, the sources for Assyrian history cease . . .
No explanation can be given for this curious blackout. With
appalling suddenness, the Empire disintegrated.[108]

Who was behind the fall of Assyria? The names of the
rebellious Babylonian kings provide a clue. The chief
instigator of the rebellion was *Nabo*polassar, who was
followed on the throne by his son *Nebu*chadnezzar, both
names signifying the god Nabu, a son of Marduk.[109]

Did the gods intervene to bring the tyranny of the
arrogant and barbaric Assyrians to an end? Had the
Assyrians pushed the tolerance of the gods to the limit?
Significantly, one of their last acts, in 640 BC, was to
crush the Elamite kingdom (worshippers of Ninurta),
having earlier carried out a brutal assault on Egypt
(664 BC NC). The Assyrians thus had few allies amongst
the gods.

Until the historians provide some alternative explanations, we must seriously consider the possibility that the
divine hand of Nabu was directly or indirectly behind the
Assyrians' sudden demise.

Ezekiel and the New Temple

We may never know whether Nabu did provide support to Babylon, but what we *do* know is that the Babylonians went on to gain control over the rival city of Jerusalem. In 597 BC, the kings of Jerusalem became Babylonian appointees and the Israelite elite were exiled. This was followed in 586 BC by a major Jewish revolt, which was ruthlessly suppressed by the Babylonian king Nebuchadnezzar II. He burned Jerusalem's 'temple', demolished its buildings and city walls, and carried off its treasures. In the meantime, Nebuchadnezzar brought the city of Babylon to new heights of grandeur, including its famous hanging gardens. It is surprising that the rival gods allowed Jerusalem and Babylon to experience such contrasting fates.

One of the Israelites deported from Jerusalem to Babylon in 597 BC was a priest named Ezekiel – the same priest whose 'visions' of a spacecraft were described in chapter 1. The highly technical descriptions provided by Ezekiel testify to the reality of his experiences. In 572 BC, Ezekiel was lifted up by the Lord's 'Spirit' and transported to a 'temple'.[110] Biblical translations give the impression that he was taken to Solomon's Temple in Jerusalem, but that temple had of course been destroyed fourteen years earlier. In addition, several of the features described by Ezekiel, such as a river running from the temple towards the sea, clearly do not describe the geography of Jerusalem. In fact, a reading of the Biblical text in the original Hebrew makes it quite apparent that Ezekiel was *totally unfamiliar* with his new surroundings.[111] So where was the temple to which Ezekiel was taken?

A temple which does match Ezekiel's description exists at Chavin de Huantar in the Andes. Several scholars have pointed out the amazing series of similarities between

Chavin and the Biblical location, most obviously Chavin's situation on a *very* high mountain at a height of 10,430 feet.[112] The second similarity is that the temple at Chavin is precisely aligned to the cardinal points of the compass, with its main gate facing east, just as described by Ezekiel. Finally, Ezekiel observed a river which ran 'from under' the threshold of the temple from its south side towards the east, and ultimately onwards to a sea in the east. As described in chapter 3, excavations at Chavin have uncovered a subterranean network of tunnels that were used to divert water from the Wacheqsa river *through* the site and downwards towards the Mosna river, which closely skirts the sunken plaza on its southern side (see Illustration 4). The latter river then connects to the Puchka, which flows in turn to the Maranon and finally into the Amazon, taking it to a *sea in the east*, just as described by Ezekiel.

The astounding conclusion is that Yahweh was attempting to build in Peru a replica of his 'temple' which had been destroyed in Jerusalem fourteen years earlier. Furthermore, his ambitious plan extended far beyond Chavin, otherwise why would be bring Ezekiel thousands of miles to give him hundreds of precise measurements from the Chavin temple? Yahweh's full intentions are quite clearly recorded in Ezekiel verse 43:

> 'Son of man, describe the temple to the people of Israel . . . Let them consider the plan, and if they are ashamed of all they have done, make known to them the design . . . Write these down before them so that they may be faithful to its design . . .'[113]

Unless we believe in coincidences, the picture which emerges from this analysis is a dramatic attempt by Ishkur/Yahweh to reassert his authority among the gods, perhaps prompted by the contrasting fortunes of Jerusalem and Babylon. Did his attempt fail? As far as we know, Ezekiel's compatriots never succeeded in following his instructions to build a Chavin replica. As for Chavin itself, whatever might have once existed there may have been destroyed and built over by later constructions dating from the era 500–200 BC.[114] It would be particularly interesting to excavate *beneath* its sunken plaza.

What exactly was the so-called 'temple' which Ishkur built at Chavin? If the Biblical account of the temple of Jerusalem is a guide, then we are dealing not with a temple in any conventional sense, but with some kind of technical construction for a specific purpose. A possible clue is contained in the Raymondi Stele (Figure 23, black-and-white section), which is thought to have been carved at Chavin *c.* 500 BC, when it emerged as a sacred centre not long after Ezekiel's visit. The stele shows Ishkur, symbolised by a bull-god, standing beneath what we might now interpret as a stylised rocket . . .

Day of the Jaguar

I would now like to focus on the culture, legends and artefacts of the American continent which consistently recollect a ruthless destruction of men by their gods. I will attempt to demonstrate that these traditions have their origins in the events at Chavin de Huantar in the sixth century BC.

The most famous Aztec artefact is the great 'Sun Stone', found at the Aztec capital of Tenochtitlan and now exhibited in the Museum at Mexico City (Plate 61, colour section). The four rectangular panels which surround the central face are thought to represent the four great periods (or 'suns') of Aztec history.[115] Each sun is identified by the phenomenon that brought it to an end. According to the Aztec tradition, the first sun was destroyed by water, the second by strong winds, the third by quakes and storms, and the fourth by the jaguar. The Aztecs considered themselves to be living in the fifth sun, at the beginning of which they had migrated to their present land, led by their god Huitzilpochtli.

There have been many attempts to confirm the validity of the Aztec suns, all of which have suffered from conflicting data on the length of each period. Putting this data to one side, the solution to the first three suns strikes me as quite simple. The first sun was ended by water, thus representing the great Flood in 10983 BC. The second sun was ended by wind, representing the nuclear destruction in 2024 BC in the lands from which the first Americans came. And the third sun was ended by quakes and storms, representing the cosmic event in 1390 BC that halted the Earth's rotation and caused massive 'hailstones' to crash down from the sky.[116] Aztec traditions maintained that the feathered serpent god, Quetzalcoatl, had arrived near the beginning of the fourth sun, i.e. around 1390 BC. This is consistent with my hypothesis that the gods had moved to the New World following the climactic events c. 1450 BC.

Some time after 1390 BC, the fourth sun was ended by the 'jaguar'. This tradition is commemorated throughout the Americas in the form of numerous religious cults involving various fanged animals. Maya priests, for example, were depicted wearing jaguar skins, and one of the most famous priests was called Balam, literally meaning 'jaguar' in the local language. Experts believe that this cult first began at Chavin de Huantar, where according to the National Geographic Society, 'the Chavin venerated jaguars and other jungle predators as gods'.[117] This cult is indeed depicted in the graphic Chavin representations of ferocious bull-like creatures with snarling teeth, as seen in Figures 6 and 23 (see black-and-white section).

The legend of the jaguar is connected chronologically to another legend according to which mankind was over-run by 'wild animals' at a time of chaos and warfare between the gods. This legend of the 'wild animals' has been commemorated in numerous enigmatic stone carvings, which have always puzzled the experts. A particularly good example can be found at El Baul in Guatemala. 'Monument 27' at El Baul depicts a figure breathing fire and holding what appear to be grenades in each hand (Figure 30, black-and-white section). Its human-like body is joined to a helmeted head, featuring goggles and the snarling face of a wild beast. At its feet crouches a much smaller figure of a man, making an offering to the jaguar-like beast.

Close to El Baul, at Santa Lucia Cotzumalhuapa, a similar sacrificial scene has been found on a stele, now in the Berlin Museum. This stele shows various races of men looking skywards and offering an unidentifiable sacrifice to a diving god. This image of a diving or descending god is commonplace in later Mesoamerican culture, with two Mayan examples being shown in Illustration 26. Although experts dismiss these images as 'the setting Sun' or 'bee gods' (seriously!), it seems more likely to symbolise a menacing threat from the skies.

Illustration 26   a.   b.

A similar threat from the skies was depicted at the Aztec capital of Tenochtitlan, where archaeologists found two large statues guarding the Temple of the Eagles. These imposing statues are of frightening bird-men (or gods), their human faces peering out from inside the beaks of giant eagles.

This artistic combination of man and animal (called zoomorphism) crops up again and again in the ancient American cultures. At Quirigua, a Mayan site in southern Guatemala, an outdoor museum contains one of the world's weirdest collections of carved stones. The zoomorphic images on these stones also present a third aspect – that of machines. One visitor to the site has described his impressions of:

> A huge monster of unknown animal origin, with enormous sharp claws, and always with the head or torso of a human being in its mouth, not as though it were devouring the person, but rather it appears that the person is *riding in* the monster.[118] (emphasis added)

At San Agustin, Colombia, several dozen related sites from an unknown culture are dominated by 320 monolithic stone sculptures. These sculptures are so horrific that, in 1758, a Franciscan priest branded them 'works of the devil'. Fortunately they have survived, and now comprise one of the world's scariest open-air museums. Many of the statues are two-storeyed, such as Figure 31 (see black-and-white section) which shows a 6-feet high jaguar-man surmounted by a jaguar-bird with fierce teeth. Elsewhere a terrifying figure sits under a stone roof with a human skull dangling from its neck. whilst many other statues depict monsters feeding small human figures into their mouths. One text book sums up the scholarly consensus on San Agustin as follows:

> The most striking sculptures are the statues of humans with feline features, particularly fangs, which have been connected by scholars with jaguar shamanism.[119]

Another fantastic combination of machine and man was

found on the Peruvian coast. A small ceramic figurine from the Moche culture depicts a monstrous looking animal on two legs, with a machine-like chimney on its head (Figure 32, black-and-white section). The monster is shown in the act of decapitating a man, and is typical of numerous similar depictions in this region.

The Olmecs of Mesoamerica also appear to have been involved in the attack by wild animals. Archaeologists believe that the Olmecs practised a jaguar cult at the site of Teopantecuanitlan, and some authorities refer to them as 'the people of the jaguar'.[120] A common aspect of Olmec art was an infantile form with a cleft head and fanged snarling mouth, such as the jade figurine shown in Figure 33 (see black-and-white section).

What are the ancient artists trying to tell us? Did terror literally come from the skies, and did the depictions of 'wild animals' represent gods attacking man with aerial vehicles? In short, was mankind caught up in a war between the gods in the Americas?

There is no doubt that both South American and Mesoamerican cultures preserve the records of an Enlilite victory over Enkiite gods in the relatively recent past. The national emblem of modern-day Mexico is an eagle grasping a snake with its beak and claw (Figure 34, black-and-white section), the snake being an Enkiite symbol.

In Maya country, a mask was discovered showing snakes firmly held by the teeth of a jaguar god (Figure 35, black-and-white section).

Meanwhile, at the site of San Agustin in central Colombia, one of the most prominent statues is of a stone bird clutching a snake (Figure 36, black-and-white section). All of these images provide a strikingly consistent symbolism.

The pyramid at Chichen Itza (Plate 62, colour section) also reflects the same symbolism. At 5 p.m. on the spring and autumn equinoxes, a shadow moves down the pyramid like the rippling body of a serpent. Having reached the bottom, it then wriggles its way back to the top. This is thought to symbolise the serpent god descending to Earth and then departing. Meanwhile, inside the pyramid at the top of a flight of narrow stairs, the Toltecs built a small shrine to the jaguar. A possible interpretation of this is, once again, the superiority of the jaguar over the serpents of the Enkiites.

When did this war of the gods occur? The fifth Aztec sun, marked by the jaguar, began some time after the fourth sun in 1390 BC, but when exactly? Can we link it chronologically to Ishkur/Yahweh, the destruction of the Temple of Jerusalem and Ezekiel's visit to the new temple at Chavin?

Our first clue comes from Aztec legend. The Aztec war god was known as Huitzilpochtli. He was usually shown holding a powerful weapon and he had, according to one legend, won a battle against four hundred lesser gods. Another legend, possibly referring to the same event and the same god, states that a god named 'Smoking Mirror' fought the feathered serpent god, Quetzalcoatl, at Tula, just north of Teotihuacan, and thereby brought his reign to an end. Archaeologists excavating at Teotihuacan have found images of the Storm God, Ishkur, everywhere, indicating that he and Huitzilpochtli were one and the same victorious god.

The legend of the Smoking Mirror corresponds with another tale, according to which Quetzalcoatl left Meso-america following the outbreak of wars between the gods. The serpent god set out with a band of followers from Tula towards Yucatan, from where he sailed eastward on a 'serpent raft'.[121] This event is one of the most significant in the history of the Americas, since Quetzalcoatl left with a promise to return. The return date was fixed according to a sacred calendar of 260 days which combined with a 365-day calendar to produce a sacred round of 52 years. Thereafter, all of the Mesoamerican cultures counted the years and awaited the return of Quetzalcoatl every time the 52-year cycle was completed.

Since Quetzalcoatl's promise is of central importance to the sacred round, it is highly likely that the 260-day sacred calendar (on which the sacred round depended) was set in motion at the date he left. It may therefore be highly significant that the earliest sacred round date yet found in Mexico equates to 500 BC, which suggests that Quetzalcoatl may have left Mesoamerica in 552 BC. Can it be a coincidence that this date, marking the battle of the gods, is a mere 18 years after Ezekiel's trip to Chavin?

Our other chronological evidence comes from archaeology. Whilst the dates are admittedly rather vague, the established chronology for San Agustin and Chavin de Huantar are both entirely consistent with the period around 550 BC,[122] which is the earliest established date for the jaguar cult. This period coincides *exactly* with a phenomenon known as 'El Nino' which caused massive social and cultural changes in South America.[123] In particular, the Peruvian coastal settlements suddenly declined whilst Chavin, in stark contrast, suddenly arose as a powerful religious centre. Archaeologists are unsure exactly what was behind El Nino, but if we put all of the clues together, then the war of the gods becomes the force behind El Nino and Chavin de Huantar emerges as the catalyst that started the war of the gods.

How did mankind get caught up in this conflict? Whilst we cannot be certain, a possible clue appears within the later Chavin temple. As suggested in chapter 3, the *El Lanzon* carving has been positioned at the heart of the temple to protect it from an unknown enemy. Furthermore, the walls of the temple are designed to obstruct access for men of *large stature*. Could this enemy have been a group of the Negroes who arrived at Chavin *c.* 1450 BC? According to the pre-Incan legend cited in the previous chapter, 'giants' had marched into the mountains, upset their god, and been destroyed. It is possible that these people, close relations of the Olmecs, were forced by Ishkur to build his 'temple', but then subsequently sabotaged it. If that act of sabotage was incited by a rival god, then we can understand why both men *and* gods became involved in the ensuing conflict.

This analysis implies that it was Ishkur/Yahweh who unleashed the fury of the 'wild animals' upon mankind, an attack which made a long-lasting impression on the survivors. Among these survivors were almost certainly the ancestors of the Aztecs, the latter being renowned for their bloodthirsty sacrificial rites, which seem so alien to us. We can begin to empathise with the Aztecs, however, when we study one of their ceremonial daggers shown in Plate 60 (see colour section). This dagger, which was used for cutting out the hearts of their human sacrificial victims, has a handle decorated with the image of the diving Storm God.

Another New World Order

Whilst wild animals were over-running man in the Americas, the kingdom of Babylon was on its last knees. Its last ruler, Nabonidos, ascended the throne in 555 BC.[124] Amid signs of increasing disillusionment, no doubt caused by the continuing absence of the gods, Nabonidos declared Nannar/Sin to be the supreme god. This, however, was no more than a desperate call on an absent god, for Nannar/Sin did not help Babylon to resist the invasion of the Persian army, commanded by Cyrus, in 539 BC. Nor, for that matter, did Marduk or Nabu. The handover of power was suspiciously smooth.

Thus began a new phase in the history of mankind. The power of the Sumerians, Babylonians and Assyrians had waned. Within fourteen years, the pharaonic dynasties in Egypt would also be ended by the Persians. For the first time in history, an empire arose which was neither Hamitic nor Shemitic in race, for both the Persians and the Medes (their subservient allies) were from the tribe of Noah's third son, Japheth. When the Persian empire gave way to Alexander the Great in 330 BC, it was again a Japhethite kingdom. And world power has been exercised in the name of Japheth ever since.

The age of Cyrus also marked a turning point in world religion. All of the peoples subdued by Babylon, including the Jews, were allowed to return to the worship of their former gods and rebuild their temples. Cyrus thus encouraged a new age of paganism, based on the idols of gods who had not been seen for a thousand years. All of these gods, however, were made subservient to Ahura-Mazda, the 'God of Truth and Light', who was depicted as a deity of heaven rather than of Earth.

This new era of religious freedom paved the way for the emergence of powerful new religions, which represented a unique experience for mankind. In the period 550–500 BC, idol worship began to fall out of favour and some of the world's greatest thinkers began to seek a higher spiritual realm, promoting new ideals such as peace and compassion. The influence of Buddha in India and Confucius in China, during this period, cannot be understated. It is noteworthy that Buddha regarded the gods as mere flesh-and-blood beings who were not to be worshipped, since they were caught up in the same problems as mankind; he thus sought a spiritual enlightenment, or nirvana, that was higher than the gods.[125]

Is it a coincidence that all of these political and religious changes occurred in the direct aftermath of the war of the gods on the opposite side of the world? Could the serpent god, who was forced to leave the Americas in 552 BC, have had something to do with these changes? The evidence suggests that the serpent god was Enki and that he did indeed return to the continent of Asia.

Enki's nickname Ea meant 'He Whose Home is Water'. Scholars believe that he can also be identified with the mythical Oannes, an amphibious 'fish-man' who emerged from the Erythrean Sea and taught civilisation to the Sumerians. The presence of Enki in Mesoamerica can be determined from the Mayan word 'uaana', which is virtually identical to Oannes and means 'He Whose Home is Water'.[126] Just off the Yucatan coast, from where Quetzalcoatl allegedly left Mesoamerica, there lies an island named Jaina. The Itzas, a people who occupied that region in later times (and gave their name to Chichen Itza), recognised Jaina as the final resting place of Itzamna, the god of the Itzas. The meaning of Itzamna was, once again, 'He Whose Home is Water'.[127] According to legend, Quetzalcoatl (alias Ea/Enki) sailed away from Jaina and went eastwards on a 'serpent raft'.

The same serpent raft and the same god turn up in the east, c. 500 BC, at a sacred site called Budhanilkantha in Nepal! Plate 63 (see colour section) shows the statue of a god, known as 'the Sleeping Vishnu', lying on a bed of snakes inside a water tank. This statue is a mystery, even to experts on Hindu religion, since it bears all the hallmarks of the god Vishnu, and yet the name Budhanilkantha means 'Old Blue Throat', a name signifying a different god, Shiva. This presents the experts with a strange contradiction, since Vishnu is the preserver and Shiva the destroyer. Whatever this duality signifies, the statue on the raft of snakes is definitely Vishnu, and that god is also commonly known in Nepal as 'Narayan'. The name Narayan means 'the one who looks after the people', and one of his nicknames was, amazingly, 'He Whose Home is Water'![128]

It would thus seem that Enki (and possibly his clan) were forced to leave South America c. 550 BC and consequently returned to Asia. In the light of this dramatic relocation, it is quite possible that the Enkiite gods decided to rid the

Near East of the rival Shemitic and Hamitic powers which had fought so bitterly for 1,500 years, by bringing about a new world order through a Japhethite empire.

Chapter Fifteen Conclusions

* An escalating conflict between Marduk and Inanna caused the destruction of Mari, Crete and Mohenjo-daro *c.* 1450 BC. This conflict brought about large-scale migrations, particularly to the Americas. The gods, too, decided to relocate to the New World and agreed a policy of non-interference in the Old World.

* Yahweh, the god of the Old Testament, was a flesh-and-blood god, known to the Sumerians as Ishkur. He broke the policy of non-interference by attempting to build a new monotheistic kingdom via the Israelites in Canaan.

* Ishkur/Yahweh used King David to reacquire Jerusalem, the site of the old mission control centre. The 'temple' which was built at Jerusalem in 953 BC was not a temple in the conventional sense. It was destroyed by Ramesses on the instructions of Marduk.

* Ezekiel was flown to Yahweh's new 'temple' at Chavin de Huantar in 572 BC. Ishkur's plans for Chavin and a further duplicate of that temple elsewhere were thwarted by an incident at Chavin which led to a war of the gods in the Americas *c.* 550 BC.

* As a result of the war, one group of gods relocated to Asia and may have conspired to bring about a new world order in 539 BC.

CHAPTER SIXTEEN

GODS OF
THE NEW MILLENNIUM

Nibiru's Return

Around 200 BC,[1] the planet Nibiru made another of its 3,600-year returns into the heart of the Solar System – the most recent in a series that had spanned 11000, 7400 and 3800 BC.

If we could travel back in time to observe Nibiru's most recent return, what exactly would we see? According to the ancient texts, Nibiru emerges from the depths of space and loops around the Sun in an orbit *beyond* the planet Mars – a considerable distance from the Earth. If Nibiru was large enough, we might see it appearing as a very bright star, just as the planet Venus appears as the 'Morning Star'. But is Nibiru large enough? According to the scientists, it is around three times the size of Earth, and hence three times the size of Venus. This greater size, relative to Venus, does not compensate, however, for its much greater distance from the Earth. Consequently, using Venus as a bench-mark, Nibiru would appear only as a *very tiny point of light*. This tiny point of light would appear to be fixed in position, but would in fact be moving slowly across the Earth's skies over a period of several years. In summary, Nibiru would be very difficult to spot. Our trip back in time would thus be a waste of time, because we wouldn't see anything unless we knew exactly when and where to look.

Did the astronomers of 200 BC know where to look? In my view, it is almost certain that remnants of Sumerian astronomical knowledge from 3,600 years earlier *did* survive, and in all probability Nibiru's return was eagerly awaited, detected and carefully logged by Chinese and Babylonian astronomers. Why then have the astronomical records of this sighting never been found? The answer almost certainly lies in the fact that many ancient records have never been properly translated, in addition to which there is a tremendous reluctance to acknowledge their scientific content.

In the few cases where scholars *have* attempted to correlate Chinese and Babylonian texts to modern astronomy, they have all focused on the non-controversial area of comets, whose orbits are scientifically proven. If one of these scholars was to find an entry describing the appearance of a 'star' called Nibiru which slowly moved and then disappeared several years later, it would be dismissed as an anomaly, since there is no currently recognised scientific theory to account for a 'star' which moves of its own accord. Consequently, there would be absolutely no incentive for any scholar to bring such an interesting translation to our attention!

In the light of the above, there is no reason to assume that Nibiru did not turn up on schedule. After all, the evidence in chapter 7 indicates that it has been orbiting the Sun for 4 *billion* years, so it is unlikely to have missed its most recent rendezvous.

In addition, two highly significant things did occur *c.* 200 BC. The first occurred at the ceremonial centre of Chavin de Huantar, which had been constantly occupied since the temple incident nearly four hundred years earlier. One authority comments that:

About 200 BC, Chavin culture suddenly went into decline. Experts still do not fully understand the reasons for this abrupt change.[2]

Meanwhile, a similar change occurred at Teotihuacan, where the industrial activities came to a halt and the 'City of the Gods' became the city of men alone:

Circa 200 BC, whoever had lorded over Teotihuacan picked up and left, and the place became a Toltec city.[3]

The evidence suggests that the gods withdrew from the New World coinciding with the return of Nibiru. Indeed, since 200 BC there have been no obvious signs of any physical presence of the gods on Earth. There may have been bright lights, visions and miracles, but there has been nothing to compare with the direct personal presence of the gods which mankind experienced for nigh on 200,000 years.

It is particularly important for us to appreciate that the return of Nibiru c. 200 BC marked a unique moment in history, for it was the first occasion on which its orbit had coincided (approximately) with the end of a 2,160-year precessional age.[4] Could this symbolic event account for the apparent absence of the gods ever since? Did the chief god Anu perhaps take the opportunity to bring the warring gods on Earth to heel? In this chapter, I shall be suggesting that the gods did indeed make a conscious decision to withdraw from the affairs of mankind.

Did the gods return to Nibiru, did they go elsewhere, or did they enter a reclusive period on Earth? Wherever they went, indeed wherever they are now, we should not assume that they are in permanent retirement. On the contrary, the activities of the gods have been driven, ever since the Flood, by periods of Lordship determined by the 2,160-year divisions of the precessional cycle. According to my analysis in chapter 11, the current era of Pisces belongs to

Ereshkigal, a little-known goddess, who was never ambitious for power. Consequently, it is possible that mankind is presently in a 'hands-off' period which will expire imminently with the new precessional era of Aquarius. At the end of this chapter, I will be returning to the exact timing of this new era and its possible implications for mankind.

Stars in the East

It is a curious fact that the *current* precessional era of Pisces, symbolised by the zodiac depiction of fishes, matches the era of Christianity and its almost identical symbol of the fishes. I do not believe that this is a coincidence. In the New Testament, the timing of the birth of Jesus, the new messiah, was identified *in the stars*. The Magi[5] were not astrologers, as some religions like to suggest, but *astronomers*:

> Magi from the east came to Jerusalem and asked, 'Where is the one who has been born king of the Jews? We saw his star [rising] in the east and have come to worship him.'[6]

According to the Biblical record, the Magi saw a star in the east but headed west. They did not follow a star, but followed a *sign* that indicated the beginning of a new precessional age, for it was almost exactly 2,160 years since the compromise date of Marduk's return to Babylon.

The impression is sometimes given that the Magi were led to their destination by a moving star (or UFO as some have interpreted it) but this is almost certainly a mythological embellishment of the story. On the contrary, the Magi's dialogue with King Herod indicates that their search was targeted towards a child born at a specific time:

> Then Herod called the Magi secretly and found out from them the exact time the star had appeared . . . he gave orders to kill all the boys in Bethlehem and its vicinity who were two years old and under, in accordance with the time he had learned from the Magi.[7]

This extreme action can be attributed to Herod's familiarity with Jewish prophecy, which predicted the emergence of a messiah who would break the Roman yoke and reign over a restored kingdom of Israel.[8] Herod was thus acting to eliminate a political threat and avert a possible military uprising.

Why were Jewish expectations of a messiah so high? It would seem that many of Jesus's contemporaries were living in fear of 'End Times' and of an imminent apocalyptic event.[9] The timing and circumstances of Jesus's emergence, at the end of a precessional era, together with his comments of a second coming at 'the end of an age' and the beginning of a new era, all point towards the gods' sacred precessional calendar. It is a fact that the use of the zodiac was commonplace in the land of the Nazareans in the first century AD.

As we shall see, the importance of precession, as well as the 3,600-year orbit of Nibiru, both feature prominently in the traditions of the Bible and the Koran. These two religious books are the cornerstones of a monotheistic movement that has dominated our thinking for more than a thousand years, but are they ultimately based on the traditions of *plural gods*? Before we embark on that discussion, we must first complete our round-up of world history with a brief review of how Christianity and Islam began.

As many commentators have pointed out, the personality of Jesus has been obscured by the powerful religious movement that was begun in his name, and it has thus become difficult in many instances to discern fact from myth. Nevertheless, certain myths can be dispelled with some confidence. One such myth is exposed by Karen Armstrong, who points out that Jesus never claimed to be the Son of God, only the 'Son of Man'.[10] A second myth has been exploded by Baigent, Leigh and Lincoln (among others), who have clearly demonstrated that Jesus never intended to create a new religion. They stress that Christianity owes its roots not to Jesus but to Paul, who began to spread 'the word' with his own missionary zeal. What was the 'word' that Paul preached? According to Baigent *et al*:

> Instead of making converts to Judaism, Paul makes converts to his own personal and 'pagan' cult of Jesus ... The basic requirements for conversion to Judaism, such as circumcision, observance of the Sabbath and adherence to dietary laws, are abandoned in the process.[11]

In effect, Paul was replacing the worship of God in the Judaic sense (Yahweh) with the worship of Jesus *as God* – an act that was so blasphemous to the Nazareans that they sent missionaries in Paul's wake (including Jesus's own brother James) to undo his teachings! What were Paul's motives? Baigent *et al* describe him as an *agent provocateur*, who undermined the potential for a Jewish uprising by transferring the blame for Jesus's death onto the Jews themselves:

> In order to diffuse itself through the Romanised world, Christianity transmuted itself ... Jesus himself had to be divorced from his historical context, turned into a non-political figure – an other-worldly, spiritual Messiah who posed no challenge whatever to Caesar. Thus, all trace of Jesus's political activity was de-emphasised, diluted or excised. And, as far as possible, all trace of his Jewishness was deliberately obscured, ignored or rendered irrelevant.[12]

Despite the opposition of the Nazareans. Paul's idea of Christianity spread quickly, winning a wide body of support throughout Asia Minor, Greece, Italy and the Aegean

Islands. It would seem that the promise of ultimate resurrection from death in a Kingdom of God was a big attraction for the downtrodden masses.

In the third century AD, having survived various persecutions, Christianity became the state religion of the Roman empire under the emperor Constantine. In AD 325, Constantine held the first ever general council of Church bishops at Nicaea, to discuss the unification of religious beliefs under the umbrella of Christianity. This was a debate on theology (a systematic, academic study of divine belief) and its result was the official pronouncement that Jesus was the 'Son of God'[13] – a decision described by one modern authority as a 'victory for theology, defeat for the scriptures themselves'.[14] Almost three hundred years later, however, a prophet named Muhammad received a series of 'visions' which fundamentally challenged this central tenet of Christianity.

The visions of the prophet Muhammad were written down to form the holy book known as the Koran, which became the 'Bible' of Islamic religion.[15] Despite drawing on the same sources as the Old Testament, this book fundamentally rejected the interpretation of the Jewish scriptures. In particular, the claim that Jesus was the son of God was met with utter disdain. In the Koran, Allah himself stated that Jesus was a prophet. In fact He was quite indignant at the thought of having sons or daughters, which was a totally blasphemous idea.

Significantly, there was no mention in the Koran of physical intervention by flesh-and-blood gods. Muslims would undoubtedly argue that it was unnecessary for Allah to mention these gods, since they were only carrying out His divine will. Whilst the omission is certainly odd, my thoughts must remain private, since it is not for me (or any of us) to question what Allah chooses to say or not to say.

From a general perspective, Islam can be seen as part of a

definite historical trend. Many of its messages followed similar themes to Buddhism, Confucianism and Christianity, and its central notion of One Spiritual God followed on from Second Isaiah's concept of a composite deity known as Elohim. Like the Elohim, Allah, too, was omnipotent and omniscient, the creator of the Earth, the heavens and mankind.

Initially, monotheism fought an uphill struggle against the old polytheistic traditions and, contrary to popular belief, Islam was no exception.[16]

Nevertheless, the death of the ancient traditions of flesh-and-blood gods can be seen, with hindsight, as inevitable. By the time monotheism began to emerge, the memories of the gods were fading, for in some parts of the world they had been absent for over a thousand years. At that time, the traditions of the gods had already been filtered by the Greeks and Romans. Subsequently, the worship of the gods was eradicated by the Christianisation of pagan temples and by the relentless spread of monotheism from Islam and Judaism. The paradigms which we have today have been fundamentally shaped by these historical influences.

By taking an overview of world history, we can see how so-called mythology has its roots in reality and how many human cultures and archetypes can be traced back to the activities and culture of the gods themselves. I have already shown how this approach works in numerous ways – the pyramid cult of the pharaohs, the Aztec obsession with blood sacrifice, the archetypal images of 'giants' and 'the fountain of youth', even in the modern-day practices of numerology and astrology.

Can a similar approach explain the origins of modern religious symbolism? We have already seen how one of those symbols – the cross – has its roots in the history of the planet Nibiru, but there is more – much more – to come. In the following sections, I will examine concepts such as heaven and hell, the immortality of the soul, and the Day of Judgement, and explain the origins of all these ideas.

I am not the first to suggest a common pool of knowledge from which different religions have drawn their ideas, but no-one has ever succeeded in finding it. It is a search which most have regarded as futile, discouraged perhaps by Voltaire's famous remark that 'if God did not exist, it would be necessary to invent him'. One authority categorically states that 'the modern historian of religions knows that it is impossible to reach the sources of religion'.[17] What a defeatist attitude! I suggest that we have given up the search far too easily.

Heaven and Hell

Most of us believe in a 'heaven', but who can define what it is, or where it is? We aspire to go there, but we are not too sure of the qualifications for entry. We rely on religion to tell us, but which religion should we believe? Do any of these religions contain a divinely revealed secret, or is the idea of heaven 'made on Earth'?

Our modern scientific minds can understand heaven only as an invisible world, perhaps existing alongside the physical world, but in a different 'dimension'. However, when we study the Biblical concept of heaven with the original Hebrew terms, we find something entirely different:

> So God [Elohim] made the expanse/firmament [*Raki'a*] and separated the water under the expanse from the water above it. And it was so. God called the expanse 'sky/heaven' [*Shama'im*].[18]

What is this badly translated text trying to say? The key lies in the recognition of *Raki'a* in its more literal translation as the 'hammered-out bracelet' – a clear reference to the Asteroid Belt. The Elohim is therefore a substitute for the role of the planet Nibiru in creating the Asteroid Belt. As for the waters, they are the watery inner planets and the watery outer planets, which were separated by Nibiru's act of 'creation'.

What is the significance of heaven receiving a new name, *Shama'im*? This Hebrew term was originally written out as two words, *sham* and *ma'im*, meaning literally 'where the waters were'.[19] It is almost certainly a reference to Tiamat, the watery planet from which Earth and the Asteroid Belt were created. The 'heaven' of Genesis is thus the physical place – the orbit – where Tiamat used to be. Amazingly, the Koran says exactly the same thing:

> Are the disbelievers unaware that the heavens and the Earth were one solid mass which we tore asunder, and that we made every living thing *out of water*.[20] (emphasis added)

Does this mean that heaven is a mythical place that no longer exists – a memory of an earlier Earth at the beginning of creation? On the contrary, heaven was a location to which a few fortunate men were allowed to travel. One such man was Adapa who was provided with a *shem* by Enki who:

> Made him take the road to Heaven,
> and to Heaven he went up.
> When he had ascended to Heaven,
> he approached the gate of Anu.
> Tammuz and Gizzida were standing guard
> at the Gate of Anu.[21]

The abode of Anu was, according to the Sumerians, Nibiru. And Nibiru, the Planet of Crossing, intersected the former orbit of Tiamat in the Asteroid Belt. Thus we can geographically pinpoint an exact location in the Asteroid Belt which is the 'heaven' of the ancient scriptures. This idea of heaven has been passed down over thousands of years to represent a 'good thing', and it is indeed a place to which mankind has always aspired. Symbolically, there is little difference between the obelisks, which the Egyptians raised to the sky, and the spires of modern churches and cathedrals which echo the same theme. There is little difference between ancient kings such as Gilgamesh who tried to reach heaven by pleasing his gods, and modern-day priests who try to reach heaven by pleasing God. Mankind has always yearned to ascend, literally, to the heavens.

Is there any truth in the rumours of 'hell', the eternal fire to torment the sinners? Hell features particularly strongly in the Koran, where it appears as a fiery place guarded by nineteen mighty angels. According to the Koran, mankind was created in order to put him to the test. All our good and bad deeds are observed by invisible angels and recorded in books called 'Illiyun' and 'Sidjeen' respectively. Upon death, those souls which are doomed enter the fire of hell immediately. Other souls get a further chance to prove their worth, prior to a final Day of Resurrection, when all souls are restored to their bodies and judged by Allah.

The Biblical concept of hell is contained in the New Testament and is seen by many as an integral and essential part of Christianity, on the basis that Jesus must have died to save us from *something*. Compared to the Koran, the Biblical description of hell is somewhat vague, but this has not stopped the Bible-thumping preacher from scaring us all with tales of sadistic torture.

Other sectors of Christendom take a more relaxed view. A recent report by the Church of England abolished hell in the traditional sense and replaced it by a concept of 'total non-being'.[22] However, changes to the definition of hell only raise our suspicions that flexible theology cannot possibly provide the answers. On the contrary, we must examine the original scriptures to see what they have to say.

One religion which takes this approach, and is therefore useful for academic study, is that of the Jehovah's Witnesses. Here is their definition of hell:

> [Hell] stands for the Hebrew Sheol of the Old Testament and the Greek Hades of the Septuagint and New Testament. Since Sheol in Old Testament times referred simply to the abode of the dead, and suggested no moral distinctions, the word 'hell', as understood today, is not a happy translation.[23]

The alarm bells are immediately beginning to ring. Let us first examine the meaning of the term Hades, which is translated ten times as 'hell' in the Authorised Version of the Bible. Hades is generally known as the Greek god of the underworld, but the underworld was, as we have already discussed several times, the Lower World in Africa. The concept of an underworld or land of the dead is thus a simple misunderstanding. As for the origin of the name Hades, it derives from the Greek *haides*, whose meaning is identical to that of the Hebrew *she'ohl*.

What then does *she'ohl* mean? The Bible uses the term 34 times, translated 3 times as 'pit' and 31 times as 'grave'. Some religions interpret *she'ohl* as 'the common grave of mankind', from which the resurrection will take place when the Kingdom of God arrives. This, however, is just an interpretation that fits a particular religious scenario. In reality, both *she'ohl* and *haides* literally mean 'the hollow place' and 'the unseen place' respectively. And both terms are used in the same context to convey a common idea – a place of the dead.[24]

The etymological origin of the world *she'ohl* has been the subject of intensive academic debate. Although it is used primarily in the context of a grave, it is also used symbolically to represent the underworld.[25] Just as the underworld is described as a physical location in Africa, so too is *she'ohl* described as a physical location with bars and gates,[26] a place of darkness[27] and a place of torment.[28] Furthermore, the Bible cites God's power as extending from the heights of heaven to the depths of *she'ohl*, where his wrath could 'devour the earth and its produce and set on fire the foundations of the mountains'.[29] It was also renowned as a dry and thirst-inducing place, causing Hammurabi to warn anyone against perverting his codes of law with the following curse: 'Below, in the underworld, may he [Shamash] deprive his spirit of water!'.[30]

Could the idea of *she'ohl* have originated from a physical place, which has come to signify 'hell'? In chapter 14, I identified the underworld, Africa, as the land of the mines. These mines were dark and hollow pits, located in the lowest depths of the Earth. The work of the slaves in those mines was indeed tormenting and thirst-inducing. Many slaves died in those mines, hence the legend that the underworld was for men (but not gods) a 'place of no return'. This aspect of death in the mines, combined with their being underground and hollow, would naturally have led to the double-use of *she'ohl* to define a grave or tomb, as well as underground mines. Consider, for instance, the way the English refer to a modern underground railway as 'the underground' in everyday conversation; just as the defining noun 'railway' is dropped in modern times, so too did the reference to 'mines' fall out of usage in ancient times. There is no doubt whatsoever in my mind that the idea of hell originated from the African mines.

The mistress of those mines was Ereshkigal, also known as the 'Lady of the Great Place Below'.[31] Her scribe Belitseri was called the 'Book-keeper of Heaven and Earth' or the 'Book-keeper of the Great Gods'. The historian Alexander Heidel deduced that her role was to write down the names of the new arrivals which were announced by the gatekeeper.[32] There was even a ferry which had to be crossed to reach Ereshkigal's abode.[33] There can surely be no question that the idea of Hades has evolved from this source.

If hell does not exist in the religious sense that we have come to know and fear it, does that mean that the devil, Satan, is out of a job?

The word devil has its roots in the Greek *diabolos*, meaning 'accuser/slanderer', whilst the name Satan comes from a Hebrew term meaning 'resister/adversary'.[34] These origins do not indicate any sense of pure evil. Rather, they convey the idea of one god opposing another. The image of Satan as an evil spirit, tempting mankind astray, undoubtedly has its roots in the Garden of Eden story. And we have already seen how that story was simply a political put-down of the serpent god Enki, by his rival Enlil.

Immortal Souls?

Where do we go when we die? Do we go anywhere? The question is intimately bound up with the distinction between body and soul. Many of us intuitively believe in a separate soul, reflecting perhaps our self-awareness as a species. Science, however, has yet to provide the definitive answer on whether we truly are a 'special' species, or whether our sense of the human soul is simply a biological illusion. In fact, the whole subject of death is a taboo area for science.

We have therefore traditionally looked to religion to provide the answers to the enigma of death. Due to our all-too-short life spans, we need to believe in *something*, and this has proved an extremely fertile ground for religion. Given this need, or should I say vulnerability, it is not surprising that concepts such as heaven and hell have arisen without any logical foundation whatsoever. My analysis indicates that these concepts are the invention of man, drawn from the history and culture of the gods. This does not mean, however, that some kind of afterlife does not exist, and the concept of an immortal soul is the central issue.

It is a matter of some debate whether the Bible supports the concept of an immortal soul or not. To the man-in-the-street, any religion that speaks of heaven and hell must implicitly accept the idea of a soul. But this is actually not the case. Readers may be surprised to find that the Bible does not mention an immortal soul *per se*, but refers instead to a 'resurrection'.[35] The Jehovah's Witnesses believe that this refers to a *physical* resurrection, which is not dissimilar to that described in the Koran. They thus argue that the Bible does not support the idea of an immortal soul, and attribute its origin to a 'pagan intrusion into Christianity'.[36]

Where then did the pagan idea of an afterlife come from? Terms such as Hades, purgatory, paradise and limbo are not found in the Bible but come from Greek philosophy. And it is a well-known fact that the Greeks, in turn, obtained their ideas from earlier cultures, and in particular from Egypt.

As we have seen in earlier chapters, the Egyptian pharaohs' belief in the afterlife was one of the strongest religious beliefs in the history of any civilisation. Egyptian tombs were unique, far surpassing anything from the Sumerian civilisation. Their beliefs were so strong that they buried their dead with unprecedented possessions and treasures for use in the next life. It is fair to conclude that the concept of the immortal soul was an Egyptian first, which later spread throughout the ancient world.

How did the Egyptian beliefs come about? At the centre of the Egyptian afterlife cult was the myth of Osiris.[37] The essence of this tale is that Osiris died and was reborn. He was reborn in the sense that his seed was used by his wife Isis to create the son, Horus. And he was reborn, according to one version of the tale, after he ascended the stairway to heaven. Through these legends, Osiris came to represent the hope of eternal life to the Egyptians, who made pilgrimages to his cult centre at Abydos and re-enacted his life cycle.

As I have repeatedly described, the Egyptian concept of heaven was a physical place, which we can now identify as Nibiru. The Duat from which Osiris ascended to heaven was also a physical place, a space centre in the Sinai. And the route to the Duat was marked first by the Pyramids and then later by Heliopolis. The pharaohs' religion was based on emulating the journey of Osiris using their own pyramids and Osiris-style mummification rites. The procedures were even supervised by a 'shem' priest, the meaning of the name signifying the symbolic rocket which is so graphically depicted in ancient Egyptian art (Figure 3, black-and-white section). The reason why this cultural revolution took place in Egypt is simply geography – the pharaohs were much closer to the comings and goings of the gods in Sinai than the Sumerians were.

This geography may also account for the archetypal image of the phoenix rising from the ashes, which also has its origin in Egypt. The phoenix cult, centred significantly in Heliopolis, involved a cycle of rebirth which was closely connected to the idea of an afterlife. It is believed that the Temple of the Phoenix in Heliopolis contained an obelisk, capped by a conical or pyramid-shaped apex stone, known as the Benben Stone. Whilst the origins of this myth are lost in time, there is almost certainly a link to a physical return of a god or gods in Egypt, and possibly to the *shems* which we discussed in chapter 6.

It is these events – the Osiris ascent to heaven and the phoenix cycle of rebirth – which have caused the idea of an afterlife and an immortal soul to be passed down over thousands of years.

I would now like to shift to the closely related concept of *physical resurrection*, which also has its origins in Egypt. This idea has featured prominently in the history of religion, via the claimed resurrection from death of Jesus (disputed by the Koran), which is absolutely fundamental to Christian beliefs. Even more important is the idea of a *future* physical resurrection at a Day of Judgement. The Koran spells this out quite explicitly, and the Bible, too, can be interpreted in this sense. Both the Bible and the Koran claim that this physical resurrection will occur in a coming Kingdom of God. According to the New Testament, the Kingdom of God will come when the 'times of the Gentiles are fulfilled'.[38] When that appointed time comes, all that have lived on Earth will be physically resurrected from death, and will be judged whether they are fit to enter the Kingdom of God.

Where do these resurrection ideas come from? Ancient Egyptian folklore is brimming with resurrection myths, with Osiris, already mentioned, being the most famous example of physical resurrection from death. Another legend describes how his son Horus decapitated his own mother, who was then brought back to life by the god of magic, Thoth. Then there is the imprisonment and escape by Marduk from his death sentence in the Great Pyramid. We discussed that incident in great detail in chapter 9 and concluded that it was a genuine historic event. It is curious that, in the Babylonian myth, the resurrected Marduk had to be judged by the other gods whether he was fit to return to Babylon and assume Lordship over the gods. The religious parallel is striking.

It is also possible that our archetypal obsession with rebirth and resurrection may have its roots in an event 4 billion years ago. It was at that time that the planet Tiamat was split apart by Nibiru, with one half being reborn as the Earth, with an entirely new orbit. It was the mother of all resurrections.

Even more intriguing are the Biblical references to the *timing* of the resurrection. According to the New Testament, the Kingdom of God would come at an exact time, at the 'end of an age'.[39] Jesus said that this would occur when the 'times' of the nations were fulfilled, and a close reading suggests that the reference to 'times' implied a fixed or definite period.[40] Someone seems to have acquired the idea that God is working to a very precise timetable. Could the reference to an 'age' therefore represent a precessional period of 2,160 years, or could it perhaps represent Nibiru's orbital period of 3,600 years?

Judgement Day

The Babylonian epic of creation attributes the creation of heaven and Earth not to God but to the planet Nibiru. This story, known as the *Enuma Elish*, must have been familiar to the Jewish exiles in Babylon, where the role of Nibiru was celebrated in the name of the chief god Marduk. More than five hundred years after the exiles had returned to Jerusalem, Jesus described a Day of Judgement – our first record of this concept. But did Jesus and other earlier Jewish prophets obtain this idea from the legends of the planet Nibiru? There is certainly no mistaking Nibiru as the Lord in the following Biblical passage describing the Flood:

> The voice of the Lord is over the waters;
> the God of glory thunders,
> the Lord thunders over the mighty waters.
> The voice of the Lord is powerful;
> the voice of the Lord is majestic . . .
> The voice of the Lord strikes
> with flashes of lightning.
> The voice of the Lord shakes the desert . . .
> The Lord sits enthroned over the flood.[41]

The psalmists were clearly familiar with the idea of Nibiru causing the Flood, even though they ascribed it to a manifestation of God. Psalm 104 even describes the location of Nibiru in space:

> 'O Lord my God, you are very great;
> you are clothed with splendour and majesty.'
> He wraps himself in light as with a garment;
> he stretches out the heavens like a tent . . .

Simon Peter, an apostle of Jesus, clearly puts the Day of Judgement in the same category as the Flood:

> By these waters also the world of that time was deluged and destroyed. By the same word [of God] the present heavens and earth are reserved for fire, being kept for the day of judgement and destruction of ungodly men . . . With the Lord a day is like a thousand years . . . But the day of the Lord will come like a thief. The heavens will disappear with a roar; the elements will be destroyed by fire, and the earth and everything in it will be burned up.[42]

This passage is remarkable, since it alludes to a celestial event that affects the heavens as well as Earth. This is confirmed by references to the Day of Judgement in both the Koran and the Book of Isaiah:

> A fateful hour it shall be both in the heavens and on Earth. It will come without warning.[43]

> The floodgates of the heavens are opened, the foundations of the earth shake. The earth is broken up, the earth is split asunder, the earth is thoroughly shaken . . . In that day the Lord will punish the powers in the heavens above and the kings on the earth below.[44]

Zechariah even alludes to a celestial event which will arrest the Earth's spin:

> On that day there will be no light, no cold or frost. It will be a unique day, without daytime or night-time – a day known to the Lord. When evening comes, there will be light.[45]

If we apply our new understanding of 'heaven', the Biblical claim that the Kingdom of God will be accompanied by a new Earth *and a new heaven*[46] becomes highly significant. According to the religious interpretation, the Day of Judgement is concerned with the rights and wrongs of mankind on Earth. If so, why is there a need to shake the heavens as well?

In chapter 7, I set out the scientific evidence to suggest that the Flood was the latest in a cycle of periodic cataclysms. Could this relatively recent event in mankind's history have triggered the archetypal myth of the apocalypse? If so, the Biblical warnings of 'End Times', together with similar dire warnings from other cultures all around the world, may have a common point of origin.

The Aztecs believed that the present age or 'sun' will be destroyed by fire; Buddhist scriptures describe similar suns, with the present era being ended when the Earth bursts into flames; the Hopi Indians have a similar prophecy of the world being ended by fire. These traditions are echoed by the Bible, where Isaiah describes a day accompanied by 'flames of a devouring fire', along with 'thunder and earthquake and great noise'.[47] Psalm 97 states that the Lord will be accompanied by fire and lightning, which will melt the mountains like wax. Jesus himself cited earthquakes as one of the signs that would mark the end of the age.[48]

These legends and prophecies were not invented out of thin air, but surely have a historical basis. By recognising Nibiru as the cause of the catastrophic phenomenon, we can begin to consider a scientific prediction of the date of the next cataclysm on Earth.

When might the next cataclysm, known to religions as the Day of Judgement, threaten mankind? The last catastrophe, the Flood in 10983 BC, can be seen as a very recent event in the context of hundreds of millions of years of the Earth's history (see chapter 7). If these cataclysms operate in fixed cycles, as seems likely, then the next one must be a long way off. The good news is that there is unlikely to be a cataclysm in the year 2013 as predicted rather melodramatically by Graham Hancock using the Mayan Long Count.

How far off might the next cataclysm be? I will offer a guess, but that is all it is. The foremost number of the Sumerian mathematical system was 12,960,000. Since there should by now be no doubt regarding the Sumerians' astronomical knowledge and the source of that knowledge, could this enormous figure represent another extremely long astronomical cycle? Could it be the countdown to the next close passing of Nibiru and the next great cataclysm?

As described in chapter 7, the Flood cataclysm occurred as a result of an unusual alignment of the outer planets which forced Nibiru off course. Let us assume that each catastrophic encounter forces Nibiru into a slightly different orbit. How long would it take for the planets to once again form an alignment which coincides with a return of Nibiru? In December 1995, a team of US scientists experimenting with chaos theory announced a rather interesting result. Computer simulations showed that an array of identical pendula, subjected to the same electronic impulse, displayed chaotic behaviour over space and time; however, when each pendulum was given a different length and different impulse, organised behaviour patterns emerged.[49]

The scientist Maurice Chatelain, as part of his studies of Nibiru's orbital period, found an amazing series of 3,600-year alignments of three or more planets occurring within the Solar System.[50] Could it be possible that, from an initial state of chaos, each return of Nibiru gradually brings these planets back into a cosmic equilibrium? Could this process evolve over 3,600 returns of Nibiru?

Returning to Sumerian mathematics, it is curious that the number 60, which forms the basis of our 'short count' of seconds and minutes, when squared gives us 3,600 – a 'medium count' of the return of Nibiru. If we then square 3,600, the result is the sacred Sumerian number of 12,960,000. This period represents exactly 500 Earth precessional cycles of 25,920 years. Since Nibiru was the force that caused the Earth's wobble, there is a distinct possibility that the Earth may be wobbling in a cosmic equilibrium with Nibiru. By the same token, since Nibiru shaped the Solar System as we see it today, is it not possible that the outer planets are also orbiting in an equilibrium determined by Nibiru?

This 'long count' of 12,960,000 years would bring a risk of cataclysm but not a guarantee. If Nibiru was to make an unusual orbit into the inner Solar System, we must also consider the additional effects of the planet Mars, and furthermore, we must consider the position of Earth in its solar orbit. Some multiples of 13 million years might therefore be riskier than others. Whilst far from being a proof of this hypothesis, it is interesting that the cataclysm which destroyed the dinosaurs has been dated to 65 million years ago – that is 65 million years before the most recent cataclysm known as the Flood. The elapsed time is an exact multiple of 13 million years.

Speculation aside, it would seem that the Day of Judgement is not of immediate concern, but nor should it be misinterpreted as a symbolic religious event, for it is clearly nothing of the sort. Religions have persistently fallen into the trap of assuming that the words of the prophets are gospel, whereas it is more likely that the prophets were simply men such as ourselves, who were trying equally hard to figure out the truth of our existence. The memories of the flesh-and-blood gods were remote for them, just as they are even more remote for us today.

In summary, religions can shed little divine light on our destiny after death. We should therefore treat the established concepts of resurrection, heaven and hell with a high degree of scepticism.

The Interventionist's Day in Court

Did the gods intervene in the evolution of mankind? At the beginning of this book, I made a very bold claim that I would offer *scientific proof* of flesh-and-blood gods. How then might I claim such a scientific proof? The word 'science' is derived from the Latin verb *scire*, meaning 'to know' and thus science is the pursuit of 'knowledge'. But few sciences are exact and knowledge rarely comes with a cast-iron guarantee. Instead, it comes *beyond reasonable doubt*. This is the approach taken by the judicial system, for the simple reason that it is not practical to expect any higher degree of certainty.

At the end of the first chapter, I drew an analogy with a Day in Court, and asked you the reader to act as the jury. The role of the jury is to establish truth and make convictions based on the principle of reasonable doubt. If I can convince you the reader, beyond reasonable doubt, then the case is closed and the mysteries are solved. What then is 'the case' and how does this book meet the burden of proof required by the judicial system?

The interventionist's case is that flesh-and-blood gods created mankind in their own image through genetic engineering 200,000 years ago. Considerable evidence has been presented in chapter 2 of this book to establish genetic intervention as an *exclusive* solution to the mystery of mankind's origins. Everything else in this book represents detailed corroboration of this central claim.

In order to bring a conviction, the accused must be firmly identified. I have indeed identified the gods by name and by address – their cities on Earth and the planet Nibiru via which they came to Earth.

The next requirement is to place the accused at the scene of the 'crime'. I have established this via a chronology that links the arrival of the gods on Earth to the emergence of *Homo sapiens*. For the first time ever, we have a chronological methodology which can be confirmed by double-checking against the Biblical record dating back to Adam. Expert witnesses have been called upon to confirm the scientific basis of Biblical longevity and the Sumerian Kings Lists have also been entered into evidence to validate the Biblical time scale.

Further expert witnesses have confirmed the appearance of anatomically modern man *c*. 200,000 years ago, via fossil and mtDNA evidence. These witnesses lend further credibility to the new chronology which dates the genetic creation of *Homo sapiens* to 180,183 BC.

Finally, I have entered into evidence the testimonies of the ancient scribes, who witnessed the first-hand confessions of those gods who *were* actually present at the scene of the creation of man. These testimonies are highly consistent and uncontradicted by any contemporary witnesses.

The Interventionist's Day in Court requires not a 'weapon', as in a murder trial, but a *capability*. In order to illustrate the point, let us suppose that a murder was committed by a short sharp karate chop. We would then seek not a weapon but a suspect with the capability of inflicting the damage – a suspect trained in the martial arts. The 'crime' of which the gods stand accused is genetic intervention, the evidence being the mysterious fusion of man's chromosomes, an uplift in his brain size and all of the other enigmas outlined in chapter 2. We must therefore prove the capability of the accused to carry out the act.

Have I successfully proved the capability of the gods for genetic engineering 200,000 years ago? What I have done is repeatedly demonstrate a level of technology equivalent to that now being discovered in the twentieth century – space travel, ultrasonic machining and astronomy, as well as some skills that are still totally beyond us (how *did* they move those stones?). These skills can be physically verified and are thus solid evidence. Based on this evidence, we can reasonably conclude that the gods were aware of genetics. In support of this conclusion, we have heard the ancient scribes testifying to various acts of genetic manipulation – the cloning of Horus, the unusual birth of Noah, and indeed the first intervention to create the LU.LU. Another factor which supports this conclusion is the physical evidence of the different races of mankind alive today – a mystery which has yet to be explained by any other scientific theory.

In order to press charges against the accused, we also need *exclusivity of suspect*. The jury must ask itself *who else* might have had the capability 200,000 years ago to genetically create *Homo sapiens*? The answer is that there is not a scrap of evidence that places *any* other suspects anywhere near the scene of the 'crime' (suggestions of a Supernatural God would, I think, be ruled inadmissible in court!).

Finally, we must satisfy one last element of the judicial system to establish the case 'beyond reasonable doubt'. That element is *motive*. In chapter 14, witnesses were called upon to testify that man was created as a slave to carry out the gods' toil. I have corroborated this very strong motive by a detailed examination of the master-servant relationship that existed between man and his gods after the Flood, and I have identified the toil as a variety of activities including the mining and processing of various minerals.

During the Interventionist's Day in Court, a great deal of time has been spent in establishing the reliability of the witnesses. This is a standard legal procedure, and a very important one. I have focused in particular on the Sumerian witnesses who have provided the bulk of the testimony. I have cited detailed examples of texts which are supported word-for-word by physical evidence – in particular the damage to the Great Pyramid, Jebel Barkal and the Sinai peninsula. I have also demonstrated the amazing geographical evidence which supports the Sumerian accounts of the gods and their cities. Finally, I have described the Sumerian culture – intelligent, serious, pious and righteous.

What legal arguments might be raised in opposition to the interventionist's case? The only possible argument is the evolutionist's claim that no 'crime' has been committed, on the basis that Darwin's natural selection explains our existence. Mankind himself is therefore the battleground and the evidence of chapter 2 goes right to the heart of the issue. If the evolutionists are going to mount a serious argument, then they must exit their 'intellectual cul-de-sac' and come up with some radical adaptations to Darwin's ideas. As things stand, the Darwinian argument is weak and it is reasonable to conclude that a 'crime' has indeed been committed. As to the guilty party, the evidence is damning.

Missing Evidence

The most common attack on interventionism is to suggest that there is no physical evidence to support it. The evidence presented in this book demonstrates that these claims are without foundation. Nevertheless, critics will continue to cite the lack of this or that artefact, the non-existence of which is supposed to disprove the interventionist theory. Such an approach has no scientific merit whatsoever, and speaks only to the motives of those who would prevent us from upsetting the establishment paradigms. Nevertheless it does open up an interesting area which I would briefly like to discuss.

In 1987, Gene Phillips, the founder of the Ancient Astronaut Society, addressed the question of the missing evidence in his opening conference speech:

> The new evidence is, of course, still buried in the jungles, beneath the oceans, under the sands and in remote mountain

regions, and this brings us to a major problem which we face today – the science of archaeology is at a virtual standstill throughout the world. Very little is being done by the archaeological community to unearth the remains of ancient cultures, and they will not let anyone else do it. Archaeologists have complete control over who digs for artefacts and where. It is impossible for the lay person, or even for organisations such as ours, to 'dig' for new evidence.[51]

Let us examine Gene Phillips' claim, beginning in Mesoamerica. In 1994, *National Geographic* reported that:

Archaeologists of the five modern nations of Mexico, Belize, Guatemala, Honduras and El Salvador – and many foreigners as well – have studied its past in this century, but *thousands upon thousands of unexcavated sites await attention.[52] (emphasis added)*

In particular, *National Geographic* highlighted how little is known about the Olmecs, the earliest American civilisation, noting that 'excavation almost anywhere in Mesoamerica may enrich the treasury of Olmec art'. However, even where sites are already known, archaeological progress proceeds at a snail's pace. For example, at the famous Mayan site of Palenque, only a very small part of the complex has been excavated. Many further structures are known, which may contain relics like the beautiful and intriguing Pacal sarcophagus (Plate 58, colour section), but archaeologists have not even begun to explore them.

In South America, further clues to the mysterious functions of Tiwanaku lie buried underground. Archaeology has only belatedly realised the extent of flooding that has covered the area, and the significance of what might still lie beneath the ground. The Bolivians, short of archaeological resources, are crying out for an international team to carry out a thorough, professional excavation of the site.

In Egypt, the picture is the same. At the important site of Memphis, the capital founded by the first pharaoh Menes, only a limited amount of archaeological work has ever been carried out. Although there is little to be seen above ground, what vital clues to the beginning of Egyptian civilisation might lie buried below? Why has it taken so long to explore such a key site? Another important city in Egyptian mythology is Edfu, the city of Horus. Tradition has it that the temple which still stands at Edfu, marks the spot where a 'creation' took place. It was also at Edfu that the god Horus allegedly established a 'foundry of divine iron'. Archaeologists suspect that many ancient religious structures are buried deep beneath the present town, but no effort has been made to penetrate the lower levels. If they did, they might shed light on the apparent cloning of the god from the seed of Osiris, and they might even find the winged disc of Horus, sitting in a hangar buried beneath the ground.

Further south, close to the first cataract of the River Nile at Aswan, two other important Egyptian sites remain relatively untouched by archaeology. One is the island of Elephantine, where the god Ptah (Enki) allegedly controlled the level of the Nile from subterranean caverns. Needless to say, no underground explorations have officially taken place. Nearby, the highly sacred island of Bigeh marks the alleged place of eternal sleep for Osiris, but it is nowadays partially submerged, preventing scientific confirmation of the legend.

In Turkey, the mysterious site of Catal Huyuk dates back to around 6500 BC, making it one of the earliest known settlements. One would therefore expect it to have been thoroughly excavated, to shed light on the origins of civilisation. On the contrary, only a small fraction of the site has been excavated. Prior to the resumption of work in 1993, archaeology had stopped with the excavation of one acre out of 32 by Mellaart in the 1960s.

Why is there such a backlog of archaeological work when it would pay dividends in increased international tourism?

One reason is the prioritisation of funds and skilled archaeologists. During the last one hundred years, tremendous progress has been made by focusing resources in ancient Mesopotamia, where more than thirty sites have been extensively excavated. There are simply too many potential sites and too few trained archaeologists.

Therein lies another problem. Archaeology is by its very nature a destructive science, and modern archaeologists are paranoid about the use of proper digging and recording procedures. This approach, by necessity, makes the whole process interminably slow. One almost longs for the days when amateurs such as Schliemann vandalised (allegedly) the site of ancient Troy – at least he got something done! However, I am not seriously suggesting that as a way forward.

Another factor which slows down the rate of discovery is the obsession of modern archaeology with extensive field surveys. Valuable resources are thus focused on one site for vast lengths of time, in order to obtain a detailed understanding of that particular culture. As a result they can tell us what the Maya used to eat for breakfast, but they cannot tell us where the Maya came from! If we genuinely wish to understand more about our past, this kind of research must be deferred until we have successfully gained an overview of ancient cultures.

To be fair, not all of the missing evidence is the fault of archaeologists. We cannot blame them for the fact that ancient Babylon lies beneath the water table. We cannot blame them for the civil unrest which has hampered further excavation of the world's oldest settlement at Jericho, along with other ancient sites in Lebanon. Nor can we blame them for the modern roads and military base which prevent a thorough excavation of Teotihuacan.

Another factor which prevents archaeologists from uncovering the past is religion. It is religion which prevents what would surely be a highly revealing exploration beneath

Jerusalem. Similarly, we cannot fully excavate the ancient city of Harran, due to the Muslim temples which have been built on the site. The same archaeological block exists with hundreds of prime religious sites, which have arisen where they are for good reasons – to reflect a spot of sacred historical importance. This is a classic 'catch 22', which would frustrate even an Interventionist Institute of Archaeology if we were fortunate enough to have such a body.

Religion is also to blame for the destruction of many valuable ancient texts, which were once regarded as works of the devil by over-zealous missionaries. The destruction of these texts, however, pales into insignificance compared to the untold damage caused by thousands of years of human warfare. We can only guess at what artefacts were destroyed in the battles which razed city after city to the ground.

If warfare is public enemy number one, then vandalism must rate a close second, with few sites having escaped the looting which has continued unabated over the past few millennia. One almost weeps at the clinical efficiency with which the Spanish conquistadores melted down thousands of Incan and Aztec artefacts into gold ingots. Almost an entire cultural legacy vanished in that brief period of history.

Most of us know all about the ancient Egyptian tomb-robbers, but how many of us are aware of the alleged thefts of antiquities from Giza and Saqqara even in recent times? In March 1995, the British police arrested five leading art dealers in an attempt to break a multi-million pound trade in looted Egyptian treasures.[53] Priceless artefacts are disappearing from under the very noses of the archaeologists as they discover them.

At Tiwanaku, early explorers reported seeing bronze objects which long ago disappeared, presumably plundered by the local population. In Mesoamerica, inscriptions which might unlock the Maya's past have been hacked off temple facades and broken up, forever preventing any attempt to decode their meaning. Thousands of valuable Mayan relics have disappeared into the hands of thieves who have sold them into private collections, where they are permanently hidden from public view.

Some of the oldest private collections in the world belong to the secret societies. I would include in this category the Vatican, who have been one of the most active supporters of archaeological research in the twentieth century. Unfortunately, it is not difficult to imagine what would happen to any controversial discoveries which were made by the Catholic Church. As the old saying goes, 'turkeys don't vote for Christmas', and the Vatican is hardly going to announce a find that undermines its monotheistic position.

The most famous secret society of modern times is Freemasonry. The origins of this society begin with the Knights Templars, a group founded *c*. AD 1100 at the time of the Christian crusades to oust the Muslims from the Holy Land. Around AD 1300, the Knights Templars was declared an illegal organisation by the King of France. The fleeing Templars eventually settled in the Western Isles of Scotland, from where they founded the society which is now known as Freemasonry.[54]

The Knights Templars spent many years excavating at Jerusalem, and studies of their history suggest that they secretly recovered a technological device – either the Ark of the Covenant or a 'Manna Machine'.[55] Rumour has it that the secret location of the Ark of the Covenant may be revealed very shortly. As the best-documented technological artefact from ancient times, its public debut would cause quite a stir. Unfortunately, its secret has been kept safe for so long, that the technology behind it may no longer seem so amazing. Therefore, even if the real Ark were revealed tomorrow, scientists would denounce it as a fake.

Secret societies appear in the most unlikely places. For instance, what should we make of the Egyptian authorities' continuing delays to explore beyond the doorway that was discovered by Rudolf Gantenbrink inside the Great Pyramid? The discovery of the mysterious doorway was made on 22nd March 1993. A week later not a word had been said to the press. Frustrated by repeated stonewalling and cancelled press conferences, Gantenbrink decided to go it alone and break the story to the press. After the discovery was announced by the Daily Telegraph on 7th April 1993, it quickly became obvious that the world was not supposed to know. The German Archaeological Institute in Cairo, which had been involved in the find, told Reuters news agency that nothing of significance had been discovered![56] Officials from the Institute attempted to kill any interest by confidently telling journalists that 'there is no chamber behind the door'. On 20th April 1993, the Egyptian Gazette even carried the headline 'German scientist's claim a hoax'.

Two months after the discovery, an ex-Giza official, Dr Mohammed Ibrahim Bakr told the press that an organised 'mafia' were attempting to impede the archaeological work for their own purposes. Bakr's claim may be true or may be the accusations of an embittered man. Whichever is the case, the fact is that Rudolf Gantenbrink could easily have modified his robot to slip an endoscope underneath the doorway and resolve the matter once and for all. After *three years* of stonewalling by the Egyptian authorities, it would now seem (at the time of writing) that the opening of the doorway is imminent. But the simple truth is that the world would never have known about the Pyramid's hidden doorway, if Gantenbrink had not been present and recorded a video to prove it.

The Paradigm is Wrong!

It is time to take stock of what I have been saying. Perhaps some readers still have a nagging doubt that 'it's all so unbelievable'. In the course of researching and writing this book, I have continually tried to rationalise *why* it might seem so unbelievable. Mankind *is* here, despite the lack of evolutionary time, a fact which is quite unbelievable in itself. The Great Pyramid *is* there, in Egypt, with technology which is equally unbelievable. I have visited the sites in this book and seen 'impossible' feats of engineering with my own eyes, and so can you. These are the hard-hitting facts which should make us reassess our beliefs.

Is it really so unbelievable that we were created by flesh-and-blood gods, when the only alternatives are a Divine Creation or a Darwinian evolution? If we put our preconceptions to one side, it is the latter two scenarios which are the unbelievable ones.

The evidence I have presented is like the strands of a rope, attached to every area of human knowledge. Let us return to the mysteries which conventional scientists cannot explain:

1 It is fact that Jericho was built *c.* 8000 BC. No-one can explain why.

2 It is fact that the first civilisation emerged suddenly with advanced mathematics, astronomy and other sciences. No-one can explain how they got their knowledge and why they needed it.

3 It is fact that the Egyptian pharaohs were obsessed with the afterlife. No-one can explain what triggered their beliefs.

4 It is fact that the Great Pyramid was built with advanced technology. No-one can explain how the ancient Egyptians could have acquired such technology, and no-one can explain why the pyramid shape was so important to them.

5 It is fact that in ancient times megalithic stones weighing hundreds of tons were cut, miraculously transported into position and fitted together so accurately that one cannot fit the thinnest knife-blade between them. Some such constructions would be extremely difficult even with twentieth century technology.

6 It is fact that ancient cultures were obsessed with the calendar and the Earth's precessional wobble. No-one can explain why.

7 It is fact that the Mayan calendar began in 3113 BC, at least a thousand years before they emerged in Mesoamerica. No-one can explain why.

8 It is fact that the advanced civilisation of the Olmecs suddenly appeared in Mesoamerica, as if from nowhere. No-one can explain how a Negroid people crossed thousands of miles of ocean 3,500 years ago. No-one can understand their culture or explain their mysterious activities.

9 It is fact that an ancient and highly sophisticated people carried out mysterious activities at Tiwanaku, at a height of 13,000 feet in the Andes. No-one can explain why they were there or what they were doing.

10 It is fact that the Nazca Lines exist, and can only be properly appreciated from the air. No-one can explain how they were drawn or what they mean.

11 It is fact that the Easter Island statues could not have been cut with stone tools. No-one can explain who carved them, why they erected them, or where the artists disappeared to.

12 It is fact that the Sumerian civilisation suddenly disappeared *c*. 2000 BC. Historians have not explained why this occurred.

13 It is fact that a sudden upsurge in technology occurred all around the world *c*. 2000 BC. No-one has explained why.

14 It is fact that both Crete and Mohenjo-daro suffered cataclysms *c*. 1450 BC. No-one has explained the cause of these destructions.

15 It is fact that the mighty kingdom of Assyria collapsed in mysterious circumstances. No-one has explained what happened.

Isn't it odd that, despite the rate of technological progress, and the fantastic achievements in space exploration, our top scientists are still unable to explain all of the down-to-earth mysteries listed above. In complete contrast, the interventionist approach explains every single one of them, as part of a logical, comprehensive and fully integrated solution. As opposed to the scientists' complex arguments and contrived theories, the interventionist offers (by way of example) precise geographical relationships, supported by physical evidence – pyramids, platforms, a geological scar and blackened rocks – and all supported, in turn, by detailed textual evidence.

In addition, the interventionist approach enables us to understand, from a scientific point of view, the many prehistoric accounts which have become enshrined in myth. Thus the apparent immortality of the gods can be explained by genetic science. The Garden of Eden incident and the cursing of the serpent can be seen as a bitter dispute between two gods. The Tower of Babel incident can be understood as a controversial attempt by Marduk to rebuild his pre-Flood city in Babylon. And the Exodus represents a carefully timed evacuation by a disillusioned god.

A by-product of this study is the identification of Planet X as Nibiru, the Planet of Crossing which played a major role in the formation of the Solar System. The scientific recognition of this planet allows us to solve the fundamental unanswered questions of the Solar System. In particular, the collision of Tiamat with Nibiru can explain why the Earth's land mass is concentrated on only one side, whilst the oceanic crust appears relatively young. It can also explain why the Moon is so large in relation to Earth. It can explain where the comets and Asteroid Belt came from, and much much more. Scientists are bitterly divided, indeed confused, on all of these points, hence the extremely contrived theories which currently prevail.

As if this was not enough, the existence of a recurring cataclysmic cycle on Earth, caused by Nibiru, can explain not only how life began on Earth, but why it has also suffered a mysterious sequence of mass extinctions. The most recent such cataclysm was the Flood, an event which is so widely recorded in legend that its recognition has only been delayed by a lack of possible cause. That cause can now be scientifically identified as Nibiru.

Nibiru can also explain much of the world's religious symbolism. Its orbital path and collision course with Tiamat were commemorated in the sign of the cross. The position of the collision became known as 'heaven'. Its first two orbits were recorded as Day One and Day Two of the Biblical tale of creation. The recurring cycle of cataclysms which it caused on Earth was the origin of the belief in a Day of Judgement. As the twelfth member of the Solar System, Nibiru explains the use of '12' as a sacred number. And finally, it may also account for the importance of the sacred '7', for Earth was the seventh planet counting inwards from Nibiru.

This stark contrast between establishment confusion and interventionist solution is a sure sign that conventional studies of the Earth's past have been based on a wrong paradigm.

Nevertheless, entrenched views are not easily dislodged. Despite the overwhelming evidence in this book (and the masses of additional evidence which has been left out due to lack of space),[57] various experts will no doubt join forces to dismiss my conclusions out-of-hand. We should not be misled by these so-called experts, who outside their speciality are all amateurs. They will stop at nothing to defend their precious reputations and chronologies. These are the people who are fighting tooth-and-nail the *undeniable* geological proof that the Sphinx is thousands of years older than previously believed. Most readers of this book, as non-specialists, are in a much better position to take the wider perspective and recognise the truth of mankind's past.

Return of the Gods?

The god Quetzalcoatl left the Maya in 550 BC with a promise to return. After waiting patiently for around 1,300 years, he still hadn't shown up. A conference of Maya astronomer-priests was held in AD 763, presumably to discuss what had gone wrong. How long could the people keep faith in a long-lost god who was known only to their ancient ancestors? A hundred years or so later, the Maya gradually began to abandon their ceremonial centres, and within a few more centuries their civilisation had fallen apart. It was as if they had simply given up waiting.

The Maya probably made the right decision, because one thousand years later there is still no sign of Quetzalcoatl.

However, as we stand at the brink of the new millennium, could that return now be imminent?

As reluctant as I am to predict the unknowable future, I can nevertheless offer some scientific guidance on a range of possible chronologies. Readers can then attach their own probabilities to each possible outcome.

At the heart of this book is the theory that the gods took 'turns' for Lordship based on a division of the Earth's precessional cycle. This cycle, caused by the Earth's wobble, is an established scientific fact. The length of the precessional cycle cannot be an exact science, however, since the Earth has yet to complete such a cycle since the Flood. The latest estimates suggest a period of 25,776 years, representing twelve ages of 2,148 years. This suggests that the Sumerian mathematical system was deliberately structured on *rounded* figures of 25,920 and 2,160. In the calculations which follow, I have sometimes cited 2,160 for the sake of simplicity, but the actual figure can be read as 2,148 or an approximation thereof.

At the beginning of this chapter, I suggested that mankind might currently be experiencing a 2,160 year 'hands off' period. If this is so, then the implications are extremely urgent, for that period will shortly end.

How strong is my scientific *theory* that the gods operated in eras of 2,160 years? We have strong evidence dating the Flood to 10983 BC, and textual evidence associating the Flood with the zodiac sign of Leo. It may be a coincidence that the Sphinx was carved as a lion, but I think not. Its geological dating is admittedly not precise, but is consistent with the period 11000–8700 BC. Then we have Manetho's chronology of Egyptian gods dating the beginning of Thoth's reign to around 8700 BC, and textual evidence relating Thoth's appointment to the war of the gods. Again, it could be coincidence that the war of the gods occurred at the end of a precessional period, but I doubt it. As for the next two precessional periods, commencing 6540 BC and 4380 BC, they were relatively uneventful, but I have offered evidence that the latter, the age of Taurus, matches the era of the god Ishkur in South America.

The changeover from Taurus to the new period of Aries, from c. 2200 BC, has been commemorated throughout the ancient world, as noted by the famous Carl Jung himself. I have set out detailed evidence that this period marked the scheduled return of Marduk to Babylon, which was delayed first by Inanna and then by Ninurta. At this time, the stars were being watched all around the world, the physical evidence existing at Machu Picchu and Stonehenge in particular. Conventional science can offer no explanation for these ancient observatories, nor the ancient civilisations' widespread obsession with astronomy. Finally, I have suggested that 2,160 years later, the birth of Jesus coincided with the period of Pisces, explaining the significance of the stars which brought the Magi to Jerusalem.

When does the current precessional age end? If we count 2,160 years from the time of Jesus, we arrive in the mid 21st century, but this chronology is not based on a reliable starting point. It would seem that the Magi counted 2,160 years from Marduk's *compromise* return date to Babylon, but Marduk had in fact anticipated an *earlier* start to his era. The activity at Stonehenge, leading up to 2300 BC, marked his intended return which was only prevented by the military conquests of Inanna and Sargon. When Marduk did try to return to Babylon, his brother Nergal convinced him that his time had not yet come.

In chapter 11, I suggested that Marduk had counted from the Flood, whereas the precessional cycle had officially begun 108 years (one and a half celestial degrees) later. I then suggested that a compromise was reached, allowing the earlier starting point, but postponing his return from 2391 BC by 3 degrees (215 years) to 2176 BC.

If, however, we remove the artificial insertion of the compromise (which was only a delaying tactic), Marduk's precessional age should have been begun in 2284 BC.[58] Calculating forward from that date points to the next precessional age occurring much earlier in the 21st century – either AD 2036 or AD 2012 (based on 2,160 and 2,148 years respectively).

Other dates are also possible, depending on the assumptions used. For instance, when did the precessional cycle officially begin? If it was reset to point zero when Nibiru returned c. 200 BC, then we are already in the 'new' era, which began some time earlier in the twentieth century. The other variable is the precessional cycle – do we use 25,920, 25,776 or some other figure? One possibility, based on sacred Egyptian and Sumerian knowledge is 25,747.5 years, leading to the start of a new era in AD 1998.[59]

On the other hand, it must be stressed that the system which the gods used cannot be mimicked by the use of a calculator. If it could, why would Stonehenge have been built? The cycles of the Moon and Earth's movements around the Sun were already known. The measurement of these cycles could only have been for the correlation of something else, namely the rate of precessional change. This is of fundamental importance, because it signifies that the cycle was not regarded as a given numeric constant and Lordship could only be determined by direct observation of the heavens.

The historical significance of the precessional cycle strongly suggests that, if the gods do return, it will be within the range of dates given above. It might equally be argued that their return will not occur until Nibiru's next return c. AD 3400. And it can additionally be argued that the gods are no longer based on Nibiru and might never return.

Although I have tried to take a scientific approach to the question of when and whether the gods will return, it is difficult to ignore the tremendous expectations that are building up as we approach the new millennium. Some Jews still expect a personal messiah to come before AD 2000. Both Muslims and Christians are expecting the return of Jesus. Muslims believe that the hidden imam Muhammad al-Muntazar will reappear to restore true Islam, conquer the world and usher in a short millennium before the end of all things.[60] The Jehovah's Witnesses expect God's Kingdom to arrive imminently, since all of the features of 'End Times' are being experienced by the current generation. The ancient Maya had a great cycle of 13 Baktuns which can be used to predict the end of an era on 23rd December AD 2013.[61] Admittedly, there have been many prophets of 'End Times' during the last two thousand years, but never before has there been a scientific basis to support it.

If the gods reassume control over the Earth, how might we expect them to go about it? Will they come en masse in fleets of flying saucers, or will they announce themselves via Reuters? And how could they prove themselves to a sceptical public? Anyone could turn up claiming to be Jesus or Yahweh.

On the contrary, there may be little advantage to the gods immediately announcing themselves to the masses. News of their return might be disseminated on a need-to-know basis, with only a few world leaders permitted to approach them. Life might appear to carry on as normal, but with a new political agenda. We might detect their presence in inexplicable events, changes in government policy or acts of war that don't quite make sense, and perhaps an increase in government secrecy.

Eventually, these covert operations might give way to an openly declared presence, but only when the time is right. We should look for a manipulation of events that would facilitate a handover of sovereignty to the gods. This could best be achieved by bringing the Earth to a crisis point from which the gods themselves would emerge as saviours. We might thus expect a breakdown of the social order and a widespread disillusionment with mankind's existing institutions – governments, religions and industry. Then, when the masses are frustrated, frightened, desperate and vulnerable, they would rally to the cry of a new world order under the gods.

Should we live in fear or in hope of our returning gods? The actions of the American government seem to indicate a perceived threat. In 1996, the Pentagon announced a plan, sponsored by the US Air Force, to save the world by deploying missiles which would intercept 'asteroids' in deep space.[62] Politicians have indicated their intent to pass legislation which would force America to deploy this missile defence system, codenamed 'Clementine 2', by AD 2003. Why the sudden haste? Is it part of the same hidden agenda that is attempting to place incredibly sensitive telescopes into deep space?

In the difficult times that lie ahead, many of us may be tempted to sit back and wait for the return of our ancient gods. This would be a dangerous strategy for the return of the gods is by no means certain, and we cannot rely on them to save the Earth from all of its problems. On the other hand, many of us will see this as a time to restore our faith in a Spiritual God, an Ultimate Creator who may even have directly created the gods who created us. But whatever our inner religious thoughts might be, I would suggest that we all keep a wary eye on developments both on Earth and in space; for mankind may literally be about to meet his makers in a rendezvous which represents the greatest scientific secret of modern times.

Author's Note

It is intended to set up an Internet site for discussion of, and updates on, subjects arising from *Gods of the New Millennium*. Interested parties should search under http://www.eridu.co.uk for further information. In addition, correspondence from readers is welcomed and should be e-mailed to: alford@eridu.co.uk.

APPENDIX A

———◆———

Chronology from
Abraham to the Exodus

Abraham's year of birth has been the subject of much dispute. The Jehovah's Witnesses place it in 2018 BC, whilst most Muslim scholars believe it to be *c*. 2400–2300 BC. The date that the Israelites left Egypt on the Exodus is also much disputed, although within a tighter range of 1513–1430 BC.

The chronology which I have used in this book dates Abraham's birth to 2123 BC and the beginning of the Exodus to 1433 BC. This Appendix justifies the use of both of these dates and shows how they reconcile to each other.

The dating of Abraham's birth to 2123 BC is based on the 2024 BC date of Sodom and Gomorrah, when Abraham was 99 years old (see Genesis 17:24 and 21:5). The dating of Sodom and Gomorrah to 2024 BC is based on an identification of the Biblical Amraphel (Genesis 14 Battle of the Kings) with the Sumerian king Amar-Sin, whose reign is generally accepted to be 2046–2038 BC.[1] Although the Bible does not give Abraham's age at the Battle of the Kings, it does indicate that he was between 75 and 86 years old (Genesis 12:4 and 16:16). This pinpoints Sodom and Gomorrah to between 2027–2016 BC (because the Battle of the Kings occurred in Amar-Sin's 7th year). The sequence of Sumerian inscriptions up to 2024 BC, when they abruptly ceased, confirms the correct date of Sodom and Gomorrah (within the range just stated) to be 2024 BC. Thus Abraham was born 99 years earlier in 2123 BC.

The dating of the Exodus at 1433 BC is a backwards calculation from an astronomical event in 1391 BC, 'the day the Sun stood still',[2] which occurred *very shortly after* the Exodus ended (Joshua 10). Since the Exodus lasted 40 years (Exodus 5:6), the date that it began must have been *c*. 1435–1431 BC.

The chronology which I have used neatly reconciles an Exodus date of 1433 BC (within the range just mentioned) to Abraham's birth in 2123 BC. This reconciliation is based on a 400-year sojourn by the Israelites in Egypt. It is sometimes claimed (based on Exodus 12:40) that these 'years of sojourn' were 430 rather than 400, but such a claim conflicts with the 400 years stated in Genesis 15:13–14 and in Acts 7:6. The confusion is probably due to the inclusion of 30 years for Joseph's stay in Egypt before the sojourn of the Israelites in Egypt generally.[3] The reconciliation of the two key dates is as follows:

Abraham born	2123 BC
Abraham had Isaac (Genesis 21:5)	100
Isaac had Jacob (Genesis 25:26)	60
Jacob's age when entered Egypt (Genesis 47:9)	130
Years of sojourn	400
	1433 BC

It should be noted that the above chronology is supported by several prominent Biblical scholars, including Zecharia Sitchin and the archaeologists John Bimson and David Livingston.[4]

As mentioned earlier, the Jehovah's Witnesses date Abraham's birth to 2018 BC. This assumes, based on Galatians 3:17, that the Israelites left Egypt 430 years *after the covenant* (when Abraham left Harran). They reconcile their figures by claiming that the Israelites only lived in Egypt for 215 years instead of 430.[5] This claim is based on the Septuagint version of Exodus 12:40, which attributes the sojourn to 'Egypt *and Canaan*'. In my view, however, the Masoretic text should be preferred to the Septuagint. Moreover, Genesis 15:13 clearly suggests that the whole 400 years will be spent in an alien country, which is unlikely to mean Canaan since Abraham had already made that land his home.

As for the Jehovah's Witnesses' dating of the Exodus to 1513 BC, they reconcile this to the reign of Saul in 1117 BC and other, later, established dates. However, they admit that this is only '*one of a number of ways* in which the chronological periods stated in the Book of Judges *could* fit within the span of time indicated elsewhere in the Biblical record'[6] (emphasis added). Their time frame includes several pieces of guesswork and several rounded numbers of 40 years. It is my conclusion that their estimate is out by exactly 80 years.

APPENDIX B

Chronology of Gods and Men

270,183 BC The 'gods' arrive on Earth via the planet Nibiru.

252,183 BC Eridu, the first city of the gods, is completed – Alulim is appointed as governor.

226,983 BC Enki moves to Africa to supervise the mining activities.

183,783 BC The rank-and-file gods rebel.

180,183 BC The LU.LU slave is created by genetic engineering.

176,583 BC The Garden of Eden incident. Adam and Eve are given, by genetic engineering, the ability to procreate.

130,000 BC The days of Enosh, when mankind spreads out of Africa into Asia and 'calls upon the name of the Lord'.

107,900 –
77900 BC Enoch walks with 'God' and testifies against the 'sons of God' who have slept with the daughters of man.

70983 BC Noah is born with a genetically engineered skin colour. Mankind suffers from the

	onset of an ice age combined with the hardships inflicted by Enlil.
40000 BC	Migrations northwards cause modern behaviour to be seen in Europe for the first time. Neanderthal man is crowded out.
20983 BC	Shem, Ham and Japheth are born to Noah via wives from three different ethnic groups.
10983 BC	The Flood.
10875 BC	Lordship of the gods begins, based on 12 periods of the Earth's precessional cycle.
10450 BC	The Pyramids of Giza are built.
c. 8700 BC	War of the gods. The Great Pyramid is vandalised and replaced by a beacon at Heliopolis. The Sphinx is carved to commemorate the end of the war and the first precessional era. Space facilities are built at Jerusalem and in the Sinai peninsula. Jericho and other sites are established as defensive fortifications. Stonehenge is marked out as an astronomical observatory.
c. 4050 BC	Tiwanaku is established as a centre for the production of bronze. The first use of Chavin de Huantar and Teotihuacan for mineral processing may also date to this era.
c. 3800 BC	Civilisation is given to mankind in Sumer.
c. 3450 BC	Nimrod builds the 'Tower of Babel' for his god Marduk. It is destroyed by Enlil.
3113 BC	Civilisation is given to Egypt and Crete.
c. 3000 BC	Stonehenge is built by Thoth for Marduk as a star-clock. It measures the rate of precessional change against a lunar calendar.
2900 BC	Thoth builds star-clock at Machu Picchu. Andean calendar begins.

c. 2800 BC	Civilisation is given to Indus Valley. The Indo-European language is created by Enki.
c. 2630 BC	Egyptian pharaohs begin to construct pyramids.
27–2500 BC	Sarsen Circle and Avenue are constructed at Stonehenge.
c. 2400 BC	Akkadian empire under Inanna and Sargon the Great.
c. 2300 BC	Marduk returns to Babylon, but is persuaded to leave.
c. 2200 BC	Tiwanaku is shut down. The Nazca Incident.
2024 BC	Sodom and Gomorrah are destroyed along with the Sinai space centre. Human migrations carry technology around the world.
c. 1628 BC	Santorini erupts.
c. 1565 BC	The era of Hammurabi begins; he destroys Mari in 1531 BC.
c. 1450 BC	Minoan palaces are destroyed by Inanna. Mohenjo-daro is destroyed in retaliation. The gods leave the Old World and move to the New World. Human migrations cause upheaval worldwide. The Easter Islanders are rescued; Chavin de Huantar is occupied and the Olmecs appear in Mesoamerica.
1433 BC	Yahweh defeats Egypt and takes Israelites into Sinai safe haven.
1391 BC	The Day the Sun Stood Still. Teotihuacan pyramids are built.
1003 BC	King David captures Jerusalem.
946 BC	Solomon completes the 'Temple' of Jerusalem for Yahweh.
925 BC	Temple of Jerusalem is destroyed by Ramesses the Great.

639 BC   Assyria collapses in mysterious
          circumstances.

572 BC   Ezekiel is taken to Yahweh's new 'temple'
          at Chavin de Huantar.

c. 560 BC The Chavin temple is destroyed, leading to
          hostilities between both gods and men. The
          jaguar cult begins in the Americas.

552 BC   Quetzalcoatl leaves Mesoamerica and
          arrives in Nepal.

c. 550 BC The era of enlightenment – Buddha and
          Confucius. A new world order begins
          under the Medes and Persians.

c. 200 BC The planet Nibiru returns. Chavin de
          Huantar and Teotihuacan are abandoned.

c.200–130BC Man is left alone as the gods enter a
          hands-off precessional era.

ACKNOWLEDGEMENTS

———◆———

Many influences have come together to facilitate the discoveries which I have presented in this book. Special thanks are due to: Johan Reinhard for inspiring me to climb Huayna Picchu mountain, where I confirmed my Machu Picchu star-clock theory; Rudolf Gantenbrink, Bernd Hartmann and Zecharia Sitchin for providing the vital clues which prompted my theory of the Great Pyramid's functionality; Zecharia Sitchin for highlighting the 'sars' which underlie my new chronology; Robert Bauval and Adrian Gilbert for their discovery that the three pyramids of Giza exactly mirrored the three stars of Orion's Belt in 10450 BC; Robert Schoch for highlighting the antiquity of the Sphinx; and all of the archaeologists, linguists and other scientists whose accumulated efforts have brought human knowledge to a point where our understanding of these mysteries is finally possible.

A special mention is due to Erich von Daniken, who was the first person to stimulate my interest in the anomalous history of mankind. However, it is equally important to thank the Ancient Astronaut Society and its founder Gene Phillips, for maintaining my interest, and indeed enhancing it, ever since. The society's address is shown below for readers who wish to become members.

I would never have questioned the paradigms of history

without an open mind and a lack of prejudice. For this, I must particularly thank my parents, who never forced any ideas upon me and encouraged me to think for myself from an early age. My enthusiasm for foreign travel is also due in no small part to my parents, who sent me on two school educational cruises, when I am sure they could not really afford to do so. I am indebted to them.

The writing of this book was a major project, and indeed a somewhat daunting task. The very tight deadlines which I set myself could never have been achieved without the help of others. In particular, I would mention Geoff Bannister and Neil Gould, who assisted with the typesetting, diagrams and cover art. Thanks are also due to Eryl Powell for proofreading my draft manuscripts and offering constructive criticisms.

Finally, I would like to offer the biggest thank you to my wife, Sumu, who has provided endless support, even in the latter days when I was working 100 hours a week! Without Sumu's strength of character, I feel sure that *Gods of the New Millennium* would never have been published in the 2nd millennium AD . . .

Photographic credits: 28, 29, 30 Copyright Robert Bauval; 34 Copyright Egyptian Museum, Cairo; 39 Copyright Dean Conger, National Geographic Image Collection; 40 Copyright Staatliche Museen zu Berlin – Preussischer Kulturbesitz Vorderasiatisches Museum; 41 Copyright British Museum; 43 Copyright Enrico Ferorelli c/o Colorific; 44 Landsat MSS, NRSC Limited; 45, 46 Copyright WARA, Centro Camuno di Studi Preistorici, 25044 Capo di Ponte, Italy; 51 Copyright Reunion des Musees Nationaux, Paris; 52 Copyright Photo Garo Nalbandian; 54, 56, 57, 58 Copyright Gene Phillips, Ancient Astronaut Society; 59, 61 Copyright Wania and Mark Liddell.

All other photographs were taken by the author.

Illustration credits: Illustration 1 Copyright Josef F. Blumrich; Illustration 7 Copyright American Philosophical Society; Figure 16 Copyright Rudolf Gantenbrink; Figure 21 Copyright Wania and Mark Liddell.

Ancient Astronaut Society: this society is a non-profit, tax exempt organisation, operated exclusively for scientific, literary and educational purposes. Its activities include the publication of a bi-monthly journal, *Ancient Skies*, and regular expeditions to archaeological sites and other places of interest. For membership information contact Gene Phillips c/o 1921 St Johns Avenue, Highland Park, Illinois, 60035-3178, USA.

Notes and Bibliography

———◆———

Chapter One:
Believing the Unbelievable

1 N. Copernicus, *De revolutionibus orbium coelestium* (Concerning the Movement of the Heavenly Bodies), 1543.
2 K. Armstrong, *A History of God*, Mandarin 1993, chapter 5.
3 *Collins Dictionary of the English Language*, London & Glasgow, 1979.
4 Genesis 1:1–2.
5 Examples of apocryphal books include the Book of Enoch, the further books of Ezra, the Ascension of Moses, the Book of Jubilees and the Acts and Gospel of Thomas.
6 The Pentateuch consists of Genesis, Exodus, Leviticus, Numbers and Deuteronomy. A historical background to the Pentateuch can be found in Armstrong, op. cit., chapters 1 & 2.
7 See chapter 7 dealing with the similarities to the Babylonian *Enuma Elish*.
8 See for example chapter 12 re God's creation of male and female.
9 Genesis 6:5–7.
10 Genesis 18:20–21.
11 See the Book of Joshua. In the Book of Numbers, 21:14, there is even reference to the existence at that time of a 'Book of the Wars of the Lord'.
12 See Genesis 18 (with Abraham), Book of Exodus (with Moses), Genesis 26:24 (with Isaac).

13 The Lord wrestles Jacob in Genesis 32:24–30.
14 The Lord shows what we would regard today as unacceptable discrimination against homosexuals (Leviticus 20), hunchbacks and dwarfs (Leviticus 21:18–23).
15 K. Armstrong, op. cit., chapter 1, p. 31. See also Joshua 24.
16 Ibid., chapter 2, p. 65.
17 Genesis 1:26.
18 K. Armstrong, op. cit., chapter 2.
19 The name Mesopotamia has a Greek origin, meaning 'the land between the rivers'.
20 The *Enuma Elish* is also known as the 'Epic of Creation'. The tablet in Figure 1 is on display in the British Museum, exhibit W A K 3473, Later Mesopotamia Gallery.
21 *Enuma Elish*, Tablet V, line 65.
22 Cited in Z. Sitchin, *The Twelfth Planet*, Avon Books, New York, 1976, chapter 12, p. 349.
23 Genesis 2:7.
24 Z. Sitchin, *The Twelfth Planet*, op. cit., chapter 12, p. 357.
25 Genesis 2:21–22.
26 Z. Sitchin, *Genesis Revisited*, Avon Books, New York, 1990, chapter 9, p. 185. The operation sounds quite complex, and it has therefore been suggested that something else, perhaps the bone marrow, was also required.
27 The *Atra-Hasis* text has been pieced together from both Babylonian and Assyrian sources. See A. Heidel, *The Gilgamesh Epic and Old Testament Parallels*, University of Chicago Press, 2nd ed., 1949, p. 106.
28 See A. Heidel, op. cit., pp. 115–6. This translation cited in Z. Sitchin, *The Twelfth Planet*, op. cit., chapter 12, p. 354 & p. 358.
29 Z. Sitchin, *Genesis Revisited*, op. cit., chapter 8, pp. 161–2.
30 Genesis 2:5.
31 Cited in Z. Sitchin, *The Twelfth Planet*, op. cit., chapter 11, p. 331.
32 Ibid., p. 334.
33 For a detailed analysis of *The Epic of Gilgamesh*, see A. Heidel, op. cit.. Illustration 2 shows the 11th tablet from the British Museum, exhibit W A K 3375, in the Later Mesopotamia Gallery.
34 K. Armstrong, op. cit., chapter 5, pp. 171–2.
35 For more detail on the Cargo Cult see P. Worsley, *The Trumpet Shall Sound – A Study of 'Cargo' Cults in Melanesia*, Schocken Books, New York, 1968; also K.

Calvert, 'Cargo Cult Mentality and Development in the New Hebrides Today' in A. Mamak & G. McCall (eds), *Paradise Postponed*, Oxford Pergamon Press, 1978.

36 The term hieroglyph comes from the Greek *hieros* (sacred) and *gluphos* (carved sign).

37 The Pyramid Texts are repetitive verses, embossed or painted on the walls and passages of the pyramids of Unas, Teti, Pepi I, Merenra and Pepi II *c.* 2350–2180 BC.

38 The Egyptian term translated as 'perch' means a high-up resting place, usually of birds.

39 For numerous similar examples see R. Faulkner, *The Ancient Egyptian Coffin Texts Volume II*, Aris & Phillips Ltd, Warminster, 1977. This particular verse is cited in Z. Sitchin, *The Stairway to Heaven*. Avon Books, New York, 1980, chapter IV, pp. 63–4.

40 Exodus 19:16–18.

41 Exodus 24:16–17.

42 Exodus 34:29–30.

43 Exodus 19:12–13.

44 Exodus 25:8–9.

45 Exodus 25:22.

46 Exodus 33:3.

47 Exodus 40:21.

48 The power of the Ark was felt by Uzzah in Samuel II, 6:6–7; the Philistines in Samuel I, 4 & 5:10–12; and the men from Beth Shemesh in Samuel I, 6:19.

49 Some religions do argue that the Book of Exodus was written at the time of the Exodus *c.* 1400 BC, but less biased commentators attribute a date *c.* 800 BC, along with the rest of the Pentateuch, which was finally collated *c.* 500 BC.

50 Etana, Adapa, Enoch, Elijah, Ezekiel, Moses and Samson all claim to have soared heavenward with the permission of their god. See also the ancient Indian tales of flying 'vimanas' – R. Thompson. *Alien Identities*, Govardhan Hill, San Diego, 1993.

51 D. Dennett, *Darwin's Dangerous Idea*, Penguin, 1995, introductory comment.

52 R. Penrose, *The Emperor's New Mind Concerning Computers, Minds, and the Laws of Physics*, Oxford University Press, 1989, p. 414.

53 S. Gould, *Wonderful Life: The Burgess Shale and the Nature of History*, New York:Norton, 1989, introductory comment.

54 Kings I, 19:11–13.
55 The SETI plan subsequently hit budget problems and was scaled back in 1993. It now continues largely with private funding.
56 Some experts believe the Book of Ezekiel may be the work of more than one author, due to the alternating pattern between strange, technical visions of 'God' and apparently unrelated prophecies concerning Israel.
57 Excerpted from Ezekiel 1:4–21. Chrysolite is a brown or yellowish-green, naturally formed, hard glassy crystal, used as a gemstone.
58 J. Blumrich, *The Spaceships of Ezekiel*, Bantam Books, 1973.
59 Ibid.
60 *Homo sapiens* was so named due to his very large brain – see chapter 2.
61 E. von Daniken, *Chariots of the Gods*, Souvenir Press, 1969, first published in German 1968. Other early writers include Brinsley Le Poer Trench, *The Sky People*, Neville Spearman, 1960; and W. Drake, *Gods or Spacemen?*, Amherst Press, 1964.

Chapter Two:
Man the Evolutionary Misfit

1 C. Darwin, *On the Origin of Species by Means of Natural Selection*, London:Murray, 1859.
2 In fact, Darwin admitted some difficulty in explaining highly sophisticated organs such as the human eye and brain.
3 Alfred Wallace allowed Darwin to take the full public limelight.
4 Sir A. Keith in *Nature*, 85:2155 (1911), p. 59.
5 The 2 per cent DNA difference includes changes in the junk DNA which have no effect. From the nine or so human protein chains so far compared to chimpanzees, scientists have been unable to establish exactly where in the human genome any of the important DNA changes took place.
6 S. Jones, *The Language of the Genes*, Flamingo, 1993, chapter 6, p. 128.

7 U. Knatterbusch in *Ancient Skies* 20:2 (1993).

8 S. Jones, op. cit., chapter 4, p. 95.

9 R. Dawkins, *River Out Of Eden*, Weidenfeld & Nicolson, London, 1995, p. 11.

10 Dennett cites the fabulous example of 'Am I my brother's keeper?'

11 D. Dennett, *Darwin's Dangerous Idea*, op. cit., pp. 292 & 296.

12 R. Dawkins, op. cit.

13 This amazing similarity is seen as evidence to support Darwin's idea of a common origin for all life on Earth. See chapter 7.

14 R. Dawkins, op. cit., p. 6.

15 Ibid., p. 8.

16 For example, see R. Leakey & R. Lewin. *The Sixth Extinction*, Weidenfeld, 1996.

17 Darwin himself could not find any examples of changing species. Where major changes have been found in a species, it has been due to artificial environmental changes such as smoke and pesticides.

18 D. Dennett, op. cit., p. 292.

19 J. Gorman, 'The tortoise or the hare?' in *Discover*, October 1980, p. 89.

20 T. Huxley, cited in N. Macbeth, *Darwin Retried*, Gambit Inc., Boston, 1971, p. 141.

21 R. Dawkins, op. cit., pp. 79–80.

22 Ibid., pp. 105–6.

23 A. Wallace, cited in M. Flindt & O. Binder, *Mankind – Child of the Stars*, Fawcett, 1974, chapter 1.

24 Alan Wilson and Vincent Sarich, from the University of California at Berkeley, have used molecular genetics to 'prove' that the split from the chimpanzee occurred 5 million years ago. Other scientists believe it took place between 6–8 million years ago.

25 Research in 1995 by Professor Frans de Waal of Emory University at Yerkes Regional Primate Centre, Atlanta, Georgia.

26 She was named Lucy after the Beatles' song 'Lucy in the Sky with Diamonds', which was playing when her remains were brought back to camp by Donald Johanson!

27 *The Sunday Times News Review*, 19th March 1995.

28 *The Sunday Times*, 20th August 1995.

29 S. Jones, op. cit., chapter 6, p. 127.

30 *National Geographic*, 187:6 (1995).
31 Ibid.
32 *The Sunday Times*, 20th August 1995.
33 Standing up puts the brain in the cool wind. It also cools the body generally by reducing the body's exposure to the Sun by 40 per cent.
34 D. Falk, *Braindance*, Holt, 1992.
35 O. Lovejoy, anatomist at Kent State University.
36 J. Diamond. *The Rise and Fall of the Third Chimpanzee*, Vintage, 1991, chapter 1, p. 20.
37 The name Cro-Magnon comes from the region in France where his remains were first discovered.
38 Neanderthal man is named after the place where his remains were first found, near Dusseldorf in 1856. F. Clark Howell & T. White, of the University of California at Berkeley, state that 'the utter, almost abrupt disappearance of Neanderthal people remains one of the enigmas and critical problems in studies of human evolution'. Whilst some anthropologists believe that Neanderthal's genes are with us today via interbreeding with other *Homo sapiens*, the majority such as Chris Stringer of the British Museum, believe he was a separate species, which simply died out.
39 *Wonders of the Ancient World*, National Geographic Society, 1994, pp. 28–9.
40 See E. Trinkhaus & P. Shipman, *The Neanderthals: Changing the Image of Mankind*, Jonathan Cape, London, 1993.
41 B. Arensburg et al, 'A Middle Palaeolithic Human Hyoid Bone' in *Nature*, 338:27 (1989). The hyoid bone is positioned between the chin and the larynx and anchors the muscles that move the tongue, lower jaw and larynx.
42 See F. Hoyle, *The Intelligent Universe*, Michael Joseph, London 1983. Hoyle describes a genetic error, which causes human feet to resemble bird claws, in a small African tribe known as the 'Ostrich People'.
43 E. Trinkhaus ed., *The Emergence of Modern Humans*, Cambridge University Press, 1989.
44 M. Aitken, C. Stringer & P. Mellars (eds), *The Origin of Modern Humans and the Impact of Chronometric Dating*, Princeton University Press, 1993 (discussion held 26–27th February 1992).
45 H. Schwarcz and R. Grun, 'ESR Dating of the Origin of Modern Man' in Aitken, Stringer & Mellars, op. cit., p. 40.
46 J. Desmond Clark, 'African and Asian Perspectives on the

Origins of Modern Humans' in Aitken, Stringer & Mellars, op. cit.

47 Neanderthal date cited in *National Geographic*, 189.1 (1996). For a more balanced view concerning the uncertainty of their origins, see J. Diamond, op. cit., p. 35.

48 J. Hawkes (ed.), *Atlas of Ancient Archaeology*, Michael O'Mara, 1994, p. 9.

49 R. Lewin, *Human Evolution*, Blackwell Scientific Publications, Oxford, 1984, p. 74.

50 *National Geographic*, 187.6 (1995).

51 According to the engineer Max Flindt in Flindt & Binder, op. cit., chapter 11, p. 157.

52 R. Dawkins, op. cit., p. 124.

53 Roger Penrose is investigating quantum physics as a possible mechanism per D. Dennett, op. cit., pp. 444 & 446.

54 See D. Dennett, op. cit., p. 371 and J. Diamond, op. cit., chapter 2, p. 47 & chapter 8, p. 127.

55 D. Dennett, op. cit., p. 389.

56 Cited in D. Dennett, op. cit., pp. 384 & 387. Chomsky's ideas on a genetic blueprint for language are shared by the linguist D. Bickerton – see Diamond, op. cit., chapter 8.

57 S. Gould, 'Tires to Sandals' in *Natural History*, April 1989, p. 14.

58 P. Lieberman, *Uniquely Human: The Evolution of Speech, Thought and Selfless Behaviour*, Harvard University Press, 1991.

59 A. Koestler, 'Man – One of Evolution's Mistakes?' in *New York Times Magazine*, 19th October 1969, p. 112.

60 D. Morris, *The Naked Ape*, Triad Grafton, 1977, chapter 1, p. 38.

61 D. Morris, cited in Flindt & Binder, op. cit., chapter 7, p. 111.

62 It has been suggested that man may have had an aquatic phase in his evolution. Suggested reading: Sir Alaister Hardy, 'Was Man more aquatic in the past?' in *The New Scientist*, 17th March 1960; E. Morgan, *The Aquatic Ape – A Theory of Human Evolution*, Souvenir Press, London, 1982; E. Morgan, *The Scars of Evolution: What our Bodies Tell Us About Human Origins*, Souvenir, London, 1990; M. Roede, J. Wind, J. Patrick & V. Reynolds (eds), *The Aquatic Ape: Fact Or Fiction*, Souvenir, London, 1991.

63 D. Morris, op. cit., chapter 2, pp. 49 & 56.

64 J. Diamond, op. cit., chapter 3, p. 66.

65 S. Jones, op. cit., chapter 5, p. 109.

66 J. Diamond, op. cit., chapter 3, pp. 63–4.

67 D. Morris, op. cit., chapter 2.

68 M. Flindt & O. Binder, op. cit., chapter 8, p. 123.

69 A, G, C & T stand for adenine, guanine, cytosine and thymine.

70 Nature would normally merge two single sets of chromosomes from the male and female sex cells respectively, leading to a random combination of the genes.

71 *Financial Times*, 20th December 1993.

Chapter Three: Signs of the Gods

1 The term prehistory refers to the era before written records began; it thus denotes different periods in different geographical areas.

2 M. Barnes et al, *Secrets of Lost Empires*, BBC Books, 1996, pp. 95–135; also shown on BBC2 television 5th June 1996.

3 M. Alouf, *History of Baalbek*, 25th edition, p. 92.

4 Ibid.

5 A Boeing 747 aircraft weighs in at 337,840 kg.

6 Prof. Daniel Krencker, German Archaeological Mission, cited in Alouf, op. cit., p. 80.

7 M. Alouf, op. cit., pp. 27–8.

8 Ibid., p. 26.

9 N. Jidejian, *Baalbek Heliopolis 'City of the Sun'*, Dar El-Machreq, Beirut, 1975, p. 7. Also M. Alouf, op. cit., p. 26.

10 D. Urquhart, *The Lebanon Diary*, cited in M. Alouf, op. cit., p. 26.

11 G. Hancock, *Fingerprints of the Gods*, Mandarin, 1995, chapter 39, p. 362. Also Z. Sitchin, *The Stairway to Heaven*, op. cit., chapter IX, p. 179.

12 The Gottwald AK912 crane uses a 10.7-metre square outrigger base, a 35 metre maxiboom, a 43 metre maximast, a 117-ton upper counterweight and a 400-ton maxi-counterweight.

13 Estimate by Monsieur F. Caignart de Saulcy, cited in M. Alouf, op. cit., p. 101.

14 M. Alouf, op. cit., p. 32.

15 Ephraim George Squier, *Tiahuanaco – Baalbek del Nuevo Mondo*, 1909.

16 A. Kolata, *The Tiwanaku: Portrait of an Andean Civilisation*, Blackwell, 1993, chapters 6 & 8.

17 A. Kolata, op. cit., pp. 179–80, citing T. Weil, *Area Handbook for Bolivia*, Washington DC, US Government Printing Office, 1974.

18 A. Kolata, op. cit., chapter 6, especially pp. 190–98.

19 Ibid., citing Carlos Ponce Sangines.

20 A. Kolata, op. cit., p. 111.

21 Ibid., p. 115.

22 Ibid., pp. 129 & 131.

23 Ibid., p. 115.

24 Ibid., pp. 133 & 160.

25 Pedro de Cieza de Leon, cited in A. Kolata, op. cit., p. 3.

26 See A. Posnansky, *Tiahuanacu: The Cradle of American Man*, 2 vols, New York: J. J. Augustin, 1945.

27 The Earth's obliquity (the angle between the plane of the Earth's orbit and that of the celestial equator) changes through time, causing the Sun to shift in position on the horizon. Scientists have prepared detailed tables of the Earth's past obliquity, according to which the *Kalasasaya* must have been aligned to the Sun in either 4050 BC or 10050 BC. These dates have been jointly agreed by Posnansky (op. cit.) and Dr Rolf Muller of the Astrophysical Observatory in Potsdam.

28 Pedro de Cieza de Leon, cited in A. Kolata, op. cit., pp. 3–4.

29 A. Kolata pp. 83 & 85.

30 Ibid., pp. 90 & 93–4.

31 N. Abanto de Hoogendoorn, *Chavin de Huantar – A Short Eternity*, Lima, 1990, p. 39.

32 Ibid., p. 13.

33 Ibid., p. 54.

34 Ibid., p. 30.

35 Ibid., p. 74.

36 Z. Sitchin, *The Lost Realms*, Avon Books, New York, 1990, chapter 9, p. 189, chapter 11, p. 248 and chapter 12, p. 274.

37 N. Abanto de Hoogendoorn, op. cit., pp. 48–9.

38 J. Rowe, 'The Incas', section of *The Handbook of South American Indians*, Washington, 1946.

39 S. Hagar, *Cuzco the Celestial City*; also R. Muller, *Sonne, Mond und Sterne uber dem Reich der Inka*, Springer Verlag, Berlin, 1982.

40 M. Barnes et al, op. cit., pp. 181–221; also shown on BBC2

television 19th June 1996. See also P. Frost, *Exploring Cuzco*, Nuevas Imagenes, 1989, pp. 67–71.

41 P. Frost, op. cit., p. 58.

42 Garcilaso de la Vega, *Royal Commentaries of the Incas*, Orion Press, New York, 1961.

43 P. Frost, op. cit., pp. 103 & 106.

44 M. Barnes et al, op. cit., pp. 190–99; also shown on BBC2 television 19th June 1996.

45 Garcilaso de la Vega, op. cit.

46 J. Reinhard, *Machu Picchu The Sacred Center*, Nuevas Imagenes, Lima, 1991, p. 6.

47 S. Waisbard, 'Enigmatic Messages of the Nazcas' in *The World's Last Mysteries*, 8th edition, Reader's Digest, 1982, pp. 281–7.

48 Only a few of the Nazca geoglyphs can be seen from the ground observation tower or adjacent hillsides.

49 E. von Daniken, *Chariots of the Gods*, op. cit.

50 This is the judgement of Maria Reiche, although it has never been put to the test!

51 J. Nickell, 'The Nazca Drawings Revisited: Creation of a Full-Sized Duplicate' in *The Sceptical Inquirer* 7:3 (1983), pp. 36–44; also A. Aveni, 'The Nazca Lines: Patterns in the Desert' in *Archaeology* 39:4 (1986), pp. 32–9.

52 M. Reiche, *Mystery on the Desert*, 1st edition, Heinrich Fink GmbH, Stuttgart, 1968.

53 *National Geographic*, May 1975, p. 716. Furthermore, it should be noted that the position of the stars on the horizon is not constant, so any alignments that are found may be illusory, since no-one knows when the lines were drawn.

54 G. Hawkins, *Beyond Stonehenge*, Harper & Row, New York, 1973.

55 A. Aveni, *Report on the Analysis of Data Obtained on the Nazca Project*, National Geographic Society, 1982.

56 G. Petersen, *Evolucion y Desaparicion de las Altas Culturas Paracas-Cahuachi*, Lima, 1980.

57 J. Reinhard, *The Nazca Lines*, 5th edition, Lima, 1993, p. 31.

58 Ibid., pp. 12–56.

59 Ibid., p. 17 (eagles) & pp. 41–2 (condors).

60 Ibid., p. 56.

61 H. Silverman, 'Cahuachi: Non-Urban Cultural Complexity

on the South Coast of Peru' in *Journal of Field Archaeology*, Winter 1988.
62 J. Reinhard, op. cit., pp. 22–32.

Chapter Four: The Pyramids of Giza

1 J. Hawkes (ed.), *Atlas of Ancient Archaeology*, op. cit., p. 150.

2 P. Lemesurier, *The Great Pyramid Decoded*, Element, 1977, p. 23.

3 J. West, *The Serpent in the Sky: The High Wisdom of Ancient Egypt*, Harper & Row, New York, 1979.

4 Manetho was an Egyptian priest *c.* 300 BC. The papyrus on which his history of Egypt was written was probably destroyed in the burning of the great library of Alexandria in AD 642; fortunately it was referred to by several other contemporary historians, whose accounts have survived.

5 In particular, mummification, based on the Isis and Osiris tale. See later chapters.

6 According to the Cole Survey commissioned by the Egyptian government in 1925.

7 Sir W. Flinders Petrie, *Pyramids and Temples of Gizeh*, 1881. True North is measured along the terrestrial polar axis, as opposed to magnetic north, which fluctuates.

8 *The World's Last Mysteries*, Reader's Digest, op. cit., p. 196.

9 It is also *claimed* that the Pyramid is positioned at the exact geometric centre and southern extremity of the quadrant formed by the Nile Delta; also that its position is at the geographical centre of the Earth's entire land mass.

10 E. Powell in *Ancient Skies* 21:2 (1994).

11 *The World's Last Mysteries*, op. cit., p. 192.

12 This angle in fact works out at just under 52 degrees.

13 This ratio is expressed mathematically as $1/(2\,pi)$. The height can also be expressed as $H = 4 \times S/(2\,Pi)$, where H is the height and S is the side.

14 The golden section is known as phi, defined as 'the proportion of the two divisions of a straight line, being such that the smaller is to the larger as the larger is to the sum of the two'. This mathematically elegant ratio equals

approximately 0.618, sometimes referred to by its inverse of 1.61803.

15 The 43.5 degree angle results from the formula in note 13, where the multiplication factor of 4 is replaced by 3.

16 I cannot subscribe, for example, to the interpretation that the Pyramid is a prophecy in stone, as claimed by P. Lemesurier, op. cit.!

17 P. Lemesurier, op. cit., p. 4.

18 Sir W. Flinders Petrie, op. cit.

19 Ibid.

20 C. Dunn, 'Hi-tech Pharaohs?' (part one) in *Amateur Astronomy & Earth Sciences*, Issue Two (1995).

21 Ibid.

22 Ibid. The dead give-aways were artefacts with lips and ridges, caused by improper recentring of the lathe between two separate operations.

23 C. Dunn, 'Hi-tech Pharaohs?' (part two) in *Amateur Astronomy & Earth Sciences*, Issue Three (1996).

24 *The World's Last Mysteries*, op. cit., p. 196.

25 In fact, Herodotus acknowledged that Khufu's real tomb lay elsewhere: 'the Nile water, introduced through an artificial duct, surrounds an island where the body of Cheops is said to lie', *History*, vol. II, p. 127.

26 Z. Sitchin, *The Stairway To Heaven*, op. cit., chapter XIII. pp. 259–82. Updated in Z. Sitchin, *The Wars of Gods and Men*, Avon Books, 1985, chapter 7, p. 136.

27 The British Egyptologist Martin Stower has published a denial of the mis-spelling allegation, but his bitter attack on Sitchin does call into question his objectivity. *If* the spelling should one day be proven correct, it would then follow that Vyse *did* find a genuine hieroglyph, but *outside* the Pyramid, and that he copied (i.e. forged) it inside.

28 Z. Sitchin, *The Stairway To Heaven*, op. cit., chapter XIII, pp. 266 & 276.

29 Vyse Diary, 27.1.1837, see Sitchin, *The Stairway to Heaven*, op. cit., ch. XIII, p. 261.

30 The assistance of Imhotep was recorded in an inscription found close to the site.

31 The mummies which were found in Djoser's pyramid are now believed to have been 'intrusive burials' by later generations.

32 This pyramid's association with Sekhemkhet has been thrown into doubt by the radiocarbon dating of dried

flowers on top of the sarcophagus to a time 600 years before he lived.

33 As for the Giza pyramids, Khufu's had been ransacked by the Arabs when it was 'discovered' by the archaeologists, so it is not possible to say whether anything was originally in the sarcophagus. Menkaura's pyramid was reported to have contained an empty basal sarcophagus, which was magnificently decorated (allegedly) but was subsequently removed and lost at sea.

34 This pyramid once again contained an empty burial chamber.

35 The Egyptologists have tried in vain to find a pyramid to attribute to Shepseskaf.

36 The ownership of these latter pyramids is much more certain than the uninscribed pyramids of the Third and Fourth Dynasties.

37 Archaeological missions directed by George Reisner of Harvard University.

38 Compare the alternative theory espoused by R. Bauval and A. Gilbert that 'it was presumably built in a hurry' (*The Orion Mystery* p. 30)!

39 As suggested by Z. Sitchin, *The Stairway to Heaven*, op. cit., chapter XIII, p. 255.

40 Although there is no evidence that the pyramids themselves belonged to Khafra and Menkaura, there is evidence that Menkaura built the causeway to the third pyramid.

41 Z. Sitchin, *The Wars of Gods and Men*, op. cit., chapter 7, p. 137.

42 Whilst step-pyramids were known in Mesopotamia, there is no trace of any smooth-sided pyramids comparable to those in Egypt.

43 This is not the only example; a depiction found in the tomb of Huy shows a rocket in an underground silo. See Sitchin, *The Stairway to Heaven*, op. cit., chapter V, p. 88.

Chapter Five: Impossible Science

1 Flavius Philostratus of Athens (AD 175–249), in *Life of Apollonius of Tyana*.

2 *The World's Last Mysteries*, Reader's Digest, op. cit., p. 271.

3 The Maya's Long Count calendar had clocked up more than 4,000 years since Day One, using cycles called baktuns, which amounted to 144,000 days (395 years).

4 Magellan took the short cut through the Strait of Magellan rather than rounding the Patagonian tip at Cape Horn.

5 The prior existence of this lost map is deduced from the other two maps which are partly torn and which appear to be portions of a larger map.

6 C. Hapgood, *Maps of the Ancient Sea Kings*, Chilton Books, Philadelphia & New York, 1966.

7 The Antarctic ice cap is thought to have formed around 4000 BC. See C. Hapgood, op. cit., pp. 96 & 98.

8 A survey in 1957 (the International Geophysical Year) was followed by that of the Swedish-British-Antarctic Expedition in 1960.

9 These small discrepancies could be accounted for by the continued copying of the maps through the ages; it is feasible that an original map of perfect accuracy might once have existed.

10 Spherical trigonometry is the method of projecting global features onto a flat surface.

11 Mr Warren, the organiser of the conference, cited in E. von Daniken, *In Search of Ancient Gods*, Souvenir Press, 1973, pp. 136–7.

12 The Phoenicians were based in modern day Lebanon and Syria; their voyages are said to have included Cornwall, the Scilly Islands and the circumnavigation of Africa.

13 C. Hapgood, op. cit.

14 The first satisfactory marine chronometer was designed and built in England by John Harrison; in 1761, it was successfully tested en route to Jamaica.

15 Advanced astronomical tables have been found recorded by the Sumerians nearly 6,000 years ago. The tables included data for the motions of the Sun and Moon, listed for up to fifty years in advance.

16 M. Chatelain, *Our Ancestors Came from Outer Space*, Pan Books, 1979, chapter 6, p. 116.

17 An astrolabe simply consists of a graduated circular disc with a movable sighting device. It was used by early astronomers to measure the altitude of stars and planets.

18 D. de Solla Price in *Natural History*, March 1962.

19 Ibid.

616 NOTES AND BIBLIOGRAPHY

20 The device is displayed at the Athens Museum, catalogue reference X.15087.
21 R. Cleal, K. Walker & R. Montague, *Stonehenge in its Landscape: the 20th Century Excavations*, English Heritage, 1995. See also http:www.eng-h.gov/uk/stoneh.
22 No datings have proved possible for the holes themselves.
23 The dating is based on a single sample, but the authorities are confident that this construction followed the bluestone settings and preceded the trilithons.
24 Sir N. Lockyer, *Stonehenge and Other British Stone Monuments*, 1906.
25 C. Newham, *The Enigma of Stonehenge*, 1964; *The Astronomical Significance of Stonehenge*, 1972; and subsequently *Supplement to the Enigma of Stonehenge and its Astronomical and Geometrical Significance*.
26 G. Hawkins, *Stonehenge Decoded*, 1965.
27 A. Thom, *Megalithic Sites in Britain*, 1967; also *Megalithic Lunar Observations*.
28 Sir F. Hoyle, 'Stonehenge – An Eclipse Predictor' in *Nature*.
29 R. Muller, *Sonne, Mond und Sterne uber dem Reich der Inka*, op. cit.; also *Die Intiwatana (Sonnenwarten) im Alten Peru*.
30 D. Dearborn & R. White, *Archaeoastronomy at Machu Picchu*.
31 Z. Sitchin, *When Time Began*, Avon Books, 1993, chapter 9, p. 226.
32 Ibid., chapter 9, pp. 227 & 234.
33 It should be noted that calculating the Earth's changing obliquity backwards in time is not an exact science!
34 A. Kolata, *The Tiwanaku*, op. cit., p. 57.
35 Bishop Diego de Landa, *Relacion de las cosas de Yucatan*, 1562.
36 Lord Kingsborough recorded his travels, 1830–1848, in *Antiquities of Mexico*. John Lloyd Stephens recorded his expeditions in 1839 and 1842 in *Incidents of Travel in Central America, Chiapas and Yucatan*; and *Incidents of Travel in Yucatan*.
37 Around 70 per cent of Mayan texts have now been translated. Recent progress has been encouraging, under a new initiative by Dr David Stewart. Many glyphs, however, still remain to be deciphered.
38 G. & G. Stuart, *The Mysterious Maya*, National Geographic Society, 1977, flap introduction.
39 A fourth 'original' book is disputed; in addition, there are

two books of oral traditions written in the Latin script: Chilam Balam ('Utterings of Balam'); and the Popol Vuh ('Council Book').

40 Z. Sitchin, *The Lost Realms*, op. cit., chapter 5, p. 97.

41 The coincidence occurs upon 73 cycles of 260 days and 52 cycles of 365 days.

42 *The World's Last Mysteries*, op. cit., p. 272.

43 J. & O. Tickell, *Tikal, City of the Maya*, Tauris Parke Books, London, 1991.

44 Ibid., p. 16.

45 R. Temple, *The Sirius Mystery*, St Martin's Press, 1976.

46 M. Griaule & G. Dieterlen, 'A Sudanese Sirius System' in *Journal de la Societe des Africanistes*, XX, fasc. I, 1950; also see their book, *Le Renard Pale*, Paris 1965.

47 As for Sirius C, the third star mentioned by the Dogon, its existence has not yet been proved by modern astronomers.

48 Sirius A is clearly visible in the constellation Canis Major, just below Orion.

49 R. Temple, op. cit., p. 1.

50 This point in the heavens is sometimes referred to as the 'celestial pole' and the star nearest to it as the 'pole star'.

51 This is the original concept of the zodiac; it is now used in a much simpler manner to divide the Earth's *annual* orbit around the Sun into twelve *monthly* houses.

52 Radiocarbon dating works on organic matter and is useless for dating stone constructions; confusion has often been caused by dating organic materials left in temples long after they were built.

53 *Kabbalah* literally means 'that which was received'.

Chapter Six:
Civilisation – A Gift of the Gods

1 *Splendors of The Past*, National Geographic Society, 1981, p. 6.

2 *Wonders of the Ancient World*, NGS, op. cit., p. 48.

3 *Splendors of The Past*, op. cit., pp. 39–40.

4 A. Parrot, *Sumer*, 2nd ed., 1981.

5 J. Campbell, *The Masks of God – Primitive Mythology*, chapter 3.

6 T. Jones (ed.), *The Sumerian Problem*, New York 1969; A. Parrot, *Archeologie Mesopotamienne*, II, pp. 308–31, Paris 1946–53. The lack of awareness is certainly compounded by the difficulty of tourist travel to modern-day Iraq, and the poor state of preservation of the Sumerian ruins.

7 *The Times Atlas of World History*, 4th ed., BCA/Times Books, 1993, pp. 52–5.

8 *Splendors of The Past*, op. cit., p. 41.

9 G. Roux, *Ancient Iraq*, 3rd ed., Penguin Books, 1992, chapters 4–5.

10 *The Times Atlas of World History*, op. cit., p. 52.

11 Shinar is mentioned in Genesis 11:2, following the Flood, as the location of the Tower of Babel incident.

12 Uruk's modern name is Warka. It is referred to in the Bible (Genesis 10:10) as Erech.

13 Many English words are borrowed directly from the archaic Latin language, e.g. '*et cetera*'; a modern example of a loan-word is the French use of 'le weekend'.

14 S. Kramer, *History Begins at Sumer*, Penguin, New York, 1954.

15 Geography provided little in the way of stone, whilst Sumer's overseas trade focused on higher value and more easily transportable materials.

16 R. Forbes, *Studies in Ancient Technology*, I, Leiden, 1955; R. Forbes, *Bitumen and Petroleum in Antiquity*, Leiden, 1936; L. Aitchison, *A History of Metals*.

17 O. Neugebauer, *Astronomical Cuneiform Texts*, 3 vols, London, 1955.

18 Z. Sitchin, *When Time Began*, op. cit., chapter 3, pp. 72–3.

19 The Sumerian calendar is still in use today as the Jewish calendar, which records 1996 as the year 5756.

20 The actual shortfall each year is 10 days, 21 hours, 6 minutes and about 45.5 seconds, such that exactly seven lunar months will coincide with 19 solar years.

21 For instance, the holidays in the Muslim calendar slip back 1 month in every 3 years.

22 Simpler calendars have been based on either the Moon's cycles (e.g. the Muslim calendar) or on a division of the solar year into 12 months totalling 365 days.

23 Th. Pinches, *Some Mathematical Tablets of the British Museum*; Professor H. Hilprecht, *The Babylonian Expedition of the University of Pennsylvania*.

24 A. Jeremias, *The Old Testament in the Light of the Ancient Near East*, 1911.

25 W. Andrae, cited in C. Walker, *Wonders of the Ancient World*, Popular Press, 1988, p. 44.

26 S. Kramer, cited in E. von Daniken, *Signs of the Gods*, Putnam's, New York, 1980, chapter 6, p. 199.

27 Suggested reading: S. Kramer, *Sumerian Mythology*, New York, 1961; T. Jacobsen, *The Treasure of Darkness: A History of Mesopotamian Religion*, London 1976.

28 Z. Sitchin, *When Time Began*, op. cit., chapter 1, p. 10.

29 Z. Sitchin, *The Twelfth Planet*, op. cit., chapter 5, p. 170.

30 Ibid., p. 169.

31 G. Redslob in *Zeitschrift der Deutschen Morgenlandischen Gesellschaft* more than one hundred years previously.

32 According to Redslob, when the Old Testament reported that King David had 'made a shem' to commemorate his victory over the Arameans, he had actually erected a monument pointing skyward.

33 G. Barton, *The Royal Inscriptions of Sumer and Akkad*.

34 Genesis 11:3–4.

35 Z. Sitchin, *Divine Encounters*, Avon Books, 1995, chapter 4, p. 73.

36 Genesis 6:1–4.

37 References such as these confirm the idea that the eagle (GIR) was distinct from a shem (MU).

38 Z. Sitchin, *The Stairway to Heaven*, op. cit., chapter X, p. 203.

39 Z. Sitchin, *The Twelfth Planet*, op. cit., chapter 4, pp. 103–5.

40 Genesis 20:12.

41 Compare G. Roux, op. cit., chapter 6, p. 88, to Z. Sitchin, *The Twelfth Planet*, op. cit., chapter 10, pp. 297–8.

42 The Sumerian term KUR means mountain; see G. Roux, op. cit., chapter 7, p. 105.

43 G. Roux, op. cit., chapter 6, p. 89; Z. Sitchin, *The Twelfth Planet*, op. cit., chapter 10, p. 290.

44 The creation of man was Enki's idea and, according to one Sumerian text, he even offered his own spouse, Ninki, for the initial role as birth goddess. Cited in Z. Sitchin, *Genesis Revisited*, op. cit., chapter 8, p. 169.

45 The Sumerian words are NIN (lady), HAR or HUR (another term for mountain) and SAG (head).

46 Cited in Z. Sitchin, *The Twelfth Planet*, op. cit., chapter 12, p. 347.

47 For a full discussion of the very detailed etymological evidence, see Z. Sitchin, *Genesis Revisited*, op. cit.

48   G. Roux, op. cit., notes to chapter 5.
49   Z. Sitchin, *The Stairway to Heaven*, op. cit., chapter VI, p. 111; *neter* appears in the Akkadian language with the meaning 'watchers'.
50   E. Wallis-Budge, *Egyptian Literature Volume I*, 1912 p. xl.
51   Z. Sitchin, *The Wars of Gods and Men*, op. cit., chapter 8.
52   The Levant is equivalent to the area of present-day Israel, Lebanon, Jordan and Syria.
53   Z. Sitchin, *The Wars of Gods and Men*, op. cit., chapter 6, pp. 126–8.
54   Ibid., chapter 7 & *The Twelfth Planet*, op. cit., chapter 15, p. 415, citing *Epic of Etana*.
55   Z. Sitchin, *The Wars of Gods and Men*, op. cit., chapter 8.
56   J. Hertz (ed.), *The Pentateuch and Haftorahs*.
57   Z. Sitchin, *The Wars of Gods and Men*, op. cit., chapter 8, p. 157.
58   R. Faulkner, *The Ancient Egyptian Coffin Texts Volume II*, op. cit., p. 2 (spell 358).
59   Z. Sitchin, *The Wars of Gods and Men*, op. cit., chapter 8, pp. 160–1.
60   The name Canaan, stemming from the Hebrew *kana*, means 'to be humble'.
61   I use the term 'Shemitic' to refer to the race descended from Noah's son Shem. It should not be confused with a similar term, 'Semitic', which denotes a spoken language.
62   Genesis 9:25–27.
63   Z. Sitchin, *The Wars of Gods and Men*, chapter 10, pp. 216–9.
64   Dumuzi's offence was in much later times emulated by Amnon who raped his half-sister Tamar – see Samuel II, 13.
65   G. Roux, op. cit., chapter 6, pp. 92–3.
66   S. Kramer, *Inanna and Ebih*, cited in Z. Sitchin, *The Wars of Gods and Men*, chapter 10, p. 221.
67   Z. Sitchin, *The Wars of Gods and Men*, chapter 11, pp. 232–3.
68   Suggested reading: Sir M. Wheeler, *The Indus Civilization*, 3rd ed., Cambridge Press, 1968; S. Rao, *Lothal and the Indus Civilization*, Asia Publishing House, 1973.
69   *The World's Last Mysteries*, Reader's Digest, op. cit., p. 123.
70   This may be the source of Egyptian intoxication festivals such as that held at Dendera once a year.

71 G. Roux, op. cit., chapter 6, p. 89. A list of the 'ME' objects can be found in S. Kramer, *The Sumerians*, Chicago, 1963, p. 116.

72 We will ignore for the moment the inevitable subjective biases that are always contained in any historical account – we are concerned here with the fundamental message of the gods being our creators and teachers.

73 C. Sagan & I. Shklovskii, *Intelligent Life in the Universe*, New York:Dell, 1967.

Chapter Seven:
Passing Time on Planet X

1   G. Smith, *The Chaldean Genesis*, 1876. The most complete version of the *Enuma Elish* is an Akkadian text discovered by Layard in Nineveh; other copies have also been found, including fragments of an earlier Sumerian original.

2   Z. Sitchin, *The Twelfth Planet*, op. cit., chapter 7.

3   The term usually translated as 'winds' carries the literal meaning 'those that are by the side', hence satellites.

4   Apsu literally means 'one who exists from the beginning'.

5   Cited in G. Roux, op. cit., chapter 6, p. 97.

6   Cited in Z. Sitchin, *The Twelfth Planet*, op. cit., chapter 7, p. 223.

7   Ibid., pp. 223–6.

8   Ibid., pp. 226–7.

9   Ibid., p. 227.

10 Z. Sitchin, *Genesis Revisited*, op. cit., chapter 3, pp. 40–50. The Biblical account is in Genesis 1:1–8.

11 The Koran, chapter 21:30. English translation in *The Koran*, Penguin Books, London, 4th ed., 1974, p. 298.

12 E. Larson & P. Birkeland, *Putnam's Geology*, 1982, p. 66.

13 Z. Sitchin, *Genesis Revisited*, op. cit., chapter 5, p. 95.

14 Ibid., pp. 88–90. The word 'geo' and hence geography, geology etc comes from the Sumerian root KI.

15 J. Vervoort, in *Nature* 379:6566 (1996), pp. 624–7.

16 R. Carlson, 'Where has all the old crust gone?' in *Nature* 379:6566 (1996), pp. 581–2.

17 R. Hutchinson, *The Search for Our Beginning*, Oxford University Press, 1983.

18 The size of these impacts can be judged relative to the Arizona meteor crater on Earth which measures 1 mile in diameter; on the Moon, the Theophilus crater is 64 miles in diameter, whilst another shallower crater, Bailly, is 180 miles in diameter!

19 T. Van Flandern, *Dark Matter, Missing Planets & New Comets*, North Atlantic Books, Berkeley, California, 1993, p. 262: capture is only possible if another body of appreciable size was involved.

20 Ibid., pp. 264–5.

21 P. Moore, *Guide to the Moon*, Lutterworth Press, Guildford & London, 1976.

22 Z. Sitchin, *Genesis Revisited*, op. cit., chapter 6, pp. 125–131.

23 P. Lucey, G. Taylor & E. Malaret, 'Abundance and Distribution of Iron on the Moon' in *Science* (USA) 268:5214 (1995), pp. 1150–3.

24 T. Van Flandern, op. cit., p. 264.

25 Ibid., p. 157. Bode's Law was proposed by Daniel Titius, but named after Johann Bode who published it in 1778; the Law comprises a combined arithmetical and geometrical progression which predicts with reasonable accuracy the distances of the planets from the Sun. Z. Sitchin, *Genesis Revisited*, op. cit., chapter 2, p. 39, cites a modification to Bode's Law which removes Earth from its artificially induced location and produces even better results based only on a geometrical progression.

26 In 1972, the astronomer Michael Ovenden put forward a sophisticated support of Bode's Law, which predicted that the missing planet in the Asteroid Belt would have been the size of Saturn, and thus much larger than the combined mass of asteroids.

27 The theory of the French astronomer Louis Lagrange in 1814.

28 The Oort cloud was named after its discoverer, the Dutch astronomer Jan Oort (1950).

29 W. Hartmann, *Astronomy, The Cosmic Journey*, Wadsworth, California, 1987.

30 T. Van Flandern, op. cit., p. 179.

31 Ibid., p. 179. Van Flandern actually concludes that there was an explosion 3 million years ago (pp. 159–60), but he cites evidence that *does not* fit this timing (pp. 234–6). Van Flandern struggles to suggest what force caused the planet to explode.

32 H. Brown & C. Patterson, 'The Composition of Meteoritic Matter III: Phase Equilibria, Genetic Relationships and Planet Structure' in *Journal of Geology* 56, pp. 85–111.

33 T. Van Flandern, op. cit., pp. 298–300. Also A. Brunini, 'A possible constraint to Uranus' great collision' in *Planetary and Space Science* (UK) 43:8, August 1995, pp. 1019–21.

34 T. Van Flandern, op. cit., p. 293.

35 Ibid., chapter 13.

36 Ibid., p. 252.

37 Re Charon, see T. Van Flandern, op. cit., p. 312; also H. Levison & S. Stern, 'Possible Origin and Early Dynamical Evolution of the Pluto-Charon Binary' in *Icarus* (USA) 116:2 (1995), pp. 315–39. Re other satellite systems, see T. Van Flandern and Z. Sitchin, *Genesis Revisited*, op. cit., chapters 1–3.

38 T. Van Flandern, op. cit., p. 213.

39 What do we mean by life? Not simply existence, but the ability of an organism to replicate itself.

40 For example, the primitive bacterium *E. coli* consists of almost 4,000 different genes!

41 F. Crick & L. Orgel in *Icarus*, September 1973.

42 F. Hoyle & C. Wickramasinghe, *Evolution from Space*, J.M. Dent & Sons, London 1981; also F. Hoyle, *The Intelligent Universe*, op. cit.

43 Such seeding was once considered impossible due to the hostile environment of outer space, but scientists now recognise the existence of micro-organisms in extreme conditions on Earth; for example, within rock strata hundreds of metres deep or in volcanic hot springs at temperatures above boiling point.

44 See *Nature*, 9th November 1989.

45 Z. Sitchin, *The Twelfth Planet*, op. cit., chapter 14, pp. 406 & 409.

46 Many planets in the Solar System are hotter than can be accounted for by the heat of the Sun. Neptune, for instance, is far more distant from the Sun than Uranus, but has a similar temperature. Scientists believe that this heat must be internal, and related to the planet's size. It is therefore scientifically possible that a large planet, which Nibiru appears to be, could retain sufficient heat from internal sources to generate a hospitable climate. It should also be noted that the cataclysmic event which was

necessary to expel Nibiru into the depths of space more than 4 billion years ago might well have bestowed the planet with an exceptional internal heat.

47 R. Leakey & R. Lewin, *The Sixth Extinction*, Weidenfeld & Nicolson, London, 1996.

48 S. Gould, *Dinosaurs in a Haystack*, 1996.

49 V. Alekseev, 'A Catastrophe in Space: 520 or 350 million years ago?' in *Solar System Research* (USA) 29:5 (1995), pp. 412–16.

50 S. Luria & S. Gould, *A View of Life*, 1981, pp. 638 & 649.

51 D. Whitmire in *Newsweek*, 13th July 1987, p. 45.

52 This subject is thoroughly covered by G. Hancock, *Fingerprints of the Gods*, op. cit., pp. 201–214.

53 A. Heidel, *The Gilgamesh Epic and Old Testament Parallels*, op. cit.; also W. Lambert & A. Millard, *Atra-Hasis. The Babylonian Story of the Flood*, Oxford, 1969.

54 G. Roux, op. cit., chapter 7, p. 111.

55 *The Epic of Gilgamesh*, Tablet XI, cited in Z. Sitchin, *The Twelfth Planet*, op. cit., chapter 14, p. 397.

56 P. Martin & R. Klein (eds), *Quaternary Extinctions: A Prehistoric Revolution*, University of Arizona Press, 1984, pp. 360–1.

57 Ibid., p. 358.

58 D. Hopkins et al, *The Palaeoecology of Beringia*, Academic Press, New York, 1982.

59 F. Hibben, *The Lost Americas*, cited in C. Hapgood, *Path of the Pole*, op, cit., p. 275.

60 Ibid.

61 I. Sanderson, 'Riddle of the Quick-Frozen Giants' in *Saturday Evening Post*, 16th January 1960, p. 82. See also the works of C. Hapgood. The extent of the mammoth deaths is such that a huge trade in ivory resulted from the mining of their tusks – see D. Patten, *The Biblical Flood and the Ice Epoch: A Study in Scientific History*, Pacific Meridian, Seattle, 1966, pp. 107–8.

62 P. Martin & R. Klein (eds), op. cit., p. 357.

63 J. Imbrie & K. Palmer Imbrie, *Ice Ages: Solving the Mystery*, Enslow Publishers, New Jersey, 1979. Also C. Langway and B. Lyle Hansen, *The Frozen Future: A Prophetic Report from Antarctica*, Quadrangle, New York, 1973. Also C. Hapgood, op. cit.

64 A. Posnansky, *Tiahuanacu: The Cradle of American Man*, op. cit., Vol I, p. 28.

65 G. Phillips, 'Titicaca – Cradle of Civilization?' in *Ancient Skies* 7:6 (1981).

66 C. Hapgood, op. cit. See also I. Velikovsky, *Earth in Upheaval*, Pocket Books, New York 1977, p. 63; and G. Price, *The New Geology*, 1923, p. 579.

67 Z. Sitchin, *The Twelfth Planet*, chapter 14, p. 407.

68 Samuel II, 22:16. See also Psalms 18:15.

69 A. Jeremias, *The Old Testament in the Light of the Ancient Near East*, op. cit., cited in Z. Sitchin, *The Twelfth Planet*, op. cit., chapter 9, p. 268.

70 Berossus, cited in S. Burstein, 'The Babyloniaca of Berossus' in *Sources for the Ancient Near East* 1:5 Malibu, California, 1978.

71 Cited in C. Kang & E. Nelson, *The Discovery of Genesis*, St Louis: Concordia Publishing House, 1979.

72 Scientists believed that Venus underwent a short period of intense tectonic and volcanic activity at a relatively recent date of 500–300 million years ago.

73 J. Hollin of the University of Maine, cited in Z. Sitchin, *The Twelfth Planet*, op. cit., chapter 14, pp. 402–5.

74 Genesis 7:11.

75 Cited in Z. Sitchin, *When Time Began*, op. cit., chapter 11, p. 314. There is much evidence in support of such changes – see I. Velikovsky, *Worlds in Collision*, 1950.

76 N. Morner, J. Lanser & J. Hospers in *New Scientist*, 6th January 1972, p. 7.

77 P. Warlow, *The Reversing Earth*, JM Dent & Sons, 1982.

78 T. Van Flandern, op. cit., p. 251.

79 S. Greenwood, 'Babylonian Venus Observations' in *Ancient Skies* 19:5 (1992).

80 Venus is often referred to as a 'star' on account of its dense atmosphere of carbon dioxide, which reflects solar radiation and causes a very bright visual effect.

81 It should be noted that computer modelling of planetary positions *c.* 11000 BC may not necessarily confirm the alignments discussed in this chapter; the ephemerides for the planets are based on the orbits computed in modern times; these orbits would have been disturbed by the encounter with Nibiru 13,000 years ago; the present planetary relationships are thus not representative of their positioning *immediately prior to* the appearance of Nibiru 13,000 years ago.

82 Z. Sitchin, *The Twelfth Planet*, op. cit., chapter 8, pp. 237–8.

83 According to Z. Sitchin's interpretation of the *Enuma Elish* in *The Twelfth Planet*, op. cit., chapter 7, pp. 206 & 214.
84 Ibid., chapter 8, p. 238.
85 Z. Sitchin, *Genesis Revisited*, op. cit., chapter 2, pp. 36–8.
86 Z. Sitchin, *The Twelfth Planet*, op. cit., chapter 8, pp. 247–8.
87 For a history of the early search, see C. Tombaugh, 'Plates, Pluto and Planet X' in *Sky Telescope* (USA), 81:4 (1991), p. 360–1. The name Planet X was first suggested by Lowell in *Memoir on a Trans-Neptunian Planet*, Mem. Lowell Observatory, 1915.
88 R. Harrington & T. Van Flandern, 'The satellites of Neptune and the origin of Pluto' in *Icarus* 39 (1979), pp. 131–6. See also T. Van flandern, op. cit., pp. 305–14 & 416.
89 T. Van Flandern, op. cit., p. 312.
90 NASA Press Release, Ames Research Centre, 17th June 1982.
91 *Washington Post*, 30th December 1983.
92 R. Harrington in *The Astronomical Journal*, October 1988; see also Notes of the American Astronomical Society meeting, Arlington, Virginia, 16th January 1990.
93 *Newsweek*, 13th July 1987, p. 45.
94 The timing of these moves is significant, but beyond the scope of this book.
95 K. Croswell, 'The Hunt for Planet X' in *New Scientist* (UK) 128: 1748–9 (1990), pp. 34–7.
96 M. Littman, 'Where is Planet X?' in *Sky Telescope* (USA) 78:6 (1989), pp. 596–9.
97 E. Standish Jnr, 'Planet X: No Dynamical Evidence in the Optical Observations' in *The Astronomical Journal* (USA) 105:5 (1993), pp. 2000–6.
98 D. Hughes, 'Some cosmogonical reasons why Planet X does not exist' in *Quarterly Journal of the Royal Astronomical Society* (UK) 34:4 (1993), pp. 461–79.
99 The older data is vitally important because of the length of time taken by Uranus and Neptune to orbit the Sun. T. Van Flandern cites evidence in support of the earlier observations, op. cit., p. 322.
100 T. Van Flandern, op. cit., p. 312.
101 Ibid., p. 322.
102 Planets speed up when they get closer to the sun; Planet X may be at the slowest point in its orbit.
103 It is worth emphasising that the gods did not regard Anu as

a Divine Being; he was listed as the latest in a series of 21
previous rulers who had resided on Nibiru.

104 Z. Sitchin, *The Twelfth Planet*, op. cit.

105 The papyrus is in the Cairo Museum, reference 30646.

106 Z. Sitchin, *The Twelfth Planet*, op. cit., chapter 9, pp. 261–
2.

107 The disc is in the British Museum's Later Mesopotamia
Gallery, exhibit WA K 8538.

108 Z. Sitchin, *The Twelfth Planet*, op. cit., chapter 9, p. 275.

109 Ibid., pp. 266–7.

110 The *McGraw-Hill Encyclopedia of Astronomy*, 1983,
describes gaps in the Asteroid Belt that were probably
created by 'catastrophic collisions'. Also see T. Van
Flandern, op. cit., pp. 186–7.

111 See for example R. Hoagland, *The Monuments of Mars*,
North Atlantic Books, Berkeley, California, 1987.

112 V. Di Pietro, G. Molenaar & J. Brandenburg, *Unusual
Mars Surface Features*, 1982.

113 M. Cremo & R. Thompson, *Forbidden Archaeology: The
Hidden History of the Human Race*, San Diego,
Bhaktivedanta Institute, 1993.

Chapter Eight:
Proofs of Divine Guidance

1 Z. Sitchin, *Genesis Revisited*, op. cit., chapter 5, p. 88.

2 S. Kramer cited in Z. Sitchin, *The Twelfth Planet*, op. cit.,
chapter 10, p. 290.

3 Z. Sitchin, *The Twelfth Planet*, chapter 10, p. 304.

4 Ibid, p. 303. The modern-day locations are as follows:
Shuruppak is Tell Fara, about 64 km south-east of
Diwaniyah; Larak might be Tell el Wilaya, near Kut-el-
Imara; Larsa is Senkereh, 48 km north-west of Nasriyah;
Bad-Tibira is Tell Medain near Telloh; Lagash is al-Hiba;
Sippar is Abu Habba, about 32 km south-west of Baghdad
and 10 km east of Mahmudiya; Eridu is Abu Shahrain 19
km south-west of Ur (el-Mughayir).

5 G. Roux, *Ancient Iraq*, op. cit., chapter 5, p. 66.

6 Ibid., p. 111.

7 *The Epic of Gilgamesh*, Tablet III column iv, Old

Babylonian version. See A. Heidel, *The Gilgamesh Epic and Old Testament Parallels*, op. cit., p. 36.

8 *The Epic of Gilgamesh*, Tablet IV column vi, Assyrian version. See A. Heidel, op. cit., p. 44.

9 Ibid., Tablet V column i, A. Heidel, op. cit., p. 45.

10 Ibid., Tablet V column iv, A. Heidel, op. cit., p. 48.

11 R. Rogers, *The Religion of Babylonia and Assyria*, New York & Cincinnati, 1908, p. 205. Also A. Heidel, op. cit., pp. 256 & 259.

12 *The Middle East*, Hachette, 1966, p. 209.

13 Genesis 9:20.

14 S. Kramer, *Sumerische Literarische aus Nippur*, cited in Z. Sitchin, *The Wars of Gods and Men*, chapter 6, p. 121.

15 M. Chatelain, *Our Ancestors Came from Outer Space*, op. cit., chapter 3, p. 73.

16 Cited in Z. Sitchin, *The Wars of Gods and Men*, chapter 7, p. 143. See also A. Sjoeberg and E. Bergmann, *The Collection of the Sumerian Temple Hymns*.

17 *Ludlul Bel Nemeqi* ('I Praise the Lord of Wisdom'). See W. Lambert, *Babylonian Wisdom Literature*, Oxford, 1960. The Lower World was the lower hemisphere.

18 Cited in Z. Sitchin, *The Wars of Gods and Men*, chapter 7, p. 143.

19 Ibid., pp. 143–5.

20 Ibid., chapter 8.

21 The blinding of Horus is almost certainly the origin of the cults of the 'All-Seeing Eye', which is, for example, shown with a pyramid on the reverse of the American dollar bill. Compare also Samuel I, 11 where Nahash, king of the Ammonites, agrees peace terms subject to boring out the right eye of each of his enemies!

22 *I Sing the Song of the Mother of the Gods*; see P. Dhorme, *La Souveraine des Dieux*.

23 *National Geographic* 178:5 (1990), p. 107.

24 G. Barton, *Miscellaneous Babylonian Texts*, cited in Z. Sitchin, *The Wars of Gods and Men*, op. cit., chapter 8, pp. 163–4.

25 Tablets 10–13 of the *Lugal-e Ud Melam-bi* text; also known as 'The Book of the Feats and Exploits of Ninurta'; see collation edited by S. Geller in *Altorientalische Texte und Untersuchungen*; also in Barton op. cit. Cited in Z. Sitchin, *The Wars of Gods and Men*, chapter 8.

26 Z. Sitchin, *The Wars of Gods and Men*, op. cit., chapter 8, p. 168.

27 Ibid., p. 171.

28 Ibid.

29 Ibid., p. 165.

30 Ibid., chapter 7, p. 145 (from poem to Ninharsag).

31 The modern name of the village where Heliopolis was located is Matariyah.

32 It is claimed that the bearing of a line drawn through the south-east corners of the first and third pyramids at Giza takes one exactly to the site of the obelisk in Heliopolis. New York, London and Rome all possess obelisks which were once at Heliopolis.

33 S. Mercer, *The Religion of Ancient Egypt*, p. 127.

34 For example, in the Hathor Temple relief at Dendera.

35 Z. Sitchin, *The Wars of Gods and Men*, op. cit., chapter 9, p. 182.

36 The detailed detective work is in Z. Sitchin, *The Wars of Gods and Men*, op. cit.

37 The gods divided the Earth's surface into three latitudinal areas – the Way of Anu, the Way of Enlil and the Way of Ea – each comprising 60 degrees; the central band extended from the 30th parallel north to the 30th parallel south.

38 *The Epic of Gilgamesh*, cited in Z. Sitchin, *The Stairway to Heaven*, op. cit., chapter VII, p. 131.

39 A. Heidel, op. cit., p. 65.

40 Z. Sitchin, *The Stairway to Heaven*, op. cit., chapter XI, p. 208.

41 *The Epic of Gilgamesh*, Tablet IX column ii, cited in A. Heidel, op. cit., p. 65.

42 Z. Sitchin, *The Wars of Gods and Men*, chapter 14, p. 338.

43 M. Rice, *Egypt's Making*, Guild Publishing, 1990, pp. 247–54.

44 Z. Sitchin, *The Stairway to Heaven*, op. cit., chapter X, pp. 197–207.

45 *The Epic of Gilgamesh*; see A. Heidel, op. cit., p. 105; also M. Rice, op. cit., p. 247.

46 Ancient texts describe a TIL being used to vanquish the flying god Zu, whilst its pictographic sign resembles a missile; see Z. Sitchin, *The Twelfth Planet*, op. cit., chapter 4, p. 109.

47 S. Kramer, *Enki and Ninhursag: A Paradise Myth* in J.

Pritchard (ed.), *Ancient Near Eastern Texts Relating to the Old Testament*, Princeton NJ, 1950, pp. 37–41.

48 *Aid to Bible Understanding*, Watchtower Publications, 1971 ed., p. 472.

49 Ibid.

50 J. Kinnier Wilson, *The Legend of Etana: A New Edition*, Warminster, 1985. See also G. Roux, op. cit., chapter 7, pp. 114–5.

51 It is for this reason that scholars find Sumerian references to a 'Har Sag' mountain in Sinai.

52 Z. Sitchin, *The Wars of Gods and Men*, op. cit., chapter 7, p. 145.

53 Ibid., chapter 9, p. 179.

54 Z. Sitchin, *The Stairway to Heaven*, op. cit., chapter X, p. 194.

55 This was the final stage in Muhammad's 'night journey' (sura 17 of the Koran), in which he allegedly started at Mecca and stopped en route at Mount Sinai!

56 Z. Sitchin, *The Stairway to Heaven*, op. cit., chapter XIV, p. 292.

57 Ibid., p. 291.

58 *Aid to Bible Understanding*, op. cit., p. 633.

59 Ibid., p. 908.

60 Ibid., p. 909.

61 The 'Most High God' is an unusual Biblical reference to God; it indicates literally the highest position by rank, probably Enlil himself.

62 There is a Jewish legend, recorded in the Targums, that Melchizedek was Shem, the son of Noah, but there is no historical evidence to corroborate this.

63 Hebrews 7:1–2.

64 Book of Jubilees, cited in Z. Sitchin, *The Stairway to Heaven*, op. cit., chapter XIV, pp. 296–7.

65 *Wonders of the Ancient World*, NGS, op. cit., pp. 36–7.

66 *The World's Last Mysteries*, op. cit., p. 152.

67 Genesis 28:19. Beth El was originally called Luz, but was renamed by Jacob after he saw the 'Ladder'.

68 *Encyclopaedia Biblica*, Volume I, col. 552.

69 Z. Sitchin, *The Wars of Gods and Men*, op. cit., chapter 12, p. 277.

70 For example, that undertaken by Thutmosis IV *c.* 1400 BC.

71 M. Rice, op. cit., p. 203.

72 Annual Meeting of Geological Society of America, 1991;

Annual Meeting of the American Association for the Advancement of Science, Chicago 1992. Nearly three hundred geologists endorsed Schoch's conclusions.

73 M. Hoffman, *Egypt Before The Pharaohs*, Michael O'Mara Books, 1991, pp. 86–98.

Chapter Nine:
The Great Pyramid Revisited

1 Z. Sitchin, *The Wars of Gods and Men*, op. cit., chapter 9, p. 177.

2 Limestone is formed over millions of years by coral and other oceanic life forms. It thus contains salt which will migrate to the surface when exposed to moisture. The same process has occurred with the Sphinx – see *National Geographic* 179:4 (1991), p. 38.

3 S. Langdon, *The Death and Resurrection of Bel-Marduk*, 1923. Also H. Zimmern, 1921.

4 Z. Sitchin, *The Wars of Gods and Men*, op. cit.

5 S. Kramer, 'Inanna and Ebih' in *Sumerian Mythology*, New York, 1961.

6 Z. Sitchin, *The Wars of Gods and Men*, op. cit., chapter 10, pp. 221–2.

7 Ibid., p. 223, citing a fragmented text published by the Babylonian Section of the Museum of the University of Pennsylvania.

8 Discussed in G. Hancock, *Fingerprints of the Gods*, op. cit., chapter 37.

9 P. Lemesurier, *The Great Pyramid Decoded*, op. cit., pp. 49–51.

10 Ibid., pp. 86 & 88.

11 Z. Sitchin, *The Wars of Gods and Men*, op. cit., chapter 10, p. 226.

12 A. Rutherford, *Pyramidology* (4 vols), Institute of Pyramidology, 1957 onwards.

13 Z. Sitchin, *The Wars of Gods and Men*, op. cit., chapter 10.

14 *Aid to Bible Understanding*, op. cit., p. 69.

15 *The Independent*, 16th April 1993.

16 B. Hartmann, *The Great Pyramid – the way to the fire within*, Alberta, Canada, 1991.

17 Cited in Z. Sitchin, *The Wars of Gods and Men*, op. cit., chapter 8, p. 164.

18 Ibid.

19 Ibid., chapter 7, p. 143.

20 Ibid., chapter 10, p. 223.

21 Ibid., chapter 8, p. 169.

22 R. Bauval & A. Gilbert, *The Orion Mystery*, William Heinemann, 1994, p. 97, citing J. Greaves, *Pyramidographia*, 1646, p. 73.

23 P. Lemesurier, op. cit., p. 72, notes the existence of a rough 'pilaster' (a shallow rectangular column) at the entrance to the Queen's Chamber, on the western wall. It indicated to him that there had once been some kind of obstruction at this entrance.

24 R. Bauval & A. Gilbert, op. cit., pp. 208–9.

25 A photograph of the kink can be seen in R. Bauval & G. Hancock, *Keepers of Genesis*, William Heinemann, 1996, Plate 16.

26 C. Smyth, *The Great Pyramid*, p. 248.

27 Since three of the Pyramid's 'airshafts' were vandalised (two sealed and one valve removed), there is every likelihood that this shaft too was vandalised, for example by pouring liquid cement down into it. Unfortunately, there are no surveys of the excavated hole, and a casual inspection is simply out of the question.

28 P. Lemesurier, op. cit., p. 121.

29 R. Bauval & A. Gilbert, op. cit.; see also clarification by R. Bauval in *Amateur Astronomy & Space Sciences*, Issue Four (1996), p. 14.

30 R. Bauval reconciles the two dates (10450 BC and 2450 BC) by suggesting that construction was started in 10450 BC and took 8,000 years to complete! (cited in G. Hancock, op. cit., chapter 49).

31 Z. Sitchin, *The Stairway to Heaven*, op. cit., chapter XIII, p. 256.

Chapter Ten:
Nuclear Catastrophe 2024 BC

1 Z. Sitchin, *The Wars of Gods and Men*, op. cit.

2 S. Kramer, 'Lamentation over the destruction of Ur' in J.

Pritchard (ed.), *Ancient Near Eastern Texts Relating to the Old Testament*, Princeton NJ, 2nd ed., 1955, pp. 455–63. S. Kramer, 'Lamentation over the destruction of Sumer and Ur', in ibid., pp. 611–9. Also S. Kramer, 'The weeping goddess: Sumerian prototype of the Mater Dolorosa' in *Biblical Archaeologist*, 1983, pp. 69–80.

3 *The Uruk Lament*, cited in Z. Sitchin, *The Wars of Gods and Men*, op. cit., chapter 14, p. 339.

4 *The Eridu Lament*, cited in Z. Sitchin, *The Wars of Gods and Men*, op. cit., chapter 14, p. 340.

5 T. Jacobsen, 'The Reign of Ibbi-Suen' in *Journal of Cuneiform Studies*, VII, 1953, pp. 36–44.

6 P. Haupt article in *Beitrage zur Assyriologie*, 1918, cited in Z. Sitchin, *The Wars of Gods and Men*, chapter 14, p. 313.

7 Sumerian text K.5001, published in *The Oxford Editions of Cuneiform Texts*, vol. VI., cited in Z. Sitchin, *The Wars of Gods and Men*, chapter 14, p. 330.

8 Z. Sitchin, *The Wars of Gods and Men*, op. cit., chapters 13 & 14.

9 Two extensive translations of the *Erra Epic* have been made: P. Gossman, *Das Erra-Epos*, Wurzburg, 1955; and L. Cagni, *L'epopea di Erra*, Rome 1969.

10 Cited in Z. Sitchin, *The Wars of Gods and Men*, op. cit., chapter 14, p. 326.

11 Ibid.

12 Ibid., p. 327.

13 *Aid to Bible Understanding*, op. cit. Note that ER.RA is a derogatory term meaning 'the servant of Ra', reflecting the bias of the text's authorship in Babylonia.

14 *Erra Epic*, cited in Z. Sitchin, *The Wars of Gods and Men*, op. cit., chapter 14, p. 328.

15 Ibid., p. 327. Compare Genesis 18:23–25.

16 Ibid., p. 329.

17 These are Babylonian texts dealing with the acts of the famous Elamite chieftain, Khedorlaomer.

18 *Khedorlaomer Texts*, cited in Z. Sitchin, *The Wars of Gods and Men*, op. cit., chapter 14, p. 331.

19 *Erra Epic*, cited in ibid., p. 329.

20 *The Epic of Gilgamesh*, Tablet X column iv, Assyrian version. See A. Heidel, *The Gilgamesh Epic and Old Testament Parallels*, op. cit., p. 77.

21 Genesis 14:3. The Valley of Siddim means the 'valley of the fields'.

22 Deuteronomy 3:17. Hebrew meanings from *Aid to Bible Understanding*, op. cit. The name Arabah was later extended to the entire rift valley. A further etymological connection exists to Arabia, but on account of that country's hot climate.

23 Genesis 19:26 (salt), Genesis 14:10 (bitumen), Genesis 13:10 (well-watered).

24 I. Blake, 'Joshua's Curse and Elisha's Miracle' in *The Palestine Exploration Quarterly*, cited by Z. Sitchin.

25 *Accountancy* magazine, December 1995, pp. 34–5. The level of the Dead Sea is steadily falling due to continued over-abstraction from the River Jordan; its surface area has now shrunk by 30 per cent.

26 E. von Daniken, *The Gold of the Gods*, Putnam's, New York, 1973, chapter 5, p. 131.

27 J. Siegel 'Scientists to Probe Dead Sea Bed' in *The Jerusalem Post*, 30.10.93.

28 Z. Sitchin, *The Wars of Gods and Men*, op. cit., chapter 14, especially Figures 105–7.

29 N. Glueck, *Rivers in the Desert*, 1959, pp. 236–8.

30 E. Anati, *The Mountain of God*, Rizzoli, New York, 1986.

31 Sumerian lamentations texts, cited in Z. Sitchin, *The Wars of Gods and Men*, op. cit., chapter 14, pp. 337–9.

32 Ibid.

33 *Babel* is Hebrew for Babylon.

34 Genesis 11:4.

35 Akkadian text, tablet K-3657, translation by G. Smith, *The Chaldean Genesis*, 1876; also retranslation by W. Boscawen in *Transactions of the Society of Biblical Archaeology*, volume V.

36 Ibid., cited in Z. Sitchin, *The Wars of Gods and Men*, op. cit., chapter 9, p. 199.

37 The date 3100 BC is generally accepted for the beginning of Egyptian civilisation under Menes. The previous 350 years of chaos was recorded by Manetho.

38 B. Lewis, *The Sargon Legend*, Cambridge, Mass., 1980.

39 *Wonders of the Ancient World*, NGS, op. cit., p. 52.

40 A. Heidel, op. cit., p. 262: approximately 6 inches of rainfall per year.

41 Z. Sitchin, *When Time Began*, op. cit., pp. 311–4.

42 Z. Sitchin, *The Wars of Gods and Men*, op. cit., chapter 12, p. 253.

43 Naram-Sin literally means 'Beloved of Sin', per G. Roux, *Ancient Iraq*, op. cit., chapter 9, p. 156.

44 J. Hawkes (ed.), *Atlas of Ancient Archaeology*, op. cit., p. 198.

45 M. Rice, *Egypt's Making*, op. cit., p. 226; also R. Bauval & A. Gilbert, *The Orion Mystery*, op. cit., pp. 214–5.

46 The 6.5-feet high stele supposedly depicts Naram-Sin's victory over the Lullubu, a people of the Zagros Mountains. There is no known mountain with such a profile.

47 *The Curse of Agade*, cited in Z. Sitchin, *The Wars of Gods and Men*, op. cit., chapter 12, p. 259; see also J. Cooper, *The Curse of Agade*, Baltimore/London, 1983.

48 Z. Sitchin, *The Wars of Gods and Men*, op. cit., chapter 12, pp. 258–9.

49 J. Cooper, *The Curse of Agade*, op. cit., cited in Roux, op. cit., chapter 9, pp. 158–9.

50 *Hymn to Enlil*, in J. Pritchard (ed.), *Ancient Near Eastern Texts Relating to the Old Testament*, op. cit.

51 For a list of possible locations of Agade, see *Repertoire Geographique des Textes Cuneiformes*, I, p. 9 and II, p. 6, Wiesbaden.

52 G. Roux, op. cit., chapter 9, p. 158.

53 Suggested reading on the Guti: C. Gadd, *Cambridge Ancient History* (Revised Edition), Cambridge, I, 2, pp. 457–63.

54 G. Roux, op. cit., chapter 9, pp. 157–8.

55 Ibid., chapter 10, p. 166.

56 Ibid., chapter 5, p. 68 and chapter 10, pp. 161–5.

57 Z. Sitchin, *The Wars of Gods and Men*, op. cit., chapter 12, p. 276.

58 S. Kramer, 'The death of Ur-Nammu and his descent to the Netherworld' in *Journal of Cuneiform Studies* XXI (1967), pp. 104–22.

59 G. Roux, op. cit., chapter 10, p. 168.

60 Ibid., p. 169.

61 Ibid.

62 Z. Sitchin, *The Wars of Gods and Men*, op. cit., chapter 14, pp. 321–2.

63 J. Hawkes, op. cit., p. 141.

64 Amar-Sin literally means 'bull-calf of the god Sin', per G. Roux, op. cit., chapter 10, p. 170.

65 Z. Sitchin, *The Wars of Gods and Men*, op. cit., chapter 12, p. 280.

66 Genesis 14. In the Biblical account, the king of Shinar (Sumer) is 'Amraphel'. Z. Sitchin has identified him as Amar-Sin and thus dated the rebellion to his reign 2046–2038 BC; see *The Wars of Gods and Men*, op. cit., chapter 13, pp. 281–303.

67 *Khedorlaomer Texts*, cited in Z. Sitchin, *The Wars of Gods and Men*, op. cit., chapter 13, pp. 306–7.

68 *Aid to Bible Understanding*, op. cit.

69 Genesis 14:5–7.

70 A detailed study of this issue appears in H. Trumbull, *Kadesh-Barnea* (late 19th century). Trumbull was mystified as to why a military expedition was launched towards a remote Sinai oasis town.

71 Z. Sitchin, *The Wars of Gods and Men*, op. cit., chapter 13, p. 308. Sitchin believes there was actually a battle at the space centre, in which the patriarch Abraham successfully defended it from attack.

72 Genesis 14:8–12.

73 G. Roux, op. cit., chapter 10, p. 175. Shu-Sin literally means 'the one of the god Sin'.

74 Ibid., p. 176. Ibbi-Sin literally means 'the god Sin has called'.

75 Ibid., p. 175.

76 Ibid., pp. 176–7. See also T. Jacobsen, 'The Reign of Ibbi-Suen' in *Journal of Cuneiform Studies* VII (1953), pp. 36–44.

77 P. Michalowski, 'Foreign tribute to Sumer during the Ur III period' in *Zeitschrift fur Assyriologie* LXVIII (1978), pp. 34–49.

78 G. Roux, op. cit., chapter 10, p. 177.

79 *Aid to Bible Understanding*, op. cit., and Genesis 10, especially 10:15–16. Suggested reading on Amorites: A. Haldar, *Who were the Amorites?*, Leiden, 1971.

80 The Elamites were from the line of Shem – see Genesis 10:22.

81 Although under David Rohl's 'new chronology' of Egypt, the FIP was *c.* 1830 BC.

82 J. Hawkes, op. cit., p. 146.

83 Cited in Z. Sitchin, *The Wars of Gods and Men*, op. cit., chapter 13, p. 298 & chapter 14, p. 322; also Z. Sitchin, *When Time Began*, op. cit., chapter 12, p. 339.

84 Genesis 18:21.

85 *The Middle East*, Hachette, op. cit., p.573.

86 A. Jeremias, *Das Alte testament im Lichte des Alten Orients*; also Z. Sitchin, *The Wars of Gods and Men*, op. cit.

87 Abram's name was changed to Abraham ('Father of a Multitude of Nations') through the covenant and circumcision in Genesis 17.

88 The term *Ibri* is used for example in Genesis 14:13.

89 Z. Sitchin, *The Wars of Gods and Men*, op. cit., chapter 13, pp. 294-5.

90 Ibid., p. 295.

91 Ibid., p. 296; the name of Abraham's father Terah carried the Sumerian meaning 'Pronouncer of Oracles'.

92 Genesis 12-14.

93 Harran was the mirror image of Ur and Sin was the god of both cities. Harran may have been named after Abraham's brother Haran (Genesis 11). Curiously, *haran* means 'mountaineer' per *Aid to Bible Understanding*, op. cit.

94 Genesis 12:4.

95 Genesis 12:6-7.

96 Genesis 12:9-10.

97 Genesis 13:3-4.

98 Genesis 21:5.

99 Z. Sitchin, *The Wars of Gods and Men*, op. cit., chapter 13, pp. 301 & 307-8.

100 Genesis 18:20-21.

101 Genesis 19:30-32.

102 Genesis 14.

103 *The Middle East*, Hachette, op. cit., p. 560.

104 Ibid., p. 558.

105 C. Walker, *Wonders of the Ancient World*, op. cit., p. 48.

106 I. Browning, *Petra*, 3rd ed., Jordan/Chatto & Windus, 1989.

107 S. Jones, *The Language of the Genes*, op. cit., chapter 9, p. 176.

Chapter Eleven: The Star-Clock

1 J. Sellers, *The Death of Gods in Ancient Egypt*, Penguin, London, 1992, p. 193.

2 Cited in M. Rice, *Egypt's Making*, op. cit., p. 274.

3 C. Jung, *Letters*, Volume 2, p. 225.

4 The age of Taurus is possibly the origin of the 'Apis' bull cult.

5 Exhibit WA 122200 in the British Museum.

6 A. Jeremias, *The Old Testament in the Light of the Ancient Near East*, 1911. See Z. Sitchin, *When Time Began*, op. cit., chapter 7, p. 187.

7 In the Berlin Vorderasiatisches Museum, exhibit VAT. 7847.

8 Cited in Z. Sitchin, *The Twelfth Planet*, op. cit., chapter 14, p. 409.

9 Ibid., citing tablet from Ashur, translated by E. Ebeling, *Tod und Leben*.

10 It has been suggested by Z. Sitchin that the signs of the zodiac were used before the Flood. If so (and the evidence presented is tenuous), the Earth's wobble would have been substantially different from that of today.

11 Z. Sitchin, *The Wars of Gods and Men*, op. cit., chapter 9.

12 Ibid., p. 192.

13 Ibid., chapter 8, p. 165.

14 Z. Sitchin, *The Twelfth Planet*, op. cit., chapter 6, p. 189.

15 Z. Sitchin, *The Wars of Gods and Men*, op. cit., chapter 5.

16 Z. Sitchin, *The Twelfth Planet*, op. cit., chapter 6, p. 189.

17 Ibid., and *The Wars of Gods and Men*, chapter 6, p. 127.

18 Z. Sitchin, *The Twelfth Planet*, op. cit., chapter 6, p. 189.

19 A. Heidel, *The Gilgamesh Epic and Old Testament Parallels*, op. cit., p. 172; and Z. Sitchin, *The Twelfth Planet*, op. cit., chapter 11, pp. 322–3.

20 J. Diamond, *The Rise and Fall of the Third Chimpanzee*, op. cit., chapter 1, p. 23 and chapter 19, pp. 322 & 334.

21 Z. Sitchin, *The Wars of Gods and Men*, op. cit., chapter 14, p. 325.

22 Z. Sitchin, *The Twelfth Planet*, op. cit., chapter 6, p. 189.

23 *The Epic of Gilgamesh*, Tablet IX column ii, Assyrian version. See A. Heidel, op. cit., p. 65. The Sumerian king Amar-Sin was killed by a scorpion sting in Sinai – see Z. Sitchin, *The Wars of Gods and Men*, op. cit., chapter 12, p. 280.

24 Cited in Z. Sitchin, *When Time Began*, op. cit., chapter 11, pp. 315–6.

25 Ibid., chapter 1, pp.23–4.

26 J. Sellers, op. cit., p. 205.

27 I also suspect that an angle of 33 degrees might have been used when a temporary beacon was set up to work alongside the new beacon at Heliopolis *c*. 8700 BC.

28 R. Cleal, K. Walker & R. Montague, *Stonehenge in its Landscape*, op. cit. and http://www.eng-h.gov/uk/stoneh.

29 Book of the Dead, also known as the Papyrus of Ani, cited in Z. Sitchin, *When Time Began*, op. cit., chapter 11, p. 308.

30 Z. Sitchin, *When Time Began*, op. cit., chapter 11, pp. 308–9.

31 Studies have shown that the earliest Egyptian calendar was based on the Moon, with 12 months averaging 29.5 days plus a thirteenth intercalary month.

32 Z. Sitchin, *When Time Began*, op. cit., chapter 11, p. 207.

33 The Aubrey hole theory was first suggested by G. Hawkins.

34 The 56 Aubrey holes were marked off in sections as follows: 10–7–22–7–10; the first ten holes acted as a decimal counter from 1 to 10; the next 36 holes enabled the recording of units of ten up to a value of 360; and the final ten holes enabled the recording of units of 360 up to a value of 3,600; this was a multi-purpose counting mechanism for any unit of measure – solar years or lunar years.

35 See discussion in Z. Sitchin, *When Time Began*, op. cit., chapters 8 & 11.

36 *Daily Mail*, 28th June 1996.

37 J. Reinhard, *Machu Picchu The Sacred Centre*, op. cit., pp. 33 & 49.

38 Ibid., pp. 13–20 & 76.

39 Ibid., p. 33.

40 Ibid., pp. 34 & 51.

41 Ibid., pp. 49 & 53.

42 Ibid., pp. 21–5; also see P. Frost, *Exploring Cuzco*, op. cit., pp. 76–8.

43 J. Reinhard, *Machu Picchu The Sacred Centre*, op. cit., pp. 20 & 22.

44 Ibid., p. 20.

45 Ibid., pp. 20–1.

46 Ibid., p. 30.

47 Ibid., pp. 45–6.

48 Z. Sitchin, *When Time Began*, op. cit. chapter 11, pp. 308–9.

49 F. Montesinos, *Memorias Antiguas del Peru*. English edition by P. Means (ed.), Hakluyt Society, London, 1920. Cited in Z. Sitchin, *The Lost Realms*, op. cit., chapter 7, p. 138.

50 Book of the Dead, cited in Z. Sitchin, *When Time Began*, chapter 11, p. 308.

51 A. Tomas, 'Cosmic Tradition in the Cultures of Asia' in *Ancient Skies* 18:3 (1991). Other authorities cite a date of 2852 BC, see A.Christie, *Chinese Mythology*, Chancellor Press, 1996, p. 15.

52 C. Thubron, *Behind The Wall*, Penguin, 1988, chapter 2, p. 55; also D. Maitland, *The Insider's Guide to China*, Merehurst Press, 1987, pp. 153–4.

53 D. Maitland, ibid.

54 Ningishzidda means literally 'Lord of the Artefact of Life'; for a discussion of his identity as Thoth, see Z. Sitchin, *The Wars of Gods and Men*, op. cit., chapter 9, and *When Time Began*, op. cit., chapter 6.

55 See G. Roux, op. cit., pp. 165–8.

56 Z. Sitchin, *When Time Began*, op. cit., chapter 6, pp. 140–58 & 164–6.

57 The name of the mountain which dominates Machu Picchu is Salcantay, derived from the Quechua word *salqa* meaning 'wild/uncivilised'. The god of this mountain was a god of wrath and a god of storms. These clues suggest that Ishkur was the god of Machu Picchu.

58 Z. Sitchin, *When Time Began*, op. cit., chapter 7, pp. 196–7.

59 M. Rice, op. cit., pp. 261–2 and photographs.

60 *Mankind's Search for God*, Watchtower Publications, p. 58.

61 Genesis 6:3.

62 A. Heidel, op. cit., p. 230.

63 Z. Sitchin, *The Twelfth Planet*, op. cit., chapter 8, p. 252.

64 Ibid., pp. 251–2.

65 This tale is probably the source of the saying '40 days and 40 nights', meaning a very long time.

66 *When the gods like men bore the work*, cited in Z. Sitchin, *The Twelfth Planet*, op. cit., chapter 12, p. 340; and background in chapter 11.

67 See W. Lambert & A. Millard, *Atra-Hasis; The Babylonian Story of the Flood*, 1970.

68 Z. Sitchin, *The Twelfth Planet*, op. cit., chapter 12, p. 340.

69 Z. Sitchin, *Divine Encounters*, op. cit., chapter 2.

70 F. Ruehl, 'What was the secret of Methuselah's Longevity?' in *Ancient Skies* 17:3 (1990).

71 D. Fasold, *The Ark of Noah*, Wynwood, New York, 1988, p. 61.

72 The fishes cited in evidence by Z. Sitchin are more likely to represent a splash-down landing by the gods in the ocean (compare Apollo space missions).

73 J. Desmond Clark, 'African and Asian Perspectives on the Origins of Modern Humans' in Aitken, Stringer & Mellars, *The Origin of Modern Humans and the Impact of Chronometric Dating*, op cit.

74 M. Aitken, C. Stringer & P. Mellars, op. cit.

75 R. Cann, M. Stoneking & A. Wilson, 'Mitochondrial DNA and Human Evolution' in *Nature* 325 (1987), pp. 31–6.

76 Alas, mtDNA can tell us nothing about the male line; however, research is in its early stages to date a common male ancestor using y-chromosomes as a genetic marker.

77 M. Stoneking, S. Sherry, A. Redd & L. Vigilant, 'New Approaches to Dating Suggest a Recent Age for the Human mtDNA Ancestor' in Aitken, Stringer & Mellars, op. cit.

78 R. Dawkins, *River Out of Eden*, op. cit., p. 52.

79 Z. Sitchin, *The Twelfth Planet*, op. cit., chapter 11, p. 334.

Chapter Twelve:
Adam's Designer Genes

1 Genesis 5:2.

2 Genesis 2:8.

3 *Atra-Hasis*, cited in A. Heidel, *The Gilgamesh Epic and Old Testament Parallels*, op. cit., p. 115. Due to a break in the tablets, it is sometimes thought, incorrectly, that this act of creation followed the Flood (Heidel p. 259).

4 S. Kramer, *The Myth of the Pickaxe*. Composite citation from Z. Sitchin, *The Wars of Gods and Men*, op. cit., chapter 5, p. 105, and Z. Sitchin, *The Twelfth Planet*, op. cit., chapter 12, p. 360. AL.ANI literally means 'axe that produces power'.

5 Z. Sitchin, *The Twelfth Planet*, op. cit., chapter 12, pp. 349–50.

6 W. Davis, *The Serpent and the Rainbow*, Collins, London, 1986, p. 177.

7 *Wonders of the Ancient World*, NGS, op. cit., pp. 240–1.

8 The Yezidis occupy the mountain region of Jebel Sinjar to the north and east of Mosul. See *The Middle East*, Hachette, op. cit., pp. 705 & 717.

9 *Wonders of the Ancient World*, NGS, op. cit., p. 214.

10 C. Singer & E. Ashworth Underwood, *A Short History of Medicine*, 2nd ed., Oxford at the Clarendon Press, 1962, p. 25.

11 Regarding the origin of the symbol, see Schouten: *The rod and serpent of Asklepios*.

12 *Splendors of The Past*, NGS, op. cit., pp. 148, 151, 166. Also *National Geographic*, 178.5 (1990), p. 98.

13 Genesis 3:14–15.

14 D. Morris, *The Naked Ape*, op. cit., chapter 8, p. 204.

15 S. Kramer, 'Enki and the World Order' in *Sumerian Mythology*, op. cit., pp. 59–62. Cited in Z. Sitchin, *The Twelfth Planet*, op. cit., chapter 10, p. 291.

16 The watery marshes of Eridu may be a clue to the origin of Enki's nickname E.A., 'He Whose Home Is Water'.

17 Z. Sitchin, *The Twelfth Planet*, op. cit., chapter 13, p. 371.

18 *Art and History of Egypt*, Bonechi, 1994, p. 5.

19 R. Bauval & A. Gilbert, *The Orion Mystery*, op. cit., p. 10.

20 *Accountancy* magazine, December 1995.

21 Herodotus, II, 5.

22 Readers are reminded that this division of lands took place after the Flood; Enki, and later Marduk, did rebuild their original cities in Mesopotamia, but this does not detract from the fact that Africa was their only *exclusive* land.

23 *The Epic of Gilgamesh*, Old Babylonian version, Tablet III column iv, lines 6–8, translation by E. Speiser in J. Pritchard (ed.), *Ancient Near Eastern Texts Relating to the Old Testament*, op. cit., p. 79.

24 A. Heidel, op. cit., p. 143.

25 It is sometimes argued, from a strict reading of the Bible, that Genesis 1:28 implies the pre-existence of sexual knowledge; however, a recognition of the Bible's imperfect origins suggests that the passage in Genesis 1:28 has been copied from its proper place in Genesis 9:1, where almost identical wording appears immediately after the Flood. Also, note that the term 'knowing' used in the Garden of Eden is consistently used elsewhere in the Bible with the connotation of sexual intercourse.

26 Z. Sitchin, *The Stairway to Heaven*, op. cit., chapter VIII, p. 160.

27 S. Jones, *The Language of the Genes*, op. cit., chapter 4, p. 93.

28 *Daily Mail*, 29th January 1996.

29 S. Jones, op. cit., chapter 4, p. 87; D. Dennett, *Darwin's*

Dangerous Idea, op. cit., p. 194; M. Eigen, *Steps Towards Life*, Oxford University Press, 1992, p. 36.

30 S. Jones op. cit., chapter 4, p. 87.

31 Ibid., p. 93.

32 Ibid., p. 91. Some examples are cited in J. Diamond. *The Rise and Fall of the Third Chimpanzee*, op. cit., chapter 7, p. 109.

33 S. Jones, op. cit., chapter 4, p. 87.

34 Ibid., pp. 91 & 93.

35 *National Geographic*, 187.6 (1995), pp. 2–41.

36 S. Jones, op. cit., chapter 4, p. 94.

37 Human cells placed in culture will stop dividing after about a hundred years; cell deaths follow within another twenty years.

38 *The Sunday Times*, 10th December 1995; *Nature*, December 1995.

39 *Daily Mail*, 29th January 1996.

40 For example, how will the body's immune system react to the insertion of foreign genes?

41 *The Sunday Times* 22nd October 1995; also S. Jones, op. cit., chapter 15, pp. 291–8.

42 *Daily Mail*, 29th January 1996.

43 S. Kramer, *Enki and Ninhursag*, op. cit. It would seem that 'in vitro' fertilisation was against the rules!

44 Since we were created in their image we should not underestimate our ability to predict their behaviour! Textual evidence indeed indicates that the higher gods did not treat the rank-and-file gods with much more respect than was reserved for man.

45 Z. Sitchin, *The Wars of Gods and Men*, op. cit., chapter 6, p. 127.

46 Genesis 20:12.

47 A. Heidel, op. cit., pp. 164–5.

48 *The Epic of Gilgamesh*, Tablet XI, Assyrian version. See A. Heidel, op. cit., p. 91.

49 G. Roux, *Ancient Iraq*, op. cit., chapter 7, pp. 105–7.

50 Genesis 3:1–5.

51 Most English dictionaries still retain this archaic definition of 'knowing'.

52 Z. Sitchin, *The Twelfth Planet*, op. cit., chapter 13, p. 370.

53 S. Jones, op. cit., chapter 6, p. 128.

54 Z. Sitchin, *The Twelfth Planet*, op. cit., chapter 12, pp. 336–7.

55 Ibid., p. 349.
56 Z. Sitchin, *The Wars of Gods and Men*, op. cit., chapter 5.
57 Genesis 3:8.
58 Genesis 3:24.
59 Z. Sitchin, *The Wars of Gods and Men*, op. cit., chapter 5, pp. 107–8.
60 Genesis 4:1.
61 Note that, in Egypt, Ninharsag was known as Hathor. The Temple of Hathor at Dendera was the place where 'birth mysteries' were celebrated in ancient times.
62 Z. Sitchin, *Divine Encounters*, op. cit., chapter 1, p. 18.

Chapter Thirteen: A New Chronology

1 M. Coe, *The Maya*, Thames and Hudson, London, 1991, pp. 108–9.
2 This Masoretic chronology differs from the Septuagint, which allowed 2,242 years from Adam to the Flood. The Masoretic chronology is widely preferred. *M'Clintock and Strong's Cyclopaedia*, Vol. II, p. 299 states: 'There is every reason to think that the Rabbins have been scrupulous in the extreme in making alterations; the Septuagint, on the other hand, shows signs of a carelessness that would almost permit change'. Furthermore, *The Critical Doctrinal and Homiletical Commentary* by Schaff-Lange comments: 'The Hebrew has the best claim to be regarded as the original text, from the well-known scrupulous, and even superstitious, care with which it has been textually preserved'.
3 Genesis 4:25–26.
4 *Aid to Bible Understanding*, op. cit., p. 971; also see Leviticus 25.
5 The Hebrew term used for fatherhood in Genesis 11:10–25 literally means 'became the ancestor of'.
6 *Aid to Bible Understanding*, op. cit., p. 279.
7 Ibid., pp. 1233 & 1255.
8 Use Table C right hand column, starting from a Flood date of 10983 BC.
9 Book of Jubilees, cited in Sitchin, *The Stairway to Heaven*, op. cit., chapter VI, p. 109.

10 Genesis 6:2 and 6:4 respectively.
11 Book of Enoch, cited in Sitchin, *The Stairway to Heaven*, op. cit., chapter VI, p. 110.
12 Ibid.
13 *Atra-Hasis*, Fragment No. IV column iii. Cited in A. Heidel, *The Gilgamesh Epic and Old Testament Parallels*, op. cit., p. 113.
14 Genesis 6:5.
15 *Atra-Hasis*, Fragment No. IV column iii. Cited in A. Heidel, op. cit., p. 114.
16 Ibid., p. 112.
17 A. Heidel, op. cit., pp. 231–2.
18 Particularly finer blades and weapons; see *National Geographic* 189:1 (1996) p. 30.
19 Ibid.
20 S. Jones, *The Language of the Genes*, op. cit., pp. 70, 82, 83.
21 J. Diamond, *The Rise and Fall of the Third Chimpanzee*, op. cit., chapter 6, p. 96.
22 The Koran, Sura Houd 50, cited in D. Fasold, *The Ark of Noah*, op. cit., p. 80.
23 A. Heidel, op. cit., p. 237.
24 Ibid., pp. 110 & 238–9.
25 J. Diamond, op. cit., chapter 6, pp. 97–105.
26 One religious view is that the Flood came from a watery canopy in the upper atmosphere, and that prior to the Flood, this canopy had protected us from harmful radiation.
27 The Bible is unfortunately not interested in the life spans of Ham and Japheth which go unrecorded.
28 *The Epic of Gilgamesh*, Tablet XI, Assyrian version, cited in Heidel, op. cit., pp. 80–1.
29 Z. Sitchin, *The Twelfth Planet*, op. cit., chapter 10, p. 290; and Z. Sitchin, *The Wars of Gods and Men*, op. cit., chapter 7, p. 131. Note also the reference to SUD in the name ZI.U.SUD.RA given to Noah in one Flood legend.
30 It has been suggested that Noah carried a gene for albinism; this cannot have been so, otherwise albinos would not be as rare today as they are.
31 Cited in Z. Sitchin, *The Twelfth Planet*, op. cit., chapter 13, pp. 385–6.
32 *Atra Hasis*, cited by G. Roux, *Ancient Iraq*, op. cit., chapter 7, p. 113. See also A. Kilmer, 'The Mesopotamian concept

of overpopulation and its solution reflected in mythology' in *Orientalia* XLI (1972), pp. 160–77.

33 Genesis 3:16. The preceding passage in Genesis 3:15 appears as a complete non-sequitur and makes little sense: 'he will crush your head and you will strike his heel'. It seems to me that this is an encrypted repeat of 3:16, indicating first the increased childbearing difficulties and secondly the domination of man over woman. Both passages belong after the Flood, not in Eden. Genesis 3:14 also appears as a non-sequitur and properly belongs with Genesis 2:19–20.

34 Genesis 5:32.

35 Genesis 11:10.

36 Cited in Fasold, op. cit., pp. 38–9. Fasold calls this sleight of hand 'the Shem shuffle'!

37 Genesis 25:8.

38 Genesis 11:26.

39 A. Polyhistor, cited in Z. Sitchin, *The Twelfth Planet*, op. cit., chapter 8, p. 248.

40 T. Jacobsen, *The Sumerian King List*, Chicago 1939. Cited in E. von Daniken, *Signs of the Gods*, op. cit., pp. 201–2; see also G. Roux, op. cit., chapter 7, pp. 108–9.

41 Z. Sitchin, *The Twelfth Planet*, op. cit., chapter 8, p. 250, first paragraph.

42 Ibid., chapter 10, p. 295.

43 References to Manetho's work were made by Sextus Africanus and Eusebius of Caesarea, 3rd–4th century AD.

44 Z. Sitchin, *The Lost Realms*, op. cit., chapter 4, p. 76.

Chapter Fourteen: The Toil of Gods and Men

1 Genesis 2:5.

2 *Splendors of the Past*, NGS, op. cit., p. 56.

3 Genesis 10:8–12; Calah is thought to be the city later named Nimrud; the location of Calneh is uncertain, and it may simply mean 'all of them'.

4 *Aid to Bible Understanding*, Watchtower Publications, op. cit. Also, the African lands are associated with Ham in Genesis 10.

5 *International Standard Bible Encyclopaedia*, vol IV, 1939

ed., p. 2147, cited in *Aid to Bible Understanding*, op. cit., p. 179.

6 *M'Clintock and Strong, Cyclopaedia*, Vol. VII, p. 109, cited in *Aid to Bible Understanding*, op. cit., p. 1227.

7 For example, *liph-neh* in used in Numbers 16:2 and Chronicles I, 14:8; the historian Josephus also supports this understanding in *Antiquities of the Jews*, as do the Jewish Targums themselves.

8 A. Hislop, *The Two Babylons*; indeed the very name Nimrod is thought to have taken on the meaning 'let us rebel'.

9 This should not be a particularly shocking conclusion; slavery was common practice thousands of years ago; for example, the Israelites were forced to build Pithom and Rameses for Pharaoh (Exodus 1:11) and Solomon later enslaved the Canaanite tribes (Kings I, 9:20–21).

10 Archaeologists have dated an impressive temple to Ishtar at Nineveh *c*. 2300 BC.

11 The name Olmec means 'Rubber People' and comes from the rubber trees in the Gulf Coast area.

12 Another six heads can be seen at the Museo de Arqueologia at Xalapa.

13 N. Davis, *The Ancient Kingdoms of Mexico*, Penguin Books, London 1990, p. 55; S. Fiedel, *The Prehistory of the Americas*, Cambridge University Press, 1992, pp. 267–8.

14 *National Geographic*, 184:5 (1993).

15 M. Coe, *Breaking the Maya Code*, Thames & Hudson, London, 1992, p. 61.

16 J & O. Tickell, *Tikal, City of the Maya*, op. cit., p. 16.

17 I am not the first to make that comparison. See J. Soustelle, *The Olmecs*.

18 W. Krickeberg, *Altamerikanische Kulturen*, Berlin 1975, translation in E. von Daniken, *The Gods and Their Grand Design*, Putnam's, New York, 1984, p. 57.

19 *The World's Last Mysteries*, Reader's Digest, op. cit., p. 259.

20 The Zapotecs are named after an Olmec city, Tres Zapotes; it is also believed that the main Zapotec city of Monte Alban may have been taken over from an earlier Olmec settlement.

21 Were the Olmecs miners? It is not at all clear what they might have been mining, but the Olmec presence has never been subject to a study from this perspective. It is possible

that they were a retired mining community who had moved to the Gulf Coast from activities elsewhere.

22   I am not the first to suggest an African connection to ancient Mesoamerica; in addition to the ideas of popular writers, similar conclusions have been reached by academic studies, e.g. A. von Wuthenau, *Unexpected Faces in Ancient America*; and L. Wiener, *Africa and the Discovery of America*, 1920; sadly, all scholarly contributions to this subject have been overlooked by the establishment.

23   *National Geographic* 188:6 (1995), p. 14.

24   Notably at Tikal and Copan 4th-5th centuries AD; one building in Tikal is half-jokingly called the 'Teotihuacan Embassy'.

25   *National Geographic* 188:6 (1995), p. 35.

26   The Toltec city of Tula is partly modelled on Teotihuacan and its development parallels the same era in which Teotihuacan was gradually collapsing.

27   *National Geographic* 188:6 (1995) p. 7.

28   Z. Sitchin, *The Lost Realms*, op. cit., chapter 3, p. 45.

29   *National Geographic* 188:6 (1995) p. 11–2.

30   H. Harleston Jnr, *A Mathematical Analysis of Teotihuacan*, XLI International Congress of Americanists, 3rd October 1974.

31   *National Geographic* 188:6 (1995), pp. 18, 22, 24.

32   *National Geographic* 188:6 (1995), p. 25.

33   *Encyclopaedia Britannica*, 8:90.

34   Z. Sitchin, *The Lost Realms*, op. cit., chapter 7, pp. 151–4.

35   Joshua 10:12–13.

36   Z. Sitchin, *The Lost Realms*, op. cit., chapter 7, p. 153.

37   *Wonders of the Ancient World*, NGS, op cit., p. 262, based on a radiocarbon dating at Cuello.

38   *National Geographic* 188:6 (1995), p. 20.

39   *Wonders of the Ancient World*, NGS, op. cit., p. 259.

40   Joshua 10:14.

41   J. de Mesa and T. Gisbert, *Akapana, la Piramide de Tiwanacu*; they noted that the ground plans of Akapana and the Teotihuacan pyramid were square with a protruding access-way and similar base measurements.

42   There is also evidence of gold production, but possibly for ceremonial purposes only.

43   A. Kolata, *The Tiwanaku*, op. cit., pp. 108–11.

44   Z. Sitchin, *The Lost Realms*, op. cit., chapter 11, p. 236.

45   A. Kolata, op. cit., pp. 238–40. The Uru's name for

themselves is *Kot'suns*, 'people of the lake'. See also *National Geographic*, February 1971.

46 This assumption is made based on Posnansky's conclusion that a gold phase preceded bronze at Tiwanaku, and Sitchin's conclusion that the gold phase coincided with the *Kalasasaya c.* 4050 BC, in preparation for a visit from Anu/Nibiru *c.* 3800 BC.

47 Research by Carnegie Institute, Washington DC; cited in C. Hapgood, *Maps of the Ancient Sea Kings*, op. cit., p. 98.

48 The term *barbaros* is used by Paul in Corinthians I, 14:11, where it is translated as 'foreigner'.

49 Z. Sitchin, *The Lost Realms*, op. cit., chapter 11, pp. 243–4.

50 G. Roux, *Ancient Iraq*, op. cit., chapter 15, p. 246.

51 *The Middle East*, Hachette, op cit., p. 841.

52 *The New Funk & Wagnalls Encyclopaedia*, Vol. XII, 1950–1, pp. 4199–4200; also see *The International Standard Bible Encyclopaedia*, Vol. II, p. 918.

53 *Journal of Near Eastern Studies*, Vol. XVIII No 1 (1959), pp. 49–53.

54 G. Roux, op. cit., chapter 14, p. 225 and chapter 15, p. 247.

55 R. Charroux, 'The Candelabra of the Andes' in *Ancient Skies* 5:1 (1978).

56 This Storm God was known to the Greeks as Zeus Heliopolitanus.

57 Macrobius, *Saturnalia* 1.23.10–12, cited in Jidejian, *Baalbek Heliopolis*, op. cit., p. 17.

58 Ramman comes from the Hebrew word *raam*, meaning to rage, to roar, to thunder.

59 The Raymondi Stele is in the Museo Nacional de Arqueologia Antropologia, Lima; it is thought to have originally been located in the sunken plaza at Chavin de Huantar.

60 The Paracas trident has no known alignments to anything important.

61 G. Hancock, *Fingerprints of the Gods*, op. cit., chapter 4, p. 38.

62 Ibid., p. 41.

63 G. Lang, 'More on Easter Island' in *Ancient Skies* 14:4 (1987).

64 G. Phillips, *Ancient Skies* 17:6 (1991). The best examples of Easter Island masonry can be seen at Ahu Tahira, Vinapu on the south-west coast of the island.

65 F. Montesinos, *Memorias Antiguas del Peru*, op. cit.; cited in Z. Sitchin, *The Lost Realms*, op. cit., chapter 9, pp. 191–2.

66 Z. Sitchin, *The Lost Realms*, op. cit., chapter 9, pp. 177–9.

67 *National Geographic* 184:5 (1993).

68 Ibid.

69 The original saying is 'plurality is not to be assumed without necessity' – from William of Occam, an English philosopher *c.* 1300–1349.

70 Samuel I, 17:4.

71 Chronicles I, 20:5.

72 Chronicles I, 20.

73 Joshua 9:10, 12:4.

74 Deuteronomy 3:11.

75 Joshua 9:10.

76 Joshua 12:4, 13:12.

77 Deuteronomy 3:11.

78 Samuel II, 21:16, Chronicles I, 20.

79 A. Heidel, *The Gilgamesh Epic and Old Testament Parallels*, op. cit., p. 195; also *Aid to Bible Understanding*, op. cit.

80 *Wonders of the Ancient World*, NGS, op. cit., p. 259.

81 *The World's Last Mysteries*, op. cit., pp. 258–9.

82 Numbers 13:22.

83 *Aid to Bible Understanding*, op. cit., p. 105.

84 Numbers 13:33.

85 In addition to the legend cited earlier, a Mochica legend states that giants landed on the coast and raped the native women; cited in Z. Sitchin, *The Lost Realms*, op. cit., chapter 9, p. 193.

86 It is curious that hardly any tombs or skeletons have been found despite the long occupations at Tiwanaku, Easter Island and in the Olmec regions of Mesoamerica.

87 Cited in *Ancient Skies* 7:6 (1981).

88 A. Posnansky, *Tiahuanacu: The Cradle of American Man*, op. cit., Vol I, p. 39.

89 Z. Sitchin, *The Twelfth Planet*, op. cit., chapter 11, p. 319.

90 Ibid.

91 Z. Sitchin, *The Wars of Gods and Men*, op. cit., chapter 5, pp. 102–6.

92 Ibid., chapter 4, p. 85.

93 Ibid., chapter 5, pp. 107–8.

94 E. Wallis-Budge, *The Gods of the Egyptians*; also Z. Sitchin, *The Lost Realms*, op. cit., chapter 12, p. 271.

95 The English word 'abyss' traces back to ABZU via the Akkadian *apsu* and the Greek *abyssos*.

96 Z. Sitchin, *The Twelfth Planet*, op. cit., chapter 11, p. 318.

97 R. Shepherd, *Prehistoric Mining and Allied Industries*, Academic Press, 1980.

98 One such case, in Swaziland, has been dated to a staggering 60000 BC. Anglo-American Corporation, one of South Africa's leading mining companies, have allowed archaeologists to examine ancient mining shafts in Swaziland and other areas; they concluded that mining was carried out 'during much of the period subsequent to 100,000 BC' (cited in Z. Sitchin, *The Twelfth Planet*, op. cit., chapter 11, p. 324).

99 Cited in Z. Sitchin, *The Twelfth Planet*, op. cit., chapter 12, p. 358.

100 R. Cann, M. Stoneking & A. Wilson, 'mtDNA and Human Evolution', op. cit.

101 L. Cavalli-Sforza, 'Genes, Peoples and Languages' in *Scientific American* Nov. 1991.

102 M. Aitken, C. Stringer & P. Mellars, *The Origin of Modern Humans and the Impact of Chronometric Dating*, op. cit.

Chapter Fifteen:
Gods of a New World Order

1 D. Rohl, *A Test of Time*, Vol. 1, Century, 1995.

2 According to J. Hawkes (ed.), *Atlas of Ancient Archaeology*, op cit., Knossos was a thriving centre as early as 6000 BC and 'was transformed soon after 3000 BC by the incipient knowledge of metal working . . .' (pp. 113 & 124). See also S. Hood, *The Minoans: Crete in the Bronze Age*, London, 1971.

3 A new capital city was built at Memphis – its ancient sacred name was *H(w)t-k-Pth*, 'House of the Ka (*shem?*) of Ptah'; it was the earliest religious centre in Egypt.

4 Minos, who gave his name to the Minoan culture, was referred to by the Greek writers Homer, Herodotus and Aristotle.

5 According to Genesis 10:13–14, Mizraim was the father of the Caphtorites. The Caphtorites were the Cretans per *Aid to Bible Understanding*, op. cit., p. 491 (the Egyptians called them by a similar name, *keftiou*). The Arabian name for Egypt is *Misr*; the Amarna letters refer to Egypt as *Misri*; the Hebrew name for Egypt is *Mits-rayim*; these names all spell out a clear link to Mizraim, the second son of Ham.

6 The role of the Indus as provider of grain is attested by ancient texts and confirmed by the archaeological discoveries of massive riverside granaries in Harappa and Mohenjo-daro.

7 S. Rao, *Lothal and the Indus Civilization*, op. cit., p. 55.

8 Trade between the Indus and Sargon has been confirmed by archaeology; see S. Rao, op. cit., p. 163.

9 The term Amorite simply means 'westerners' to someone living in Mesopotamia. The Table of Nations in Genesis 10:15–16 lists the Amorites as Canaanites, among whom they would appear to have been the dominant tribe. However, despite their Hamitic race, they were forced by their geographic location to speak a Semitic language, as evidenced by the ease with which Abraham conversed with them.

10 S. Rao, op. cit., pp. 18, 58–61, 73 & 179–80.

11 Ibid., p. 180; see also *The Egyptian Mining Temple at Timna* by B. Rothenberg, Institute of Archaeology, University College, London 1988; Timna is just to the north of the Gulf of Aqaba; Rothenberg reported that 'in the summer of 1976, the detailed geological and geomorphological mapping of the Model Area was completed and produced irrevocable evidence for widespread and rather intensive, deep-going geomorphological changes in the Timna landscape within the time span between the ancient mining activities (3rd millennium BC) and the present . . .'. Also see E. Anati, *The Mountain of God*, op. cit. – Anati notes that the sacred mountain of Jebel Ideid in Sinai is gradually crumbling away, another sign of geological shock.

12 *Wonders of the Ancient World*, NGS, op. cit., pp. 148–50; see also W. Watson, *China*, describing 'a mysteriously abrupt change'.

13 J. Hawkes, op. cit., p. 215; see also R. Forbes, *Studies in Ancient Technology*, dating the bronze period in China to 1800 BC.

14 C. Ball, *Chinese and Sumerian*, Oxford University, 1913; this was a major study comparing more than 100 pairs of pictographs; the Sumerian legacy is visible in many modern Chinese terms, for example Tiananmen, which in Sumerian spells out TI.AN.AN.MEN (Life-Heaven-Heaven-Peace).

15 P. Kolosimo, *Timeless Earth*, Bantam, 1975, chapter 7, pp. 68–70.

16 S. Langdon, *The Babylonian Epic of Creation*; also Z. Sitchin, *When Time Began*, op. cit., chapter 13, pp. 352–6.

17 The Akkadian name *Bab-Ili* means 'Gateway of the Gods'.

18 G. Roux, *Ancient Iraq*, op. cit., chapter 24, p. 395.

19 M. Dunand, *Byblos*, Beirut, 1973, pp. 23–6.

20 Exodus 1:11; Pithom means the gateway of Tem, a name by which Marduk was sometimes known; Rameses, however, is an anachronism, identifying a location in hindsight with its more recently acquired name; see D. Rohl, op. cit., chapter 4.

21 *Nub* means gold in Egyptian, hence the origin of the name Nubia.

22 The clues to the origin of the Dogon include their Nilo-Saharan tongue, and the significance of Sirius, whose cycle was used by the ancient Egyptians to monitor the cycles of the rising of the Nile.

23 The peaceful presence of these early Assyrians in the Hittite lands of Anatolia has been established as early as 1950 BC at Kultepe; see J. Hawkes, op. cit., p. 136. The Assyrians are sometimes linked to the person Asshur, the son of Shem, who is thought to have been their forefather; indeed, the same Hebrew word means both Asshur and Assyria. Suggested further reading on Assyrian origins: D. Oates, *Studies in the Ancient History of Northern Iraq*, London, 1968, pp. 19–41.

24 Suggested reading on the Hittites: O. Gurney, *The Hittites*, London, 1980; J. MacQueen, *The Hittites and their Contemporaries in Asia Minor*, London, 1986.

25 The Biblical Hittites of Genesis 10:15 were possibly the earliest occupants of the Anatolian plateau.

26 Suggested reading on the Hurrians: I. Gelb, *Hurrians and Subarians*, Chicago, 1944; G. Wilhelm, *The Hurrians*, Warminster, 1989.

27 J. Diamond, *The Rise and Fall of the Third Chimpanzee*, op. cit., chapter 15, p. 225.

28 Semitic refers to the language spoken primarily by the

descendants of Shem, who settled in the lands of Mesopotamia.

29 J. Mallory, *In Search of the Indo-Europeans*, London, 1989.

30 J. Diamond, op. cit., chapter 15 especially pp. 237–9.

31 S. Kramer, *Enmerkar and the Lord of Aratta: a Sumerian Epic Tale of Iraq and Iran*, Philadelphia, 1952.

32 Z. Sitchin, *Divine Encounters*, op. cit., chapter 6, p. 130. Aratta has been identified with the Indus city Harappa – see Z. Sitchin, *The Wars of Gods and Men*, op. cit., chapter 11, pp. 233–6.

33 The earliest Hittite temple at Kultepe was dedicated to 'Anitta', the name meaning 'beloved of Anu', a well-known nickname for Inanna. Hittite kings adopted similar names in commemoration of the goddess; see G. Roux, op. cit., chapter 14, p. 233 and J. Hawkes, op. cit., p. 136.

34 Z. Sitchin, *The Lost Realms*, op. cit., chapter 7, p. 150.

35 Hurrian worship of Teshub is evident in the name given to their later capital, Teishebaini (modern-day Karmir-Blur).

36 The explosion of Santorini was once linked chronologically to the cataclysms on Crete *c.* 1450 BC. In 1989, the Third International Thera Congress agreed on a date between 1680–1670 BC. This date was subsequently refined to 1628 BC in 1995.

37 D. Rohl, op. cit., pp. 335–42.

38 It has recently been claimed that this pinpoints the Biblical famine predicted by Joseph; such a claim has no foundation since Egypt undoubtedly suffered many famines during its long history.

39 Hammurabi is conventionally dated to a 'middle chronology' of 1792–1750 BC; D. Rohl, however, dates Hammurabi's reign to 1565–1522 BC (op. cit., p. 247). It is possible that there were two rulers by the name Hammurabi, and we are dealing here with Hammurabi II. Note that Hammurabi means 'the god Hammu is a healer' (G. Roux, op. cit., p. 195), whilst the words Ham and *mu* suggest an etymological connection to aerial vehicles from Africa!

40 Hammurabi's Law Code cited the god Shamash, which might at first seem unusual, but Sippar had been the city of Shamash since its very beginning. The Law Code at Sippar explains why Shamash was later cited as the god of justice.

41 G. Roux, op. cit., chapter 12, p. 204.

42 Cited in Z. Sitchin, *The Wars of Gods and Men*, chapter 1, p. 13.

43 *The Middle East*, Hachette, op. cit., p. 34; D. Rohl, op. cit., p. 247; J. Hawkes, op. cit., p. 176.

44 An earthquake or tidal wave from the Santorini eruption was once suggested as the cause of the Crete disaster, but both have now been discounted by the re-dating of Santorini.

45 *The Times Atlas of World History*, op. cit., p. 66.

46 *Wonders of the Ancient World*, NGS, op. cit., p. 78.

47 Ibid., p. 157.

48 Sir M. Wheeler, *The Indus Civilization*, op. cit., p. 131. Childe reached a similar conclusion in *New Light on the Most Ancient East*, London, 1952.

49 S. Rao, op. cit., chapter XVI.

50 D. Davenport & E. Vincenti, *2000 AC Distruzione Atomica*, Milano 1979; see also I. Mosin, R.Furdui & C. Burgansky, 'An Ancient Enigma' in *Soviet News* 14.7.88. The latter high-powered team comprised a geologist, a mineralogist and an engineer.

51 The possibility of a volcanic eruption at Mohenjo-daro is excluded because there is no hardened lava or volcanic ash in or anywhere near the site.

52 Cited by R. Collyns in *Ancient Skies* 21.1 (1994).

53 *The World's Last Mysteries*, Reader's Digest, op. cit., p. 122; *Wonders of the Ancient World*, NGS, op. cit., p. 156.

54 Seaward trade, on which the Indus had depended, had largely vanished after 1900 BC; see M. Wheeler, op. cit., p. 129.

55 As mentioned earlier, some experts date the earliest Mayan city at Dzibilchaltun to 2000 BC, but the dating is not exact and could equally well be 1500 BC.

56 Jeremiah 47:4, Amos 9:7.

57 *Aid to Bible Understanding*, op. cit., p. 395.

58 M. Dunand, op. cit., p. 30; *The Middle East*, op. cit., p. 40.

59 D. Rohl, op. cit., p. 203.

60 The military strength of these invaders is evidenced by excavations of tombs which demonstrate a sudden escalation in arms; see M. Dunand, op. cit., p. 28.

61 The name Phoenician may well originate from Crete, where an ancient harbour named Phoenix once existed, see Acts 27:12; palm trees were indigenous to that area according to the Greek writer Theophrastus, 4th-3rd century BC.

62 Genesis 10:15.

63 A. Kolata, *The Tiwanaku*, op. cit., p. 58.

64 Most history books on South America do little justice to the numerous similar cultures that emerged *c.* 1500 BC. For a full and proper appreciation, visit the Museum of Anthropology, Lima.

65 W. Krickeberg, *Altamerikanische Kulturen*, op. cit.

66 Cited in Z. Sitchin, *The Lost Realms*, op. cit., chapter 12, pp. 265–6. The identity of Atau (simply meaning 'Lord') is unknown. One legend suggests that his son went to Machu Picchu and founded the non-divine dynasty of the Incas. Prior to this, there had been 16 semi-divine Incan kings dating from 2400 BC (per Montesinos); the 15th of these can be dated to *c.* 1400 BC, suggesting that the new dynasty began *c.* 1350 BC. Thus Atau would have arrived *c.* 1400 BC.

67 *Wonders of the Ancient World*, NGS, op. cit., p. 216.

68 K. Armstrong, *A History of God*, op. cit., chapter 1, p. 30. The root word *hayah* means 'to be'.

69 M. Dunand, op. cit., pp. 27–8.

70 Exodus 9:16.

71 Exodus 3:21–22 and Exodus 25.

72 Yahweh knew that Pharaoh would not let them go easily, see Exodus 3:19.

73 Exodus 5:2.

74 Exodus 9:6 and 9:25 (livestock); Exodus 9:31 and 10:15 (crops and fruit trees). It is scientifically possible that the Passover was an actual event that targeted the young, perhaps via a plague of mosquitoes; Exodus 12 records how the Israelites were given detailed instructions on how to spread a noxious substance around the doors of their homes for protection from what was about to come!

75 Exodus 14. This 'miracle' can be scientifically explained, because the Red Sea can be crossed via submerged ridges if the wind blows in the right direction; the existence of these ridges was confirmed by the Suez Canal engineering survey in 1867.

76 Exodus 6:2–3.

77 Genesis 17:1–2.

78 This is also the view of K. Armstrong, op. cit., chapter 1, pp. 21 & 29.

79 *Aid to Bible Understanding*, op. cit. It is apparent from Kings I, 20:28 that the Hebrew god was recognised as a god of mountains 3,000 years ago; this confirms that the origin of *Shaddai* is *shadu*.

80 The name Hadad is related to the Hebrew word *shadhadh*

which means 'powerful/strong' (*Unger's Bible Dictionary* p. 1000); Hadad and *El Shaddai* are thus etymologically related.

81 Exodus 9:23–24.

82 Samuel I, 7:10.

83 Exodus 20:5.

84 Exodus 33:3; see also Exodus 32, 33 and Leviticus 26:14–39.

85 Numbers 25:3–4, Exodus 32:27–28.

86 Numbers 11:1–3, Numbers 14:37, Numbers 16:35.

87 Exodus 33:20.

88 The Hebrew word translated as 'glory' is *kabod*. It is derived from the root KBD meaning 'to be heavy', and thus *kabod* means a heavy object. It undoubtedly refers to Yahweh's aerial vehicle. See G. Sassoon, 'The Glory of the Lord' in *Ancient Skies* 17:1 (1990).

89 Exodus 13:21.

90 The Biblical term most commonly translated as 'angel' is *mal'akhim*, literally meaning 'an emissary'. See Z. Sitchin, *Divine Encounters*, op. cit., chapter 11.

91 Joshua 6. According to David Rohl, op. cit. pp. 304–5, the archaeologists have been searching in the wrong era and hence strata of the Jericho mound.

92 Deuteronomy 20:16–18.

93 G. Roux, op. cit., chapter 14, p. 240. Hyksos comes from the Egyptian *hiqkhase*.

94 Ibid., chapter 15, pp. 242 & 246.

95 D. Rohl, op. cit., p. 242.

96 The Amarna Letters comprise nearly 400 small clay tablets, named after the site of Tell el-Amarna where they were found in 1887. Suggested reading: S. Mercer, *The Tell el-Amarna Tablets*, Toronto, 1939.

97 G. Roux, op. cit., pp. 258–9.

98 This alliance occurred via inter-marriage in the period 1060–1000 BC, coinciding with the back-door attempt by the Indo-Europeans to take control of Egypt via Akhenaten. The Hurrians were otherwise not natural allies of Egypt, for at times they allied with the Hittites *against* Egypt. The Hurrians were influential, but more interested in trade and commerce than in military power; they thus became trapped between the two mighty powers of Egypt in the south and the Hittites in the north, and formed alliances with whichever could offer the best economic advantage.

99   D. Rohl, op. cit., pp. 200–2.

100 Manetho, cited by Josephus in *Against Apion*. It should be
     noted that the Jebusites had controlled Jerusalem from at
     least the time of Joshua per Judges 1.

101 Chronicles I, 13:3, states 'let us bring the ark of our God
     back to us, for we did not enquire of it during the reign of
     Saul'. Furthermore, in Samuel I, 14 & 28, Saul's calls to the
     Lord are almost certainly *not* via the Ark, and he does not
     receive a reply.

102 Samuel I, 30 & 23. In Exodus 39, the *ephod* is described as
     a special garment required by those who operate the Ark.
     In David's time, the Ark had been captured by the
     Philistines and then returned; it was then hidden away in
     the town of Kiriath Jearim – see Samuel I, 7:1 and
     Chronicles I, 13:5.

103 Kings I, 6; the temple was begun in the 480th year after the
     Exodus (1433 BC, see Appendix A).

104 Kings I, 14:25–26; see D. Rohl, op. cit., chapter 7, for
     identification of Ramesses with the Biblical Shishak. The
     temple took 7 years to build according to Kings I, 6:38.

105 Kings II, 19:35.

106 Kings II, 19:15–16.

107 G. Roux, op. cit., pp. 322–3.

108 *The Interpreter's Dictionary of the Bible*, Vol. 1, p. 257.

109 Nebuchadnezzar literally means 'Nabu defend the
     boundary'. Suggested reading: W. Lambert, 'The reign of
     Nebuchadnezzar I; a turning point in the history of ancient
     Mesopotamian religion' in W. McCullough (ed), *The Seed
     of Wisdom*, Toronto, 1964.

110 Ezekiel 40. The 'Spirit' of the Lord can rise above the
     mountains, see Ezekiel 11:23. Compare earlier note on the
     Lord's 'Glory' or *Kabod*.

111 W. Langbein, 'Ezekiel's Spaceships' in *Ancient Skies* 20:3
     (1993). Note for instance the vague reference to 'some
     buildings that look like a city' in Ezekiel 40:2. Langbein
     and others claim that the Biblical editors have deliberately
     twisted the translation to give the impression that the site
     was Jerusalem, and changed the verbs to future tense!

112 Particularly E. von Daniken, *The Gods and their Grand
     Design*, op. cit.; von Daniken lists 16 similarities.

113 Ezekiel 43:10–11.

114 N. Abanto de Hoogendoorn, *Chavin de Huantar – A Short
     Eternity*, op. cit. Some temples may have been built *c.* 900

BC, but the main phase, including the sunken plaza date to after 500 BC.

115 The Aztec traditions may not have been Aztec in origin. It is believed that the Aztecs were latecomers on the scene and learned much from the earlier Toltecs; the Toltecs in turn would have inherited traditions from earlier cultures.

116 Joshua 10.

117 *Wonders of the Ancient World*, NGS, op. cit., p. 283.

118 G. Phillips, 'Quirigua' in *Ancient Skies* 19:3 (1992).

119 J. Hawkes, op. cit., p. 258.

120 P. Furst, anthropologist at University Museum, Philadelphia, in *National Geographic* 184:5 (1993).

121 *Berlitz Guide to Mexico*, Oxford, 1992, p. 77.

122 *Wonders of the Ancient World*, NGS, op. cit., p. 278.

123 N. Abanto de Hoogendoorn, op. cit., pp. 31–3.

124 Nabonidos literally means 'the god Nabu is exalted'.

125 K. Armstrong, op. cit., chapter 1, p. 42.

126 G. Hancock, *Fingerprints of the Gods*, op. cit., chapter 19, p. 156.

127 Z. Sitchin, *The Lost Realms*, op. cit., chapter 5, p. 92.

128 D. Reed, *The Rough Guide to Nepal*, Harrap-Columbus, London, p. 89.

Chapter Sixteen:
Gods of the New Millennium

1 Using a Flood date of 10983 BC, Nibiru would have returned at 183 BC, assuming orbits of exactly 3,600 years. On the other hand, it is possible that 3,600 was a rounded figure. If, for example, the orbit took 3,590 years, then the return date would have been 213 BC. The date 200 BC is thus a good approximation.

2 *Wonders of the Ancient World*, NGS, op. cit., p. 283.

3 Z. Sitchin, *The Lost Realms*, op. cit., chapter 3, p. 54.

4 Three periods of 3,600 = 10,800; 5 periods of 2,160 = 10,800.

5 Magi means 'wise men'. According to Herodotus, the Magi were a tribe of the Medes. If so, they were a diplomatic mission, since the Medes would surely not have worshipped a Shemitic messiah.

6 Matthew 2:1–2.

7 Matthew 2:7 and 16.

8 *Encyclopaedia Judaica*, cited in *Mankind's Search for God*, Watchtower Publications, op. cit., p. 233.

9 M. Baigent, R. Leigh & H. Lincoln, *The Messianic Legacy*, Jonathan Cape, London, 1986, pp. 111–5.

10 K. Armstrong, *A History of God*, op. cit., chapter 3, p. 98.

11 M. Baigent et al, op. cit., p. 69.

12 Ibid., p. 71. For example, the Bible states that 'a band of men' came to the Garden of Gethsemane to arrest Jesus; Baigent et al point out that this conjures up an image of 10–30 soldiers, whereas it should have been translated 'cohort', involving a major rebellion and perhaps 500 soldiers (pp. 46–50).

13 K. Armstrong, op. cit., chapter 4.

14 *Mankind's Search for God*, op. cit., p. 276.

15 Islam means submission or commitment (to Allah); Muslim means one who makes or does Islam.

16 K. Armstrong, op. cit., chapter 5, contains an excellent review of the development of Islam.

17 *World Religions – From Ancient History to the Present*, cited in *Mankind's Search for God*, op. cit., p. 26.

18 Genesis 1:7–8.

19 Z. Sitchin, *Genesis Revisited*, op. cit., chapter 3, p. 50.

20 *The Koran*, Penguin Books, op. cit., p. 298.

21 *Tale of Adapa*, cited in Z. Sitchin, *The Twelfth Planet*, chapter 6, p. 174.

22 Church of England Doctrine Commission, 'The Mystery of Salvation', 11.1.96.

23 Citing *Collier's Encyclopaedia*, 1965 ed., Vol. 12, p. 27. Note that the 'abyss' in the Septuagint comes from the Greek *abyssos* and means the 'unfathomable', the 'infinite void' or more literally the 'watery deep'; it is a translation of *tehom* and thus a reference to the planet Tiamat. The abyss of the Book of Revelations is thus not under the earth but out in space. Abyss should therefore not be confused with the terms *she'ohl* and Hades.

24 A. Heidel, *The Gilgamesh Epic and Old Testament Parallels*, op. cit., p. 173. It is claimed that Acts 2:27 proves that Hades and *she'ohl* are identical.

25 For a comprehensive discussion see A. Heidel, op. cit., pp. 173–223.

26 Job 17:16 and Isaiah 38:10.

27 Job 10:21–22.

28 A. Heidel, op. cit., p. 185.

29 Deuteronomy 32:22.

30 Cited in A. Heidel, op. cit., p. 192.

31 Ibid. p. 171. Ereshkigal means 'Lady of the *kigal*', where *kigal* means 'the great place below.'

32 Ibid., pp. 172–3.

33 G. Roux, *Ancient Iraq*, op. cit., chapter 6, p. 101.

34 *Aid to Bible Understanding*, op. cit., p. 446.

35 The Greek term for resurrection is *a-na'sta-sis*, which occurs 42 times in the Bible: *Mankind's Search for God*, op. cit., p. 266.

36 Ibid., pp. 250 & 265.

37 See E. Wallis-Budge, *Osiris and the Egyptian Resurrection*, vol. I., for a detailed discussion.

38 Luke 21:24.

39 Matthew 28:18–20; the Greek Septuagint uses the term *aion*, meaning a long period.

40 The term for 'times' appears in Greek as *kairos*, meaning a fixed or definite period: *Aid to Bible Understanding*, op. cit., p. 94.

41 Psalm 29.

42 Peter II, 3.

43 *The Koran*, op. cit., p. 262.

44 Isaiah 24.

45 Zechariah 14:6–7.

46 Isaiah 65:17 and 66:22.

47 Isaiah 29:6.

48 Luke 21.

49 *Financial Times*, 7th December 1995; and *Nature*, December 1995.

50 M. Chatelain, 'The Marduk Mystery' in *Ancient Skies* 18:4 (1991).

51 G. Phillips, *Ancient Skies* 14:2 (1987).

52 *Wonders of the Ancient World*, NGS, op. cit., p. 255.

53 *The Sunday Times*, 12th March 1995; also *The Sunday Telegraph*, 1st January 1995.

54 See the excellent article by G. Sassoon in *Ancient Skies* 16:4 (1989); also S. Knight, *The Brotherhood*, Granada, London, 1984, p. 168.

55 G. Sassoon & R. Dale, *The Manna Machine*, Sidgwick & Jackson, London, 1978; the machine was also known as 'the Ancient of Days'.

56 Telex Reuter and sda, 16th April 1993.
57 In particular, see the highly detailed Earth Chronicles by Z. Sitchin.
58 Calculated as follows: 10983 BC − 107 = 10876 BC − (4 × 2148) = 2284 BC.
59 A precessional cycle of 25,747.5 years is arrived at assuming that the orbit of Nibiru is a multiple of 52. The latter was a sacred number to Thoth, the Egyptian god of wisdom, who was obsessed with *accurate measurement*. We might thus assume an orbital period of 3,588 instead of 3,600 years. We can then use the Sumerian mathematical principle that 3,588 squared equals 500 precessional cycles. Thus the cycle is 12,873,744 divided by 500, i.e. 25,747.5. AD 1998 is based on this cycle beginning 107 years after the Flood, i.e. 10876 BC.
60 Muhammad al-Muntazar disappeared *c.* AD 878 in a cave of the great mosque at Samarra.
61 G. Hancock, *Fingerprints of the Gods*, op. cit., uses a start point of 3114 BC to predict the end of the world on 23rd December AD 2012. However, other authorities use a Mayan start point of 3113 BC, leading to a completed cycle in AD 2013.
62 *The Sunday Times*, 24th March 1996.

Appendix A: Chronology from Abraham to the Exodus

1 Amar-Sin's reign can be dated from a total lunar eclipse during the reign of his successor, Shu-Sin. According to modern astronomical computers, this eclipse must have occurred in 2031 BC.
2 Z. Sitchin, *The Lost Realms*, op. cit., chapter 7.
3 Joseph's 30 years comprised: 13 years prior to entering Pharaoh's service (Genesis 37:2 and 41:46); followed by 7 years of plenty, 7 years of famine, and another 3 years before his kinsfolk joined him.
4 J. Bimson & D. Livingston, in *Biblical Archaeology Review*, Sept-Oct 1987.
5 *Aid to Bible Understanding*, op. cit., p. 541.
6 Ibid., pp. 336–7.

Index